Natural Language Processing with Python

Natural Language Processing with Python

Steven Bird, Ewan Klein, and Edward Loper

O'REILLY®

Beijing · Cambridge · Farnham · Köln · Sebastopol · Taipei · Tokyo

Natural Language Processing with Python

by Steven Bird, Ewan Klein, and Edward Loper

Copyright © 2009 Steven Bird, Ewan Klein, and Edward Loper. All rights reserved.
Printed in the United States of America.

Published by O'Reilly Media, Inc., 1005 Gravenstein Highway North, Sebastopol, CA 95472.

O'Reilly books may be purchased for educational, business, or sales promotional use. Online editions
are also available for most titles (*http://my.safaribooksonline.com*). For more information, contact our
corporate/institutional sales department: (800) 998-9938 or *corporate@oreilly.com*.

Editor: Julie Steele	**Indexer:** Ellen Troutman Zaig
Production Editor: Loranah Dimant	**Cover Designer:** Karen Montgomery
Copyeditor: Genevieve d'Entremont	**Interior Designer:** David Futato
Proofreader: Loranah Dimant	**Illustrator:** Robert Romano

Printing History:

June 2009:   First Edition.

ISBN: 978-0-596-51649-9

[M]

1244663349

Table of Contents

Preface

This is a book about Natural Language Processing. By "natural language" we mean a language that is used for everyday communication by humans; languages such as English, Hindi, or Portuguese. In contrast to artificial languages such as programming languages and mathematical notations, natural languages have evolved as they pass from generation to generation, and are hard to pin down with explicit rules. We will take Natural Language Processing—or NLP for short—in a wide sense to cover any kind of computer manipulation of natural language. At one extreme, it could be as simple as counting word frequencies to compare different writing styles. At the other extreme, NLP involves "understanding" complete human utterances, at least to the extent of being able to give useful responses to them.

Technologies based on NLP are becoming increasingly widespread. For example, phones and handheld computers support predictive text and handwriting recognition; web search engines give access to information locked up in unstructured text; machine translation allows us to retrieve texts written in Chinese and read them in Spanish. By providing more natural human-machine interfaces, and more sophisticated access to stored information, language processing has come to play a central role in the multilingual information society.

This book provides a highly accessible introduction to the field of NLP. It can be used for individual study or as the textbook for a course on natural language processing or computational linguistics, or as a supplement to courses in artificial intelligence, text mining, or corpus linguistics. The book is intensely practical, containing hundreds of fully worked examples and graded exercises.

The book is based on the Python programming language together with an open source library called the *Natural Language Toolkit* (NLTK). NLTK includes extensive software, data, and documentation, all freely downloadable from *http://www.nltk.org/*. Distributions are provided for Windows, Macintosh, and Unix platforms. We strongly encourage you to download Python and NLTK, and try out the examples and exercises along the way.

Audience

NLP is important for scientific, economic, social, and cultural reasons. NLP is experiencing rapid growth as its theories and methods are deployed in a variety of new language technologies. For this reason it is important for a wide range of people to have a working knowledge of NLP. Within industry, this includes people in human-computer interaction, business information analysis, and web software development. Within academia, it includes people in areas from humanities computing and corpus linguistics through to computer science and artificial intelligence. (To many people in academia, NLP is known by the name of "Computational Linguistics.")

This book is intended for a diverse range of people who want to learn how to write programs that analyze written language, regardless of previous programming experience:

New to programming?
> The early chapters of the book are suitable for readers with no prior knowledge of programming, so long as you aren't afraid to tackle new concepts and develop new computing skills. The book is full of examples that you can copy and try for yourself, together with hundreds of graded exercises. If you need a more general introduction to Python, see the list of Python resources at *http://docs.python.org/*.

New to Python?
> Experienced programmers can quickly learn enough Python using this book to get immersed in natural language processing. All relevant Python features are carefully explained and exemplified, and you will quickly come to appreciate Python's suitability for this application area. The language index will help you locate relevant discussions in the book.

Already dreaming in Python?
> Skim the Python examples and dig into the interesting language analysis material that starts in Chapter 1. You'll soon be applying your skills to this fascinating domain.

Emphasis

This book is a **practical** introduction to NLP. You will learn by example, write real programs, and grasp the value of being able to test an idea through implementation. If you haven't learned already, this book will teach you **programming**. Unlike other programming books, we provide extensive illustrations and exercises from NLP. The approach we have taken is also **principled**, in that we cover the theoretical underpinnings and don't shy away from careful linguistic and computational analysis. We have tried to be **pragmatic** in striking a balance between theory and application, identifying the connections and the tensions. Finally, we recognize that you won't get through this unless it is also **pleasurable**, so we have tried to include many applications and examples that are interesting and entertaining, and sometimes whimsical.

Note that this book is not a reference work. Its coverage of Python and NLP is selective, and presented in a tutorial style. For reference material, please consult the substantial quantity of searchable resources available at *http://python.org/* and *http://www.nltk .org/*.

This book is not an advanced computer science text. The content ranges from introductory to intermediate, and is directed at readers who want to learn how to analyze text using Python and the Natural Language Toolkit. To learn about advanced algorithms implemented in NLTK, you can examine the Python code linked from *http:// www.nltk.org/*, and consult the other materials cited in this book.

What You Will Learn

By digging into the material presented here, you will learn:

- How simple programs can help you manipulate and analyze language data, and how to write these programs
- How key concepts from NLP and linguistics are used to describe and analyze language
- How data structures and algorithms are used in NLP
- How language data is stored in standard formats, and how data can be used to evaluate the performance of NLP techniques

Depending on your background, and your motivation for being interested in NLP, you will gain different kinds of skills and knowledge from this book, as set out in Table P-1.

Table P-1. Skills and knowledge to be gained from reading this book, depending on readers' goals and background

Goals	Background in arts and humanities	Background in science and engineering
Language analysis	Manipulating large corpora, exploring linguistic models, and testing empirical claims.	Using techniques in data modeling, data mining, and knowledge discovery to analyze natural language.
Language technology	Building robust systems to perform linguistic tasks with technological applications.	Using linguistic algorithms and data structures in robust language processing software.

Organization

The early chapters are organized in order of conceptual difficulty, starting with a practical introduction to language processing that shows how to explore interesting bodies of text using tiny Python programs (Chapters 1–3). This is followed by a chapter on structured programming (Chapter 4) that consolidates the programming topics scattered across the preceding chapters. After this, the pace picks up, and we move on to a series of chapters covering fundamental topics in language processing: tagging, classification, and information extraction (Chapters 5–7). The next three chapters look at ways to parse a sentence, recognize its syntactic structure, and construct representations of meaning (Chapters 8–10). The final chapter is devoted to linguistic data and how it can be managed effectively (Chapter 11). The book concludes with an Afterword, briefly discussing the past and future of the field.

Within each chapter, we switch between different styles of presentation. In one style, natural language is the driver. We analyze language, explore linguistic concepts, and use programming examples to support the discussion. We often employ Python constructs that have not been introduced systematically, so you can see their purpose before delving into the details of how and why they work. This is just like learning idiomatic expressions in a foreign language: you're able to buy a nice pastry without first having learned the intricacies of question formation. In the other style of presentation, the programming language will be the driver. We'll analyze programs, explore algorithms, and the linguistic examples will play a supporting role.

Each chapter ends with a series of graded exercises, which are useful for consolidating the material. The exercises are graded according to the following scheme: ○ is for easy exercises that involve minor modifications to supplied code samples or other simple activities; ◑ is for intermediate exercises that explore an aspect of the material in more depth, requiring careful analysis and design; ● is for difficult, open-ended tasks that will challenge your understanding of the material and force you to think independently (readers new to programming should skip these).

Each chapter has a further reading section and an online "extras" section at *http://www.nltk.org/*, with pointers to more advanced materials and online resources. Online versions of all the code examples are also available there.

Why Python?

Python is a simple yet powerful programming language with excellent functionality for processing linguistic data. Python can be downloaded for free from *http://www.python.org/*. Installers are available for all platforms.

Here is a five-line Python program that processes *file.txt* and prints all the words ending in ing:

```
>>> for line in open("file.txt"):
...     for word in line.split():
...         if word.endswith('ing'):
...             print word
```

This program illustrates some of the main features of Python. First, whitespace is used to *nest* lines of code; thus the line starting with if falls inside the scope of the previous line starting with for; this ensures that the ing test is performed for each word. Second, Python is *object-oriented*; each variable is an entity that has certain defined attributes and methods. For example, the value of the variable line is more than a sequence of characters. It is a string object that has a "method" (or operation) called split() that we can use to break a line into its words. To apply a method to an object, we write the object name, followed by a period, followed by the method name, i.e., `line.split()`. Third, methods have *arguments* expressed inside parentheses. For instance, in the example, `word.endswith('ing')` had the argument `'ing'` to indicate that we wanted words ending with *ing* and not something else. Finally—and most importantly—Python is highly readable, so much so that it is fairly easy to guess what this program does even if you have never written a program before.

We chose Python because it has a shallow learning curve, its syntax and semantics are transparent, and it has good string-handling functionality. As an interpreted language, Python facilitates interactive exploration. As an object-oriented language, Python permits data and methods to be encapsulated and re-used easily. As a dynamic language, Python permits attributes to be added to objects on the fly, and permits variables to be typed dynamically, facilitating rapid development. Python comes with an extensive standard library, including components for graphical programming, numerical processing, and web connectivity.

Python is heavily used in industry, scientific research, and education around the world. Python is often praised for the way it facilitates productivity, quality, and maintainability of software. A collection of Python success stories is posted at *http://www .python.org/about/success/*.

NLTK defines an infrastructure that can be used to build NLP programs in Python. It provides basic classes for representing data relevant to natural language processing; standard interfaces for performing tasks such as part-of-speech tagging, syntactic parsing, and text classification; and standard implementations for each task that can be combined to solve complex problems.

NLTK comes with extensive documentation. In addition to this book, the website at *http://www.nltk.org/* provides API documentation that covers every module, class, and function in the toolkit, specifying parameters and giving examples of usage. The website also provides many HOWTOs with extensive examples and test cases, intended for users, developers, and instructors.

Software Requirements

To get the most out of this book, you should install several free software packages. Current download pointers and instructions are available at *http://www.nltk.org/*.

Python
> The material presented in this book assumes that you are using Python version 2.4 or 2.5. We are committed to porting NLTK to Python 3.0 once the libraries that NLTK depends on have been ported.

NLTK
> The code examples in this book use NLTK version 2.0. Subsequent releases of NLTK will be backward-compatible.

NLTK-Data
> This contains the linguistic corpora that are analyzed and processed in the book.

NumPy (recommended)
> This is a scientific computing library with support for multidimensional arrays and linear algebra, required for certain probability, tagging, clustering, and classification tasks.

Matplotlib (recommended)
> This is a 2D plotting library for data visualization, and is used in some of the book's code samples that produce line graphs and bar charts.

NetworkX (optional)
> This is a library for storing and manipulating network structures consisting of nodes and edges. For visualizing semantic networks, also install the Graphviz library.

Prover9 (optional)
> This is an automated theorem prover for first-order and equational logic, used to support inference in language processing.

Natural Language Toolkit (NLTK)

NLTK was originally created in 2001 as part of a computational linguistics course in the Department of Computer and Information Science at the University of Pennsylvania. Since then it has been developed and expanded with the help of dozens of contributors. It has now been adopted in courses in dozens of universities, and serves as the basis of many research projects. Table P-2 lists the most important NLTK modules.

Table P-2. Language processing tasks and corresponding NLTK modules with examples of functionality

Language processing task	NLTK modules	Functionality
Accessing corpora	nltk.corpus	Standardized interfaces to corpora and lexicons
String processing	nltk.tokenize, nltk.stem	Tokenizers, sentence tokenizers, stemmers
Collocation discovery	nltk.collocations	t-test, chi-squared, point-wise mutual information
Part-of-speech tagging	nltk.tag	n-gram, backoff, Brill, HMM, TnT
Classification	nltk.classify, nltk.cluster	Decision tree, maximum entropy, naive Bayes, EM, k-means
Chunking	nltk.chunk	Regular expression, n-gram, named entity
Parsing	nltk.parse	Chart, feature-based, unification, probabilistic, dependency
Semantic interpretation	nltk.sem, nltk.inference	Lambda calculus, first-order logic, model checking
Evaluation metrics	nltk.metrics	Precision, recall, agreement coefficients
Probability and estimation	nltk.probability	Frequency distributions, smoothed probability distributions
Applications	nltk.app, nltk.chat	Graphical concordancer, parsers, WordNet browser, chatbots

Language processing task	NLTK modules	Functionality
Linguistic fieldwork	nltk.toolbox	Manipulate data in SIL Toolbox format

NLTK was designed with four primary goals in mind:

Simplicity
> To provide an intuitive framework along with substantial building blocks, giving users a practical knowledge of NLP without getting bogged down in the tedious house-keeping usually associated with processing annotated language data

Consistency
> To provide a uniform framework with consistent interfaces and data structures, and easily guessable method names

Extensibility
> To provide a structure into which new software modules can be easily accommodated, including alternative implementations and competing approaches to the same task

Modularity
> To provide components that can be used independently without needing to understand the rest of the toolkit

Contrasting with these goals are three non-requirements—potentially useful qualities that we have deliberately avoided. First, while the toolkit provides a wide range of functions, it is not encyclopedic; it is a toolkit, not a system, and it will continue to evolve with the field of NLP. Second, while the toolkit is efficient enough to support meaningful tasks, it is not highly optimized for runtime performance; such optimizations often involve more complex algorithms, or implementations in lower-level programming languages such as C or C++. This would make the software less readable and more difficult to install. Third, we have tried to avoid clever programming tricks, since we believe that clear implementations are preferable to ingenious yet indecipherable ones.

For Instructors

Natural Language Processing is often taught within the confines of a single-semester course at the advanced undergraduate level or postgraduate level. Many instructors have found that it is difficult to cover both the theoretical and practical sides of the subject in such a short span of time. Some courses focus on theory to the exclusion of practical exercises, and deprive students of the challenge and excitement of writing programs to automatically process language. Other courses are simply designed to teach programming for linguists, and do not manage to cover any significant NLP content. NLTK was originally developed to address this problem, making it feasible to cover a substantial amount of theory and practice within a single-semester course, even if students have no prior programming experience.

A significant fraction of any NLP syllabus deals with algorithms and data structures. On their own these can be rather dry, but NLTK brings them to life with the help of interactive graphical user interfaces that make it possible to view algorithms step-by-step. Most NLTK components include a demonstration that performs an interesting task without requiring any special input from the user. An effective way to deliver the materials is through interactive presentation of the examples in this book, entering them in a Python session, observing what they do, and modifying them to explore some empirical or theoretical issue.

This book contains hundreds of exercises that can be used as the basis for student assignments. The simplest exercises involve modifying a supplied program fragment in a specified way in order to answer a concrete question. At the other end of the spectrum, NLTK provides a flexible framework for graduate-level research projects, with standard implementations of all the basic data structures and algorithms, interfaces to dozens of widely used datasets (corpora), and a flexible and extensible architecture. Additional support for teaching using NLTK is available on the NLTK website.

We believe this book is unique in providing a comprehensive framework for students to learn about NLP in the context of learning to program. What sets these materials apart is the tight coupling of the chapters and exercises with NLTK, giving students— even those with no prior programming experience—a practical introduction to NLP. After completing these materials, students will be ready to attempt one of the more advanced textbooks, such as *Speech and Language Processing*, by Jurafsky and Martin (Prentice Hall, 2008).

This book presents programming concepts in an unusual order, beginning with a non-trivial data type—lists of strings—then introducing non-trivial control structures such as comprehensions and conditionals. These idioms permit us to do useful language processing from the start. Once this motivation is in place, we return to a systematic presentation of fundamental concepts such as strings, loops, files, and so forth. In this way, we cover the same ground as more conventional approaches, without expecting readers to be interested in the programming language for its own sake.

Two possible course plans are illustrated in Table P-3. The first one presumes an arts/humanities audience, whereas the second one presumes a science/engineering audience. Other course plans could cover the first five chapters, then devote the remaining time to a single area, such as text classification (Chapters 6 and 7), syntax (Chapters 8 and 9), semantics (Chapter 10), or linguistic data management (Chapter 11).

Table P-3. Suggested course plans; approximate number of lectures per chapter

Chapter	Arts and Humanities	Science and Engineering
Chapter 1, *Language Processing and Python*	2–4	2
Chapter 2, *Accessing Text Corpora and Lexical Resources*	2–4	2
Chapter 3, *Processing Raw Text*	2–4	2
Chapter 4, *Writing Structured Programs*	2–4	1–2

Chapter	Arts and Humanities	Science and Engineering
Chapter 5, *Categorizing and Tagging Words*	2–4	2–4
Chapter 6, *Learning to Classify Text*	0–2	2–4
Chapter 7, *Extracting Information from Text*	2	2–4
Chapter 8, *Analyzing Sentence Structure*	2–4	2–4
Chapter 9, *Building Feature-Based Grammars*	2–4	1–4
Chapter 10, *Analyzing the Meaning of Sentences*	1–2	1–4
Chapter 11, *Managing Linguistic Data*	1–2	1–4
Total	18–36	18–36

Conventions Used in This Book

The following typographical conventions are used in this book:

Bold
> Indicates new terms.

Italic
> Used within paragraphs to refer to linguistic examples, the names of texts, and URLs; also used for filenames and file extensions.

`Constant width`
> Used for program listings, as well as within paragraphs to refer to program elements such as variable or function names, statements, and keywords; also used for program names.

`Constant width italic`
> Shows text that should be replaced with user-supplied values or by values determined by context; also used for metavariables within program code examples.

 This icon signifies a tip, suggestion, or general note.

 This icon indicates a warning or caution.

Using Code Examples

This book is here to help you get your job done. In general, you may use the code in this book in your programs and documentation. You do not need to contact us for permission unless you're reproducing a significant portion of the code. For example, writing a program that uses several chunks of code from this book does not require permission. Selling or distributing a CD-ROM of examples from O'Reilly books does require permission. Answering a question by citing this book and quoting example code does not require permission. Incorporating a significant amount of example code from this book into your product's documentation does require permission.

We appreciate, but do not require, attribution. An attribution usually includes the title, author, publisher, and ISBN. For example: "*Natural Language Processing with Python*, by Steven Bird, Ewan Klein, and Edward Loper. Copyright 2009 Steven Bird, Ewan Klein, and Edward Loper, 978-0-596-51649-9."

If you feel your use of code examples falls outside fair use or the permission given above, feel free to contact us at *permissions@oreilly.com*.

Safari® Books Online

Safari When you see a Safari® Books Online icon on the cover of your favorite technology book, that means the book is available online through the O'Reilly Network Safari Bookshelf.

Safari offers a solution that's better than e-books. It's a virtual library that lets you easily search thousands of top tech books, cut and paste code samples, download chapters, and find quick answers when you need the most accurate, current information. Try it for free at *http://my.safaribooksonline.com*.

How to Contact Us

Please address comments and questions concerning this book to the publisher:

> O'Reilly Media, Inc.
> 1005 Gravenstein Highway North
> Sebastopol, CA 95472
> 800-998-9938 (in the United States or Canada)
> 707-829-0515 (international or local)
> 707-829-0104 (fax)

We have a web page for this book, where we list errata, examples, and any additional information. You can access this page at:

> *http://www.oreilly.com/catalog/9780596516499*

The authors provide additional materials for each chapter via the NLTK website at:

http://www.nltk.org/

To comment or ask technical questions about this book, send email to:

bookquestions@oreilly.com

For more information about our books, conferences, Resource Centers, and the O'Reilly Network, see our website at:

http://www.oreilly.com

Acknowledgments

The authors are indebted to the following people for feedback on earlier drafts of this book: Doug Arnold, Michaela Atterer, Greg Aumann, Kenneth Beesley, Steven Bethard, Ondrej Bojar, Chris Cieri, Robin Cooper, Grev Corbett, James Curran, Dan Garrette, Jean Mark Gawron, Doug Hellmann, Nitin Indurkhya, Mark Liberman, Peter Ljunglöf, Stefan Müller, Robin Munn, Joel Nothman, Adam Przepiorkowski, Brandon Rhodes, Stuart Robinson, Jussi Salmela, Kyle Schlansker, Rob Speer, and Richard Sproat. We are thankful to many students and colleagues for their comments on the class materials that evolved into these chapters, including participants at NLP and linguistics summer schools in Brazil, India, and the USA. This book would not exist without the members of the `nltk-dev` developer community, named on the NLTK website, who have given so freely of their time and expertise in building and extending NLTK.

We are grateful to the U.S. National Science Foundation, the Linguistic Data Consortium, an Edward Clarence Dyason Fellowship, and the Universities of Pennsylvania, Edinburgh, and Melbourne for supporting our work on this book.

We thank Julie Steele, Abby Fox, Loranah Dimant, and the rest of the O'Reilly team, for organizing comprehensive reviews of our drafts from people across the NLP and Python communities, for cheerfully customizing O'Reilly's production tools to accommodate our needs, and for meticulous copyediting work.

Finally, we owe a huge debt of gratitude to our partners, Kay, Mimo, and Jee, for their love, patience, and support over the many years that we worked on this book. We hope that our children—Andrew, Alison, Kirsten, Leonie, and Maaike—catch our enthusiasm for language and computation from these pages.

Royalties

Royalties from the sale of this book are being used to support the development of the Natural Language Toolkit.

Figure P-1. Edward Loper, Ewan Klein, and Steven Bird, Stanford, July 2007

## CHAPTER 1

Language Processing and Python

It is easy to get our hands on millions of words of text. What can we do with it, assuming we can write some simple programs? In this chapter, we'll address the following questions:

1. What can we achieve by combining simple programming techniques with large quantities of text?

2. How can we automatically extract key words and phrases that sum up the style and content of a text?

3. What tools and techniques does the Python programming language provide for such work?

4. What are some of the interesting challenges of natural language processing?

This chapter is divided into sections that skip between two quite different styles. In the "computing with language" sections, we will take on some linguistically motivated programming tasks without necessarily explaining how they work. In the "closer look at Python" sections we will systematically review key programming concepts. We'll flag the two styles in the section titles, but later chapters will mix both styles without being so up-front about it. We hope this style of introduction gives you an authentic taste of what will come later, while covering a range of elementary concepts in linguistics and computer science. If you have basic familiarity with both areas, you can skip to Section 1.5; we will repeat any important points in later chapters, and if you miss anything you can easily consult the online reference material at *http://www.nltk.org/*. If the material is completely new to you, this chapter will raise more questions than it answers, questions that are addressed in the rest of this book.

1.1 Computing with Language: Texts and Words

We're all very familiar with text, since we read and write it every day. Here we will treat text as *raw data* for the programs we write, programs that manipulate and analyze it in a variety of interesting ways. But before we can do this, we have to get started with the Python interpreter.

Getting Started with Python

One of the friendly things about Python is that it allows you to type directly into the interactive **interpreter**—the program that will be running your Python programs. You can access the Python interpreter using a simple graphical interface called the Interactive DeveLopment Environment (IDLE). On a Mac you can find this under Applications→MacPython, and on Windows under All Programs→Python. Under Unix you can run Python from the shell by typing `idle` (if this is not installed, try typing `python`). The interpreter will print a blurb about your Python version; simply check that you are running Python 2.4 or 2.5 (here it is 2.5.1):

```
Python 2.5.1 (r251:54863, Apr 15 2008, 22:57:26)
[GCC 4.0.1 (Apple Inc. build 5465)] on darwin
Type "help", "copyright", "credits" or "license" for more information.
>>>
```

 If you are unable to run the Python interpreter, you probably don't have Python installed correctly. Please visit *http://python.org/* for detailed instructions.

The >>> prompt indicates that the Python interpreter is now waiting for input. When copying examples from this book, don't type the ">>>" yourself. Now, let's begin by using Python as a calculator:

```
>>> 1 + 5 * 2 - 3
8
>>>
```

Once the interpreter has finished calculating the answer and displaying it, the prompt reappears. This means the Python interpreter is waiting for another instruction.

 Your Turn: Enter a few more expressions of your own. You can use asterisk (*) for multiplication and slash (/) for division, and parentheses for bracketing expressions. Note that division doesn't always behave as you might expect—it does integer division (with rounding of fractions downwards) when you type `1/3` and "floating-point" (or decimal) division when you type `1.0/3.0`. In order to get the expected behavior of division (standard in Python 3.0), you need to type: `from __future__ import division`.

The preceding examples demonstrate how you can work interactively with the Python interpreter, experimenting with various expressions in the language to see what they do. Now let's try a non-sensical expression to see how the interpreter handles it:

```
>>> 1 +
  File "<stdin>", line 1
    1 +
      ^
SyntaxError: invalid syntax
>>>
```

This produced a **syntax error**. In Python, it doesn't make sense to end an instruction with a plus sign. The Python interpreter indicates the line where the problem occurred (line 1 of <stdin>, which stands for "standard input").

Now that we can use the Python interpreter, we're ready to start working with language data.

Getting Started with NLTK

Before going further you should install NLTK, downloadable for free from *http://www .nltk.org/*. Follow the instructions there to download the version required for your platform.

Once you've installed NLTK, start up the Python interpreter as before, and install the data required for the book by typing the following two commands at the Python prompt, then selecting the book collection as shown in Figure 1-1.

```
>>> import nltk
>>> nltk.download()
```

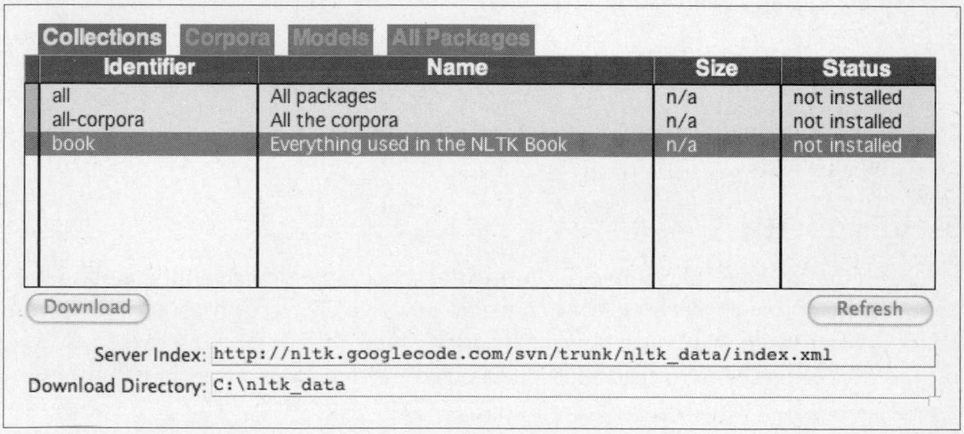

Figure 1-1. Downloading the NLTK Book Collection: Browse the available packages using nltk.download(). *The **Collections** tab on the downloader shows how the packages are grouped into sets, and you should select the line labeled **book** to obtain all data required for the examples and exercises in this book. It consists of about 30 compressed files requiring about 100Mb disk space. The full collection of data (i.e., **all** in the downloader) is about five times this size (at the time of writing) and continues to expand.*

Once the data is downloaded to your machine, you can load some of it using the Python interpreter. The first step is to type a special command at the Python prompt, which tells the interpreter to load some texts for us to explore: `from nltk.book import *`. This says "from NLTK's book module, load all items." The book module contains all the data you will need as you read this chapter. After printing a welcome message, it loads the text of several books (this will take a few seconds). Here's the command again, together with the output that you will see. Take care to get spelling and punctuation right, and remember that you don't type the >>>.

```
>>> from nltk.book import *
*** Introductory Examples for the NLTK Book ***
Loading text1, ..., text9 and sent1, ..., sent9
Type the name of the text or sentence to view it.
Type: 'texts()' or 'sents()' to list the materials.
text1: Moby Dick by Herman Melville 1851
text2: Sense and Sensibility by Jane Austen 1811
text3: The Book of Genesis
text4: Inaugural Address Corpus
text5: Chat Corpus
text6: Monty Python and the Holy Grail
text7: Wall Street Journal
text8: Personals Corpus
text9: The Man Who Was Thursday by G . K . Chesterton 1908
>>>
```

Any time we want to find out about these texts, we just have to enter their names at the Python prompt:

```
>>> text1
<Text: Moby Dick by Herman Melville 1851>
>>> text2
<Text: Sense and Sensibility by Jane Austen 1811>
>>>
```

Now that we can use the Python interpreter, and have some data to work with, we're ready to get started.

Searching Text

There are many ways to examine the context of a text apart from simply reading it. A concordance view shows us every occurrence of a given word, together with some context. Here we look up the word *monstrous* in *Moby Dick* by entering `text1` followed by a period, then the term `concordance`, and then placing `"monstrous"` in parentheses:

```
>>> text1.concordance("monstrous")
Building index...
Displaying 11 of 11 matches:
ong the former , one was of a most monstrous size . ... This came towards us ,
ON OF THE PSALMS . " Touching that monstrous bulk of the whale or ork we have r
ll over with a heathenish array of monstrous clubs and spears . Some were thick
d as you gazed , and wondered what monstrous cannibal and savage could ever hav
that has survived the flood ; most monstrous and most mountainous ! That Himmal
they might scout at Moby Dick as a monstrous fable , or still worse and more de
th of Radney .'" CHAPTER 55 Of the monstrous Pictures of Whales . I shall ere l
ing Scenes . In connexion with the monstrous pictures of whales , I am strongly
ere to enter upon those still more monstrous stories of them which are to be fo
```

```
ght have been rummaged out of this monstrous cabinet there is no telling . But
of Whale - Bones ; for Whales of a monstrous size are oftentimes cast up dead u
>>>
```

 Your Turn: Try searching for other words; to save re-typing, you might be able to use up-arrow, Ctrl-up-arrow, or Alt-p to access the previous command and modify the word being searched. You can also try searches on some of the other texts we have included. For example, search *Sense and Sensibility* for the word *affection*, using `text2.concord ance("affection")`. Search the book of Genesis to find out how long some people lived, using: `text3.concordance("lived")`. You could look at `text4`, the *Inaugural Address Corpus*, to see examples of English going back to 1789, and search for words like *nation*, *terror*, *god* to see how these words have been used differently over time. We've also included `text5`, the *NPS Chat Corpus*: search this for unconventional words like *im*, *ur*, *lol*. (Note that this corpus is uncensored!)

Once you've spent a little while examining these texts, we hope you have a new sense of the richness and diversity of language. In the next chapter you will learn how to access a broader range of text, including text in languages other than English.

A concordance permits us to see words in context. For example, we saw that *monstrous* occurred in contexts such as *the ___ pictures* and *the ___ size*. What other words appear in a similar range of contexts? We can find out by appending the term `similar` to the name of the text in question, then inserting the relevant word in parentheses:

```
>>> text1.similar("monstrous")
Building word-context index...
subtly impalpable pitiable curious imperial perilous trustworthy
abundant untoward singular lamentable few maddens horrible loving lazy
mystifying christian exasperate puzzled
>>> text2.similar("monstrous")
Building word-context index...
very exceedingly so heartily a great good amazingly as sweet
remarkably extremely vast
>>>
```

Observe that we get different results for different texts. Austen uses this word quite differently from Melville; for her, *monstrous* has positive connotations, and sometimes functions as an intensifier like the word *very*.

The term `common_contexts` allows us to examine just the contexts that are shared by two or more words, such as *monstrous* and *very*. We have to enclose these words by square brackets as well as parentheses, and separate them with a comma:

```
>>> text2.common_contexts(["monstrous", "very"])
be_glad am_glad a_pretty is_pretty a_lucky
>>>
```

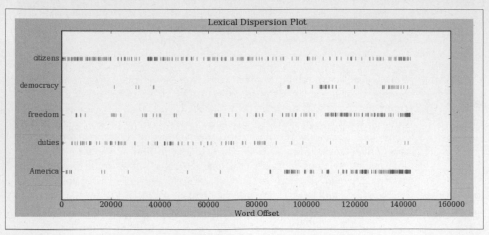

Figure 1-2. Lexical dispersion plot for words in U.S. Presidential Inaugural Addresses: This can be used to investigate changes in language use over time.

Your Turn: Pick another pair of words and compare their usage in two different texts, using the `similar()` and `common_contexts()` functions.

It is one thing to automatically detect that a particular word occurs in a text, and to display some words that appear in the same context. However, we can also determine the *location* of a word in the text: how many words from the beginning it appears. This positional information can be displayed using a **dispersion plot**. Each stripe represents an instance of a word, and each row represents the entire text. In Figure 1-2 we see some striking patterns of word usage over the last 220 years (in an artificial text constructed by joining the texts of the Inaugural Address Corpus end-to-end). You can produce this plot as shown below. You might like to try more words (e.g., *liberty*, *constitution*) and different texts. Can you predict the dispersion of a word before you view it? As before, take care to get the quotes, commas, brackets, and parentheses exactly right.

```
>>> text4.dispersion_plot(["citizens", "democracy", "freedom", "duties", "America"])
>>>
```

Important: You need to have Python's NumPy and Matplotlib packages installed in order to produce the graphical plots used in this book. Please see *http://www.nltk.org/* for installation instructions.

Now, just for fun, let's try generating some random text in the various styles we have just seen. To do this, we type the name of the text followed by the term `generate`. (We need to include the parentheses, but there's nothing that goes between them.)

```
>>> text3.generate()
In the beginning of his brother is a hairy man , whose top may reach
unto heaven ; and ye shall sow the land of Egypt there was no bread in
all that he was taken out of the month , upon the earth . So shall thy
wages be ? And they made their father ; and Isaac was old , and kissed
him : and Laban with his cattle in the midst of the hands of Esau thy
first born , and Phichol the chief butler unto his son Isaac , she
>>>
```

Note that the first time you run this command, it is slow because it gathers statistics about word sequences. Each time you run it, you will get different output text. Now try generating random text in the style of an inaugural address or an Internet chat room. Although the text is random, it reuses common words and phrases from the source text and gives us a sense of its style and content. (What is lacking in this randomly generated text?)

 When `generate` produces its output, punctuation is split off from the preceding word. While this is not correct formatting for English text, we do it to make clear that words and punctuation are independent of one another. You will learn more about this in Chapter 3.

Counting Vocabulary

The most obvious fact about texts that emerges from the preceding examples is that they differ in the vocabulary they use. In this section, we will see how to use the computer to count the words in a text in a variety of useful ways. As before, you will jump right in and experiment with the Python interpreter, even though you may not have studied Python systematically yet. Test your understanding by modifying the examples, and trying the exercises at the end of the chapter.

Let's begin by finding out the length of a text from start to finish, in terms of the words and punctuation symbols that appear. We use the term `len` to get the length of something, which we'll apply here to the book of Genesis:

```
>>> len(text3)
44764
>>>
```

So Genesis has 44,764 words and punctuation symbols, or "tokens." A **token** is the technical name for a sequence of characters—such as `hairy`, `his`, or `:)`—that we want to treat as a group. When we count the number of tokens in a text, say, the phrase *to be or not to be*, we are counting occurrences of these sequences. Thus, in our example phrase there are two occurrences of *to*, two of *be*, and one each of *or* and *not*. But there are only four distinct vocabulary items in this phrase. How many distinct words does the book of Genesis contain? To work this out in Python, we have to pose the question slightly differently. The vocabulary of a text is just the *set* of tokens that it uses, since in a set, all duplicates are collapsed together. In Python we can obtain the vocabulary items of `text3` with the command: `set(text3)`. When you do this, many screens of words will fly past. Now try the following:

```
>>> sorted(set(text3)) ❶
['!', "'", '(', ')', ',', ',)', '.', '.)', ':', ';', ';)', '?', '?)',
'A', 'Abel', 'Abelmizraim', 'Abidah', 'Abide', 'Abimael', 'Abimelech',
'Abr', 'Abrah', 'Abraham', 'Abram', 'Accad', 'Achbor', 'Adah', ...]
>>> len(set(text3)) ❷
2789
>>>
```

By wrapping `sorted()` around the Python expression `set(text3)` ❶, we obtain a sorted list of vocabulary items, beginning with various punctuation symbols and continuing with words starting with *A*. All capitalized words precede lowercase words. We discover the size of the vocabulary indirectly, by asking for the number of items in the set, and again we can use `len` to obtain this number ❷. Although it has 44,764 tokens, this book has only 2,789 distinct words, or "word types." A **word type** is the form or spelling of the word independently of its specific occurrences in a text—that is, the word considered as a unique item of vocabulary. Our count of 2,789 items will include punctuation symbols, so we will generally call these unique items **types** instead of word types.

Now, let's calculate a measure of the lexical richness of the text. The next example shows us that each word is used 16 times on average (we need to make sure Python uses floating-point division):

```
>>> from __future__ import division
>>> len(text3) / len(set(text3))
16.050197203298673
>>>
```

Next, let's focus on particular words. We can count how often a word occurs in a text, and compute what percentage of the text is taken up by a specific word:

```
>>> text3.count("smote")
5
>>> 100 * text4.count('a') / len(text4)
1.4643016433938312
>>>
```

 Your Turn: How many times does the word *lol* appear in `text5`? How much is this as a percentage of the total number of words in this text?

You may want to repeat such calculations on several texts, but it is tedious to keep retyping the formula. Instead, you can come up with your own name for a task, like "lexical_diversity" or "percentage", and associate it with a block of code. Now you only have to type a short name instead of one or more complete lines of Python code, and you can reuse it as often as you like. The block of code that does a task for us is called a **function**, and we define a short name for our function with the keyword `def`. The next example shows how to define two new functions, `lexical_diversity()` and `percentage()`:

```
>>> def lexical_diversity(text): ❶
...     return len(text) / len(set(text)) ❷
...
>>> def percentage(count, total): ❸
...     return 100 * count / total
...
```

Caution!

The Python interpreter changes the prompt from `>>>` to `...` after encountering the colon at the end of the first line. The `...` prompt indicates that Python expects an **indented code block** to appear next. It is up to you to do the indentation, by typing four spaces or hitting the Tab key. To finish the indented block, just enter a blank line.

In the definition of `lexical diversity()` ❶, we specify a **parameter** labeled `text`. This parameter is a "placeholder" for the actual text whose lexical diversity we want to compute, and reoccurs in the block of code that will run when the function is used, in line ❷. Similarly, `percentage()` is defined to take two parameters, labeled `count` and `total` ❸.

Once Python knows that `lexical_diversity()` and `percentage()` are the names for specific blocks of code, we can go ahead and use these functions:

```
>>> lexical_diversity(text3)
16.050197203298673
>>> lexical_diversity(text5)
7.4200461589185629
>>> percentage(4, 5)
80.0
>>> percentage(text4.count('a'), len(text4))
1.4643016433938312
>>>
```

To recap, we use or **call** a function such as `lexical_diversity()` by typing its name, followed by an open parenthesis, the name of the text, and then a close parenthesis. These parentheses will show up often; their role is to separate the name of a task—such as `lexical_diversity()`—from the data that the task is to be performed on—such as `text3`. The data value that we place in the parentheses when we call a function is an **argument** to the function.

You have already encountered several functions in this chapter, such as `len()`, `set()`, and `sorted()`. By convention, we will always add an empty pair of parentheses after a function name, as in `len()`, just to make clear that what we are talking about is a function rather than some other kind of Python expression. Functions are an important concept in programming, and we only mention them at the outset to give newcomers a sense of the power and creativity of programming. Don't worry if you find it a bit confusing right now.

Later we'll see how to use functions when tabulating data, as in Table 1-1. Each row of the table will involve the same computation but with different data, and we'll do this repetitive work using a function.

Table 1-1. Lexical diversity of various genres in the Brown Corpus

Genre	Tokens	Types	Lexical diversity
skill and hobbies	82345	11935	6.9
humor	21695	5017	4.3
fiction: science	14470	3233	4.5
press: reportage	100554	14394	7.0
fiction: romance	70022	8452	8.3
religion	39399	6373	6.2

1.2 A Closer Look at Python: Texts as Lists of Words

You've seen some important elements of the Python programming language. Let's take a few moments to review them systematically.

Lists

What is a text? At one level, it is a sequence of symbols on a page such as this one. At another level, it is a sequence of chapters, made up of a sequence of sections, where each section is a sequence of paragraphs, and so on. However, for our purposes, we will think of a text as nothing more than a sequence of words and punctuation. Here's how we represent text in Python, in this case the opening sentence of *Moby Dick*:

```
>>> sent1 = ['Call', 'me', 'Ishmael', '.']
>>>
```

After the prompt we've given a name we made up, sent1, followed by the equals sign, and then some quoted words, separated with commas, and surrounded with brackets. This bracketed material is known as a **list** in Python: it is how we store a text. We can inspect it by typing the name ❶. We can ask for its length ❷. We can even apply our own lexical_diversity() function to it ❸.

```
>>> sent1 ❶
['Call', 'me', 'Ishmael', '.']
>>> len(sent1) ❷
4
>>> lexical_diversity(sent1) ❸
1.0
>>>
```

Some more lists have been defined for you, one for the opening sentence of each of our texts, `sent2` ... `sent9`. We inspect two of them here; you can see the rest for yourself using the Python interpreter (if you get an error saying that `sent2` is not defined, you need to first type `from nltk.book import *`).

```
>>> sent2
['The', 'family', 'of', 'Dashwood', 'had', 'long',
'been', 'settled', 'in', 'Sussex', '.']
>>> sent3
['In', 'the', 'beginning', 'God', 'created', 'the',
'heaven', 'and', 'the', 'earth', '.']
>>>
```

 Your Turn: Make up a few sentences of your own, by typing a name, equals sign, and a list of words, like this: ex1 = ['Monty', 'Python', 'and', 'the', 'Holy', 'Grail']. Repeat some of the other Python operations we saw earlier in Section 1.1, e.g., sorted(ex1), len(set(ex1)), ex1.count('the').

A pleasant surprise is that we can use Python's addition operator on lists. Adding two lists ❶ creates a new list with everything from the first list, followed by everything from the second list:

```
>>> ['Monty', 'Python'] + ['and', 'the', 'Holy', 'Grail'] ❶
['Monty', 'Python', 'and', 'the', 'Holy', 'Grail']
```

 This special use of the addition operation is called **concatenation**; it combines the lists together into a single list. We can concatenate sentences to build up a text.

We don't have to literally type the lists either; we can use short names that refer to predefined lists.

```
>>> sent4 + sent1
['Fellow', '-', 'Citizens', 'of', 'the', 'Senate', 'and', 'of', 'the',
'House', 'of', 'Representatives', ':', 'Call', 'me', 'Ishmael', '.']
>>>
```

What if we want to add a single item to a list? This is known as **appending**. When we append() to a list, the list itself is updated as a result of the operation.

```
>>> sent1.append("Some")
>>> sent1
['Call', 'me', 'Ishmael', '.', 'Some']
>>>
```

Indexing Lists

As we have seen, a text in Python is a list of words, represented using a combination of brackets and quotes. Just as with an ordinary page of text, we can count up the total number of words in text1 with len(text1), and count the occurrences in a text of a particular word—say, *heaven*—using text1.count('heaven').

With some patience, we can pick out the 1st, 173rd, or even 14,278th word in a printed text. Analogously, we can identify the elements of a Python list by their order of occurrence in the list. The number that represents this position is the item's **index**. We instruct Python to show us the item that occurs at an index such as 173 in a text by writing the name of the text followed by the index inside square brackets:

```
>>> text4[173]
'awaken'
>>>
```

We can do the converse; given a word, find the index of when it first occurs:

```
>>> text4.index('awaken')
173
>>>
```

Indexes are a common way to access the words of a text, or, more generally, the elements of any list. Python permits us to access sublists as well, extracting manageable pieces of language from large texts, a technique known as **slicing**.

```
>>> text5[16715:16735]
['U86', 'thats', 'why', 'something', 'like', 'gamefly', 'is', 'so', 'good',
'because', 'you', 'can', 'actually', 'play', 'a', 'full', 'game', 'without',
'buying', 'it']
>>> text6[1600:1625]
['We', "'", 're', 'an', 'anarcho', '-', 'syndicalist', 'commune', '.', 'We',
'take', 'it', 'in', 'turns', 'to', 'act', 'as', 'a', 'sort', 'of', 'executive',
'officer', 'for', 'the', 'week']
>>>
```

Indexes have some subtleties, and we'll explore these with the help of an artificial sentence:

```
>>> sent = ['word1', 'word2', 'word3', 'word4', 'word5',
...          'word6', 'word7', 'word8', 'word9', 'word10']
>>> sent[0]
'word1'
>>> sent[9]
'word10'
>>>
```

Notice that our indexes start from zero: sent element zero, written sent[0], is the first word, 'word1', whereas sent element 9 is 'word10'. The reason is simple: the moment Python accesses the content of a list from the computer's memory, it is already at the first element; we have to tell it how many elements forward to go. Thus, zero steps forward leaves it at the first element.

This practice of counting from zero is initially confusing, but typical of modern programming languages. You'll quickly get the hang of it if you've mastered the system of counting centuries where 19XY is a year in the 20th century, or if you live in a country where the floors of a building are numbered from 1, and so walking up *n-1* flights of stairs takes you to level *n*.

Now, if we accidentally use an index that is too large, we get an error:

```
>>> sent[10]
Traceback (most recent call last):
  File "<stdin>", line 1, in ?
IndexError: list index out of range
>>>
```

This time it is not a syntax error, because the program fragment is syntactically correct. Instead, it is a **runtime error**, and it produces a Traceback message that shows the context of the error, followed by the name of the error, IndexError, and a brief explanation.

Let's take a closer look at slicing, using our artificial sentence again. Here we verify that the slice 5:8 includes sent elements at indexes 5, 6, and 7:

```
>>> sent[5:8]
['word6', 'word7', 'word8']
>>> sent[5]
'word6'
>>> sent[6]
'word7'
>>> sent[7]
'word8'
>>>
```

By convention, m:n means elements *m...n-1*. As the next example shows, we can omit the first number if the slice begins at the start of the list ❶, and we can omit the second number if the slice goes to the end ❷:

```
>>> sent[:3] ❶
['word1', 'word2', 'word3']
>>> text2[141525:] ❷
['among', 'the', 'merits', 'and', 'the', 'happiness', 'of', 'Elinor', 'and', 'Marianne',
',', 'let', 'it', 'not', 'be', 'ranked', 'as', 'the', 'least', 'considerable', ',',
'that', 'though', 'sisters', ',', 'and', 'living', 'almost', 'within', 'sight', 'of',
'each', 'other', ',', 'they', 'could', 'live', 'without', 'disagreement', 'between',
'themselves', ',', 'or', 'producing', 'coolness', 'between', 'their', 'husbands', '.',
'THE', 'END']
>>>
```

We can modify an element of a list by assigning to one of its index values. In the next example, we put sent[0] on the left of the equals sign ❶. We can also replace an entire slice with new material ❷. A consequence of this last change is that the list only has four elements, and accessing a later value generates an error ❸.

```
>>> sent[0] = 'First'  ❶
>>> sent[9] = 'Last'
>>> len(sent)
10
>>> sent[1:9] = ['Second', 'Third']  ❷
>>> sent
['First', 'Second', 'Third', 'Last']
>>> sent[9]  ❸
Traceback (most recent call last):
  File "<stdin>", line 1, in ?
IndexError: list index out of range
>>>
```

 Your Turn: Take a few minutes to define a sentence of your own and modify individual words and groups of words (slices) using the same methods used earlier. Check your understanding by trying the exercises on lists at the end of this chapter.

Variables

From the start of Section 1.1, you have had access to texts called text1, text2, and so on. It saved a lot of typing to be able to refer to a 250,000-word book with a short name like this! In general, we can make up names for anything we care to calculate. We did this ourselves in the previous sections, e.g., defining a **variable** sent1, as follows:

```
>>> sent1 = ['Call', 'me', 'Ishmael', '.']
>>>
```

Such lines have the form: *variable = expression*. Python will evaluate the expression, and save its result to the variable. This process is called **assignment**. It does not generate any output; you have to type the variable on a line of its own to inspect its contents. The equals sign is slightly misleading, since information is moving from the right side to the left. It might help to think of it as a left-arrow. The name of the variable can be anything you like, e.g., my_sent, sentence, xyzzy. It must start with a letter, and can include numbers and underscores. Here are some examples of variables and assignments:

```
>>> my_sent = ['Bravely', 'bold', 'Sir', 'Robin', ',', 'rode',
... 'forth', 'from', 'Camelot', '.']
>>> noun_phrase = my_sent[1:4]
>>> noun_phrase
['bold', 'Sir', 'Robin']
>>> wOrDs = sorted(noun_phrase)
>>> wOrDs
['Robin', 'Sir', 'bold']
>>>
```

Remember that capitalized words appear before lowercase words in sorted lists.

Notice in the previous example that we split the definition of `my_sent` over two lines. Python expressions can be split across multiple lines, so long as this happens within any kind of brackets. Python uses the `...` prompt to indicate that more input is expected. It doesn't matter how much indentation is used in these continuation lines, but some indentation usually makes them easier to read.

It is good to choose meaningful variable names to remind you—and to help anyone else who reads your Python code—what your code is meant to do. Python does not try to make sense of the names; it blindly follows your instructions, and does not object if you do something confusing, such as `one = 'two'` or `two = 3`. The only restriction is that a variable name cannot be any of Python's reserved words, such as `def`, `if`, `not`, and `import`. If you use a reserved word, Python will produce a syntax error:

```
>>> not = 'Camelot'
File "<stdin>", line 1
    not = 'Camelot'
        ^
SyntaxError: invalid syntax
>>>
```

We will often use variables to hold intermediate steps of a computation, especially when this makes the code easier to follow. Thus `len(set(text1))` could also be written:

```
>>> vocab = set(text1)
>>> vocab_size = len(vocab)
>>> vocab_size
19317
>>>
```

 Caution!

Take care with your choice of names (or **identifiers**) for Python variables. First, you should start the name with a letter, optionally followed by digits (`0` to `9`) or letters. Thus, `abc23` is fine, but `23abc` will cause a syntax error. Names are case-sensitive, which means that `myVar` and `myvar` are distinct variables. Variable names cannot contain whitespace, but you can separate words using an underscore, e.g., `my_var`. Be careful not to insert a hyphen instead of an underscore: `my-var` is wrong, since Python interprets the `-` as a minus sign.

Strings

Some of the methods we used to access the elements of a list also work with individual words, or **strings**. For example, we can assign a string to a variable ❶, index a string ❷, and slice a string ❸.

```
>>> name = 'Monty'  ❶
>>> name[0]  ❷
'M'
>>> name[:4]  ❸
'Mont'
>>>
```

We can also perform multiplication and addition with strings:

```
>>> name * 2
'MontyMonty'
>>> name + '!'
'Monty!'
>>>
```

We can join the words of a list to make a single string, or split a string into a list, as follows:

```
>>> ' '.join(['Monty', 'Python'])
'Monty Python'
>>> 'Monty Python'.split()
['Monty', 'Python']
>>>
```

We will come back to the topic of strings in Chapter 3. For the time being, we have two important building blocks—lists and strings—and are ready to get back to some language analysis.

1.3 Computing with Language: Simple Statistics

Let's return to our exploration of the ways we can bring our computational resources to bear on large quantities of text. We began this discussion in Section 1.1, and saw how to search for words in context, how to compile the vocabulary of a text, how to generate random text in the same style, and so on.

In this section, we pick up the question of what makes a text distinct, and use automatic methods to find characteristic words and expressions of a text. As in Section 1.1, you can try new features of the Python language by copying them into the interpreter, and you'll learn about these features systematically in the following section.

Before continuing further, you might like to check your understanding of the last section by predicting the output of the following code. You can use the interpreter to check whether you got it right. If you're not sure how to do this task, it would be a good idea to review the previous section before continuing further.

```
>>> saying = ['After', 'all', 'is', 'said', 'and', 'done',
...           'more', 'is', 'said', 'than', 'done']
>>> tokens = set(saying)
>>> tokens = sorted(tokens)
>>> tokens[-2:]
what output do you expect here?
>>>
```

Frequency Distributions

How can we automatically identify the words of a text that are most informative about the topic and genre of the text? Imagine how you might go about finding the 50 most frequent words of a book. One method would be to keep a tally for each vocabulary item, like that shown in Figure 1-3. The tally would need thousands of rows, and it would be an exceedingly laborious process—so laborious that we would rather assign the task to a machine.

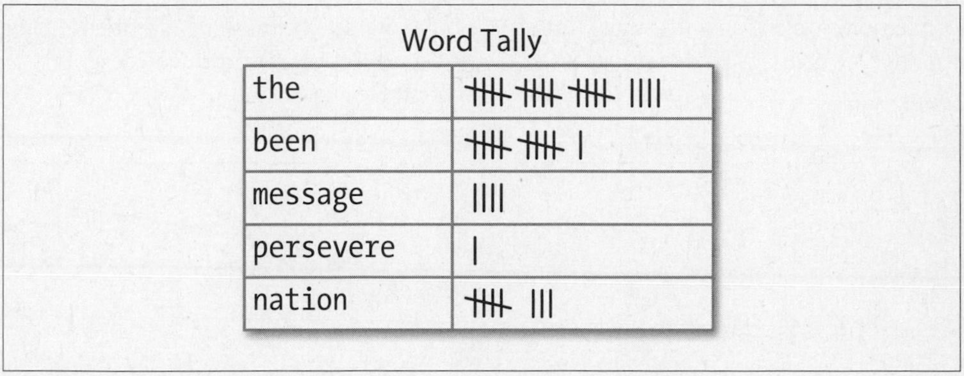

Word Tally	
the	︙︙︙︙ ︙︙︙︙ ︙︙︙︙ ‖‖
been	︙︙︙︙ ︙︙︙︙ ╎
message	‖‖
persevere	╎
nation	︙︙︙︙ ‖╎

Figure 1-3. Counting words appearing in a text (a frequency distribution).

The table in Figure 1-3 is known as a **frequency distribution** , and it tells us the frequency of each vocabulary item in the text. (In general, it could count any kind of observable event.) It is a "distribution" since it tells us how the total number of word tokens in the text are distributed across the vocabulary items. Since we often need frequency distributions in language processing, NLTK provides built-in support for them. Let's use a `FreqDist` to find the 50 most frequent words of *Moby Dick*. Try to work out what is going on here, then read the explanation that follows.

```
>>> fdist1 = FreqDist(text1) ❶
>>> fdist1 ❷
<FreqDist with 260819 outcomes>
>>> vocabulary1 = fdist1.keys() ❸
>>> vocabulary1[:50] ❹
[',', 'the', '.', 'of', 'and', 'a', 'to', ';', 'in', 'that', "'", '-',
'his', 'it', 'I', 's', 'is', 'he', 'with', 'was', 'as', '"', 'all', 'for',
'this', '!', 'at', 'by', 'but', 'not', '--', 'him', 'from', 'be', 'on',
'so', 'whale', 'one', 'you', 'had', 'have', 'there', 'But', 'or', 'were',
'now', 'which', '?', 'me', 'like']
>>> fdist1['whale']
906
>>>
```

When we first invoke `FreqDist`, we pass the name of the text as an argument ❶. We can inspect the total number of words ("outcomes") that have been counted up ❷ — 260,819 in the case of *Moby Dick*. The expression `keys()` gives us a list of all the distinct types in the text ❸, and we can look at the first 50 of these by slicing the list ❹.

Your Turn: Try the preceding frequency distribution example for your-self, for `text2`. Be careful to use the correct parentheses and uppercase letters. If you get an error message `NameError: name 'FreqDist' is not defined`, you need to start your work with `from nltk.book import *`.

Do any words produced in the last example help us grasp the topic or genre of this text? Only one word, *whale*, is slightly informative! It occurs over 900 times. The rest of the words tell us nothing about the text; they're just English "plumbing." What proportion of the text is taken up with such words? We can generate a cumulative frequency plot for these words, using `fdist1.plot(50, cumulative=True)`, to produce the graph in Figure 1-4. These 50 words account for nearly half the book!

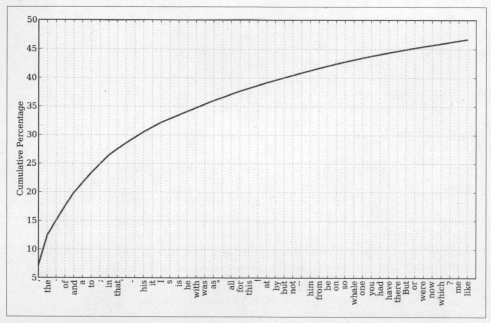

Figure 1-4. Cumulative frequency plot for the 50 most frequently used words in Moby Dick, *which account for nearly half of the tokens.*

If the frequent words don't help us, how about the words that occur once only, the so-called **hapaxes**? View them by typing `fdist1.hapaxes()`. This list contains *lexicographer*, *cetological*, *contraband*, *expostulations*, and about 9,000 others. It seems that there are too many rare words, and without seeing the context we probably can't guess what half of the hapaxes mean in any case! Since neither frequent nor infrequent words help, we need to try something else.

Fine-Grained Selection of Words

Next, let's look at the *long* words of a text; perhaps these will be more characteristic and informative. For this we adapt some notation from set theory. We would like to find the words from the vocabulary of the text that are more than 15 characters long. Let's call this property P, so that $P(w)$ is true if and only if w is more than 15 characters long. Now we can express the words of interest using mathematical set notation as shown in (1a). This means "the set of all w such that w is an element of V (the vocabulary) and w has property P."

(1)   a. $\{w \mid w \in V \,\&\, P(w)\}$

       b. `[w for w in V if p(w)]`

The corresponding Python expression is given in (1b). (Note that it produces a list, not a set, which means that duplicates are possible.) Observe how similar the two notations are. Let's go one more step and write executable Python code:

```
>>> V = set(text1)
>>> long_words = [w for w in V if len(w) > 15]
>>> sorted(long_words)
['CIRCUMNAVIGATION', 'Physiognomically', 'apprehensiveness', 'cannibalistically',
'characteristically', 'circumnavigating', 'circumnavigation', 'circumnavigations',
'comprehensiveness', 'hermaphroditical', 'indiscriminately', 'indispensableness',
'irresistibleness', 'physiognomically', 'preternaturalness', 'responsibilities',
'simultaneousness', 'subterraneousness', 'supernaturalness', 'superstitiousness',
'uncomfortableness', 'uncompromisedness', 'undiscriminating', 'uninterpenetratingly']
>>>
```

For each word `w` in the vocabulary `V`, we check whether `len(w)` is greater than 15; all other words will be ignored. We will discuss this syntax more carefully later.

Your Turn: Try out the previous statements in the Python interpreter, and experiment with changing the text and changing the length condition. Does it make an difference to your results if you change the variable names, e.g., using `[word for word in vocab if ...]`?

Let's return to our task of finding words that characterize a text. Notice that the long words in `text4` reflect its national focus—*constitutionally*, *transcontinental*—whereas those in `text5` reflect its informal content: *booooooooooooglyyyyyy* and *yuuuuuuuuuuuuummmmmmmmmmmmm*. Have we succeeded in automatically extracting words that typify a text? Well, these very long words are often hapaxes (i.e., unique) and perhaps it would be better to find *frequently occurring* long words. This seems promising since it eliminates frequent short words (e.g., *the*) and infrequent long words (e.g., *antiphilosophists*). Here are all words from the chat corpus that are longer than seven characters, that occur more than seven times:

```
>>> fdist5 = FreqDist(text5)
>>> sorted([w for w in set(text5) if len(w) > 7 and fdist5[w] > 7])
['#14-19teens', '#talkcity_adults', '((((((((((((', '........', 'Question',
'actually', 'anything', 'computer', 'cute.-ass', 'everyone', 'football',
'innocent', 'listening', 'remember', 'seriously', 'something', 'together',
'tomorrow', 'watching']
>>>
```

Notice how we have used two conditions: `len(w) > 7` ensures that the words are longer than seven letters, and `fdist5[w] > 7` ensures that these words occur more than seven times. At last we have managed to automatically identify the frequently occurring content-bearing words of the text. It is a modest but important milestone: a tiny piece of code, processing tens of thousands of words, produces some informative output.

Collocations and Bigrams

A **collocation** is a sequence of words that occur together unusually often. Thus *red wine* is a collocation, whereas *the wine* is not. A characteristic of collocations is that they are resistant to substitution with words that have similar senses; for example, *maroon wine* sounds very odd.

To get a handle on collocations, we start off by extracting from a text a list of word pairs, also known as **bigrams**. This is easily accomplished with the function `bigrams()`:

```
>>> bigrams(['more', 'is', 'said', 'than', 'done'])
[('more', 'is'), ('is', 'said'), ('said', 'than'), ('than', 'done')]
>>>
```

Here we see that the pair of words *than-done* is a bigram, and we write it in Python as `('than', 'done')`. Now, collocations are essentially just frequent bigrams, except that we want to pay more attention to the cases that involve rare words. In particular, we want to find bigrams that occur more often than we would expect based on the frequency of individual words. The `collocations()` function does this for us (we will see how it works later):

```
>>> text4.collocations()
Building collocations list
United States; fellow citizens; years ago; Federal Government; General
Government; American people; Vice President; Almighty God; Fellow
citizens; Chief Magistrate; Chief Justice; God bless; Indian tribes;
public debt; foreign nations; political parties; State governments;
```

```
National Government; United Nations; public money
>>> text8.collocations()
Building collocations list
medium build; social drinker; quiet nights; long term; age open;
financially secure; fun times; similar interests; Age open; poss
rship; single mum; permanent relationship; slim build; seeks lady;
Late 30s; Photo pls; Vibrant personality; European background; ASIAN
LADY; country drives
>>>
```

The collocations that emerge are very specific to the genre of the texts. In order to find *red wine* as a collocation, we would need to process a much larger body of text.

Counting Other Things

Counting words is useful, but we can count other things too. For example, we can look at the distribution of word lengths in a text, by creating a `FreqDist` out of a long list of numbers, where each number is the length of the corresponding word in the text:

```
>>> [len(w) for w in text1] ❶
[1, 4, 4, 2, 6, 8, 4, 1, 9, 1, 1, 8, 2, 1, 4, 11, 5, 2, 1, 7, 6, 1, 3, 4, 5, 2, ...]
>>> fdist = FreqDist([len(w) for w in text1]) ❷
>>> fdist ❸
<FreqDist with 260819 outcomes>
>>> fdist.keys()
[3, 1, 4, 2, 5, 6, 7, 8, 9, 10, 11, 12, 13, 14, 15, 16, 17, 18, 20]
>>>
```

We start by deriving a list of the lengths of words in `text1` ❶, and the `FreqDist` then counts the number of times each of these occurs ❷. The result ❸ is a distribution containing a quarter of a million items, each of which is a number corresponding to a word token in the text. But there are only 20 distinct items being counted, the numbers 1 through 20, because there are only 20 different word lengths. I.e., there are words consisting of just 1 character, 2 characters, ..., 20 characters, but none with 21 or more characters. One might wonder how frequent the different lengths of words are (e.g., how many words of length 4 appear in the text, are there more words of length 5 than length 4, etc.). We can do this as follows:

```
>>> fdist.items()
[(3, 50223), (1, 47933), (4, 42345), (2, 38513), (5, 26597), (6, 17111), (7, 14399),
(8, 9966), (9, 6428), (10, 3528), (11, 1873), (12, 1053), (13, 567), (14, 177),
(15, 70), (16, 22), (17, 12), (18, 1), (20, 1)]
>>> fdist.max()
3
>>> fdist[3]
50223
>>> fdist.freq(3)
0.19255882431878046
>>>
```

From this we see that the most frequent word length is 3, and that words of length 3 account for roughly 50,000 (or 20%) of the words making up the book. Although we will not pursue it here, further analysis of word length might help us understand differences between authors, genres, or languages. Table 1-2 summarizes the functions defined in frequency distributions.

Table 1-2. Functions defined for NLTK's frequency distributions

Example	Description
`fdist = FreqDist(samples)`	Create a frequency distribution containing the given samples
`fdist.inc(sample)`	Increment the count for this sample
`fdist['monstrous']`	Count of the number of times a given sample occurred
`fdist.freq('monstrous')`	Frequency of a given sample
`fdist.N()`	Total number of samples
`fdist.keys()`	The samples sorted in order of decreasing frequency
`for sample in fdist:`	Iterate over the samples, in order of decreasing frequency
`fdist.max()`	Sample with the greatest count
`fdist.tabulate()`	Tabulate the frequency distribution
`fdist.plot()`	Graphical plot of the frequency distribution
`fdist.plot(cumulative=True)`	Cumulative plot of the frequency distribution
`fdist1 < fdist2`	Test if samples in `fdist1` occur less frequently than in `fdist2`

Our discussion of frequency distributions has introduced some important Python concepts, and we will look at them systematically in Section 1.4.

1.4 Back to Python: Making Decisions and Taking Control

So far, our little programs have had some interesting qualities: the ability to work with language, and the potential to save human effort through automation. A key feature of programming is the ability of machines to make decisions on our behalf, executing instructions when certain conditions are met, or repeatedly looping through text data until some condition is satisfied. This feature is known as **control**, and is the focus of this section.

Conditionals

Python supports a wide range of operators, such as < and >=, for testing the relationship between values. The full set of these **relational operators** are shown in Table 1-3.

Table 1-3. Numerical comparison operators

Operator	Relationship
<	Less than
<=	Less than or equal to
==	Equal to (note this is two "="signs, not one)

Operator	Relationship
!=	Not equal to
>	Greater than
>=	Greater than or equal to

We can use these to select different words from a sentence of news text. Here are some examples—notice only the operator is changed from one line to the next. They all use `sent7`, the first sentence from `text7` (*Wall Street Journal*). As before, if you get an error saying that `sent7` is undefined, you need to first type: `from nltk.book import *`.

```
>>> sent7
['Pierre', 'Vinken', ',', '61', 'years', 'old', ',', 'will', 'join', 'the',
'board', 'as', 'a', 'nonexecutive', 'director', 'Nov.', '29', '.']
>>> [w for w in sent7 if len(w) < 4]
[',', '61', 'old', ',', 'the', 'as', 'a', '29', '.']
>>> [w for w in sent7 if len(w) <= 4]
[',', '61', 'old', ',', 'will', 'join', 'the', 'as', 'a', 'Nov.', '29', '.']
>>> [w for w in sent7 if len(w) == 4]
['will', 'join', 'Nov.']
>>> [w for w in sent7 if len(w) != 4]
['Pierre', 'Vinken', ',', '61', 'years', 'old', ',', 'the', 'board',
'as', 'a', 'nonexecutive', 'director', '29', '.']
>>>
```

There is a common pattern to all of these examples: `[w for w in text if condition]`, where *condition* is a Python "test" that yields either true or false. In the cases shown in the previous code example, the condition is always a numerical comparison. However, we can also test various properties of words, using the functions listed in Table 1-4.

Table 1-4. Some word comparison operators

Function	Meaning
s.startswith(t)	Test if s starts with t
s.endswith(t)	Test if s ends with t
t in s	Test if t is contained inside s
s.islower()	Test if all cased characters in s are lowercase
s.isupper()	Test if all cased characters in s are uppercase
s.isalpha()	Test if all characters in s are alphabetic
s.isalnum()	Test if all characters in s are alphanumeric
s.isdigit()	Test if all characters in s are digits
s.istitle()	Test if s is titlecased (all words in s have initial capitals)

Here are some examples of these operators being used to select words from our texts: words ending with *-ableness*; words containing *gnt*; words having an initial capital; and words consisting entirely of digits.

```
>>> sorted([w for w in set(text1) if w.endswith('ableness')])
['comfortableness', 'honourableness', 'immutableness', 'indispensableness', ...]
>>> sorted([term for term in set(text4) if 'gnt' in term])
['Sovereignty', 'sovereignties', 'sovereignty']
>>> sorted([item for item in set(text6) if item.istitle()])
['A', 'Aaaaaaaaah', 'Aaaaaaaah', 'Aaaaaah', 'Aaaah', 'Aaaaugh', 'Aaagh', ...]
>>> sorted([item for item in set(sent7) if item.isdigit()])
['29', '61']
>>>
```

We can also create more complex conditions. If *c* is a condition, then not *c* is also a condition. If we have two conditions c_1 and c_2, then we can combine them to form a new condition using conjunction and disjunction: c_1 and c_2, c_1 or c_2.

Your Turn: Run the following examples and try to explain what is going on in each one. Next, try to make up some conditions of your own.

```
>>> sorted([w for w in set(text7) if '-' in w and 'index' in w])
>>> sorted([wd for wd in set(text3) if wd.istitle() and len(wd) > 10])
>>> sorted([w for w in set(sent7) if not w.islower()])
>>> sorted([t for t in set(text2) if 'cie' in t or 'cei' in t])
```

Operating on Every Element

In Section 1.3, we saw some examples of counting items other than words. Let's take a closer look at the notation we used:

```
>>> [len(w) for w in text1]
[1, 4, 4, 2, 6, 8, 4, 1, 9, 1, 1, 8, 2, 1, 4, 11, 5, 2, 1, 7, 6, 1, 3, 4, 5, 2, ...]
>>> [w.upper() for w in text1]
['[', 'MOBY', 'DICK', 'BY', 'HERMAN', 'MELVILLE', '1851', ']', 'ETYMOLOGY', '.', ...]
>>>
```

These expressions have the form [f(w) for ...] or [w.f() for ...], where f is a function that operates on a word to compute its length, or to convert it to uppercase. For now, you don't need to understand the difference between the notations f(w) and w.f(). Instead, simply learn this Python idiom which performs the same operation on every element of a list. In the preceding examples, it goes through each word in text1, assigning each one in turn to the variable w and performing the specified operation on the variable.

The notation just described is called a "list comprehension." This is our first example of a Python idiom, a fixed notation that we use habitually without bothering to analyze each time. Mastering such idioms is an important part of becoming a fluent Python programmer.

Let's return to the question of vocabulary size, and apply the same idiom here:

```
>>> len(text1)
260819
```

```
>>> len(set(text1))
19317
>>> len(set([word.lower() for word in text1]))
17231
>>>
```

Now that we are not double-counting words like *This* and *this*, which differ only in capitalization, we've wiped 2,000 off the vocabulary count! We can go a step further and eliminate numbers and punctuation from the vocabulary count by filtering out any non-alphabetic items:

```
>>> len(set([word.lower() for word in text1 if word.isalpha()]))
16948
>>>
```

This example is slightly complicated: it lowercases all the purely alphabetic items. Perhaps it would have been simpler just to count the lowercase-only items, but this gives the wrong answer (why?).

Don't worry if you don't feel confident with list comprehensions yet, since you'll see many more examples along with explanations in the following chapters.

Nested Code Blocks

Most programming languages permit us to execute a block of code when a **conditional expression**, or if statement, is satisfied. We already saw examples of conditional tests in code like [w for w in sent7 if len(w) < 4]. In the following program, we have created a variable called word containing the string value 'cat'. The if statement checks whether the test len(word) < 5 is true. It is, so the body of the if statement is invoked and the print statement is executed, displaying a message to the user. Remember to indent the print statement by typing four spaces.

```
>>> word = 'cat'
>>> if len(word) < 5:
...     print 'word length is less than 5'
...     ❶
word length is less than 5
>>>
```

When we use the Python interpreter we have to add an extra blank line ❶ in order for it to detect that the nested block is complete.

If we change the conditional test to len(word) >= 5, to check that the length of word is greater than or equal to 5, then the test will no longer be true. This time, the body of the if statement will not be executed, and no message is shown to the user:

```
>>> if len(word) >= 5:
...     print 'word length is greater than or equal to 5'
...
>>>
```

An `if` statement is known as a **control structure** because it controls whether the code in the indented block will be run. Another control structure is the `for` loop. Try the following, and remember to include the colon and the four spaces:

```
>>> for word in ['Call', 'me', 'Ishmael', '.']:
...     print word
...
Call
me
Ishmael
.
>>>
```

This is called a loop because Python executes the code in circular fashion. It starts by performing the assignment `word` = `'Call'`, effectively using the `word` variable to name the first item of the list. Then, it displays the value of `word` to the user. Next, it goes back to the `for` statement, and performs the assignment `word` = `'me'` before displaying this new value to the user, and so on. It continues in this fashion until every item of the list has been processed.

Looping with Conditions

Now we can combine the `if` and `for` statements. We will loop over every item of the list, and print the item only if it ends with the letter *l*. We'll pick another name for the variable to demonstrate that Python doesn't try to make sense of variable names.

```
>>> sent1 = ['Call', 'me', 'Ishmael', '.']
>>> for xyzzy in sent1:
...     if xyzzy.endswith('l'):
...         print xyzzy
...
Call
Ishmael
>>>
```

You will notice that `if` and `for` statements have a colon at the end of the line, before the indentation begins. In fact, all Python control structures end with a colon. The colon indicates that the current statement relates to the indented block that follows.

We can also specify an action to be taken if the condition of the `if` statement is not met. Here we see the `elif` (else if) statement, and the `else` statement. Notice that these also have colons before the indented code.

```
>>> for token in sent1:
...     if token.islower():
...         print token, 'is a lowercase word'
...     elif token.istitle():
...         print token, 'is a titlecase word'
...     else:
...         print token, 'is punctuation'
...
Call is a titlecase word
me is a lowercase word
```

```
Ishmael is a titlecase word
. is punctuation
>>>
```

As you can see, even with this small amount of Python knowledge, you can start to build multiline Python programs. It's important to develop such programs in pieces, testing that each piece does what you expect before combining them into a program. This is why the Python interactive interpreter is so invaluable, and why you should get comfortable using it.

Finally, let's combine the idioms we've been exploring. First, we create a list of *cie* and *cei* words, then we loop over each item and print it. Notice the comma at the end of the print statement, which tells Python to produce its output on a single line.

```
>>> tricky = sorted([w for w in set(text2) if 'cie' in w or 'cei' in w])
>>> for word in tricky:
...     print word,
ancient ceiling conceit conceited conceive conscience
conscientious conscientiously deceitful deceive ...
>>>
```

1.5 Automatic Natural Language Understanding

We have been exploring language bottom-up, with the help of texts and the Python programming language. However, we're also interested in exploiting our knowledge of language and computation by building useful language technologies. We'll take the opportunity now to step back from the nitty-gritty of code in order to paint a bigger picture of natural language processing.

At a purely practical level, we all need help to navigate the universe of information locked up in text on the Web. Search engines have been crucial to the growth and popularity of the Web, but have some shortcomings. It takes skill, knowledge, and some luck, to extract answers to such questions as: *What tourist sites can I visit between Philadelphia and Pittsburgh on a limited budget? What do experts say about digital SLR cameras? What predictions about the steel market were made by credible commentators in the past week?* Getting a computer to answer them automatically involves a range of language processing tasks, including information extraction, inference, and summarization, and would need to be carried out on a scale and with a level of robustness that is still beyond our current capabilities.

On a more philosophical level, a long-standing challenge within artificial intelligence has been to build intelligent machines, and a major part of intelligent behavior is understanding language. For many years this goal has been seen as too difficult. However, as NLP technologies become more mature, and robust methods for analyzing unrestricted text become more widespread, the prospect of natural language understanding has re-emerged as a plausible goal.

In this section we describe some language understanding technologies, to give you a sense of the interesting challenges that are waiting for you.

Word Sense Disambiguation

In **word sense disambiguation** we want to work out which sense of a word was intended in a given context. Consider the ambiguous words *serve* and *dish*:

(2)   a. *serve*: help with food or drink; hold an office; put ball into play

        b. *dish*: plate; course of a meal; communications device

In a sentence containing the phrase: *he served the dish*, you can detect that both *serve* and *dish* are being used with their food meanings. It's unlikely that the topic of discussion shifted from sports to crockery in the space of three words. This would force you to invent bizarre images, like a tennis pro taking out his frustrations on a china tea-set laid out beside the court. In other words, we automatically disambiguate words using context, exploiting the simple fact that nearby words have closely related meanings. As another example of this contextual effect, consider the word *by*, which has several meanings, for example, *the book by Chesterton* (agentive—Chesterton was the author of the book); *the cup by the stove* (locative—the stove is where the cup is); and *submit by Friday* (temporal—Friday is the time of the submitting). Observe in (3) that the meaning of the italicized word helps us interpret the meaning of *by*.

(3)   a. The lost children were found by the *searchers* (agentive)

        b. The lost children were found by the *mountain* (locative)

        c. The lost children were found by the *afternoon* (temporal)

Pronoun Resolution

A deeper kind of language understanding is to work out "who did what to whom," i.e., to detect the subjects and objects of verbs. You learned to do this in elementary school, but it's harder than you might think. In the sentence *the thieves stole the paintings*, it is easy to tell who performed the stealing action. Consider three possible following sentences in (4), and try to determine what was sold, caught, and found (one case is ambiguous).

(4)   a. The thieves stole the paintings. They were subsequently *sold*.

        b. The thieves stole the paintings. They were subsequently *caught*.

        c. The thieves stole the paintings. They were subsequently *found*.

Answering this question involves finding the **antecedent** of the pronoun *they*, either thieves or paintings. Computational techniques for tackling this problem include **anaphora resolution**—identifying what a pronoun or noun phrase refers to—and

semantic role labeling—identifying how a noun phrase relates to the verb (as agent, patient, instrument, and so on).

Generating Language Output

If we can automatically solve such problems of language understanding, we will be able to move on to tasks that involve generating language output, such as **question answering** and **machine translation**. In the first case, a machine should be able to answer a user's questions relating to collection of texts:

(5)   a. *Text:* ... The thieves stole the paintings. They were subsequently sold. ...

     b. *Human:* Who or what was sold?

     c. *Machine:* The paintings.

The machine's answer demonstrates that it has correctly worked out that *they* refers to paintings and not to thieves. In the second case, the machine should be able to translate the text into another language, accurately conveying the meaning of the original text. In translating the example text into French, we are forced to choose the gender of the pronoun in the second sentence: *ils* (masculine) if the thieves are sold, and *elles* (feminine) if the paintings are sold. Correct translation actually depends on correct understanding of the pronoun.

(6)   a. The thieves stole the paintings. They were subsequently found.

     b. Les voleurs ont volé les peintures. Ils ont été trouvés plus tard. (the thieves)

     c. Les voleurs ont volé les peintures. Elles ont été trouvées plus tard. (the paintings)

In all of these examples, working out the sense of a word, the subject of a verb, and the antecedent of a pronoun are steps in establishing the meaning of a sentence, things we would expect a language understanding system to be able to do.

Machine Translation

For a long time now, machine translation (MT) has been the holy grail of language understanding, ultimately seeking to provide high-quality, idiomatic translation between any pair of languages. Its roots go back to the early days of the Cold War, when the promise of automatic translation led to substantial government sponsorship, and with it, the genesis of NLP itself.

Today, practical translation systems exist for particular pairs of languages, and some are integrated into web search engines. However, these systems have some serious shortcomings. We can explore them with the help of NLTK's "babelizer" (which is automatically loaded when you import this chapter's materials using `from nltk.book import *`). This program submits a sentence for translation into a specified language, then submits the resulting sentence for translation back into English. It stops after 12 iterations, or if it receives a translation that was produced already (indicating a loop):

```
>>> babelize_shell()
NLTK Babelizer: type 'help' for a list of commands.
Babel> how long before the next flight to Alice Springs?
Babel> german
Babel> run
0> how long before the next flight to Alice Springs?
1> wie lang vor dem folgenden Flug zu Alice Springs?
2> how long before the following flight to Alice jump?
3> wie lang vor dem folgenden Flug zu Alice springen Sie?
4> how long before the following flight to Alice do you jump?
5> wie lang, bevor der folgende Flug zu Alice tun, Sie springen?
6> how long, before the following flight to Alice does, do you jump?
7> wie lang bevor der folgende Flug zu Alice tut, tun Sie springen?
8> how long before the following flight to Alice does, do you jump?
9> wie lang, bevor der folgende Flug zu Alice tut, tun Sie springen?
10> how long, before the following flight does to Alice, do do you jump?
11> wie lang bevor der folgende Flug zu Alice tut, Sie tun Sprung?
12> how long before the following flight does leap to Alice, does you?
```

Observe that the system correctly translates *Alice Springs* from English to German (in the line starting 1>), but on the way back to English, this ends up as *Alice jump* (line 2). The preposition *before* is initially translated into the corresponding German preposition *vor*, but later into the conjunction *bevor* (line 5). After line 5 the sentences become non-sensical (but notice the various phrasings indicated by the commas, and the change from *jump* to *leap*). The translation system did not recognize when a word was part of a proper name, and it misinterpreted the grammatical structure. The grammatical problems are more obvious in the following example. Did John find the pig, or did the pig find John?

```
>>> babelize_shell()
Babel> The pig that John found looked happy
Babel> german
Babel> run
0> The pig that John found looked happy
1> Das Schwein, das John fand, schaute gl?cklich
2> The pig, which found John, looked happy
```

Machine translation is difficult because a given word could have several possible translations (depending on its meaning), and because word order must be changed in keeping with the grammatical structure of the target language. Today these difficulties are being faced by collecting massive quantities of parallel texts from news and government websites that publish documents in two or more languages. Given a document in German and English, and possibly a bilingual dictionary, we can automatically pair up the sentences, a process called **text alignment**. Once we have a million or more sentence pairs, we can detect corresponding words and phrases, and build a model that can be used for translating new text.

Spoken Dialogue Systems

In the history of artificial intelligence, the chief measure of intelligence has been a linguistic one, namely the **Turing Test**: can a dialogue system, responding to a user's text input, perform so naturally that we cannot distinguish it from a human-generated response? In contrast, today's commercial dialogue systems are very limited, but still perform useful functions in narrowly defined domains, as we see here:

    S: How may I help you?
    U: When is Saving Private Ryan playing?
    S: For what theater?
    U: The Paramount theater.
    S: Saving Private Ryan is not playing at the Paramount theater, but
    it's playing at the Madison theater at 3:00, 5:30, 8:00, and 10:30.

You could not ask this system to provide driving instructions or details of nearby restaurants unless the required information had already been stored and suitable question-answer pairs had been incorporated into the language processing system.

Observe that this system seems to understand the user's goals: the user asks when a movie is showing and the system correctly determines from this that the user wants to see the movie. This inference seems so obvious that you probably didn't notice it was made, yet a natural language system needs to be endowed with this capability in order to interact naturally. Without it, when asked, *Do you know when* Saving Private Ryan *is playing*?, a system might unhelpfully respond with a cold *Yes*. However, the developers of commercial dialogue systems use contextual assumptions and business logic to ensure that the different ways in which a user might express requests or provide information are handled in a way that makes sense for the particular application. So, if you type *When is ...*, or *I want to know when ...*, or *Can you tell me when ...*, simple rules will always yield screening times. This is enough for the system to provide a useful service.

Dialogue systems give us an opportunity to mention the commonly assumed pipeline for NLP. Figure 1-5 shows the architecture of a simple dialogue system. Along the top of the diagram, moving from left to right, is a "pipeline" of some language understanding **components**. These map from speech input via syntactic parsing to some kind of meaning representation. Along the middle, moving from right to left, is the reverse pipeline of components for converting concepts to speech. These components make up the dynamic aspects of the system. At the bottom of the diagram are some representative bodies of static information: the repositories of language-related data that the processing components draw on to do their work.

 Your Turn: For an example of a primitive dialogue system, try having a conversation with an NLTK chatbot. To see the available chatbots, run `nltk.chat.chatbots()`. (Remember to `import nltk` first.)

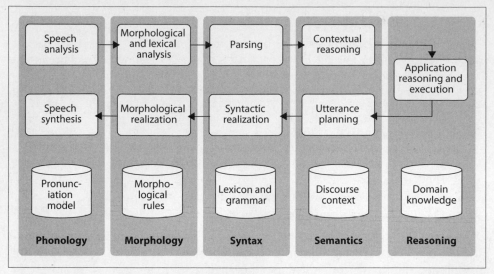

Figure 1-5. Simple pipeline architecture for a spoken dialogue system: Spoken input (top left) is analyzed, words are recognized, sentences are parsed and interpreted in context, application-specific actions take place (top right); a response is planned, realized as a syntactic structure, then to suitably inflected words, and finally to spoken output; different types of linguistic knowledge inform each stage of the process.

Textual Entailment

The challenge of language understanding has been brought into focus in recent years by a public "shared task" called Recognizing Textual Entailment (RTE). The basic scenario is simple. Suppose you want to find evidence to support the hypothesis: *Sandra Goudie was defeated by Max Purnell*, and that you have another short text that seems to be relevant, for example, *Sandra Goudie was first elected to Parliament in the 2002 elections, narrowly winning the seat of Coromandel by defeating Labour candidate Max Purnell and pushing incumbent Green MP Jeanette Fitzsimons into third place*. Does the text provide enough evidence for you to accept the hypothesis? In this particular case, the answer will be "No." You can draw this conclusion easily, but it is very hard to come up with automated methods for making the right decision. The RTE Challenges provide data that allow competitors to develop their systems, but not enough data for "brute force" machine learning techniques (a topic we will cover in Chapter 6). Consequently, some linguistic analysis is crucial. In the previous example, it is important for the system to note that *Sandra Goudie* names the person being defeated in the hypothesis, not the person doing the defeating in the text. As another illustration of the difficulty of the task, consider the following text-hypothesis pair:

(7) a. Text: David Golinkin is the editor or author of 18 books, and over 150 responsa, articles, sermons and books

     b. Hypothesis: Golinkin has written 18 books

In order to determine whether the hypothesis is supported by the text, the system needs the following background knowledge: (i) if someone is an author of a book, then he/she has written that book; (ii) if someone is an editor of a book, then he/she has not written (all of) that book; (iii) if someone is editor or author of 18 books, then one cannot conclude that he/she is author of 18 books.

Limitations of NLP

Despite the research-led advances in tasks such as RTE, natural language systems that have been deployed for real-world applications still cannot perform common-sense reasoning or draw on world knowledge in a general and robust manner. We can wait for these difficult artificial intelligence problems to be solved, but in the meantime it is necessary to live with some severe limitations on the reasoning and knowledge capabilities of natural language systems. Accordingly, right from the beginning, an important goal of NLP research has been to make progress on the difficult task of building technologies that "understand language," using superficial yet powerful techniques instead of unrestricted knowledge and reasoning capabilities. Indeed, this is one of the goals of this book, and we hope to equip you with the knowledge and skills to build useful NLP systems, and to contribute to the long-term aspiration of building intelligent machines.

1.6 Summary

- Texts are represented in Python using lists: `['Monty', 'Python']`. We can use indexing, slicing, and the `len()` function on lists.
- A word "token" is a particular appearance of a given word in a text; a word "type" is the unique form of the word as a particular sequence of letters. We count word tokens using `len(text)` and word types using `len(set(text))`.
- We obtain the vocabulary of a text t using `sorted(set(t))`.
- We operate on each item of a text using `[f(x) for x in text]`.
- To derive the vocabulary, collapsing case distinctions and ignoring punctuation, we can write `set([w.lower() for w in text if w.isalpha()])`.
- We process each word in a text using a `for` statement, such as `for w in t:` or `for word in text:`. This must be followed by the colon character and an indented block of code, to be executed each time through the loop.
- We test a condition using an `if` statement: `if len(word) < 5:`. This must be followed by the colon character and an indented block of code, to be executed only if the condition is true.
- A frequency distribution is a collection of items along with their frequency counts (e.g., the words of a text and their frequency of appearance).

- A function is a block of code that has been assigned a name and can be reused. Functions are defined using the `def` keyword, as in `def mult(x, y)`; *x* and *y* are parameters of the function, and act as placeholders for actual data values.
- A function is called by specifying its name followed by one or more arguments inside parentheses, like this: `mult(3, 4)`, e.g., `len(text1)`.

1.7 Further Reading

This chapter has introduced new concepts in programming, natural language processing, and linguistics, all mixed in together. Many of them are consolidated in the following chapters. However, you may also want to consult the online materials provided with this chapter (at *http://www.nltk.org/*), including links to additional background materials, and links to online NLP systems. You may also like to read up on some linguistics and NLP-related concepts in Wikipedia (e.g., collocations, the Turing Test, the type-token distinction).

You should acquaint yourself with the Python documentation available at *http://docs .python.org/*, including the many tutorials and comprehensive reference materials linked there. A *Beginner's Guide to Python* is available at *http://wiki.python.org/moin/ BeginnersGuide*. Miscellaneous questions about Python might be answered in the FAQ at *http://www.python.org/doc/faq/general/*.

As you delve into NLTK, you might want to subscribe to the mailing list where new releases of the toolkit are announced. There is also an NLTK-Users mailing list, where users help each other as they learn how to use Python and NLTK for language analysis work. Details of these lists are available at *http://www.nltk.org/*.

For more information on the topics covered in Section 1.5, and on NLP more generally, you might like to consult one of the following excellent books:

- Indurkhya, Nitin and Fred Damerau (eds., 2010) *Handbook of Natural Language Processing* (second edition), Chapman & Hall/CRC.
- Jurafsky, Daniel and James Martin (2008) *Speech and Language Processing* (second edition), Prentice Hall.
- Mitkov, Ruslan (ed., 2002) *The Oxford Handbook of Computational Linguistics*. Oxford University Press. (second edition expected in 2010).

The Association for Computational Linguistics is the international organization that represents the field of NLP. The ACL website (*http://www.aclweb.org/*) hosts many useful resources, including: information about international and regional conferences and workshops; the *ACL Wiki* with links to hundreds of useful resources; and the *ACL Anthology*, which contains most of the NLP research literature from the past 50 years, fully indexed and freely downloadable.

Some excellent introductory linguistics textbooks are: (Finegan, 2007), (O'Grady et al., 2004), (OSU, 2007). You might like to consult *LanguageLog*, a popular linguistics blog with occasional posts that use the techniques described in this book.

1.8 Exercises

1. ○ Try using the Python interpreter as a calculator, and typing expressions like `12 / (4 + 1)`.

2. ○ Given an alphabet of 26 letters, there are 26 to the power 10, or `26 ** 10`, 10-letter strings we can form. That works out to `141167095653376L` (the `L` at the end just indicates that this is Python's long-number format). How many hundred-letter strings are possible?

3. ○ The Python multiplication operation can be applied to lists. What happens when you type `['Monty', 'Python'] * 20`, or `3 * sent1`?

4. ○ Review Section 1.1 on computing with language. How many words are there in `text2`? How many distinct words are there?

5. ○ Compare the lexical diversity scores for humor and romance fiction in Table 1-1. Which genre is more lexically diverse?

6. ○ Produce a dispersion plot of the four main protagonists in *Sense and Sensibility*: Elinor, Marianne, Edward, and Willoughby. What can you observe about the different roles played by the males and females in this novel? Can you identify the couples?

7. ○ Find the collocations in `text5`.

8. ○ Consider the following Python expression: `len(set(text4))`. State the purpose of this expression. Describe the two steps involved in performing this computation.

9. ○ Review Section 1.2 on lists and strings.

   a. Define a string and assign it to a variable, e.g., `my_string = 'My String'` (but put something more interesting in the string). Print the contents of this variable in two ways, first by simply typing the variable name and pressing Enter, then by using the `print` statement.

   b. Try adding the string to itself using `my_string + my_string`, or multiplying it by a number, e.g., `my_string * 3`. Notice that the strings are joined together without any spaces. How could you fix this?

10. ○ Define a variable `my_sent` to be a list of words, using the syntax `my_sent = ["My", "sent"]` (but with your own words, or a favorite saying).

    a. Use `' '.join(my_sent)` to convert this into a string.

    b. Use `split()` to split the string back into the list form you had to start with.

11. ○ Define several variables containing lists of words, e.g., `phrase1`, `phrase2`, and so on. Join them together in various combinations (using the plus operator) to form

whole sentences. What is the relationship between `len(phrase1 + phrase2)` and `len(phrase1) + len(phrase2)`?

12. ○ Consider the following two expressions, which have the same value. Which one will typically be more relevant in NLP? Why?

    a. `"Monty Python"[6:12]`

    b. `["Monty", "Python"][1]`

13. ○ We have seen how to represent a sentence as a list of words, where each word is a sequence of characters. What does `sent1[2][2]` do? Why? Experiment with other index values.

14. ○ The first sentence of `text3` is provided to you in the variable `sent3`. The index of *the* in `sent3` is 1, because `sent3[1]` gives us `'the'`. What are the indexes of the two other occurrences of this word in `sent3`?

15. ○ Review the discussion of conditionals in Section 1.4. Find all words in the Chat Corpus (`text5`) starting with the letter *b*. Show them in alphabetical order.

16. ○ Type the expression `range(10)` at the interpreter prompt. Now try `range(10, 20)`, `range(10, 20, 2)`, and `range(20, 10, -2)`. We will see a variety of uses for this built-in function in later chapters.

17. ◑ Use `text9.index()` to find the index of the word *sunset*. You'll need to insert this word as an argument between the parentheses. By a process of trial and error, find the slice for the complete sentence that contains this word.

18. ◑ Using list addition, and the `set` and `sorted` operations, compute the vocabulary of the sentences `sent1 ... sent8`.

19. ◑ What is the difference between the following two lines? Which one will give a larger value? Will this be the case for other texts?

```
>>> sorted(set([w.lower() for w in text1]))
>>> sorted([w.lower() for w in set(text1)])
```

20. ◑ What is the difference between the following two tests: `w.isupper()` and `not w.islower()`?

21. ◑ Write the slice expression that extracts the last two words of `text2`.

22. ◑ Find all the four-letter words in the Chat Corpus (`text5`). With the help of a frequency distribution (`FreqDist`), show these words in decreasing order of frequency.

23. ◑ Review the discussion of looping with conditions in Section 1.4. Use a combination of `for` and `if` statements to loop over the words of the movie script for *Monty Python and the Holy Grail* (`text6`) and `print` all the uppercase words, one per line.

24. ◑ Write expressions for finding all words in `text6` that meet the following conditions. The result should be in the form of a list of words: `['word1', 'word2', ...]`.

a. Ending in *ize*

b. Containing the letter *z*

c. Containing the sequence of letters *pt*

d. All lowercase letters except for an initial capital (i.e., `titlecase`)

25. ◑ Define `sent` to be the list of words `['she', 'sells', 'sea', 'shells', 'by', 'the', 'sea', 'shore']`. Now write code to perform the following tasks:

    a. Print all words beginning with *sh*.

    b. Print all words longer than four characters

26. ◑ What does the following Python code do? `sum([len(w) for w in text1])` Can you use it to work out the average word length of a text?

27. ◑ Define a function called `vocab_size(text)` that has a single parameter for the text, and which returns the vocabulary size of the text.

28. ◑ Define a function `percent(word, text)` that calculates how often a given word occurs in a text and expresses the result as a percentage.

29. ◑ We have been using sets to store vocabularies. Try the following Python expression: `set(sent3) < set(text1)`. Experiment with this using different arguments to `set()`. What does it do? Can you think of a practical application for this?

## CHAPTER 2

Accessing Text Corpora and Lexical Resources

Practical work in Natural Language Processing typically uses large bodies of linguistic data, or **corpora**. The goal of this chapter is to answer the following questions:

1. What are some useful text corpora and lexical resources, and how can we access them with Python?

2. Which Python constructs are most helpful for this work?

3. How do we avoid repeating ourselves when writing Python code?

This chapter continues to present programming concepts by example, in the context of a linguistic processing task. We will wait until later before exploring each Python construct systematically. Don't worry if you see an example that contains something unfamiliar; simply try it out and see what it does, and—if you're game—modify it by substituting some part of the code with a different text or word. This way you will associate a task with a programming idiom, and learn the hows and whys later.

2.1 Accessing Text Corpora

As just mentioned, a text corpus is a large body of text. Many corpora are designed to contain a careful balance of material in one or more genres. We examined some small text collections in Chapter 1, such as the speeches known as the US Presidential Inaugural Addresses. This particular corpus actually contains dozens of individual texts—one per address—but for convenience we glued them end-to-end and treated them as a single text. Chapter 1 also used various predefined texts that we accessed by typing `from book import *`. However, since we want to be able to work with other texts, this section examines a variety of text corpora. We'll see how to select individual texts, and how to work with them.

Gutenberg Corpus

NLTK includes a small selection of texts from the Project Gutenberg electronic text archive, which contains some 25,000 free electronic books, hosted at *http://www.gutenberg.org/*. We begin by getting the Python interpreter to load the NLTK package, then ask to see `nltk.corpus.gutenberg.fileids()`, the file identifiers in this corpus:

```
>>> import nltk
>>> nltk.corpus.gutenberg.fileids()
['austen-emma.txt', 'austen-persuasion.txt', 'austen-sense.txt', 'bible-kjv.txt',
'blake-poems.txt', 'bryant-stories.txt', 'burgess-busterbrown.txt',
'carroll-alice.txt', 'chesterton-ball.txt', 'chesterton-brown.txt',
'chesterton-thursday.txt', 'edgeworth-parents.txt', 'melville-moby_dick.txt',
'milton-paradise.txt', 'shakespeare-caesar.txt', 'shakespeare-hamlet.txt',
'shakespeare-macbeth.txt', 'whitman-leaves.txt']
```

Let's pick out the first of these texts—*Emma* by Jane Austen—and give it a short name, `emma`, then find out how many words it contains:

```
>>> emma = nltk.corpus.gutenberg.words('austen-emma.txt')
>>> len(emma)
192427
```

> In Section 1.1, we showed how you could carry out concordancing of a text such as `text1` with the command `text1.concordance()`. However, this assumes that you are using one of the nine texts obtained as a result of doing `from nltk.book import *`. Now that you have started examining data from `nltk.corpus`, as in the previous example, you have to employ the following pair of statements to perform concordancing and other tasks from Section 1.1:
>
> ```
> >>> emma = nltk.Text(nltk.corpus.gutenberg.words('austen-emma.txt'))
> >>> emma.concordance("surprize")
> ```

When we defined `emma`, we invoked the `words()` function of the `gutenberg` object in NLTK's `corpus` package. But since it is cumbersome to type such long names all the time, Python provides another version of the `import` statement, as follows:

```
>>> from nltk.corpus import gutenberg
>>> gutenberg.fileids()
['austen-emma.txt', 'austen-persuasion.txt', 'austen-sense.txt', ...]
>>> emma = gutenberg.words('austen-emma.txt')
```

Let's write a short program to display other information about each text, by looping over all the values of `fileid` corresponding to the `gutenberg` file identifiers listed earlier and then computing statistics for each text. For a compact output display, we will make sure that the numbers are all integers, using `int()`.

```
>>> for fileid in gutenberg.fileids():
...     num_chars = len(gutenberg.raw(fileid))     ❶
...     num_words = len(gutenberg.words(fileid))
...     num_sents = len(gutenberg.sents(fileid))
```

```
...        num_vocab = len(set([w.lower() for w in gutenberg.words(fileid)]))
...        print int(num_chars/num_words), int(num_words/num_sents), int(num_words/num_vocab),
           fileid
...
4 21 26 austen-emma.txt
4 23 16 austen-persuasion.txt
4 24 22 austen-sense.txt
4 33 79 bible-kjv.txt
4 18 5 blake-poems.txt
4 17 14 bryant-stories.txt
4 17 12 burgess-busterbrown.txt
4 16 12 carroll-alice.txt
4 17 11 chesterton-ball.txt
4 19 11 chesterton-brown.txt
4 16 10 chesterton-thursday.txt
4 18 24 edgeworth-parents.txt
4 24 15 melville-moby_dick.txt
4 52 10 milton-paradise.txt
4 12 8 shakespeare-caesar.txt
4 13 7 shakespeare-hamlet.txt
4 13 6 shakespeare-macbeth.txt
4 35 12 whitman-leaves.txt
```

This program displays three statistics for each text: average word length, average sentence length, and the number of times each vocabulary item appears in the text on average (our lexical diversity score). Observe that average word length appears to be a general property of English, since it has a recurrent value of 4. (In fact, the average word length is really 3, not 4, since the num_chars variable counts space characters.) By contrast average sentence length and lexical diversity appear to be characteristics of particular authors.

The previous example also showed how we can access the "raw" text of the book ❶, not split up into tokens. The raw() function gives us the contents of the file without any linguistic processing. So, for example, len(gutenberg.raw('blake-poems.txt')) tells us how many *letters* occur in the text, including the spaces between words. The sents() function divides the text up into its sentences, where each sentence is a list of words:

```
>>> macbeth_sentences = gutenberg.sents('shakespeare-macbeth.txt')
>>> macbeth_sentences
[['[', 'The', 'Tragedie', 'of', 'Macbeth', 'by', 'William', 'Shakespeare',
'1603', ']'], ['Actus', 'Primus', '.'], ...]
>>> macbeth_sentences[1037]
['Double', ',', 'double', ',', 'toile', 'and', 'trouble', ';',
'Fire', 'burne', ',', 'and', 'Cauldron', 'bubble']
>>> longest_len = max([len(s) for s in macbeth_sentences])
>>> [s for s in macbeth_sentences if len(s) == longest_len]
[['Doubtfull', 'it', 'stood', ',', 'As', 'two', 'spent', 'Swimmers', ',', 'that',
'doe', 'cling', 'together', ',', 'And', 'choake', 'their', 'Art', ':', 'The',
'mercilesse', 'Macdonwald', ...], ...]
```

Most NLTK corpus readers include a variety of access methods apart from words(), raw(), and sents(). Richer linguistic content is available from some corpora, such as part-of-speech tags, dialogue tags, syntactic trees, and so forth; we will see these in later chapters.

Web and Chat Text

Although Project Gutenberg contains thousands of books, it represents established literature. It is important to consider less formal language as well. NLTK's small collection of web text includes content from a Firefox discussion forum, conversations overheard in New York, the movie script of *Pirates of the Carribean*, personal advertisements, and wine reviews:

```
>>> from nltk.corpus import webtext
>>> for fileid in webtext.fileids():
...     print fileid, webtext.raw(fileid)[:65], '...'
...
firefox.txt Cookie Manager: "Don't allow sites that set removed cookies to se...
grail.txt SCENE 1: [wind] [clop clop clop] KING ARTHUR: Whoa there! [clop...
overheard.txt White guy: So, do you have any plans for this evening? Asian girl...
pirates.txt PIRATES OF THE CARRIBEAN: DEAD MAN'S CHEST, by Ted Elliott & Terr...
singles.txt 25 SEXY MALE, seeks attrac older single lady, for discreet encoun...
wine.txt Lovely delicate, fragrant Rhone wine. Polished leather and strawb...
```

There is also a corpus of instant messaging chat sessions, originally collected by the Naval Postgraduate School for research on automatic detection of Internet predators. The corpus contains over 10,000 posts, anonymized by replacing usernames with generic names of the form "UserNNN", and manually edited to remove any other identifying information. The corpus is organized into 15 files, where each file contains several hundred posts collected on a given date, for an age-specific chatroom (teens, 20s, 30s, 40s, plus a generic adults chatroom). The filename contains the date, chatroom, and number of posts; e.g., **10-19-20s_706posts.xml** contains 706 posts gathered from the 20s chat room on 10/19/2006.

```
>>> from nltk.corpus import nps_chat
>>> chatroom = nps_chat.posts('10-19-20s_706posts.xml')
>>> chatroom[123]
['i', 'do', "n't", 'want', 'hot', 'pics', 'of', 'a', 'female', ',',
'I', 'can', 'look', 'in', 'a', 'mirror', '.']
```

Brown Corpus

The Brown Corpus was the first million-word electronic corpus of English, created in 1961 at Brown University. This corpus contains text from 500 sources, and the sources have been categorized by genre, such as *news*, *editorial*, and so on. Table 2-1 gives an example of each genre (for a complete list, see *http://icame.uib.no/brown/bcm-los.html*).

Table 2-1. Example document for each section of the Brown Corpus

ID	File	Genre	Description
A16	ca16	news	Chicago Tribune: *Society Reportage*
B02	cb02	editorial	Christian Science Monitor: *Editorials*
C17	cc17	reviews	Time Magazine: *Reviews*
D12	cd12	religion	Underwood: *Probing the Ethics of Realtors*
E36	ce36	hobbies	Norling: *Renting a Car in Europe*
F25	cf25	lore	Boroff: *Jewish Teenage Culture*
G22	cg22	belles_lettres	Reiner: *Coping with Runaway Technology*
H15	ch15	government	US Office of Civil and Defence Mobilization: *The Family Fallout Shelter*
J17	cj19	learned	Mosteller: *Probability with Statistical Applications*
K04	ck04	fiction	W.E.B. Du Bois: *Worlds of Color*
L13	cl13	mystery	Hitchens: *Footsteps in the Night*
M01	cm01	science_fiction	Heinlein: *Stranger in a Strange Land*
N14	cn15	adventure	Field: *Rattlesnake Ridge*
P12	cp12	romance	Callaghan: *A Passion in Rome*
R06	cr06	humor	Thurber: *The Future, If Any, of Comedy*

We can access the corpus as a list of words or a list of sentences (where each sentence is itself just a list of words). We can optionally specify particular categories or files to read:

```
>>> from nltk.corpus import brown
>>> brown.categories()
['adventure', 'belles_lettres', 'editorial', 'fiction', 'government', 'hobbies',
'humor', 'learned', 'lore', 'mystery', 'news', 'religion', 'reviews', 'romance',
'science_fiction']
>>> brown.words(categories='news')
['The', 'Fulton', 'County', 'Grand', 'Jury', 'said', ...]
>>> brown.words(fileids=['cg22'])
['Does', 'our', 'society', 'have', 'a', 'runaway', ',', ...]
>>> brown.sents(categories=['news', 'editorial', 'reviews'])
[['The', 'Fulton', 'County'...], ['The', 'jury', 'further'...], ...]
```

The Brown Corpus is a convenient resource for studying systematic differences between genres, a kind of linguistic inquiry known as **stylistics**. Let's compare genres in their usage of modal verbs. The first step is to produce the counts for a particular genre. Remember to import nltk before doing the following:

```
>>> from nltk.corpus import brown
>>> news_text = brown.words(categories='news')
>>> fdist = nltk.FreqDist([w.lower() for w in news_text])
>>> modals = ['can', 'could', 'may', 'might', 'must', 'will']
>>> for m in modals:
...     print m + ':', fdist[m],
```

```
...
can: 94 could: 87 may: 93 might: 38 must: 53 will: 389
```

 Your Turn: Choose a different section of the Brown Corpus, and adapt the preceding example to count a selection of *wh* words, such as *what*, *when*, *where*, *who* and *why*.

Next, we need to obtain counts for each genre of interest. We'll use NLTK's support for conditional frequency distributions. These are presented systematically in Section 2.2, where we also unpick the following code line by line. For the moment, you can ignore the details and just concentrate on the output.

```
>>> cfd = nltk.ConditionalFreqDist(
...         (genre, word)
...         for genre in brown.categories()
...         for word in brown.words(categories=genre))
>>> genres = ['news', 'religion', 'hobbies', 'science_fiction', 'romance', 'humor']
>>> modals = ['can', 'could', 'may', 'might', 'must', 'will']
>>> cfd.tabulate(conditions=genres, samples=modals)
```

	can	could	may	might	must	will
news	93	86	66	38	50	389
religion	82	59	78	12	54	71
hobbies	268	58	131	22	83	264
science_fiction	16	49	4	12	8	16
romance	74	193	11	51	45	43
humor	16	30	8	8	9	13

Observe that the most frequent modal in the news genre is *will*, while the most frequent modal in the romance genre is *could*. Would you have predicted this? The idea that word counts might distinguish genres will be taken up again in Chapter 6.

Reuters Corpus

The Reuters Corpus contains 10,788 news documents totaling 1.3 million words. The documents have been classified into 90 topics, and grouped into two sets, called "training" and "test"; thus, the text with fileid `'test/14826'` is a document drawn from the test set. This split is for training and testing algorithms that automatically detect the topic of a document, as we will see in Chapter 6.

```
>>> from nltk.corpus import reuters
>>> reuters.fileids()
['test/14826', 'test/14828', 'test/14829', 'test/14832', ...]
>>> reuters.categories()
['acq', 'alum', 'barley', 'bop', 'carcass', 'castor-oil', 'cocoa',
'coconut', 'coconut-oil', 'coffee', 'copper', 'copra-cake', 'corn',
'cotton', 'cotton-oil', 'cpi', 'cpu', 'crude', 'dfl', 'dlr', ...]
```

Unlike the Brown Corpus, categories in the Reuters Corpus overlap with each other, simply because a news story often covers multiple topics. We can ask for the topics covered by one or more documents, or for the documents included in one or more categories. For convenience, the corpus methods accept a single fileid or a list of fileids.

```
>>> reuters.categories('training/9865')
['barley', 'corn', 'grain', 'wheat']
>>> reuters.categories(['training/9865', 'training/9880'])
['barley', 'corn', 'grain', 'money-fx', 'wheat']
>>> reuters.fileids('barley')
['test/15618', 'test/15649', 'test/15676', 'test/15728', 'test/15871', ...]
>>> reuters.fileids(['barley', 'corn'])
['test/14832', 'test/14858', 'test/15033', 'test/15043', 'test/15106',
'test/15287', 'test/15341', 'test/15618', 'test/15618', 'test/15648', ...]
```

Similarly, we can specify the words or sentences we want in terms of files or categories. The first handful of words in each of these texts are the titles, which by convention are stored as uppercase.

```
>>> reuters.words('training/9865')[:14]
['FRENCH', 'FREE', 'MARKET', 'CEREAL', 'EXPORT', 'BIDS',
'DETAILED', 'French', 'operators', 'have', 'requested', 'licences', 'to', 'export']
>>> reuters.words(['training/9865', 'training/9880'])
['FRENCH', 'FREE', 'MARKET', 'CEREAL', 'EXPORT', ...]
>>> reuters.words(categories='barley')
['FRENCH', 'FREE', 'MARKET', 'CEREAL', 'EXPORT', ...]
>>> reuters.words(categories=['barley', 'corn'])
['THAI', 'TRADE', 'DEFICIT', 'WIDENS', 'IN', 'FIRST', ...]
```

Inaugural Address Corpus

In Section 1.1, we looked at the Inaugural Address Corpus, but treated it as a single text. The graph in Figure 1-2 used "word offset" as one of the axes; this is the numerical index of the word in the corpus, counting from the first word of the first address. However, the corpus is actually a collection of 55 texts, one for each presidential address. An interesting property of this collection is its time dimension:

```
>>> from nltk.corpus import inaugural
>>> inaugural.fileids()
['1789-Washington.txt', '1793-Washington.txt', '1797-Adams.txt', ...]
>>> [fileid[:4] for fileid in inaugural.fileids()]
['1789', '1793', '1797', '1801', '1805', '1809', '1813', '1817', '1821', ...]
```

Notice that the year of each text appears in its filename. To get the year out of the filename, we extracted the first four characters, using `fileid[:4]`.

Let's look at how the words *America* and *citizen* are used over time. The following code converts the words in the Inaugural corpus to lowercase using `w.lower()` ❶, then checks whether they start with either of the "targets" `america` or `citizen` using `startswith()` ❶. Thus it will count words such as *American's* and *Citizens*. We'll learn about conditional frequency distributions in Section 2.2; for now, just consider the output, shown in Figure 2-1.

```
>>> cfd = nltk.ConditionalFreqDist(
...           (target, file[:4])
...           for fileid in inaugural.fileids()
...           for w in inaugural.words(fileid)
...           for target in ['america', 'citizen']
...           if w.lower().startswith(target)) ❶
>>> cfd.plot()
```

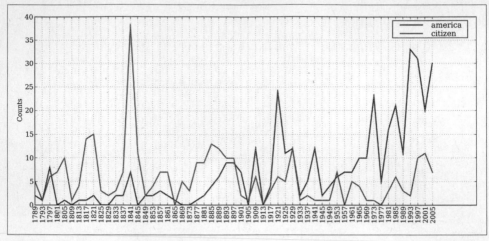

Figure 2-1. Plot of a conditional frequency distribution: All words in the Inaugural Address Corpus that begin with america *or* citizen *are counted; separate counts are kept for each address; these are plotted so that trends in usage over time can be observed; counts are not normalized for document length.*

Annotated Text Corpora

Many text corpora contain linguistic annotations, representing part-of-speech tags, named entities, syntactic structures, semantic roles, and so forth. NLTK provides convenient ways to access several of these corpora, and has data packages containing corpora and corpus samples, freely downloadable for use in teaching and research. Table 2-2 lists some of the corpora. For information about downloading them, see *http://www.nltk.org/data*. For more examples of how to access NLTK corpora, please consult the Corpus HOWTO at *http://www.nltk.org/howto*.

Table 2-2. Some of the corpora and corpus samples distributed with NLTK

Corpus	Compiler	Contents
Brown Corpus	Francis, Kucera	15 genres, 1.15M words, tagged, categorized
CESS Treebanks	CLiC-UB	1M words, tagged and parsed (Catalan, Spanish)
Chat-80 Data Files	Pereira & Warren	World Geographic Database
CMU Pronouncing Dictionary	CMU	127k entries
CoNLL 2000 Chunking Data	CoNLL	270k words, tagged and chunked

Corpus	Compiler	Contents
CoNLL 2002 Named Entity	CoNLL	700k words, POS and named entity tagged (Dutch, Spanish)
CoNLL 2007 Dependency Parsed Tree-banks (selections)	CoNLL	150k words, dependency parsed (Basque, Catalan)
Dependency Treebank	Narad	Dependency parsed version of Penn Treebank sample
Floresta Treebank	Diana Santos et al.	9k sentences, tagged and parsed (Portuguese)
Gazetteer Lists	Various	Lists of cities and countries
Genesis Corpus	Misc web sources	6 texts, 200k words, 6 languages
Gutenberg (selections)	Hart, Newby, et al.	18 texts, 2M words
Inaugural Address Corpus	CSpan	U.S. Presidential Inaugural Addresses (1789–present)
Indian POS Tagged Corpus	Kumaran et al.	60k words, tagged (Bangla, Hindi, Marathi, Telugu)
MacMorpho Corpus	NILC, USP, Brazil	1M words, tagged (Brazilian Portuguese)
Movie Reviews	Pang, Lee	2k movie reviews with sentiment polarity classification
Names Corpus	Kantrowitz, Ross	8k male and female names
NIST 1999 Info Extr (selections)	Garofolo	63k words, newswire and named entity SGML markup
NPS Chat Corpus	Forsyth, Martell	10k IM chat posts, POS and dialogue-act tagged
Penn Treebank (selections)	LDC	40k words, tagged and parsed
PP Attachment Corpus	Ratnaparkhi	28k prepositional phrases, tagged as noun or verb modifiers
Proposition Bank	Palmer	113k propositions, 3,300 verb frames
Question Classification	Li, Roth	6k questions, categorized
Reuters Corpus	Reuters	1.3M words, 10k news documents, categorized
Roget's Thesaurus	Project Gutenberg	200k words, formatted text
RTE Textual Entailment	Dagan et al.	8k sentence pairs, categorized
SEMCOR	Rus, Mihalcea	880k words, POS and sense tagged
Senseval 2 Corpus	Pedersen	600k words, POS and sense tagged
Shakespeare texts (selections)	Bosak	8 books in XML format
State of the Union Corpus	CSpan	485k words, formatted text
Stopwords Corpus	Porter et al.	2,400 stopwords for 11 languages
Swadesh Corpus	Wiktionary	Comparative wordlists in 24 languages
Switchboard Corpus (selections)	LDC	36 phone calls, transcribed, parsed
TIMIT Corpus (selections)	NIST/LDC	Audio files and transcripts for 16 speakers
Univ Decl of Human Rights	United Nations	480k words, 300+ languages
VerbNet 2.1	Palmer et al.	5k verbs, hierarchically organized, linked to WordNet
Wordlist Corpus	OpenOffice.org et al.	960k words and 20k affixes for 8 languages
WordNet 3.0 (English)	Miller, Fellbaum	145k synonym sets

Corpora in Other Languages

NLTK comes with corpora for many languages, though in some cases you will need to learn how to manipulate character encodings in Python before using these corpora (see Section 3.3).

```
>>> nltk.corpus.cess_esp.words()
['El', 'grupo', 'estatal', 'Electricit\xe9_de_France', ...]
>>> nltk.corpus.floresta.words()
['Um', 'revivalismo', 'refrescante', 'O', '7_e_Meio', ...]
>>> nltk.corpus.indian.words('hindi.pos')
['\xe0\xa4\xaa\xe0\xa5\x82\xe0\xa4\xb0\xe0\xa5\x8d\xe0\xa4\xa3',
'\xe0\xa4\xaa\xe0\xa5\x8d\xe0\xa4\xb0\xe0\xa4\xa4\xe0\xa4\xbf\xe0\xa4\xac\xe0\xa4
\x82\xe0\xa4\xa7', ...]
>>> nltk.corpus.udhr.fileids()
['Abkhaz-Cyrillic+Abkh', 'Abkhaz-UTF8', 'Achehnese-Latin1', 'Achuar-Shiwiar-Latin1',
'Adja-UTF8', 'Afaan_Oromo_Oromiffa-Latin1', 'Afrikaans-Latin1', 'Aguaruna-Latin1',
'Akuapem_Twi-UTF8', 'Albanian_Shqip-Latin1', 'Amahuaca', 'Amahuaca-Latin1', ...]
>>> nltk.corpus.udhr.words('Javanese-Latin1')[11:]
[u'Saben', u'umat', u'manungsa', u'lair', u'kanthi', ...]
```

The last of these corpora, udhr, contains the Universal Declaration of Human Rights in over 300 languages. The fileids for this corpus include information about the character encoding used in the file, such as UTF8 or Latin1. Let's use a conditional frequency distribution to examine the differences in word lengths for a selection of languages included in the udhr corpus. The output is shown in Figure 2-2 (run the program yourself to see a color plot). Note that True and False are Python's built-in Boolean values.

```
>>> from nltk.corpus import udhr
>>> languages = ['Chickasaw', 'English', 'German_Deutsch',
...     'Greenlandic_Inuktikut', 'Hungarian_Magyar', 'Ibibio_Efik']
>>> cfd = nltk.ConditionalFreqDist(
...           (lang, len(word))
...           for lang in languages
...           for word in udhr.words(lang + '-Latin1'))
>>> cfd.plot(cumulative=True)
```

 Your Turn: Pick a language of interest in udhr.fileids(), and define a variable raw_text = udhr.raw(*Language-Latin1*). Now plot a frequency distribution of the letters of the text using

```
nltk.FreqDist(raw_text).plot().
```

Unfortunately, for many languages, substantial corpora are not yet available. Often there is insufficient government or industrial support for developing language resources, and individual efforts are piecemeal and hard to discover or reuse. Some languages have no established writing system, or are endangered. (See Section 2.7 for suggestions on how to locate language resources.)

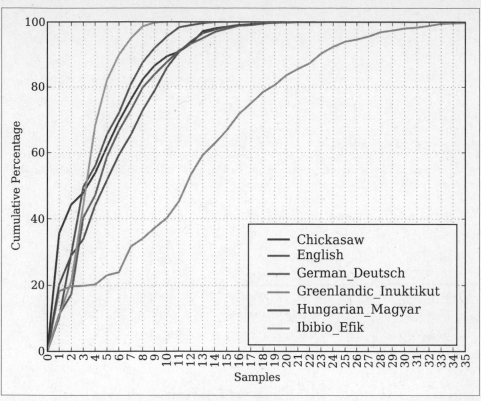

Figure 2-2. Cumulative word length distributions: Six translations of the Universal Declaration of Human Rights are processed; this graph shows that words having five or fewer letters account for about 80% of Ibibio text, 60% of German text, and 25% of Inuktitut text.

Text Corpus Structure

We have seen a variety of corpus structures so far; these are summarized in Figure 2-3. The simplest kind lacks any structure: it is just a collection of texts. Often, texts are grouped into categories that might correspond to genre, source, author, language, etc. Sometimes these categories overlap, notably in the case of topical categories, as a text can be relevant to more than one topic. Occasionally, text collections have temporal structure, news collections being the most common example.

NLTK's corpus readers support efficient access to a variety of corpora, and can be used to work with new corpora. Table 2-3 lists functionality provided by the corpus readers.

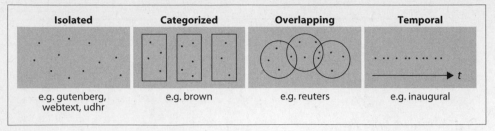

Isolated	Categorized	Overlapping	Temporal
e.g. gutenberg, webtext, udhr	e.g. brown	e.g. reuters	e.g. inaugural

Figure 2-3. Common structures for text corpora: The simplest kind of corpus is a collection of isolated texts with no particular organization; some corpora are structured into categories, such as genre (Brown Corpus); some categorizations overlap, such as topic categories (Reuters Corpus); other corpora represent language use over time (Inaugural Address Corpus).

Table 2-3. Basic corpus functionality defined in NLTK: More documentation can be found using help(nltk.corpus.reader) and by reading the online Corpus HOWTO at http://www.nltk.org/howto.

Example	Description
fileids()	The files of the corpus
fileids([categories])	The files of the corpus corresponding to these categories
categories()	The categories of the corpus
categories([fileids])	The categories of the corpus corresponding to these files
raw()	The raw content of the corpus
raw(fileids=[f1,f2,f3])	The raw content of the specified files
raw(categories=[c1,c2])	The raw content of the specified categories
words()	The words of the whole corpus
words(fileids=[f1,f2,f3])	The words of the specified fileids
words(categories=[c1,c2])	The words of the specified categories
sents()	The sentences of the specified categories
sents(fileids=[f1,f2,f3])	The sentences of the specified fileids
sents(categories=[c1,c2])	The sentences of the specified categories
abspath(fileid)	The location of the given file on disk
encoding(fileid)	The encoding of the file (if known)
open(fileid)	Open a stream for reading the given corpus file
root()	The path to the root of locally installed corpus
readme()	The contents of the README file of the corpus

We illustrate the difference between some of the corpus access methods here:

```
>>> raw = gutenberg.raw("burgess-busterbrown.txt")
>>> raw[1:20]
'The Adventures of B'
>>> words = gutenberg.words("burgess-busterbrown.txt")
>>> words[1:20]
```

```
['The', 'Adventures', 'of', 'Buster', 'Bear', 'by', 'Thornton', 'W', '.',
'Burgess', '1920', ']', 'I', 'BUSTER', 'BEAR', 'GOES', 'FISHING', 'Buster',
'Bear']
>>> sents = gutenberg.sents("burgess-busterbrown.txt")
>>> sents[1:20]
[['I'], ['BUSTER', 'BEAR', 'GOES', 'FISHING'], ['Buster', 'Bear', 'yawned', 'as',
'he', 'lay', 'on', 'his', 'comfortable', 'bed', 'of', 'leaves', 'and', 'watched',
'the', 'first', 'early', 'morning', 'sunbeams', 'creeping', 'through', ...], ...]
```

Loading Your Own Corpus

If you have a your own collection of text files that you would like to access using the
methods discussed earlier, you can easily load them with the help of NLTK's Plain
textCorpusReader. Check the location of your files on your file system; in the following
example, we have taken this to be the directory */usr/share/dict*. Whatever the location,
set this to be the value of corpus_root ❶. The second parameter of the PlaintextCor
pusReader initializer ❷ can be a list of fileids, like ['a.txt', 'test/b.txt'], or a pattern
that matches all fileids, like '[abc]/.*\.txt' (see Section 3.4 for information about
regular expressions).

```
>>> from nltk.corpus import PlaintextCorpusReader
>>> corpus_root = '/usr/share/dict' ❶
>>> wordlists = PlaintextCorpusReader(corpus_root, '.*') ❷
>>> wordlists.fileids()
['README', 'connectives', 'propernames', 'web2', 'web2a', 'words']
>>> wordlists.words('connectives')
['the', 'of', 'and', 'to', 'a', 'in', 'that', 'is', ...]
```

As another example, suppose you have your own local copy of Penn Treebank (release
3), in C:\corpora. We can use the BracketParseCorpusReader to access this corpus. We
specify the corpus_root to be the location of the parsed *Wall Street Journal* component
of the corpus ❶, and give a file_pattern that matches the files contained within its
subfolders ❷ (using forward slashes).

```
>>> from nltk.corpus import BracketParseCorpusReader
>>> corpus_root = r"C:\corpora\penntreebank\parsed\mrg\wsj" ❶
>>> file_pattern = r".*/wsj_.*\.mrg" ❷
>>> ptb = BracketParseCorpusReader(corpus_root, file_pattern)
>>> ptb.fileids()
['00/wsj_0001.mrg', '00/wsj_0002.mrg', '00/wsj_0003.mrg', '00/wsj_0004.mrg', ...]
>>> len(ptb.sents())
49208
>>> ptb.sents(fileids='20/wsj_2013.mrg')[19]
['The', '55-year-old', 'Mr.', 'Noriega', 'is', "n't", 'as', 'smooth', 'as', 'the',
'shah', 'of', 'Iran', ',', 'as', 'well-born', 'as', 'Nicaragua', "'s", 'Anastasio',
'Somoza', ',', 'as', 'imperial', 'as', 'Ferdinand', 'Marcos', 'of', 'the', 'Philippines',
'or', 'as', 'bloody', 'as', 'Haiti', "'s", 'Baby', 'Doc', 'Duvalier', '.']
```

2.2 Conditional Frequency Distributions

We introduced frequency distributions in Section 1.3. We saw that given some list `mylist` of words or other items, `FreqDist(mylist)` would compute the number of occurrences of each item in the list. Here we will generalize this idea.

When the texts of a corpus are divided into several categories (by genre, topic, author, etc.), we can maintain separate frequency distributions for each category. This will allow us to study systematic differences between the categories. In the previous section, we achieved this using NLTK's `ConditionalFreqDist` data type. A **conditional frequency distribution** is a collection of frequency distributions, each one for a different "condition." The condition will often be the category of the text. Figure 2-4 depicts a fragment of a conditional frequency distribution having just two conditions, one for news text and one for romance text.

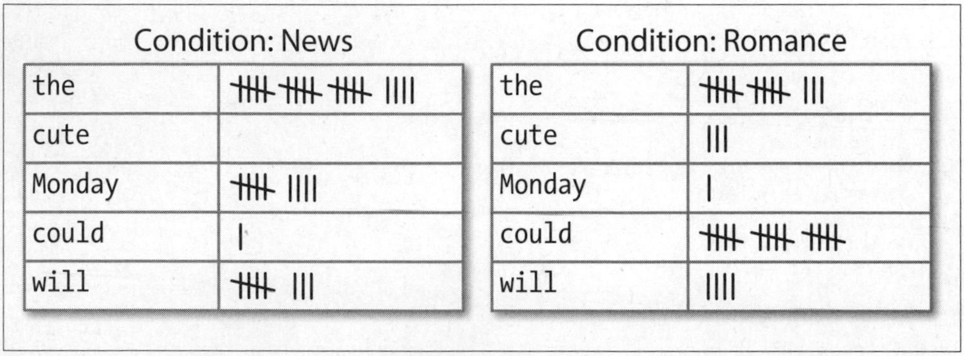

Condition: News		Condition: Romance	
the	ⴕⴕ ⴕⴕ ⴕⴕ ||||	the	ⴕⴕ ⴕⴕ |||
cute		cute	|||
Monday	ⴕⴕ ||||	Monday	|
could	|	could	ⴕⴕ ⴕⴕ ⴕⴕ
will	ⴕⴕ |||	will	||||

Figure 2-4. Counting words appearing in a text collection (a conditional frequency distribution).

Conditions and Events

A frequency distribution counts observable events, such as the appearance of words in a text. A conditional frequency distribution needs to pair each event with a condition. So instead of processing a sequence of words ❶, we have to process a sequence of pairs ❷:

```
>>> text = ['The', 'Fulton', 'County', 'Grand', 'Jury', 'said', ...] ❶
>>> pairs = [('news', 'The'), ('news', 'Fulton'), ('news', 'County'), ...] ❷
```

Each pair has the form (*condition*, *event*). If we were processing the entire Brown Corpus by genre, there would be 15 conditions (one per genre) and 1,161,192 events (one per word).

Counting Words by Genre

In Section 2.1, we saw a conditional frequency distribution where the condition was the section of the Brown Corpus, and for each condition we counted words. Whereas `FreqDist()` takes a simple list as input, `ConditionalFreqDist()` takes a list of pairs.

```
>>> from nltk.corpus import brown
>>> cfd = nltk.ConditionalFreqDist(
...             (genre, word)
...             for genre in brown.categories()
...             for word in brown.words(categories=genre))
```

Let's break this down, and look at just two genres, news and romance. For each genre ❷, we loop over every word in the genre ❸, producing pairs consisting of the genre and the word ❶:

```
>>> genre_word = [(genre, word) ❶
...                 for genre in ['news', 'romance'] ❷
...                 for word in brown.words(categories=genre)] ❸
>>> len(genre_word)
170576
```

So, as we can see in the following code, pairs at the beginning of the list genre_word will be of the form ('news', *word*) ❶, whereas those at the end will be of the form ('romance', *word*) ❷.

```
>>> genre_word[:4]
[('news', 'The'), ('news', 'Fulton'), ('news', 'County'), ('news', 'Grand')] ❶
>>> genre_word[-4:]
[('romance', 'afraid'), ('romance', 'not'), ('romance', "''"), ('romance', '.')] ❷
```

We can now use this list of pairs to create a ConditionalFreqDist, and save it in a variable cfd. As usual, we can type the name of the variable to inspect it ❶, and verify it has two conditions ❷:

```
>>> cfd = nltk.ConditionalFreqDist(genre_word)
>>> cfd ❶
<ConditionalFreqDist with 2 conditions>
>>> cfd.conditions()
['news', 'romance'] ❷
```

Let's access the two conditions, and satisfy ourselves that each is just a frequency distribution:

```
>>> cfd['news']
<FreqDist with 100554 outcomes>
>>> cfd['romance']
<FreqDist with 70022 outcomes>
>>> list(cfd['romance'])
[',', '.', 'the', 'and', 'to', 'a', 'of', '``', "''", 'was', 'I', 'in', 'he', 'had',
'?', 'her', 'that', 'it', 'his', 'she', 'with', 'you', 'for', 'at', 'He', 'on', 'him',
'said', '!', '--', 'be', 'as', ';', 'have', 'but', 'not', 'would', 'She', 'The', ...]
>>> cfd['romance']['could']
193
```

Plotting and Tabulating Distributions

Apart from combining two or more frequency distributions, and being easy to initialize, a ConditionalFreqDist provides some useful methods for tabulation and plotting.

The plot in Figure 2-1 was based on a conditional frequency distribution reproduced in the following code. The condition is either of the words *america* or *citizen* ❷, and the counts being plotted are the number of times the word occurred in a particular speech. It exploits the fact that the filename for each speech—for example, *1865-Lincoln.txt*—contains the year as the first four characters ❶. This code generates the pair (`'america'`, `'1865'`) for every instance of a word whose lowercased form starts with *america*—such as *Americans*—in the file *1865-Lincoln.txt*.

```
>>> from nltk.corpus import inaugural
>>> cfd = nltk.ConditionalFreqDist(
...           (target, fileid[:4]) ❶
...           for fileid in inaugural.fileids()
...           for w in inaugural.words(fileid)
...           for target in ['america', 'citizen'] ❷
...           if w.lower().startswith(target))
```

The plot in Figure 2-2 was also based on a conditional frequency distribution, reproduced in the following code. This time, the condition is the name of the language, and the counts being plotted are derived from word lengths ❶. It exploits the fact that the filename for each language is the language name followed by `'-Latin1'` (the character encoding).

```
>>> from nltk.corpus import udhr
>>> languages = ['Chickasaw', 'English', 'German_Deutsch',
...      'Greenlandic_Inuktikut', 'Hungarian_Magyar', 'Ibibio_Efik']
>>> cfd = nltk.ConditionalFreqDist(
...           (lang, len(word)) ❶
...           for lang in languages
...           for word in udhr.words(lang + '-Latin1'))
```

In the `plot()` and `tabulate()` methods, we can optionally specify which conditions to display with a `conditions=` parameter. When we omit it, we get all the conditions. Similarly, we can limit the samples to display with a `samples=` parameter. This makes it possible to load a large quantity of data into a conditional frequency distribution, and then to explore it by plotting or tabulating selected conditions and samples. It also gives us full control over the order of conditions and samples in any displays. For example, we can tabulate the cumulative frequency data just for two languages, and for words less than 10 characters long, as shown next. We interpret the last cell on the top row to mean that 1,638 words of the English text have nine or fewer letters.

```
>>> cfd.tabulate(conditions=['English', 'German_Deutsch'],
...              samples=range(10), cumulative=True)
                  0    1    2    3    4    5    6    7    8    9
        English   0  185  525  883  997 1166 1283 1440 1558 1638
 German_Deutsch   0  171  263  614  717  894 1013 1110 1213 1275
```

Your Turn: Working with the news and romance genres from the Brown Corpus, find out which days of the week are most newsworthy, and which are most romantic. Define a variable called `days` containing a list of days of the week, i.e., `['Monday', ...]`. Now tabulate the counts for these words using `cfd.tabulate(samples=days)`. Now try the same thing using `plot` in place of `tabulate`. You may control the output order of days with the help of an extra parameter: `condi tions=['Monday', ...]`.

You may have noticed that the multiline expressions we have been using with conditional frequency distributions look like list comprehensions, but without the brackets. In general, when we use a list comprehension as a parameter to a function, like `set([w.lower for w in t])`, we are permitted to omit the square brackets and just write `set(w.lower() for w in t)`. (See the discussion of "generator expressions" in Section 4.2 for more about this.)

Generating Random Text with Bigrams

We can use a conditional frequency distribution to create a table of bigrams (word pairs, introduced in Section 1.3). The `bigrams()` function takes a list of words and builds a list of consecutive word pairs:

```
>>> sent = ['In', 'the', 'beginning', 'God', 'created', 'the', 'heaven',
...     'and', 'the', 'earth', '.']
>>> nltk.bigrams(sent)
[('In', 'the'), ('the', 'beginning'), ('beginning', 'God'), ('God', 'created'),
('created', 'the'), ('the', 'heaven'), ('heaven', 'and'), ('and', 'the'),
('the', 'earth'), ('earth', '.')]
```

In Example 2-1, we treat each word as a condition, and for each one we effectively create a frequency distribution over the following words. The function `gener ate_model()` contains a simple loop to generate text. When we call the function, we choose a word (such as `'living'`) as our initial context. Then, once inside the loop, we print the current value of the variable `word`, and reset `word` to be the most likely token in that context (using `max()`); next time through the loop, we use that word as our new context. As you can see by inspecting the output, this simple approach to text generation tends to get stuck in loops. Another method would be to randomly choose the next word from among the available words.

Example 2-1. Generating random text: This program obtains all bigrams from the text of the book of Genesis, then constructs a conditional frequency distribution to record which words are most likely to follow a given word; e.g., after the word living, *the most likely word is* creature; *the* `generate_model()` *function uses this data, and a seed word, to generate random text.*

```
def generate_model(cfdist, word, num=15):
    for i in range(num):
        print word,
        word = cfdist[word].max()
```

```
text = nltk.corpus.genesis.words('english-kjv.txt')
bigrams = nltk.bigrams(text)
cfd = nltk.ConditionalFreqDist(bigrams) ❶
```

```
>>> print cfd['living']
<FreqDist: 'creature': 7, 'thing': 4, 'substance': 2, ',': 1, '.': 1, 'soul': 1>
>>> generate_model(cfd, 'living')
living creature that he said , and the land of the land of the land
```

Conditional frequency distributions are a useful data structure for many NLP tasks. Their commonly used methods are summarized in Table 2-4.

Table 2-4. NLTK's conditional frequency distributions: Commonly used methods and idioms for defining, accessing, and visualizing a conditional frequency distribution of counters

Example	Description
cfdist = ConditionalFreqDist(pairs)	Create a conditional frequency distribution from a list of pairs
cfdist.conditions()	Alphabetically sorted list of conditions
cfdist[condition]	The frequency distribution for this condition
cfdist[condition][sample]	Frequency for the given sample for this condition
cfdist.tabulate()	Tabulate the conditional frequency distribution
cfdist.tabulate(samples, conditions)	Tabulation limited to the specified samples and conditions
cfdist.plot()	Graphical plot of the conditional frequency distribution
cfdist.plot(samples, conditions)	Graphical plot limited to the specified samples and conditions
cfdist1 < cfdist2	Test if samples in cfdist1 occur less frequently than in cfdist2

2.3 More Python: Reusing Code

By this time you've probably typed and retyped a lot of code in the Python interactive interpreter. If you mess up when retyping a complex example, you have to enter it again. Using the arrow keys to access and modify previous commands is helpful but only goes so far. In this section, we see two important ways to reuse code: text editors and Python functions.

Creating Programs with a Text Editor

The Python interactive interpreter performs your instructions as soon as you type them. Often, it is better to compose a multiline program using a text editor, then ask Python to run the whole program at once. Using IDLE, you can do this by going to the File menu and opening a new window. Try this now, and enter the following one-line program:

```
print 'Monty Python'
```

Save this program in a file called *monty.py*, then go to the Run menu and select the command Run Module. (We'll learn what modules are shortly.) The result in the main IDLE window should look like this:

```
>>> ============================= RESTART =================================
>>>
Monty Python
>>>
```

You can also type `from monty import *` and it will do the same thing.

From now on, you have a choice of using the interactive interpreter or a text editor to create your programs. It is often convenient to test your ideas using the interpreter, revising a line of code until it does what you expect. Once you're ready, you can paste the code (minus any `>>>` or `...` prompts) into the text editor, continue to expand it, and finally save the program in a file so that you don't have to type it in again later. Give the file a short but descriptive name, using all lowercase letters and separating words with underscore, and using the *.py* filename extension, e.g., *monty_python.py*.

 Important: Our inline code examples include the `>>>` and `...` prompts as if we are interacting directly with the interpreter. As they get more complicated, you should instead type them into the editor, without the prompts, and run them from the editor as shown earlier. When we provide longer programs in this book, we will leave out the prompts to remind you to type them into a file rather than using the interpreter. You can see this already in Example 2-1. Note that the example still includes a couple of lines with the Python prompt; this is the interactive part of the task where you inspect some data and invoke a function. Remember that all code samples like Example 2-1 are downloadable from *http://www.nltk.org/*.

Functions

Suppose that you work on analyzing text that involves different forms of the same word, and that part of your program needs to work out the plural form of a given singular noun. Suppose it needs to do this work in two places, once when it is processing some texts and again when it is processing user input.

Rather than repeating the same code several times over, it is more efficient and reliable to localize this work inside a **function**. A function is just a named block of code that performs some well-defined task, as we saw in Section 1.1. A function is usually defined to take some inputs, using special variables known as **parameters**, and it may produce a result, also known as a **return value**. We define a function using the keyword `def` followed by the function name and any input parameters, followed by the body of the function. Here's the function we saw in Section 1.1 (including the `import` statement that makes division behave as expected):

```
>>> from __future__ import division
>>> def lexical_diversity(text):
...     return len(text) / len(set(text))
```

We use the keyword `return` to indicate the value that is produced as output by the function. In this example, all the work of the function is done in the `return` statement. Here's an equivalent definition that does the same work using multiple lines of code. We'll change the parameter name from `text` to `my_text_data` to remind you that this is an arbitrary choice:

```
>>> def lexical_diversity(my_text_data):
...     word_count = len(my_text_data)
...     vocab_size = len(set(my_text_data))
...     diversity_score = word_count / vocab_size
...     return diversity_score
```

Notice that we've created some new variables inside the body of the function. These are **local variables** and are not accessible outside the function. So now we have defined a function with the name `lexical_diversity`. But just defining it won't produce any output! Functions do nothing until they are "called" (or "invoked").

Let's return to our earlier scenario, and actually define a simple function to work out English plurals. The function `plural()` in Example 2-2 takes a singular noun and generates a plural form, though it is not always correct. (We'll discuss functions at greater length in Section 4.4.)

Example 2-2. A Python function: This function tries to work out the plural form of any English noun; the keyword def (define) is followed by the function name, then a parameter inside parentheses, and a colon; the body of the function is the indented block of code; it tries to recognize patterns within the word and process the word accordingly; e.g., if the word ends with y, delete the y and add ies.

```
def plural(word):
    if word.endswith('y'):
        return word[:-1] + 'ies'
    elif word[-1] in 'sx' or word[-2:] in ['sh', 'ch']:
        return word + 'es'
    elif word.endswith('an'):
        return word[:-2] + 'en'
    else:
        return word + 's'
>>> plural('fairy')
'fairies'
>>> plural('woman')
'women'
```

The `endswith()` function is always associated with a string object (e.g., `word` in Example 2-2). To call such functions, we give the name of the object, a period, and then the name of the function. These functions are usually known as **methods**.

Modules

Over time you will find that you create a variety of useful little text-processing functions, and you end up copying them from old programs to new ones. Which file contains the latest version of the function you want to use? It makes life a lot easier if you can collect your work into a single place, and access previously defined functions without making copies.

To do this, save your function(s) in a file called (say) *textproc.py*. Now, you can access your work simply by importing it from the file:

```
>>> from textproc import plural
>>> plural('wish')
wishes
>>> plural('fan')
fen
```

Our plural function obviously has an error, since the plural of *fan* is *fans*. Instead of typing in a new version of the function, we can simply edit the existing one. Thus, at every stage, there is only one version of our plural function, and no confusion about which one is being used.

A collection of variable and function definitions in a file is called a Python **module**. A collection of related modules is called a **package**. NLTK's code for processing the Brown Corpus is an example of a module, and its collection of code for processing all the different corpora is an example of a package. NLTK itself is a set of packages, sometimes called a **library**.

Caution!

If you are creating a file to contain some of your Python code, do *not* name your file *nltk.py*: it may get imported in place of the "real" NLTK package. When it imports modules, Python first looks in the current directory (folder).

2.4 Lexical Resources

A lexicon, or lexical resource, is a collection of words and/or phrases along with associated information, such as part-of-speech and sense definitions. Lexical resources are secondary to texts, and are usually created and enriched with the help of texts. For example, if we have defined a text `my_text`, then `vocab = sorted(set(my_text))` builds the vocabulary of `my_text`, whereas `word_freq = FreqDist(my_text)` counts the frequency of each word in the text. Both `vocab` and `word_freq` are simple lexical resources. Similarly, a concordance like the one we saw in Section 1.1 gives us information about word usage that might help in the preparation of a dictionary. Standard terminology for lexicons is illustrated in Figure 2-5. A **lexical entry** consists of a **headword** (also known as a **lemma**) along with additional information, such as the part-of-speech and

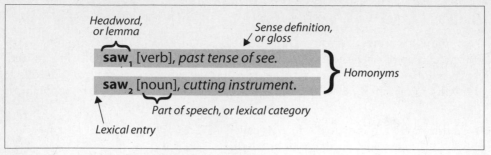

Figure 2-5. Lexicon terminology: Lexical entries for two lemmas having the same spelling (homonyms), providing part-of-speech and gloss information.

the sense definition. Two distinct words having the same spelling are called **homonyms**.

The simplest kind of lexicon is nothing more than a sorted list of words. Sophisticated lexicons include complex structure within and across the individual entries. In this section, we'll look at some lexical resources included with NLTK.

Wordlist Corpora

NLTK includes some corpora that are nothing more than wordlists. The Words Corpus is the */usr/dict/words* file from Unix, used by some spellcheckers. We can use it to find unusual or misspelled words in a text corpus, as shown in Example 2-3.

Example 2-3. Filtering a text: This program computes the vocabulary of a text, then removes all items that occur in an existing wordlist, leaving just the uncommon or misspelled words.

```
def unusual_words(text):
    text_vocab = set(w.lower() for w in text if w.isalpha())
    english_vocab = set(w.lower() for w in nltk.corpus.words.words())
    unusual = text_vocab.difference(english_vocab)
    return sorted(unusual)
>>> unusual_words(nltk.corpus.gutenberg.words('austen-sense.txt'))
['abbeyland', 'abhorrence', 'abominably', 'abridgement', 'accordant', 'accustomary',
'adieus', 'affability', 'affectedly', 'aggrandizement', 'alighted', 'allenham',
'amiably', 'annamaria', 'annuities', 'apologising', 'arbour', 'archness', ...]
>>> unusual_words(nltk.corpus.nps_chat.words())
['aaaaaaaaaaaaaaaaa', 'aaahhhh', 'abou', 'abourted', 'abs', 'ack', 'acros',
'actualy', 'adduser', 'addy', 'adoted', 'adreniline', 'ae', 'afe', 'affari', 'afk',
'agaibn', 'agurlwithbigguns', 'ahah', 'ahahah', 'ahahh', 'ahahha', 'ahem', 'ahh', ...]
```

There is also a corpus of **stopwords**, that is, high-frequency words such as *the*, *to*, and *also* that we sometimes want to filter out of a document before further processing. Stopwords usually have little lexical content, and their presence in a text fails to distinguish it from other texts.

```
>>> from nltk.corpus import stopwords
>>> stopwords.words('english')
['a', "a's", 'able', 'about', 'above', 'according', 'accordingly', 'across',
```

```
'actually', 'after', 'afterwards', 'again', 'against', "ain't", 'all', 'allow',
'allows', 'almost', 'alone', 'along', 'already', 'also', 'although', 'always', ...]
```

Let's define a function to compute what fraction of words in a text are *not* in the stop-words list:

```
>>> def content_fraction(text):
...     stopwords = nltk.corpus.stopwords.words('english')
...     content = [w for w in text if w.lower() not in stopwords]
...     return len(content) / len(text)
...
>>> content_fraction(nltk.corpus.reuters.words())
0.65997695393285261
```

Thus, with the help of stopwords, we filter out a third of the words of the text. Notice that we've combined two different kinds of corpus here, using a lexical resource to filter the content of a text corpus.

E	G	I	
V	R	V	How many words of four letters or more can you make from those shown here? Each letter may be used once per word. Each word must contain the center letter and there must be at least one nine-letter word. No plurals ending in "s"; no foreign words; no proper names. 21 words, good; 32 words, very good; 42 words, excellent.
O	N	L	

Figure 2-6. A word puzzle: A grid of randomly chosen letters with rules for creating words out of the letters; this puzzle is known as "Target."

A wordlist is useful for solving word puzzles, such as the one in Figure 2-6. Our program iterates through every word and, for each one, checks whether it meets the conditions. It is easy to check obligatory letter ❷ and length ❶ constraints (and we'll only look for words with six or more letters here). It is trickier to check that candidate solutions only use combinations of the supplied letters, especially since some of the supplied letters appear twice (here, the letter *v*). The FreqDist comparison method ❸ permits us to check that the frequency of each *letter* in the candidate word is less than or equal to the frequency of the corresponding letter in the puzzle.

```
>>> puzzle_letters = nltk.FreqDist('egivrvonl')
>>> obligatory = 'r'
>>> wordlist = nltk.corpus.words.words()
>>> [w for w in wordlist if len(w) >= 6 ❶
...                         and obligatory in w ❷
...                         and nltk.FreqDist(w) <= puzzle_letters] ❸
['glover', 'gorlin', 'govern', 'grovel', 'ignore', 'involver', 'lienor',
'linger', 'longer', 'lovering', 'noiler', 'overling', 'region', 'renvoi',
'revolving', 'ringle', 'roving', 'violer', 'virole']
```

One more wordlist corpus is the Names Corpus, containing 8,000 first names categorized by gender. The male and female names are stored in separate files. Let's find names that appear in both files, i.e., names that are ambiguous for gender:

```
>>> names = nltk.corpus.names
>>> names.fileids()
['female.txt', 'male.txt']
>>> male_names = names.words('male.txt')
>>> female_names = names.words('female.txt')
>>> [w for w in male_names if w in female_names]
['Abbey', 'Abbie', 'Abby', 'Addie', 'Adrian', 'Adrien', 'Ajay', 'Alex', 'Alexis',
'Alfie', 'Ali', 'Alix', 'Allie', 'Allyn', 'Andie', 'Andrea', 'Andy', 'Angel',
'Angie', 'Ariel', 'Ashley', 'Aubrey', 'Augustine', 'Austin', 'Averil', ...]
```

It is well known that names ending in the letter *a* are almost always female. We can see this and some other patterns in the graph in Figure 2-7, produced by the following code. Remember that name[-1] is the last letter of name.

```
>>> cfd = nltk.ConditionalFreqDist(
...          (fileid, name[-1])
...          for fileid in names.fileids()
...          for name in names.words(fileid))
>>> cfd.plot()
```

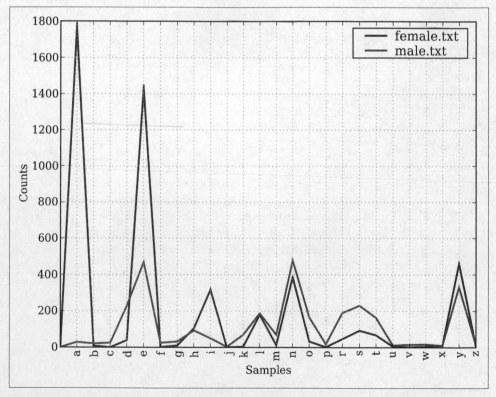

Figure 2-7. Conditional frequency distribution: This plot shows the number of female and male names ending with each letter of the alphabet; most names ending with a, e, or i are female; names ending in h and l are equally likely to be male or female; names ending in k, o, r, s, and t are likely to be male.

A Pronouncing Dictionary

A slightly richer kind of lexical resource is a table (or spreadsheet), containing a word plus some properties in each row. NLTK includes the CMU Pronouncing Dictionary for U.S. English, which was designed for use by speech synthesizers.

```
>>> entries = nltk.corpus.cmudict.entries()
>>> len(entries)
127012
>>> for entry in entries[39943:39951]:
...     print entry
...
('fir', ['F', 'ER1'])
('fire', ['F', 'AY1', 'ER0'])
('fire', ['F', 'AY1', 'R'])
('firearm', ['F', 'AY1', 'ER0', 'AA2', 'R', 'M'])
('firearm', ['F', 'AY1', 'R', 'AA2', 'R', 'M'])
('firearms', ['F', 'AY1', 'ER0', 'AA2', 'R', 'M', 'Z'])
('firearms', ['F', 'AY1', 'R', 'AA2', 'R', 'M', 'Z'])
('fireball', ['F', 'AY1', 'ER0', 'B', 'AO2', 'L'])
```

For each word, this lexicon provides a list of phonetic codes—distinct labels for each contrastive sound—known as *phones*. Observe that *fire* has two pronunciations (in U.S. English): the one-syllable F AY1 R, and the two-syllable F AY1 ER0. The symbols in the CMU Pronouncing Dictionary are from the *Arpabet*, described in more detail at *http://en.wikipedia.org/wiki/Arpabet*.

Each entry consists of two parts, and we can process these individually using a more complex version of the for statement. Instead of writing for entry in entries:, we replace entry with *two* variable names, word, pron ❶. Now, each time through the loop, word is assigned the first part of the entry, and pron is assigned the second part of the entry:

```
>>> for word, pron in entries:           ❶
...     if len(pron) == 3:               ❷
...         ph1, ph2, ph3 = pron         ❸
...         if ph1 == 'P' and ph3 == 'T':
...             print word, ph2,
...
pait EY1 pat AE1 pate EY1 patt AE1 peart ER1 peat IY1 peet IY1 peete IY1 pert ER1
pet EH1 pete IY1 pett EH1 piet IY1 piette IY1 pit IH1 pitt IH1 pot AA1 pote OW1
pott AA1 pout AW1 puett UW1 purt ER1 put UH1 putt AH1
```

The program just shown scans the lexicon looking for entries whose pronunciation consists of three phones ❷. If the condition is true, it assigns the contents of pron to three new variables: ph1, ph2, and ph3. Notice the unusual form of the statement that does that work ❸.

Here's another example of the same for statement, this time used inside a list comprehension. This program finds all words whose pronunciation ends with a syllable sounding like *nicks*. You could use this method to find rhyming words.

```
>>> syllable = ['N', 'IHO', 'K', 'S']
>>> [word for word, pron in entries if pron[-4:] == syllable]
["atlantic's", 'audiotronics', 'avionics', 'beatniks', 'calisthenics', 'centronics',
'chetniks', "clinic's", 'clinics', 'conics', 'cynics', 'diasonics', "dominic's",
'ebonics', 'electronics', "electronics'", 'endotronics', "endotronics'", 'enix', ...]
```

Notice that the one pronunciation is spelled in several ways: *nics, niks, nix,* and even
ntic's with a silent *t,* for the word *atlantic's.* Let's look for some other mismatches
between pronunciation and writing. Can you summarize the purpose of the following
examples and explain how they work?

```
>>> [w for w, pron in entries if pron[-1] == 'M' and w[-1] == 'n']
['autumn', 'column', 'condemn', 'damn', 'goddamn', 'hymn', 'solemn']
>>> sorted(set(w[:2] for w, pron in entries if pron[0] == 'N' and w[0] != 'n'))
['gn', 'kn', 'mn', 'pn']
```

The phones contain digits to represent primary stress (1), secondary stress (2), and no
stress (0). As our final example, we define a function to extract the stress digits and then
scan our lexicon to find words having a particular stress pattern.

```
>>> def stress(pron):
...     return [char for phone in pron for char in phone if char.isdigit()]
>>> [w for w, pron in entries if stress(pron) == ['0', '1', '0', '2', '0']]
['abbreviated', 'abbreviating', 'accelerated', 'accelerating', 'accelerator',
'accentuated', 'accentuating', 'accommodated', 'accommodating', 'accommodative',
'accumulated', 'accumulating', 'accumulative', 'accumulator', 'accumulators', ...]
>>> [w for w, pron in entries if stress(pron) == ['0', '2', '0', '1', '0']]
['abbreviation', 'abbreviations', 'abomination', 'abortifacient', 'abortifacients',
'academicians', 'accommodation', 'accommodations', 'accreditation', 'accreditations',
'accumulation', 'accumulations', 'acetylcholine', 'acetylcholine', 'adjudication', ...]
```

 A subtlety of this program is that our user-defined function **stress()** is
invoked inside the condition of a list comprehension. There is also a
doubly nested **for** loop. There's a lot going on here, and you might want
to return to this once you've had more experience using list comprehensions.

We can use a conditional frequency distribution to help us find minimally contrasting
sets of words. Here we find all the *p* words consisting of three sounds ❷, and group
them according to their first and last sounds ❶.

```
>>> p3 = [(pron[0]+'-'+pron[2], word) ❶
...       for (word, pron) in entries
...       if pron[0] == 'P' and len(pron) == 3] ❷
>>> cfd = nltk.ConditionalFreqDist(p3)
>>> for template in cfd.conditions():
...     if len(cfd[template]) > 10:
...         words = cfd[template].keys()
...         wordlist = ' '.join(words)
...         print template, wordlist[:70] + "..."
...
P-CH perch puche poche peach petsche poach pietsch putsch pautsch piche pet...
```

```
P-K pik peek pic pique paque polk perc poke perk pac pock poch purk pak pa...
P-L pil poehl pille pehl pol pall pohl pahl paul perl pale paille perle po...
P-N paine payne pon pain pin pawn pinn pun pine paign pen pyne pane penn p...
P-P pap paap pipp paup pape pup pep poop pop pipe paape popp pip peep pope...
P-R paar poor par poore pear pare pour peer pore parr por pair porr pier...
P-S pearse piece posts pasts peace perce pos pers pace puss pesce pass pur...
P-T pot puett pit pete putt pat purt pet peart pott pett pait pert pote pa...
P-Z pays p.s pao's pais paws p.'s pas pez paz pei's pose poise peas paiz p...
```

Rather than iterating over the whole dictionary, we can also access it by looking up particular words. We will use Python's dictionary data structure, which we will study systematically in Section 5.3. We look up a dictionary by specifying its name, followed by a **key** (such as the word `'fire'`) inside square brackets ❶.

```
>>> prondict = nltk.corpus.cmudict.dict()
>>> prondict['fire'] ❶
[['F', 'AY1', 'ER0'], ['F', 'AY1', 'R']]
>>> prondict['blog'] ❷
Traceback (most recent call last):
  File "<stdin>", line 1, in <module>
KeyError: 'blog'
>>> prondict['blog'] = [['B', 'L', 'AA1', 'G']] ❸
>>> prondict['blog']
[['B', 'L', 'AA1', 'G']]
```

If we try to look up a non-existent key ❷, we get a `KeyError`. This is similar to what happens when we index a list with an integer that is too large, producing an `IndexError ror`. The word *blog* is missing from the pronouncing dictionary, so we tweak our version by assigning a value for this key ❸ (this has no effect on the NLTK corpus; next time we access it, *blog* will still be absent).

We can use any lexical resource to process a text, e.g., to filter out words having some lexical property (like nouns), or mapping every word of the text. For example, the following text-to-speech function looks up each word of the text in the pronunciation dictionary:

```
>>> text = ['natural', 'language', 'processing']
>>> [ph for w in text for ph in prondict[w][0]]
['N', 'AE1', 'CH', 'ER0', 'AH0', 'L', 'L', 'AE1', 'NG', 'G', 'W', 'AH0', 'JH',
 'P', 'R', 'AA1', 'S', 'EH0', 'S', 'IH0', 'NG']
```

Comparative Wordlists

Another example of a tabular lexicon is the **comparative wordlist**. NLTK includes so-called **Swadesh wordlists**, lists of about 200 common words in several languages. The languages are identified using an ISO 639 two-letter code.

```
>>> from nltk.corpus import swadesh
>>> swadesh.fileids()
['be', 'bg', 'bs', 'ca', 'cs', 'cu', 'de', 'en', 'es', 'fr', 'hr', 'it', 'la', 'mk',
 'nl', 'pl', 'pt', 'ro', 'ru', 'sk', 'sl', 'sr', 'sw', 'uk']
>>> swadesh.words('en')
['I', 'you (singular), thou', 'he', 'we', 'you (plural)', 'they', 'this', 'that',
```

```
'here', 'there', 'who', 'what', 'where', 'when', 'how', 'not', 'all', 'many', 'some',
'few', 'other', 'one', 'two', 'three', 'four', 'five', 'big', 'long', 'wide', ...]
```

We can access cognate words from multiple languages using the `entries()` method, specifying a list of languages. With one further step we can convert this into a simple dictionary (we'll learn about `dict()` in Section 5.3).

```
>>> fr2en = swadesh.entries(['fr', 'en'])
>>> fr2en
[('je', 'I'), ('tu, vous', 'you (singular), thou'), ('il', 'he'), ...]
>>> translate = dict(fr2en)
>>> translate['chien']
'dog'
>>> translate['jeter']
'throw'
```

We can make our simple translator more useful by adding other source languages. Let's get the German-English and Spanish-English pairs, convert each to a dictionary using `dict()`, then *update* our original `translate` dictionary with these additional mappings:

```
>>> de2en = swadesh.entries(['de', 'en'])    # German-English
>>> es2en = swadesh.entries(['es', 'en'])    # Spanish-English
>>> translate.update(dict(de2en))
>>> translate.update(dict(es2en))
>>> translate['Hund']
'dog'
>>> translate['perro']
'dog'
```

We can compare words in various Germanic and Romance languages:

```
>>> languages = ['en', 'de', 'nl', 'es', 'fr', 'pt', 'la']
>>> for i in [139, 140, 141, 142]:
...     print swadesh.entries(languages)[i]
...
('say', 'sagen', 'zeggen', 'decir', 'dire', 'dizer', 'dicere')
('sing', 'singen', 'zingen', 'cantar', 'chanter', 'cantar', 'canere')
('play', 'spielen', 'spelen', 'jugar', 'jouer', 'jogar, brincar', 'ludere')
('float', 'schweben', 'zweven', 'flotar', 'flotter', 'flutuar, boiar', 'fluctuare')
```

Shoebox and Toolbox Lexicons

Perhaps the single most popular tool used by linguists for managing data is *Toolbox*, previously known as *Shoebox* since it replaces the field linguist's traditional shoebox full of file cards. Toolbox is freely downloadable from *http://www.sil.org/computing/toolbox/*.

A Toolbox file consists of a collection of entries, where each entry is made up of one or more fields. Most fields are optional or repeatable, which means that this kind of lexical resource cannot be treated as a table or spreadsheet.

Here is a dictionary for the Rotokas language. We see just the first entry, for the word *kaa*, meaning "to gag":

```
>>> from nltk.corpus import toolbox
>>> toolbox.entries('rotokas.dic')
[('kaa', [('ps', 'V'), ('pt', 'A'), ('ge', 'gag'), ('tkp', 'nek i pas'),
('dcsv', 'true'), ('vx', '1'), ('sc', '???'), ('dt', '29/Oct/2005'),
('ex', 'Apoka ira kaaroi aioa-ia reoreopaoro.'),
('xp', 'Kaikai i pas long nek bilong Apoka bikos em i kaikai na toktok.'),
('xe', 'Apoka is gagging from food while talking.')]), ...]
```

Entries consist of a series of attribute-value pairs, such as ('ps', 'V') to indicate that the part-of-speech is 'V' (verb), and ('ge', 'gag') to indicate that the gloss-into-English is 'gag'. The last three pairs contain an example sentence in Rotokas and its translations into Tok Pisin and English.

The loose structure of Toolbox files makes it hard for us to do much more with them at this stage. XML provides a powerful way to process this kind of corpus, and we will return to this topic in Chapter 11.

The Rotokas language is spoken on the island of Bougainville, Papua New Guinea. This lexicon was contributed to NLTK by Stuart Robinson. Rotokas is notable for having an inventory of just 12 phonemes (contrastive sounds); see *http://en.wikipedia.org/wiki/Rotokas_language*

2.5 WordNet

WordNet is a semantically oriented dictionary of English, similar to a traditional thesaurus but with a richer structure. NLTK includes the English WordNet, with 155,287 words and 117,659 synonym sets. We'll begin by looking at synonyms and how they are accessed in WordNet.

Senses and Synonyms

Consider the sentence in (1a). If we replace the word *motorcar* in (1a) with *automobile*, to get (1b), the meaning of the sentence stays pretty much the same:

(1) a. Benz is credited with the invention of the motorcar.

  b. Benz is credited with the invention of the automobile.

Since everything else in the sentence has remained unchanged, we can conclude that the words *motorcar* and *automobile* have the same meaning, i.e., they are **synonyms**. We can explore these words with the help of WordNet:

```
>>> from nltk.corpus import wordnet as wn
>>> wn.synsets('motorcar')
[Synset('car.n.01')]
```

Thus, *motorcar* has just one possible meaning and it is identified as car.n.01, the first noun sense of *car*. The entity car.n.01 is called a **synset**, or "synonym set," a collection of synonymous words (or "lemmas"):

```
>>> wn.synset('car.n.01').lemma_names
['car', 'auto', 'automobile', 'machine', 'motorcar']
```

Each word of a synset can have several meanings, e.g., *car* can also signify a train carriage, a gondola, or an elevator car. However, we are only interested in the single meaning that is common to all words of this synset. Synsets also come with a prose definition and some example sentences:

```
>>> wn.synset('car.n.01').definition
'a motor vehicle with four wheels; usually propelled by an internal combustion engine'
>>> wn.synset('car.n.01').examples
['he needs a car to get to work']
```

Although definitions help humans to understand the intended meaning of a synset, the *words* of the synset are often more useful for our programs. To eliminate ambiguity, we will identify these words as `car.n.01.automobile`, `car.n.01.motorcar`, and so on. This pairing of a synset with a word is called a lemma. We can get all the lemmas for a given synset ❶, look up a particular lemma ❷, get the synset corresponding to a lemma ❸, and get the "name" of a lemma ❹:

```
>>> wn.synset('car.n.01').lemmas ❶
[Lemma('car.n.01.car'), Lemma('car.n.01.auto'), Lemma('car.n.01.automobile'),
Lemma('car.n.01.machine'), Lemma('car.n.01.motorcar')]
>>> wn.lemma('car.n.01.automobile') ❷
Lemma('car.n.01.automobile')
>>> wn.lemma('car.n.01.automobile').synset ❸
Synset('car.n.01')
>>> wn.lemma('car.n.01.automobile').name ❹
'automobile'
```

Unlike the words *automobile* and *motorcar*, which are unambiguous and have one synset, the word *car* is ambiguous, having five synsets:

```
>>> wn.synsets('car')
[Synset('car.n.01'), Synset('car.n.02'), Synset('car.n.03'), Synset('car.n.04'),
Synset('cable_car.n.01')]
>>> for synset in wn.synsets('car'):
...     print synset.lemma_names
...
['car', 'auto', 'automobile', 'machine', 'motorcar']
['car', 'railcar', 'railway_car', 'railroad_car']
['car', 'gondola']
['car', 'elevator_car']
['cable_car', 'car']
```

For convenience, we can access all the lemmas involving the word *car* as follows:

```
>>> wn.lemmas('car')
[Lemma('car.n.01.car'), Lemma('car.n.02.car'), Lemma('car.n.03.car'),
Lemma('car.n.04.car'), Lemma('cable_car.n.01.car')]
```

Your Turn: Write down all the senses of the word *dish* that you can think of. Now, explore this word with the help of WordNet, using the same operations shown earlier.

The WordNet Hierarchy

WordNet synsets correspond to abstract concepts, and they don't always have corresponding words in English. These concepts are linked together in a hierarchy. Some concepts are very general, such as *Entity*, *State*, *Event*; these are called **unique beginners** or root synsets. Others, such as *gas guzzler* and *hatchback*, are much more specific. A small portion of a concept hierarchy is illustrated in Figure 2-8.

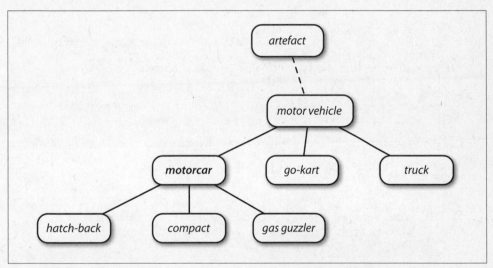

Figure 2-8. Fragment of WordNet concept hierarchy: Nodes correspond to synsets; edges indicate the hypernym/hyponym relation, i.e., the relation between superordinate and subordinate concepts.

WordNet makes it easy to navigate between concepts. For example, given a concept like *motorcar*, we can look at the concepts that are more specific—the (immediate) **hyponyms**.

```
>>> motorcar = wn.synset('car.n.01')
>>> types_of_motorcar = motorcar.hyponyms()
>>> types_of_motorcar[26]
Synset('ambulance.n.01')
>>> sorted([lemma.name for synset in types_of_motorcar for lemma in synset.lemmas])
['Model_T', 'S.U.V.', 'SUV', 'Stanley_Steamer', 'ambulance', 'beach_waggon',
'beach_wagon', 'bus', 'cab', 'compact', 'compact_car', 'convertible',
'coupe', 'cruiser', 'electric', 'electric_automobile', 'electric_car',
'estate_car', 'gas_guzzler', 'hack', 'hardtop', 'hatchback', 'heap',
'horseless_carriage', 'hot-rod', 'hot_rod', 'jalopy', 'jeep', 'landrover',
'limo', 'limousine', 'loaner', 'minicar', 'minivan', 'pace_car', 'patrol_car',
```

```
'phaeton', 'police_car', 'police_cruiser', 'prowl_car', 'race_car', 'racer',
'racing_car', 'roadster', 'runabout', 'saloon', 'secondhand_car', 'sedan',
'sport_car', 'sport_utility', 'sport_utility_vehicle', 'sports_car', 'squad_car',
'station_waggon', 'station_wagon', 'stock_car', 'subcompact', 'subcompact_car',
'taxi', 'taxicab', 'tourer', 'touring_car', 'two-seater', 'used-car', 'waggon',
'wagon']
```

We can also navigate up the hierarchy by visiting hypernyms. Some words have multiple paths, because they can be classified in more than one way. There are two paths between car.n.01 and entity.n.01 because wheeled_vehicle.n.01 can be classified as both a vehicle and a container.

```
>>> motorcar.hypernyms()
[Synset('motor_vehicle.n.01')]
>>> paths = motorcar.hypernym_paths()
>>> len(paths)
2
>>> [synset.name for synset in paths[0]]
['entity.n.01', 'physical_entity.n.01', 'object.n.01', 'whole.n.02', 'artifact.n.01',
'instrumentality.n.03', 'container.n.01', 'wheeled_vehicle.n.01',
'self-propelled_vehicle.n.01', 'motor_vehicle.n.01', 'car.n.01']
>>> [synset.name for synset in paths[1]]
['entity.n.01', 'physical_entity.n.01', 'object.n.01', 'whole.n.02', 'artifact.n.01',
'instrumentality.n.03', 'conveyance.n.03', 'vehicle.n.01', 'wheeled_vehicle.n.01',
'self-propelled_vehicle.n.01', 'motor_vehicle.n.01', 'car.n.01']
```

We can get the most general hypernyms (or root hypernyms) of a synset as follows:

```
>>> motorcar.root_hypernyms()
[Synset('entity.n.01')]
```

 Your Turn: Try out NLTK's convenient graphical WordNet browser: nltk.app.wordnet(). Explore the WordNet hierarchy by following the hypernym and hyponym links.

More Lexical Relations

Hypernyms and hyponyms are called **lexical relations** because they relate one synset to another. These two relations navigate up and down the "is-a" hierarchy. Another important way to navigate the WordNet network is from items to their components (**meronyms**) or to the things they are contained in (**holonyms**). For example, the parts of a *tree* are its *trunk*, *crown*, and so on; these are the part_meronyms(). The *substance* a tree is made of includes *heartwood* and *sapwood*, i.e., the substance_meronyms(). A collection of trees forms a *forest*, i.e., the member_holonyms():

```
>>> wn.synset('tree.n.01').part_meronyms()
[Synset('burl.n.02'), Synset('crown.n.07'), Synset('stump.n.01'),
Synset('trunk.n.01'), Synset('limb.n.02')]
>>> wn.synset('tree.n.01').substance_meronyms()
[Synset('heartwood.n.01'), Synset('sapwood.n.01')]
```

```
>>> wn.synset('tree.n.01').member_holonyms()
[Synset('forest.n.01')]
```

To see just how intricate things can get, consider the word *mint*, which has several closely related senses. We can see that `mint.n.04` is part of `mint.n.02` and the substance from which `mint.n.05` is made.

```
>>> for synset in wn.synsets('mint', wn.NOUN):
...     print synset.name + ':', synset.definition
...
batch.n.02: (often followed by `of') a large number or amount or extent
mint.n.02: any north temperate plant of the genus Mentha with aromatic leaves and
           small mauve flowers
mint.n.03: any member of the mint family of plants
mint.n.04: the leaves of a mint plant used fresh or candied
mint.n.05: a candy that is flavored with a mint oil
mint.n.06: a plant where money is coined by authority of the government
>>> wn.synset('mint.n.04').part_holonyms()
[Synset('mint.n.02')]
>>> wn.synset('mint.n.04').substance_holonyms()
[Synset('mint.n.05')]
```

There are also relationships between verbs. For example, the act of *walking* involves the act of *stepping*, so walking **entails** stepping. Some verbs have multiple entailments:

```
>>> wn.synset('walk.v.01').entailments()
[Synset('step.v.01')]
>>> wn.synset('eat.v.01').entailments()
[Synset('swallow.v.01'), Synset('chew.v.01')]
>>> wn.synset('tease.v.03').entailments()
[Synset('arouse.v.07'), Synset('disappoint.v.01')]
```

Some lexical relationships hold between lemmas, e.g., **antonymy**:

```
>>> wn.lemma('supply.n.02.supply').antonyms()
[Lemma('demand.n.02.demand')]
>>> wn.lemma('rush.v.01.rush').antonyms()
[Lemma('linger.v.04.linger')]
>>> wn.lemma('horizontal.a.01.horizontal').antonyms()
[Lemma('vertical.a.01.vertical'), Lemma('inclined.a.02.inclined')]
>>> wn.lemma('staccato.r.01.staccato').antonyms()
[Lemma('legato.r.01.legato')]
```

You can see the lexical relations, and the other methods defined on a synset, using `dir()`. For example, try `dir(wn.synset('harmony.n.02'))`.

Semantic Similarity

We have seen that synsets are linked by a complex network of lexical relations. Given a particular synset, we can traverse the WordNet network to find synsets with related meanings. Knowing which words are semantically related is useful for indexing a collection of texts, so that a search for a general term such as *vehicle* will match documents containing specific terms such as *limousine*.

Recall that each synset has one or more hypernym paths that link it to a root hypernym such as `entity.n.01`. Two synsets linked to the same root may have several hypernyms in common (see Figure 2-8). If two synsets share a very specific hypernym—one that is low down in the hypernym hierarchy—they must be closely related.

```
>>> right = wn.synset('right_whale.n.01')
>>> orca = wn.synset('orca.n.01')
>>> minke = wn.synset('minke_whale.n.01')
>>> tortoise = wn.synset('tortoise.n.01')
>>> novel = wn.synset('novel.n.01')
>>> right.lowest_common_hypernyms(minke)
[Synset('baleen_whale.n.01')]
>>> right.lowest_common_hypernyms(orca)
[Synset('whale.n.02')]
>>> right.lowest_common_hypernyms(tortoise)
[Synset('vertebrate.n.01')]
>>> right.lowest_common_hypernyms(novel)
[Synset('entity.n.01')]
```

Of course we know that *whale* is very specific (and *baleen whale* even more so), whereas *vertebrate* is more general and *entity* is completely general. We can quantify this concept of generality by looking up the depth of each synset:

```
>>> wn.synset('baleen_whale.n.01').min_depth()
14
>>> wn.synset('whale.n.02').min_depth()
13
>>> wn.synset('vertebrate.n.01').min_depth()
8
>>> wn.synset('entity.n.01').min_depth()
0
```

Similarity measures have been defined over the collection of WordNet synsets that incorporate this insight. For example, `path_similarity` assigns a score in the range 0–1 based on the shortest path that connects the concepts in the hypernym hierarchy (`-1` is returned in those cases where a path cannot be found). Comparing a synset with itself will return 1. Consider the following similarity scores, relating *right whale* to *minke whale*, *orca*, *tortoise*, and *novel*. Although the numbers won't mean much, they decrease as we move away from the semantic space of sea creatures to inanimate objects.

```
>>> right.path_similarity(minke)
0.25
>>> right.path_similarity(orca)
0.16666666666666666
>>> right.path_similarity(tortoise)
0.076923076923076927
>>> right.path_similarity(novel)
0.043478260869565216
```

Several other similarity measures are available; you can type `help(wn)` for more information. NLTK also includes VerbNet, a hierarchical verb lexicon linked to WordNet. It can be accessed with `nltk.corpus.verb net`.

2.6 Summary

- A text corpus is a large, structured collection of texts. NLTK comes with many corpora, e.g., the Brown Corpus, `nltk.corpus.brown`.

- Some text corpora are categorized, e.g., by genre or topic; sometimes the categories of a corpus overlap each other.

- A conditional frequency distribution is a collection of frequency distributions, each one for a different condition. They can be used for counting word frequencies, given a context or a genre.

- Python programs more than a few lines long should be entered using a text editor, saved to a file with a *.py* extension, and accessed using an `import` statement.

- Python functions permit you to associate a name with a particular block of code, and reuse that code as often as necessary.

- Some functions, known as "methods," are associated with an object, and we give the object name followed by a period followed by the method name, like this: `x.funct(y)`, e.g., `word.isalpha()`.

- To find out about some variable v, type `help(v)` in the Python interactive interpreter to read the help entry for this kind of object.

- WordNet is a semantically oriented dictionary of English, consisting of synonym sets—or synsets—and organized into a network.

- Some functions are not available by default, but must be accessed using Python's `import` statement.

2.7 Further Reading

Extra materials for this chapter are posted at *http://www.nltk.org/*, including links to freely available resources on the Web. The corpus methods are summarized in the Corpus HOWTO, at *http://www.nltk.org/howto*, and documented extensively in the online API documentation.

Significant sources of published corpora are the *Linguistic Data Consortium* (LDC) and the *European Language Resources Agency* (ELRA). Hundreds of annotated text and speech corpora are available in dozens of languages. Non-commercial licenses permit the data to be used in teaching and research. For some corpora, commercial licenses are also available (but for a higher fee).

These and many other language resources have been documented using OLAC Metadata, and can be searched via the OLAC home page at *http://www.language-archives .org/*. *Corpora List* (see *http://gandalf.aksis.uib.no/corpora/sub.html*) is a mailing list for discussions about corpora, and you can find resources by searching the list archives or posting to the list. The most complete inventory of the world's languages is *Ethnologue*, *http://www.ethnologue.com/*. Of 7,000 languages, only a few dozen have substantial digital resources suitable for use in NLP.

This chapter has touched on the field of **Corpus Linguistics**. Other useful books in this area include (Biber, Conrad, & Reppen, 1998), (McEnery, 2006), (Meyer, 2002), (Sampson & McCarthy, 2005), and (Scott & Tribble, 2006). Further readings in quantitative data analysis in linguistics are: (Baayen, 2008), (Gries, 2009), and (Woods, Fletcher, & Hughes, 1986).

The original description of WordNet is (Fellbaum, 1998). Although WordNet was originally developed for research in psycholinguistics, it is now widely used in NLP and Information Retrieval. WordNets are being developed for many other languages, as documented at *http://www.globalwordnet.org/*. For a study of WordNet similarity measures, see (Budanitsky & Hirst, 2006).

Other topics touched on in this chapter were phonetics and lexical semantics, and we refer readers to Chapters 7 and 20 of (Jurafsky & Martin, 2008).

2.8 Exercises

1. ○ Create a variable `phrase` containing a list of words. Experiment with the operations described in this chapter, including addition, multiplication, indexing, slicing, and sorting.

2. ○ Use the corpus module to explore `austen-persuasion.txt`. How many word tokens does this book have? How many word types?

3. ○ Use the Brown Corpus reader `nltk.corpus.brown.words()` or the Web Text Corpus reader `nltk.corpus.webtext.words()` to access some sample text in two different genres.

4. ○ Read in the texts of the *State of the Union* addresses, using the `state_union` corpus reader. Count occurrences of `men`, `women`, and `people` in each document. What has happened to the usage of these words over time?

5. ○ Investigate the holonym-meronym relations for some nouns. Remember that there are three kinds of holonym-meronym relation, so you need to use `member_mer onyms()`, `part_meronyms()`, `substance_meronyms()`, `member_holonyms()`, `part_holonyms()`, and `substance_holonyms()`.

6. ○ In the discussion of comparative wordlists, we created an object called `trans late`, which you could look up using words in both German and Italian in order

to get corresponding words in English. What problem might arise with this approach? Can you suggest a way to avoid this problem?

7. ○ According to Strunk and White's *Elements of Style*, the word *however*, used at the start of a sentence, means "in whatever way" or "to whatever extent," and not "nevertheless." They give this example of correct usage: *However you advise him, he will probably do as he thinks best.* (*http://www.bartleby.com/141/strunk3.html*) Use the concordance tool to study actual usage of this word in the various texts we have been considering. See also the *LanguageLog* posting "Fossilized prejudices about 'however'" at *http://itre.cis.upenn.edu/~myl/languagelog/archives/001913 .html*.

8. ◑ Define a conditional frequency distribution over the Names Corpus that allows you to see which *initial* letters are more frequent for males versus females (see Figure 2-7).

9. ◑ Pick a pair of texts and study the differences between them, in terms of vocabulary, vocabulary richness, genre, etc. Can you find pairs of words that have quite different meanings across the two texts, such as *monstrous* in *Moby Dick* and in *Sense and Sensibility*?

10. ◑ Read the BBC News article: "UK's Vicky Pollards 'left behind'" at *http://news .bbc.co.uk/1/hi/education/6173441.stm*. The article gives the following statistic about teen language: "the top 20 words used, including yeah, no, but and like, account for around a third of all words." How many word types account for a third of all word tokens, for a variety of text sources? What do you conclude about this statistic? Read more about this on *LanguageLog*, at *http://itre.cis.upenn.edu/~myl/ languagelog/archives/003993.html*.

11. ◑ Investigate the table of modal distributions and look for other patterns. Try to explain them in terms of your own impressionistic understanding of the different genres. Can you find other closed classes of words that exhibit significant differences across different genres?

12. ◑ The CMU Pronouncing Dictionary contains multiple pronunciations for certain words. How many distinct words does it contain? What fraction of words in this dictionary have more than one possible pronunciation?

13. ◑ What percentage of noun synsets have no hyponyms? You can get all noun synsets using `wn.all_synsets('n')`.

14. ◑ Define a function `supergloss(s)` that takes a synset `s` as its argument and returns a string consisting of the concatenation of the definition of `s`, and the definitions of all the hypernyms and hyponyms of `s`.

15. ◑ Write a program to find all words that occur at least three times in the Brown Corpus.

16. ◑ Write a program to generate a table of lexical diversity scores (i.e., token/type ratios), as we saw in Table 1-1. Include the full set of Brown Corpus genres

(`nltk.corpus.brown.categories()`). Which genre has the lowest diversity (greatest number of tokens per type)? Is this what you would have expected?

17. ◑ Write a function that finds the 50 most frequently occurring words of a text that are not stopwords.

18. ◑ Write a program to print the 50 most frequent bigrams (pairs of adjacent words) of a text, omitting bigrams that contain stopwords.

19. ◑ Write a program to create a table of word frequencies by genre, like the one given in Section 2.1 for modals. Choose your own words and try to find words whose presence (or absence) is typical of a genre. Discuss your findings.

20. ◑ Write a function `word_freq()` that takes a word and the name of a section of the Brown Corpus as arguments, and computes the frequency of the word in that section of the corpus.

21. ◑ Write a program to guess the number of syllables contained in a text, making use of the CMU Pronouncing Dictionary.

22. ◑ Define a function `hedge(text)` that processes a text and produces a new version with the word `'like'` between every third word.

23. ● **Zipf's Law**: Let $f(w)$ be the frequency of a word w in free text. Suppose that all the words of a text are ranked according to their frequency, with the most frequent word first. Zipf's Law states that the frequency of a word type is inversely proportional to its rank (i.e., $f \times r = k$, for some constant k). For example, the 50th most common word type should occur three times as frequently as the 150th most common word type.

    a. Write a function to process a large text and plot word frequency against word rank using `pylab.plot`. Do you confirm Zipf's law? (Hint: it helps to use a logarithmic scale.) What is going on at the extreme ends of the plotted line?

    b. Generate random text, e.g., using `random.choice("abcdefg ")`, taking care to include the space character. You will need to `import random` first. Use the string concatenation operator to accumulate characters into a (very) long string. Then tokenize this string, generate the Zipf plot as before, and compare the two plots. What do you make of Zipf's Law in the light of this?

24. ● Modify the text generation program in Example 2-1 further, to do the following tasks:

a. Store the *n* most likely words in a list `words`, then randomly choose a word from the list using `random.choice()`. (You will need to `import random` first.)

b. Select a particular genre, such as a section of the Brown Corpus or a Genesis translation, one of the Gutenberg texts, or one of the Web texts. Train the model on this corpus and get it to generate random text. You may have to experiment with different start words. How intelligible is the text? Discuss the strengths and weaknesses of this method of generating random text.

c. Now train your system using two distinct genres and experiment with generating text in the hybrid genre. Discuss your observations.

25. ● Define a function `find_language()` that takes a string as its argument and returns a list of languages that have that string as a word. Use the `udhr` corpus and limit your searches to files in the Latin-1 encoding.

26. ● What is the branching factor of the noun hypernym hierarchy? I.e., for every noun synset that has hyponyms—or children in the hypernym hierarchy—how many do they have on average? You can get all noun synsets using `wn.all_syn sets('n')`.

27. ● The polysemy of a word is the number of senses it has. Using WordNet, we can determine that the noun *dog* has seven senses with `len(wn.synsets('dog', 'n'))`. Compute the average polysemy of nouns, verbs, adjectives, and adverbs according to WordNet.

28. ● Use one of the predefined similarity measures to score the similarity of each of the following pairs of words. Rank the pairs in order of decreasing similarity. How close is your ranking to the order given here, an order that was established experimentally by (Miller & Charles, 1998): car-automobile, gem-jewel, journey-voyage, boy-lad, coast-shore, asylum-madhouse, magician-wizard, midday-noon, furnace-stove, food-fruit, bird-cock, bird-crane, tool-implement, brother-monk, lad-brother, crane-implement, journey-car, monk-oracle, cemetery-woodland, food-rooster, coast-hill, forest-graveyard, shore-woodland, monk-slave, coast-forest, lad-wizard, chord-smile, glass-magician, rooster-voyage, noon-string.

## CHAPTER 3

Processing Raw Text

The most important source of texts is undoubtedly the Web. It's convenient to have existing text collections to explore, such as the corpora we saw in the previous chapters. However, you probably have your own text sources in mind, and need to learn how to access them.

The goal of this chapter is to answer the following questions:

1. How can we write programs to access text from local files and from the Web, in order to get hold of an unlimited range of language material?

2. How can we split documents up into individual words and punctuation symbols, so we can carry out the same kinds of analysis we did with text corpora in earlier chapters?

3. How can we write programs to produce formatted output and save it in a file?

In order to address these questions, we will be covering key concepts in NLP, including tokenization and stemming. Along the way you will consolidate your Python knowledge and learn about strings, files, and regular expressions. Since so much text on the Web is in HTML format, we will also see how to dispense with markup.

 Important: From this chapter onwards, our program samples will assume you begin your interactive session or your program with the following import statements:

```
>>> from __future__ import division
>>> import nltk, re, pprint
```

3.1 Accessing Text from the Web and from Disk

Electronic Books

A small sample of texts from Project Gutenberg appears in the NLTK corpus collection. However, you may be interested in analyzing other texts from Project Gutenberg. You can browse the catalog of 25,000 free online books at *http://www.gutenberg.org/cata log/*, and obtain a URL to an ASCII text file. Although 90% of the texts in Project Gutenberg are in English, it includes material in over 50 other languages, including Catalan, Chinese, Dutch, Finnish, French, German, Italian, Portuguese, and Spanish (with more than 100 texts each).

Text number 2554 is an English translation of *Crime and Punishment*, and we can access it as follows.

```
>>> from urllib import urlopen
>>> url = "http://www.gutenberg.org/files/2554/2554.txt"
>>> raw = urlopen(url).read()
>>> type(raw)
<type 'str'>
>>> len(raw)
1176831
>>> raw[:75]
'The Project Gutenberg EBook of Crime and Punishment, by Fyodor Dostoevsky\r\n'
```

 The read() process will take a few seconds as it downloads this large book. If you're using an Internet proxy that is not correctly detected by Python, you may need to specify the proxy manually as follows:

```
>>> proxies = {'http': 'http://www.someproxy.com:3128'}
>>> raw = urlopen(url, proxies=proxies).read()
```

The variable raw contains a string with 1,176,831 characters. (We can see that it is a string, using type(raw).) This is the raw content of the book, including many details we are not interested in, such as whitespace, line breaks, and blank lines. Notice the \r and \n in the opening line of the file, which is how Python displays the special carriage return and line-feed characters (the file must have been created on a Windows machine). For our language processing, we want to break up the string into words and punctuation, as we saw in Chapter 1. This step is called **tokenization**, and it produces our familiar structure, a list of words and punctuation.

```
>>> tokens = nltk.word_tokenize(raw)
>>> type(tokens)
<type 'list'>
>>> len(tokens)
255809
>>> tokens[:10]
['The', 'Project', 'Gutenberg', 'EBook', 'of', 'Crime', 'and', 'Punishment', ',', 'by']
```

Notice that NLTK was needed for tokenization, but not for any of the earlier tasks of opening a URL and reading it into a string. If we now take the further step of creating an NLTK text from this list, we can carry out all of the other linguistic processing we saw in Chapter 1, along with the regular list operations, such as slicing:

```
>>> text = nltk.Text(tokens)
>>> type(text)
<type 'nltk.text.Text'>
>>> text[1020:1060]
['CHAPTER', 'I', 'On', 'an', 'exceptionally', 'hot', 'evening', 'early', 'in',
'July', 'a', 'young', 'man', 'came', 'out', 'of', 'the', 'garret', 'in',
'which', 'he', 'lodged', 'in', 'S', '.', 'Place', 'and', 'walked', 'slowly',
',', 'as', 'though', 'in', 'hesitation', ',', 'towards', 'K', '.', 'bridge', '.']
>>> text.collocations()
Katerina Ivanovna; Pulcheria Alexandrovna; Avdotya Romanovna; Pyotr
Petrovitch; Project Gutenberg; Marfa Petrovna; Rodion Romanovitch;
Sofya Semyonovna; Nikodim Fomitch; did not; Hay Market; Andrey
Semyonovitch; old woman; Literary Archive; Dmitri Prokofitch; great
deal; United States; Praskovya Pavlovna; Porfiry Petrovitch; ear rings
```

Notice that *Project Gutenberg* appears as a collocation. This is because each text downloaded from Project Gutenberg contains a header with the name of the text, the author, the names of people who scanned and corrected the text, a license, and so on. Sometimes this information appears in a footer at the end of the file. We cannot reliably detect where the content begins and ends, and so have to resort to manual inspection of the file, to discover unique strings that mark the beginning and the end, before trimming raw to be just the content and nothing else:

```
>>> raw.find("PART I")
5303
>>> raw.rfind("End of Project Gutenberg's Crime")
1157681
>>> raw = raw[5303:1157681] ❶
>>> raw.find("PART I")
0
```

The find() and rfind() ("reverse find") methods help us get the right index values to use for slicing the string ❶. We overwrite raw with this slice, so now it begins with "PART I" and goes up to (but not including) the phrase that marks the end of the content.

This was our first brush with the reality of the Web: texts found on the Web may contain unwanted material, and there may not be an automatic way to remove it. But with a small amount of extra work we can extract the material we need.

Dealing with HTML

Much of the text on the Web is in the form of HTML documents. You can use a web browser to save a page as text to a local file, then access this as described in the later section on files. However, if you're going to do this often, it's easiest to get Python to do the work directly. The first step is the same as before, using urlopen. For fun we'll pick a BBC News story called "Blondes to die out in 200 years," an urban legend passed along by the BBC as established scientific fact:

```
>>> url = "http://news.bbc.co.uk/2/hi/health/2284783.stm"
>>> html = urlopen(url).read()
>>> html[:60]
'<!doctype html public "-//W3C//DTD HTML 4.0 Transitional//EN'
```

You can type print html to see the HTML content in all its glory, including meta tags, an image map, JavaScript, forms, and tables.

Getting text out of HTML is a sufficiently common task that NLTK provides a helper function nltk.clean_html(), which takes an HTML string and returns raw text. We can then tokenize this to get our familiar text structure:

```
>>> raw = nltk.clean_html(html)
>>> tokens = nltk.word_tokenize(raw)
>>> tokens
['BBC', 'NEWS', '|', 'Health', '|', 'Blondes', "'", 'to', 'die', 'out', ...]
```

This still contains unwanted material concerning site navigation and related stories. With some trial and error you can find the start and end indexes of the content and select the tokens of interest, and initialize a text as before.

```
>>> tokens = tokens[96:399]
>>> text = nltk.Text(tokens)
>>> text.concordance('gene')
 they say too few people now carry the gene for blondes to last beyond the next tw
 t blonde hair is caused by a recessive gene . In order for a child to have blonde
 to have blonde hair , it must have the gene on both sides of the family in the gra
 there is a disadvantage of having that gene or by chance . They don ' t disappear
 ondes would disappear is if having the gene was a disadvantage and I do not think
```

 For more sophisticated processing of HTML, use the *Beautiful Soup* package, available at *http://www.crummy.com/software/BeautifulSoup/*.

Processing Search Engine Results

The Web can be thought of as a huge corpus of unannotated text. Web search engines provide an efficient means of searching this large quantity of text for relevant linguistic examples. The main advantage of search engines is size: since you are searching such a large set of documents, you are more likely to find any linguistic pattern you are interested in. Furthermore, you can make use of very specific patterns, which would match only one or two examples on a smaller example, but which might match tens of thousands of examples when run on the Web. A second advantage of web search engines is that they are very easy to use. Thus, they provide a very convenient tool for quickly checking a theory, to see if it is reasonable. See Table 3-1 for an example.

Table 3-1. Google hits for collocations: The number of hits for collocations involving the words absolutely *or* definitely, *followed by one of* adore, love, like, *or* prefer. *(Liberman, in LanguageLog, 2005)*

Google hits	adore	love	like	prefer
absolutely	289,000	905,000	16,200	644
definitely	1,460	51,000	158,000	62,600
ratio	198:1	18:1	1:10	1:97

Unfortunately, search engines have some significant shortcomings. First, the allowable range of search patterns is severely restricted. Unlike local corpora, where you write programs to search for arbitrarily complex patterns, search engines generally only allow you to search for individual words or strings of words, sometimes with wildcards. Second, search engines give inconsistent results, and can give widely different figures when used at different times or in different geographical regions. When content has been duplicated across multiple sites, search results may be boosted. Finally, the markup in the result returned by a search engine may change unpredictably, breaking any pattern-based method of locating particular content (a problem which is ameliorated by the use of search engine APIs).

 Your Turn: Search the Web for "the of" (inside quotes). Based on the large count, can we conclude that *the of* is a frequent collocation in English?

Processing RSS Feeds

The blogosphere is an important source of text, in both formal and informal registers. With the help of a third-party Python library called the *Universal Feed Parser*, freely downloadable from *http://feedparser.org/*, we can access the content of a blog, as shown here:

```
>>> import feedparser
>>> llog = feedparser.parse("http://languagelog.ldc.upenn.edu/nll/?feed=atom")
>>> llog['feed']['title']
u'Language Log'
>>> len(llog.entries)
15
>>> post = llog.entries[2]
>>> post.title
u"He's My BF"
>>> content = post.content[0].value
>>> content[:70]
u'<p>Today I was chatting with three of our visiting graduate students f'
>>> nltk.word_tokenize(nltk.html_clean(content))
>>> nltk.word_tokenize(nltk.clean_html(llog.entries[2].content[0].value))
[u'Today', u'I', u'was', u'chatting', u'with', u'three', u'of', u'our', u'visiting',
u'graduate', u'students', u'from', u'the', u'PRC', u'.', u'Thinking', u'that', u'I',
```

```
u'was', u'being', u'au', u'courant', u',', u'I', u'mentioned', u'the', u'expression',
u'DUI4XIANG4', u'\u5c0d\u8c61', u'("', u'boy', u'/', u'girl', u'friend', u'"', ...]
```

Note that the resulting strings have a u prefix to indicate that they are Unicode strings
(see Section 3.3). With some further work, we can write programs to create a small
corpus of blog posts, and use this as the basis for our NLP work.

Reading Local Files

In order to read a local file, we need to use Python's built-in open() function, followed
by the read() method. Supposing you have a file *document.txt*, you can load its contents
like this:

```
>>> f = open('document.txt')
>>> raw = f.read()
```

Your Turn: Create a file called *document.txt* using a text editor, and
type in a few lines of text, and save it as plain text. If you are using IDLE,
select the New Window command in the File menu, typing the required
text into this window, and then saving the file as *document.txt* inside
the directory that IDLE offers in the pop-up dialogue box. Next, in the
Python interpreter, open the file using f = open('document.txt'), then
inspect its contents using print f.read().

Various things might have gone wrong when you tried this. If the interpreter couldn't
find your file, you would have seen an error like this:

```
>>> f = open('document.txt')
Traceback (most recent call last):
  File "<pyshell#7>", line 1, in -toplevel-
    f = open('document.txt')
IOError: [Errno 2] No such file or directory: 'document.txt'
```

To check that the file that you are trying to open is really in the right directory, use
IDLE's Open command in the File menu; this will display a list of all the files in the
directory where IDLE is running. An alternative is to examine the current directory
from within Python:

```
>>> import os
>>> os.listdir('.')
```

Another possible problem you might have encountered when accessing a text file is the
newline conventions, which are different for different operating systems. The built-in
open() function has a second parameter for controlling how the file is opened: open('do
cument.txt', 'rU'). 'r' means to open the file for reading (the default), and 'U' stands
for "Universal", which lets us ignore the different conventions used for marking newlines.

Assuming that you can open the file, there are several methods for reading it. The
read() method creates a string with the contents of the entire file:

```
>>> f.read()
'Time flies like an arrow.\nFruit flies like a banana.\n'
```

Recall that the '\n' characters are **newlines**; this is equivalent to pressing Enter on a keyboard and starting a new line.

We can also read a file one line at a time using a for loop:

```
>>> f = open('document.txt', 'rU')
>>> for line in f:
...     print line.strip()
Time flies like an arrow.
Fruit flies like a banana.
```

Here we use the strip() method to remove the newline character at the end of the input line.

NLTK's corpus files can also be accessed using these methods. We simply have to use nltk.data.find() to get the filename for any corpus item. Then we can open and read it in the way we just demonstrated:

```
>>> path = nltk.data.find('corpora/gutenberg/melville-moby_dick.txt')
>>> raw = open(path, 'rU').read()
```

Extracting Text from PDF, MSWord, and Other Binary Formats

ASCII text and HTML text are human-readable formats. Text often comes in binary formats—such as PDF and MSWord—that can only be opened using specialized software. Third-party libraries such as pypdf and pywin32 provide access to these formats. Extracting text from multicolumn documents is particularly challenging. For one-off conversion of a few documents, it is simpler to open the document with a suitable application, then save it as text to your local drive, and access it as described below. If the document is already on the Web, you can enter its URL in Google's search box. The search result often includes a link to an HTML version of the document, which you can save as text.

Capturing User Input

Sometimes we want to capture the text that a user inputs when she is interacting with our program. To prompt the user to type a line of input, call the Python function raw_input(). After saving the input to a variable, we can manipulate it just as we have done for other strings.

```
>>> s = raw_input("Enter some text: ")
Enter some text: On an exceptionally hot evening early in July
>>> print "You typed", len(nltk.word_tokenize(s)), "words."
You typed 8 words.
```

The NLP Pipeline

Figure 3-1 summarizes what we have covered in this section, including the process of building a vocabulary that we saw in Chapter 1. (One step, normalization, will be discussed in Section 3.6.)

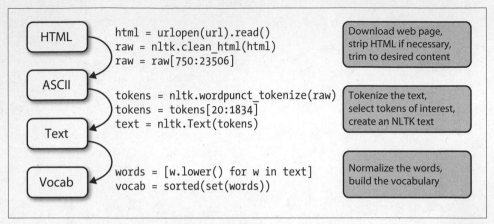

Figure 3-1. The processing pipeline: We open a URL and read its HTML content, remove the markup and select a slice of characters; this is then tokenized and optionally converted into an nltk.Text *object; we can also lowercase all the words and extract the vocabulary.*

There's a lot going on in this pipeline. To understand it properly, it helps to be clear about the type of each variable that it mentions. We find out the type of any Python object *x* using type(*x*); e.g., type(1) is <int> since 1 is an integer.

When we load the contents of a URL or file, and when we strip out HTML markup, we are dealing with strings, Python's <str> data type (we will learn more about strings in Section 3.2):

```
>>> raw = open('document.txt').read()
>>> type(raw)
<type 'str'>
```

When we tokenize a string we produce a list (of words), and this is Python's <list> type. Normalizing and sorting lists produces other lists:

```
>>> tokens = nltk.word_tokenize(raw)
>>> type(tokens)
<type 'list'>
>>> words = [w.lower() for w in tokens]
>>> type(words)
<type 'list'>
>>> vocab = sorted(set(words))
>>> type(vocab)
<type 'list'>
```

The type of an object determines what operations you can perform on it. So, for example, we can append to a list but not to a string:

```
>>> vocab.append('blog')
>>> raw.append('blog')
Traceback (most recent call last):
  File "<stdin>", line 1, in <module>
AttributeError: 'str' object has no attribute 'append'
```

Similarly, we can concatenate strings with strings, and lists with lists, but we cannot concatenate strings with lists:

```
>>> query = 'Who knows?'
>>> beatles = ['john', 'paul', 'george', 'ringo']
>>> query + beatles
Traceback (most recent call last):
  File "<stdin>", line 1, in <module>
TypeError: cannot concatenate 'str' and 'list' objects
```

In the next section, we examine strings more closely and further explore the relationship between strings and lists.

3.2 Strings: Text Processing at the Lowest Level

It's time to study a fundamental data type that we've been studiously avoiding so far. In earlier chapters we focused on a text as a list of words. We didn't look too closely at words and how they are handled in the programming language. By using NLTK's corpus interface we were able to ignore the files that these texts had come from. The contents of a word, and of a file, are represented by programming languages as a fundamental data type known as a **string**. In this section, we explore strings in detail, and show the connection between strings, words, texts, and files.

Basic Operations with Strings

Strings are specified using single quotes ❶ or double quotes ❷, as shown in the following code example. If a string contains a single quote, we must backslash-escape the quote ❸ so Python knows a literal quote character is intended, or else put the string in double quotes ❷. Otherwise, the quote inside the string ❹ will be interpreted as a close quote, and the Python interpreter will report a syntax error:

```
>>> monty = 'Monty Python' ❶
>>> monty
'Monty Python'
>>> circus = "Monty Python's Flying Circus" ❷
>>> circus
"Monty Python's Flying Circus"
>>> circus = 'Monty Python\'s Flying Circus' ❸
>>> circus
"Monty Python's Flying Circus"
>>> circus = 'Monty Python's Flying Circus' ❹
  File "<stdin>", line 1
    circus = 'Monty Python's Flying Circus'
                           ^
SyntaxError: invalid syntax
```

Sometimes strings go over several lines. Python provides us with various ways of entering them. In the next example, a sequence of two strings is joined into a single string. We need to use backslash ❶ or parentheses ❷ so that the interpreter knows that the statement is not complete after the first line.

```
>>> couplet = "Shall I compare thee to a Summer's day?"\
...           "Thou are more lovely and more temperate:" ❶
>>> print couplet
Shall I compare thee to a Summer's day?Thou are more lovely and more temperate:
>>> couplet = ("Rough winds do shake the darling buds of May,"
...            "And Summer's lease hath all too short a date:") ❷
>>> print couplet
Rough winds do shake the darling buds of May,And Summer's lease hath all too short a date:
```

Unfortunately these methods do not give us a newline between the two lines of the sonnet. Instead, we can use a triple-quoted string as follows:

```
>>> couplet = """Shall I compare thee to a Summer's day?
... Thou are more lovely and more temperate:"""
>>> print couplet
Shall I compare thee to a Summer's day?
Thou are more lovely and more temperate:
>>> couplet = '''Rough winds do shake the darling buds of May,
... And Summer's lease hath all too short a date:'''
>>> print couplet
Rough winds do shake the darling buds of May,
And Summer's lease hath all too short a date:
```

Now that we can define strings, we can try some simple operations on them. First let's look at the + operation, known as **concatenation** ❶. It produces a new string that is a copy of the two original strings pasted together end-to-end. Notice that concatenation doesn't do anything clever like insert a space between the words. We can even multiply strings ❷:

```
>>> 'very' + 'very' + 'very' ❶
'veryveryvery'
>>> 'very' * 3 ❷
'veryveryvery'
```

 Your Turn: Try running the following code, then try to use your understanding of the string + and * operations to figure out how it works. Be careful to distinguish between the string ' ', which is a single whitespace character, and '', which is the empty string.

```
>>> a = [1, 2, 3, 4, 5, 6, 7, 6, 5, 4, 3, 2, 1]
>>> b = [' ' * 2 * (7 - i) + 'very' * i for i in a]
>>> for line in b:
...     print b
```

We've seen that the addition and multiplication operations apply to strings, not just numbers. However, note that we cannot use subtraction or division with strings:

```
>>> 'very' - 'y'
Traceback (most recent call last):
  File "<stdin>", line 1, in <module>
TypeError: unsupported operand type(s) for -: 'str' and 'str'
>>> 'very' / 2
Traceback (most recent call last):
  File "<stdin>", line 1, in <module>
TypeError: unsupported operand type(s) for /: 'str' and 'int'
```

These error messages are another example of Python telling us that we have got our data types in a muddle. In the first case, we are told that the operation of subtraction (i.e., -) cannot apply to objects of type `str` (strings), while in the second, we are told that division cannot take `str` and `int` as its two operands.

Printing Strings

So far, when we have wanted to look at the contents of a variable or see the result of a calculation, we have just typed the variable name into the interpreter. We can also see the contents of a variable using the `print` statement:

```
>>> print monty
Monty Python
```

Notice that there are no quotation marks this time. When we inspect a variable by typing its name in the interpreter, the interpreter prints the Python representation of its value. Since it's a string, the result is quoted. However, when we tell the interpreter to `print` the contents of the variable, we don't see quotation characters, since there are none inside the string.

The `print` statement allows us to display more than one item on a line in various ways, as shown here:

```
>>> grail = 'Holy Grail'
>>> print monty + grail
Monty PythonHoly Grail
>>> print monty, grail
Monty Python Holy Grail
>>> print monty, "and the", grail
Monty Python and the Holy Grail
```

Accessing Individual Characters

As we saw in Section 1.2 for lists, strings are indexed, starting from zero. When we index a string, we get one of its characters (or letters). A single character is nothing special—it's just a string of length 1.

```
>>> monty[0]
'M'
>>> monty[3]
't'
>>> monty[5]
' '
```

As with lists, if we try to access an index that is outside of the string, we get an error:

```
>>> monty[20]
Traceback (most recent call last):
  File "<stdin>", line 1, in ?
IndexError: string index out of range
```

Again as with lists, we can use negative indexes for strings, where -1 is the index of the last character ❶. Positive and negative indexes give us two ways to refer to any position in a string. In this case, when the string had a length of 12, indexes 5 and -7 both refer to the same character (a space). (Notice that 5 = len(monty) - 7.)

```
>>> monty[-1] ❶
'n'
>>> monty[5]
' '
>>> monty[-7]
' '
```

We can write for loops to iterate over the characters in strings. This print statement ends with a trailing comma, which is how we tell Python not to print a newline at the end.

```
>>> sent = 'colorless green ideas sleep furiously'
>>> for char in sent:
...     print char,
...
c o l o r l e s s   g r e e n   i d e a s   s l e e p   f u r i o u s l y
```

We can count individual characters as well. We should ignore the case distinction by normalizing everything to lowercase, and filter out non-alphabetic characters:

```
>>> from nltk.corpus import gutenberg
>>> raw = gutenberg.raw('melville-moby_dick.txt')
>>> fdist = nltk.FreqDist(ch.lower() for ch in raw if ch.isalpha())
>>> fdist.keys()
['e', 't', 'a', 'o', 'n', 'i', 's', 'h', 'r', 'l', 'd', 'u', 'm', 'c', 'w',
'f', 'g', 'p', 'b', 'y', 'v', 'k', 'q', 'j', 'x', 'z']
```

This gives us the letters of the alphabet, with the most frequently occurring letters listed first (this is quite complicated and we'll explain it more carefully later). You might like to visualize the distribution using fdist.plot(). The relative character frequencies of a text can be used in automatically identifying the language of the text.

Accessing Substrings

A substring is any continuous section of a string that we want to pull out for further processing. We can easily access substrings using the same slice notation we used for lists (see Figure 3-2). For example, the following code accesses the substring starting at index 6, up to (but not including) index 10:

```
>>> monty[6:10]
'Pyth'
```

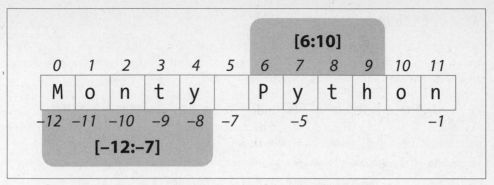

Figure 3-2. String slicing: The string Monty Python *is shown along with its positive and negative indexes; two substrings are selected using "slice" notation. The slice* [m,n] *contains the characters from position m through n-1.*

Here we see the characters are 'P', 'y', 't', and 'h', which correspond to monty[6] ... monty[9] but not monty[10]. This is because a slice *starts* at the first index but finishes *one before* the end index.

We can also slice with negative indexes—the same basic rule of starting from the start index and stopping one before the end index applies; here we stop before the space character.

```
>>> monty[-12:-7]
'Monty'
```

As with list slices, if we omit the first value, the substring begins at the start of the string. If we omit the second value, the substring continues to the end of the string:

```
>>> monty[:5]
'Monty'
>>> monty[6:]
'Python'
```

We test if a string contains a particular substring using the in operator, as follows:

```
>>> phrase = 'And now for something completely different'
>>> if 'thing' in phrase:
...     print 'found "thing"'
found "thing"
```

We can also find the position of a substring within a string, using find():

```
>>> monty.find('Python')
6
```

 Your Turn: Make up a sentence and assign it to a variable, e.g., sent = 'my sentence...'. Now write slice expressions to pull out individual words. (This is obviously not a convenient way to process the words of a text!)

More Operations on Strings

Python has comprehensive support for processing strings. A summary, including some operations we haven't seen yet, is shown in Table 3-2. For more information on strings, type help(str) at the Python prompt.

Table 3-2. Useful string methods: Operations on strings in addition to the string tests shown in Table 1-4; all methods produce a new string or list

Method	Functionality
s.find(t)	Index of first instance of string t inside s (-1 if not found)
s.rfind(t)	Index of last instance of string t inside s (-1 if not found)
s.index(t)	Like s.find(t), except it raises ValueError if not found
s.rindex(t)	Like s.rfind(t), except it raises ValueError if not found
s.join(text)	Combine the words of the text into a string using s as the glue
s.split(t)	Split s into a list wherever a t is found (whitespace by default)
s.splitlines()	Split s into a list of strings, one per line
s.lower()	A lowercased version of the string s
s.upper()	An uppercased version of the string s
s.titlecase()	A titlecased version of the string s
s.strip()	A copy of s without leading or trailing whitespace
s.replace(t, u)	Replace instances of t with u inside s

The Difference Between Lists and Strings

Strings and lists are both kinds of **sequence**. We can pull them apart by indexing and slicing them, and we can join them together by concatenating them. However, we cannot join strings and lists:

```
>>> query = 'Who knows?'
>>> beatles = ['John', 'Paul', 'George', 'Ringo']
>>> query[2]
'o'
>>> beatles[2]
'George'
>>> query[:2]
'Wh'
>>> beatles[:2]
['John', 'Paul']
>>> query + " I don't"
"Who knows? I don't"
>>> beatles + 'Brian'
Traceback (most recent call last):
  File "<stdin>", line 1, in <module>
TypeError: can only concatenate list (not "str") to list
>>> beatles + ['Brian']
['John', 'Paul', 'George', 'Ringo', 'Brian']
```

When we open a file for reading into a Python program, we get a string corresponding to the contents of the whole file. If we use a `for` loop to process the elements of this string, all we can pick out are the individual characters—we don't get to choose the granularity. By contrast, the elements of a list can be as big or small as we like: for example, they could be paragraphs, sentences, phrases, words, characters. So lists have the advantage that we can be flexible about the elements they contain, and correspondingly flexible about any downstream processing. Consequently, one of the first things we are likely to do in a piece of NLP code is tokenize a string into a list of strings (Section 3.7). Conversely, when we want to write our results to a file, or to a terminal, we will usually format them as a string (Section 3.9).

Lists and strings do not have exactly the same functionality. Lists have the added power that you can change their elements:

```
>>> beatles[0] = "John Lennon"
>>> del beatles[-1]
>>> beatles
['John Lennon', 'Paul', 'George']
```

On the other hand, if we try to do that with a *string*—changing the 0th character in `query` to `'F'`—we get:

```
>>> query[0] = 'F'
Traceback (most recent call last):
  File "<stdin>", line 1, in ?
TypeError: object does not support item assignment
```

This is because strings are **immutable**: you can't change a string once you have created it. However, lists are **mutable**, and their contents can be modified at any time. As a result, lists support operations that modify the original value rather than producing a new value.

 Your Turn: Consolidate your knowledge of strings by trying some of the exercises on strings at the end of this chapter.

3.3 Text Processing with Unicode

Our programs will often need to deal with different languages, and different character sets. The concept of "plain text" is a fiction. If you live in the English-speaking world you probably use ASCII, possibly without realizing it. If you live in Europe you might use one of the extended Latin character sets, containing such characters as "ø" for Danish and Norwegian, "ő" for Hungarian, "ñ" for Spanish and Breton, and "ň" for Czech and Slovak. In this section, we will give an overview of how to use Unicode for processing texts that use non-ASCII character sets.

What Is Unicode?

Unicode supports over a million characters. Each character is assigned a number, called a **code point**. In Python, code points are written in the form \u*XXXX*, where *XXXX* is the number in four-digit hexadecimal form.

Within a program, we can manipulate Unicode strings just like normal strings. However, when Unicode characters are stored in files or displayed on a terminal, they must be encoded as a stream of bytes. Some encodings (such as ASCII and Latin-2) use a single byte per code point, so they can support only a small subset of Unicode, enough for a single language. Other encodings (such as UTF-8) use multiple bytes and can represent the full range of Unicode characters.

Text in files will be in a particular encoding, so we need some mechanism for translating it into Unicode—translation into Unicode is called **decoding**. Conversely, to write out Unicode to a file or a terminal, we first need to translate it into a suitable encoding—this translation out of Unicode is called **encoding**, and is illustrated in Figure 3-3.

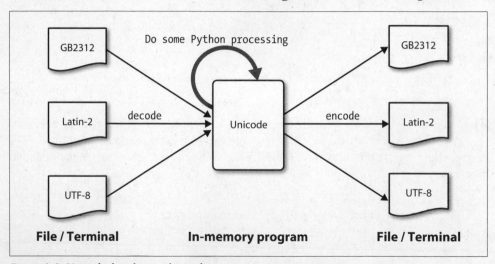

Figure 3-3. Unicode decoding and encoding.

From a Unicode perspective, characters are abstract entities that can be realized as one or more **glyphs**. Only glyphs can appear on a screen or be printed on paper. A font is a mapping from characters to glyphs.

Extracting Encoded Text from Files

Let's assume that we have a small text file, and that we know how it is encoded. For example, *polish-lat2.txt*, as the name suggests, is a snippet of Polish text (from the Polish Wikipedia; see *http://pl.wikipedia.org/wiki/Biblioteka_Pruska*). This file is encoded as Latin-2, also known as ISO-8859-2. The function `nltk.data.find()` locates the file for us.

```
>>> path = nltk.data.find('corpora/unicode_samples/polish-lat2.txt')
```

The Python `codecs` module provides functions to read encoded data into Unicode strings, and to write out Unicode strings in encoded form. The `codecs.open()` function takes an encoding parameter to specify the encoding of the file being read or written. So let's import the `codecs` module, and call it with the encoding `'latin2'` to open our Polish file as Unicode:

```
>>> import codecs
>>> f = codecs.open(path, encoding='latin2')
```

For a list of encoding parameters allowed by `codecs`, see *http://docs.python.org/lib/standard-encodings.html*. Note that we can write Unicode-encoded data to a file using `f = codecs.open(path, 'w', encoding='utf-8')`.

Text read from the file object `f` will be returned in Unicode. As we pointed out earlier, in order to view this text on a terminal, we need to encode it, using a suitable encoding. The Python-specific encoding `unicode_escape` is a dummy encoding that converts all non-ASCII characters into their \u*XXXX* representations. Code points above the ASCII 0–127 range but below 256 are represented in the two-digit form \x*XX*.

```
>>> for line in f:
...     line = line.strip()
...     print line.encode('unicode_escape')
Pruska Biblioteka Pa\u0144stwowa. Jej dawne zbiory znane pod nazw\u0105
"Berlinka" to skarb kultury i sztuki niemieckiej. Przewiezione przez
Niemc\xf3w pod koniec II wojny \u015bwiatowej na Dolny \u015al\u0105sk, zosta\u0142y
odnalezione po 1945 r. na terytorium Polski. Trafi\u0142y do Biblioteki
Jagiello\u0144skiej w Krakowie, obejmuj\u0105 ponad 500 tys. zabytkowych
archiwali\xf3w, m.in. manuskrypty Goethego, Mozarta, Beethovena, Bacha.
```

The first line in this output illustrates a Unicode escape string preceded by the \u escape string, namely \u0144. The relevant Unicode character will be displayed on the screen as the glyph ń. In the third line of the preceding example, we see \xf3, which corresponds to the glyph ó, and is within the 128–255 range.

In Python, a Unicode string literal can be specified by preceding an ordinary string literal with a `u`, as in `u'hello'`. Arbitrary Unicode characters are defined using the \u*XXXX* escape sequence inside a Unicode string literal. We find the integer ordinal of a character using `ord()`. For example:

```
>>> ord('a')
97
```

The hexadecimal four-digit notation for 97 is 0061, so we can define a Unicode string literal with the appropriate escape sequence:

```
>>> a = u'\u0061'
>>> a
u'a'
>>> print a
a
```

Notice that the Python `print` statement is assuming a default encoding of the Unicode character, namely ASCII. However, ń is outside the ASCII range, so cannot be printed unless we specify an encoding. In the following example, we have specified that `print` should use the `repr()` of the string, which outputs the UTF-8 escape sequences (of the form \xXX) rather than trying to render the glyphs.

```
>>> nacute = u'\u0144'
>>> nacute
u'\u0144'
>>> nacute_utf = nacute.encode('utf8')
>>> print repr(nacute_utf)
'\xc5\x84'
```

If your operating system and locale are set up to render UTF-8 encoded characters, you ought to be able to give the Python command `print nacute_utf` and see ń on your screen.

 There are many factors determining what glyphs are rendered on your screen. If you are sure that you have the correct encoding, but your Python code is still failing to produce the glyphs you expected, you should also check that you have the necessary fonts installed on your system.

The module `unicodedata` lets us inspect the properties of Unicode characters. In the following example, we select all characters in the third line of our Polish text outside the ASCII range and print their UTF-8 escaped value, followed by their code point integer using the standard Unicode convention (i.e., prefixing the hex digits with U+), followed by their Unicode name.

```
>>> import unicodedata
>>> lines = codecs.open(path, encoding='latin2').readlines()
>>> line = lines[2]
>>> print line.encode('unicode_escape')
Niemc\xf3w pod koniec II wojny \u015bwiatowej na Dolny \u015al\u0105sk, zosta\u0142y\n
>>> for c in line:
...     if ord(c) > 127:
...         print '%r U+%04x %s' % (c.encode('utf8'), ord(c), unicodedata.name(c))
'\xc3\xb3' U+00f3 LATIN SMALL LETTER O WITH ACUTE
'\xc5\x9b' U+015b LATIN SMALL LETTER S WITH ACUTE
'\xc5\x9a' U+015a LATIN CAPITAL LETTER S WITH ACUTE
'\xc4\x85' U+0105 LATIN SMALL LETTER A WITH OGONEK
'\xc5\x82' U+0142 LATIN SMALL LETTER L WITH STROKE
```

If you replace the `%r` (which yields the `repr()` value) by `%s` in the format string of the preceding code sample, and if your system supports UTF-8, you should see an output like the following:

```
ó U+00f3 LATIN SMALL LETTER O WITH ACUTE
ś U+015b LATIN SMALL LETTER S WITH ACUTE
Ś U+015a LATIN CAPITAL LETTER S WITH ACUTE
```

```
ą U+0105 LATIN SMALL LETTER A WITH OGONEK
ł U+0142 LATIN SMALL LETTER L WITH STROKE
```

Alternatively, you may need to replace the encoding `'utf8'` in the example by `'latin2'`, again depending on the details of your system.

The next examples illustrate how Python string methods and the `re` module accept Unicode strings.

```
>>> line.find(u'zosta\u0142y')
54
>>> line = line.lower()
>>> print line.encode('unicode_escape')
niemc\xf3w pod koniec ii wojny \u015bwiatowej na dolny \u015bl\u0105sk, zosta\u0142y\n
>>> import re
>>> m = re.search(u'\u015b\w*', line)
>>> m.group()
u'\u015bwiatowej'
```

NLTK tokenizers allow Unicode strings as input, and correspondingly yield Unicode strings as output.

```
>>> nltk.word_tokenize(line)
[u'niemc\xf3w', u'pod', u'koniec', u'ii', u'wojny', u'\u015bwiatowej',
u'na', u'dolny', u'\u015bl\u0105sk', u'zosta\u0142y']
```

Using Your Local Encoding in Python

If you are used to working with characters in a particular local encoding, you probably want to be able to use your standard methods for inputting and editing strings in a Python file. In order to do this, you need to include the string `'# -*- coding: <coding> -*-'` as the first or second line of your file. Note that `<coding>` has to be a string like `'latin-1'`, `'big5'`, or `'utf-8'` (see Figure 3-4).

Figure 3-4 also illustrates how regular expressions can use encoded strings.

3.4 Regular Expressions for Detecting Word Patterns

Many linguistic processing tasks involve pattern matching. For example, we can find words ending with *ed* using `endswith('ed')`. We saw a variety of such "word tests" in Table 1-4. Regular expressions give us a more powerful and flexible method for describing the character patterns we are interested in.

There are many other published introductions to regular expressions, organized around the syntax of regular expressions and applied to searching text files. Instead of doing this again, we focus on the use of regular expressions at different stages of linguistic processing. As usual, we'll adopt a problem-based approach and present new features only as they are needed to solve practical problems. In our discussion we will mark regular expressions using chevrons like this: «patt».

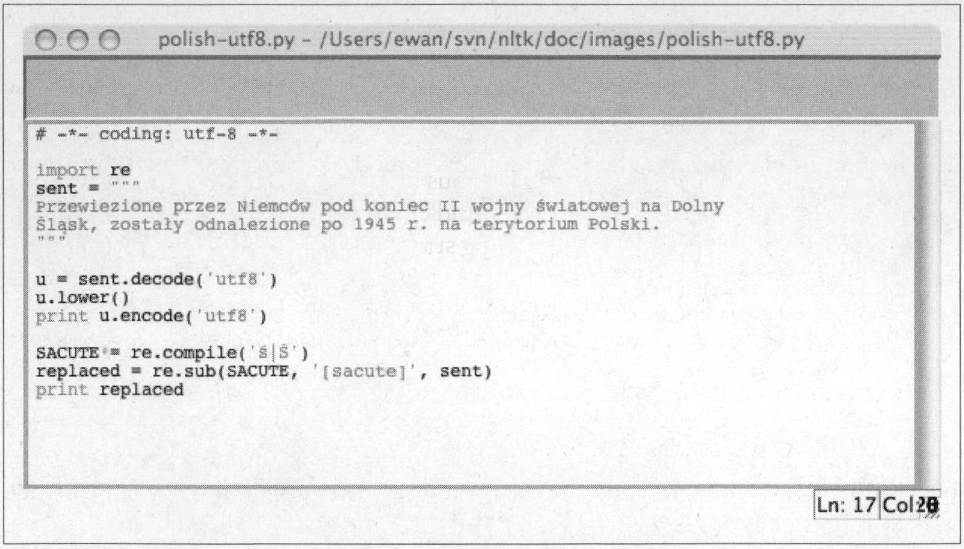

```
polish-utf8.py – /Users/ewan/svn/nltk/doc/images/polish-utf8.py

# -*- coding: utf-8 -*-

import re
sent = """
Przewiezione przez Niemców pod koniec II wojny światowej na Dolny
Śląsk, zostały odnalezione po 1945 r. na terytorium Polski.
"""

u = sent.decode('utf8')
u.lower()
print u.encode('utf8')

SACUTE = re.compile('ś|Ś')
replaced = re.sub(SACUTE, '[sacute]', sent)
print replaced
```

`Ln: 17 Col: 28`

Figure 3-4. Unicode and IDLE: UTF-8 encoded string literals in the IDLE editor; this requires that an appropriate font is set in IDLE's preferences; here we have chosen Courier CE.

To use regular expressions in Python, we need to import the `re` library using: `import re`. We also need a list of words to search; we'll use the Words Corpus again (Section 2.4). We will preprocess it to remove any proper names.

```
>>> import re
>>> wordlist = [w for w in nltk.corpus.words.words('en') if w.islower()]
```

Using Basic Metacharacters

Let's find words ending with *ed* using the regular expression «ed$». We will use the `re.search(p, s)` function to check whether the pattern `p` can be found somewhere inside the string `s`. We need to specify the characters of interest, and use the dollar sign, which has a special behavior in the context of regular expressions in that it matches the end of the word:

```
>>> [w for w in wordlist if re.search('ed$', w)]
['abaissed', 'abandoned', 'abased', 'abashed', 'abatised', 'abed', 'aborted', ...]
```

The **. wildcard** symbol matches any single character. Suppose we have room in a crossword puzzle for an eight-letter word, with *j* as its third letter and *t* as its sixth letter. In place of each blank cell we use a period:

```
>>> [w for w in wordlist if re.search('^..j..t..$', w)]
['abjectly', 'adjuster', 'dejected', 'dejectly', 'injector', 'majestic', ...]
```

Your Turn: The caret symbol ^ matches the start of a string, just like the $ matches the end. What results do we get with the example just shown if we leave out both of these, and search for «..j..t..»?

Finally, the ? symbol specifies that the previous character is optional. Thus «^e-?mail $» will match both *email* and *e-mail*. We could count the total number of occurrences of this word (in either spelling) in a text using sum(1 for w in text if re.search('^e-? mail$', w)).

Ranges and Closures

The **T9** system is used for entering text on mobile phones (see Figure 3-5). Two or more words that are entered with the same sequence of keystrokes are known as **textonyms**. For example, both *hole* and *golf* are entered by pressing the sequence 4653. What other words could be produced with the same sequence? Here we use the regular expression «^[ghi][mno][jlk][def]$»:

```
>>> [w for w in wordlist if re.search('^[ghi][mno][jlk][def]$', w)]
['gold', 'golf', 'hold', 'hole']
```

The first part of the expression, «^[ghi]», matches the start of a word followed by *g*, *h*, or *i*. The next part of the expression, «[mno]», constrains the second character to be *m*, *n*, or *o*. The third and fourth characters are also constrained. Only four words satisfy all these constraints. Note that the order of characters inside the square brackets is not significant, so we could have written «^[hig][nom][ljk][fed]$» and matched the same words.

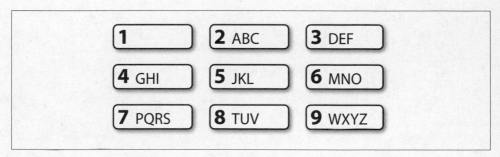

Figure 3-5. T9: Text on 9 keys.

 Your Turn: Look for some "finger-twisters," by searching for words that use only part of the number-pad. For example «^[ghijklmno]+$», or more concisely, «^[g-o]+$», will match words that only use keys 4, 5, 6 in the center row, and «^[a-fj-o]+$» will match words that use keys 2, 3, 5, 6 in the top-right corner. What do - and + mean?

Let's explore the + symbol a bit further. Notice that it can be applied to individual letters, or to bracketed sets of letters:

```
>>> chat_words = sorted(set(w for w in nltk.corpus.nps_chat.words()))
>>> [w for w in chat_words if re.search('^m+i+n+e+$', w)]
['miiiiiiiiiiiiiiinnnnnnnnnneeeeeeeee', 'miiiiiinnnnnnnnnneeeeeeee', 'mine',
'mmmmmmmmiiiiiiiiiiinnnnnnnnnneeeeeeee']
>>> [w for w in chat_words if re.search('^[ha]+$', w)]
['a', 'aaaaaaaaaaaaaaaaaa', 'aaahhhh', 'ah', 'ahah', 'ahahah', 'ahh',
'ahhahahaha', 'ahhh', 'ahhhh', 'ahhhhhh', 'ahhhhhhhhhhhhh', 'h', 'ha', 'haaa',
'hah', 'haha', 'hahaaa', 'hahah', 'hahaha', 'hahahaa', 'hahahah', 'hahahaha', ...]
```

It should be clear that + simply means "one or more instances of the preceding item," which could be an individual character like m, a set like [fed], or a range like [d-f]. Now let's replace + with *, which means "zero or more instances of the preceding item." The regular expression «^m*i*n*e*$» will match everything that we found using «^m+i +n+e+$», but also words where some of the letters don't appear at all, e.g., *me*, *min*, and *mmmmm*. Note that the + and * symbols are sometimes referred to as **Kleene closures**, or simply **closures**.

The ^ operator has another function when it appears as the first character inside square brackets. For example, «[^aeiouAEIOU]» matches any character other than a vowel. We can search the NPS Chat Corpus for words that are made up entirely of non-vowel characters using «^[^aeiouAEIOU]+$» to find items like these: :):):), grrr, cyb3r, and zzzzzzzz. Notice this includes non-alphabetic characters.

Here are some more examples of regular expressions being used to find tokens that match a particular pattern, illustrating the use of some new symbols: \, {}, (), and |.

```
>>> wsj = sorted(set(nltk.corpus.treebank.words()))
>>> [w for w in wsj if re.search('^[0-9]+\.[0-9]+$', w)]
['0.0085', '0.05', '0.1', '0.16', '0.2', '0.25', '0.28', '0.3', '0.4', '0.5',
'0.50', '0.54', '0.56', '0.60', '0.7', '0.82', '0.84', '0.9', '0.95', '0.99',
'1.01', '1.1', '1.125', '1.14', '1.1650', '1.17', '1.18', '1.19', '1.2', ...]
>>> [w for w in wsj if re.search('^[A-Z]+\$$', w)]
['C$', 'US$']
>>> [w for w in wsj if re.search('^[0-9]{4}$', w)]
['1614', '1637', '1787', '1901', '1903', '1917', '1925', '1929', '1933', ...]
>>> [w for w in wsj if re.search('^[0-9]+-[a-z]{3,5}$', w)]
['10-day', '10-lap', '10-year', '100-share', '12-point', '12-year', ...]
>>> [w for w in wsj if re.search('^[a-z]{5,}-[a-z]{2,3}-[a-z]{,6}$', w)]
['black-and-white', 'bread-and-butter', 'father-in-law', 'machine-gun-toting',
'savings-and-loan']
>>> [w for w in wsj if re.search('(ed|ing)$', w)]
['62%-owned', 'Absorbed', 'According', 'Adopting', 'Advanced', 'Advancing', ...]
```

 Your Turn: Study the previous examples and try to work out what the \, {}, (), and | notations mean before you read on.

You probably worked out that a backslash means that the following character is deprived of its special powers and must literally match a specific character in the word. Thus, while . is special, \. only matches a period. The braced expressions, like {3,5}, specify the number of repeats of the previous item. The pipe character indicates a choice between the material on its left or its right. Parentheses indicate the scope of an operator, and they can be used together with the pipe (or disjunction) symbol like this: «w(i|e|ai|oo)t», matching *wit*, *wet*, *wait*, and *woot*. It is instructive to see what happens when you omit the parentheses from the last expression in the example, and search for «ed|ing$».

The metacharacters we have seen are summarized in Table 3-3.

Table 3-3. Basic regular expression metacharacters, including wildcards, ranges, and closures

Operator	Behavior
.	Wildcard, matches any character
^abc	Matches some pattern *abc* at the start of a string
abc$	Matches some pattern *abc* at the end of a string
[abc]	Matches one of a set of characters
[A-Z0-9]	Matches one of a range of characters
ed|ing|s	Matches one of the specified strings (disjunction)
*	Zero or more of previous item, e.g., a*, [a-z]* (also known as *Kleene Closure*)
+	One or more of previous item, e.g., a+, [a-z]+
?	Zero or one of the previous item (i.e., optional), e.g., a?, [a-z]?
{n}	Exactly *n* repeats where *n* is a non-negative integer
{n,}	At least *n* repeats
{,n}	No more than *n* repeats
{m,n}	At least *m* and no more than *n* repeats
a(b|c)+	Parentheses that indicate the scope of the operators

To the Python interpreter, a regular expression is just like any other string. If the string contains a backslash followed by particular characters, it will interpret these specially. For example, \b would be interpreted as the backspace character. In general, when using regular expressions containing backslash, we should instruct the interpreter not to look inside the string at all, but simply to pass it directly to the re library for processing. We do this by prefixing the string with the letter r, to indicate that it is a **raw string**. For example, the raw string r'\band\b' contains two \b symbols that are interpreted by the re library as matching word boundaries instead of backspace characters. If you get into the habit of using r'...' for regular expressions—as we will do from now on—you will avoid having to think about these complications.

3.5 Useful Applications of Regular Expressions

The previous examples all involved searching for words *w* that match some regular expression *regexp* using re.search(regexp, w). Apart from checking whether a regular expression matches a word, we can use regular expressions to extract material from words, or to modify words in specific ways.

Extracting Word Pieces

The re.findall() ("find all") method finds all (non-overlapping) matches of the given regular expression. Let's find all the vowels in a word, then count them:

```
>>> word = 'supercalifragilisticexpialidocious'
>>> re.findall(r'[aeiou]', word)
['u', 'e', 'a', 'i', 'a', 'i', 'i', 'i', 'e', 'i', 'a', 'i', 'o', 'i', 'o', 'u']
>>> len(re.findall(r'[aeiou]', word))
16
```

Let's look for all sequences of two or more vowels in some text, and determine their relative frequency:

```
>>> wsj = sorted(set(nltk.corpus.treebank.words()))
>>> fd = nltk.FreqDist(vs for word in wsj
...                         for vs in re.findall(r'[aeiou]{2,}', word))
>>> fd.items()
[('io', 549), ('ea', 476), ('ie', 331), ('ou', 329), ('ai', 261), ('ia', 253),
('ee', 217), ('oo', 174), ('ua', 109), ('au', 106), ('ue', 105), ('ui', 95),
('ei', 86), ('oi', 65), ('oa', 59), ('eo', 39), ('iou', 27), ('eu', 18), ...]
```

 Your Turn: In the W3C Date Time Format, dates are represented like this: 2009-12-31. Replace the ? in the following Python code with a regular expression, in order to convert the string '2009-12-31' to a list of integers [2009, 12, 31]:

```
[int(n) for n in re.findall(?, '2009-12-31')]
```

Doing More with Word Pieces

Once we can use re.findall() to extract material from words, there are interesting things to do with the pieces, such as glue them back together or plot them.

It is sometimes noted that English text is highly redundant, and it is still easy to read when word-internal vowels are left out. For example, *declaration* becomes *dclrtn*, and *inalienable* becomes *inlnble*, retaining any initial or final vowel sequences. The regular expression in our next example matches initial vowel sequences, final vowel sequences, and all consonants; everything else is ignored. This three-way disjunction is processed left-to-right, and if one of the three parts matches the word, any later parts of the regular expression are ignored. We use re.findall() to extract all the matching pieces, and ''.join() to join them together (see Section 3.9 for more about the join operation).

```
>>> regexp = r'^[AEIOUaeiou]+|[AEIOUaeiou]+$|[^AEIOUaeiou]'
>>> def compress(word):
...     pieces = re.findall(regexp, word)
...     return ''.join(pieces)
...
>>> english_udhr = nltk.corpus.udhr.words('English-Latin1')
>>> print nltk.tokenwrap(compress(w) for w in english_udhr[:75])
Unvrsl Dclrtn of Hmn Rghts Prmble Whrs rcgntn of the inhrnt dgnty and
of the eql and inlnble rghts of all mmbrs of the hmn fmly is the fndtn
of frdm , jstce and pce in the wrld , Whrs dsrgrd and cntmpt fr hmn
rghts hve rsltd in brbrs acts whch hve outrgd the cnscnce of mnknd ,
and the advnt of a wrld in whch hmn bngs shll enjy frdm of spch and
```

Next, let's combine regular expressions with conditional frequency distributions. Here we will extract all consonant-vowel sequences from the words of Rotokas, such as *ka* and *si*. Since each of these is a pair, it can be used to initialize a conditional frequency distribution. We then tabulate the frequency of each pair:

```
>>> rotokas_words = nltk.corpus.toolbox.words('rotokas.dic')
>>> cvs = [cv for w in rotokas_words for cv in re.findall(r'[ptksvr][aeiou]', w)]
>>> cfd = nltk.ConditionalFreqDist(cvs)
>>> cfd.tabulate()
    a   e   i   o   u
k 418 148  94 420 173
p  83  31 105  34  51
r 187  63  84  89  79
s   0   0 100   2   1
t  47   8   0 148  37
v  93  27 105  48  49
```

Examining the rows for *s* and *t*, we see they are in partial "complementary distribution," which is evidence that they are not distinct phonemes in the language. Thus, we could conceivably drop *s* from the Rotokas alphabet and simply have a pronunciation rule that the letter *t* is pronounced *s* when followed by *i*. (Note that the single entry having *su*, namely *kasuari*, 'cassowary' is borrowed from English).

If we want to be able to inspect the words behind the numbers in that table, it would be helpful to have an index, allowing us to quickly find the list of words that contains a given consonant-vowel pair. For example, cv_index['su'] should give us all words containing *su*. Here's how we can do this:

```
>>> cv_word_pairs = [(cv, w) for w in rotokas_words
...                          for cv in re.findall(r'[ptksvr][aeiou]', w)]
>>> cv_index = nltk.Index(cv_word_pairs)
>>> cv_index['su']
['kasuari']
>>> cv_index['po']
['kaapo', 'kaapopato', 'kaipori', 'kaiporipie', 'kaiporivira', 'kapo', 'kapoa',
'kapokao', 'kapokapo', 'kapokapo', 'kapokapoa', 'kapokapoa', 'kapokapora', ...]
```

This program processes each word w in turn, and for each one, finds every substring that matches the regular expression «[ptksvr][aeiou]». In the case of the word *ka-suari*, it finds *ka*, *su*, and *ri*. Therefore, the cv_word_pairs list will contain ('ka', 'ka

suari'), ('su', 'kasuari'), and ('ri', 'kasuari'). One further step, using
nltk.Index(), converts this into a useful index.

Finding Word Stems

When we use a web search engine, we usually don't mind (or even notice) if the words
in the document differ from our search terms in having different endings. A query for
laptops finds documents containing *laptop* and vice versa. Indeed, *laptop* and *laptops*
are just two forms of the same dictionary word (or lemma). For some language processing tasks we want to ignore word endings, and just deal with word stems.

There are various ways we can pull out the stem of a word. Here's a simple-minded
approach that just strips off anything that looks like a suffix:

```
>>> def stem(word):
...     for suffix in ['ing', 'ly', 'ed', 'ious', 'ies', 'ive', 'es', 's', 'ment']:
...         if word.endswith(suffix):
...             return word[:-len(suffix)]
...     return word
```

Although we will ultimately use NLTK's built-in stemmers, it's interesting to see how
we can use regular expressions for this task. Our first step is to build up a disjunction
of all the suffixes. We need to enclose it in parentheses in order to limit the scope of
the disjunction.

```
>>> re.findall(r'^.*(ing|ly|ed|ious|ies|ive|es|s|ment)$', 'processing')
['ing']
```

Here, re.findall() just gave us the suffix even though the regular expression matched
the entire word. This is because the parentheses have a second function, to select substrings to be extracted. If we want to use the parentheses to specify the scope of the
disjunction, but not to select the material to be output, we have to add ?:, which is just
one of many arcane subtleties of regular expressions. Here's the revised version.

```
>>> re.findall(r'^.*(?:ing|ly|ed|ious|ies|ive|es|s|ment)$', 'processing')
['processing']
```

However, we'd actually like to split the word into stem and suffix. So we should just
parenthesize both parts of the regular expression:

```
>>> re.findall(r'^(.*)(ing|ly|ed|ious|ies|ive|es|s|ment)$', 'processing')
[('process', 'ing')]
```

This looks promising, but still has a problem. Let's look at a different word, *processes*:

```
>>> re.findall(r'^(.*)(ing|ly|ed|ious|ies|ive|es|s|ment)$', 'processes')
[('processe', 's')]
```

The regular expression incorrectly found an -*s* suffix instead of an -*es* suffix. This demonstrates another subtlety: the star operator is "greedy" and so the .* part of the expression tries to consume as much of the input as possible. If we use the "non-greedy"
version of the star operator, written *?, we get what we want:

```
>>> re.findall(r'^(.*?)(ing|ly|ed|ious|ies|ive|es|s|ment)$', 'processes')
[('process', 'es')]
```

This works even when we allow an empty suffix, by making the content of the second parentheses optional:

```
>>> re.findall(r'^(.*?)(ing|ly|ed|ious|ies|ive|es|s|ment)?$', 'language')
[('language', '')]
```

This approach still has many problems (can you spot them?), but we will move on to define a function to perform stemming, and apply it to a whole text:

```
>>> def stem(word):
...     regexp = r'^(.*?)(ing|ly|ed|ious|ies|ive|es|s|ment)?$'
...     stem, suffix = re.findall(regexp, word)[0]
...     return stem
...
>>> raw = """DENNIS: Listen, strange women lying in ponds distributing swords
... is no basis for a system of government.  Supreme executive power derives from
... a mandate from the masses, not from some farcical aquatic ceremony."""
>>> tokens = nltk.word_tokenize(raw)
>>> [stem(t) for t in tokens]
['DENNIS', ':', 'Listen', ',', 'strange', 'women', 'ly', 'in', 'pond',
'distribut', 'sword', 'i', 'no', 'basi', 'for', 'a', 'system', 'of', 'govern',
'.', 'Supreme', 'execut', 'power', 'deriv', 'from', 'a', 'mandate', 'from',
'the', 'mass', ',', 'not', 'from', 'some', 'farcical', 'aquatic', 'ceremony', '.']
```

Notice that our regular expression removed the *s* from *ponds* but also from *is* and *basis*. It produced some non-words, such as *distribut* and *deriv*, but these are acceptable stems in some applications.

Searching Tokenized Text

You can use a special kind of regular expression for searching across multiple words in a text (where a text is a list of tokens). For example, "<a> <man>" finds all instances of *a man* in the text. The angle brackets are used to mark token boundaries, and any whitespace between the angle brackets is ignored (behaviors that are unique to NLTK's findall() method for texts). In the following example, we include <.*> ❶, which will match any single token, and enclose it in parentheses so only the matched word (e.g., *monied*) and not the matched phrase (e.g., *a monied man*) is produced. The second example finds three-word phrases ending with the word *bro* ❷. The last example finds sequences of three or more words starting with the letter *l* ❸.

```
>>> from nltk.corpus import gutenberg, nps_chat
>>> moby = nltk.Text(gutenberg.words('melville-moby_dick.txt'))
>>> moby.findall(r"<a> (<.*>) <man>")        ❶
monied; nervous; dangerous; white; white; white; pious; queer; good;
mature; white; Cape; great; wise; wise; butterless; white; fiendish;
pale; furious; better; certain; complete; dismasted; younger; brave;
brave; brave; brave
>>> chat = nltk.Text(nps_chat.words())
>>> chat.findall(r"<.*> <.*> <bro>")         ❷
you rule bro; telling you bro; u twizted bro
```

```
>>> chat.findall(r"<l.*>{3,}") ❸
lol lol lol; lmao lol lol; lol lol lol; la la la la la; la la la; la
la la; lovely lol lol love; lol lol lol.; la la la; la la la
```

Your Turn: Consolidate your understanding of regular expression patterns and substitutions using `nltk.re_show(p, s)`, which annotates the string *s* to show every place where pattern *p* was matched, and `nltk.app.nemo()`, which provides a graphical interface for exploring regular expressions. For more practice, try some of the exercises on regular expressions at the end of this chapter.

It is easy to build search patterns when the linguistic phenomenon we're studying is tied to particular words. In some cases, a little creativity will go a long way. For instance, searching a large text corpus for expressions of the form *x and other ys* allows us to discover hypernyms (see Section 2.5):

```
>>> from nltk.corpus import brown
>>> hobbies_learned = nltk.Text(brown.words(categories=['hobbies', 'learned']))
>>> hobbies_learned.findall(r"<\w*> <and> <other> <\w*s>")
speed and other activities; water and other liquids; tomb and other
landmarks; Statues and other monuments; pearls and other jewels;
charts and other items; roads and other features; figures and other
objects; military and other areas; demands and other factors;
abstracts and other compilations; iron and other metals
```

With enough text, this approach would give us a useful store of information about the taxonomy of objects, without the need for any manual labor. However, our search results will usually contain false positives, i.e., cases that we would want to exclude. For example, the result *demands and other factors* suggests that *demand* is an instance of the type *factor*, but this sentence is actually about wage demands. Nevertheless, we could construct our own ontology of English concepts by manually correcting the output of such searches.

This combination of automatic and manual processing is the most common way for new corpora to be constructed. We will return to this in Chapter 11.

Searching corpora also suffers from the problem of false negatives, i.e., omitting cases that we would want to include. It is risky to conclude that some linguistic phenomenon doesn't exist in a corpus just because we couldn't find any instances of a search pattern. Perhaps we just didn't think carefully enough about suitable patterns.

Your Turn: Look for instances of the pattern *as x as y* to discover information about entities and their properties.

3.6 Normalizing Text

In earlier program examples we have often converted text to lowercase before doing anything with its words, e.g., `set(w.lower() for w in text)`. By using `lower()`, we have **normalized** the text to lowercase so that the distinction between *The* and *the* is ignored. Often we want to go further than this and strip off any affixes, a task known as stemming. A further step is to make sure that the resulting form is a known word in a dictionary, a task known as lemmatization. We discuss each of these in turn. First, we need to define the data we will use in this section:

```
>>> raw = """DENNIS: Listen, strange women lying in ponds distributing swords
... is no basis for a system of government.  Supreme executive power derives from
... a mandate from the masses, not from some farcical aquatic ceremony."""
>>> tokens = nltk.word_tokenize(raw)
```

Stemmers

NLTK includes several off-the-shelf stemmers, and if you ever need a stemmer, you should use one of these in preference to crafting your own using regular expressions, since NLTK's stemmers handle a wide range of irregular cases. The Porter and Lancaster stemmers follow their own rules for stripping affixes. Observe that the Porter stemmer correctly handles the word *lying* (mapping it to *lie*), whereas the Lancaster stemmer does not.

```
>>> porter = nltk.PorterStemmer()
>>> lancaster = nltk.LancasterStemmer()
>>> [porter.stem(t) for t in tokens]
['DENNI', ':', 'Listen', ',', 'strang', 'women', 'lie', 'in', 'pond',
'distribut', 'sword', 'is', 'no', 'basi', 'for', 'a', 'system', 'of', 'govern',
'.', 'Suprem', 'execut', 'power', 'deriv', 'from', 'a', 'mandat', 'from',
'the', 'mass', ',', 'not', 'from', 'some', 'farcic', 'aquat', 'ceremoni', '.']
>>> [lancaster.stem(t) for t in tokens]
['den', ':', 'list', ',', 'strange', 'wom', 'lying', 'in', 'pond', 'distribut',
'sword', 'is', 'no', 'bas', 'for', 'a', 'system', 'of', 'govern', '.', 'suprem',
'execut', 'pow', 'der', 'from', 'a', 'mand', 'from', 'the', 'mass', ',', 'not',
'from', 'som', 'farc', 'aqu', 'ceremony', '.']
```

Stemming is not a well-defined process, and we typically pick the stemmer that best suits the application we have in mind. The Porter Stemmer is a good choice if you are indexing some texts and want to support search using alternative forms of words (illustrated in Example 3-1, which uses *object-oriented* programming techniques that are outside the scope of this book, string formatting techniques to be covered in Section 3.9, and the `enumerate()` function to be explained in Section 4.2).

Example 3-1. Indexing a text using a stemmer.

```
class IndexedText(object):

    def __init__(self, stemmer, text):
        self._text = text
        self._stemmer = stemmer
```

```
        self._index = nltk.Index((self._stem(word), i)
                                 for (i, word) in enumerate(text))

    def concordance(self, word, width=40):
        key = self._stem(word)
        wc = width/4                     # words of context
        for i in self._index[key]:
            lcontext = ' '.join(self._text[i-wc:i])
            rcontext = ' '.join(self._text[i:i+wc])
            ldisplay = '%*s'  % (width, lcontext[-width:])
            rdisplay = '%-*s' % (width, rcontext[:width])
            print ldisplay, rdisplay

    def _stem(self, word):
        return self._stemmer.stem(word).lower()

>>> porter = nltk.PorterStemmer()
>>> grail = nltk.corpus.webtext.words('grail.txt')
>>> text = IndexedText(porter, grail)
>>> text.concordance('lie')
r king ! DENNIS : Listen , strange women lying in ponds distributing swords is no
 beat a very brave retreat . ROBIN : All lies ! MINSTREL : [ singing ] Bravest of
     Nay . Nay . Come . Come . You may lie here . Oh , but you are wounded !
doctors immediately ! No , no , please ! Lie down . [ clap clap ] PIGLET : Well
ere is much danger , for beyond the cave lies the Gorge of Eternal Peril , which
   you . Oh ... TIM : To the north there lies a cave -- the cave of Caerbannog --
h it and lived ! Bones of full fifty men lie strewn about its lair . So , brave k
not stop our fight ' til each one of you lies dead , and the Holy Grail returns t
```

Lemmatization

The WordNet lemmatizer removes affixes only if the resulting word is in its dictionary. This additional checking process makes the lemmatizer slower than the stemmers just mentioned. Notice that it doesn't handle *lying*, but it converts *women* to *woman*.

```
>>> wnl = nltk.WordNetLemmatizer()
>>> [wnl.lemmatize(t) for t in tokens]
['DENNIS', ':', 'Listen', ',', 'strange', 'woman', 'lying', 'in', 'pond',
'distributing', 'sword', 'is', 'no', 'basis', 'for', 'a', 'system', 'of',
'government', '.', 'Supreme', 'executive', 'power', 'derives', 'from', 'a',
'mandate', 'from', 'the', 'mass', ',', 'not', 'from', 'some', 'farcical',
'aquatic', 'ceremony', '.']
```

The WordNet lemmatizer is a good choice if you want to compile the vocabulary of some texts and want a list of valid lemmas (or lexicon headwords).

> Another normalization task involves identifying **non-standard words**, including numbers, abbreviations, and dates, and mapping any such tokens to a special vocabulary. For example, every decimal number could be mapped to a single token 0.0, and every acronym could be mapped to AAA. This keeps the vocabulary small and improves the accuracy of many language modeling tasks.

3.7 Regular Expressions for Tokenizing Text

Tokenization is the task of cutting a string into identifiable linguistic units that constitute a piece of language data. Although it is a fundamental task, we have been able to delay it until now because many corpora are already tokenized, and because NLTK includes some tokenizers. Now that you are familiar with regular expressions, you can learn how to use them to tokenize text, and to have much more control over the process.

Simple Approaches to Tokenization

The very simplest method for tokenizing text is to split on whitespace. Consider the following text from *Alice's Adventures in Wonderland*:

```
>>> raw = """'When I'M a Duchess,' she said to herself, (not in a very hopeful tone
... though), 'I won't have any pepper in my kitchen AT ALL. Soup does very
... well without--Maybe it's always pepper that makes people hot-tempered,'..."""
```

We could split this raw text on whitespace using `raw.split()`. To do the same using a regular expression, it is not enough to match any space characters in the string ❶, since this results in tokens that contain a \n newline character; instead, we need to match any number of spaces, tabs, or newlines ❷:

```
>>> re.split(r' ', raw) ❶
["'When", "I'M", 'a', "Duchess,'", 'she', 'said', 'to', "herself,'", '(not', 'in',
'a', 'very', 'hopeful', 'tone\nthough),', "'I", "won't", 'have', 'any', 'pepper',
'in', 'my', 'kitchen', 'AT', 'ALL.', 'Soup', 'does', 'very\nwell', 'without--Maybe',
"it's", 'always', 'pepper', 'that', 'makes', 'people', "hot-tempered,'..."]
>>> re.split(r'[ \t\n]+', raw) ❷
["'When", "I'M", 'a', "Duchess,'", 'she', 'said', 'to', "herself,'", '(not', 'in',
'a', 'very', 'hopeful', 'tone', 'though),', "'I", "won't", 'have', 'any', 'pepper',
'in', 'my', 'kitchen', 'AT', 'ALL.', 'Soup', 'does', 'very', 'well', 'without--Maybe',
"it's", 'always', 'pepper', 'that', 'makes', 'people', "hot-tempered,'..."]
```

The regular expression «[\t\n]+» matches one or more spaces, tabs (\t), or newlines (\n). Other whitespace characters, such as carriage return and form feed, should really be included too. Instead, we will use a built-in `re` abbreviation, \s, which means any whitespace character. The second statement in the preceding example can be rewritten as `re.split(r'\s+', raw)`.

 Important: Remember to prefix regular expressions with the letter r (meaning "raw"), which instructs the Python interpreter to treat the string literally, rather than processing any backslashed characters it contains.

Splitting on whitespace gives us tokens like `'(not'` and `'herself,'`. An alternative is to use the fact that Python provides us with a character class \w for word characters, equivalent to [a-zA-Z0-9_]. It also defines the complement of this class, \W, i.e., all characters other than letters, digits, or underscore. We can use \W in a simple regular expression to split the input on anything *other* than a word character:

```
>>> re.split(r'\W+', raw)
['', 'When', 'I', 'M', 'a', 'Duchess', 'she', 'said', 'to', 'herself', 'not', 'in',
'a', 'very', 'hopeful', 'tone', 'though', 'I', 'won', 't', 'have', 'any', 'pepper',
'in', 'my', 'kitchen', 'AT', 'ALL', 'Soup', 'does', 'very', 'well', 'without',
'Maybe', 'it', 's', 'always', 'pepper', 'that', 'makes', 'people', 'hot', 'tempered',
'']
```

Observe that this gives us empty strings at the start and the end (to understand why, try doing 'xx'.split('x')). With re.findall(r'\w+', raw), we get the same tokens, but without the empty strings, using a pattern that matches the words instead of the spaces. Now that we're matching the words, we're in a position to extend the regular expression to cover a wider range of cases. The regular expression «\w+|\S\w*» will first try to match any sequence of word characters. If no match is found, it will try to match any *non*-whitespace character (\S is the complement of \s) followed by further word characters. This means that punctuation is grouped with any following letters (e.g., *'s*) but that sequences of two or more punctuation characters are separated.

```
>>> re.findall(r'\w+|\S\w*', raw)
["'When", 'I', "'M", 'a', 'Duchess', ',', "'", 'she', 'said', 'to', 'herself', ',',
'(not', 'in', 'a', 'very', 'hopeful', 'tone', 'though', ')', ',', "'I", 'won', "'t",
'have', 'any', 'pepper', 'in', 'my', 'kitchen', 'AT', 'ALL', '.', 'Soup', 'does',
'very', 'well', 'without', '-', '-Maybe', 'it', "'s", 'always', 'pepper', 'that',
'makes', 'people', 'hot', '-tempered', ',', "'", '.', '.', '.']
```

Let's generalize the \w+ in the preceding expression to permit word-internal hyphens and apostrophes: «\w+([-']\w+)*». This expression means \w+ followed by zero or more instances of [-']\w+; it would match *hot-tempered* and *it's*. (We need to include ?: in this expression for reasons discussed earlier.) We'll also add a pattern to match quote characters so these are kept separate from the text they enclose.

```
>>> print re.findall(r"\w+(?:[-']\w+)*|'|[-.(]+|\S\w*", raw)
["'", 'When', "I'M", 'a', 'Duchess', ',', "'", 'she', 'said', 'to', 'herself', ',',
'(', 'not', 'in', 'a', 'very', 'hopeful', 'tone', 'though', ')', ',', "'", 'I',
"won't", 'have', 'any', 'pepper', 'in', 'my', 'kitchen', 'AT', 'ALL', '.', 'Soup',
'does', 'very', 'well', 'without', '--', 'Maybe', "it's", 'always', 'pepper',
'that', 'makes', 'people', 'hot-tempered', ',', "'", '...']
```

The expression in this example also included «[-.(]+», which causes the double hyphen, ellipsis, and open parenthesis to be tokenized separately.

Table 3-4 lists the regular expression character class symbols we have seen in this section, in addition to some other useful symbols.

Table 3-4. Regular expression symbols

Symbol	Function
\b	Word boundary (zero width)
\d	Any decimal digit (equivalent to [0-9])

Symbol	Function
\D	Any non-digit character (equivalent to [^0-9])
\s	Any whitespace character (equivalent to [\t\n\r\f\v]
\S	Any non-whitespace character (equivalent to [^ \t\n\r\f\v])
\w	Any alphanumeric character (equivalent to [a-zA-Z0-9_])
\W	Any non-alphanumeric character (equivalent to [^a-zA-Z0-9_])
\t	The tab character
\n	The newline character

NLTK's Regular Expression Tokenizer

The function `nltk.regexp_tokenize()` is similar to `re.findall()` (as we've been using it for tokenization). However, `nltk.regexp_tokenize()` is more efficient for this task, and avoids the need for special treatment of parentheses. For readability we break up the regular expression over several lines and add a comment about each line. The special `(?x)` "verbose flag" tells Python to strip out the embedded whitespace and comments.

```
>>> text = 'That U.S.A. poster-print costs $12.40...'
>>> pattern = r'''(?x)    # set flag to allow verbose regexps
...     ([A-Z]\.)+        # abbreviations, e.g. U.S.A.
...   | \w+(-\w+)*        # words with optional internal hyphens
...   | \$?\d+(\.\d+)?%?  # currency and percentages, e.g. $12.40, 82%
...   | \.\.\.            # ellipsis
...   | [][.,;"'?():-_`]  # these are separate tokens
... '''
>>> nltk.regexp_tokenize(text, pattern)
['That', 'U.S.A.', 'poster-print', 'costs', '$12.40', '...']
```

When using the verbose flag, you can no longer use ' ' to match a space character; use `\s` instead. The `regexp_tokenize()` function has an optional `gaps` parameter. When set to `True`, the regular expression specifies the gaps between tokens, as with `re.split()`.

 We can evaluate a tokenizer by comparing the resulting tokens with a wordlist, and then report any tokens that don't appear in the wordlist, using `set(tokens).difference(wordlist)`. You'll probably want to lowercase all the tokens first.

Further Issues with Tokenization

Tokenization turns out to be a far more difficult task than you might have expected. No single solution works well across the board, and we must decide what counts as a token depending on the application domain.

When developing a tokenizer it helps to have access to raw text which has been manually tokenized, in order to compare the output of your tokenizer with high-quality (or "gold-standard") tokens. The NLTK corpus collection includes a sample of Penn Treebank data, including the raw *Wall Street Journal* text (`nltk.corpus.tree bank_raw.raw()`) and the tokenized version (`nltk.corpus.treebank.words()`).

A final issue for tokenization is the presence of contractions, such as *didn't*. If we are analyzing the meaning of a sentence, it would probably be more useful to normalize this form to two separate forms: *did* and *n't* (or *not*). We can do this work with the help of a lookup table.

3.8 Segmentation

This section discusses more advanced concepts, which you may prefer to skip on the first time through this chapter.

Tokenization is an instance of a more general problem of **segmentation**. In this section, we will look at two other instances of this problem, which use radically different techniques to the ones we have seen so far in this chapter.

Sentence Segmentation

Manipulating texts at the level of individual words often presupposes the ability to divide a text into individual sentences. As we have seen, some corpora already provide access at the sentence level. In the following example, we compute the average number of words per sentence in the Brown Corpus:

```
>>> len(nltk.corpus.brown.words()) / len(nltk.corpus.brown.sents())
20.250994070456922
```

In other cases, the text is available only as a stream of characters. Before tokenizing the text into words, we need to segment it into sentences. NLTK facilitates this by including the Punkt sentence segmenter (Kiss & Strunk, 2006). Here is an example of its use in segmenting the text of a novel. (Note that if the segmenter's internal data has been updated by the time you read this, you will see different output.)

```
>>> sent_tokenizer=nltk.data.load('tokenizers/punkt/english.pickle')
>>> text = nltk.corpus.gutenberg.raw('chesterton-thursday.txt')
>>> sents = sent_tokenizer.tokenize(text)
>>> pprint.pprint(sents[171:181])
['"Nonsense!',
 '" said Gregory, who was very rational when anyone else\nattempted paradox.',
 '"Why do all the clerks and navvies in the\nrailway trains look so sad and tired,...',
 'I will\ntell you.',
 'It is because they know that the train is going right.',
 'It\nis because they know that whatever place they have taken a ticket\nfor that ...',
 'It is because after they have\npassed Sloane Square they know that the next stat...',
 'Oh, their wild rapture!',
 'oh,\ntheir eyes like stars and their souls again in Eden, if the next\nstation w...'
 '"\n\n"It is you who are unpoetical," replied the poet Syme.']
```

Notice that this example is really a single sentence, reporting the speech of Mr. Lucian Gregory. However, the quoted speech contains several sentences, and these have been split into individual strings. This is reasonable behavior for most applications.

Sentence segmentation is difficult because a period is used to mark abbreviations, and some periods simultaneously mark an abbreviation and terminate a sentence, as often happens with acronyms like *U.S.A.*

For another approach to sentence segmentation, see Section 6.2.

Word Segmentation

For some writing systems, tokenizing text is made more difficult by the fact that there is no visual representation of word boundaries. For example, in Chinese, the three-character string: 爱国人 (ai4 "love" [verb], guo3 "country", ren2 "person") could be tokenized as 爱国 / 人, "country-loving person," or as 爱 / 国人, "love country-person."

A similar problem arises in the processing of spoken language, where the hearer must segment a continuous speech stream into individual words. A particularly challenging version of this problem arises when we don't know the words in advance. This is the problem faced by a language learner, such as a child hearing utterances from a parent. Consider the following artificial example, where word boundaries have been removed:

(1)　　a. doyouseethekitty

　　　　b. seethedoggy

　　　　c. doyoulikethekitty

　　　　d. likethedoggy

Our first challenge is simply to represent the problem: we need to find a way to separate text content from the segmentation. We can do this by annotating each character with a boolean value to indicate whether or not a word-break appears after the character (an idea that will be used heavily for "chunking" in Chapter 7). Let's assume that the learner is given the utterance breaks, since these often correspond to extended pauses. Here is a possible representation, including the initial and target segmentations:

```
>>> text = "doyouseethekittyseethedoggydoyoulikethekittylikethedoggy"
>>> seg1 = "0000000000000001000000000010000000000000000100000000000"
>>> seg2 = "0100100100100001001001000010100100010010000100010010000"
```

Observe that the segmentation strings consist of zeros and ones. They are one character shorter than the source text, since a text of length n can be broken up in only $n-1$ places. The segment() function in Example 3-2 demonstrates that we can get back to the original segmented text from its representation.

Example 3-2. Reconstruct segmented text from string representation: seg1 *and* seg2 *represent the initial and final segmentations of some hypothetical child-directed speech; the* segment() *function can use them to reproduce the segmented text.*

```
def segment(text, segs):
    words = []
    last = 0
    for i in range(len(segs)):
        if segs[i] == '1':
            words.append(text[last:i+1])
            last = i+1
    words.append(text[last:])
    return words
>>> text = "doyouseethekittyseethedoggydoyoulikethekittylikethedoggy"
>>> seg1 = "0000000000000001000000000010000000000000000100000000000"
>>> seg2 = "0100100100100001001001000010100100010010000100010010000"
>>> segment(text, seg1)
['doyouseethekitty', 'seethedoggy', 'doyoulikethekitty', 'likethedoggy']
>>> segment(text, seg2)
['do', 'you', 'see', 'the', 'kitty', 'see', 'the', 'doggy', 'do', 'you',
 'like', 'the', kitty', 'like', 'the', 'doggy']
```

Now the segmentation task becomes a search problem: find the bit string that causes the text string to be correctly segmented into words. We assume the learner is acquiring words and storing them in an internal lexicon. Given a suitable lexicon, it is possible to reconstruct the source text as a sequence of lexical items. Following (Brent & Cartwright, 1995), we can define an **objective function**, a scoring function whose value we will try to optimize, based on the size of the lexicon and the amount of information needed to reconstruct the source text from the lexicon. We illustrate this in Figure 3-6.

Figure 3-6. Calculation of objective function: Given a hypothetical segmentation of the source text (on the left), derive a lexicon and a derivation table that permit the source text to be reconstructed, then total up the number of characters used by each lexical item (including a boundary marker) and each derivation, to serve as a score of the quality of the segmentation; smaller values of the score indicate a better segmentation.

It is a simple matter to implement this objective function, as shown in Example 3-3.

Example 3-3. Computing the cost of storing the lexicon and reconstructing the source text.

```
def evaluate(text, segs):
    words = segment(text, segs)
    text_size = len(words)
    lexicon_size = len(' '.join(list(set(words))))
    return text_size + lexicon_size

>>> text = "doyouseethekittyseethedoggydoyoulikethekittylikethedoggy"
>>> seg1 = "0000000000000001000000000010000000000000000100000000000"
>>> seg2 = "0100100100100001001001000010100100010010000100010010000"
>>> seg3 = "0000100100000011001000000110000100010000001100010000001"
>>> segment(text, seg3)
['doyou', 'see', 'thekitt', 'y', 'see', 'thedogg', 'y', 'doyou', 'like',
 'thekitt', 'y', 'like', 'thedogg', 'y']
>>> evaluate(text, seg3)
46
>>> evaluate(text, seg2)
47
>>> evaluate(text, seg1)
63
```

The final step is to search for the pattern of zeros and ones that maximizes this objective function, shown in Example 3-4. Notice that the best segmentation includes "words" like *thekitty*, since there's not enough evidence in the data to split this any further.

Example 3-4. Non-deterministic search using simulated annealing: Begin searching with phrase segmentations only; randomly perturb the zeros and ones proportional to the "temperature"; with each iteration the temperature is lowered and the perturbation of boundaries is reduced.

```
from random import randint

def flip(segs, pos):
    return segs[:pos] + str(1-int(segs[pos])) + segs[pos+1:]

def flip_n(segs, n):
    for i in range(n):
        segs = flip(segs, randint(0,len(segs)-1))
    return segs

def anneal(text, segs, iterations, cooling_rate):
    temperature = float(len(segs))
    while temperature > 0.5:
        best_segs, best = segs, evaluate(text, segs)
        for i in range(iterations):
            guess = flip_n(segs, int(round(temperature)))
            score = evaluate(text, guess)
            if score < best:
                best, best_segs = score, guess
        score, segs = best, best_segs
        temperature = temperature / cooling_rate
        print evaluate(text, segs), segment(text, segs)
```

```
    print
    return segs

>>> text = "doyouseethekittyseethedoggydoyoulikethekittylikethedoggy"
>>> seg1 = "0000000000000001000000000010000000000000000100000000000"
>>> anneal(text, seg1, 5000, 1.2)
60 ['doyouseetheki', 'tty', 'see', 'thedoggy', 'doyouliketh', 'ekittylike', 'thedoggy']
58 ['doy', 'ouseetheki', 'ttysee', 'thedoggy', 'doy', 'o', 'ulikethekittylike', 'thedoggy']
56 ['doyou', 'seetheki', 'ttysee', 'thedoggy', 'doyou', 'liketh', 'ekittylike', 'thedoggy']
54 ['doyou', 'seethekit', 'tysee', 'thedoggy', 'doyou', 'likethekittylike', 'thedoggy']
53 ['doyou', 'seethekit', 'tysee', 'thedoggy', 'doyou', 'like', 'thekitty', 'like', 'thedoggy']
51 ['doyou', 'seethekittysee', 'thedoggy', 'doyou', 'like', 'thekitty', 'like', 'thedoggy']
42 ['doyou', 'see', 'thekitty', 'see', 'thedoggy', 'doyou', 'like', 'thekitty', 'like', 'thedoggy']
'000010010000000100100000001000010001000000010001000000'
```

With enough data, it is possible to automatically segment text into words with a reasonable degree of accuracy. Such methods can be applied to tokenization for writing systems that don't have any visual representation of word boundaries.

3.9 Formatting: From Lists to Strings

Often we write a program to report a single data item, such as a particular element in a corpus that meets some complicated criterion, or a single summary statistic such as a word-count or the performance of a tagger. More often, we write a program to produce a structured result; for example, a tabulation of numbers or linguistic forms, or a reformatting of the original data. When the results to be presented are linguistic, textual output is usually the most natural choice. However, when the results are numerical, it may be preferable to produce graphical output. In this section, you will learn about a variety of ways to present program output.

From Lists to Strings

The simplest kind of structured object we use for text processing is lists of words. When we want to output these to a display or a file, we must convert these lists into strings. To do this in Python we use the `join()` method, and specify the string to be used as the "glue":

```
>>> silly = ['We', 'called', 'him', 'Tortoise', 'because', 'he', 'taught', 'us', '.']
>>> ' '.join(silly)
'We called him Tortoise because he taught us .'
>>> ';'.join(silly)
'We;called;him;Tortoise;because;he;taught;us;.'
>>> ''.join(silly)
'WecalledhimTortoisebecausehetaughtus.'
```

So `' '.join(silly)` means: take all the items in `silly` and concatenate them as one big string, using `' '` as a spacer between the items. I.e., `join()` is a method of the string that you want to use as the glue. (Many people find this notation for `join()` counterintuitive.) The `join()` method only works on a list of strings—what we have been calling a text—a complex type that enjoys some privileges in Python.

Strings and Formats

We have seen that there are two ways to display the contents of an object:

```
>>> word = 'cat'
>>> sentence = """hello
... world"""
>>> print word
cat
>>> print sentence
hello
world
>>> word
'cat'
>>> sentence
'hello\nworld'
```

The `print` command yields Python's attempt to produce the most human-readable form of an object. The second method—naming the variable at a prompt—shows us a string that can be used to recreate this object. It is important to keep in mind that both of these are just strings, displayed for the benefit of you, the user. They do not give us any clue as to the actual internal representation of the object.

There are many other useful ways to display an object as a string of characters. This may be for the benefit of a human reader, or because we want to **export** our data to a particular file format for use in an external program.

Formatted output typically contains a combination of variables and pre-specified strings. For example, given a frequency distribution `fdist`, we could do:

```
>>> fdist = nltk.FreqDist(['dog', 'cat', 'dog', 'cat', 'dog', 'snake', 'dog', 'cat'])
>>> for word in fdist:
...     print word, '->', fdist[word], ';',
dog -> 4 ; cat -> 3 ; snake -> 1 ;
```

Apart from the problem of unwanted whitespace, print statements that contain alternating variables and constants can be difficult to read and maintain. A better solution is to use **string formatting expressions**.

```
>>> for word in fdist:
...     print '%s->%d;' % (word, fdist[word]),
dog->4; cat->3; snake->1;
```

To understand what is going on here, let's test out the string formatting expression on its own. (By now this will be your usual method of exploring new syntax.)

```
>>> '%s->%d;' % ('cat', 3)
'cat->3;'
>>> '%s->%d;' % 'cat'
Traceback (most recent call last):
  File "<stdin>", line 1, in <module>
TypeError: not enough arguments for format string
```

The special symbols %s and %d are placeholders for strings and (decimal) integers. We can embed these inside a string, then use the % operator to combine them. Let's unpack this code further, in order to see this behavior up close:

```
>>> '%s->' % 'cat'
'cat->'
>>> '%d' % 3
'3'
>>> 'I want a %s right now' % 'coffee'
'I want a coffee right now'
```

We can have a number of placeholders, but following the % operator we need to specify a tuple with exactly the same number of values:

```
>>> "%s wants a %s %s" % ("Lee", "sandwich", "for lunch")
'Lee wants a sandwich for lunch'
```

We can also provide the values for the placeholders indirectly. Here's an example using a for loop:

```
>>> template = 'Lee wants a %s right now'
>>> menu = ['sandwich', 'spam fritter', 'pancake']
>>> for snack in menu:
...     print template % snack
...
Lee wants a sandwich right now
Lee wants a spam fritter right now
Lee wants a pancake right now
```

The %s and %d symbols are called **conversion specifiers**. They start with the % character and end with a conversion character such as s (for string) or d (for decimal integer) The string containing conversion specifiers is called a **format string**. We combine a format string with the % operator and a tuple of values to create a complete string formatting expression.

Lining Things Up

So far our formatting strings generated output of arbitrary width on the page (or screen), such as %s and %d. We can specify a width as well, such as %6s, producing a string that is padded to width 6. It is right-justified by default ❶, but we can include a minus sign to make it left-justified ❷. In case we don't know in advance how wide a displayed value should be, the width value can be replaced with a star in the formatting string, then specified using a variable ❸.

```
>>> '%6s' % 'dog' ❶
'   dog'
>>> '%-6s' % 'dog' ❷
'dog   '
>>> width = 6
>>> '%-*s' % (width, 'dog') ❸
'dog   '
```

Other control characters are used for decimal integers and floating-point numbers. Since the percent character % has a special interpretation in formatting strings, we have to precede it with another % to get it in the output.

```
>>> count, total = 3205, 9375
>>> "accuracy for %d words: %2.4f%%" % (total, 100 * count / total)
'accuracy for 9375 words: 34.1867%'
```

An important use of formatting strings is for tabulating data. Recall that in Section 2.1 we saw data being tabulated from a conditional frequency distribution. Let's perform the tabulation ourselves, exercising full control of headings and column widths, as shown in Example 3-5. Note the clear separation between the language processing work, and the tabulation of results.

Example 3-5. Frequency of modals in different sections of the Brown Corpus.

```
def tabulate(cfdist, words, categories):
    print '%-16s' % 'Category',
    for word in words:                                # column headings
        print '%6s' % word,
    print
    for category in categories:
        print '%-16s' % category,                     # row heading
        for word in words:                            # for each word
            print '%6d' % cfdist[category][word],     # print table cell
        print                                         # end the row

>>> from nltk.corpus import brown
>>> cfd = nltk.ConditionalFreqDist(
...           (genre, word)
...           for genre in brown.categories()
...           for word in brown.words(categories=genre))
>>> genres = ['news', 'religion', 'hobbies', 'science_fiction', 'romance', 'humor']
>>> modals = ['can', 'could', 'may', 'might', 'must', 'will']
>>> tabulate(cfd, modals, genres)
```

Category	can	could	may	might	must	will
news	93	86	66	38	50	389
religion	82	59	78	12	54	71
hobbies	268	58	131	22	83	264
science_fiction	16	49	4	12	8	16
romance	74	193	11	51	45	43
humor	16	30	8	8	9	13

Recall from the listing in Example 3-1 that we used a formatting string "%*s". This allows us to specify the width of a field using a variable.

```
>>> '%*s' % (15, "Monty Python")
'   Monty Python'
```

We could use this to automatically customize the column to be just wide enough to accommodate all the words, using width = max(len(w) for w in words). Remember that the comma at the end of print statements adds an extra space, and this is sufficient to prevent the column headings from running into each other.

Writing Results to a File

We have seen how to read text from files (Section 3.1). It is often useful to write output to files as well. The following code opens a file *output.txt* for writing, and saves the program output to the file.

```
>>> output_file = open('output.txt', 'w')
>>> words = set(nltk.corpus.genesis.words('english-kjv.txt'))
>>> for word in sorted(words):
...     output_file.write(word + "\n")
```

 Your Turn: What is the effect of appending \n to each string before we write it to the file? If you're using a Windows machine, you may want to use word + "\r\n" instead. What happens if we do

```
output_file.write(word)
```

When we write non-text data to a file, we must convert it to a string first. We can do this conversion using formatting strings, as we saw earlier. Let's write the total number of words to our file, before closing it.

```
>>> len(words)
2789
>>> str(len(words))
'2789'
>>> output_file.write(str(len(words)) + "\n")
>>> output_file.close()
```

 Caution!
You should avoid filenames that contain space characters, such as *output file.txt*, or that are identical except for case distinctions, e.g., *Output.txt* and *output.TXT*.

Text Wrapping

When the output of our program is text-like, instead of tabular, it will usually be necessary to wrap it so that it can be displayed conveniently. Consider the following output, which overflows its line, and which uses a complicated `print` statement:

```
>>> saying = ['After', 'all', 'is', 'said', 'and', 'done', ',',
...           'more', 'is', 'said', 'than', 'done', '.']
>>> for word in saying:
...     print word, '(' + str(len(word)) + '),',
After (5), all (3), is (2), said (4), and (3), done (4), , (1), more (4), is (2), said (4),
```

We can take care of line wrapping with the help of Python's `textwrap` module. For maximum clarity we will separate each step onto its own line:

```
>>> from textwrap import fill
>>> format = '%s (%d),'
```

```
>>> pieces = [format % (word, len(word)) for word in saying]
>>> output = ' '.join(pieces)
>>> wrapped = fill(output)
>>> print wrapped
After (5), all (3), is (2), said (4), and (3), done (4), , (1), more
(4), is (2), said (4), than (4), done (4), . (1),
```

Notice that there is a linebreak between more and its following number. If we wanted to avoid this, we could redefine the formatting string so that it contained no spaces (e.g., '%s_(%d),'), then instead of printing the value of wrapped, we could print wrapped.replace('_', ' ').

3.10 Summary

- In this book we view a text as a list of words. A "raw text" is a potentially long string containing words and whitespace formatting, and is how we typically store and visualize a text.

- A string is specified in Python using single or double quotes: 'Monty Python', "Monty Python".

- The characters of a string are accessed using indexes, counting from zero: 'Monty Python'[0] gives the value M. The length of a string is found using len().

- Substrings are accessed using slice notation: 'Monty Python'[1:5] gives the value onty. If the start index is omitted, the substring begins at the start of the string; if the end index is omitted, the slice continues to the end of the string.

- Strings can be split into lists: 'Monty Python'.split() gives ['Monty', 'Python']. Lists can be joined into strings: '/'.join(['Monty', 'Python']) gives 'Monty/Python'.

- We can read text from a file f using text = open(f).read(). We can read text from a URL u using text = urlopen(u).read(). We can iterate over the lines of a text file using for line in open(f).

- Texts found on the Web may contain unwanted material (such as headers, footers, and markup), that need to be removed before we do any linguistic processing.

- Tokenization is the segmentation of a text into basic units—or tokens—such as words and punctuation. Tokenization based on whitespace is inadequate for many applications because it bundles punctuation together with words. NLTK provides an off-the-shelf tokenizer nltk.word_tokenize().

- Lemmatization is a process that maps the various forms of a word (such as *appeared*, *appears*) to the canonical or citation form of the word, also known as the lexeme or lemma (e.g., *appear*).

- Regular expressions are a powerful and flexible method of specifying patterns. Once we have imported the re module, we can use re.findall() to find all substrings in a string that match a pattern.

- If a regular expression string includes a backslash, you should tell Python not to preprocess the string, by using a raw string with an `r` prefix: `r'regexp'`.

- When backslash is used before certain characters, e.g., `\n`, this takes on a special meaning (newline character); however, when backslash is used before regular expression wildcards and operators, e.g., `\.`, `\|`, `\$`, these characters *lose* their special meaning and are matched literally.

- A string formatting expression `template % arg_tuple` consists of a format string `template` that contains conversion specifiers like `%-6s` and `%0.2d`.

3.11 Further Reading

Extra materials for this chapter are posted at *http://www.nltk.org/*, including links to freely available resources on the Web. Remember to consult the Python reference materials at *http://docs.python.org/*. (For example, this documentation covers "universal newline support," explaining how to work with the different newline conventions used by various operating systems.)

For more examples of processing words with NLTK, see the tokenization, stemming, and corpus HOWTOs at *http://www.nltk.org/howto*. Chapters 2 and 3 of (Jurafsky & Martin, 2008) contain more advanced material on regular expressions and morphology. For more extensive discussion of text processing with Python, see (Mertz, 2003). For information about normalizing non-standard words, see (Sproat et al., 2001).

There are many references for regular expressions, both practical and theoretical. For an introductory tutorial to using regular expressions in Python, see Kuchling's *Regular Expression HOWTO*, *http://www.amk.ca/python/howto/regex/*. For a comprehensive and detailed manual in using regular expressions, covering their syntax in most major programming languages, including Python, see (Friedl, 2002). Other presentations include Section 2.1 of (Jurafsky & Martin, 2008), and Chapter 3 of (Mertz, 2003).

There are many online resources for Unicode. Useful discussions of Python's facilities for handling Unicode are:

- PEP-100 *http://www.python.org/dev/peps/pep-0100/*
- Jason Orendorff, *Unicode for Programmers*, *http://www.jorendorff.com/articles/unicode/*
- A. M. Kuchling, *Unicode HOWTO*, *http://www.amk.ca/python/howto/unicode*
- Frederik Lundh, *Python Unicode Objects*, *http://effbot.org/zone/unicode-objects.htm*
- Joel Spolsky, *The Absolute Minimum Every Software Developer Absolutely, Positively Must Know About Unicode and Character Sets (No Excuses!)*, *http://www.joelonsoftware.com/articles/Unicode.html*

The problem of tokenizing Chinese text is a major focus of SIGHAN, the ACL Special Interest Group on Chinese Language Processing (*http://sighan.org/*). Our method for segmenting English text follows (Brent & Cartwright, 1995); this work falls in the area of language acquisition (Niyogi, 2006).

Collocations are a special case of multiword expressions. A **multiword expression** is a small phrase whose meaning and other properties cannot be predicted from its words alone, e.g., *part-of-speech* (Baldwin & Kim, 2010).

Simulated annealing is a heuristic for finding a good approximation to the optimum value of a function in a large, discrete search space, based on an analogy with annealing in metallurgy. The technique is described in many Artificial Intelligence texts.

The approach to discovering hyponyms in text using search patterns like *x and other ys* is described by (Hearst, 1992).

3.12 Exercises

1. ○ Define a string s = 'colorless'. Write a Python statement that changes this to "colourless" using only the slice and concatenation operations.

2. ○ We can use the slice notation to remove morphological endings on words. For example, 'dogs'[:-1] removes the last character of dogs, leaving dog. Use slice notation to remove the affixes from these words (we've inserted a hyphen to indicate the affix boundary, but omit this from your strings): dish-es, run-ning, nation-ality, un-do, pre-heat.

3. ○ We saw how we can generate an IndexError by indexing beyond the end of a string. Is it possible to construct an index that goes too far to the left, before the start of the string?

4. ○ We can specify a "step" size for the slice. The following returns every second character within the slice: monty[6:11:2]. It also works in the reverse direction: monty[10:5:-2]. Try these for yourself, and then experiment with different step values.

5. ○ What happens if you ask the interpreter to evaluate monty[::-1]? Explain why this is a reasonable result.

6. ○ Describe the class of strings matched by the following regular expressions:

    a. [a-zA-Z]+

    b. [A-Z][a-z]*

    c. p[aeiou]{,2}t

    d. \d+(\.\d+)?

    e. ([^aeiou][aeiou][^aeiou])*

    f. \w+|[^\w\s]+

    Test your answers using nltk.re_show().

7. ○ Write regular expressions to match the following classes of strings:

    a. A single determiner (assume that *a*, *an*, and *the* are the only determiners)

    b. An arithmetic expression using integers, addition, and multiplication, such as `2*3+8`

8. ○ Write a utility function that takes a URL as its argument, and returns the contents of the URL, with all HTML markup removed. Use `urllib.urlopen` to access the contents of the URL, e.g.:

```
raw_contents = urllib.urlopen('http://www.nltk.org/').read()
```

9. ○ Save some text into a file *corpus.txt*. Define a function `load(f)` that reads from the file named in its sole argument, and returns a string containing the text of the file.

    a. Use `nltk.regexp_tokenize()` to create a tokenizer that tokenizes the various kinds of punctuation in this text. Use one multiline regular expression inline comments, using the verbose flag (`?x`).

    b. Use `nltk.regexp_tokenize()` to create a tokenizer that tokenizes the following kinds of expressions: monetary amounts; dates; names of people and organizations.

10. ○ Rewrite the following loop as a list comprehension:

```
>>> sent = ['The', 'dog', 'gave', 'John', 'the', 'newspaper']
>>> result = []
>>> for word in sent:
...     word_len = (word, len(word))
...     result.append(word_len)
>>> result
[('The', 3), ('dog', 3), ('gave', 4), ('John', 4), ('the', 3), ('newspaper', 9)]
```

11. ○ Define a string `raw` containing a sentence of your own choosing. Now, split `raw` on some character other than space, such as `'s'`.

12. ○ Write a `for` loop to print out the characters of a string, one per line.

13. ○ What is the difference between calling `split` on a string with no argument and one with `' '` as the argument, e.g., `sent.split()` versus `sent.split(' ')`? What happens when the string being split contains tab characters, consecutive space characters, or a sequence of tabs and spaces? (In IDLE you will need to use `'\t'` to enter a tab character.)

14. ○ Create a variable `words` containing a list of words. Experiment with `words.sort()` and `sorted(words)`. What is the difference?

15. ○ Explore the difference between strings and integers by typing the following at a Python prompt: `"3" * 7` and `3 * 7`. Try converting between strings and integers using `int("3")` and `str(3)`.

16. ○ Earlier, we asked you to use a text editor to create a file called *test.py*, containing the single line `monty = 'Monty Python'`. If you haven't already done this (or can't find the file), go ahead and do it now. Next, start up a new session with the Python

interpreter, and enter the expression `monty` at the prompt. You will get an error from the interpreter. Now, try the following (note that you have to leave off the *.py* part of the filename):

```
>>> from test import msg
>>> msg
```

This time, Python should return with a value. You can also try `import test`, in which case Python should be able to evaluate the expression `test.monty` at the prompt.

17. ○ What happens when the formatting strings `%6s` and `%-6s` are used to display strings that are longer than six characters?

18. ◑ Read in some text from a corpus, tokenize it, and print the list of all *wh*-word types that occur. (*wh*-words in English are used in questions, relative clauses, and exclamations: *who*, *which*, *what*, and so on.) Print them in order. Are any words duplicated in this list, because of the presence of case distinctions or punctuation?

19. ◑ Create a file consisting of words and (made up) frequencies, where each line consists of a word, the space character, and a positive integer, e.g., `fuzzy 53`. Read the file into a Python list using `open(filename).readlines()`. Next, break each line into its two fields using `split()`, and convert the number into an integer using `int()`. The result should be a list of the form: `[['fuzzy', 53], ...]`.

20. ◑ Write code to access a favorite web page and extract some text from it. For example, access a weather site and extract the forecast top temperature for your town or city today.

21. ◑ Write a function `unknown()` that takes a URL as its argument, and returns a list of unknown words that occur on that web page. In order to do this, extract all substrings consisting of lowercase letters (using `re.findall()`) and remove any items from this set that occur in the Words Corpus (`nltk.corpus.words`). Try to categorize these words manually and discuss your findings.

22. ◑ Examine the results of processing the URL *http://news.bbc.co.uk/* using the regular expressions suggested above. You will see that there is still a fair amount of non-textual data there, particularly JavaScript commands. You may also find that sentence breaks have not been properly preserved. Define further regular expressions that improve the extraction of text from this web page.

23. ◑ Are you able to write a regular expression to tokenize text in such a way that the word *don't* is tokenized into *do* and *n't*? Explain why this regular expression won't work: «n't|\w+».

24. ◑ Try to write code to convert text into *hAck3r*, using regular expressions and substitution, where e → 3, i → 1, o → 0, l → |, s → 5, . → 5w33t!, ate → 8. Normalize the text to lowercase before converting it. Add more substitutions of your own. Now try to map s to two different values: $ for word-initial s, and 5 for word-internal s.

25. ◑ *Pig Latin* is a simple transformation of English text. Each word of the text is converted as follows: move any consonant (or consonant cluster) that appears at the start of the word to the end, then append *ay*, e.g., *string* → *ingstray*, *idle* → *idleay* (see *http://en.wikipedia.org/wiki/Pig_Latin*).

    a. Write a function to convert a word to Pig Latin.

    b. Write code that converts text, instead of individual words.

    c. Extend it further to preserve capitalization, to keep `qu` together (so that `quiet` becomes `ietquay`, for example), and to detect when `y` is used as a consonant (e.g., `yellow`) versus a vowel (e.g., `style`).

26. ◑ Download some text from a language that has vowel harmony (e.g., Hungarian), extract the vowel sequences of words, and create a vowel bigram table.

27. ◑ Python's `random` module includes a function `choice()` which randomly chooses an item from a sequence; e.g., `choice("aehh ")` will produce one of four possible characters, with the letter `h` being twice as frequent as the others. Write a generator expression that produces a sequence of 500 randomly chosen letters drawn from the string `"aehh "`, and put this expression inside a call to the `''.join()` function, to concatenate them into one long string. You should get a result that looks like uncontrolled sneezing or maniacal laughter: `he haha ee heheeh eha`. Use `split()` and `join()` again to normalize the whitespace in this string.

28. ◑ Consider the numeric expressions in the following sentence from the MedLine Corpus: *The corresponding free cortisol fractions in these sera were 4.53 +/- 0.15% and 8.16 +/- 0.23%, respectively.* Should we say that the numeric expression *4.53 +/- 0.15%* is three words? Or should we say that it's a single compound word? Or should we say that it is actually *nine* words, since it's read "four point five three, plus or minus fifteen percent"? Or should we say that it's not a "real" word at all, since it wouldn't appear in any dictionary? Discuss these different possibilities. Can you think of application domains that motivate at least two of these answers?

29. ◑ Readability measures are used to score the reading difficulty of a text, for the purposes of selecting texts of appropriate difficulty for language learners. Let us define μ_w to be the average number of letters per word, and μ_s to be the average number of words per sentence, in a given text. The Automated Readability Index (ARI) of the text is defined to be: $4.71 \mu_w + 0.5 \mu_s - 21.43$. Compute the ARI score for various sections of the Brown Corpus, including section `f` (popular lore) and `j` (learned). Make use of the fact that `nltk.corpus.brown.words()` produces a sequence of words, whereas `nltk.corpus.brown.sents()` produces a sequence of sentences.

30. ◑ Use the Porter Stemmer to normalize some tokenized text, calling the stemmer on each word. Do the same thing with the Lancaster Stemmer, and see if you observe any differences.

31. ◑ Define the variable `saying` to contain the list `['After', 'all', 'is', 'said', 'and', 'done', ',', 'more', 'is', 'said', 'than', 'done', '.']`. Process the list

using a `for` loop, and store the result in a new list `lengths`. Hint: begin by assigning the empty list to `lengths`, using `lengths = []`. Then each time through the loop, use `append()` to add another length value to the list.

32. ◑ Define a variable `silly` to contain the string: `'newly formed bland ideas are inexpressible in an infuriating way'`. (This happens to be the legitimate interpretation that bilingual English-Spanish speakers can assign to Chomsky's famous nonsense phrase *colorless green ideas sleep furiously*, according to Wikipedia). Now write code to perform the following tasks:

    a. Split `silly` into a list of strings, one per word, using Python's `split()` operation, and save this to a variable called `bland`.

    b. Extract the second letter of each word in `silly` and join them into a string, to get `'eoldrnnnna'`.

    c. Combine the words in `bland` back into a single string, using `join()`. Make sure the words in the resulting string are separated with whitespace.

    d. Print the words of `silly` in alphabetical order, one per line.

33. ◑ The `index()` function can be used to look up items in sequences. For example, `'inexpressible'.index('e')` tells us the index of the first position of the letter `e`.

    a. What happens when you look up a substring, e.g., `'inexpressible'.index('re')`?

    b. Define a variable `words` containing a list of words. Now use `words.index()` to look up the position of an individual word.

    c. Define a variable `silly` as in Exercise 32. Use the `index()` function in combination with list slicing to build a list `phrase` consisting of all the words up to (but not including) `in` in `silly`.

34. ◑ Write code to convert nationality adjectives such as *Canadian* and *Australian* to their corresponding nouns *Canada* and *Australia* (see *http://en.wikipedia.org/wiki/List_of_adjectival_forms_of_place_names*).

35. ◑ Read the LanguageLog post on phrases of the form *as best as p can* and *as best p can*, where *p* is a pronoun. Investigate this phenomenon with the help of a corpus and the `findall()` method for searching tokenized text described in Section 3.5. The post is at *http://itre.cis.upenn.edu/~myl/languagelog/archives/002733.html*.

36. ◑ Study the *lolcat* version of the book of Genesis, accessible as `nltk.corpus.genesis.words('lolcat.txt')`, and the rules for converting text into *lolspeak* at *http://www.lolcatbible.com/index.php?title=How_to_speak_lolcat*. Define regular expressions to convert English words into corresponding lolspeak words.

37. ◑ Read about the `re.sub()` function for string substitution using regular expressions, using `help(re.sub)` and by consulting the further readings for this chapter. Use `re.sub` in writing code to remove HTML tags from an HTML file, and to normalize whitespace.

38. • An interesting challenge for tokenization is words that have been split across a linebreak. E.g., if *long-term* is split, then we have the string `long-\nterm`.

   a. Write a regular expression that identifies words that are hyphenated at a line-break. The expression will need to include the `\n` character.

   b. Use `re.sub()` to remove the `\n` character from these words.

   c. How might you identify words that should not remain hyphenated once the newline is removed, e.g., `'encyclo-\npedia'`?

39. • Read the Wikipedia entry on *Soundex*. Implement this algorithm in Python.

40. • Obtain raw texts from two or more genres and compute their respective reading difficulty scores as in the earlier exercise on reading difficulty. E.g., compare ABC Rural News and ABC Science News (`nltk.corpus.abc`). Use Punkt to perform sentence segmentation.

41. • Rewrite the following nested loop as a nested list comprehension:

```
>>> words = ['attribution', 'confabulation', 'elocution',
...          'sequoia', 'tenacious', 'unidirectional']
>>> vsequences = set()
>>> for word in words:
...     vowels = []
...     for char in word:
...         if char in 'aeiou':
...             vowels.append(char)
...     vsequences.add(''.join(vowels))
>>> sorted(vsequences)
['aiuio', 'eaiou', 'eouio', 'euoia', 'oauaio', 'uiieioa']
```

42. • Use WordNet to create a semantic index for a text collection. Extend the concordance search program in Example 3-1, indexing each word using the offset of its first synset, e.g., `wn.synsets('dog')[0].offset` (and optionally the offset of some of its ancestors in the hypernym hierarchy).

43. • With the help of a multilingual corpus such as the Universal Declaration of Human Rights Corpus (`nltk.corpus.udhr`), along with NLTK's frequency distribution and rank correlation functionality (`nltk.FreqDist`, `nltk.spearman_correlation`), develop a system that guesses the language of a previously unseen text. For simplicity, work with a single character encoding and just a few languages.

44. • Write a program that processes a text and discovers cases where a word has been used with a novel sense. For each word, compute the WordNet similarity between all synsets of the word and all synsets of the words in its context. (Note that this is a crude approach; doing it well is a difficult, open research problem.)

45. • Read the article on normalization of non-standard words (Sproat et al., 2001), and implement a similar system for text normalization.

## CHAPTER 4

Writing Structured Programs

By now you will have a sense of the capabilities of the Python programming language for processing natural language. However, if you're new to Python or to programming, you may still be wrestling with Python and not feel like you are in full control yet. In this chapter we'll address the following questions:

1. How can you write well-structured, readable programs that you and others will be able to reuse easily?

2. How do the fundamental building blocks work, such as loops, functions, and assignment?

3. What are some of the pitfalls with Python programming, and how can you avoid them?

Along the way, you will consolidate your knowledge of fundamental programming constructs, learn more about using features of the Python language in a natural and concise way, and learn some useful techniques in visualizing natural language data. As before, this chapter contains many examples and exercises (and as before, some exercises introduce new material). Readers new to programming should work through them carefully and consult other introductions to programming if necessary; experienced programmers can quickly skim this chapter.

In the other chapters of this book, we have organized the programming concepts as dictated by the needs of NLP. Here we revert to a more conventional approach, where the material is more closely tied to the structure of the programming language. There's not room for a complete presentation of the language, so we'll just focus on the language constructs and idioms that are most important for NLP.

4.1 Back to the Basics

Assignment

Assignment would seem to be the most elementary programming concept, not deserving a separate discussion. However, there are some surprising subtleties here. Consider the following code fragment:

```
>>> foo = 'Monty'
>>> bar = foo ❶
>>> foo = 'Python' ❷
>>> bar
'Monty'
```

This behaves exactly as expected. When we write bar = foo in the code ❶, the value of foo (the string 'Monty') is assigned to bar. That is, bar is a **copy** of foo, so when we overwrite foo with a new string 'Python' on line ❷, the value of bar is not affected.

However, assignment statements do not always involve making copies in this way. Assignment always copies the value of an expression, but a value is not always what you might expect it to be. In particular, the "value" of a structured object such as a list is actually just a *reference* to the object. In the following example, ❶ assigns the reference of foo to the new variable bar. Now when we modify something inside foo on line ❷, we can see that the contents of bar have also been changed.

```
>>> foo = ['Monty', 'Python']
>>> bar = foo ❶
>>> foo[1] = 'Bodkin' ❷
>>> bar
['Monty', 'Bodkin']
```

The line bar = foo ❶ does not copy the contents of the variable, only its "object reference." To understand what is going on here, we need to know how lists are stored in the computer's memory. In Figure 4-1, we see that a list foo is a reference to an object stored at location 3133 (which is itself a series of pointers to other locations holding strings). When we assign bar = foo, it is just the object reference 3133 that gets copied. This behavior extends to other aspects of the language, such as parameter passing (Section 4.4).

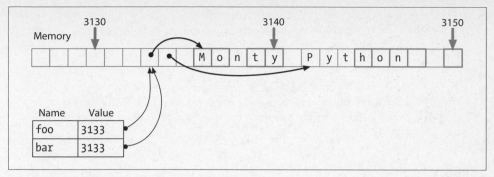

Figure 4-1. List assignment and computer memory: Two list objects foo and bar reference the same location in the computer's memory; updating foo will also modify bar, and vice versa.

Let's experiment some more, by creating a variable `empty` holding the empty list, then using it three times on the next line.

```
>>> empty = []
>>> nested = [empty, empty, empty]
>>> nested
[[], [], []]
>>> nested[1].append('Python')
>>> nested
[['Python'], ['Python'], ['Python']]
```

Observe that changing one of the items inside our nested list of lists changed them all. This is because each of the three elements is actually just a reference to one and the same list in memory.

 Your Turn: Use multiplication to create a list of lists: `nested = [[]] * 3`. Now modify one of the elements of the list, and observe that all the elements are changed. Use Python's `id()` function to find out the numerical identifier for any object, and verify that `id(nested[0])`, `id(nested[1])`, and `id(nested[2])` are all the same.

Now, notice that when we assign a new value to one of the elements of the list, it does not propagate to the others:

```
>>> nested = [[]] * 3
>>> nested[1].append('Python')
>>> nested[1] = ['Monty']
>>> nested
[['Python'], ['Monty'], ['Python']]
```

We began with a list containing three references to a single empty list object. Then we modified that object by appending `'Python'` to it, resulting in a list containing three references to a single list object `['Python']`. Next, we *overwrote* one of those references with a reference to a new object `['Monty']`. This last step modified one of the three object references inside the nested list. However, the `['Python']` object wasn't changed, and is still referenced from two places in our nested list of lists. It is crucial to appreciate this difference between modifying an object via an object reference and overwriting an object reference.

 Important: To copy the items from a list foo to a new list bar, you can write bar = foo[:]. This copies the object references inside the list. To copy a structure without copying any object references, use copy.deep copy().

Equality

Python provides two ways to check that a pair of items are the same. The `is` operator tests for object identity. We can use it to verify our earlier observations about objects. First, we create a list containing several copies of the same object, and demonstrate that they are not only identical according to ==, but also that they are one and the same object:

```
>>> size = 5
>>> python = ['Python']
>>> snake_nest = [python] * size
>>> snake_nest[0] == snake_nest[1] == snake_nest[2] == snake_nest[3] == snake_nest[4]
True
>>> snake_nest[0] is snake_nest[1] is snake_nest[2] is snake_nest[3] is snake_nest[4]
True
```

Now let's put a new python in this nest. We can easily show that the objects are not all identical:

```
>>> import random
>>> position = random.choice(range(size))
>>> snake_nest[position] = ['Python']
>>> snake_nest
[['Python'], ['Python'], ['Python'], ['Python'], ['Python']]
>>> snake_nest[0] == snake_nest[1] == snake_nest[2] == snake_nest[3] == snake_nest[4]
True
>>> snake_nest[0] is snake_nest[1] is snake_nest[2] is snake_nest[3] is snake_nest[4]
False
```

You can do several pairwise tests to discover which position contains the interloper, but the `id()` function makes detection is easier:

```
>>> [id(snake) for snake in snake_nest]
[513528, 533168, 513528, 513528, 513528]
```

This reveals that the second item of the list has a distinct identifier. If you try running this code snippet yourself, expect to see different numbers in the resulting list, and don't be surprised if the interloper is in a different position.

Having two kinds of equality might seem strange. However, it's really just the type-token distinction, familiar from natural language, here showing up in a programming language.

Conditionals

In the condition part of an `if` statement, a non-empty string or list is evaluated as true, while an empty string or list evaluates as false.

```
>>> mixed = ['cat', '', ['dog'], []]
>>> for element in mixed:
...     if element:
...         print element
...
cat
['dog']
```

That is, we *don't* need to say `if len(element) > 0:` in the condition.

What's the difference between using `if...elif` as opposed to using a couple of `if` statements in a row? Well, consider the following situation:

```
>>> animals = ['cat', 'dog']
>>> if 'cat' in animals:
...     print 1
... elif 'dog' in animals:
...     print 2
...
1
```

Since the `if` clause of the statement is satisfied, Python never tries to evaluate the `elif` clause, so we never get to print out 2. By contrast, if we replaced the `elif` by an `if`, then we would print out both 1 and 2. So an `elif` clause potentially gives us more information than a bare `if` clause; when it evaluates to true, it tells us not only that the condition is satisfied, but also that the condition of the main `if` clause was *not* satisfied.

The functions `all()` and `any()` can be applied to a list (or other sequence) to check whether all or any items meet some condition:

```
>>> sent = ['No', 'good', 'fish', 'goes', 'anywhere', 'without', 'a', 'porpoise', '.']
>>> all(len(w) > 4 for w in sent)
False
>>> any(len(w) > 4 for w in sent)
True
```

4.2 Sequences

So far, we have seen two kinds of sequence object: strings and lists. Another kind of sequence is called a **tuple**. Tuples are formed with the comma operator ❶, and typically enclosed using parentheses. We've actually seen them in the previous chapters, and sometimes referred to them as "pairs," since there were always two members. However, tuples can have any number of members. Like lists and strings, tuples can be indexed ❷ and sliced ❸, and have a length ❹.

```
>>> t = 'walk', 'fem', 3 ❶
>>> t
('walk', 'fem', 3)
```

```
>>> t[0]  ❷
'walk'
>>> t[1:]  ❸
('fem', 3)
>>> len(t)  ❹
```

Caution!

Tuples are constructed using the comma operator. Parentheses are a more general feature of Python syntax, designed for grouping. A tuple containing the single element 'snark' is defined by adding a trailing comma, like this: 'snark',. The empty tuple is a special case, and is defined using empty parentheses ().

Let's compare strings, lists, and tuples directly, and do the indexing, slice, and length operation on each type:

```
>>> raw = 'I turned off the spectroroute'
>>> text = ['I', 'turned', 'off', 'the', 'spectroroute']
>>> pair = (6, 'turned')
>>> raw[2], text[3], pair[1]
('t', 'the', 'turned')
>>> raw[-3:], text[-3:], pair[-3:]
('ute', ['off', 'the', 'spectroroute'], (6, 'turned'))
>>> len(raw), len(text), len(pair)
(29, 5, 2)
```

Notice in this code sample that we computed multiple values on a single line, separated by commas. These comma-separated expressions are actually just tuples—Python allows us to omit the parentheses around tuples if there is no ambiguity. When we print a tuple, the parentheses are always displayed. By using tuples in this way, we are implicitly aggregating items together.

Your Turn: Define a set, e.g., using set(text), and see what happens when you convert it to a list or iterate over its members.

Operating on Sequence Types

We can iterate over the items in a sequence s in a variety of useful ways, as shown in Table 4-1.

Table 4-1. Various ways to iterate over sequences

Python expression	Comment
for item in s	Iterate over the items of s
for item in sorted(s)	Iterate over the items of s in order
for item in set(s)	Iterate over unique elements of s

Python expression	Comment
`for item in reversed(s)`	Iterate over elements of s in reverse
`for item in set(s).difference(t)`	Iterate over elements of s not in t
`for item in random.shuffle(s)`	Iterate over elements of s in random order

The sequence functions illustrated in Table 4-1 can be combined in various ways; for example, to get unique elements of s sorted in reverse, use `reversed(sorted(set(s)))`.

We can convert between these sequence types. For example, `tuple(s)` converts any kind of sequence into a tuple, and `list(s)` converts any kind of sequence into a list. We can convert a list of strings to a single string using the `join()` function, e.g., `':'.join(words)`.

Some other objects, such as a `FreqDist`, can be converted into a sequence (using `list()`) and support iteration:

```
>>> raw = 'Red lorry, yellow lorry, red lorry, yellow lorry.'
>>> text = nltk.word_tokenize(raw)
>>> fdist = nltk.FreqDist(text)
>>> list(fdist)
['lorry', ',', 'yellow', '.', 'Red', 'red']
>>> for key in fdist:
...     print fdist[key],
...
4 3 2 1 1 1
```

In the next example, we use tuples to re-arrange the contents of our list. (We can omit the parentheses because the comma has higher precedence than assignment.)

```
>>> words = ['I', 'turned', 'off', 'the', 'spectroroute']
>>> words[2], words[3], words[4] = words[3], words[4], words[2]
>>> words
['I', 'turned', 'the', 'spectroroute', 'off']
```

This is an idiomatic and readable way to move items inside a list. It is equivalent to the following traditional way of doing such tasks that does not use tuples (notice that this method needs a temporary variable `tmp`).

```
>>> tmp = words[2]
>>> words[2] = words[3]
>>> words[3] = words[4]
>>> words[4] = tmp
```

As we have seen, Python has sequence functions such as `sorted()` and `reversed()` that rearrange the items of a sequence. There are also functions that modify the *structure* of a sequence, which can be handy for language processing. Thus, `zip()` takes the items of two or more sequences and "zips" them together into a single list of pairs. Given a sequence s, `enumerate(s)` returns pairs consisting of an index and the item at that index.

```
>>> words = ['I', 'turned', 'off', 'the', 'spectroroute']
>>> tags = ['noun', 'verb', 'prep', 'det', 'noun']
>>> zip(words, tags)
```

```
[('I', 'noun'), ('turned', 'verb'), ('off', 'prep'),
('the', 'det'), ('spectroroute', 'noun')]
>>> list(enumerate(words))
[(0, 'I'), (1, 'turned'), (2, 'off'), (3, 'the'), (4, 'spectroroute')]
```

For some NLP tasks it is necessary to cut up a sequence into two or more parts. For instance, we might want to "train" a system on 90% of the data and test it on the remaining 10%. To do this we decide the location where we want to cut the data ❶, then cut the sequence at that location ❷.

```
>>> text = nltk.corpus.nps_chat.words()
>>> cut = int(0.9 * len(text))  ❶
>>> training_data, test_data = text[:cut], text[cut:]  ❷
>>> text == training_data + test_data  ❸
True
>>> len(training_data) / len(test_data)  ❹
9
```

We can verify that none of the original data is lost during this process, nor is it duplicated ❸. We can also verify that the ratio of the sizes of the two pieces is what we intended ❹.

Combining Different Sequence Types

Let's combine our knowledge of these three sequence types, together with list comprehensions, to perform the task of sorting the words in a string by their length.

```
>>> words = 'I turned off the spectroroute'.split()  ❶
>>> wordlens = [(len(word), word) for word in words]  ❷
>>> wordlens.sort()  ❸
>>> ' '.join(w for (_, w) in wordlens)  ❹
'I off the turned spectroroute'
```

Each of the preceding lines of code contains a significant feature. A simple string is actually an object with methods defined on it, such as split() ❶. We use a list comprehension to build a list of tuples ❷, where each tuple consists of a number (the word length) and the word, e.g., (3, 'the'). We use the sort() method ❸ to sort the list in place. Finally, we discard the length information and join the words back into a single string ❹. (The underscore ❹ is just a regular Python variable, but we can use underscore by convention to indicate that we will not use its value.)

We began by talking about the commonalities in these sequence types, but the previous code illustrates important differences in their roles. First, strings appear at the beginning and the end: this is typical in the context where our program is reading in some text and producing output for us to read. Lists and tuples are used in the middle, but for different purposes. A list is typically a sequence of objects all having the *same type*, of *arbitrary length*. We often use lists to hold sequences of words. In contrast, a tuple is typically a collection of objects of *different types*, of *fixed length*. We often use a tuple to hold a **record**, a collection of different **fields** relating to some entity. This distinction between the use of lists and tuples takes some getting used to, so here is another example:

```
>>> lexicon = [
...     ('the', 'det', ['Di:', 'D@']),
...     ('off', 'prep', ['Qf', 'O:f'])
... ]
```

Here, a lexicon is represented as a list because it is a collection of objects of a single type—lexical entries—of no predetermined length. An individual entry is represented as a tuple because it is a collection of objects with different interpretations, such as the orthographic form, the part-of-speech, and the pronunciations (represented in the SAMPA computer-readable phonetic alphabet; see *http://www.phon.ucl.ac.uk/home/ sampa/*). Note that these pronunciations are stored using a list. (Why?)

A good way to decide when to use tuples versus lists is to ask whether the interpretation of an item depends on its position. For example, a tagged token combines two strings having different interpretations, and we choose to interpret the first item as the token and the second item as the tag. Thus we use tuples like this: ('grail', 'noun'). A tuple of the form ('noun', 'grail') would be non-sensical since it would be a word noun tagged grail. In contrast, the elements of a text are all tokens, and position is not significant. Thus we use lists like this: ['venetian', 'blind']. A list of the form ['blind', 'venetian'] would be equally valid. The linguistic meaning of the words might be different, but the interpretation of list items as tokens is unchanged.

The distinction between lists and tuples has been described in terms of usage. However, there is a more fundamental difference: in Python, lists are **mutable**, whereas tuples are **immutable**. In other words, lists can be modified, whereas tuples cannot. Here are some of the operations on lists that do in-place modification of the list:

```
>>> lexicon.sort()
>>> lexicon[1] = ('turned', 'VBD', ['t3:nd', 't3`nd'])
>>> del lexicon[0]
```

Your Turn: Convert lexicon to a tuple, using lexicon = tuple(lexicon), then try each of the operations, to confirm that none of them is permitted on tuples.

Generator Expressions

We've been making heavy use of list comprehensions, for compact and readable processing of texts. Here's an example where we tokenize and normalize a text:

```
>>> text = '''"When I use a word," Humpty Dumpty said in rather a scornful tone,
... "it means just what I choose it to mean - neither more nor less."'''
>>> [w.lower() for w in nltk.word_tokenize(text)]
['"', 'when', 'i', 'use', 'a', 'word', ',', '"', 'humpty', 'dumpty', 'said', ...]
```

Suppose we now want to process these words further. We can do this by inserting the preceding expression inside a call to some other function ❶, but Python allows us to omit the brackets ❷.

```
>>> max([w.lower() for w in nltk.word_tokenize(text)]) ❶
'word'
>>> max(w.lower() for w in nltk.word_tokenize(text)) ❷
'word'
```

The second line uses a **generator expression**. This is more than a notational convenience: in many language processing situations, generator expressions will be more efficient. In ❶, storage for the list object must be allocated before the value of `max()` is computed. If the text is very large, this could be slow. In ❷, the data is streamed to the calling function. Since the calling function simply has to find the maximum value—the word that comes latest in lexicographic sort order—it can process the stream of data without having to store anything more than the maximum value seen so far.

4.3 Questions of Style

Programming is as much an art as a science. The undisputed "bible" of programming, a 2,500 page multivolume work by Donald Knuth, is called *The Art of Computer Programming*. Many books have been written on *Literate Programming*, recognizing that humans, not just computers, must read and understand programs. Here we pick up on some issues of programming style that have important ramifications for the readability of your code, including code layout, procedural versus declarative style, and the use of loop variables.

Python Coding Style

When writing programs you make many subtle choices about names, spacing, comments, and so on. When you look at code written by other people, needless differences in style make it harder to interpret the code. Therefore, the designers of the Python language have published a style guide for Python code, available at *http://www.python .org/dev/peps/pep-0008/*. The underlying value presented in the style guide is *consistency*, for the purpose of maximizing the readability of code. We briefly review some of its key recommendations here, and refer readers to the full guide for detailed discussion with examples.

Code layout should use four spaces per indentation level. You should make sure that when you write Python code in a file, you avoid tabs for indentation, since these can be misinterpreted by different text editors and the indentation can be messed up. Lines should be less than 80 characters long; if necessary, you can break a line inside parentheses, brackets, or braces, because Python is able to detect that the line continues over to the next line, as in the following examples:

```
>>> cv_word_pairs = [(cv, w) for w in rotokas_words
...                         for cv in re.findall('[ptksvr][aeiou]', w)]
```

```
>>> cfd = nltk.ConditionalFreqDist(
...           (genre, word)
...           for genre in brown.categories()
...           for word in brown.words(categories=genre))
>>> ha_words = ['aaahhhh', 'ah', 'ahah', 'ahahah', 'ahh', 'ahhahahaha',
...             'ahhh', 'ahhhh', 'ahhhhhh', 'ahhhhhhhhhhhhhh', 'ha',
...             'haaa', 'hah', 'haha', 'hahaaa', 'hahah', 'hahaha']
```

If you need to break a line outside parentheses, brackets, or braces, you can often add extra parentheses, and you can always add a backslash at the end of the line that is broken:

```
>>> if (len(syllables) > 4 and len(syllables[2]) == 3 and
...     syllables[2][2] in [aeiou] and syllables[2][3] == syllables[1][3]):
...       process(syllables)
>>> if len(syllables) > 4 and len(syllables[2]) == 3 and \
...     syllables[2][2] in [aeiou] and syllables[2][3] == syllables[1][3]:
...       process(syllables)
```

 Typing spaces instead of tabs soon becomes a chore. Many programming editors have built-in support for Python, and can automatically indent code and highlight any syntax errors (including indentation errors). For a list of Python-aware editors, please see *http://wiki.python .org/moin/PythonEditors*.

Procedural Versus Declarative Style

We have just seen how the same task can be performed in different ways, with implications for efficiency. Another factor influencing program development is *programming style*. Consider the following program to compute the average length of words in the Brown Corpus:

```
>>> tokens = nltk.corpus.brown.words(categories='news')
>>> count = 0
>>> total = 0
>>> for token in tokens:
...     count += 1
...     total += len(token)
>>> print total / count
4.2765382469
```

In this program we use the variable count to keep track of the number of tokens seen, and total to store the combined length of all words. This is a low-level style, not far removed from machine code, the primitive operations performed by the computer's CPU. The two variables are just like a CPU's registers, accumulating values at many intermediate stages, values that are meaningless until the end. We say that this program is written in a *procedural* style, dictating the machine operations step by step. Now consider the following program that computes the same thing:

```
>>> total = sum(len(t) for t in tokens)
>>> print total / len(tokens)
4.2765382469
```

The first line uses a generator expression to sum the token lengths, while the second line computes the average as before. Each line of code performs a complete, meaningful task, which can be understood in terms of high-level properties like: "total is the sum of the lengths of the tokens." Implementation details are left to the Python interpreter. The second program uses a built-in function, and constitutes programming at a more abstract level; the resulting code is more declarative. Let's look at an extreme example:

```
>>> word_list = []
>>> len_word_list = len(word_list)
>>> i = 0
>>> while i < len(tokens):
...     j = 0
...     while j < len_word_list and word_list[j] < tokens[i]:
...         j += 1
...     if j == 0 or tokens[i] != word_list[j]:
...         word_list.insert(j, tokens[i])
...         len_word_list += 1
...     i += 1
```

The equivalent declarative version uses familiar built-in functions, and its purpose is instantly recognizable:

```
>>> word_list = sorted(set(tokens))
```

Another case where a loop counter seems to be necessary is for printing a counter with each line of output. Instead, we can use enumerate(), which processes a sequence s and produces a tuple of the form (i, s[i]) for each item in s, starting with (0, s[0]). Here we enumerate the keys of the frequency distribution, and capture the integer-string pair in the variables rank and word. We print rank+1 so that the counting appears to start from 1, as required when producing a list of ranked items.

```
>>> fd = nltk.FreqDist(nltk.corpus.brown.words())
>>> cumulative = 0.0
>>> for rank, word in enumerate(fd):
...     cumulative += fd[word] * 100 / fd.N()
...     print "%3d %6.2f%% %s" % (rank+1, cumulative, word)
...     if cumulative > 25:
...         break
...
  1   5.40% the
  2  10.42% ,
  3  14.67% .
  4  17.78% of
  5  20.19% and
  6  22.40% to
  7  24.29% a
  8  25.97% in
```

It's sometimes tempting to use loop variables to store a maximum or minimum value seen so far. Let's use this method to find the longest word in a text.

```
>>> text = nltk.corpus.gutenberg.words('milton-paradise.txt')
>>> longest = ''
>>> for word in text:
...     if len(word) > len(longest):
...         longest = word
>>> longest
'unextinguishable'
```

However, a more transparent solution uses two list comprehensions, both having forms that should be familiar by now:

```
>>> maxlen = max(len(word) for word in text)
>>> [word for word in text if len(word) == maxlen]
['unextinguishable', 'transubstantiate', 'inextinguishable', 'incomprehensible']
```

Note that our first solution found the first word having the longest length, while the second solution found *all* of the longest words (which is usually what we would want). Although there's a theoretical efficiency difference between the two solutions, the main overhead is reading the data into main memory; once it's there, a second pass through the data is effectively instantaneous. We also need to balance our concerns about program efficiency with programmer efficiency. A fast but cryptic solution will be harder to understand and maintain.

Some Legitimate Uses for Counters

There are cases where we still want to use loop variables in a list comprehension. For example, we need to use a loop variable to extract successive overlapping n-grams from a list:

```
>>> sent = ['The', 'dog', 'gave', 'John', 'the', 'newspaper']
>>> n = 3
>>> [sent[i:i+n] for i in range(len(sent)-n+1)]
[['The', 'dog', 'gave'],
 ['dog', 'gave', 'John'],
 ['gave', 'John', 'the'],
 ['John', 'the', 'newspaper']]
```

It is quite tricky to get the range of the loop variable right. Since this is a common operation in NLP, NLTK supports it with functions bigrams(text) and trigrams(text), and a general-purpose ngrams(text, n).

Here's an example of how we can use loop variables in building multidimensional structures. For example, to build an array with *m* rows and *n* columns, where each cell is a set, we could use a nested list comprehension:

```
>>> m, n = 3, 7
>>> array = [[set() for i in range(n)] for j in range(m)]
>>> array[2][5].add('Alice')
>>> pprint.pprint(array)
[[set([]), set([]), set([]), set([]), set([]), set([]), set([])],
 [set([]), set([]), set([]), set([]), set([]), set([]), set([])],
 [set([]), set([]), set([]), set([]), set([]), set(['Alice']), set([])]]
```

Observe that the loop variables i and j are not used anywhere in the resulting object; they are just needed for a syntactically correct for statement. As another example of this usage, observe that the expression ['very' for i in range(3)] produces a list containing three instances of 'very', with no integers in sight.

Note that it would be incorrect to do this work using multiplication, for reasons concerning object copying that were discussed earlier in this section.

```
>>> array = [[set()] * n] * m
>>> array[2][5].add(7)
>>> pprint.pprint(array)
[[set([7]), set([7]), set([7]), set([7]), set([7]), set([7]), set([7])],
 [set([7]), set([7]), set([7]), set([7]), set([7]), set([7]), set([7])],
 [set([7]), set([7]), set([7]), set([7]), set([7]), set([7]), set([7])]]
```

Iteration is an important programming device. It is tempting to adopt idioms from other languages. However, Python offers some elegant and highly readable alternatives, as we have seen.

4.4 Functions: The Foundation of Structured Programming

Functions provide an effective way to package and reuse program code, as already explained in Section 2.3. For example, suppose we find that we often want to read text from an HTML file. This involves several steps: opening the file, reading it in, normalizing whitespace, and stripping HTML markup. We can collect these steps into a function, and give it a name such as get_text(), as shown in Example 4-1.

Example 4-1. Read text from a file.

```
import re
def get_text(file):
    """Read text from a file, normalizing whitespace and stripping HTML markup."""
    text = open(file).read()
    text = re.sub('\s+', ' ', text)
    text = re.sub(r'<.*?>', ' ', text)
    return text
```

Now, any time we want to get cleaned-up text from an HTML file, we can just call get_text() with the name of the file as its only argument. It will return a string, and we can assign this to a variable, e.g., contents = get_text("test.html"). Each time we want to use this series of steps, we only have to call the function.

Using functions has the benefit of saving space in our program. More importantly, our choice of name for the function helps make the program *readable*. In the case of the preceding example, whenever our program needs to read cleaned-up text from a file we don't have to clutter the program with four lines of code; we simply need to call get_text(). This naming helps to provide some "semantic interpretation"—it helps a reader of our program to see what the program "means."

Notice that this example function definition contains a string. The first string inside a function definition is called a **docstring**. Not only does it document the purpose of the function to someone reading the code, it is accessible to a programmer who has loaded the code from a file:

```
>>> help(get_text)
Help on function get_text:

get_text(file)
    Read text from a file, normalizing whitespace
    and stripping HTML markup.
```

We have seen that functions help to make our work reusable and readable. They also help make it *reliable*. When we reuse code that has already been developed and tested, we can be more confident that it handles a variety of cases correctly. We also remove the risk of forgetting some important step or introducing a bug. The program that calls our function also has increased reliability. The author of that program is dealing with a shorter program, and its components behave transparently.

To summarize, as its name suggests, a function captures functionality. It is a segment of code that can be given a meaningful name and which performs a well-defined task. Functions allow us to abstract away from the details, to see a bigger picture, and to program more effectively.

The rest of this section takes a closer look at functions, exploring the mechanics and discussing ways to make your programs easier to read.

Function Inputs and Outputs

We pass information to functions using a function's parameters, the parenthesized list of variables and constants following the function's name in the function definition. Here's a complete example:

```
>>> def repeat(msg, num):      ❶
...     return ' '.join([msg] * num)
>>> monty = 'Monty Python'
>>> repeat(monty, 3) ❷
'Monty Python Monty Python Monty Python'
```

We first define the function to take two parameters, msg and num ❶. Then, we call the function and pass it two arguments, monty and 3 ❷; these arguments fill the "placeholders" provided by the parameters and provide values for the occurrences of msg and num in the function body.

It is not necessary to have any parameters, as we see in the following example:

```
>>> def monty():
...     return "Monty Python"
>>> monty()
'Monty Python'
```

A function usually communicates its results back to the calling program via the return statement, as we have just seen. To the calling program, it looks as if the function call had been replaced with the function's result:

```
>>> repeat(monty(), 3)
'Monty Python Monty Python Monty Python'
>>> repeat('Monty Python', 3)
'Monty Python Monty Python Monty Python'
```

A Python function is not required to have a return statement. Some functions do their work as a side effect, printing a result, modifying a file, or updating the contents of a parameter to the function (such functions are called "procedures" in some other programming languages).

Consider the following three sort functions. The third one is dangerous because a programmer could use it without realizing that it had modified its input. In general, functions should modify the contents of a parameter (my_sort1()), or return a value (my_sort2()), but not both (my_sort3()).

```
>>> def my_sort1(mylist):      # good: modifies its argument, no return value
...     mylist.sort()
>>> def my_sort2(mylist):      # good: doesn't touch its argument, returns value
...     return sorted(mylist)
>>> def my_sort3(mylist):      # bad: modifies its argument and also returns it
...     mylist.sort()
...     return mylist
```

Parameter Passing

Back in Section 4.1, you saw that assignment works on values, but that the value of a structured object is a *reference* to that object. The same is true for functions. Python interprets function parameters as values (this is known as **call-by-value**). In the following code, set_up() has two parameters, both of which are modified inside the function. We begin by assigning an empty string to w and an empty dictionary to p. After calling the function, w is unchanged, while p is changed:

```
>>> def set_up(word, properties):
...     word = 'lolcat'
...     properties.append('noun')
...     properties = 5
...
>>> w = ''
>>> p = []
>>> set_up(w, p)
>>> w
''
>>> p
['noun']
```

Notice that w was not changed by the function. When we called set_up(w, p), the value of w (an empty string) was assigned to a new variable word. Inside the function, the value

---

of word was modified. However, that change did not propagate to w. This parameter passing is identical to the following sequence of assignments:

```
>>> w = ''
>>> word = w
>>> word = 'lolcat'
>>> w
''
```

Let's look at what happened with the list p. When we called set_up(w, p), the value of p (a reference to an empty list) was assigned to a new local variable properties, so both variables now reference the same memory location. The function modifies properties, and this change is also reflected in the value of p, as we saw. The function also assigned a new value to properties (the number 5); this did not modify the contents at that memory location, but created a new local variable. This behavior is just as if we had done the following sequence of assignments:

```
>>> p = []
>>> properties = p
>>> properties.append['noun']
>>> properties = 5
>>> p
['noun']
```

Thus, to understand Python's call-by-value parameter passing, it is enough to understand how assignment works. Remember that you can use the id() function and is operator to check your understanding of object identity after each statement.

Variable Scope

Function definitions create a new local **scope** for variables. When you assign to a new variable inside the body of a function, the name is defined only within that function. The name is not visible outside the function, or in other functions. This behavior means you can choose variable names without being concerned about collisions with names used in your other function definitions.

When you refer to an existing name from within the body of a function, the Python interpreter first tries to resolve the name with respect to the names that are local to the function. If nothing is found, the interpreter checks whether it is a global name within the module. Finally, if that does not succeed, the interpreter checks whether the name is a Python built-in. This is the so-called **LGB rule** of name resolution: local, then global, then built-in.

Caution!

A function can create a new global variable, using the global declaration. However, this practice should be avoided as much as possible. Defining global variables inside a function introduces dependencies on context and limits the portability (or reusability) of the function. In general you should use parameters for function inputs and return values for function outputs.

Checking Parameter Types

Python does not force us to declare the type of a variable when we write a program, and this permits us to define functions that are flexible about the type of their arguments. For example, a tagger might expect a sequence of words, but it wouldn't care whether this sequence is expressed as a list, a tuple, or an iterator (a new sequence type that we'll discuss later).

However, often we want to write programs for later use by others, and want to program in a defensive style, providing useful warnings when functions have not been invoked correctly. The author of the following tag() function assumed that its argument would always be a string.

```
>>> def tag(word):
...     if word in ['a', 'the', 'all']:
...         return 'det'
...     else:
...         return 'noun'
...
>>> tag('the')
'det'
>>> tag('knight')
'noun'
>>> tag(["'Tis", 'but', 'a', 'scratch'])   ❶
'noun'
```

The function returns sensible values for the arguments 'the' and 'knight', but look what happens when it is passed a list ❶—it fails to complain, even though the result which it returns is clearly incorrect. The author of this function could take some extra steps to ensure that the word parameter of the tag() function is a string. A naive approach would be to check the type of the argument using if not type(word) is str, and if word is not a string, to simply return Python's special empty value, None. This is a slight improvement, because the function is checking the type of the argument, and trying to return a "special" diagnostic value for the wrong input. However, it is also dangerous because the calling program may not detect that None is intended as a "special" value, and this diagnostic return value may then be propagated to other parts of the program with unpredictable consequences. This approach also fails if the word is a Unicode string, which has type unicode, not str. Here's a better solution, using an assert statement together with Python's basestring type that generalizes over both unicode and str.

```
>>> def tag(word):
...     assert isinstance(word, basestring), "argument to tag() must be a string"
...     if word in ['a', 'the', 'all']:
...         return 'det'
...     else:
...         return 'noun'
```

If the assert statement fails, it will produce an error that cannot be ignored, since it halts program execution. Additionally, the error message is easy to interpret. Adding assertions to a program helps you find logical errors, and is a kind of **defensive programming**. A more fundamental approach is to document the parameters to each function using docstrings, as described later in this section.

Functional Decomposition

Well-structured programs usually make extensive use of functions. When a block of program code grows longer than 10–20 lines, it is a great help to readability if the code is broken up into one or more functions, each one having a clear purpose. This is analogous to the way a good essay is divided into paragraphs, each expressing one main idea.

Functions provide an important kind of abstraction. They allow us to group multiple actions into a single, complex action, and associate a name with it. (Compare this with the way we combine the actions of *go* and *bring back* into a single more complex action *fetch*.) When we use functions, the main program can be written at a higher level of abstraction, making its structure transparent, as in the following:

```
>>> data = load_corpus()
>>> results = analyze(data)
>>> present(results)
```

Appropriate use of functions makes programs more readable and maintainable. Additionally, it becomes possible to reimplement a function—replacing the function's body with more efficient code—without having to be concerned with the rest of the program.

Consider the `freq_words` function in Example 4-2. It updates the contents of a frequency distribution that is passed in as a parameter, and it also prints a list of the *n* most frequent words.

Example 4-2. Poorly designed function to compute frequent words.

```
def freq_words(url, freqdist, n):
    text = nltk.clean_url(url)
    for word in nltk.word_tokenize(text):
        freqdist.inc(word.lower())
    print freqdist.keys()[:n]
>>> constitution = "http://www.archives.gov/national-archives-experience" \
...                 "/charters/constitution_transcript.html"
>>> fd = nltk.FreqDist()
>>> freq_words(constitution, fd, 20)
['the', 'of', 'charters', 'bill', 'constitution', 'rights', ',',
'declaration', 'impact', 'freedom', '-', 'making', 'independence']
```

This function has a number of problems. The function has two side effects: it modifies the contents of its second parameter, and it prints a selection of the results it has computed. The function would be easier to understand and to reuse elsewhere if we initialize the `FreqDist()` object inside the function (in the same place it is populated), and if we moved the selection and display of results to the calling program. In Example 4-3 we **refactor** this function, and simplify its interface by providing a single `url` parameter.

Example 4-3. Well-designed function to compute frequent words.

```
def freq_words(url):
    freqdist = nltk.FreqDist()
    text = nltk.clean_url(url)
    for word in nltk.word_tokenize(text):
        freqdist.inc(word.lower())
    return freqdist
```

```
>>> fd = freq_words(constitution)
>>> print fd.keys()[:20]
['the', 'of', 'charters', 'bill', 'constitution', 'rights', ',',
'declaration', 'impact', 'freedom', '-', 'making', 'independence']
```

Note that we have now simplified the work of freq_words to the point that we can do its work with three lines of code:

```
>>> words = nltk.word_tokenize(nltk.clean_url(constitution))
>>> fd = nltk.FreqDist(word.lower() for word in words)
>>> fd.keys()[:20]
['the', 'of', 'charters', 'bill', 'constitution', 'rights', ',',
'declaration', 'impact', 'freedom', '-', 'making', 'independence']
```

Documenting Functions

If we have done a good job at decomposing our program into functions, then it should be easy to describe the purpose of each function in plain language, and provide this in the docstring at the top of the function definition. This statement should not explain how the functionality is implemented; in fact, it should be possible to reimplement the function using a different method without changing this statement.

For the simplest functions, a one-line docstring is usually adequate (see Example 4-1). You should provide a triple-quoted string containing a complete sentence on a single line. For non-trivial functions, you should still provide a one-sentence summary on the first line, since many docstring processing tools index this string. This should be followed by a blank line, then a more detailed description of the functionality (see *http:// www.python.org/dev/peps/pep-0257/* for more information on docstring conventions).

Docstrings can include a **doctest block**, illustrating the use of the function and the expected output. These can be tested automatically using Python's docutils module. Docstrings should document the type of each parameter to the function, and the return type. At a minimum, that can be done in plain text. However, note that NLTK uses the "epytext" markup language to document parameters. This format can be automatically converted into richly structured API documentation (see *http://www.nltk.org/*), and includes special handling of certain "fields," such as @param, which allow the inputs and outputs of functions to be clearly documented. Example 4-4 illustrates a complete docstring.

Example 4-4. Illustration of a complete docstring, consisting of a one-line summary, a more detailed explanation, a doctest example, and epytext markup specifying the parameters, types, return type, and exceptions.

```
def accuracy(reference, test):
    """
    Calculate the fraction of test items that equal the corresponding reference items.

    Given a list of reference values and a corresponding list of test values,
    return the fraction of corresponding values that are equal.
    In particular, return the fraction of indexes
    {0<i<=len(test)} such that C{test[i] == reference[i]}.

    >>> accuracy(['ADJ', 'N', 'V', 'N'], ['N', 'N', 'V', 'ADJ'])
    0.5

    @param reference: An ordered list of reference values.
    @type reference: C{list}
    @param test: A list of values to compare against the corresponding
        reference values.
    @type test: C{list}
    @rtype: C{float}
    @raise ValueError: If C{reference} and C{length} do not have the
        same length.
    """

    if len(reference) != len(test):
        raise ValueError("Lists must have the same length.")
    num_correct = 0
    for x, y in izip(reference, test):
        if x == y:
            num_correct += 1
    return float(num_correct) / len(reference)
```

4.5 Doing More with Functions

This section discusses more advanced features, which you may prefer to skip on the first time through this chapter.

Functions As Arguments

So far the arguments we have passed into functions have been simple objects, such as strings, or structured objects, such as lists. Python also lets us pass a function as an argument to another function. Now we can abstract out the operation, and apply a *different operation* on the *same data*. As the following examples show, we can pass the built-in function len() or a user-defined function last_letter() as arguments to another function:

```
>>> sent = ['Take', 'care', 'of', 'the', 'sense', ',', 'and', 'the',
...         'sounds', 'will', 'take', 'care', 'of', 'themselves', '.']
>>> def extract_property(prop):
...     return [prop(word) for word in sent]
...
```

```
>>> extract_property(len)
[4, 4, 2, 3, 5, 1, 3, 3, 6, 4, 4, 4, 2, 10, 1]
>>> def last_letter(word):
...     return word[-1]
>>> extract_property(last_letter)
['e', 'e', 'f', 'e', 'e', ',', 'd', 'e', 's', 'l', 'e', 'e', 'f', 's', '.']
```

The objects len and last_letter can be passed around like lists and dictionaries. Notice that parentheses are used after a function name only if we are invoking the function; when we are simply treating the function as an object, these are omitted.

Python provides us with one more way to define functions as arguments to other functions, so-called **lambda expressions**. Supposing there was no need to use the last_letter() function in multiple places, and thus no need to give it a name. Let's suppose we can equivalently write the following:

```
>>> extract_property(lambda w: w[-1])
['e', 'e', 'f', 'e', 'e', ',', 'd', 'e', 's', 'l', 'e', 'e', 'f', 's', '.']
```

Our next example illustrates passing a function to the sorted() function. When we call the latter with a single argument (the list to be sorted), it uses the built-in comparison function cmp(). However, we can supply our own sort function, e.g., to sort by decreasing length.

```
>>> sorted(sent)
[',', '.', 'Take', 'and', 'care', 'care', 'of', 'of', 'sense', 'sounds',
'take', 'the', 'the', 'themselves', 'will']
>>> sorted(sent, cmp)
[',', '.', 'Take', 'and', 'care', 'care', 'of', 'of', 'sense', 'sounds',
'take', 'the', 'the', 'themselves', 'will']
>>> sorted(sent, lambda x, y: cmp(len(y), len(x)))
['themselves', 'sounds', 'sense', 'Take', 'care', 'will', 'take', 'care',
'the', 'and', 'the', 'of', 'of', ',', '.']
```

Accumulative Functions

These functions start by initializing some storage, and iterate over input to build it up, before returning some final object (a large structure or aggregated result). A standard way to do this is to initialize an empty list, accumulate the material, then return the list, as shown in function **search1()** in Example 4-5.

Example 4-5. Accumulating output into a list.

```
def search1(substring, words):
    result = []
    for word in words:
        if substring in word:
            result.append(word)
    return result

def search2(substring, words):
    for word in words:
        if substring in word:
            yield word
```

```
print "search1:"
for item in search1('zz', nltk.corpus.brown.words()):
    print item
print "search2:"
for item in search2('zz', nltk.corpus.brown.words()):
    print item
```

The function `search2()` is a generator. The first time this function is called, it gets as far as the `yield` statement and pauses. The calling program gets the first word and does any necessary processing. Once the calling program is ready for another word, execution of the function is continued from where it stopped, until the next time it encounters a `yield` statement. This approach is typically more efficient, as the function only generates the data as it is required by the calling program, and does not need to allocate additional memory to store the output (see the earlier discussion of generator expressions).

Here's a more sophisticated example of a generator which produces all permutations of a list of words. In order to force the `permutations()` function to generate all its output, we wrap it with a call to `list()` ❶.

```
>>> def permutations(seq):
...     if len(seq) <= 1:
...         yield seq
...     else:
...         for perm in permutations(seq[1:]):
...             for i in range(len(perm)+1):
...                 yield perm[:i] + seq[0:1] + perm[i:]
...
>>> list(permutations(['police', 'fish', 'buffalo']))     ❶
[['police', 'fish', 'buffalo'], ['fish', 'police', 'buffalo'],
 ['fish', 'buffalo', 'police'], ['police', 'buffalo', 'fish'],
 ['buffalo', 'police', 'fish'], ['buffalo', 'fish', 'police']]
```

The `permutations` function uses a technique called recursion, discussed later in Section 4.7. The ability to generate permutations of a set of words is useful for creating data to test a grammar (Chapter 8).

Higher-Order Functions

Python provides some higher-order functions that are standard features of functional programming languages such as Haskell. We illustrate them here, alongside the equivalent expression using list comprehensions.

Let's start by defining a function `is_content_word()` which checks whether a word is from the open class of content words. We use this function as the first parameter of `filter()`, which applies the function to each item in the sequence contained in its second parameter, and retains only the items for which the function returns `True`.

```
>>> def is_content_word(word):
...     return word.lower() not in ['a', 'of', 'the', 'and', 'will', ',', '.']
>>> sent = ['Take', 'care', 'of', 'the', 'sense', ',', 'and', 'the',
...         'sounds', 'will', 'take', 'care', 'of', 'themselves', '.']
>>> filter(is_content_word, sent)
['Take', 'care', 'sense', 'sounds', 'take', 'care', 'themselves']
>>> [w for w in sent if is_content_word(w)]
['Take', 'care', 'sense', 'sounds', 'take', 'care', 'themselves']
```

Another higher-order function is `map()`, which applies a function to every item in a sequence. It is a general version of the `extract_property()` function we saw earlier in this section. Here is a simple way to find the average length of a sentence in the news section of the Brown Corpus, followed by an equivalent version with list comprehension calculation:

```
>>> lengths = map(len, nltk.corpus.brown.sents(categories='news'))
>>> sum(lengths) / len(lengths)
21.7508111616
>>> lengths = [len(w) for w in nltk.corpus.brown.sents(categories='news'))]
>>> sum(lengths) / len(lengths)
21.7508111616
```

In the previous examples, we specified a user-defined function `is_content_word()` and a built-in function `len()`. We can also provide a lambda expression. Here's a pair of equivalent examples that count the number of vowels in each word.

```
>>> map(lambda w: len(filter(lambda c: c.lower() in "aeiou", w)), sent)
[2, 2, 1, 1, 2, 0, 1, 1, 2, 1, 2, 2, 1, 3, 0]
>>> [len([c for c in w if c.lower() in "aeiou"]) for w in sent]
[2, 2, 1, 1, 2, 0, 1, 1, 2, 1, 2, 2, 1, 3, 0]
```

The solutions based on list comprehensions are usually more readable than the solutions based on higher-order functions, and we have favored the former approach throughout this book.

Named Arguments

When there are a lot of parameters it is easy to get confused about the correct order. Instead we can refer to parameters by name, and even assign them a default value just in case one was not provided by the calling program. Now the parameters can be specified in any order, and can be omitted.

```
>>> def repeat(msg='<empty>', num=1):
...     return msg * num
>>> repeat(num=3)
'<empty><empty><empty>'
>>> repeat(msg='Alice')
'Alice'
>>> repeat(num=5, msg='Alice')
'AliceAliceAliceAliceAlice'
```

These are called **keyword arguments**. If we mix these two kinds of parameters, then we must ensure that the unnamed parameters precede the named ones. It has to be this way, since unnamed parameters are defined by position. We can define a function that takes an arbitrary number of unnamed and named parameters, and access them via an in-place list of arguments `*args` and an in-place dictionary of keyword arguments `**kwargs`.

```
>>> def generic(*args, **kwargs):
...     print args
...     print kwargs
...
>>> generic(1, "African swallow", monty="python")
(1, 'African swallow')
{'monty': 'python'}
```

When `*args` appears as a function parameter, it actually corresponds to all the unnamed parameters of the function. As another illustration of this aspect of Python syntax, consider the `zip()` function, which operates on a variable number of arguments. We'll use the variable name `*song` to demonstrate that there's nothing special about the name `*args`.

```
>>> song = [['four', 'calling', 'birds'],
...         ['three', 'French', 'hens'],
...         ['two', 'turtle', 'doves']]
>>> zip(song[0], song[1], song[2])
[('four', 'three', 'two'), ('calling', 'French', 'turtle'), ('birds', 'hens', 'doves')]
>>> zip(*song)
[('four', 'three', 'two'), ('calling', 'French', 'turtle'), ('birds', 'hens', 'doves')]
```

It should be clear from this example that typing `*song` is just a convenient shorthand, and equivalent to typing out `song[0]`, `song[1]`, `song[2]`.

Here's another example of the use of keyword arguments in a function definition, along with three equivalent ways to call the function:

```
>>> def freq_words(file, min=1, num=10):
...     text = open(file).read()
...     tokens = nltk.word_tokenize(text)
...     freqdist = nltk.FreqDist(t for t in tokens if len(t) >= min)
...     return freqdist.keys()[:num]
>>> fw = freq_words('ch01.rst', 4, 10)
>>> fw = freq_words('ch01.rst', min=4, num=10)
>>> fw = freq_words('ch01.rst', num=10, min=4)
```

A side effect of having named arguments is that they permit optionality. Thus we can leave out any arguments where we are happy with the default value: `freq_words('ch01.rst', min=4)`, `freq_words('ch01.rst', 4)`. Another common use of optional arguments is to permit a flag. Here's a revised version of the same function that reports its progress if a `verbose` flag is set:

```
>>> def freq_words(file, min=1, num=10, verbose=False):
...     freqdist = FreqDist()
...     if trace: print "Opening", file
...     text = open(file).read()
...     if trace: print "Read in %d characters" % len(file)
...     for word in nltk.word_tokenize(text):
```

```
...          if len(word) >= min:
...              freqdist.inc(word)
...                  if trace and freqdist.N() % 100 == 0: print "."
...      if trace: print
...      return freqdist.keys()[:num]
```

Caution!

Take care not to use a mutable object as the default value of a parameter.
A series of calls to the function will use the same object, sometimes with
bizarre results, as we will see in the discussion of debugging later.

4.6 Program Development

Programming is a skill that is acquired over several years of experience with a variety
of programming languages and tasks. Key high-level abilities are *algorithm design* and
its manifestation in *structured programming*. Key low-level abilities include familiarity
with the syntactic constructs of the language, and knowledge of a variety of diagnostic
methods for trouble-shooting a program which does not exhibit the expected behavior.

This section describes the internal structure of a program module and how to organize
a multi-module program. Then it describes various kinds of error that arise during
program development, what you can do to fix them and, better still, to avoid them in
the first place.

Structure of a Python Module

The purpose of a program module is to bring logically related definitions and functions
together in order to facilitate reuse and abstraction. Python modules are nothing more
than individual *.py* files. For example, if you were working with a particular corpus
format, the functions to read and write the format could be kept together. Constants
used by both formats, such as field separators, or a EXTN = ".inf" filename extension,
could be shared. If the format was updated, you would know that only one file needed
to be changed. Similarly, a module could contain code for creating and manipulating
a particular data structure such as syntax trees, or code for performing a particular
processing task such as plotting corpus statistics.

When you start writing Python modules, it helps to have some examples to emulate.
You can locate the code for any NLTK module on your system using the __file__
variable:

```
>>> nltk.metrics.distance.__file__
'/usr/lib/python2.5/site-packages/nltk/metrics/distance.pyc'
```

This returns the location of the compiled *.pyc* file for the module, and you'll probably
see a different location on your machine. The file that you will need to open is the
corresponding *.py* source file, and this will be in the same directory as the *.pyc* file.

Alternatively, you can view the latest version of this module on the Web at *http://code .google.com/p/nltk/source/browse/trunk/nltk/nltk/metrics/distance.py*.

Like every other NLTK module, *distance.py* begins with a group of comment lines giving a one-line title of the module and identifying the authors. (Since the code is distributed, it also includes the URL where the code is available, a copyright statement, and license information.) Next is the module-level docstring, a triple-quoted multiline string containing information about the module that will be printed when someone types `help(nltk.metrics.distance)`.

```
# Natural Language Toolkit: Distance Metrics
#
# Copyright (C) 2001-2009 NLTK Project
# Author: Edward Loper <edloper@gradient.cis.upenn.edu>
#         Steven Bird <sb@csse.unimelb.edu.au>
#         Tom Lippincott <tom@cs.columbia.edu>
# URL: <http://www.nltk.org/>
# For license information, see LICENSE.TXT
#

"""
Distance Metrics.

Compute the distance between two items (usually strings).
As metrics, they must satisfy the following three requirements:

1. d(a, a) = 0
2. d(a, b) >= 0
3. d(a, c) <= d(a, b) + d(b, c)
"""
```

After this comes all the import statements required for the module, then any global variables, followed by a series of function definitions that make up most of the module. Other modules define "classes," the main building blocks of object-oriented programming, which falls outside the scope of this book. (Most NLTK modules also include a `demo()` function, which can be used to see examples of the module in use.)

 Some module variables and functions are only used within the module. These should have names beginning with an underscore, e.g., `_helper()`, since this will hide the name. If another module imports this one, using the idiom: `from module import *`, these names will not be imported. You can optionally list the externally accessible names of a module using a special built-in variable like this: `__all__ = ['edit_dis tance', 'jaccard_distance']`.

Multimodule Programs

Some programs bring together a diverse range of tasks, such as loading data from a corpus, performing some analysis tasks on the data, then visualizing it. We may already have stable modules that take care of loading data and producing visualizations. Our work might involve coding up the analysis task, and just invoking functions from the existing modules. This scenario is depicted in Figure 4-2.

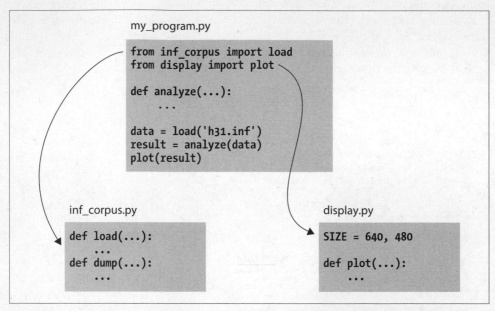

Figure 4-2. Structure of a multimodule program: The main program my_program.py *imports functions from two other modules; unique analysis tasks are localized to the main program, while common loading and visualization tasks are kept apart to facilitate reuse and abstraction.*

By dividing our work into several modules and using `import` statements to access functions defined elsewhere, we can keep the individual modules simple and easy to maintain. This approach will also result in a growing collection of modules, and make it possible for us to build sophisticated systems involving a hierarchy of modules. Designing such systems well is a complex software engineering task, and beyond the scope of this book.

Sources of Error

Mastery of programming depends on having a variety of problem-solving skills to draw upon when the program doesn't work as expected. Something as trivial as a misplaced symbol might cause the program to behave very differently. We call these "bugs" because they are tiny in comparison to the damage they can cause. They creep into our code unnoticed, and it's only much later when we're running the program on some new data that their presence is detected. Sometimes, fixing one bug only reveals another, and we get the distinct impression that the bug is on the move. The only reassurance we have is that bugs are spontaneous and not the fault of the programmer.

Flippancy aside, debugging code is hard because there are so many ways for it to be faulty. Our understanding of the input data, the algorithm, or even the programming language, may be at fault. Let's look at examples of each of these.

First, the input data may contain some unexpected characters. For example, WordNet synset names have the form `tree.n.01`, with three components separated using periods. The NLTK WordNet module initially decomposed these names using `split('.')`. However, this method broke when someone tried to look up the word *PhD*, which has the synset name `ph.d..n.01`, containing four periods instead of the expected two. The solution was to use `rsplit('.', 2)` to do at most two splits, using the rightmost instances of the period, and leaving the `ph.d.` string intact. Although several people had tested the module before it was released, it was some weeks before someone detected the problem (see *http://code.google.com/p/nltk/issues/detail?id=297*).

Second, a supplied function might not behave as expected. For example, while testing NLTK's interface to WordNet, one of the authors noticed that no synsets had any antonyms defined, even though the underlying database provided a large quantity of antonym information. What looked like a bug in the WordNet interface turned out to be a misunderstanding about WordNet itself: antonyms are defined for lemmas, not for synsets. The only "bug" was a misunderstanding of the interface (see *http://code .google.com/p/nltk/issues/detail?id=98*).

Third, our understanding of Python's semantics may be at fault. It is easy to make the wrong assumption about the relative scope of two operators. For example, `"%s.%s. %02d" % "ph.d.", "n", 1` produces a runtime error `TypeError: not enough arguments for format string`. This is because the percent operator has higher precedence than the comma operator. The fix is to add parentheses in order to force the required scope. As another example, suppose we are defining a function to collect all tokens of a text having a given length. The function has parameters for the text and the word length, and an extra parameter that allows the initial value of the result to be given as a parameter:

```
>>> def find_words(text, wordlength, result=[]):
...     for word in text:
...         if len(word) == wordlength:
...             result.append(word)
...     return result
>>> find_words(['omg', 'teh', 'lolcat', 'sitted', 'on', 'teh', 'mat'], 3) ❶
['omg', 'teh', 'teh', 'mat']
>>> find_words(['omg', 'teh', 'lolcat', 'sitted', 'on', 'teh', 'mat'], 2, ['ur']) ❷
['ur', 'on']
>>> find_words(['omg', 'teh', 'lolcat', 'sitted', 'on', 'teh', 'mat'], 3) ❸
['omg', 'teh', 'teh', 'mat', 'omg', 'teh', 'teh', 'mat']
```

The first time we call `find_words()` ❶, we get all three-letter words as expected. The second time we specify an initial value for the result, a one-element list `['ur']`, and as expected, the result has this word along with the other two-letter word in our text. Now, the next time we call `find_words()` ❸ we use the same parameters as in ❶, but we get a different result! Each time we call `find_words()` with no third parameter, the result will simply extend the result of the previous call, rather than start with the empty result list as specified in the function definition. The program's behavior is not as expected because we incorrectly assumed that the default value was created at the time the function was invoked. However, it is created just once, at the time the Python interpreter loads the function. This one list object is used whenever no explicit value is provided to the function.

Debugging Techniques

Since most code errors result from the programmer making incorrect assumptions, the first thing to do when you detect a bug is to *check your assumptions*. Localize the problem by adding print statements to the program, showing the value of important variables, and showing how far the program has progressed.

If the program produced an "exception"—a runtime error—the interpreter will print a **stack trace**, pinpointing the location of program execution at the time of the error. If the program depends on input data, try to reduce this to the smallest size while still producing the error.

Once you have localized the problem to a particular function or to a line of code, you need to work out what is going wrong. It is often helpful to recreate the situation using the interactive command line. Define some variables, and then copy-paste the offending line of code into the session and see what happens. Check your understanding of the code by reading some documentation and examining other code samples that purport to do the same thing that you are trying to do. Try explaining your code to someone else, in case she can see where things are going wrong.

Python provides a **debugger** which allows you to monitor the execution of your program, specify line numbers where execution will stop (i.e., **breakpoints**), and step through sections of code and inspect the value of variables. You can invoke the debugger on your code as follows:

```
>>> import pdb
>>> import mymodule
>>> pdb.run('mymodule.myfunction()')
```

It will present you with a prompt (Pdb) where you can type instructions to the debugger. Type help to see the full list of commands. Typing step (or just s) will execute the current line and stop. If the current line calls a function, it will enter the function and stop at the first line. Typing next (or just n) is similar, but it stops execution at the next line in the current function. The break (or b) command can be used to create or list breakpoints. Type continue (or c) to continue execution as far as the next breakpoint. Type the name of any variable to inspect its value.

We can use the Python debugger to locate the problem in our find_words() function. Remember that the problem arose the second time the function was called. We'll start by calling the function without using the debugger ❶, using the smallest possible input. The second time, we'll call it with the debugger ❷.

```
>>> import pdb
>>> find_words(['cat'], 3)  ❶
['cat']
>>> pdb.run("find_words(['dog'], 3)")  ❷
> <string>(1)<module>()
(Pdb) step
--Call--
> <stdin>(1)find_words()
(Pdb) args
text = ['dog']
wordlength = 3
result = ['cat']
```

Here we typed just two commands into the debugger: `step` took us inside the function, and `args` showed the values of its arguments (or parameters). We see immediately that `result` has an initial value of `['cat']`, and not the empty list as expected. The debugger has helped us to localize the problem, prompting us to check our understanding of Python functions.

Defensive Programming

In order to avoid some of the pain of debugging, it helps to adopt some defensive programming habits. Instead of writing a 20-line program and then testing it, build the program bottom-up out of small pieces that are known to work. Each time you combine these pieces to make a larger unit, test it carefully to see that it works as expected. Consider adding `assert` statements to your code, specifying properties of a variable, e.g., `assert(isinstance(text, list))`. If the value of the `text` variable later becomes a string when your code is used in some larger context, this will raise an `AssertionError` and you will get immediate notification of the problem.

Once you think you've found the bug, view your solution as a hypothesis. Try to predict the effect of your bugfix before re-running the program. If the bug isn't fixed, don't fall into the trap of blindly changing the code in the hope that it will magically start working again. Instead, for each change, try to articulate a hypothesis about what is wrong and why the change will fix the problem. Then undo the change if the problem was not resolved.

As you develop your program, extend its functionality, and fix any bugs, it helps to maintain a suite of test cases. This is called **regression testing**, since it is meant to detect situations where the code "regresses"—where a change to the code has an unintended side effect of breaking something that used to work. Python provides a simple regression-testing framework in the form of the `doctest` module. This module searches a file of code or documentation for blocks of text that look like an interactive Python session, of the form you have already seen many times in this book. It executes the Python commands it finds, and tests that their output matches the output supplied in the original file. Whenever there is a mismatch, it reports the expected and actual values. For details, please consult the `doctest` documentation at *http://docs.python.org/library/doctest.html*. Apart from its value for regression testing, the `doctest` module is useful for ensuring that your software documentation stays in sync with your code.

Perhaps the most important defensive programming strategy is to set out your code clearly, choose meaningful variable and function names, and simplify the code wherever possible by decomposing it into functions and modules with well-documented interfaces.

4.7 Algorithm Design

This section discusses more advanced concepts, which you may prefer to skip on the first time through this chapter.

A major part of algorithmic problem solving is selecting or adapting an appropriate algorithm for the problem at hand. Sometimes there are several alternatives, and choosing the best one depends on knowledge about how each alternative performs as the size of the data grows. Whole books are written on this topic, and we only have space to introduce some key concepts and elaborate on the approaches that are most prevalent in natural language processing.

The best-known strategy is known as **divide-and-conquer**. We attack a problem of size *n* by dividing it into two problems of size *n/2*, solve these problems, and combine their results into a solution of the original problem. For example, suppose that we had a pile of cards with a single word written on each card. We could sort this pile by splitting it in half and giving it to two other people to sort (they could do the same in turn). Then, when two sorted piles come back, it is an easy task to merge them into a single sorted pile. See Figure 4-3 for an illustration of this process.

Another example is the process of looking up a word in a dictionary. We open the book somewhere around the middle and compare our word with the current page. If it's earlier in the dictionary, we repeat the process on the first half; if it's later, we use the second half. This search method is called *binary search* since it splits the problem in half at every step.

In another approach to algorithm design, we attack a problem by transforming it into an instance of a problem we already know how to solve. For example, in order to detect duplicate entries in a list, we can **pre-sort** the list, then scan through it once to check whether any adjacent pairs of elements are identical.

Recursion

The earlier examples of sorting and searching have a striking property: to solve a problem of size *n*, we have to break it in half and then work on one or more problems of size *n/2*. A common way to implement such methods uses **recursion**. We define a function *f*, which simplifies the problem, and *calls itself* to solve one or more easier

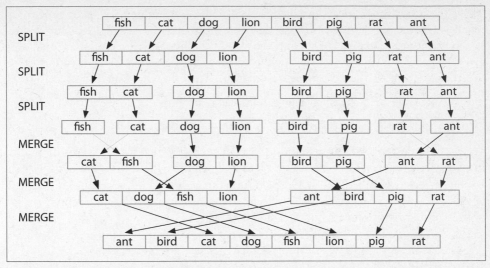

Figure 4-3. Sorting by divide-and-conquer: To sort an array, we split it in half and sort each half (recursively); we merge each sorted half back into a whole list (again recursively); this algorithm is known as "Merge Sort."

instances of the same problem. It then combines the results into a solution for the original problem.

For example, suppose we have a set of *n* words, and want to calculate how many different ways they can be combined to make a sequence of words. If we have only one word (*n*=1), there is just one way to make it into a sequence. If we have a set of two words, there are two ways to put them into a sequence. For three words there are six possibilities. In general, for *n* words, there are $n \times n\text{-}1 \times ... \times 2 \times 1$ ways (i.e., the factorial of *n*). We can code this up as follows:

```
>>> def factorial1(n):
...     result = 1
...     for i in range(n):
...         result *= (i+1)
...     return result
```

However, there is also a recursive algorithm for solving this problem, based on the following observation. Suppose we have a way to construct all orderings for *n*-1 distinct words. Then for each such ordering, there are *n* places where we can insert a new word: at the start, the end, or any of the *n*-2 boundaries between the words. Thus we simply multiply the number of solutions found for *n*-1 by the value of *n*. We also need the **base case**, to say that if we have a single word, there's just one ordering. We can code this up as follows:

```
>>> def factorial2(n):
...     if n == 1:
...         return 1
...     else:
...         return n * factorial2(n-1)
```

These two algorithms solve the same problem. One uses iteration while the other uses recursion. We can use recursion to navigate a deeply nested object, such as the Word-Net hypernym hierarchy. Let's count the size of the hypernym hierarchy rooted at a given synset *s*. We'll do this by finding the size of each hyponym of *s*, then adding these together (we will also add 1 for the synset itself). The following function `size1()` does this work; notice that the body of the function includes a recursive call to `size1()`:

```
>>> def size1(s):
...     return 1 + sum(size1(child) for child in s.hyponyms())
```

We can also design an iterative solution to this problem which processes the hierarchy in layers. The first layer is the synset itself ❶, then all the hyponyms of the synset, then all the hyponyms of the hyponyms. Each time through the loop it computes the next layer by finding the hyponyms of everything in the last layer ❸. It also maintains a total of the number of synsets encountered so far ❷.

```
>>> def size2(s):
...     layer = [s]           ❶
...     total = 0
...     while layer:
...         total += len(layer)   ❷
...         layer = [h for c in layer for h in c.hyponyms()]  ❸
...     return total
```

Not only is the iterative solution much longer, it is harder to interpret. It forces us to think procedurally, and keep track of what is happening with the `layer` and `total` variables through time. Let's satisfy ourselves that both solutions give the same result. We'll use a new form of the import statement, allowing us to abbreviate the name `wordnet` to `wn`:

```
>>> from nltk.corpus import wordnet as wn
>>> dog = wn.synset('dog.n.01')
>>> size1(dog)
190
>>> size2(dog)
190
```

As a final example of recursion, let's use it to *construct* a deeply nested object. A **letter trie** is a data structure that can be used for indexing a lexicon, one letter at a time. (The name is based on the word re*trie*val.) For example, if `trie` contained a letter trie, then `trie['c']` would be a smaller trie which held all words starting with *c*. Example 4-6 demonstrates the recursive process of building a trie, using Python dictionaries (Section 5.3). To insert the word *chien* (French for *dog*), we split off the *c* and recursively insert *hien* into the sub-trie `trie['c']`. The recursion continues until there are no letters remaining in the word, when we store the intended value (in this case, the word *dog*).

Example 4-6. Building a letter trie: A recursive function that builds a nested dictionary structure; each level of nesting contains all words with a given prefix, and a sub-trie containing all possible continuations.

```
def insert(trie, key, value):
    if key:
        first, rest = key[0], key[1:]
        if first not in trie:
            trie[first] = {}
        insert(trie[first], rest, value)
    else:
        trie['value'] = value

>>> trie = nltk.defaultdict(dict)
>>> insert(trie, 'chat', 'cat')
>>> insert(trie, 'chien', 'dog')
>>> insert(trie, 'chair', 'flesh')
>>> insert(trie, 'chic', 'stylish')
>>> trie = dict(trie)                  # for nicer printing
>>> trie['c']['h']['a']['t']['value']
'cat'
>>> pprint.pprint(trie)
{'c': {'h': {'a': {'t': {'value': 'cat'}},
             {'i': {'r': {'value': 'flesh'}}},
       'i': {'e': {'n': {'value': 'dog'}}}
             {'c': {'value': 'stylish'}}}}}
```

Caution!

Despite the simplicity of recursive programming, it comes with a cost. Each time a function is called, some state information needs to be pushed on a stack, so that once the function has completed, execution can continue from where it left off. For this reason, iterative solutions are often more efficient than recursive solutions.

Space-Time Trade-offs

We can sometimes significantly speed up the execution of a program by building an auxiliary data structure, such as an index. The listing in Example 4-7 implements a simple text retrieval system for the Movie Reviews Corpus. By indexing the document collection, it provides much faster lookup.

Example 4-7. A simple text retrieval system.

```
def raw(file):
    contents = open(file).read()
    contents = re.sub(r'<.*?>', ' ', contents)
    contents = re.sub('\s+', ' ', contents)
    return contents

def snippet(doc, term): # buggy
    text = ' '*30 + raw(doc) + ' '*30
    pos = text.index(term)
    return text[pos-30:pos+30]
```

```
print "Building Index..."
files = nltk.corpus.movie_reviews.abspaths()
idx = nltk.Index((w, f) for f in files for w in raw(f).split())

query = ''
while query != "quit":
    query = raw_input("query> ")
    if query in idx:
        for doc in idx[query]:
            print snippet(doc, query)
    else:
        print "Not found"
```

A more subtle example of a space-time trade-off involves replacing the tokens of a corpus with integer identifiers. We create a vocabulary for the corpus, a list in which each word is stored once, then invert this list so that we can look up any word to find its identifier. Each document is preprocessed, so that a list of words becomes a list of integers. Any language models can now work with integers. See the listing in Example 4-8 for an example of how to do this for a tagged corpus.

Example 4-8. Preprocess tagged corpus data, converting all words and tags to integers.

```
def preprocess(tagged_corpus):
    words = set()
    tags = set()
    for sent in tagged_corpus:
        for word, tag in sent:
            words.add(word)
            tags.add(tag)
    wm = dict((w,i) for (i,w) in enumerate(words))
    tm = dict((t,i) for (i,t) in enumerate(tags))
    return [[(wm[w], tm[t]) for (w,t) in sent] for sent in tagged_corpus]
```

Another example of a space-time trade-off is maintaining a vocabulary list. If you need to process an input text to check that all words are in an existing vocabulary, the vocabulary should be stored as a set, not a list. The elements of a set are automatically indexed, so testing membership of a large set will be much faster than testing membership of the corresponding list.

We can test this claim using the `timeit` module. The `Timer` class has two parameters: a statement that is executed multiple times, and setup code that is executed once at the beginning. We will simulate a vocabulary of 100,000 items using a list ❶ or set ❷ of integers. The test statement will generate a random item that has a 50% chance of being in the vocabulary ❸.

```
>>> from timeit import Timer
>>> vocab_size = 100000
>>> setup_list = "import random; vocab = range(%d)" % vocab_size  ❶
>>> setup_set = "import random; vocab = set(range(%d))" % vocab_size  ❷
>>> statement = "random.randint(0, %d) in vocab" % vocab_size * 2  ❸
>>> print Timer(statement, setup_list).timeit(1000)
2.78092288971
>>> print Timer(statement, setup_set).timeit(1000)
0.0037260055542
```

Performing 1,000 list membership tests takes a total of 2.8 seconds, whereas the equivalent tests on a set take a mere 0.0037 seconds, or three orders of magnitude faster!

Dynamic Programming

Dynamic programming is a general technique for designing algorithms which is widely used in natural language processing. The term "programming" is used in a different sense to what you might expect, to mean planning or scheduling. Dynamic programming is used when a problem contains overlapping subproblems. Instead of computing solutions to these subproblems repeatedly, we simply store them in a lookup table. In the remainder of this section, we will introduce dynamic programming, but in a rather different context to syntactic parsing.

Pingala was an Indian author who lived around the 5th century B.C., and wrote a treatise on Sanskrit prosody called the *Chandas Shastra*. Virahanka extended this work around the 6th century A.D., studying the number of ways of combining short and long syllables to create a meter of length n. Short syllables, marked S, take up one unit of length, while long syllables, marked L, take two. Pingala found, for example, that there are five ways to construct a meter of length 4: $V_4 = \{LL, SSL, SLS, LSS, SSSS\}$. Observe that we can split V_4 into two subsets, those starting with L and those starting with S, as shown in (1).

(1) $V_4 =$
    LL, LSS
        i.e. L prefixed to each item of $V_2 = \{L, SS\}$
    SSL, SLS, SSSS
        i.e. S prefixed to each item of $V_3 = \{SL, LS, SSS\}$

With this observation, we can write a little recursive function called virahanka1() to compute these meters, shown in Example 4-9. Notice that, in order to compute V_4 we first compute V_3 and V_2. But to compute V_3, we need to first compute V_2 and V_1. This **call structure** is depicted in (2).

Example 4-9. Four ways to compute Sanskrit meter: (i) iterative, (ii) bottom-up dynamic programming, (iii) top-down dynamic programming, and (iv) built-in memoization.

```
def virahanka1(n):
    if n == 0:
        return [""]
    elif n == 1:
        return ["S"]
    else:
        s = ["S" + prosody for prosody in virahanka1(n-1)]
        l = ["L" + prosody for prosody in virahanka1(n-2)]
        return s + l

def virahanka2(n):
    lookup = [[""], ["S"]]
    for i in range(n-1):
        s = ["S" + prosody for prosody in lookup[i+1]]
        l = ["L" + prosody for prosody in lookup[i]]
        lookup.append(s + l)
    return lookup[n]

def virahanka3(n, lookup={0:[""], 1:["S"]}):
    if n not in lookup:
        s = ["S" + prosody for prosody in virahanka3(n-1)]
        l = ["L" + prosody for prosody in virahanka3(n-2)]
        lookup[n] = s + l
    return lookup[n]

from nltk import memoize
@memoize
def virahanka4(n):
    if n == 0:
        return [""]
    elif n == 1:
        return ["S"]
    else:
        s = ["S" + prosody for prosody in virahanka4(n-1)]
        l = ["L" + prosody for prosody in virahanka4(n-2)]
        return s + l

>>> virahanka1(4)
['SSSS', 'SSL', 'SLS', 'LSS', 'LL']
>>> virahanka2(4)
['SSSS', 'SSL', 'SLS', 'LSS', 'LL']
>>> virahanka3(4)
['SSSS', 'SSL', 'SLS', 'LSS', 'LL']
>>> virahanka4(4)
['SSSS', 'SSL', 'SLS', 'LSS', 'LL']
```

(2)

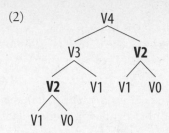

As you can see, V_2 is computed twice. This might not seem like a significant problem, but it turns out to be rather wasteful as n gets large: to compute V_{20} using this recursive technique, we would compute V_2 4,181 times; and for V_{40} we would compute V_2 63,245,986 times! A much better alternative is to store the value of V_2 in a table and look it up whenever we need it. The same goes for other values, such as V_3 and so on. Function `virahanka2()` implements a dynamic programming approach to the problem. It works by filling up a table (called `lookup`) with solutions to *all* smaller instances of the problem, stopping as soon as we reach the value we're interested in. At this point we read off the value and return it. Crucially, each subproblem is only ever solved once.

Notice that the approach taken in `virahanka2()` is to solve smaller problems on the way to solving larger problems. Accordingly, this is known as the **bottom-up** approach to dynamic programming. Unfortunately it turns out to be quite wasteful for some applications, since it may compute solutions to sub-problems that are never required for solving the main problem. This wasted computation can be avoided using the **top-down** approach to dynamic programming, which is illustrated in the function `virahanka3()` in Example 4-9. Unlike the bottom-up approach, this approach is recursive. It avoids the huge wastage of `virahanka1()` by checking whether it has previously stored the result. If not, it computes the result recursively and stores it in the table. The last step is to return the stored result. The final method, in `virahanka4()`, is to use a Python "decorator" called `memoize`, which takes care of the housekeeping work done by `virahanka3()` without cluttering up the program. This "memoization" process stores the result of each previous call to the function along with the parameters that were used. If the function is subsequently called with the same parameters, it returns the stored result instead of recalculating it. (This aspect of Python syntax is beyond the scope of this book.)

This concludes our brief introduction to dynamic programming. We will encounter it again in Section 8.4.

4.8 A Sample of Python Libraries

Python has hundreds of third-party libraries, specialized software packages that extend the functionality of Python. NLTK is one such library. To realize the full power of Python programming, you should become familiar with several other libraries. Most of these will need to be manually installed on your computer.

Matplotlib

Python has some libraries that are useful for visualizing language data. The Matplotlib package supports sophisticated plotting functions with a MATLAB-style interface, and is available from *http://matplotlib.sourceforge.net/*.

So far we have focused on textual presentation and the use of formatted print statements to get output lined up in columns. It is often very useful to display numerical data in graphical form, since this often makes it easier to detect patterns. For example, in Example 3-5, we saw a table of numbers showing the frequency of particular modal verbs in the Brown Corpus, classified by genre. The program in Example 4-10 presents the same information in graphical format. The output is shown in Figure 4-4 (a color figure in the graphical display).

Example 4-10. Frequency of modals in different sections of the Brown Corpus.

```
colors = 'rgbcmyk' # red, green, blue, cyan, magenta, yellow, black
def bar_chart(categories, words, counts):
    "Plot a bar chart showing counts for each word by category"
    import pylab
    ind = pylab.arange(len(words))
    width = 1 / (len(categories) + 1)
    bar_groups = []
    for c in range(len(categories)):
        bars = pylab.bar(ind+c*width, counts[categories[c]], width,
                         color=colors[c % len(colors)])
        bar_groups.append(bars)
    pylab.xticks(ind+width, words)
    pylab.legend([b[0] for b in bar_groups], categories, loc='upper left')
    pylab.ylabel('Frequency')
    pylab.title('Frequency of Six Modal Verbs by Genre')
    pylab.show()
>>> genres = ['news', 'religion', 'hobbies', 'government', 'adventure']
>>> modals = ['can', 'could', 'may', 'might', 'must', 'will']
>>> cfdist = nltk.ConditionalFreqDist(
...              (genre, word)
...              for genre in genres
...              for word in nltk.corpus.brown.words(categories=genre)
...              if word in modals)
...
>>> counts = {}
>>> for genre in genres:
...     counts[genre] = [cfdist[genre][word] for word in modals]
>>> bar_chart(genres, modals, counts)
```

From the bar chart it is immediately obvious that *may* and *must* have almost identical relative frequencies. The same goes for *could* and *might*.

It is also possible to generate such data visualizations on the fly. For example, a web page with form input could permit visitors to specify search parameters, submit the form, and see a dynamically generated visualization. To do this we have to specify the

Agg backend for `matplotlib`, which is a library for producing raster (pixel) images ❶. Next, we use all the same PyLab methods as before, but instead of displaying the result on a graphical terminal using `pylab.show()`, we save it to a file using `pylab.savefig()` ❷. We specify the filename and dpi, then print HTML markup that directs the web browser to load the file.

```
>>> import matplotlib
>>> matplotlib.use('Agg') ❶
>>> pylab.savefig('modals.png') ❷
>>> print 'Content-Type: text/html'
>>> print
>>> print '<html><body>'
>>> print '<img src="modals.png"/>'
>>> print '</body></html>'
```

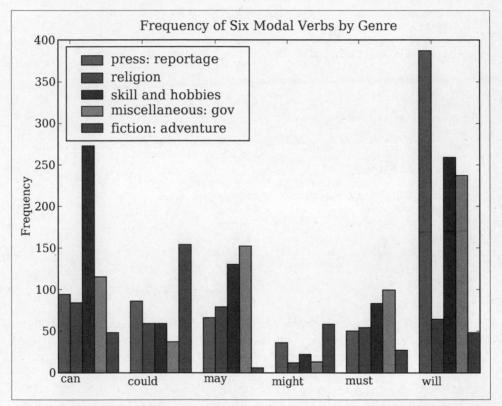

Figure 4-4. Bar chart showing frequency of modals in different sections of Brown Corpus: This visualization was produced by the program in Example 4-10.

NetworkX

The NetworkX package is for defining and manipulating structures consisting of nodes and edges, known as **graphs**. It is available from *https://networkx.lanl.gov/*. NetworkX can be used in conjunction with Matplotlib to visualize networks, such as WordNet (the semantic network we introduced in Section 2.5). The program in Example 4-11 initializes an empty graph ❸ and then traverses the WordNet hypernym hierarchy adding edges to the graph ❶. Notice that the traversal is recursive ❷, applying the programming technique discussed in Section 4.7. The resulting display is shown in Figure 4-5.

Example 4-11. Using the NetworkX and Matplotlib libraries.

```
import networkx as nx
import matplotlib
from nltk.corpus import wordnet as wn

def traverse(graph, start, node):
    graph.depth[node.name] = node.shortest_path_distance(start)
    for child in node.hyponyms():
        graph.add_edge(node.name, child.name) ❶
        traverse(graph, start, child) ❷

def hyponym_graph(start):
    G = nx.Graph() ❸
    G.depth = {}
    traverse(G, start, start)
    return G

def graph_draw(graph):
    nx.draw_graphviz(graph,
        node_size = [16 * graph.degree(n) for n in graph],
        node_color = [graph.depth[n] for n in graph],
        with_labels = False)
    matplotlib.pyplot.show()

>>> dog = wn.synset('dog.n.01')
>>> graph = hyponym_graph(dog)
>>> graph_draw(graph)
```

CSV

Language analysis work often involves data tabulations, containing information about lexical items, the participants in an empirical study, or the linguistic features extracted from a corpus. Here's a fragment of a simple lexicon, in CSV format:

```
sleep, sli:p, v.i, a condition of body and mind ...
walk, wo:k, v.intr, progress by lifting and setting down each foot ...
wake, weik, intrans, cease to sleep
```

We can use Python's CSV library to read and write files stored in this format. For example, we can open a CSV file called *lexicon.csv* ❶ and iterate over its rows ❷:

```
>>> import csv
>>> input_file = open("lexicon.csv", "rb") ❶
>>> for row in csv.reader(input_file): ❷
...     print row
['sleep', 'sli:p', 'v.i', 'a condition of body and mind ...']
```

```
['walk', 'wo:k', 'v.intr', 'progress by lifting and setting down each foot ...']
['wake', 'weik', 'intrans', 'cease to sleep']
```

Each row is just a list of strings. If any fields contain numerical data, they will appear as strings, and will have to be converted using `int()` or `float()`.

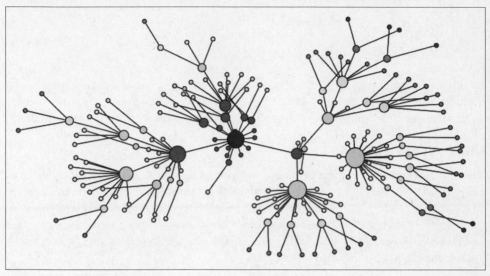

Figure 4-5. Visualization with NetworkX and Matplotlib: Part of the WordNet hypernym hierarchy is displayed, starting with dog.n.01 (the darkest node in the middle); node size is based on the number of children of the node, and color is based on the distance of the node from dog.n.01; this visualization was produced by the program in Example 4-11.

NumPy

The NumPy package provides substantial support for numerical processing in Python. NumPy has a multidimensional array object, which is easy to initialize and access:

```
>>> from numpy import array
>>> cube = array([ [[0,0,0], [1,1,1], [2,2,2]],
...                [[3,3,3], [4,4,4], [5,5,5]],
...                [[6,6,6], [7,7,7], [8,8,8]] ])
>>> cube[1,1,1]
4
>>> cube[2].transpose()
array([[6, 7, 8],
       [6, 7, 8],
       [6, 7, 8]])
>>> cube[2,1:]
array([[7, 7, 7],
       [8, 8, 8]])
```

NumPy includes linear algebra functions. Here we perform singular value decomposition on a matrix, an operation used in **latent semantic analysis** to help identify implicit concepts in a document collection:

```
>>> from numpy import linalg
>>> a=array([[4,0], [3,-5]])
>>> u,s,vt = linalg.svd(a)
>>> u
array([[-0.4472136 , -0.89442719],
       [-0.89442719,  0.4472136 ]])
>>> s
array([ 6.32455532,  3.16227766])
>>> vt
array([[-0.70710678,  0.70710678],
       [-0.70710678, -0.70710678]])
```

NLTK's clustering package `nltk.cluster` makes extensive use of NumPy arrays, and includes support for *k*-means clustering, Gaussian EM clustering, group average agglomerative clustering, and dendogram plots. For details, type `help(nltk.cluster)`.

Other Python Libraries

There are many other Python libraries, and you can search for them with the help of the Python Package Index at *http://pypi.python.org/*. Many libraries provide an interface to external software, such as relational databases (e.g., `mysql-python`) and large document collections (e.g., `PyLucene`). Many other libraries give access to file formats such as PDF, MSWord, and XML (`pypdf`, `pywin32`, `xml.etree`), RSS feeds (e.g., `feedparser`), and electronic mail (e.g., `imaplib`, `email`).

4.9 Summary

- Python's assignment and parameter passing use object references; e.g., if `a` is a list and we assign `b = a`, then any operation on `a` will modify `b`, and vice versa.

- The `is` operation tests whether two objects are identical internal objects, whereas `==` tests whether two objects are equivalent. This distinction parallels the type-token distinction.

- Strings, lists, and tuples are different kinds of sequence object, supporting common operations such as indexing, slicing, `len()`, `sorted()`, and membership testing using `in`.

- We can write text to a file by opening the file for writing

      ofile = open('output.txt', 'w'

  then adding content to the file `ofile.write("Monty Python")`, and finally closing the file `ofile.close()`.

- A declarative programming style usually produces more compact, readable code; manually incremented loop variables are usually unnecessary. When a sequence must be enumerated, use `enumerate()`.

- Functions are an essential programming abstraction: key concepts to understand are parameter passing, variable scope, and docstrings.

- A function serves as a namespace: names defined inside a function are not visible outside that function, unless those names are declared to be global.

- Modules permit logically related material to be localized in a file. A module serves as a namespace: names defined in a module—such as variables and functions—are not visible to other modules, unless those names are imported.

- Dynamic programming is an algorithm design technique used widely in NLP that stores the results of previous computations in order to avoid unnecessary recomputation.

4.10 Further Reading

This chapter has touched on many topics in programming, some specific to Python, and some quite general. We've just scratched the surface, and you may want to read more about these topics, starting with the further materials for this chapter available at *http://www.nltk.org/*.

The Python website provides extensive documentation. It is important to understand the built-in functions and standard types, described at *http://docs.python.org/library/functions.html* and *http://docs.python.org/library/stdtypes.html*. We have learned about generators and their importance for efficiency; for information about iterators, a closely related topic, see *http://docs.python.org/library/itertools.html*. Consult your favorite Python book for more information on such topics. An excellent resource for using Python for multimedia processing, including working with sound files, is (Guzdial, 2005).

When using the online Python documentation, be aware that your installed version might be different from the version of the documentation you are reading. You can easily check what version you have, with `import sys; sys.version`. Version-specific documentation is available at *http://www.python.org/doc/versions/*.

Algorithm design is a rich field within computer science. Some good starting points are (Harel, 2004), (Levitin, 2004), and (Knuth, 2006). Useful guidance on the practice of software development is provided in (Hunt & Thomas, 2000) and (McConnell, 2004).

4.11 Exercises

1. ○ Find out more about sequence objects using Python's help facility. In the interpreter, type `help(str)`, `help(list)`, and `help(tuple)`. This will give you a full list of the functions supported by each type. Some functions have special names flanked with underscores; as the help documentation shows, each such function corresponds to something more familiar. For example `x.__getitem__(y)` is just a long-winded way of saying `x[y]`.

2. ○ Identify three operations that can be performed on both tuples and lists. Identify three list operations that cannot be performed on tuples. Name a context where using a list instead of a tuple generates a Python error.

3. ○ Find out how to create a tuple consisting of a single item. There are at least two ways to do this.

4. ○ Create a list `words = ['is', 'NLP', 'fun', '?']`. Use a series of assignment statements (e.g., `words[1] = words[2]`) and a temporary variable `tmp` to transform this list into the list `['NLP', 'is', 'fun', '!']`. Now do the same transformation using tuple assignment.

5. ○ Read about the built-in comparison function `cmp`, by typing `help(cmp)`. How does it differ in behavior from the comparison operators?

6. ○ Does the method for creating a sliding window of n-grams behave correctly for the two limiting cases: $n = 1$ and $n = \text{len(sent)}$?

7. ○ We pointed out that when empty strings and empty lists occur in the condition part of an `if` clause, they evaluate to `False`. In this case, they are said to be occurring in a Boolean context. Experiment with different kinds of non-Boolean expressions in Boolean contexts, and see whether they evaluate as `True` or `False`.

8. ○ Use the inequality operators to compare strings, e.g., `'Monty' < 'Python'`. What happens when you do `'Z' < 'a'`? Try pairs of strings that have a common prefix, e.g., `'Monty' < 'Montague'`. Read up on "lexicographical sort" in order to understand what is going on here. Try comparing structured objects, e.g., `('Monty', 1) < ('Monty', 2)`. Does this behave as expected?

9. ○ Write code that removes whitespace at the beginning and end of a string, and normalizes whitespace between words to be a single-space character.

   a. Do this task using `split()` and `join()`.

   b. Do this task using regular expression substitutions.

10. ○ Write a program to sort words by length. Define a helper function `cmp_len` which uses the `cmp` comparison function on word lengths.

11. ◑ Create a list of words and store it in a variable `sent1`. Now assign `sent2 = sent1`. Modify one of the items in `sent1` and verify that `sent2` has changed.

    a. Now try the same exercise, but instead assign `sent2 = sent1[:]`. Modify `sent1` again and see what happens to `sent2`. Explain.

    b. Now define `text1` to be a list of lists of strings (e.g., to represent a text consisting of multiple sentences). Now assign `text2 = text1[:]`, assign a new value to one of the words, e.g., `text1[1][1] = 'Monty'`. Check what this did to `text2`. Explain.

    c. Load Python's `deepcopy()` function (i.e., `from copy import deepcopy`), consult its documentation, and test that it makes a fresh copy of any object.

12. ◑ Initialize an *n*-by-*m* list of lists of empty strings using list multiplication, e.g., `word_table = [[''] * n] * m`. What happens when you set one of its values, e.g., `word_table[1][2] = "hello"`? Explain why this happens. Now write an expression using `range()` to construct a list of lists, and show that it does not have this problem.

13. ◐ Write code to initialize a two-dimensional array of sets called `word_vowels` and process a list of words, adding each word to `word_vowels[l][v]` where l is the length of the word and v is the number of vowels it contains.

14. ◐ Write a function `novel10(text)` that prints any word that appeared in the last 10% of a text that had not been encountered earlier.

15. ◐ Write a program that takes a sentence expressed as a single string, splits it, and counts up the words. Get it to print out each word and the word's frequency, one per line, in alphabetical order.

16. ◐ Read up on Gematria, a method for assigning numbers to words, and for mapping between words having the same number to discover the hidden meaning of texts (*http://en.wikipedia.org/wiki/Gematria*, *http://essenes.net/gemcal.htm*).

    a. Write a function `gematria()` that sums the numerical values of the letters of a word, according to the letter values in `letter_vals`:

    ```
    >>> letter_vals = {'a':1, 'b':2, 'c':3, 'd':4, 'e':5, 'f':80, 'g':3, 'h':8,
    ... 'i':10, 'j':10, 'k':20, 'l':30, 'm':40, 'n':50, 'o':70, 'p':80, 'q':100,
    ... 'r':200, 's':300, 't':400, 'u':6, 'v':6, 'w':800, 'x':60, 'y':10, 'z':7}
    ```

    b. Process a corpus (e.g., `nltk.corpus.state_union`) and for each document, count how many of its words have the number 666.

    c. Write a function `decode()` to process a text, randomly replacing words with their Gematria equivalents, in order to discover the "hidden meaning" of the text.

17. ◐ Write a function `shorten(text, n)` to process a text, omitting the *n* most frequently occurring words of the text. How readable is it?

18. ◐ Write code to print out an index for a lexicon, allowing someone to look up words according to their meanings (or their pronunciations; whatever properties are contained in the lexical entries).

19. ◐ Write a list comprehension that sorts a list of WordNet synsets for proximity to a given synset. For example, given the synsets `minke_whale.n.01`, `orca.n.01`, `novel.n.01`, and `tortoise.n.01`, sort them according to their `path_distance()` from `right_whale.n.01`.

20. ◐ Write a function that takes a list of words (containing duplicates) and returns a list of words (with no duplicates) sorted by decreasing frequency. E.g., if the input list contained 10 instances of the word `table` and 9 instances of the word `chair`, then `table` would appear before `chair` in the output list.

21. ◐ Write a function that takes a text and a vocabulary as its arguments and returns the set of words that appear in the text but not in the vocabulary. Both arguments can be represented as lists of strings. Can you do this in a single line, using `set.difference()`?

22. ◐ Import the `itemgetter()` function from the `operator` module in Python's standard library (i.e., `from operator import itemgetter`). Create a list `words` containing sev-

eral words. Now try calling: `sorted(words, key=itemgetter(1))`, and `sorted(words, key=itemgetter(-1))`. Explain what `itemgetter()` is doing.

23. ◑ Write a recursive function `lookup(trie, key)` that looks up a key in a trie, and returns the value it finds. Extend the function to return a word when it is uniquely determined by its prefix (e.g., vanguard is the only word that starts with vang-, so `lookup(trie, 'vang')` should return the same thing as `lookup(trie, 'vanguard')`).

24. ◑ Read up on "keyword linkage" (Chapter 5 of (Scott & Tribble, 2006)). Extract keywords from NLTK's Shakespeare Corpus and using the NetworkX package, plot keyword linkage networks.

25. ◑ Read about string edit distance and the Levenshtein Algorithm. Try the implementation provided in `nltk.edit_dist()`. In what way is this using dynamic programming? Does it use the bottom-up or top-down approach? (See also *http://norvig.com/spell-correct.html*.)

26. ◑ The Catalan numbers arise in many applications of combinatorial mathematics, including the counting of parse trees (Section 8.6). The series can be defined as follows: $C_0 = 1$, and $C_{n+1} = \Sigma_{0..n} (C_i C_{n-i})$.

    a. Write a recursive function to compute nth Catalan number C_n.

    b. Now write another function that does this computation using dynamic programming.

    c. Use the `timeit` module to compare the performance of these functions as n increases.

27. ● Reproduce some of the results of (Zhao & Zobel, 2007) concerning authorship identification.

28. ● Study gender-specific lexical choice, and see if you can reproduce some of the results of *http://www.clintoneast.com/articles/words.php*.

29. ● Write a recursive function that pretty prints a trie in alphabetically sorted order, for example:

```
chair: 'flesh'
---t: 'cat'
--ic: 'stylish'
---en: 'dog'
```

30. ● With the help of the trie data structure, write a recursive function that processes text, locating the uniqueness point in each word, and discarding the remainder of each word. How much compression does this give? How readable is the resulting text?

31. ● Obtain some raw text, in the form of a single, long string. Use Python's `textwrap` module to break it up into multiple lines. Now write code to add extra spaces between words, in order to justify the output. Each line must have the same width, and spaces must be approximately evenly distributed across each line. No line can begin or end with a space.

32. • Develop a simple extractive summarization tool, that prints the sentences of a document which contain the highest total word frequency. Use `FreqDist()` to count word frequencies, and use `sum` to sum the frequencies of the words in each sentence. Rank the sentences according to their score. Finally, print the *n* highest-scoring sentences in document order. Carefully review the design of your program, especially your approach to this double sorting. Make sure the program is written as clearly as possible.

33. • Develop your own `NgramTagger` class that inherits from NLTK's class, and which encapsulates the method of collapsing the vocabulary of the tagged training and testing data that was described in Chapter 5. Make sure that the unigram and default backoff taggers have access to the full vocabulary.

34. • Read the following article on semantic orientation of adjectives. Use the NetworkX package to visualize a network of adjectives with edges to indicate same versus different semantic orientation (see *http://www.aclweb.org/anthology/P97 -1023*).

35. • Design an algorithm to find the "statistically improbable phrases" of a document collection (see *http://www.amazon.com/gp/search-inside/sipshelp.html*).

36. • Write a program to implement a brute-force algorithm for discovering word squares, a kind of *n × n*: crossword in which the entry in the *n*th row is the same as the entry in the *n*th column. For discussion, see *http://itre.cis.upenn.edu/~myl/languagelog/archives/002679.html*.

## CHAPTER 5

Categorizing and Tagging Words

Back in elementary school you learned the difference between nouns, verbs, adjectives, and adverbs. These "word classes" are not just the idle invention of grammarians, but are useful categories for many language processing tasks. As we will see, they arise from simple analysis of the distribution of words in text. The goal of this chapter is to answer the following questions:

1. What are lexical categories, and how are they used in natural language processing?
2. What is a good Python data structure for storing words and their categories?
3. How can we automatically tag each word of a text with its word class?

Along the way, we'll cover some fundamental techniques in NLP, including sequence labeling, n-gram models, backoff, and evaluation. These techniques are useful in many areas, and tagging gives us a simple context in which to present them. We will also see how tagging is the second step in the typical NLP pipeline, following tokenization.

The process of classifying words into their **parts-of-speech** and labeling them accordingly is known as **part-of-speech tagging**, **POS tagging**, or simply **tagging**. Parts-of-speech are also known as **word classes** or **lexical categories**. The collection of tags used for a particular task is known as a **tagset**. Our emphasis in this chapter is on exploiting tags, and tagging text automatically.

5.1 Using a Tagger

A part-of-speech tagger, or **POS tagger**, processes a sequence of words, and attaches a part of speech tag to each word (don't forget to `import nltk`):

```
>>> text = nltk.word_tokenize("And now for something completely different")
>>> nltk.pos_tag(text)
[('And', 'CC'), ('now', 'RB'), ('for', 'IN'), ('something', 'NN'),
('completely', 'RB'), ('different', 'JJ')]
```

Here we see that *and* is CC, a coordinating conjunction; *now* and *completely* are RB, or adverbs; *for* is IN, a preposition; *something* is NN, a noun; and *different* is JJ, an adjective.

NLTK provides documentation for each tag, which can be queried using the tag, e.g., `nltk.help.upenn_tagset('RB')`, or a regular expression, e.g., `nltk.help.upenn_brown_tagset('NN.*')`. Some corpora have README files with tagset documentation; see `nltk.`*name*`.readme()`, substituting in the name of the corpus.

Let's look at another example, this time including some homonyms:

```
>>> text = nltk.word_tokenize("They refuse to permit us to obtain the refuse permit")
>>> nltk.pos_tag(text)
[('They', 'PRP'), ('refuse', 'VBP'), ('to', 'TO'), ('permit', 'VB'), ('us', 'PRP'),
('to', 'TO'), ('obtain', 'VB'), ('the', 'DT'), ('refuse', 'NN'), ('permit', 'NN')]
```

Notice that *refuse* and *permit* both appear as a present tense verb (VBP) and a noun (NN). E.g., *refUSE* is a verb meaning "deny," while *REFuse* is a noun meaning "trash" (i.e., they are not homophones). Thus, we need to know which word is being used in order to pronounce the text correctly. (For this reason, text-to-speech systems usually perform POS tagging.)

Your Turn: Many words, like *ski* and *race*, can be used as nouns or verbs with no difference in pronunciation. Can you think of others? Hint: think of a commonplace object and try to put the word *to* before it to see if it can also be a verb, or think of an action and try to put *the* before it to see if it can also be a noun. Now make up a sentence with both uses of this word, and run the POS tagger on this sentence.

Lexical categories like "noun" and part-of-speech tags like NN seem to have their uses, but the details will be obscure to many readers. You might wonder what justification there is for introducing this extra level of information. Many of these categories arise from superficial analysis of the distribution of words in text. Consider the following analysis involving *woman* (a noun), *bought* (a verb), *over* (a preposition), and *the* (a determiner). The `text.similar()` method takes a word w, finds all contexts $w_1 w\ w_2$, then finds all words w' that appear in the same context, i.e. $w_1 w' w_2$.

```
>>> text = nltk.Text(word.lower() for word in nltk.corpus.brown.words())
>>> text.similar('woman')
Building word-context index...
man time day year car moment world family house country child boy
state job way war girl place room word
>>> text.similar('bought')
made said put done seen had found left given heard brought got been
was set told took in felt that
>>> text.similar('over')
in on to of and for with from at by that into as up out down through
is all about
>>> text.similar('the')
a his this their its her an that our any all one these my in your no
some other and
```

Observe that searching for *woman* finds nouns; searching for *bought* mostly finds verbs; searching for *over* generally finds prepositions; searching for *the* finds several determiners. A tagger can correctly identify the tags on these words in the context of a sentence, e.g., *The woman bought over $150,000 worth of clothes.*

A tagger can also model our knowledge of unknown words; for example, we can guess that *scrobbling* is probably a verb, with the root *scrobble*, and likely to occur in contexts like *he was scrobbling*.

5.2 Tagged Corpora

Representing Tagged Tokens

By convention in NLTK, a tagged token is represented using a tuple consisting of the token and the tag. We can create one of these special tuples from the standard string representation of a tagged token, using the function `str2tuple()`:

```
>>> tagged_token = nltk.tag.str2tuple('fly/NN')
>>> tagged_token
('fly', 'NN')
>>> tagged_token[0]
'fly'
>>> tagged_token[1]
'NN'
```

We can construct a list of tagged tokens directly from a string. The first step is to tokenize the string to access the individual `word/tag` strings, and then to convert each of these into a tuple (using `str2tuple()`).

```
>>> sent = '''
... The/AT grand/JJ jury/NN commented/VBD on/IN a/AT number/NN of/IN
... other/AP topics/NNS ,/, AMONG/IN them/PPO the/AT Atlanta/NP and/CC
... Fulton/NP-tl County/NN-tl purchasing/VBG departments/NNS which/WDT it/PPS
... said/VBD ``/`` ARE/BER well/QL operated/VBN and/CC follow/VB generally/RB
... accepted/VBN practices/NNS which/WDT inure/VB to/IN the/AT best/JJT
... interest/NN of/IN both/ABX governments/NNS ''/'' ./.
... '''
>>> [nltk.tag.str2tuple(t) for t in sent.split()]
[('The', 'AT'), ('grand', 'JJ'), ('jury', 'NN'), ('commented', 'VBD'),
('on', 'IN'), ('a', 'AT'), ('number', 'NN'), ... ('.', '.')]
```

Reading Tagged Corpora

Several of the corpora included with NLTK have been **tagged** for their part-of-speech. Here's an example of what you might see if you opened a file from the Brown Corpus with a text editor:

The/at Fulton/np-tl County/nn-tl Grand/jj-tl Jury/nn-tl said/vbd Friday/nr an/at investigation/nn of/in Atlanta's/np$ recent/jj primary/nn election/nn produced/vbd / no/at evidence/nn "/" that/cs any/dti irregularities/nns took/vbd place/nn ./.

Other corpora use a variety of formats for storing part-of-speech tags. NLTK's corpus readers provide a uniform interface so that you don't have to be concerned with the different file formats. In contrast with the file extract just shown, the corpus reader for the Brown Corpus represents the data as shown next. Note that part-of-speech tags have been converted to uppercase; this has become standard practice since the Brown Corpus was published.

```
>>> nltk.corpus.brown.tagged_words()
[('The', 'AT'), ('Fulton', 'NP-TL'), ('County', 'NN-TL'), ...]
>>> nltk.corpus.brown.tagged_words(simplify_tags=True)
[('The', 'DET'), ('Fulton', 'N'), ('County', 'N'), ...]
```

Whenever a corpus contains tagged text, the NLTK corpus interface will have a `tagged_words()` method. Here are some more examples, again using the output format illustrated for the Brown Corpus:

```
>>> print nltk.corpus.nps_chat.tagged_words()
[('now', 'RB'), ('im', 'PRP'), ('left', 'VBD'), ...]
>>> nltk.corpus.conll2000.tagged_words()
[('Confidence', 'NN'), ('in', 'IN'), ('the', 'DT'), ...]
>>> nltk.corpus.treebank.tagged_words()
[('Pierre', 'NNP'), ('Vinken', 'NNP'), (',', ','), ...]
```

Not all corpora employ the same set of tags; see the tagset help functionality and the `readme()` methods mentioned earlier for documentation. Initially we want to avoid the complications of these tagsets, so we use a built-in mapping to a simplified tagset:

```
>>> nltk.corpus.brown.tagged_words(simplify_tags=True)
[('The', 'DET'), ('Fulton', 'NP'), ('County', 'N'), ...]
>>> nltk.corpus.treebank.tagged_words(simplify_tags=True)
[('Pierre', 'NP'), ('Vinken', 'NP'), (',', ','), ...]
```

Tagged corpora for several other languages are distributed with NLTK, including Chinese, Hindi, Portuguese, Spanish, Dutch, and Catalan. These usually contain non-ASCII text, and Python always displays this in hexadecimal when printing a larger structure such as a list.

```
>>> nltk.corpus.sinica_treebank.tagged_words()
[('\xe4\xb8\x80', 'Neu'), ('\xe5\x8f\x8b\xe6\x83\x85', 'Nad'), ...]
>>> nltk.corpus.indian.tagged_words()
[('\xe0\xa6\xae\xe0\xa6\xb9\xe0\xa6\xbf\xe0\xa6\xb7\xe0\xa7\x87\xe0\xa6\xb0', 'NN'),
('\xe0\xa6\xb8\xe0\xa6\xa8\xe0\xa7\x8d\xe0\xa6\xa4\xe0\xa6\xbe\xe0\xa6\xa8', 'NN'),
...]
>>> nltk.corpus.mac_morpho.tagged_words()
[('Jersei', 'N'), ('atinge', 'V'), ('m\xe9dia', 'N'), ...]
>>> nltk.corpus.conll2002.tagged_words()
[('Sao', 'NC'), ('Paulo', 'VMI'), ('(', 'Fpa'), ...]
>>> nltk.corpus.cess_cat.tagged_words()
[('El', 'da0ms0'), ('Tribunal_Suprem', 'np0000o'), ...]
```

If your environment is set up correctly, with appropriate editors and fonts, you should be able to display individual strings in a human-readable way. For example, Figure 5-1 shows data accessed using `nltk.corpus.indian`.

If the corpus is also segmented into sentences, it will have a `tagged_sents()` method that divides up the tagged words into sentences rather than presenting them as one big list. This will be useful when we come to developing automatic taggers, as they are trained and tested on lists of sentences, not words.

A Simplified Part-of-Speech Tagset

Tagged corpora use many different conventions for tagging words. To help us get started, we will be looking at a simplified tagset (shown in Table 5-1).

Table 5-1. Simplified part-of-speech tagset

Tag	Meaning	Examples
ADJ	adjective	*new, good, high, special, big, local*
ADV	adverb	*really, already, still, early, now*
CNJ	conjunction	*and, or, but, if, while, although*
DET	determiner	*the, a, some, most, every, no*
EX	existential	*there, there's*
FW	foreign word	*dolce, ersatz, esprit, quo, maitre*
MOD	modal verb	*will, can, would, may, must, should*
N	noun	*year, home, costs, time, education*
NP	proper noun	*Alison, Africa, April, Washington*
NUM	number	*twenty-four, fourth, 1991, 14:24*
PRO	pronoun	*he, their, her, its, my, I, us*
P	preposition	*on, of, at, with, by, into, under*
TO	the word *to*	*to*
UH	interjection	*ah, bang, ha, whee, hmpf, oops*
V	verb	*is, has, get, do, make, see, run*
VD	past tense	*said, took, told, made, asked*
VG	present participle	*making, going, playing, working*
VN	past participle	*given, taken, begun, sung*
WH	*wh* determiner	*who, which, when, what, where, how*

```
Bangla: ক_ ̃ড়মেরগ_লরি/'NN' আকারার/'NN' বাংলারার/'NNP' বা/'CC' ভারতরের/'NNP' ?/None
ন_য়/'JJ' ?/None এ_ চলরের/'NN' প_রচল তি/'JJ' ক_ ̃ড়ট/'NN' ঘর/'NN' নয়/'VM' [কি]/'SYM'
Hindi: प_किस्तान/'NNP' की/'PREP' प_र्व/'JJ' प्रधानम त्री/'NN' बेनज़ीर/'NNPC' भ_ट्टो/'NNP'
पर/'PREP' लगे/'VFM' भ्रष्टाचार/'NN' के/'PREP' आरोपों/'NN' के/'PREP' खिलाफ/'PREP' भ_ट्टो/'NNP'
द्वारा/'PREP' दायर/'NVB' की/'VFM' गई/'VAUX' याचिका/'NN' की/'PREP' स_नवाई/'NN'
म_मलवार/'NN' को/'PREP' वकीलों/'NN' की/'PREP' हड़ताल/'NN' के/'PREP' कारण/'PREP'
स्थ गित/'JVB' कर/'VFM' दी/'VAUX' गई/'VAUX' ।/'PUNC'
Marathi: श्रमिण/'JJ' जिल्ह्य़ाच्य़ा/'NN' बाळासाहेब/'NNPC' भोसले/'NNP' य_ांच्या/'PRP' ?/None
घर्षतेखालील/'NN' पथावरी/'NN' आज/'NN' ब_?/None क/'NN' ब्बालें/'VM' ./'SYM'
Telugu: ఫలచరులు/'NN' మంద/'PREP' వచ్చిన/'VJJ' ఒ కుల/'NN' మ/'PREP' సైక్కిడా/'NN'
```

Figure 5-1. POS tagged data from four Indian languages: Bangla, Hindi, Marathi, and Telugu.

Let's see which of these tags are the most common in the news category of the Brown Corpus:

```
>>> from nltk.corpus import brown
>>> brown_news_tagged = brown.tagged_words(categories='news', simplify_tags=True)
>>> tag_fd = nltk.FreqDist(tag for (word, tag) in brown_news_tagged)
>>> tag_fd.keys()
['N', 'P', 'DET', 'NP', 'V', 'ADJ', ',', '.', 'CNJ', 'PRO', 'ADV', 'VD', ...]
```

 Your Turn: Plot the frequency distribution just shown using `tag_fd.plot(cumulative=True)`. What percentage of words are tagged using the first five tags of the above list?

We can use these tags to do powerful searches using a graphical POS-concordance tool `nltk.app.concordance()`. Use it to search for any combination of words and POS tags, e.g., N N N N, hit/VD, hit/VN, or the ADJ man.

Nouns

Nouns generally refer to people, places, things, or concepts, e.g., *woman, Scotland, book, intelligence*. Nouns can appear after determiners and adjectives, and can be the subject or object of the verb, as shown in Table 5-2.

Table 5-2. Syntactic patterns involving some nouns

Word	After a determiner	Subject of the verb
woman	*the* woman who I saw yesterday ...	the woman *sat* down
Scotland	*the* Scotland I remember as a child ...	Scotland *has* five million people
book	*the* book I bought yesterday ...	this book *recounts* the colonization of Australia
intelligence	*the* intelligence displayed by the child ...	Mary's intelligence *impressed* her teachers

The simplified noun tags are N for common nouns like *book*, and NP for proper nouns like *Scotland*.

Let's inspect some tagged text to see what parts-of-speech occur before a noun, with the most frequent ones first. To begin with, we construct a list of bigrams whose members are themselves word-tag pairs, such as (('The', 'DET'), ('Fulton', 'NP')) and (('Fulton', 'NP'), ('County', 'N')). Then we construct a FreqDist from the tag parts of the bigrams.

```
>>> word_tag_pairs = nltk.bigrams(brown_news_tagged)
>>> list(nltk.FreqDist(a[1] for (a, b) in word_tag_pairs if b[1] == 'N'))
['DET', 'ADJ', 'N', 'P', 'NP', 'NUM', 'V', 'PRO', 'CNJ', '.', ',', 'VG', 'VN', ...]
```

This confirms our assertion that nouns occur after determiners and adjectives, including numeral adjectives (tagged as NUM).

Verbs

Verbs are words that describe events and actions, e.g., *fall* and *eat*, as shown in Table 5-3. In the context of a sentence, verbs typically express a relation involving the referents of one or more noun phrases.

Table 5-3. Syntactic patterns involving some verbs

Word	Simple	With modifiers and adjuncts (italicized)
fall	Rome fell	Dot com stocks *suddenly* fell *like a stone*
eat	Mice eat cheese	John ate the pizza *with gusto*

What are the most common verbs in news text? Let's sort all the verbs by frequency:

```
>>> wsj = nltk.corpus.treebank.tagged_words(simplify_tags=True)
>>> word_tag_fd = nltk.FreqDist(wsj)
>>> [word + "/" + tag for (word, tag) in word_tag_fd if tag.startswith('V')]
['is/V', 'said/VD', 'was/VD', 'are/V', 'be/V', 'has/V', 'have/V', 'says/V',
'were/VD', 'had/VD', 'been/VN', "'s/V", 'do/V', 'say/V', 'make/V', 'did/VD',
'rose/VD', 'does/V', 'expected/VN', 'buy/V', 'take/V', 'get/V', 'sell/V',
'help/V', 'added/VD', 'including/VG', 'according/VG', 'made/VN', 'pay/V', ...]
```

Note that the items being counted in the frequency distribution are word-tag pairs. Since words and tags are paired, we can treat the word as a condition and the tag as an event, and initialize a conditional frequency distribution with a list of condition-event pairs. This lets us see a frequency-ordered list of tags given a word:

```
>>> cfd1 = nltk.ConditionalFreqDist(wsj)
>>> cfd1['yield'].keys()
['V', 'N']
>>> cfd1['cut'].keys()
['V', 'VD', 'N', 'VN']
```

We can reverse the order of the pairs, so that the tags are the conditions, and the words are the events. Now we can see likely words for a given tag:

```
>>> cfd2 = nltk.ConditionalFreqDist((tag, word) for (word, tag) in wsj)
>>> cfd2['VN'].keys()
['been', 'expected', 'made', 'compared', 'based', 'priced', 'used', 'sold',
'named', 'designed', 'held', 'fined', 'taken', 'paid', 'traded', 'said', ...]
```

To clarify the distinction between VD (past tense) and VN (past participle), let's find words that can be both VD and VN, and see some surrounding text:

```
>>> [w for w in cfd1.conditions() if 'VD' in cfd1[w] and 'VN' in cfd1[w]]
['Asked', 'accelerated', 'accepted', 'accused', 'acquired', 'added', 'adopted', ...]
>>> idx1 = wsj.index(('kicked', 'VD'))
>>> wsj[idx1-4:idx1+1]
[('While', 'P'), ('program', 'N'), ('trades', 'N'), ('swiftly', 'ADV'),
('kicked', 'VD')]
>>> idx2 = wsj.index(('kicked', 'VN'))
>>> wsj[idx2-4:idx2+1]
[('head', 'N'), ('of', 'P'), ('state', 'N'), ('has', 'V'), ('kicked', 'VN')]
```

In this case, we see that the past participle of *kicked* is preceded by a form of the auxiliary verb *have*. Is this generally true?

Your Turn: Given the list of past participles specified by cfd2['VN'].keys(), try to collect a list of all the word-tag pairs that immediately precede items in that list.

Adjectives and Adverbs

Two other important word classes are **adjectives** and **adverbs**. Adjectives describe nouns, and can be used as modifiers (e.g., *large* in *the large pizza*), or as predicates (e.g., *the pizza is large*). English adjectives can have internal structure (e.g., *fall+ing* in *the falling stocks*). Adverbs modify verbs to specify the time, manner, place, or direction of the event described by the verb (e.g., *quickly* in *the stocks fell quickly*). Adverbs may also modify adjectives (e.g., *really* in *Mary's teacher was really nice*).

English has several categories of closed class words in addition to prepositions, such as **articles** (also often called **determiners**) (e.g., *the*, *a*), **modals** (e.g., *should*, *may*), and **personal pronouns** (e.g., *she*, *they*). Each dictionary and grammar classifies these words differently.

Your Turn: If you are uncertain about some of these parts-of-speech, study them using nltk.app.concordance(), or watch some of the *Schoolhouse Rock!* grammar videos available at YouTube, or consult Section 5.9.

Unsimplified Tags

Let's find the most frequent nouns of each noun part-of-speech type. The program in Example 5-1 finds all tags starting with NN, and provides a few example words for each one. You will see that there are many variants of NN; the most important contain $ for possessive nouns, S for plural nouns (since plural nouns typically end in *s*), and P for proper nouns. In addition, most of the tags have suffix modifiers: -NC for citations, -HL for words in headlines, and -TL for titles (a feature of Brown tags).

Example 5-1. Program to find the most frequent noun tags.

```
def findtags(tag_prefix, tagged_text):
    cfd = nltk.ConditionalFreqDist((tag, word) for (word, tag) in tagged_text
                                   if tag.startswith(tag_prefix))
    return dict((tag, cfd[tag].keys()[:5]) for tag in cfd.conditions())

>>> tagdict = findtags('NN', nltk.corpus.brown.tagged_words(categories='news'))
>>> for tag in sorted(tagdict):
...     print tag, tagdict[tag]
...
NN ['year', 'time', 'state', 'week', 'man']
NN$ ["year's", "world's", "state's", "nation's", "company's"]
NN$-HL ["Golf's", "Navy's"]
NN$-TL ["President's", "University's", "League's", "Gallery's", "Army's"]
NN-HL ['cut', 'Salary', 'condition', 'Question', 'business']
NN-NC ['eva', 'ova', 'aya']
NN-TL ['President', 'House', 'State', 'University', 'City']
NN-TL-HL ['Fort', 'City', 'Commissioner', 'Grove', 'House']
NNS ['years', 'members', 'people', 'sales', 'men']
NNS$ ["children's", "women's", "men's", "janitors'", "taxpayers'"]
NNS$-HL ["Dealers'", "Idols'"]
NNS$-TL ["Women's", "States'", "Giants'", "Officers'", "Bombers'"]
NNS-HL ['years', 'idols', 'Creations', 'thanks', 'centers']
NNS-TL ['States', 'Nations', 'Masters', 'Rules', 'Communists']
NNS-TL-HL ['Nations']
```

When we come to constructing part-of-speech taggers later in this chapter, we will use the unsimplified tags.

Exploring Tagged Corpora

Let's briefly return to the kinds of exploration of corpora we saw in previous chapters, this time exploiting POS tags.

Suppose we're studying the word *often* and want to see how it is used in text. We could ask to see the words that follow *often*:

```
>>> brown_learned_text = brown.words(categories='learned')
>>> sorted(set(b for (a, b) in nltk.ibigrams(brown_learned_text) if a == 'often'))
[',', '.', 'accomplished', 'analytically', 'appear', 'apt', 'associated', 'assuming',
'became', 'become', 'been', 'began', 'call', 'called', 'carefully', 'chose', ...]
```

However, it's probably more instructive use the tagged_words() method to look at the part-of-speech tag of the following words:

```
>>> brown_lrnd_tagged = brown.tagged_words(categories='learned', simplify_tags=True)
>>> tags = [b[1] for (a, b) in nltk.ibigrams(brown_lrnd_tagged) if a[0] == 'often']
>>> fd = nltk.FreqDist(tags)
>>> fd.tabulate()
  VN    V   VD  DET  ADJ  ADV    P  CNJ    ,   TO   VG   WH  VBZ    .
  15   12    8    5    5    4    4    3    3    1    1    1    1    1
```

Notice that the most high-frequency parts-of-speech following *often* are verbs. Nouns never appear in this position (in this particular corpus).

Next, let's look at some larger context, and find words involving particular sequences of tags and words (in this case "<Verb> to <Verb>"). In Example 5-2, we consider each three-word window in the sentence ❶, and check whether they meet our criterion ❷. If the tags match, we print the corresponding words ❸.

Example 5-2. Searching for three-word phrases using POS tags.

```
from nltk.corpus import brown
def process(sentence):
    for (w1,t1), (w2,t2), (w3,t3) in nltk.trigrams(sentence): ❶
        if (t1.startswith('V') and t2 == 'TO' and t3.startswith('V')): ❷
            print w1, w2, w3 ❸

>>> for tagged_sent in brown.tagged_sents():
...        process(tagged_sent)
...
combined to achieve
continue to place
serve to protect
wanted to wait
allowed to place
expected to become
...
```

Finally, let's look for words that are highly ambiguous as to their part-of-speech tag. Understanding why such words are tagged as they are in each context can help us clarify the distinctions between the tags.

```
>>> brown_news_tagged = brown.tagged_words(categories='news', simplify_tags=True)
>>> data = nltk.ConditionalFreqDist((word.lower(), tag)
...                                 for (word, tag) in brown_news_tagged)
>>> for word in data.conditions():
...        if len(data[word]) > 3:
...            tags = data[word].keys()
...            print word, ' '.join(tags)
...
best ADJ ADV NP V
better ADJ ADV V DET
close ADV ADJ V N
cut V N VN VD
even ADV DET ADJ V
grant NP N V -
hit V VD VN N
lay ADJ V NP VD
left VD ADJ N VN
```

```
like CNJ V ADJ P -
near P ADV ADJ DET
open ADJ V N ADV
past N ADJ DET P
present ADJ ADV V N
read V VN VD NP
right ADJ N DET ADV
second NUM ADV DET N
set VN V VD N -
that CNJ V WH DET
```

 Your Turn: Open the POS concordance tool `nltk.app.concordance()` and load the complete Brown Corpus (simplified tagset). Now pick some of the words listed at the end of the previous code example and see how the tag of the word correlates with the context of the word. E.g., search for `near` to see all forms mixed together, `near/ADJ` to see it used as an adjective, `near N` to see just those cases where a noun follows, and so forth.

5.3 Mapping Words to Properties Using Python Dictionaries

As we have seen, a tagged word of the form (`word, tag`) is an association between a word and a part-of-speech tag. Once we start doing part-of-speech tagging, we will be creating programs that assign a tag to a word, the tag which is most likely in a given context. We can think of this process as **mapping** from words to tags. The most natural way to store mappings in Python uses the so-called **dictionary** data type (also known as an **associative array** or **hash array** in other programming languages). In this section, we look at dictionaries and see how they can represent a variety of language information, including parts-of-speech.

Indexing Lists Versus Dictionaries

A text, as we have seen, is treated in Python as a list of words. An important property of lists is that we can "look up" a particular item by giving its index, e.g., `text1[100]`. Notice how we specify a number and get back a word. We can think of a list as a simple kind of table, as shown in Figure 5-2.

0	Call
1	me
2	Ishmael
3	.

Figure 5-2. List lookup: We access the contents of a Python list with the help of an integer index.

Contrast this situation with frequency distributions (Section 1.3), where we specify a word and get back a number, e.g., `fdist['monstrous']`, which tells us the number of times a given word has occurred in a text. Lookup using words is familiar to anyone who has used a dictionary. Some more examples are shown in Figure 5-3.

Phone List		Domain Name Resolution		Word Frequency Table	
Alex	x154	aclweb.org	128.231.23.4	computational	25
Dana	x642	amazon.com	12.118.92.43	language	196
Kim	x911	google.com	28.31.23.124	linguistics	17
Les	x120	python.org	18.21.3.144	natural	56
Sandy	x124	sourceforge.net	51.98.23.53	processing	57

Figure 5-3. Dictionary lookup: we access the entry of a dictionary using a key such as someone's name, a web domain, or an English word; other names for dictionary are map, hashmap, hash, and associative array.

In the case of a phonebook, we look up an entry using a *name* and get back a number. When we type a domain name in a web browser, the computer looks this up to get back an IP address. A word frequency table allows us to look up a word and find its frequency in a text collection. In all these cases, we are mapping from names to numbers, rather than the other way around as with a list. In general, we would like to be able to map between arbitrary types of information. Table 5-4 lists a variety of linguistic objects, along with what they map.

Table 5-4. Linguistic objects as mappings from keys to values

Linguistic object	Maps from	Maps to
Document Index	Word	List of pages (where word is found)
Thesaurus	Word sense	List of synonyms
Dictionary	Headword	Entry (part-of-speech, sense definitions, etymology)
Comparative Wordlist	Gloss term	Cognates (list of words, one per language)
Morph Analyzer	Surface form	Morphological analysis (list of component morphemes)

Most often, we are mapping from a "word" to some structured object. For example, a document index maps from a word (which we can represent as a string) to a list of pages (represented as a list of integers). In this section, we will see how to represent such mappings in Python.

Dictionaries in Python

Python provides a **dictionary** data type that can be used for mapping between arbitrary types. It is like a conventional dictionary, in that it gives you an efficient way to look things up. However, as we see from Table 5-4, it has a much wider range of uses.

To illustrate, we define `pos` to be an empty dictionary and then add four entries to it, specifying the part-of-speech of some words. We add entries to a dictionary using the familiar square bracket notation:

```
>>> pos = {}
>>> pos
{}
>>> pos['colorless'] = 'ADJ'  ❶
>>> pos
{'colorless': 'ADJ'}
>>> pos['ideas'] = 'N'
>>> pos['sleep'] = 'V'
>>> pos['furiously'] = 'ADV'
>>> pos  ❷
{'furiously': 'ADV', 'ideas': 'N', 'colorless': 'ADJ', 'sleep': 'V'}
```

So, for example, ❶ says that the part-of-speech of *colorless* is adjective, or more specifically, that the **key** `'colorless'` is assigned the **value** `'ADJ'` in dictionary `pos`. When we inspect the value of `pos` ❷ we see a set of key-value pairs. Once we have populated the dictionary in this way, we can employ the keys to retrieve values:

```
>>> pos['ideas']
'N'
>>> pos['colorless']
'ADJ'
```

Of course, we might accidentally use a key that hasn't been assigned a value.

```
>>> pos['green']
Traceback (most recent call last):
  File "<stdin>", line 1, in ?
KeyError: 'green'
```

This raises an important question. Unlike lists and strings, where we can use `len()` to work out which integers will be legal indexes, how do we work out the legal keys for a dictionary? If the dictionary is not too big, we can simply inspect its contents by evaluating the variable `pos`. As we saw earlier in line ❷, this gives us the key-value pairs. Notice that they are not in the same order they were originally entered; this is because dictionaries are not sequences but mappings (see Figure 5-3), and the keys are not inherently ordered.

Alternatively, to just find the keys, we can either convert the dictionary to a list ❶ or use the dictionary in a context where a list is expected, as the parameter of `sorted()` ❷ or in a `for` loop ❸.

```
>>> list(pos)  ❶
['ideas', 'furiously', 'colorless', 'sleep']
>>> sorted(pos)  ❷
['colorless', 'furiously', 'ideas', 'sleep']
>>> [w for w in pos if w.endswith('s')]  ❸
['colorless', 'ideas']
```

When you type list(pos), you might see a different order to the one shown here. If you want to see the keys in order, just sort them.

As well as iterating over all keys in the dictionary with a `for` loop, we can use the `for` loop as we did for printing lists:

```
>>> for word in sorted(pos):
...     print word + ":", pos[word]
...
colorless: ADJ
furiously: ADV
sleep: V
ideas: N
```

Finally, the dictionary methods `keys()`, `values()`, and `items()` allow us to access the keys, values, and key-value pairs as separate lists. We can even sort tuples ❶, which orders them according to their first element (and if the first elements are the same, it uses their second elements).

```
>>> pos.keys()
['colorless', 'furiously', 'sleep', 'ideas']
>>> pos.values()
['ADJ', 'ADV', 'V', 'N']
>>> pos.items()
[('colorless', 'ADJ'), ('furiously', 'ADV'), ('sleep', 'V'), ('ideas', 'N')]
>>> for key, val in sorted(pos.items()): ❶
...     print key + ":", val
...
colorless: ADJ
furiously: ADV
ideas: N
sleep: V
```

We want to be sure that when we look something up in a dictionary, we get only one value for each key. Now suppose we try to use a dictionary to store the fact that the word *sleep* can be used as both a verb and a noun:

```
>>> pos['sleep'] = 'V'
>>> pos['sleep']
'V'
>>> pos['sleep'] = 'N'
>>> pos['sleep']
'N'
```

Initially, `pos['sleep']` is given the value `'V'`. But this is immediately overwritten with the new value, `'N'`. In other words, there can be only one entry in the dictionary for `'sleep'`. However, there is a way of storing multiple values in that entry: we use a list value, e.g., `pos['sleep'] = ['N', 'V']`. In fact, this is what we saw in Section 2.4 for the CMU Pronouncing Dictionary, which stores multiple pronunciations for a single word.

Defining Dictionaries

We can use the same key-value pair format to create a dictionary. There are a couple of ways to do this, and we will normally use the first:

```
>>> pos = {'colorless': 'ADJ', 'ideas': 'N', 'sleep': 'V', 'furiously': 'ADV'}
>>> pos = dict(colorless='ADJ', ideas='N', sleep='V', furiously='ADV')
```

Note that dictionary keys must be immutable types, such as strings and tuples. If we try to define a dictionary using a mutable key, we get a `TypeError`:

```
>>> pos = {['ideas', 'blogs', 'adventures']: 'N'}
Traceback (most recent call last):
  File "<stdin>", line 1, in <module>
TypeError: list objects are unhashable
```

Default Dictionaries

If we try to access a key that is not in a dictionary, we get an error. However, it's often useful if a dictionary can automatically create an entry for this new key and give it a default value, such as zero or the empty list. Since Python 2.5, a special kind of dictionary called a `defaultdict` has been available. (It is provided as `nltk.defaultdict` for the benefit of readers who are using Python 2.4.) In order to use it, we have to supply a parameter which can be used to create the default value, e.g., `int`, `float`, `str`, `list`, `dict`, `tuple`.

```
>>> frequency = nltk.defaultdict(int)
>>> frequency['colorless'] = 4
>>> frequency['ideas']
0
>>> pos = nltk.defaultdict(list)
>>> pos['sleep'] = ['N', 'V']
>>> pos['ideas']
[]
```

> These default values are actually functions that convert other objects to the specified type (e.g., `int("2")`, `list("2")`). When they are called with no parameter—say, `int()`, `list()`—they return `0` and `[]` respectively.

The preceding examples specified the default value of a dictionary entry to be the default value of a particular data type. However, we can specify any default value we like, simply by providing the name of a function that can be called with no arguments to create the required value. Let's return to our part-of-speech example, and create a dictionary whose default value for any entry is `'N'` ❶. When we access a non-existent entry ❷, it is automatically added to the dictionary ❸.

```
>>> pos = nltk.defaultdict(lambda: 'N')  ❶
>>> pos['colorless'] = 'ADJ'
>>> pos['blog']  ❷
'N'
```

```
>>> pos.items()
[('blog', 'N'), ('colorless', 'ADJ')]
```
❸

 This example used a *lambda expression*, introduced in Section 4.4. This lambda expression specifies no parameters, so we call it using parentheses with no arguments. Thus, the following definitions of f and g are equivalent:

```
>>> f = lambda: 'N'
>>> f()
'N'
>>> def g():
...     return 'N'
>>> g()
'N'
```

Let's see how default dictionaries could be used in a more substantial language processing task. Many language processing tasks—including tagging—struggle to correctly process the hapaxes of a text. They can perform better with a fixed vocabulary and a guarantee that no new words will appear. We can preprocess a text to replace low-frequency words with a special "out of vocabulary" token, UNK, with the help of a default dictionary. (Can you work out how to do this without reading on?)

We need to create a default dictionary that maps each word to its replacement. The most frequent *n* words will be mapped to themselves. Everything else will be mapped to UNK.

```
>>> alice = nltk.corpus.gutenberg.words('carroll-alice.txt')
>>> vocab = nltk.FreqDist(alice)
>>> v1000 = list(vocab)[:1000]
>>> mapping = nltk.defaultdict(lambda: 'UNK')
>>> for v in v1000:
...     mapping[v] = v
...
>>> alice2 = [mapping[v] for v in alice]
>>> alice2[:100]
['UNK', 'Alice', "'", 's', 'Adventures', 'in', 'Wonderland', 'by', 'UNK', 'UNK',
'UNK', 'UNK', 'CHAPTER', 'I', '.', 'UNK', 'the', 'Rabbit', '-', 'UNK', 'Alice',
'was', 'beginning', 'to', 'get', 'very', 'tired', 'of', 'sitting', 'by', 'her',
'sister', 'on', 'the', 'bank', ',', 'and', 'of', 'having', 'nothing', 'to', 'do',
':', 'once', 'or', 'twice', 'she', 'had', 'UNK', 'into', 'the', 'book', 'her',
'sister', 'was', 'UNK', ',', 'but', 'it', 'had', 'no', 'pictures', 'or', 'UNK',
'in', 'it', ',', "'", 'and', 'what', 'is', 'the', 'use', 'of', 'a', 'book', ',', "'",
'thought', 'Alice', "'", 'without', 'pictures', 'or', 'conversation', "?'", ...]
>>> len(set(alice2))
1001
```

Incrementally Updating a Dictionary

We can employ dictionaries to count occurrences, emulating the method for tallying words shown in Figure 1-3. We begin by initializing an empty defaultdict, then process each part-of-speech tag in the text. If the tag hasn't been seen before, it will have a zero count by default. Each time we encounter a tag, we increment its count using the `+=` operator (see Example 5-3).

Example 5-3. Incrementally updating a dictionary, and sorting by value.

```
>>> counts = nltk.defaultdict(int)
>>> from nltk.corpus import brown
>>> for (word, tag) in brown.tagged_words(categories='news'):
...     counts[tag] += 1
...
>>> counts['N']
22226
>>> list(counts)
['FW', 'DET', 'WH', "'", 'VBZ', 'VB+PPO', "'", ')', 'ADJ', 'PRO', '*', '-', ...]

>>> from operator import itemgetter
>>> sorted(counts.items(), key=itemgetter(1), reverse=True)
[('N', 22226), ('P', 10845), ('DET', 10648), ('NP', 8336), ('V', 7313), ...]
>>> [t for t, c in sorted(counts.items(), key=itemgetter(1), reverse=True)]
['N', 'P', 'DET', 'NP', 'V', 'ADJ', ',', '.', 'CNJ', 'PRO', 'ADV', 'VD', ...]
```

The listing in Example 5-3 illustrates an important idiom for sorting a dictionary by its values, to show words in decreasing order of frequency. The first parameter of `sorted()` is the items to sort, which is a list of tuples consisting of a POS tag and a frequency. The second parameter specifies the sort key using a function `itemgetter()`. In general, `itemgetter(n)` returns a function that can be called on some other sequence object to obtain the *n*th element:

```
>>> pair = ('NP', 8336)
>>> pair[1]
8336
>>> itemgetter(1)(pair)
8336
```

The last parameter of `sorted()` specifies that the items should be returned in reverse order, i.e., decreasing values of frequency.

There's a second useful programming idiom at the beginning of Example 5-3, where we initialize a `defaultdict` and then use a `for` loop to update its values. Here's a schematic version:

```
>>> my_dictionary = nltk.defaultdict(function to create default value)
>>> for item in sequence:
...     my_dictionary[item_key] is updated with information about item
```

Here's another instance of this pattern, where we index words according to their last two letters:

```
>>> last_letters = nltk.defaultdict(list)
>>> words = nltk.corpus.words.words('en')
>>> for word in words:
...     key = word[-2:]
...     last_letters[key].append(word)
...
```

```
>>> last_letters['ly']
['abactinally', 'abandonedly', 'abasedly', 'abashedly', 'abashlessly', 'abbreviately',
'abdominally', 'abhorrently', 'abidingly', 'abiogenetically', 'abiologically', ...]
>>> last_letters['zy']
['blazy', 'bleezy', 'blowzy', 'boozy', 'breezy', 'bronzy', 'buzzy', 'Chazy', ...]
```

The following example uses the same pattern to create an anagram dictionary. (You might experiment with the third line to get an idea of why this program works.)

```
>>> anagrams = nltk.defaultdict(list)
>>> for word in words:
...     key = ''.join(sorted(word))
...     anagrams[key].append(word)
...
>>> anagrams['aeilnrt']
['entrail', 'latrine', 'ratline', 'reliant', 'retinal', 'trenail']
```

Since accumulating words like this is such a common task, NLTK provides a more convenient way of creating a `defaultdict(list)`, in the form of `nltk.Index()`:

```
>>> anagrams = nltk.Index((''.join(sorted(w)), w) for w in words)
>>> anagrams['aeilnrt']
['entrail', 'latrine', 'ratline', 'reliant', 'retinal', 'trenail']
```

> `nltk.Index` is a `defaultdict(list)` with extra support for initialization. Similarly, `nltk.FreqDist` is essentially a `defaultdict(int)` with extra support for initialization (along with sorting and plotting methods).

Complex Keys and Values

We can use default dictionaries with complex keys and values. Let's study the range of possible tags for a word, given the word itself and the tag of the previous word. We will see how this information can be used by a POS tagger.

```
>>> pos = nltk.defaultdict(lambda: nltk.defaultdict(int))
>>> brown_news_tagged = brown.tagged_words(categories='news', simplify_tags=True)
>>> for ((w1, t1), (w2, t2)) in nltk.ibigrams(brown_news_tagged): ❶
...     pos[(t1, w2)][t2] += 1 ❷
...
>>> pos[('DET', 'right')] ❸
defaultdict(<type 'int'>, {'ADV': 3, 'ADJ': 9, 'N': 3})
```

This example uses a dictionary whose default value for an entry is a dictionary (whose default value is `int()`, i.e., zero). Notice how we iterated over the bigrams of the tagged corpus, processing a pair of word-tag pairs for each iteration ❶. Each time through the loop we updated our `pos` dictionary's entry for (`t1`, `w2`), a tag and its *following* word ❷. When we look up an item in `pos` we must specify a compound key ❸, and we get back a dictionary object. A POS tagger could use such information to decide that the word *right*, when preceded by a determiner, should be tagged as `ADJ`.

Inverting a Dictionary

Dictionaries support efficient lookup, so long as you want to get the value for any key. If d is a dictionary and k is a key, we type d[k] and immediately obtain the value. Finding a key given a value is slower and more cumbersome:

```
>>> counts = nltk.defaultdict(int)
>>> for word in nltk.corpus.gutenberg.words('milton-paradise.txt'):
...     counts[word] += 1
...
>>> [key for (key, value) in counts.items() if value == 32]
['brought', 'Him', 'virtue', 'Against', 'There', 'thine', 'King', 'mortal',
'every', 'been']
```

If we expect to do this kind of "reverse lookup" often, it helps to construct a dictionary that maps values to keys. In the case that no two keys have the same value, this is an easy thing to do. We just get all the key-value pairs in the dictionary, and create a new dictionary of value-key pairs. The next example also illustrates another way of initializing a dictionary pos with key-value pairs.

```
>>> pos = {'colorless': 'ADJ', 'ideas': 'N', 'sleep': 'V', 'furiously': 'ADV'}
>>> pos2 = dict((value, key) for (key, value) in pos.items())
>>> pos2['N']
'ideas'
```

Let's first make our part-of-speech dictionary a bit more realistic and add some more words to pos using the dictionary update() method, to create the situation where multiple keys have the same value. Then the technique just shown for reverse lookup will no longer work (why not?). Instead, we have to use append() to accumulate the words for each part-of-speech, as follows:

```
>>> pos.update({'cats': 'N', 'scratch': 'V', 'peacefully': 'ADV', 'old': 'ADJ'})
>>> pos2 = nltk.defaultdict(list)
>>> for key, value in pos.items():
...     pos2[value].append(key)
...
>>> pos2['ADV']
['peacefully', 'furiously']
```

Now we have inverted the pos dictionary, and can look up any part-of-speech and find all words having that part-of-speech. We can do the same thing even more simply using NLTK's support for indexing, as follows:

```
>>> pos2 = nltk.Index((value, key) for (key, value) in pos.items())
>>> pos2['ADV']
['peacefully', 'furiously']
```

A summary of Python's dictionary methods is given in Table 5-5.

Table 5-5. Python's dictionary methods: A summary of commonly used methods and idioms involving dictionaries

Example	Description
`d = {}`	Create an empty dictionary and assign it to d
`d[key] = value`	Assign a value to a given dictionary key
`d.keys()`	The list of keys of the dictionary
`list(d)`	The list of keys of the dictionary
`sorted(d)`	The keys of the dictionary, sorted
`key in d`	Test whether a particular key is in the dictionary
`for key in d`	Iterate over the keys of the dictionary
`d.values()`	The list of values in the dictionary
`dict([(k1,v1), (k2,v2), ...])`	Create a dictionary from a list of key-value pairs
`d1.update(d2)`	Add all items from d2 to d1
`defaultdict(int)`	A dictionary whose default value is zero

5.4 Automatic Tagging

In the rest of this chapter we will explore various ways to automatically add part-of-speech tags to text. We will see that the tag of a word depends on the word and its context within a sentence. For this reason, we will be working with data at the level of (tagged) sentences rather than words. We'll begin by loading the data we will be using.

```
>>> from nltk.corpus import brown
>>> brown_tagged_sents = brown.tagged_sents(categories='news')
>>> brown_sents = brown.sents(categories='news')
```

The Default Tagger

The simplest possible tagger assigns the same tag to each token. This may seem to be a rather banal step, but it establishes an important baseline for tagger performance. In order to get the best result, we tag each word with the most likely tag. Let's find out which tag is most likely (now using the unsimplified tagset):

```
>>> tags = [tag for (word, tag) in brown.tagged_words(categories='news')]
>>> nltk.FreqDist(tags).max()
'NN'
```

Now we can create a tagger that tags everything as NN.

```
>>> raw = 'I do not like green eggs and ham, I do not like them Sam I am!'
>>> tokens = nltk.word_tokenize(raw)
>>> default_tagger = nltk.DefaultTagger('NN')
>>> default_tagger.tag(tokens)
[('I', 'NN'), ('do', 'NN'), ('not', 'NN'), ('like', 'NN'), ('green', 'NN'),
('eggs', 'NN'), ('and', 'NN'), ('ham', 'NN'), (',', 'NN'), ('I', 'NN'),
```

```
('do', 'NN'), ('not', 'NN'), ('like', 'NN'), ('them', 'NN'), ('Sam', 'NN'),
('I', 'NN'), ('am', 'NN'), ('!', 'NN')]
```

Unsurprisingly, this method performs rather poorly. On a typical corpus, it will tag only about an eighth of the tokens correctly, as we see here:

```
>>> default_tagger.evaluate(brown_tagged_sents)
0.13089484257215028
```

Default taggers assign their tag to every single word, even words that have never been encountered before. As it happens, once we have processed several thousand words of English text, most new words will be nouns. As we will see, this means that default taggers can help to improve the robustness of a language processing system. We will return to them shortly.

The Regular Expression Tagger

The regular expression tagger assigns tags to tokens on the basis of matching patterns. For instance, we might guess that any word ending in *ed* is the past participle of a verb, and any word ending with *'s* is a possessive noun. We can express these as a list of regular expressions:

```
>>> patterns = [
...     (r'.*ing$', 'VBG'),              # gerunds
...     (r'.*ed$', 'VBD'),               # simple past
...     (r'.*es$', 'VBZ'),               # 3rd singular present
...     (r'.*ould$', 'MD'),              # modals
...     (r'.*\'s$', 'NN$'),              # possessive nouns
...     (r'.*s$', 'NNS'),                # plural nouns
...     (r'^-?[0-9]+(.[0-9]+)?$', 'CD'), # cardinal numbers
...     (r'.*', 'NN')                    # nouns (default)
... ]
```

Note that these are processed in order, and the first one that matches is applied. Now we can set up a tagger and use it to tag a sentence. After this step, it is correct about a fifth of the time.

```
>>> regexp_tagger = nltk.RegexpTagger(patterns)
>>> regexp_tagger.tag(brown_sents[3])
[('``', 'NN'), ('Only', 'NN'), ('a', 'NN'), ('relative', 'NN'), ('handful', 'NN'),
('of', 'NN'), ('such', 'NN'), ('reports', 'NNS'), ('was', 'NNS'), ('received', 'VBD'),
("'", 'NN'), (',', 'NN'), ('the', 'NN'), ('jury', 'NN'), ('said', 'NN'), (',', 'NN'),
('``', 'NN'), ('considering', 'VBG'), ('the', 'NN'), ('widespread', 'NN'), ...]
>>> regexp_tagger.evaluate(brown_tagged_sents)
0.20326391789486245
```

The final regular expression «.*» is a catch-all that tags everything as a noun. This is equivalent to the default tagger (only much less efficient). Instead of respecifying this as part of the regular expression tagger, is there a way to combine this tagger with the default tagger? We will see how to do this shortly.

Your Turn: See if you can come up with patterns to improve the performance of the regular expression tagger just shown. (Note that Section 6.1 describes a way to partially automate such work.)

The Lookup Tagger

A lot of high-frequency words do not have the NN tag. Let's find the hundred most frequent words and store their most likely tag. We can then use this information as the model for a "lookup tagger" (an NLTK UnigramTagger):

```
>>> fd = nltk.FreqDist(brown.words(categories='news'))
>>> cfd = nltk.ConditionalFreqDist(brown.tagged_words(categories='news'))
>>> most_freq_words = fd.keys()[:100]
>>> likely_tags = dict((word, cfd[word].max()) for word in most_freq_words)
>>> baseline_tagger = nltk.UnigramTagger(model=likely_tags)
>>> baseline_tagger.evaluate(brown_tagged_sents)
0.45578495136941344
```

It should come as no surprise by now that simply knowing the tags for the 100 most frequent words enables us to tag a large fraction of tokens correctly (nearly half, in fact). Let's see what it does on some untagged input text:

```
>>> sent = brown.sents(categories='news')[3]
>>> baseline_tagger.tag(sent)
[('``', '``'), ('Only', None), ('a', 'AT'), ('relative', None),
('handful', None), ('of', 'IN'), ('such', None), ('reports', None),
('was', 'BEDZ'), ('received', None), ("''", "''"), (',', ','),
('the', 'AT'), ('jury', None), ('said', 'VBD'), (',', ','),
('``', '``'), ('considering', None), ('the', 'AT'), ('widespread', None),
('interest', None), ('in', 'IN'), ('the', 'AT'), ('election', None),
(',', ','), ('the', 'AT'), ('number', None), ('of', 'IN'),
('voters', None), ('and', 'CC'), ('the', 'AT'), ('size', None),
('of', 'IN'), ('this', 'DT'), ('city', None), ("''", "''"), ('.', '.')]
```

Many words have been assigned a tag of None, because they were not among the 100 most frequent words. In these cases we would like to assign the default tag of NN. In other words, we want to use the lookup table first, and if it is unable to assign a tag, then use the default tagger, a process known as **backoff** (Section 5.5). We do this by specifying one tagger as a parameter to the other, as shown next. Now the lookup tagger will only store word-tag pairs for words other than nouns, and whenever it cannot assign a tag to a word, it will invoke the default tagger.

```
>>> baseline_tagger = nltk.UnigramTagger(model=likely_tags,
...                                      backoff=nltk.DefaultTagger('NN'))
```

Let's put all this together and write a program to create and evaluate lookup taggers having a range of sizes (Example 5-4).

Example 5-4. Lookup tagger performance with varying model size.

```
def performance(cfd, wordlist):
    lt = dict((word, cfd[word].max()) for word in wordlist)
    baseline_tagger = nltk.UnigramTagger(model=lt, backoff=nltk.DefaultTagger('NN'))
    return baseline_tagger.evaluate(brown.tagged_sents(categories='news'))

def display():
    import pylab
    words_by_freq = list(nltk.FreqDist(brown.words(categories='news')))
    cfd = nltk.ConditionalFreqDist(brown.tagged_words(categories='news'))
    sizes = 2 ** pylab.arange(15)
    perfs = [performance(cfd, words_by_freq[:size]) for size in sizes]
    pylab.plot(sizes, perfs, '-bo')
    pylab.title('Lookup Tagger Performance with Varying Model Size')
    pylab.xlabel('Model Size')
    pylab.ylabel('Performance')
    pylab.show()
>>> display()
```

Observe in Figure 5-4 that performance initially increases rapidly as the model size grows, eventually reaching a plateau, when large increases in model size yield little improvement in performance. (This example used the `pylab` plotting package, discussed in Section 4.8.)

Evaluation

In the previous examples, you will have noticed an emphasis on accuracy scores. In fact, evaluating the performance of such tools is a central theme in NLP. Recall the processing pipeline in Figure 1-5; any errors in the output of one module are greatly multiplied in the downstream modules.

We evaluate the performance of a tagger relative to the tags a human expert would assign. Since we usually don't have access to an expert and impartial human judge, we make do instead with **gold standard** test data. This is a corpus which has been manually annotated and accepted as a standard against which the guesses of an automatic system are assessed. The tagger is regarded as being correct if the tag it guesses for a given word is the same as the gold standard tag.

Of course, the humans who designed and carried out the original gold standard annotation were only human. Further analysis might show mistakes in the gold standard, or may eventually lead to a revised tagset and more elaborate guidelines. Nevertheless, the gold standard is by definition "correct" as far as the evaluation of an automatic tagger is concerned.

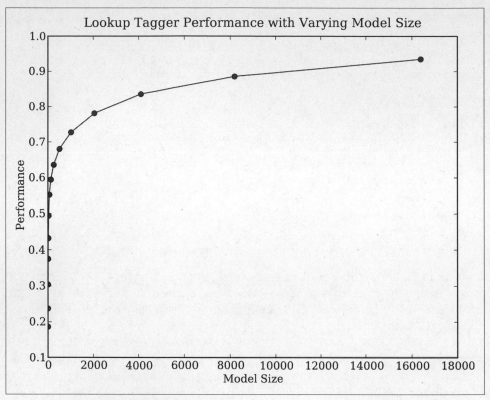

Figure 5-4. Lookup tagger

 Developing an annotated corpus is a major undertaking. Apart from the data, it generates sophisticated tools, documentation, and practices for ensuring high-quality annotation. The tagsets and other coding schemes inevitably depend on some theoretical position that is not shared by all. However, corpus creators often go to great lengths to make their work as theory-neutral as possible in order to maximize the usefulness of their work. We will discuss the challenges of creating a corpus in Chapter 11.

5.5 N-Gram Tagging

Unigram Tagging

Unigram taggers are based on a simple statistical algorithm: for each token, assign the tag that is most likely for that particular token. For example, it will assign the tag JJ to any occurrence of the word *frequent*, since *frequent* is used as an adjective (e.g., *a frequent word*) more often than it is used as a verb (e.g., *I frequent this cafe*). A unigram tagger behaves just like a lookup tagger (Section 5.4), except there is a more convenient technique for setting it up, called **training**. In the following code sample, we train a unigram tagger, use it to tag a sentence, and then evaluate:

```
>>> from nltk.corpus import brown
>>> brown_tagged_sents = brown.tagged_sents(categories='news')
>>> brown_sents = brown.sents(categories='news')
>>> unigram_tagger = nltk.UnigramTagger(brown_tagged_sents)
>>> unigram_tagger.tag(brown_sents[2007])
[('Various', 'JJ'), ('of', 'IN'), ('the', 'AT'), ('apartments', 'NNS'),
('are', 'BER'), ('of', 'IN'), ('the', 'AT'), ('terrace', 'NN'), ('type', 'NN'),
(',', ','), ('being', 'BEG'), ('on', 'IN'), ('the', 'AT'), ('ground', 'NN'),
('floor', 'NN'), ('so', 'QL'), ('that', 'CS'), ('entrance', 'NN'), ('is', 'BEZ'),
('direct', 'JJ'), ('.', '.')]
>>> unigram_tagger.evaluate(brown_tagged_sents)
0.9349006503968017
```

We **train** a UnigramTagger by specifying tagged sentence data as a parameter when we initialize the tagger. The training process involves inspecting the tag of each word and storing the most likely tag for any word in a dictionary that is stored inside the tagger.

Separating the Training and Testing Data

Now that we are training a tagger on some data, we must be careful not to test it on the same data, as we did in the previous example. A tagger that simply memorized its training data and made no attempt to construct a general model would get a perfect score, but would be useless for tagging new text. Instead, we should split the data, training on 90% and testing on the remaining 10%:

```
>>> size = int(len(brown_tagged_sents) * 0.9)
>>> size
4160
>>> train_sents = brown_tagged_sents[:size]
>>> test_sents = brown_tagged_sents[size:]
>>> unigram_tagger = nltk.UnigramTagger(train_sents)
>>> unigram_tagger.evaluate(test_sents)
0.81202033290142528
```

Although the score is worse, we now have a better picture of the usefulness of this tagger, i.e., its performance on previously unseen text.

General N-Gram Tagging

When we perform a language processing task based on unigrams, we are using one item of context. In the case of tagging, we consider only the current token, in isolation from any larger context. Given such a model, the best we can do is tag each word with its *a priori* most likely tag. This means we would tag a word such as *wind* with the same tag, regardless of whether it appears in the context *the wind* or *to wind*.

An **n-gram tagger** is a generalization of a unigram tagger whose context is the current word together with the part-of-speech tags of the $n-1$ preceding tokens, as shown in Figure 5-5. The tag to be chosen, t_n, is circled, and the context is shaded in grey. In the example of an n-gram tagger shown in Figure 5-5, we have $n=3$; that is, we consider

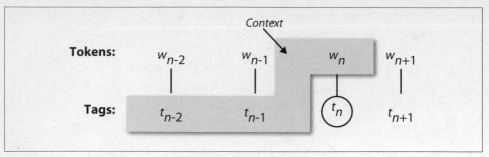

Figure 5-5. Tagger context.

the tags of the two preceding words in addition to the current word. An n-gram tagger picks the tag that is most likely in the given context.

 A 1-gram tagger is another term for a unigram tagger: i.e., the context used to tag a token is just the text of the token itself. 2-gram taggers are also called *bigram taggers*, and 3-gram taggers are called *trigram taggers*.

The NgramTagger class uses a tagged training corpus to determine which part-of-speech tag is most likely for each context. Here we see a special case of an n-gram tagger, namely a bigram tagger. First we train it, then use it to tag untagged sentences:

```
>>> bigram_tagger = nltk.BigramTagger(train_sents)
>>> bigram_tagger.tag(brown_sents[2007])
[('Various', 'JJ'), ('of', 'IN'), ('the', 'AT'), ('apartments', 'NNS'),
('are', 'BER'), ('of', 'IN'), ('the', 'AT'), ('terrace', 'NN'),
('type', 'NN'), (',', ','), ('being', 'BEG'), ('on', 'IN'), ('the', 'AT'),
('ground', 'NN'), ('floor', 'NN'), ('so', 'CS'), ('that', 'CS'),
('entrance', 'NN'), ('is', 'BEZ'), ('direct', 'JJ'), ('.', '.')]
>>> unseen_sent = brown_sents[4203]
>>> bigram_tagger.tag(unseen_sent)
[('The', 'AT'), ('population', 'NN'), ('of', 'IN'), ('the', 'AT'), ('Congo', 'NP'),
('is', 'BEZ'), ('13.5', None), ('million', None), (',', None), ('divided', None),
('into', None), ('at', None), ('least', None), ('seven', None), ('major', None),
('``', None), ('culture', None), ('clusters', None), ("'''", None), ('and', None),
('innumerable', None), ('tribes', None), ('speaking', None), ('400', None),
('separate', None), ('dialects', None), ('.', None)]
```

Notice that the bigram tagger manages to tag every word in a sentence it saw during training, but does badly on an unseen sentence. As soon as it encounters a new word (i.e., *13.5*), it is unable to assign a tag. It cannot tag the following word (i.e., *million*), even if it was seen during training, simply because it never saw it during training with a None tag on the previous word. Consequently, the tagger fails to tag the rest of the sentence. Its overall accuracy score is very low:

```
>>> bigram_tagger.evaluate(test_sents)
0.10276088906608193
```

As *n* gets larger, the specificity of the contexts increases, as does the chance that the data we wish to tag contains contexts that were not present in the training data. This is known as the *sparse data* problem, and is quite pervasive in NLP. As a consequence, there is a trade-off between the accuracy and the coverage of our results (and this is related to the **precision/recall trade-off** in information retrieval).

 Caution!

N-gram taggers should not consider context that crosses a sentence boundary. Accordingly, NLTK taggers are designed to work with lists of sentences, where each sentence is a list of words. At the start of a sentence, t_{n-1} and preceding tags are set to None.

Combining Taggers

One way to address the trade-off between accuracy and coverage is to use the more accurate algorithms when we can, but to fall back on algorithms with wider coverage when necessary. For example, we could combine the results of a bigram tagger, a unigram tagger, and a default tagger, as follows:

1. Try tagging the token with the bigram tagger.
2. If the bigram tagger is unable to find a tag for the token, try the unigram tagger.
3. If the unigram tagger is also unable to find a tag, use a default tagger.

Most NLTK taggers permit a backoff tagger to be specified. The backoff tagger may itself have a backoff tagger:

```
>>> t0 = nltk.DefaultTagger('NN')
>>> t1 = nltk.UnigramTagger(train_sents, backoff=t0)
>>> t2 = nltk.BigramTagger(train_sents, backoff=t1)
>>> t2.evaluate(test_sents)
0.84491179108940495
```

 Your Turn: Extend the preceding example by defining a TrigramTagger called t3, which backs off to t2.

Note that we specify the backoff tagger when the tagger is initialized so that training can take advantage of the backoff tagger. Thus, if the bigram tagger would assign the same tag as its unigram backoff tagger in a certain context, the bigram tagger discards the training instance. This keeps the bigram tagger model as small as possible. We can further specify that a tagger needs to see more than one instance of a context in order to retain it. For example, nltk.BigramTagger(sents, cutoff=2, backoff=t1) will discard contexts that have only been seen once or twice.

Tagging Unknown Words

Our approach to tagging unknown words still uses backoff to a regular expression tagger or a default tagger. These are unable to make use of context. Thus, if our tagger encountered the word *blog*, not seen during training, it would assign it the same tag, regardless of whether this word appeared in the context *the blog* or *to blog*. How can we do better with these unknown words, or **out-of-vocabulary** items?

A useful method to tag unknown words based on context is to limit the vocabulary of a tagger to the most frequent *n* words, and to replace every other word with a special word *UNK* using the method shown in Section 5.3. During training, a unigram tagger will probably learn that *UNK* is usually a noun. However, the n-gram taggers will detect contexts in which it has some other tag. For example, if the preceding word is *to* (tagged TO), then *UNK* will probably be tagged as a verb.

Storing Taggers

Training a tagger on a large corpus may take a significant time. Instead of training a tagger every time we need one, it is convenient to save a trained tagger in a file for later reuse. Let's save our tagger t2 to a file *t2.pkl*:

```
>>> from cPickle import dump
>>> output = open('t2.pkl', 'wb')
>>> dump(t2, output, -1)
>>> output.close()
```

Now, in a separate Python process, we can load our saved tagger:

```
>>> from cPickle import load
>>> input = open('t2.pkl', 'rb')
>>> tagger = load(input)
>>> input.close()
```

Now let's check that it can be used for tagging:

```
>>> text = """The board's action shows what free enterprise
...     is up against in our complex maze of regulatory laws ."""
>>> tokens = text.split()
>>> tagger.tag(tokens)
[('The', 'AT'), ("board's", 'NN$'), ('action', 'NN'), ('shows', 'NNS'),
('what', 'WDT'), ('free', 'JJ'), ('enterprise', 'NN'), ('is', 'BEZ'),
('up', 'RP'), ('against', 'IN'), ('in', 'IN'), ('our', 'PP$'), ('complex', 'JJ'),
('maze', 'NN'), ('of', 'IN'), ('regulatory', 'NN'), ('laws', 'NNS'), ('.', '.')]
```

Performance Limitations

What is the upper limit to the performance of an n-gram tagger? Consider the case of a trigram tagger. How many cases of part-of-speech ambiguity does it encounter? We can determine the answer to this question empirically:

```
>>> cfd = nltk.ConditionalFreqDist(
...           ((x[1], y[1], z[0]), z[1])
...           for sent in brown_tagged_sents
...           for x, y, z in nltk.trigrams(sent))
>>> ambiguous_contexts = [c for c in cfd.conditions() if len(cfd[c]) > 1]
>>> sum(cfd[c].N() for c in ambiguous_contexts) / cfd.N()
0.049297702068029296
```

Thus, 1 out of 20 trigrams is ambiguous. Given the current word and the previous two tags, in 5% of cases there is more than one tag that could be legitimately assigned to the current word according to the training data. Assuming we always pick the most likely tag in such ambiguous contexts, we can derive a lower bound on the performance of a trigram tagger.

Another way to investigate the performance of a tagger is to study its mistakes. Some tags may be harder than others to assign, and it might be possible to treat them specially by pre- or post-processing the data. A convenient way to look at tagging errors is the **confusion matrix**. It charts expected tags (the gold standard) against actual tags generated by a tagger:

```
>>> test_tags = [tag for sent in brown.sents(categories='editorial')
...               for (word, tag) in t2.tag(sent)]
>>> gold_tags = [tag for (word, tag) in brown.tagged_words(categories='editorial')]
>>> print nltk.ConfusionMatrix(gold, test)
```

Based on such analysis we may decide to modify the tagset. Perhaps a distinction between tags that is difficult to make can be dropped, since it is not important in the context of some larger processing task.

Another way to analyze the performance bound on a tagger comes from the less than 100% agreement between human annotators.

In general, observe that the tagging process collapses distinctions: e.g., lexical identity is usually lost when all personal pronouns are tagged PRP. At the same time, the tagging process introduces new distinctions and removes ambiguities: e.g., *deal* tagged as VB or NN. This characteristic of collapsing certain distinctions and introducing new distinctions is an important feature of tagging which facilitates classification and prediction. When we introduce finer distinctions in a tagset, an n-gram tagger gets more detailed information about the left-context when it is deciding what tag to assign to a particular word. However, the tagger simultaneously has to do more work to classify the current token, simply because there are more tags to choose from. Conversely, with fewer distinctions (as with the simplified tagset), the tagger has less information about context, and it has a smaller range of choices in classifying the current token.

We have seen that ambiguity in the training data leads to an upper limit in tagger performance. Sometimes more context will resolve the ambiguity. In other cases, however, as noted by (Abney, 1996), the ambiguity can be resolved only with reference to syntax or to world knowledge. Despite these imperfections, part-of-speech tagging has played a central role in the rise of statistical approaches to natural language processing. In the early 1990s, the surprising accuracy of statistical taggers was a striking demonstration that it was possible to solve one small part of the language understanding problem, namely part-of-speech disambiguation, without reference to deeper sources of linguistic knowledge. Can this idea be pushed further? In Chapter 7, we will see that it can.

Tagging Across Sentence Boundaries

An n-gram tagger uses recent tags to guide the choice of tag for the current word. When tagging the first word of a sentence, a trigram tagger will be using the part-of-speech tag of the previous two tokens, which will normally be the last word of the previous sentence and the sentence-ending punctuation. However, the lexical category that closed the previous sentence has no bearing on the one that begins the next sentence.

To deal with this situation, we can train, run, and evaluate taggers using lists of tagged sentences, as shown in Example 5-5.

Example 5-5. N-gram tagging at the sentence level.

```
brown_tagged_sents = brown.tagged_sents(categories='news')
brown_sents = brown.sents(categories='news')

size = int(len(brown_tagged_sents) * 0.9)
train_sents = brown_tagged_sents[:size]
test_sents = brown_tagged_sents[size:]

t0 = nltk.DefaultTagger('NN')
t1 = nltk.UnigramTagger(train_sents, backoff=t0)
t2 = nltk.BigramTagger(train_sents, backoff=t1)

>>> t2.evaluate(test_sents)
0.84491179108940495
```

5.6 Transformation-Based Tagging

A potential issue with n-gram taggers is the size of their n-gram table (or language model). If tagging is to be employed in a variety of language technologies deployed on mobile computing devices, it is important to strike a balance between model size and tagger performance. An n-gram tagger with backoff may store trigram and bigram tables, which are large, sparse arrays that may have hundreds of millions of entries.

A second issue concerns context. The only information an n-gram tagger considers from prior context is tags, even though words themselves might be a useful source of information. It is simply impractical for n-gram models to be conditioned on the identities of words in the context. In this section, we examine Brill tagging, an inductive tagging method which performs very well using models that are only a tiny fraction of the size of n-gram taggers.

Brill tagging is a kind of *transformation-based learning*, named after its inventor. The general idea is very simple: guess the tag of each word, then go back and fix the mistakes.

In this way, a Brill tagger successively transforms a bad tagging of a text into a better one. As with n-gram tagging, this is a *supervised learning* method, since we need annotated training data to figure out whether the tagger's guess is a mistake or not. However, unlike n-gram tagging, it does not count observations but compiles a list of transformational correction rules.

The process of Brill tagging is usually explained by analogy with painting. Suppose we were painting a tree, with all its details of boughs, branches, twigs, and leaves, against a uniform sky-blue background. Instead of painting the tree first and then trying to paint blue in the gaps, it is simpler to paint the whole canvas blue, then "correct" the tree section by over-painting the blue background. In the same fashion, we might paint the trunk a uniform brown before going back to over-paint further details with even finer brushes. Brill tagging uses the same idea: begin with broad brush strokes, and then fix up the details, with successively finer changes. Let's look at an example involving the following sentence:

(1) The President said he will ask Congress to increase grants to states for vocational rehabilitation.

We will examine the operation of two rules: (a) replace NN with VB when the previous word is TO; (b) replace TO with IN when the next tag is NNS. Table 5-6 illustrates this process, first tagging with the unigram tagger, then applying the rules to fix the errors.

Table 5-6. Steps in Brill tagging

Phrase	to	increase	grants	to	states	for	vocational	rehabilitation
Unigram	TO	*NN*	NNS	*TO*	NNS	IN	JJ	NN
Rule 1		*VB*						
Rule 2				*IN*				
Output	TO	VB	NNS	IN	NNS	IN	JJ	NN
Gold	TO	VB	NNS	IN	NNS	IN	JJ	NN

In this table, we see two rules. All such rules are generated from a template of the following form: "replace T_1 with T_2 in the context C." Typical contexts are the identity or the tag of the preceding or following word, or the appearance of a specific tag within two to three words of the current word. During its training phase, the tagger guesses values for T_1, T_2, and C, to create thousands of candidate rules. Each rule is scored according to its net benefit: the number of incorrect tags that it corrects, less the number of correct tags it incorrectly modifies.

Brill taggers have another interesting property: the rules are linguistically interpretable. Compare this with the n-gram taggers, which employ a potentially massive table of n-grams. We cannot learn much from direct inspection of such a table, in comparison to the rules learned by the Brill tagger. Example 5-6 demonstrates NLTK's Brill tagger.

Example 5-6. Brill tagger demonstration: The tagger has a collection of templates of the form X → Y if the preceding word is Z; the variables in these templates are instantiated to particular words and tags to create "rules"; the score for a rule is the number of broken examples it corrects minus the number of correct cases it breaks; apart from training a tagger, the demonstration displays residual errors.

```
>>> nltk.tag.brill.demo()
Training Brill tagger on 80 sentences...
Finding initial useful rules...
    Found 6555 useful rules.

          B   |
   S  F   r  0 |        Score = Fixed - Broken
   c  i   o  t | R      Fixed = num tags changed incorrect -> correct
   o  x   k  h | u      Broken = num tags changed correct -> incorrect
   r  e   e  e | l      Other = num tags changed incorrect -> incorrect
   e  d   n  r | e
------------------+---------------------------------------------------
  12 13   1  4 | NN -> VB if the tag of the preceding word is 'TO'
   8  9   1 23 | NN -> VBD if the tag of the following word is 'DT'
   8  8   0  9 | NN -> VBD if the tag of the preceding word is 'NNS'
   6  9   3 16 | NN -> NNP if the tag of words i-2...i-1 is '-NONE-'
   5  8   3  6 | NN -> NNP if the tag of the following word is 'NNP'
   5  6   1  0 | NN -> NNP if the text of words i-2...i-1 is 'like'
   5  5   0  3 | NN -> VBN if the text of the following word is '*-1'
   ...
>>> print(open("errors.out").read())
             left context |    word/test->gold    | right context
--------------------------+-----------------------+--------------------------
                          |    Then/NN->RB        | ,/, in/IN the/DT guests/N
 , in/IN the/DT guests/NNS |    '/VBD->POS         | honor/NN ,/, the/DT speed
 '/POS honor/NN ,/, the/DT |    speedway/JJ->NN    | hauled/VBD out/RP four/CD
 NN ,/, the/DT speedway/NN |    hauled/NN->VBD     | out/RP four/CD drivers/NN
 DT speedway/NN hauled/VBD |    out/NNP->RP        | four/CD drivers/NNS ,/, c
 dway/NN hauled/VBD out/RP |    four/NNP->CD       | drivers/NNS ,/, crews/NNS
 hauled/VBD out/RP four/CD |    drivers/NNP->NNS   | ,/, crews/NNS and/CC even
 P four/CD drivers/NNS ,/, |    crews/NN->NNS      | and/CC even/RB the/DT off
 NNS and/CC even/RB the/DT |    official/NNP->JJ   | Indianapolis/NNP 500/CD a
                          |    After/VBD->IN      | the/DT race/NN ,/, Fortun
 ter/IN the/DT race/NN ,/, |    Fortune/IN->NNP    | 500/CD executives/NNS dro
 s/NNS drooled/VBD like/IN |    schoolboys/NNP->NNS| over/IN the/DT cars/NNS a
 olboys/NNS over/IN the/DT |    cars/NN->NNS       | and/CC drivers/NNS ./.
```

5.7 How to Determine the Category of a Word

Now that we have examined word classes in detail, we turn to a more basic question: how do we decide what category a word belongs to in the first place? In general, linguists use morphological, syntactic, and semantic clues to determine the category of a word.

Morphological Clues

The internal structure of a word may give useful clues as to the word's category. For example, -*ness* is a suffix that combines with an adjective to produce a noun, e.g., *happy* → *happiness*, *ill* → *illness*. So if we encounter a word that ends in -*ness*, this is very likely to be a noun. Similarly, -*ment* is a suffix that combines with some verbs to produce a noun, e.g., *govern* → *government* and *establish* → *establishment*.

English verbs can also be morphologically complex. For instance, the **present participle** of a verb ends in -*ing*, and expresses the idea of ongoing, incomplete action (e.g., *falling*, *eating*). The -*ing* suffix also appears on nouns derived from verbs, e.g., *the falling of the leaves* (this is known as the **gerund**).

Syntactic Clues

Another source of information is the typical contexts in which a word can occur. For example, assume that we have already determined the category of nouns. Then we might say that a syntactic criterion for an adjective in English is that it can occur immediately before a noun, or immediately following the words *be* or *very*. According to these tests, *near* should be categorized as an adjective:

(2) a. the near window
     b. The end is (very) near.

Semantic Clues

Finally, the meaning of a word is a useful clue as to its lexical category. For example, the best-known definition of a noun is semantic: "the name of a person, place, or thing." Within modern linguistics, semantic criteria for word classes are treated with suspicion, mainly because they are hard to formalize. Nevertheless, semantic criteria underpin many of our intuitions about word classes, and enable us to make a good guess about the categorization of words in languages with which we are unfamiliar. For example, if all we know about the Dutch word *verjaardag* is that it means the same as the English word *birthday*, then we can guess that *verjaardag* is a noun in Dutch. However, some care is needed: although we might translate *zij is vandaag jarig* as *it's her birthday today*, the word *jarig* is in fact an adjective in Dutch, and has no exact equivalent in English.

New Words

All languages acquire new lexical items. A list of words recently added to the Oxford Dictionary of English includes *cyberslacker*, *fatoush*, *blamestorm*, *SARS*, *cantopop*, *bupkis*, *noughties*, *muggle*, and *robata*. Notice that all these new words are nouns, and this is reflected in calling nouns an **open class**. By contrast, prepositions are regarded as a **closed class**. That is, there is a limited set of words belonging to the class (e.g., *above*, *along*, *at*, *below*, *beside*, *between*, *during*, *for*, *from*, *in*, *near*, *on*, *outside*, *over*, *past, through, towards, under, up, with*), and membership of the set only changes very gradually over time.

Morphology in Part-of-Speech Tagsets

Common tagsets often capture some **morphosyntactic** information, that is, information about the kind of morphological markings that words receive by virtue of their syntactic role. Consider, for example, the selection of distinct grammatical forms of the word *go* illustrated in the following sentences:

(3)   a. *Go* away!

        b. He sometimes *goes* to the cafe.

        c. All the cakes have *gone*.

        d. We *went* on the excursion.

Each of these forms—*go*, *goes*, *gone*, and *went*—is morphologically distinct from the others. Consider the form *goes*. This occurs in a restricted set of grammatical contexts, and requires a third person singular subject. Thus, the following sentences are ungrammatical.

(4)   a. *They sometimes *goes* to the cafe.

        b. *I sometimes *goes* to the cafe.

By contrast, *gone* is the past participle form; it is required after *have* (and cannot be replaced in this context by *goes*), and cannot occur as the main verb of a clause.

(5)   a. *All the cakes have *goes*.

        b. *He sometimes *gone* to the cafe.

We can easily imagine a tagset in which the four distinct grammatical forms just discussed were all tagged as VB. Although this would be adequate for some purposes, a more fine-grained tagset provides useful information about these forms that can help other processors that try to detect patterns in tag sequences. The Brown tagset captures these distinctions, as summarized in Table 5-7.

Table 5-7. Some morphosyntactic distinctions in the Brown tagset

Form	Category	Tag
go	base	VB
goes	third singular present	VBZ
gone	past participle	VBN
going	gerund	VBG
went	simple past	VBD

In addition to this set of verb tags, the various forms of the verb *to be* have special tags: be/BE, being/BEG, am/BEM, are/BER, is/BEZ, been/BEN, were/BED, and was/BEDZ (plus extra tags for negative forms of the verb). All told, this fine-grained tagging of verbs means that an automatic tagger that uses this tagset is effectively carrying out a limited amount of **morphological analysis**.

Most part-of-speech tagsets make use of the same basic categories, such as noun, verb, adjective, and preposition. However, tagsets differ both in how finely they divide words into categories, and in how they define their categories. For example, *is* might be tagged simply as a verb in one tagset, but as a distinct form of the *lexeme be* in another tagset (as in the Brown Corpus). This variation in tagsets is unavoidable, since part-of-speech tags are used in different ways for different tasks. In other words, there is no one "right way" to assign tags, only more or less useful ways depending on one's goals.

5.8 Summary

- Words can be grouped into classes, such as nouns, verbs, adjectives, and adverbs. These classes are known as lexical categories or parts-of-speech. Parts-of-speech are assigned short labels, or tags, such as NN and VB.

- The process of automatically assigning parts-of-speech to words in text is called part-of-speech tagging, POS tagging, or just tagging.

- Automatic tagging is an important step in the NLP pipeline, and is useful in a variety of situations, including predicting the behavior of previously unseen words, analyzing word usage in corpora, and text-to-speech systems.

- Some linguistic corpora, such as the Brown Corpus, have been POS tagged.

- A variety of tagging methods are possible, e.g., default tagger, regular expression tagger, unigram tagger, and n-gram taggers. These can be combined using a technique known as backoff.

- Taggers can be trained and evaluated using tagged corpora.

- Backoff is a method for combining models: when a more specialized model (such as a bigram tagger) cannot assign a tag in a given context, we back off to a more general model (such as a unigram tagger).

- Part-of-speech tagging is an important, early example of a sequence classification task in NLP: a classification decision at any one point in the sequence makes use of words and tags in the local context.

- A dictionary is used to map between arbitrary types of information, such as a string and a number: freq['cat'] = 12. We create dictionaries using the brace notation: pos = {}, pos = {'furiously': 'adv', 'ideas': 'n', 'colorless': 'adj'}.

- N-gram taggers can be defined for large values of *n*, but once *n* is larger than 3, we usually encounter the sparse data problem; even with a large quantity of training data, we see only a tiny fraction of possible contexts.

- Transformation-based tagging involves learning a series of repair rules of the form "change tag *s* to tag *t* in context *c*," where each rule fixes mistakes and possibly introduces a (smaller) number of errors.

5.9 Further Reading

Extra materials for this chapter are posted at *http://www.nltk.org/*, including links to freely available resources on the Web. For more examples of tagging with NLTK, please see the Tagging HOWTO at *http://www.nltk.org/howto*. Chapters 4 and 5 of (Jurafsky & Martin, 2008) contain more advanced material on n-grams and part-of-speech tagging. Other approaches to tagging involve machine learning methods (Chapter 6). In Chapter 7, we will see a generalization of tagging called *chunking* in which a contiguous sequence of words is assigned a single tag.

For tagset documentation, see `nltk.help.upenn_tagset()` and `nltk.help.brown_tagset()`. Lexical categories are introduced in linguistics textbooks, including those listed in Chapter 1 of this book.

There are many other kinds of tagging. Words can be tagged with directives to a speech synthesizer, indicating which words should be emphasized. Words can be tagged with sense numbers, indicating which sense of the word was used. Words can also be tagged with morphological features. Examples of each of these kinds of tags are shown in the following list. For space reasons, we only show the tag for a single word. Note also that the first two examples use XML-style tags, where elements in angle brackets enclose the word that is tagged.

Speech Synthesis Markup Language (W3C SSML)
```
That is a <emphasis>big</emphasis> car!
```

SemCor: Brown Corpus tagged with WordNet senses
```
Space in any <wf pos="NN" lemma="form" wnsn="4">form</wf> is completely meas
ured by the three dimensions. (Wordnet form/nn sense 4: "shape, form, config-
uration, contour, conformation")
```

Morphological tagging, from the Turin University Italian Treebank
```
E' italiano , come progetto e realizzazione , il primo (PRIMO ADJ ORDIN M
SING) porto turistico dell' Albania .
```

Note that tagging is also performed at higher levels. Here is an example of dialogue act tagging, from the NPS Chat Corpus (Forsyth & Martell, 2007) included with NLTK. Each turn of the dialogue is categorized as to its communicative function:

```
Statement   User117 Dude..., I wanted some of that
ynQuestion  User120 m I missing something?
Bye         User117 I'm gonna go fix food, I'll be back later.
System      User122 JOIN
System      User2   slaps User122 around a bit with a large trout.
Statement   User121 18/m pm me if u tryin to chat
```

5.10 Exercises

1. ○ Search the Web for "spoof newspaper headlines," to find such gems as: *British Left Waffles on Falkland Islands*, and *Juvenile Court to Try Shooting Defendant*. Manually tag these headlines to see whether knowledge of the part-of-speech tags removes the ambiguity.

2. ○ Working with someone else, take turns picking a word that can be either a noun or a verb (e.g., *contest*); the opponent has to predict which one is likely to be the most frequent in the Brown Corpus. Check the opponent's prediction, and tally the score over several turns.

3. ○ Tokenize and tag the following sentence: *They wind back the clock, while we chase after the wind.* What different pronunciations and parts-of-speech are involved?

4. ○ Review the mappings in Table 5-4. Discuss any other examples of mappings you can think of. What type of information do they map from and to?

5. ○ Using the Python interpreter in interactive mode, experiment with the dictionary examples in this chapter. Create a dictionary `d`, and add some entries. What happens whether you try to access a non-existent entry, e.g., `d['xyz']`?

6. ○ Try deleting an element from a dictionary `d`, using the syntax `del d['abc']`. Check that the item was deleted.

7. ○ Create two dictionaries, `d1` and `d2`, and add some entries to each. Now issue the command `d1.update(d2)`. What did this do? What might it be useful for?

8. ○ Create a dictionary `e`, to represent a single lexical entry for some word of your choice. Define keys such as `headword`, `part-of-speech`, `sense`, and `example`, and assign them suitable values.

9. ○ Satisfy yourself that there are restrictions on the distribution of *go* and *went*, in the sense that they cannot be freely interchanged in the kinds of contexts illustrated in (3), Section 5.7.

10. ○ Train a unigram tagger and run it on some new text. Observe that some words are not assigned a tag. Why not?

11. ○ Learn about the affix tagger (type `help(nltk.AffixTagger)`). Train an affix tagger and run it on some new text. Experiment with different settings for the affix length and the minimum word length. Discuss your findings.

12. ○ Train a bigram tagger with no backoff tagger, and run it on some of the training data. Next, run it on some new data. What happens to the performance of the tagger? Why?

13. ○ We can use a dictionary to specify the values to be substituted into a formatting string. Read Python's library documentation for formatting strings (*http://docs.py*

thon.org/lib/typesseq-strings.html) and use this method to display today's date in two different formats.

14. ◑ Use `sorted()` and `set()` to get a sorted list of tags used in the Brown Corpus, removing duplicates.

15. ◑ Write programs to process the Brown Corpus and find answers to the following questions:

    a. Which nouns are more common in their plural form, rather than their singular form? (Only consider regular plurals, formed with the *-s* suffix.)

    b. Which word has the greatest number of distinct tags? What are they, and what do they represent?

    c. List tags in order of decreasing frequency. What do the 20 most frequent tags represent?

    d. Which tags are nouns most commonly found after? What do these tags represent?

16. ◑ Explore the following issues that arise in connection with the lookup tagger:

    a. What happens to the tagger performance for the various model sizes when a backoff tagger is omitted?

    b. Consider the curve in Figure 5-4; suggest a good size for a lookup tagger that balances memory and performance. Can you come up with scenarios where it would be preferable to minimize memory usage, or to maximize performance with no regard for memory usage?

17. ◑ What is the upper limit of performance for a lookup tagger, assuming no limit to the size of its table? (Hint: write a program to work out what percentage of tokens of a word are assigned the most likely tag for that word, on average.)

18. ◑ Generate some statistics for tagged data to answer the following questions:

    a. What proportion of word types are always assigned the same part-of-speech tag?

    b. How many words are ambiguous, in the sense that they appear with at least two tags?

    c. What percentage of word *tokens* in the Brown Corpus involve these ambiguous words?

19. ◑ The `evaluate()` method works out how accurately the tagger performs on this text. For example, if the supplied tagged text was [('the', 'DT'), ('dog', 'NN')] and the tagger produced the output [('the', 'NN'), ('dog', 'NN')], then the score would be 0.5. Let's try to figure out how the evaluation method works:

    a. A tagger t takes a list of words as input, and produces a list of tagged words as output. However, t.evaluate() is given correctly tagged text as its only parameter. What must it do with this input before performing the tagging?

b. Once the tagger has created newly tagged text, how might the `evaluate()` method go about comparing it with the original tagged text and computing the accuracy score?

c. Now examine the source code to see how the method is implemented. Inspect `nltk.tag.api.__file__` to discover the location of the source code, and open this file using an editor (be sure to use the *api.py* file and not the compiled *api.pyc* binary file).

20. ◑ Write code to search the Brown Corpus for particular words and phrases according to tags, to answer the following questions:

   a. Produce an alphabetically sorted list of the distinct words tagged as `MD`.

   b. Identify words that can be plural nouns or third person singular verbs (e.g., *deals*, *flies*).

   c. Identify three-word prepositional phrases of the form IN + DET + NN (e.g., *in the lab*).

   d. What is the ratio of masculine to feminine pronouns?

21. ◑ In Table 3-1, we saw a table involving frequency counts for the verbs *adore*, *love*, *like*, and *prefer*, and preceding qualifiers such as *really*. Investigate the full range of qualifiers (Brown tag `QL`) that appear before these four verbs.

22. ◑ We defined the `regexp_tagger` that can be used as a fall-back tagger for unknown words. This tagger only checks for cardinal numbers. By testing for particular prefix or suffix strings, it should be possible to guess other tags. For example, we could tag any word that ends with *-s* as a plural noun. Define a regular expression tagger (using `RegexpTagger()`) that tests for at least five other patterns in the spelling of words. (Use inline documentation to explain the rules.)

23. ◑ Consider the regular expression tagger developed in the exercises in the previous section. Evaluate the tagger using its `accuracy()` method, and try to come up with ways to improve its performance. Discuss your findings. How does objective evaluation help in the development process?

24. ◑ How serious is the sparse data problem? Investigate the performance of n-gram taggers as *n* increases from 1 to 6. Tabulate the accuracy score. Estimate the training data required for these taggers, assuming a vocabulary size of 10^5 and a tagset size of 10^2.

25. ◑ Obtain some tagged data for another language, and train and evaluate a variety of taggers on it. If the language is morphologically complex, or if there are any orthographic clues (e.g., capitalization) to word classes, consider developing a regular expression tagger for it (ordered after the unigram tagger, and before the default tagger). How does the accuracy of your tagger(s) compare with the same taggers run on English data? Discuss any issues you encounter in applying these methods to the language.

26. ◑ Example 5-4 plotted a curve showing change in the performance of a lookup tagger as the model size was increased. Plot the performance curve for a unigram tagger, as the amount of training data is varied.

27. ◑ Inspect the confusion matrix for the bigram tagger t2 defined in Section 5.5, and identify one or more sets of tags to collapse. Define a dictionary to do the mapping, and evaluate the tagger on the simplified data.

28. ◑ Experiment with taggers using the simplified tagset (or make one of your own by discarding all but the first character of each tag name). Such a tagger has fewer distinctions to make, but much less information on which to base its work. Discuss your findings.

29. ◑ Recall the example of a bigram tagger which encountered a word it hadn't seen during training, and tagged the rest of the sentence as None. It is possible for a bigram tagger to fail partway through a sentence even if it contains no unseen words (even if the sentence was used during training). In what circumstance can this happen? Can you write a program to find some examples of this?

30. ◑ Preprocess the Brown News data by replacing low-frequency words with *UNK*, but leaving the tags untouched. Now train and evaluate a bigram tagger on this data. How much does this help? What is the contribution of the unigram tagger and default tagger now?

31. ◑ Modify the program in Example 5-4 to use a logarithmic scale on the *x*-axis, by replacing pylab.plot() with pylab.semilogx(). What do you notice about the shape of the resulting plot? Does the gradient tell you anything?

32. ◑ Consult the documentation for the Brill tagger demo function, using help(nltk.tag.brill.demo). Experiment with the tagger by setting different values for the parameters. Is there any trade-off between training time (corpus size) and performance?

33. ◑ Write code that builds a dictionary of dictionaries of sets. Use it to store the set of POS tags that can follow a given word having a given POS tag, i.e., word$_i$ → tag$_i$ → tag$_{i+1}$.

34. ● There are 264 distinct words in the Brown Corpus having exactly three possible tags.

    a. Print a table with the integers 1..10 in one column, and the number of distinct words in the corpus having 1..10 distinct tags in the other column.

    b. For the word with the greatest number of distinct tags, print out sentences from the corpus containing the word, one for each possible tag.

35. ● Write a program to classify contexts involving the word *must* according to the tag of the following word. Can this be used to discriminate between the epistemic and deontic uses of *must*?

36. ● Create a regular expression tagger and various unigram and n-gram taggers, incorporating backoff, and train them on part of the Brown Corpus.

---

a. Create three different combinations of the taggers. Test the accuracy of each combined tagger. Which combination works best?

b. Try varying the size of the training corpus. How does it affect your results?

37. ● Our approach for tagging an unknown word has been to consider the letters of the word (using `RegexpTagger()`), or to ignore the word altogether and tag it as a noun (using `nltk.DefaultTagger()`). These methods will not do well for texts having new words that are not nouns. Consider the sentence *I like to blog on Kim's blog*. If *blog* is a new word, then looking at the previous tag (`TO` versus `NP$`) would probably be helpful, i.e., we need a default tagger that is sensitive to the preceding tag.

a. Create a new kind of unigram tagger that looks at the tag of the previous word, and ignores the current word. (The best way to do this is to modify the source code for `UnigramTagger()`, which presumes knowledge of object-oriented programming in Python.)

b. Add this tagger to the sequence of backoff taggers (including ordinary trigram and bigram taggers that look at words), right before the usual default tagger.

c. Evaluate the contribution of this new unigram tagger.

38. ● Consider the code in Section 5.5, which determines the upper bound for accuracy of a trigram tagger. Review Abney's discussion concerning the impossibility of exact tagging (Abney, 2006). Explain why correct tagging of these examples requires access to other kinds of information than just words and tags. How might you estimate the scale of this problem?

39. ● Use some of the estimation techniques in `nltk.probability`, such as *Lidstone* or *Laplace* estimation, to develop a statistical tagger that does a better job than n-gram backoff taggers in cases where contexts encountered during testing were not seen during training.

40. ● Inspect the diagnostic files created by the Brill tagger `rules.out` and `errors.out`. Obtain the demonstration code by accessing the source code (at *http://www.nltk.org/code*) and create your own version of the Brill tagger. Delete some of the rule templates, based on what you learned from inspecting `rules.out`. Add some new rule templates which employ contexts that might help to correct the errors you saw in `errors.out`.

41. ● Develop an n-gram backoff tagger that permits "anti-n-grams" such as `["the", "the"]` to be specified when a tagger is initialized. An anti-n-gram is assigned a count of zero and is used to prevent backoff for this n-gram (e.g., to avoid estimating $P(the \mid the)$ as just $P(the)$).

42. ● Investigate three different ways to define the split between training and testing data when developing a tagger using the Brown Corpus: genre (`category`), source (`fileid`), and sentence. Compare their relative performance and discuss which method is the most legitimate. (You might use n-fold cross validation, discussed in Section 6.3, to improve the accuracy of the evaluations.)

## CHAPTER 6

Learning to Classify Text

Detecting patterns is a central part of Natural Language Processing. Words ending in *-ed* tend to be past tense verbs (Chapter 5). Frequent use of *will* is indicative of news text (Chapter 3). These observable patterns—word structure and word frequency—happen to correlate with particular aspects of meaning, such as tense and topic. But how did we know where to start looking, which aspects of form to associate with which aspects of meaning?

The goal of this chapter is to answer the following questions:

1. How can we identify particular features of language data that are salient for classifying it?
2. How can we construct models of language that can be used to perform language processing tasks automatically?
3. What can we learn about language from these models?

Along the way we will study some important machine learning techniques, including decision trees, naive Bayes classifiers, and maximum entropy classifiers. We will gloss over the mathematical and statistical underpinnings of these techniques, focusing instead on how and when to use them (see Section 6.9 for more technical background). Before looking at these methods, we first need to appreciate the broad scope of this topic.

6.1 Supervised Classification

Classification is the task of choosing the correct **class label** for a given input. In basic classification tasks, each input is considered in isolation from all other inputs, and the set of labels is defined in advance. Some examples of classification tasks are:

- Deciding whether an email is spam or not.
- Deciding what the topic of a news article is, from a fixed list of topic areas such as "sports," "technology," and "politics."
- Deciding whether a given occurrence of the word *bank* is used to refer to a river bank, a financial institution, the act of tilting to the side, or the act of depositing something in a financial institution.

The basic classification task has a number of interesting variants. For example, in multi-class classification, each instance may be assigned multiple labels; in open-class classification, the set of labels is not defined in advance; and in sequence classification, a list of inputs are jointly classified.

A classifier is called **supervised** if it is built based on training corpora containing the correct label for each input. The framework used by supervised classification is shown in Figure 6-1.

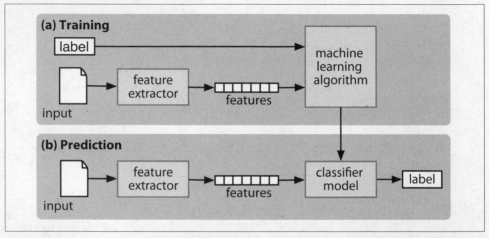

Figure 6-1. Supervised classification. (a) During training, a feature extractor is used to convert each input value to a feature set. These feature sets, which capture the basic information about each input that should be used to classify it, are discussed in the next section. Pairs of feature sets and labels are fed into the machine learning algorithm to generate a model. (b) During prediction, the same feature extractor is used to convert unseen inputs to feature sets. These feature sets are then fed into the model, which generates predicted labels.

In the rest of this section, we will look at how classifiers can be employed to solve a wide variety of tasks. Our discussion is not intended to be comprehensive, but to give a representative sample of tasks that can be performed with the help of text classifiers.

Gender Identification

In Section 2.4, we saw that male and female names have some distinctive characteristics. Names ending in *a*, *e*, and *i* are likely to be female, while names ending in *k*, *o*, *r*, *s*, and *t* are likely to be male. Let's build a classifier to model these differences more precisely.

The first step in creating a classifier is deciding what **features** of the input are relevant, and how to **encode** those features. For this example, we'll start by just looking at the final letter of a given name. The following **feature extractor** function builds a dictionary containing relevant information about a given name:

```
>>> def gender_features(word):
...     return {'last_letter': word[-1]}
>>> gender_features('Shrek')
{'last_letter': 'k'}
```

The dictionary that is returned by this function is called a **feature set** and maps from features' names to their values. Feature names are case-sensitive strings that typically provide a short human-readable description of the feature. Feature values are values with simple types, such as Booleans, numbers, and strings.

 Most classification methods require that features be encoded using simple value types, such as Booleans, numbers, and strings. But note that just because a feature has a simple type, this does not necessarily mean that the feature's value is simple to express or compute; indeed, it is even possible to use very complex and informative values, such as the output of a second supervised classifier, as features.

Now that we've defined a feature extractor, we need to prepare a list of examples and corresponding class labels:

```
>>> from nltk.corpus import names
>>> import random
>>> names = ([(name, 'male') for name in names.words('male.txt')] +
...          [(name, 'female') for name in names.words('female.txt')])
>>> random.shuffle(names)
```

Next, we use the feature extractor to process the names data, and divide the resulting list of feature sets into a **training set** and a **test set**. The training set is used to train a new "naive Bayes" classifier.

```
>>> featuresets = [(gender_features(n), g) for (n,g) in names]
>>> train_set, test_set = featuresets[500:], featuresets[:500]
>>> classifier = nltk.NaiveBayesClassifier.train(train_set)
```

We will learn more about the naive Bayes classifier later in the chapter. For now, let's just test it out on some names that did not appear in its training data:

```
>>> classifier.classify(gender_features('Neo'))
'male'
>>> classifier.classify(gender_features('Trinity'))
'female'
```

Observe that these character names from *The Matrix* are correctly classified. Although this science fiction movie is set in 2199, it still conforms with our expectations about names and genders. We can systematically evaluate the classifier on a much larger quantity of unseen data:

```
>>> print nltk.classify.accuracy(classifier, test_set)
0.758
```

Finally, we can examine the classifier to determine which features it found most effective for distinguishing the names' genders:

```
>>> classifier.show_most_informative_features(5)
Most Informative Features
             last_letter = 'a'          female : male   =     38.3 : 1.0
             last_letter = 'k'            male : female =     31.4 : 1.0
             last_letter = 'f'            male : female =     15.3 : 1.0
             last_letter = 'p'            male : female =     10.6 : 1.0
             last_letter = 'w'            male : female =     10.6 : 1.0
```

This listing shows that the names in the training set that end in *a* are female 38 times more often than they are male, but names that end in *k* are male 31 times more often than they are female. These ratios are known as **likelihood ratios**, and can be useful for comparing different feature-outcome relationships.

 Your Turn: Modify the gender_features() function to provide the classifier with features encoding the length of the name, its first letter, and any other features that seem like they might be informative. Retrain the classifier with these new features, and test its accuracy.

When working with large corpora, constructing a single list that contains the features of every instance can use up a large amount of memory. In these cases, use the function nltk.classify.apply_features, which returns an object that acts like a list but does not store all the feature sets in memory:

```
>>> from nltk.classify import apply_features
>>> train_set = apply_features(gender_features, names[500:])
>>> test_set = apply_features(gender_features, names[:500])
```

Choosing the Right Features

Selecting relevant features and deciding how to encode them for a learning method can have an enormous impact on the learning method's ability to extract a good model. Much of the interesting work in building a classifier is deciding what features might be relevant, and how we can represent them. Although it's often possible to get decent performance by using a fairly simple and obvious set of features, there are usually significant gains to be had by using carefully constructed features based on a thorough understanding of the task at hand.

Typically, feature extractors are built through a process of trial-and-error, guided by intuitions about what information is relevant to the problem. It's common to start with a "kitchen sink" approach, including all the features that you can think of, and then checking to see which features actually are helpful. We take this approach for name gender features in Example 6-1.

Example 6-1. A feature extractor that overfits gender features. The featuresets returned by this feature extractor contain a large number of specific features, leading to overfitting for the relatively small Names Corpus.

```
def gender_features2(name):
    features = {}
    features["firstletter"] = name[0].lower()
    features["lastletter"] = name[-1].lower()
    for letter in 'abcdefghijklmnopqrstuvwxyz':
        features["count(%s)" % letter] = name.lower().count(letter)
        features["has(%s)" % letter] = (letter in name.lower())
    return features

>>> gender_features2('John')
{'count(j)': 1, 'has(d)': False, 'count(b)': 0, ...}
```

However, there are usually limits to the number of features that you should use with a given learning algorithm—if you provide too many features, then the algorithm will have a higher chance of relying on idiosyncrasies of your training data that don't generalize well to new examples. This problem is known as **overfitting**, and can be especially problematic when working with small training sets. For example, if we train a naive Bayes classifier using the feature extractor shown in Example 6-1, it will overfit the relatively small training set, resulting in a system whose accuracy is about 1% lower than the accuracy of a classifier that only pays attention to the final letter of each name:

```
>>> featuresets = [(gender_features2(n), g) for (n,g) in names]
>>> train_set, test_set = featuresets[500:], featuresets[:500]
>>> classifier = nltk.NaiveBayesClassifier.train(train_set)
>>> print nltk.classify.accuracy(classifier, test_set)
0.748
```

Once an initial set of features has been chosen, a very productive method for refining the feature set is **error analysis**. First, we select a **development set**, containing the corpus data for creating the model. This development set is then subdivided into the **training set** and the **dev-test** set.

```
>>> train_names = names[1500:]
>>> devtest_names = names[500:1500]
>>> test_names = names[:500]
```

The training set is used to train the model, and the dev-test set is used to perform error analysis. The test set serves in our final evaluation of the system. For reasons discussed later, it is important that we employ a separate dev-test set for error analysis, rather than just using the test set. The division of the corpus data into different subsets is shown in Figure 6-2.

Having divided the corpus into appropriate datasets, we train a model using the training set ❶, and then run it on the dev-test set ❷.

```
>>> train_set = [(gender_features(n), g) for (n,g) in train_names]
>>> devtest_set = [(gender_features(n), g) for (n,g) in devtest_names]
>>> test_set = [(gender_features(n), g) for (n,g) in test_names]
>>> classifier = nltk.NaiveBayesClassifier.train(train_set)  ❶
```

```
>>> print nltk.classify.accuracy(classifier, devtest_set) ❷
0.765
```

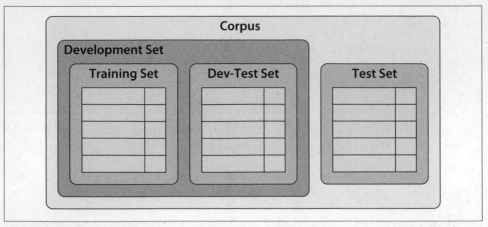

Figure 6-2. Organization of corpus data for training supervised classifiers. The corpus data is divided into two sets: the development set and the test set. The development set is often further subdivided into a training set and a dev-test set.

Using the dev-test set, we can generate a list of the errors that the classifier makes when predicting name genders:

```
>>> errors = []
>>> for (name, tag) in devtest_names:
...     guess = classifier.classify(gender_features(name))
...     if guess != tag:
...         errors.append( (tag, guess, name) )
```

We can then examine individual error cases where the model predicted the wrong label, and try to determine what additional pieces of information would allow it to make the right decision (or which existing pieces of information are tricking it into making the wrong decision). The feature set can then be adjusted accordingly. The names classifier that we have built generates about 100 errors on the dev-test corpus:

```
>>> for (tag, guess, name) in sorted(errors): # doctest: +ELLIPSIS +NORMALIZE_WHITESPACE
...     print 'correct=%-8s guess=%-8s name=%-30s' %
(tag, guess, name)
    ...
correct=female   guess=male      name=Cindelyn
    ...
correct=female   guess=male      name=Katheryn
correct=female   guess=male      name=Kathryn
    ...
correct=male     guess=female    name=Aldrich
    ...
correct=male     guess=female    name=Mitch
    ...
correct=male     guess=female    name=Rich
    ...
```

Looking through this list of errors makes it clear that some suffixes that are more than one letter can be indicative of name genders. For example, names ending in *yn* appear to be predominantly female, despite the fact that names ending in *n* tend to be male; and names ending in *ch* are usually male, even though names that end in *h* tend to be female. We therefore adjust our feature extractor to include features for two-letter suffixes:

```
>>> def gender_features(word):
...     return {'suffix1': word[-1:],
...             'suffix2': word[-2:]}
```

Rebuilding the classifier with the new feature extractor, we see that the performance on the dev-test dataset improves by almost three percentage points (from 76.5% to 78.2%):

```
>>> train_set = [(gender_features(n), g) for (n,g) in train_names]
>>> devtest_set = [(gender_features(n), g) for (n,g) in devtest_names]
>>> classifier = nltk.NaiveBayesClassifier.train(train_set)
>>> print nltk.classify.accuracy(classifier, devtest_set)
0.782
```

This error analysis procedure can then be repeated, checking for patterns in the errors that are made by the newly improved classifier. Each time the error analysis procedure is repeated, we should select a different dev-test/training split, to ensure that the classifier does not start to reflect idiosyncrasies in the dev-test set.

But once we've used the dev-test set to help us develop the model, we can no longer trust that it will give us an accurate idea of how well the model would perform on new data. It is therefore important to keep the test set separate, and unused, until our model development is complete. At that point, we can use the test set to evaluate how well our model will perform on new input values.

Document Classification

In Section 2.1, we saw several examples of corpora where documents have been labeled with categories. Using these corpora, we can build classifiers that will automatically tag new documents with appropriate category labels. First, we construct a list of documents, labeled with the appropriate categories. For this example, we've chosen the Movie Reviews Corpus, which categorizes each review as positive or negative.

```
>>> from nltk.corpus import movie_reviews
>>> documents = [(list(movie_reviews.words(fileid)), category)
...              for category in movie_reviews.categories()
...              for fileid in movie_reviews.fileids(category)]
>>> random.shuffle(documents)
```

Next, we define a feature extractor for documents, so the classifier will know which aspects of the data it should pay attention to (see Example 6-2). For document topic identification, we can define a feature for each word, indicating whether the document contains that word. To limit the number of features that the classifier needs to process, we begin by constructing a list of the 2,000 most frequent words in the overall corpus ❶. We can then define a feature extractor ❷ that simply checks whether each of these words is present in a given document.

Example 6-2. A feature extractor for document classification, whose features indicate whether or not individual words are present in a given document.

```
all_words = nltk.FreqDist(w.lower() for w in movie_reviews.words())
word_features = all_words.keys()[:2000] ❶

def document_features(document): ❷
    document_words = set(document) ❸
    features = {}
    for word in word_features:
        features['contains(%s)' % word] = (word in document_words)
    return features

>>> print document_features(movie_reviews.words('pos/cv957_8737.txt'))
{'contains(waste)': False, 'contains(lot)': False, ...}
```

 We compute the set of all words in a document in ❸, rather than just checking if word in document, because checking whether a word occurs in a set is much faster than checking whether it occurs in a list (see Section 4.7).

Now that we've defined our feature extractor, we can use it to train a classifier to label new movie reviews (Example 6-3). To check how reliable the resulting classifier is, we compute its accuracy on the test set ❶. And once again, we can use show_most_infor mative_features() to find out which features the classifier found to be most informative ❷.

Example 6-3. Training and testing a classifier for document classification.

```
featuresets = [(document_features(d), c) for (d,c) in documents]
train_set, test_set = featuresets[100:], featuresets[:100]
classifier = nltk.NaiveBayesClassifier.train(train_set)

>>> print nltk.classify.accuracy(classifier, test_set) ❶
0.81
>>> classifier.show_most_informative_features(5) ❷
Most Informative Features
     contains(outstanding) = True              pos : neg    =     11.1 : 1.0
          contains(seagal) = True              neg : pos    =      7.7 : 1.0
     contains(wonderfully) = True              pos : neg    =      6.8 : 1.0
           contains(damon) = True              pos : neg    =      5.9 : 1.0
          contains(wasted) = True              neg : pos    =      5.8 : 1.0
```

Apparently in this corpus, a review that mentions *Seagal* is almost 8 times more likely to be negative than positive, while a review that mentions *Damon* is about 6 times more likely to be positive.

Part-of-Speech Tagging

In Chapter 5, we built a regular expression tagger that chooses a part-of-speech tag for a word by looking at the internal makeup of the word. However, this regular expression tagger had to be handcrafted. Instead, we can train a classifier to work out which suffixes are most informative. Let's begin by finding the most common suffixes:

```
>>> from nltk.corpus import brown
>>> suffix_fdist = nltk.FreqDist()
>>> for word in brown.words():
...     word = word.lower()
...     suffix_fdist.inc(word[-1:])
...     suffix_fdist.inc(word[-2:])
...     suffix_fdist.inc(word[-3:])

>>> common_suffixes = suffix_fdist.keys()[:100]
>>> print common_suffixes
['e', ',', '.', 's', 'd', 't', 'he', 'n', 'a', 'of', 'the',
 'y', 'r', 'to', 'in', 'f', 'o', 'ed', 'nd', 'is', 'on', 'l',
 'g', 'and', 'ng', 'er', 'as', 'ing', 'h', 'at', 'es', 'or',
 're', 'it', '``', 'an', "''", 'm', ';', 'i', 'ly', 'ion', ...]
```

Next, we'll define a feature extractor function that checks a given word for these suffixes:

```
>>> def pos_features(word):
...     features = {}
...     for suffix in common_suffixes:
...         features['endswith(%s)' % suffix] = word.lower().endswith(suffix)
...     return features
```

Feature extraction functions behave like tinted glasses, highlighting some of the properties (colors) in our data and making it impossible to see other properties. The classifier will rely exclusively on these highlighted properties when determining how to label inputs. In this case, the classifier will make its decisions based only on information about which of the common suffixes (if any) a given word has.

Now that we've defined our feature extractor, we can use it to train a new "decision tree" classifier (to be discussed in Section 6.4):

```
>>> tagged_words = brown.tagged_words(categories='news')
>>> featuresets = [(pos_features(n), g) for (n,g) in tagged_words]

>>> size = int(len(featuresets) * 0.1)
>>> train_set, test_set = featuresets[size:], featuresets[:size]

>>> classifier = nltk.DecisionTreeClassifier.train(train_set)
>>> nltk.classify.accuracy(classifier, test_set)
0.62705121829935351

>>> classifier.classify(pos_features('cats'))
'NNS'
```

One nice feature of decision tree models is that they are often fairly easy to interpret. We can even instruct NLTK to print them out as pseudocode:

```
>>> print classifier.pseudocode(depth=4)
if endswith(,) == True: return ','
if endswith(,) == False:
  if endswith(the) == True: return 'AT'
  if endswith(the) == False:
    if endswith(s) == True:
      if endswith(is) == True: return 'BEZ'
      if endswith(is) == False: return 'VBZ'
    if endswith(s) == False:
      if endswith(.) == True: return '.'
      if endswith(.) == False: return 'NN'
```

Here, we can see that the classifier begins by checking whether a word ends with a comma—if so, then it will receive the special tag ",". Next, the classifier checks whether the word ends in "the", in which case it's almost certainly a determiner. This "suffix" gets used early by the decision tree because the word *the* is so common. Continuing on, the classifier checks if the word ends in *s*. If so, then it's most likely to receive the verb tag VBZ (unless it's the word *is*, which has the special tag BEZ), and if not, then it's most likely a noun (unless it's the punctuation mark "."). The actual classifier contains further nested if-then statements below the ones shown here, but the depth=4 argument just displays the top portion of the decision tree.

Exploiting Context

By augmenting the feature extraction function, we could modify this part-of-speech tagger to leverage a variety of other word-internal features, such as the length of the word, the number of syllables it contains, or its prefix. However, as long as the feature extractor just looks at the target word, we have no way to add features that depend on the *context* in which the word appears. But contextual features often provide powerful clues about the correct tag—for example, when tagging the word *fly*, knowing that the previous word is *a* will allow us to determine that it is functioning as a noun, not a verb.

In order to accommodate features that depend on a word's context, we must revise the pattern that we used to define our feature extractor. Instead of just passing in the word to be tagged, we will pass in a complete (untagged) sentence, along with the index of the target word. This approach is demonstrated in Example 6-4, which employs a context-dependent feature extractor to define a part-of-speech tag classifier.

Example 6-4. A part-of-speech classifier whose feature detector examines the context in which a word appears in order to determine which part-of-speech tag should be assigned. In particular, the identity of the previous word is included as a feature.

```
def pos_features(sentence, i): ❶
    features = {"suffix(1)": sentence[i][-1:],
                "suffix(2)": sentence[i][-2:],
                "suffix(3)": sentence[i][-3:]}
    if i == 0:
        features["prev-word"] = "<START>"
    else:
        features["prev-word"] = sentence[i-1]
    return features
>>> pos_features(brown.sents()[0], 8)
{'suffix(3)': 'ion', 'prev-word': 'an', 'suffix(2)': 'on', 'suffix(1)': 'n'}
>>> tagged_sents = brown.tagged_sents(categories='news')
>>> featuresets = []
>>> for tagged_sent in tagged_sents:
...     untagged_sent = nltk.tag.untag(tagged_sent)
...     for i, (word, tag) in enumerate(tagged_sent):
...         featuresets.append(
(pos_features(untagged_sent, i), tag) )

>>> size = int(len(featuresets) * 0.1)
>>> train_set, test_set = featuresets[size:], featuresets[:size]
>>> classifier = nltk.NaiveBayesClassifier.train(train_set)

>>> nltk.classify.accuracy(classifier, test_set)
0.78915962207856782
```

It's clear that exploiting contextual features improves the performance of our part-of-speech tagger. For example, the classifier learns that a word is likely to be a noun if it comes immediately after the word *large* or the word *gubernatorial*. However, it is unable to learn the generalization that a word is probably a noun if it follows an adjective, because it doesn't have access to the previous word's part-of-speech tag. In general, simple classifiers always treat each input as independent from all other inputs. In many contexts, this makes perfect sense. For example, decisions about whether names tend to be male or female can be made on a case-by-case basis. However, there are often cases, such as part-of-speech tagging, where we are interested in solving classification problems that are closely related to one another.

Sequence Classification

In order to capture the dependencies between related classification tasks, we can use **joint classifier** models, which choose an appropriate labeling for a collection of related inputs. In the case of part-of-speech tagging, a variety of different **sequence classifier** models can be used to jointly choose part-of-speech tags for all the words in a given sentence.

One sequence classification strategy, known as **consecutive classification** or **greedy sequence classification**, is to find the most likely class label for the first input, then to use that answer to help find the best label for the next input. The process can then be repeated until all of the inputs have been labeled. This is the approach that was taken by the bigram tagger from Section 5.5, which began by choosing a part-of-speech tag for the first word in the sentence, and then chose the tag for each subsequent word based on the word itself and the predicted tag for the previous word.

This strategy is demonstrated in Example 6-5. First, we must augment our feature extractor function to take a `history` argument, which provides a list of the tags that we've predicted for the sentence so far ❶. Each tag in `history` corresponds with a word in `sentence`. But note that `history` will only contain tags for words we've already classified, that is, words to the left of the target word. Thus, although it is possible to look at some features of words to the right of the target word, it is not possible to look at the tags for those words (since we haven't generated them yet).

Having defined a feature extractor, we can proceed to build our sequence classifier ❷. During training, we use the annotated tags to provide the appropriate history to the feature extractor, but when tagging new sentences, we generate the history list based on the output of the tagger itself.

Example 6-5. Part-of-speech tagging with a consecutive classifier.

```
def pos_features(sentence, i, history): ❶
    features = {"suffix(1)": sentence[i][-1:],
                "suffix(2)": sentence[i][-2:],
                "suffix(3)": sentence[i][-3:]}
    if i == 0:
        features["prev-word"] = "<START>"
        features["prev-tag"] = "<START>"
    else:
        features["prev-word"] = sentence[i-1]
        features["prev-tag"] = history[i-1]
    return features

class ConsecutivePosTagger(nltk.TaggerI): ❷
    def __init__(self, train_sents):
        train_set = []
        for tagged_sent in train_sents:
            untagged_sent = nltk.tag.untag(tagged_sent)
            history = []
            for i, (word, tag) in enumerate(tagged_sent):
                featureset = pos_features(untagged_sent, i, history)
                train_set.append( (featureset, tag) )
                history.append(tag)
        self.classifier = nltk.NaiveBayesClassifier.train(train_set)

    def tag(self, sentence):
        history = []
        for i, word in enumerate(sentence):
            featureset = pos_features(sentence, i, history)
```

```
            tag = self.classifier.classify(featureset)
            history.append(tag)
        return zip(sentence, history)
>>> tagged_sents = brown.tagged_sents(categories='news')
>>> size = int(len(tagged_sents) * 0.1)
>>> train_sents, test_sents = tagged_sents[size:], tagged_sents[:size]
>>> tagger = ConsecutivePosTagger(train_sents)
>>> print tagger.evaluate(test_sents)
0.79796012981
```

Other Methods for Sequence Classification

One shortcoming of this approach is that we commit to every decision that we make. For example, if we decide to label a word as a noun, but later find evidence that it should have been a verb, there's no way to go back and fix our mistake. One solution to this problem is to adopt a transformational strategy instead. Transformational joint classifiers work by creating an initial assignment of labels for the inputs, and then iteratively refining that assignment in an attempt to repair inconsistencies between related inputs. The Brill tagger, described in Section 5.6, is a good example of this strategy.

Another solution is to assign scores to all of the possible sequences of part-of-speech tags, and to choose the sequence whose overall score is highest. This is the approach taken by **Hidden Markov Models**. Hidden Markov Models are similar to consecutive classifiers in that they look at both the inputs and the history of predicted tags. However, rather than simply finding the single best tag for a given word, they generate a probability distribution over tags. These probabilities are then combined to calculate probability scores for tag sequences, and the tag sequence with the highest probability is chosen. Unfortunately, the number of possible tag sequences is quite large. Given a tag set with 30 tags, there are about 600 trillion (30^{10}) ways to label a 10-word sentence. In order to avoid considering all these possible sequences separately, Hidden Markov Models require that the feature extractor only look at the most recent tag (or the most recent n tags, where n is fairly small). Given that restriction, it is possible to use dynamic programming (Section 4.7) to efficiently find the most likely tag sequence. In particular, for each consecutive word index i, a score is computed for each possible current and previous tag. This same basic approach is taken by two more advanced models, called **Maximum Entropy Markov Models** and **Linear-Chain Conditional Random Field Models**; but different algorithms are used to find scores for tag sequences.

6.2 Further Examples of Supervised Classification

Sentence Segmentation

Sentence segmentation can be viewed as a classification task for punctuation: whenever we encounter a symbol that could possibly end a sentence, such as a period or a question mark, we have to decide whether it terminates the preceding sentence.

The first step is to obtain some data that has already been segmented into sentences and convert it into a form that is suitable for extracting features:

```
>>> sents = nltk.corpus.treebank_raw.sents()
>>> tokens = []
>>> boundaries = set()
>>> offset = 0
>>> for sent in nltk.corpus.treebank_raw.sents():
...     tokens.extend(sent)
...     offset += len(sent)
...     boundaries.add(offset-1)
```

Here, `tokens` is a merged list of tokens from the individual sentences, and `boundaries` is a set containing the indexes of all sentence-boundary tokens. Next, we need to specify the features of the data that will be used in order to decide whether punctuation indicates a sentence boundary:

```
>>> def punct_features(tokens, i):
...     return {'next-word-capitalized': tokens[i+1][0].isupper(),
...             'prevword': tokens[i-1].lower(),
...             'punct': tokens[i],
...             'prev-word-is-one-char': len(tokens[i-1]) == 1}
```

Based on this feature extractor, we can create a list of labeled featuresets by selecting all the punctuation tokens, and tagging whether they are boundary tokens or not:

```
>>> featuresets = [(punct_features(tokens, i), (i in boundaries))
...                 for i in range(1, len(tokens)-1)
...                 if tokens[i] in '.?!']
```

Using these featuresets, we can train and evaluate a punctuation classifier:

```
>>> size = int(len(featuresets) * 0.1)
>>> train_set, test_set = featuresets[size:], featuresets[:size]
>>> classifier = nltk.NaiveBayesClassifier.train(train_set)
>>> nltk.classify.accuracy(classifier, test_set)
0.97419354838709682
```

To use this classifier to perform sentence segmentation, we simply check each punctuation mark to see whether it's labeled as a boundary, and divide the list of words at the boundary marks. The listing in Example 6-6 shows how this can be done.

Example 6-6. Classification-based sentence segmenter.

```
def segment_sentences(words):
    start = 0
    sents = []
    for i, word in words:
        if word in '.?!' and classifier.classify(words, i) == True:
            sents.append(words[start:i+1])
            start = i+1
    if start < len(words):
        sents.append(words[start:])
```

Identifying Dialogue Act Types

When processing dialogue, it can be useful to think of utterances as a type of *action* performed by the speaker. This interpretation is most straightforward for performative statements such as *I forgive you* or *I bet you can't climb that hill*. But greetings, questions, answers, assertions, and clarifications can all be thought of as types of speech-based actions. Recognizing the **dialogue acts** underlying the utterances in a dialogue can be an important first step in understanding the conversation.

The NPS Chat Corpus, which was demonstrated in Section 2.1, consists of over 10,000 posts from instant messaging sessions. These posts have all been labeled with one of 15 dialogue act types, such as "Statement," "Emotion," "ynQuestion," and "Continuer." We can therefore use this data to build a classifier that can identify the dialogue act types for new instant messaging posts. The first step is to extract the basic messaging data. We will call xml_posts() to get a data structure representing the XML annotation for each post:

```
>>> posts = nltk.corpus.nps_chat.xml_posts()[:10000]
```

Next, we'll define a simple feature extractor that checks what words the post contains:

```
>>> def dialogue_act_features(post):
...     features = {}
...     for word in nltk.word_tokenize(post):
...         features['contains(%s)' % word.lower()] = True
...     return features
```

Finally, we construct the training and testing data by applying the feature extractor to each post (using post.get('class') to get a post's dialogue act type), and create a new classifier:

```
>>> featuresets = [(dialogue_act_features(post.text), post.get('class'))
...                 for post in posts]
>>> size = int(len(featuresets) * 0.1)
>>> train_set, test_set = featuresets[size:], featuresets[:size]
>>> classifier = nltk.NaiveBayesClassifier.train(train_set)
>>> print nltk.classify.accuracy(classifier, test_set)
0.66
```

Recognizing Textual Entailment

Recognizing textual entailment (RTE) is the task of determining whether a given piece of text *T* entails another text called the "hypothesis" (as already discussed in Section 1.5). To date, there have been four RTE Challenges, where shared development and test data is made available to competing teams. Here are a couple of examples of text/hypothesis pairs from the Challenge 3 development dataset. The label *True* indicates that the entailment holds, and *False* indicates that it fails to hold.

Challenge 3, Pair 34 (True)

> **T**: Parviz Davudi was representing Iran at a meeting of the Shanghai Co-operation Organisation (SCO), the fledgling association that binds Russia, China and four former Soviet republics of central Asia together to fight terrorism.

> **H**: China is a member of SCO.

Challenge 3, Pair 81 (False)

> **T**: According to NC Articles of Organization, the members of LLC company are H. Nelson Beavers, III, H. Chester Beavers and Jennie Beavers Stewart.

> **H**: Jennie Beavers Stewart is a share-holder of Carolina Analytical Laboratory.

It should be emphasized that the relationship between text and hypothesis is not intended to be logical entailment, but rather whether a human would conclude that the text provides reasonable evidence for taking the hypothesis to be true.

We can treat RTE as a classification task, in which we try to predict the *True/False* label for each pair. Although it seems likely that successful approaches to this task will involve a combination of parsing, semantics, and real-world knowledge, many early attempts at RTE achieved reasonably good results with shallow analysis, based on similarity between the text and hypothesis at the word level. In the ideal case, we would expect that if there is an entailment, then all the information expressed by the hypothesis should also be present in the text. Conversely, if there is information found in the hypothesis that is absent from the text, then there will be no entailment.

In our RTE feature detector (Example 6-7), we let words (i.e., word types) serve as proxies for information, and our features count the degree of word overlap, and the degree to which there are words in the hypothesis but not in the text (captured by the method hyp_extra()). Not all words are equally important—named entity mentions, such as the names of people, organizations, and places, are likely to be more significant, which motivates us to extract distinct information for words and nes (named entities). In addition, some high-frequency function words are filtered out as "stopwords."

Example 6-7. "Recognizing Text Entailment" feature extractor: The RTEFeatureExtractor *class builds a bag of words for both the text and the hypothesis after throwing away some stopwords, then calculates overlap and difference.*

```
def rte_features(rtepair):
    extractor = nltk.RTEFeatureExtractor(rtepair)
    features = {}
    features['word_overlap'] = len(extractor.overlap('word'))
    features['word_hyp_extra'] = len(extractor.hyp_extra('word'))
    features['ne_overlap'] = len(extractor.overlap('ne'))
    features['ne_hyp_extra'] = len(extractor.hyp_extra('ne'))
    return features
```

To illustrate the content of these features, we examine some attributes of the text/hypothesis Pair 34 shown earlier:

```
>>> rtepair = nltk.corpus.rte.pairs(['rte3_dev.xml'])[33]
>>> extractor = nltk.RTEFeatureExtractor(rtepair)
>>> print extractor.text_words
set(['Russia', 'Organisation', 'Shanghai', 'Asia', 'four', 'at',
'operation', 'SCO', ...])
>>> print extractor.hyp_words
set(['member', 'SCO', 'China'])
>>> print extractor.overlap('word')
set([])
>>> print extractor.overlap('ne')
set(['SCO', 'China'])
>>> print extractor.hyp_extra('word')
set(['member'])
```

These features indicate that all important words in the hypothesis are contained in the text, and thus there is some evidence for labeling this as *True*.

The module `nltk.classify.rte_classify` reaches just over 58% accuracy on the combined RTE test data using methods like these. Although this figure is not very impressive, it requires significant effort, and more linguistic processing, to achieve much better results.

Scaling Up to Large Datasets

Python provides an excellent environment for performing basic text processing and feature extraction. However, it is not able to perform the numerically intensive calculations required by machine learning methods nearly as quickly as lower-level languages such as C. Thus, if you attempt to use the pure-Python machine learning implementations (such as `nltk.NaiveBayesClassifier`) on large datasets, you may find that the learning algorithm takes an unreasonable amount of time and memory to complete.

If you plan to train classifiers with large amounts of training data or a large number of features, we recommend that you explore NLTK's facilities for interfacing with external machine learning packages. Once these packages have been installed, NLTK can transparently invoke them (via system calls) to train classifier models significantly faster than the pure-Python classifier implementations. See the NLTK web page for a list of recommended machine learning packages that are supported by NLTK.

6.3 Evaluation

In order to decide whether a classification model is accurately capturing a pattern, we must evaluate that model. The result of this evaluation is important for deciding how trustworthy the model is, and for what purposes we can use it. Evaluation can also be an effective tool for guiding us in making future improvements to the model.

The Test Set

Most evaluation techniques calculate a score for a model by comparing the labels that it generates for the inputs in a **test set** (or **evaluation set**) with the correct labels for those inputs. This test set typically has the same format as the training set. However, it is very important that the test set be distinct from the training corpus: if we simply reused the training set as the test set, then a model that simply memorized its input, without learning how to generalize to new examples, would receive misleadingly high scores.

When building the test set, there is often a trade-off between the amount of data available for testing and the amount available for training. For classification tasks that have a small number of well-balanced labels and a diverse test set, a meaningful evaluation can be performed with as few as 100 evaluation instances. But if a classification task has a large number of labels or includes very infrequent labels, then the size of the test set should be chosen to ensure that the least frequent label occurs at least 50 times. Additionally, if the test set contains many closely related instances—such as instances drawn from a single document—then the size of the test set should be increased to ensure that this lack of diversity does not skew the evaluation results. When large amounts of annotated data are available, it is common to err on the side of safety by using 10% of the overall data for evaluation.

Another consideration when choosing the test set is the degree of similarity between instances in the test set and those in the development set. The more similar these two datasets are, the less confident we can be that evaluation results will generalize to other datasets. For example, consider the part-of-speech tagging task. At one extreme, we could create the training set and test set by randomly assigning sentences from a data source that reflects a single genre, such as news:

```
>>> import random
>>> from nltk.corpus import brown
>>> tagged_sents = list(brown.tagged_sents(categories='news'))
>>> random.shuffle(tagged_sents)
>>> size = int(len(tagged_sents) * 0.1)
>>> train_set, test_set = tagged_sents[size:], tagged_sents[:size]
```

In this case, our test set will be *very* similar to our training set. The training set and test set are taken from the same genre, and so we cannot be confident that evaluation results would generalize to other genres. What's worse, because of the call to `random.shuffle()`, the test set contains sentences that are taken from the same documents that were used for training. If there is any consistent pattern within a document (say, if a given word appears with a particular part-of-speech tag especially frequently), then that difference will be reflected in both the development set and the test set. A somewhat better approach is to ensure that the training set and test set are taken from different documents:

```
>>> file_ids = brown.fileids(categories='news')
>>> size = int(len(file_ids) * 0.1)
>>> train_set = brown.tagged_sents(file_ids[size:])
>>> test_set = brown.tagged_sents(file_ids[:size])
```

If we want to perform a more stringent evaluation, we can draw the test set from documents that are less closely related to those in the training set:

```
>>> train_set = brown.tagged_sents(categories='news')
>>> test_set = brown.tagged_sents(categories='fiction')
```

If we build a classifier that performs well on this test set, then we can be confident that it has the power to generalize well beyond the data on which it was trained.

Accuracy

The simplest metric that can be used to evaluate a classifier, **accuracy**, measures the percentage of inputs in the test set that the classifier correctly labeled. For example, a name gender classifier that predicts the correct name 60 times in a test set containing 80 names would have an accuracy of 60/80 = 75%. The function `nltk.classify.accuracy()` will calculate the accuracy of a classifier model on a given test set:

```
>>> classifier = nltk.NaiveBayesClassifier.train(train_set)
>>> print 'Accuracy: %4.2f' % nltk.classify.accuracy(classifier, test_set)
0.75
```

When interpreting the accuracy score of a classifier, it is important to consider the frequencies of the individual class labels in the test set. For example, consider a classifier that determines the correct word sense for each occurrence of the word *bank*. If we evaluate this classifier on financial newswire text, then we may find that the `financial-institution` sense appears 19 times out of 20. In that case, an accuracy of 95% would hardly be impressive, since we could achieve that accuracy with a model that always returns the `financial-institution` sense. However, if we instead evaluate the classifier on a more balanced corpus, where the most frequent word sense has a frequency of 40%, then a 95% accuracy score would be a much more positive result. (A similar issue arises when measuring inter-annotator agreement in Section 11.2.)

Precision and Recall

Another instance where accuracy scores can be misleading is in "search" tasks, such as information retrieval, where we are attempting to find documents that are relevant to a particular task. Since the number of irrelevant documents far outweighs the number of relevant documents, the accuracy score for a model that labels every document as irrelevant would be very close to 100%.

It is therefore conventional to employ a different set of measures for search tasks, based on the number of items in each of the four categories shown in Figure 6-3:

- **True positives** are relevant items that we correctly identified as relevant.
- **True negatives** are irrelevant items that we correctly identified as irrelevant.
- **False positives** (or **Type I errors**) are irrelevant items that we incorrectly identified as relevant.
- **False negatives** (or **Type II errors**) are relevant items that we incorrectly identified as irrelevant.

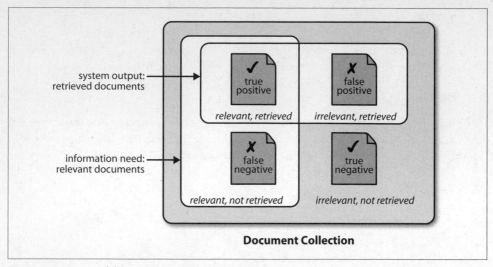

Figure 6-3. True and false positives and negatives.

Given these four numbers, we can define the following metrics:

- **Precision**, which indicates how many of the items that we identified were relevant, is $TP/(TP+FP)$.

- **Recall**, which indicates how many of the relevant items that we identified, is $TP/(TP+FN)$.

- The **F-Measure** (or **F-Score**), which combines the precision and recall to give a single score, is defined to be the harmonic mean of the precision and recall $(2 \times Precision \times Recall)/(Precision+Recall)$.

Confusion Matrices

When performing classification tasks with three or more labels, it can be informative to subdivide the errors made by the model based on which types of mistake it made. A **confusion matrix** is a table where each cell $[i,j]$ indicates how often label j was predicted when the correct label was i. Thus, the diagonal entries (i.e., cells $[i,j]$) indicate labels that were correctly predicted, and the off-diagonal entries indicate errors. In the following example, we generate a confusion matrix for the unigram tagger developed in Section 5.4:

```
>>> def tag_list(tagged_sents):
...     return [tag for sent in tagged_sents for (word, tag) in sent]
>>> def apply_tagger(tagger, corpus):
...     return [tagger.tag(nltk.tag.untag(sent)) for sent in corpus]
>>> gold = tag_list(brown.tagged_sents(categories='editorial'))
>>> test = tag_list(apply_tagger(t2, brown.tagged_sents(categories='editorial')))
>>> cm = nltk.ConfusionMatrix(gold, test)
```

```
     |                              N                         |
     |    N    I    A    J          N             V    N      |
     |    N    N    T    J    .     S    ,        B    P      |
-----+--------------------------------------------------------+
  NN | <11.8%> 0.0%    .  0.2%    .  0.0%    .  0.3% 0.0%     |
  IN |   0.0% <9.0%>   .     .    .  0.0%    .     .     .    |
  AT |     .     .  <8.6%>   .    .     .    .     .     .    |
  JJ |   1.6%    .     . <4.0%>   .     .    .  0.0% 0.0%     |
   . |     .     .     .     . <4.8%>   .    .     .     .    |
  NS |   1.5%    .     .     .    . <3.2%>   .     . 0.0%     |
   , |     .     .     .     .    .     . <4.4%>   .     .    |
   B |   0.9%    .     . 0.0%    .     .    . <2.4%>    .    |
  NP |   1.0%    .     . 0.0%    .     .    .     . <1.9%>|
-----+--------------------------------------------------------+
(row = reference; col = test)
```

The confusion matrix indicates that common errors include a substitution of NN for JJ (for 1.6% of words), and of NN for NNS (for 1.5% of words). Note that periods (.) indicate cells whose value is 0, and that the diagonal entries—which correspond to correct classifications—are marked with angle brackets.

Cross-Validation

In order to evaluate our models, we must reserve a portion of the annotated data for the test set. As we already mentioned, if the test set is too small, our evaluation may not be accurate. However, making the test set larger usually means making the training set smaller, which can have a significant impact on performance if a limited amount of annotated data is available.

One solution to this problem is to perform multiple evaluations on different test sets, then to combine the scores from those evaluations, a technique known as **cross-validation**. In particular, we subdivide the original corpus into *N* subsets called **folds**. For each of these folds, we train a model using all of the data *except* the data in that fold, and then test that model on the fold. Even though the individual folds might be too small to give accurate evaluation scores on their own, the combined evaluation score is based on a large amount of data and is therefore quite reliable.

A second, and equally important, advantage of using cross-validation is that it allows us to examine how widely the performance varies across different training sets. If we get very similar scores for all *N* training sets, then we can be fairly confident that the score is accurate. On the other hand, if scores vary widely across the *N* training sets, then we should probably be skeptical about the accuracy of the evaluation score.

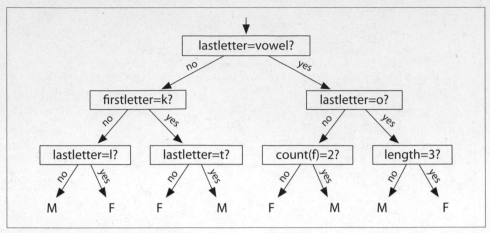

Figure 6-4. Decision Tree model for the name gender task. Note that tree diagrams are conventionally drawn "upside down," with the root at the top, and the leaves at the bottom.

6.4 Decision Trees

In the next three sections, we'll take a closer look at three machine learning methods that can be used to automatically build classification models: decision trees, naive Bayes classifiers, and Maximum Entropy classifiers. As we've seen, it's possible to treat these learning methods as black boxes, simply training models and using them for prediction without understanding how they work. But there's a lot to be learned from taking a closer look at how these learning methods select models based on the data in a training set. An understanding of these methods can help guide our selection of appropriate features, and especially our decisions about how those features should be encoded. And an understanding of the generated models can allow us to extract information about which features are most informative, and how those features relate to one another.

A **decision tree** is a simple flowchart that selects labels for input values. This flowchart consists of **decision nodes**, which check feature values, and **leaf nodes**, which assign labels. To choose the label for an input value, we begin at the flowchart's initial decision node, known as its **root node**. This node contains a condition that checks one of the input value's features, and selects a branch based on that feature's value. Following the branch that describes our input value, we arrive at a new decision node, with a new condition on the input value's features. We continue following the branch selected by each node's condition, until we arrive at a leaf node which provides a label for the input value. Figure 6-4 shows an example decision tree model for the name gender task.

Once we have a decision tree, it is straightforward to use it to assign labels to new input values. What's less straightforward is how we can build a decision tree that models a given training set. But before we look at the learning algorithm for building decision trees, we'll consider a simpler task: picking the best "decision stump" for a corpus. A

decision stump is a decision tree with a single node that decides how to classify inputs based on a single feature. It contains one leaf for each possible feature value, specifying the class label that should be assigned to inputs whose features have that value. In order to build a decision stump, we must first decide which feature should be used. The simplest method is to just build a decision stump for each possible feature, and see which one achieves the highest accuracy on the training data, although there are other alternatives that we will discuss later. Once we've picked a feature, we can build the decision stump by assigning a label to each leaf based on the most frequent label for the selected examples in the training set (i.e., the examples where the selected feature has that value).

Given the algorithm for choosing decision stumps, the algorithm for growing larger decision trees is straightforward. We begin by selecting the overall best decision stump for the classification task. We then check the accuracy of each of the leaves on the training set. Leaves that do not achieve sufficient accuracy are then replaced by new decision stumps, trained on the subset of the training corpus that is selected by the path to the leaf. For example, we could grow the decision tree in Figure 6-4 by replacing the leftmost leaf with a new decision stump, trained on the subset of the training set names that do not start with a *k* or end with a vowel or an *l*.

Entropy and Information Gain

As was mentioned before, there are several methods for identifying the most informative feature for a decision stump. One popular alternative, called **information gain**, measures how much more organized the input values become when we divide them up using a given feature. To measure how disorganized the original set of input values are, we calculate entropy of their labels, which will be high if the input values have highly varied labels, and low if many input values all have the same label. In particular, entropy is defined as the sum of the probability of each label times the log probability of that same label:

(1) $H = \Sigma_{l \in labels} P(l) \times \log_2 P(l)$.

For example, Figure 6-5 shows how the entropy of labels in the name gender prediction task depends on the ratio of male to female names. Note that if most input values have the same label (e.g., if $P(\text{male})$ is near 0 or near 1), then entropy is low. In particular, labels that have low frequency do not contribute much to the entropy (since $P(l)$ is small), and labels with high frequency also do not contribute much to the entropy (since $\log_2 P(l)$ is small). On the other hand, if the input values have a wide variety of labels, then there are many labels with a "medium" frequency, where neither $P(l)$ nor $\log_2 P(l)$ is small, so the entropy is high. Example 6-8 demonstrates how to calculate the entropy of a list of labels.

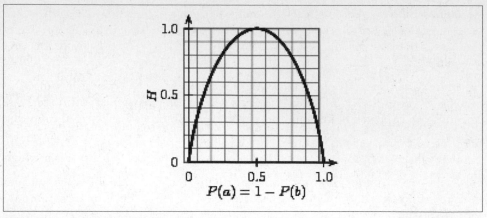

Figure 6-5. The entropy of labels in the name gender prediction task, as a function of the percentage of names in a given set that are male.

Example 6-8. Calculating the entropy of a list of labels.

```
import math
def entropy(labels):
    freqdist = nltk.FreqDist(labels)
    probs = [freqdist.freq(l) for l in nltk.FreqDist(labels)]
    return -sum([p * math.log(p,2) for p in probs])
```

```
>>> print entropy(['male', 'male', 'male', 'male'])
0.0
>>> print entropy(['male', 'female', 'male', 'male'])
0.811278124459
```

```
>>> print entropy(['female', 'male', 'female', 'male'])
1.0
>>> print entropy(['female', 'female', 'male', 'female'])
0.811278124459
>>> print entropy(['female', 'female', 'female', 'female'])
0.0
```

Once we have calculated the entropy of the labels of the original set of input values, we can determine how much more organized the labels become once we apply the decision stump. To do so, we calculate the entropy for each of the decision stump's leaves, and take the average of those leaf entropy values (weighted by the number of samples in each leaf). The information gain is then equal to the original entropy minus this new, reduced entropy. The higher the information gain, the better job the decision stump does of dividing the input values into coherent groups, so we can build decision trees by selecting the decision stumps with the highest information gain.

Another consideration for decision trees is efficiency. The simple algorithm for selecting decision stumps described earlier must construct a candidate decision stump for every possible feature, and this process must be repeated for every node in the constructed decision tree. A number of algorithms have been developed to cut down on the training time by storing and reusing information about previously evaluated examples.

Decision trees have a number of useful qualities. To begin with, they're simple to understand, and easy to interpret. This is especially true near the top of the decision tree, where it is usually possible for the learning algorithm to find very useful features. Decision trees are especially well suited to cases where many hierarchical categorical distinctions can be made. For example, decision trees can be very effective at capturing phylogeny trees.

However, decision trees also have a few disadvantages. One problem is that, since each branch in the decision tree splits the training data, the amount of training data available to train nodes lower in the tree can become quite small. As a result, these lower decision nodes may **overfit** the training set, learning patterns that reflect idiosyncrasies of the training set rather than linguistically significant patterns in the underlying problem. One solution to this problem is to stop dividing nodes once the amount of training data becomes too small. Another solution is to grow a full decision tree, but then to **prune** decision nodes that do not improve performance on a dev-test.

A second problem with decision trees is that they force features to be checked in a specific order, even when features may act relatively independently of one another. For example, when classifying documents into topics (such as sports, automotive, or murder mystery), features such as `hasword(football)` are highly indicative of a specific label, regardless of what the other feature values are. Since there is limited space near the top of the decision tree, most of these features will need to be repeated on many different branches in the tree. And since the number of branches increases exponentially as we go down the tree, the amount of repetition can be very large.

A related problem is that decision trees are not good at making use of features that are weak predictors of the correct label. Since these features make relatively small incremental improvements, they tend to occur very low in the decision tree. But by the time the decision tree learner has descended far enough to use these features, there is not enough training data left to reliably determine what effect they should have. If we could instead look at the effect of these features across the entire training set, then we might be able to make some conclusions about how they should affect the choice of label.

The fact that decision trees require that features be checked in a specific order limits their ability to exploit features that are relatively independent of one another. The naive Bayes classification method, which we'll discuss next, overcomes this limitation by allowing all features to act "in parallel."

6.5 Naive Bayes Classifiers

In **naive Bayes** classifiers, every feature gets a say in determining which label should be assigned to a given input value. To choose a label for an input value, the naive Bayes classifier begins by calculating the **prior probability** of each label, which is determined by checking the frequency of each label in the training set. The contribution from each feature is then combined with this prior probability, to arrive at a likelihood estimate for each label. The label whose likelihood estimate is the highest is then assigned to the input value. Figure 6-6 illustrates this process.

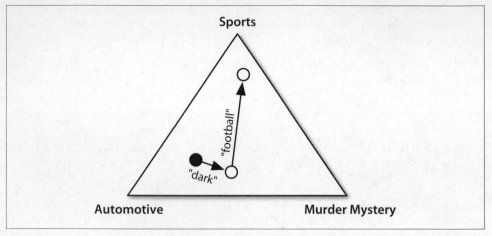

Figure 6-6. An abstract illustration of the procedure used by the naive Bayes classifier to choose the topic for a document. In the training corpus, most documents are automotive, so the classifier starts out at a point closer to the "automotive" label. But it then considers the effect of each feature. In this example, the input document contains the word dark, which is a weak indicator for murder mysteries, but it also contains the word football, which is a strong indicator for sports documents. After every feature has made its contribution, the classifier checks which label it is closest to, and assigns that label to the input.

Individual features make their contribution to the overall decision by "voting against" labels that don't occur with that feature very often. In particular, the likelihood score for each label is reduced by multiplying it by the probability that an input value with that label would have the feature. For example, if the word *run* occurs in 12% of the sports documents, 10% of the murder mystery documents, and 2% of the automotive documents, then the likelihood score for the sports label will be multiplied by 0.12, the likelihood score for the murder mystery label will be multiplied by 0.1, and the likelihood score for the automotive label will be multiplied by 0.02. The overall effect will be to reduce the score of the murder mystery label slightly more than the score of the sports label, and to significantly reduce the automotive label with respect to the other two labels. This process is illustrated in Figures 6-7 and 6-8.

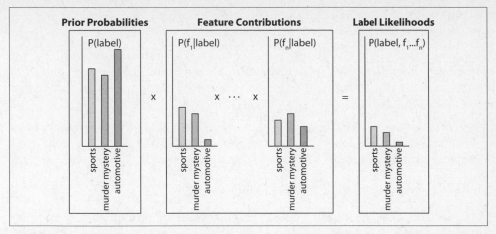

Figure 6-7. Calculating label likelihoods with naive Bayes. Naive Bayes begins by calculating the prior probability of each label, based on how frequently each label occurs in the training data. Every feature then contributes to the likelihood estimate for each label, by multiplying it by the probability that input values with that label will have that feature. The resulting likelihood score can be thought of as an estimate of the probability that a randomly selected value from the training set would have both the given label and the set of features, assuming that the feature probabilities are all independent.

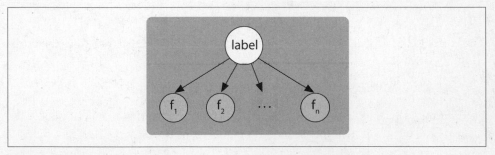

Figure 6-8. A Bayesian Network Graph illustrating the generative process that is assumed by the naive Bayes classifier. To generate a labeled input, the model first chooses a label for the input, and then it generates each of the input's features based on that label. Every feature is assumed to be entirely independent of every other feature, given the label.

Underlying Probabilistic Model

Another way of understanding the naive Bayes classifier is that it chooses the most likely label for an input, under the assumption that every input value is generated by first choosing a class label for that input value, and then generating each feature, entirely independent of every other feature. Of course, this assumption is unrealistic; features are often highly dependent on one another. We'll return to some of the consequences of this assumption at the end of this section. This simplifying assumption, known as the **naive Bayes assumption** (or **independence assumption**), makes it much easier to combine the contributions of the different features, since we don't need to worry about how they should interact with one another.

Based on this assumption, we can calculate an expression for $P(label|features)$, the probability that an input will have a particular label given that it has a particular set of features. To choose a label for a new input, we can then simply pick the label l that maximizes $P(l|features)$.

To begin, we note that $P(label|features)$ is equal to the probability that an input has a particular label *and* the specified set of features, divided by the probability that it has the specified set of features:

(2) $P(label|features) = P(features, label)/P(features)$

Next, we note that $P(features)$ will be the same for every choice of label, so if we are simply interested in finding the most likely label, it suffices to calculate $P(features, label)$, which we'll call the label likelihood.

 If we want to generate a probability estimate for each label, rather than just choosing the most likely label, then the easiest way to compute $P(features)$ is to simply calculate the sum over labels of $P(features, label)$:

(3) $P(features) = \Sigma_{label \in labels} P(features, label)$

The label likelihood can be expanded out as the probability of the label times the probability of the features given the label:

(4) $P(features, label) = P(label) \times P(features|label)$

Furthermore, since the features are all independent of one another (given the label), we can separate out the probability of each individual feature:

(5) $P(features, label) = P(label) \times \Pi_{f \in features}P(f|label)$

This is exactly the equation we discussed earlier for calculating the label likelihood: *P(label)* is the prior probability for a given label, and each *P(f|label)* is the contribution of a single feature to the label likelihood.

Zero Counts and Smoothing

The simplest way to calculate *P(f|label)*, the contribution of a feature *f* toward the label likelihood for a label *label*, is to take the percentage of training instances with the given label that also have the given feature:

(6) $P(f|label) = count(f, label)/count(label)$

However, this simple approach can become problematic when a feature *never* occurs with a given label in the training set. In this case, our calculated value for $P(f|label)$ will be zero, which will cause the label likelihood for the given label to be zero. Thus, the input will never be assigned this label, regardless of how well the other features fit the label.

The basic problem here is with our calculation of $P(f|label)$, the probability that an input will have a feature, given a label. In particular, just because we haven't seen a feature/label combination occur in the training set, doesn't mean it's impossible for that combination to occur. For example, we may not have seen any murder mystery documents that contained the word *football*, but we wouldn't want to conclude that it's completely impossible for such documents to exist.

Thus, although *count(f,label)/count(label)* is a good estimate for $P(f|label)$ when *count(f, label)* is relatively high, this estimate becomes less reliable when *count(f)* becomes smaller. Therefore, when building naive Bayes models, we usually employ more sophisticated techniques, known as **smoothing** techniques, for calculating $P(f|label)$, the probability of a feature given a label. For example, the **Expected Likelihood Estimation** for the probability of a feature given a label basically adds 0.5 to each *count(f,label)* value, and the **Heldout Estimation** uses a heldout corpus to calculate the relationship between feature frequencies and feature probabilities. The `nltk.prob ability` module provides support for a wide variety of smoothing techniques.

Non-Binary Features

We have assumed here that each feature is binary, i.e., that each input either has a feature or does not. Label-valued features (e.g., a color feature, which could be *red*, *green*, *blue*, *white*, or *orange*) can be converted to binary features by replacing them with binary features, such as "color-is-red". Numeric features can be converted to binary features by **binning**, which replaces them with features such as "4<x<6."

Another alternative is to use regression methods to model the probabilities of numeric features. For example, if we assume that the height feature has a bell curve distribution, then we could estimate $P(height|label)$ by finding the mean and variance of the heights of the inputs with each label. In this case, $P(f=v|label)$ would not be a fixed value, but would vary depending on the value of v.

The Naivete of Independence

The reason that naive Bayes classifiers are called "naive" is that it's unreasonable to assume that all features are independent of one another (given the label). In particular, almost all real-world problems contain features with varying degrees of dependence on one another. If we had to avoid any features that were dependent on one another, it would be very difficult to construct good feature sets that provide the required information to the machine learning algorithm.

So what happens when we ignore the independence assumption, and use the naive Bayes classifier with features that are not independent? One problem that arises is that the classifier can end up "double-counting" the effect of highly correlated features, pushing the classifier closer to a given label than is justified.

To see how this can occur, consider a name gender classifier that contains two identical features, f_1 and f_2. In other words, f_2 is an exact copy of f_1, and contains no new information. When the classifier is considering an input, it will include the contribution of both f_1 and f_2 when deciding which label to choose. Thus, the information content of these two features will be given more weight than it deserves.

Of course, we don't usually build naive Bayes classifiers that contain two identical features. However, we do build classifiers that contain features which are dependent on one another. For example, the features ends-with(a) and ends-with(vowel) are dependent on one another, because if an input value has the first feature, then it must also have the second feature. For features like these, the duplicated information may be given more weight than is justified by the training set.

The Cause of Double-Counting

The reason for the double-counting problem is that during training, feature contributions are computed separately; but when using the classifier to choose labels for new inputs, those feature contributions are combined. One solution, therefore, is to consider the possible interactions between feature contributions during training. We could then use those interactions to adjust the contributions that individual features make.

To make this more precise, we can rewrite the equation used to calculate the likelihood of a label, separating out the contribution made by each feature (or label):

(7) $P(features, label) = w[label] \times \prod_{f \in features} w[f, label]$

Here, $w[label]$ is the "starting score" for a given label, and $w[f, label]$ is the contribution made by a given feature towards a label's likelihood. We call these values $w[label]$ and $w[f, label]$ the **parameters** or **weights** for the model. Using the naive Bayes algorithm, we set each of these parameters independently:

(8) $w[label] = P(label)$

(9) $w[f, label] = P(f|label)$

However, in the next section, we'll look at a classifier that considers the possible interactions between these parameters when choosing their values.

6.6 Maximum Entropy Classifiers

The **Maximum Entropy** classifier uses a model that is very similar to the model employed by the naive Bayes classifier. But rather than using probabilities to set the model's parameters, it uses search techniques to find a set of parameters that will maximize the performance of the classifier. In particular, it looks for the set of parameters that maximizes the **total likelihood** of the training corpus, which is defined as:

(10) $P(features) = \Sigma_{x \in corpus} P(label(x)|features(x))$

Where $P(label|features)$, the probability that an input whose features are *features* will have class label *label*, is defined as:

(11) $P(label|features) = P(label, features)/\Sigma_{label} P(label, features)$

Because of the potentially complex interactions between the effects of related features, there is no way to directly calculate the model parameters that maximize the likelihood of the training set. Therefore, Maximum Entropy classifiers choose the model parameters using **iterative optimization** techniques, which initialize the model's parameters to random values, and then repeatedly refine those parameters to bring them closer to the optimal solution. These iterative optimization techniques guarantee that each refinement of the parameters will bring them closer to the optimal values, but do not necessarily provide a means of determining when those optimal values have been reached. Because the parameters for Maximum Entropy classifiers are selected using iterative optimization techniques, they can take a long time to learn. This is especially true when the size of the training set, the number of features, and the number of labels are all large.

 Some iterative optimization techniques are much faster than others. When training Maximum Entropy models, avoid the use of Generalized Iterative Scaling (GIS) or Improved Iterative Scaling (IIS), which are both considerably slower than the Conjugate Gradient (CG) and the BFGS optimization methods.

The Maximum Entropy Model

The Maximum Entropy classifier model is a generalization of the model used by the naive Bayes classifier. Like the naive Bayes model, the Maximum Entropy classifier calculates the likelihood of each label for a given input value by multiplying together the parameters that are applicable for the input value and label. The naive Bayes classifier model defines a parameter for each label, specifying its prior probability, and a parameter for each (feature, label) pair, specifying the contribution of individual features toward a label's likelihood.

In contrast, the Maximum Entropy classifier model leaves it up to the user to decide what combinations of labels and features should receive their own parameters. In particular, it is possible to use a single parameter to associate a feature with more than one label; or to associate more than one feature with a given label. This will sometimes allow the model to "generalize" over some of the differences between related labels or features.

Each combination of labels and features that receives its own parameter is called a **joint-feature**. Note that joint-features are properties of *labeled* values, whereas (simple) features are properties of *unlabeled* values.

 In literature that describes and discusses Maximum Entropy models, the term "features" often refers to joint-features; the term "contexts" refers to what we have been calling (simple) features.

Typically, the joint-features that are used to construct Maximum Entropy models exactly mirror those that are used by the naive Bayes model. In particular, a joint-feature is defined for each label, corresponding to w[*label*], and for each combination of (simple) feature and label, corresponding to $w[f, label]$. Given the joint-features for a Maximum Entropy model, the score assigned to a label for a given input is simply the product of the parameters associated with the joint-features that apply to that input and label:

(12) $P(input, label) = \prod_{joint\text{-}features(input,label)} w[joint\text{-}feature]$

Maximizing Entropy

The intuition that motivates Maximum Entropy classification is that we should build a model that captures the frequencies of individual joint-features, without making any unwarranted assumptions. An example will help to illustrate this principle.

Suppose we are assigned the task of picking the correct word sense for a given word, from a list of 10 possible senses (labeled A–J). At first, we are not told anything more about the word or the senses. There are many probability distributions that we could choose for the 10 senses, such as:

	A	B	C	D	E	F	G	H	I	J
(i)	10%	10%	10%	10%	10%	10%	10%	10%	10%	10%
(ii)	5%	15%	0%	30%	0%	8%	12%	0%	6%	24%
(iii)	0%	100%	0%	0%	0%	0%	0%	0%	0%	0%

Although any of these distributions *might* be correct, we are likely to choose distribution *(i)*, because without any more information, there is no reason to believe that any word sense is more likely than any other. On the other hand, distributions *(ii)* and *(iii)* reflect assumptions that are not supported by what we know.

One way to capture this intuition that distribution *(i)* is more "fair" than the other two is to invoke the concept of entropy. In the discussion of decision trees, we described entropy as a measure of how "disorganized" a set of labels was. In particular, if a single label dominates then entropy is low, but if the labels are more evenly distributed then entropy is high. In our example, we chose distribution *(i)* because its label probabilities are evenly distributed—in other words, because its entropy is high. In general, the **Maximum Entropy principle** states that, among the distributions that are consistent with what we know, we should choose the distribution whose entropy is highest.

Next, suppose that we are told that sense A appears 55% of the time. Once again, there are many distributions that are consistent with this new piece of information, such as:

	A	B	C	D	E	F	G	H	I	J
(iv)	55%	45%	0%	0%	0%	0%	0%	0%	0%	0%
(v)	55%	5%	5%	5%	5%	5%	5%	5%	5%	5%
(vi)	55%	3%	1%	2%	9%	5%	0%	25%	0%	0%

But again, we will likely choose the distribution that makes the fewest unwarranted assumptions—in this case, distribution *(v)*.

Finally, suppose that we are told that the word *up* appears in the nearby context 10% of the time, and that when it does appear in the context there's an 80% chance that sense A or C will be used. In this case, we will have a harder time coming up with an appropriate distribution by hand; however, we can verify that the following distribution looks appropriate:

		A	B	C	D	E	F	G	H	I	J
(vii)	+up	5.1%	0.25%	2.9%	0.25%	0.25%	0.25%	0.25%	0.25%	0.25%	0.25%
	−up	49.9%	4.46%	4.46%	4.46%	4.46%	4.46%	4.46%	4.46%	4.46%	4.46%

In particular, the distribution is consistent with what we know: if we add up the probabilities in column A, we get 55%; if we add up the probabilities of row 1, we get 10%; and if we add up the boxes for senses A and C in the +up row, we get 8% (or 80% of the +up cases). Furthermore, the remaining probabilities appear to be "evenly distributed."

Throughout this example, we have restricted ourselves to distributions that are consistent with what we know; among these, we chose the distribution with the highest entropy. This is exactly what the Maximum Entropy classifier does as well. In particular, for each joint-feature, the Maximum Entropy model calculates the "empirical frequency" of that feature—i.e., the frequency with which it occurs in the training set. It then searches for the distribution which maximizes entropy, while still predicting the correct frequency for each joint-feature.

Generative Versus Conditional Classifiers

An important difference between the naive Bayes classifier and the Maximum Entropy classifier concerns the types of questions they can be used to answer. The naive Bayes classifier is an example of a **generative** classifier, which builds a model that predicts $P(input, label)$, the joint probability of an $(input, label)$ pair. As a result, generative models can be used to answer the following questions:

1. What is the most likely label for a given input?
2. How likely is a given label for a given input?
3. What is the most likely input value?
4. How likely is a given input value?
5. How likely is a given input value with a given label?
6. What is the most likely label for an input that might have one of two values (but we don't know which)?

The Maximum Entropy classifier, on the other hand, is an example of a **conditional** classifier. Conditional classifiers build models that predict $P(label|input)$—the probability of a label *given* the input value. Thus, conditional models can still be used to answer questions 1 and 2. However, conditional models *cannot* be used to answer the remaining questions 3–6.

In general, generative models are strictly more powerful than conditional models, since we can calculate the conditional probability $P(label|input)$ from the joint probability $P(input, label)$, but not vice versa. However, this additional power comes at a price. Because the model is more powerful, it has more "free parameters" that need to be learned. However, the size of the training set is fixed. Thus, when using a more powerful model, we end up with less data that can be used to train each parameter's value, making it harder to find the best parameter values. As a result, a generative model may not do as good a job at answering questions 1 and 2 as a conditional model, since the conditional model can focus its efforts on those two questions. However, if we do need answers to questions like 3–6, then we have no choice but to use a generative model.

The difference between a generative model and a conditional model is analogous to the difference between a topographical map and a picture of a skyline. Although the topographical map can be used to answer a wider variety of questions, it is significantly more difficult to generate an accurate topographical map than it is to generate an accurate skyline.

6.7 Modeling Linguistic Patterns

Classifiers can help us to understand the linguistic patterns that occur in natural language, by allowing us to create explicit **models** that capture those patterns. Typically, these models are using supervised classification techniques, but it is also possible to build analytically motivated models. Either way, these explicit models serve two important purposes: they help us to understand linguistic patterns, and they can be used to make predictions about new language data.

The extent to which explicit models can give us insights into linguistic patterns depends largely on what kind of model is used. Some models, such as decision trees, are relatively transparent, and give us direct information about which factors are important in making decisions and about which factors are related to one another. Other models, such as multilevel neural networks, are much more opaque. Although it can be possible to gain insight by studying them, it typically takes a lot more work.

But all explicit models can make predictions about new **unseen** language data that was not included in the corpus used to build the model. These predictions can be evaluated to assess the accuracy of the model. Once a model is deemed sufficiently accurate, it can then be used to automatically predict information about new language data. These predictive models can be combined into systems that perform many useful language processing tasks, such as document classification, automatic translation, and question answering.

What Do Models Tell Us?

It's important to understand what we can learn about language from an automatically constructed model. One important consideration when dealing with models of language is the distinction between descriptive models and explanatory models. Descriptive models capture patterns in the data, but they don't provide any information about *why* the data contains those patterns. For example, as we saw in Table 3-1, the synonyms *absolutely* and *definitely* are not interchangeable: we say *absolutely adore* not *definitely adore*, and *definitely prefer*, not *absolutely prefer*. In contrast, explanatory models attempt to capture properties and relationships that cause the linguistic patterns. For example, we might introduce the abstract concept of "polar adjective" as an adjective that has an extreme meaning, and categorize some adjectives, such as *adore* and *detest* as polar. Our explanatory model would contain the constraint that *absolutely* can combine only with polar adjectives, and *definitely* can only combine with non-polar adjectives. In summary, descriptive models provide information about correlations in the data, while explanatory models go further to postulate causal relationships.

Most models that are automatically constructed from a corpus are descriptive models; in other words, they can tell us what features are relevant to a given pattern or construction, but they can't necessarily tell us how those features and patterns relate to one another. If our goal is to understand the linguistic patterns, then we can use this information about which features are related as a starting point for further experiments designed to tease apart the relationships between features and patterns. On the other hand, if we're just interested in using the model to make predictions (e.g., as part of a language processing system), then we can use the model to make predictions about new data without worrying about the details of underlying causal relationships.

6.8 Summary

- Modeling the linguistic data found in corpora can help us to understand linguistic patterns, and can be used to make predictions about new language data.

- Supervised classifiers use labeled training corpora to build models that predict the label of an input based on specific features of that input.

- Supervised classifiers can perform a wide variety of NLP tasks, including document classification, part-of-speech tagging, sentence segmentation, dialogue act type identification, and determining entailment relations, and many other tasks.

- When training a supervised classifier, you should split your corpus into three datasets: a training set for building the classifier model, a dev-test set for helping select and tune the model's features, and a test set for evaluating the final model's performance.

- When evaluating a supervised classifier, it is important that you use fresh data that was not included in the training or dev-test set. Otherwise, your evaluation results may be unrealistically optimistic.

- Decision trees are automatically constructed tree-structured flowcharts that are used to assign labels to input values based on their features. Although they're easy to interpret, they are not very good at handling cases where feature values interact in determining the proper label.

- In naive Bayes classifiers, each feature independently contributes to the decision of which label should be used. This allows feature values to interact, but can be problematic when two or more features are highly correlated with one another.

- Maximum Entropy classifiers use a basic model that is similar to the model used by naive Bayes; however, they employ iterative optimization to find the set of feature weights that maximizes the probability of the training set.

- Most of the models that are automatically constructed from a corpus are descriptive, that is, they let us know which features are relevant to a given pattern or construction, but they don't give any information about causal relationships between those features and patterns.

6.9 Further Reading

Please consult *http://www.nltk.org/* for further materials on this chapter and on how to install external machine learning packages, such as Weka, Mallet, TADM, and MegaM. For more examples of classification and machine learning with NLTK, please see the classification HOWTOs at *http://www.nltk.org/howto*.

For a general introduction to machine learning, we recommend (Alpaydin, 2004). For a more mathematically intense introduction to the theory of machine learning, see (Hastie, Tibshirani & Friedman, 2009). Excellent books on using machine learning

---

techniques for NLP include (Abney, 2008), (Daelemans & Bosch, 2005), (Feldman & Sanger, 2007), (Segaran, 2007), and (Weiss et al., 2004). For more on smoothing techniques for language problems, see (Manning & Schütze, 1999). For more on sequence modeling, and especially hidden Markov models, see (Manning & Schütze, 1999) or (Jurafsky & Martin, 2008). Chapter 13 of (Manning, Raghavan & Schütze, 2008) discusses the use of naive Bayes for classifying texts.

Many of the machine learning algorithms discussed in this chapter are numerically intensive, and as a result, they will run slowly when coded naively in Python. For information on increasing the efficiency of numerically intensive algorithms in Python, see (Kiusalaas, 2005).

The classification techniques described in this chapter can be applied to a very wide variety of problems. For example, (Agirre & Edmonds, 2007) uses classifiers to perform word-sense disambiguation; and (Melamed, 2001) uses classifiers to create parallel texts. Recent textbooks that cover text classification include (Manning, Raghavan & Schütze, 2008) and (Croft, Metzler & Strohman, 2009).

Much of the current research in the application of machine learning techniques to NLP problems is driven by government-sponsored "challenges," where a set of research organizations are all provided with the same development corpus and asked to build a system, and the resulting systems are compared based on a reserved test set. Examples of these challenge competitions include CoNLL Shared Tasks, the Recognizing Textual Entailment competitions, the ACE competitions, and the AQUAINT competitions. Consult *http://www.nltk.org/* for a list of pointers to the web pages for these challenges.

6.10 Exercises

1. ○ Read up on one of the language technologies mentioned in this section, such as word sense disambiguation, semantic role labeling, question answering, machine translation, or named entity recognition. Find out what type and quantity of annotated data is required for developing such systems. Why do you think a large amount of data is required?

2. ○ Using any of the three classifiers described in this chapter, and any features you can think of, build the best name gender classifier you can. Begin by splitting the Names Corpus into three subsets: 500 words for the test set, 500 words for the dev-test set, and the remaining 6,900 words for the training set. Then, starting with the example name gender classifier, make incremental improvements. Use the dev-test set to check your progress. Once you are satisfied with your classifier, check its final performance on the test set. How does the performance on the test set compare to the performance on the dev-test set? Is this what you'd expect?

3. ○ The Senseval 2 Corpus contains data intended to train word-sense disambiguation classifiers. It contains data for four words: *hard*, *interest*, *line*, and *serve*. Choose one of these four words, and load the corresponding data:

```
>>> from nltk.corpus import senseval
>>> instances = senseval.instances('hard.pos')
>>> size = int(len(instances) * 0.1)
>>> train_set, test_set = instances[size:], instances[:size]
```

Using this dataset, build a classifier that predicts the correct sense tag for a given instance. See the corpus HOWTO at *http://www.nltk.org/howto* for information on using the instance objects returned by the Senseval 2 Corpus.

4. ○ Using the movie review document classifier discussed in this chapter, generate a list of the 30 features that the classifier finds to be most informative. Can you explain why these particular features are informative? Do you find any of them surprising?

5. ○ Select one of the classification tasks described in this chapter, such as name gender detection, document classification, part-of-speech tagging, or dialogue act classification. Using the same training and test data, and the same feature extractor, build three classifiers for the task: a decision tree, a naive Bayes classifier, and a Maximum Entropy classifier. Compare the performance of the three classifiers on your selected task. How do you think that your results might be different if you used a different feature extractor?

6. ○ The synonyms *strong* and *powerful* pattern differently (try combining them with *chip* and *sales*). What features are relevant in this distinction? Build a classifier that predicts when each word should be used.

7. ◑ The dialogue act classifier assigns labels to individual posts, without considering the context in which the post is found. However, dialogue acts are highly dependent on context, and some sequences of dialogue act are much more likely than others. For example, a ynQuestion dialogue act is much more likely to be answered by a `yanswer` than by a `greeting`. Make use of this fact to build a consecutive classifier for labeling dialogue acts. Be sure to consider what features might be useful. See the code for the consecutive classifier for part-of-speech tags in Example 6-5 to get some ideas.

8. ◑ Word features can be very useful for performing document classification, since the words that appear in a document give a strong indication about what its semantic content is. However, many words occur very infrequently, and some of the most informative words in a document may never have occurred in our training data. One solution is to make use of a **lexicon**, which describes how different words relate to one another. Using the WordNet lexicon, augment the movie review document classifier presented in this chapter to use features that generalize the words that appear in a document, making it more likely that they will match words found in the training data.

9. ● The PP Attachment Corpus is a corpus describing prepositional phrase attachment decisions. Each instance in the corpus is encoded as a `PPAttachment` object:

```
>>> from nltk.corpus import ppattach
>>> ppattach.attachments('training')
[PPAttachment(sent='0', verb='join', noun1='board',
              prep='as', noun2='director', attachment='V'),
 PPAttachment(sent='1', verb='is', noun1='chairman',
              prep='of', noun2='N.V.', attachment='N'),
 ...]
>>> inst = ppattach.attachments('training')[1]
>>> (inst.noun1, inst.prep, inst.noun2)
('chairman', 'of', 'N.V.')
```

Select only the instances where `inst.attachment` is `N`:

```
>>> nattach = [inst for inst in ppattach.attachments('training')
...            if inst.attachment == 'N']
```

Using this subcorpus, build a classifier that attempts to predict which preposition is used to connect a given pair of nouns. For example, given the pair of nouns *team* and *researchers*, the classifier should predict the preposition *of*. See the corpus HOWTO at *http://www.nltk.org/howto* for more information on using the PP Attachment Corpus.

10. ● Suppose you wanted to automatically generate a prose description of a scene, and already had a word to uniquely describe each entity, such as *the book*, and simply wanted to decide whether to use *in* or *on* in relating various items, e.g., *the book is in the cupboard* versus *the book is on the shelf*. Explore this issue by looking at corpus data and writing programs as needed. Consider the following examples:

(13)   a. in the car *versus* on the train

        b. in town *versus* on campus

        c. in the picture *versus* on the screen

        d. in Macbeth *versus* on Letterman

## CHAPTER 7

Extracting Information from Text

For any given question, it's likely that someone has written the answer down somewhere. The amount of natural language text that is available in electronic form is truly staggering, and is increasing every day. However, the complexity of natural language can make it very difficult to access the information in that text. The state of the art in NLP is still a long way from being able to build general-purpose representations of meaning from unrestricted text. If we instead focus our efforts on a limited set of questions or "entity relations," such as "where are different facilities located" or "who is employed by what company," we can make significant progress. The goal of this chapter is to answer the following questions:

1. How can we build a system that extracts structured data from unstructured text?
2. What are some robust methods for identifying the entities and relationships described in a text?
3. Which corpora are appropriate for this work, and how do we use them for training and evaluating our models?

Along the way, we'll apply techniques from the last two chapters to the problems of chunking and named entity recognition.

7.1 Information Extraction

Information comes in many shapes and sizes. One important form is **structured data**, where there is a regular and predictable organization of entities and relationships. For example, we might be interested in the relation between companies and locations. Given a particular company, we would like to be able to identify the locations where it does business; conversely, given a location, we would like to discover which companies do business in that location. If our data is in tabular form, such as the example in Table 7-1, then answering these queries is straightforward.

Table 7-1. Locations data

OrgName	LocationName
Omnicom	New York
DDB Needham	New York
Kaplan Thaler Group	New York
BBDO South	Atlanta
Georgia-Pacific	Atlanta

If this location data was stored in Python as a list of tuples (*entity*, *relation*, *entity*), then the question "Which organizations operate in Atlanta?" could be translated as follows:

```
>>> print [org for (e1, rel, e2) if rel=='IN' and e2=='Atlanta']
['BBDO South', 'Georgia-Pacific']
```

Things are more tricky if we try to get similar information out of text. For example, consider the following snippet (from `nltk.corpus.ieer`, for fileid `NYT19980315.0085`).

(1) The fourth Wells account moving to another agency is the packaged paper-products division of Georgia-Pacific Corp., which arrived at Wells only last fall. Like Hertz and the History Channel, it is also leaving for an Omnicom-owned agency, the BBDO South unit of BBDO Worldwide. BBDO South in Atlanta, which handles corporate advertising for Georgia-Pacific, will assume additional duties for brands like Angel Soft toilet tissue and Sparkle paper towels, said Ken Haldin, a spokesman for Georgia-Pacific in Atlanta.

If you read through (1), you will glean the information required to answer the example question. But how do we get a machine to understand enough about (1) to return the list ['BBDO South', 'Georgia-Pacific'] as an answer? This is obviously a much harder task. Unlike Table 7-1, (1) contains no structure that links organization names with location names.

One approach to this problem involves building a very general representation of meaning (Chapter 10). In this chapter we take a different approach, deciding in advance that we will only look for very specific kinds of information in text, such as the relation between organizations and locations. Rather than trying to use text like (1) to answer the question directly, we first convert the **unstructured data** of natural language sentences into the structured data of Table 7-1. Then we reap the benefits of powerful query tools such as SQL. This method of getting meaning from text is called **Information Extraction**.

Information Extraction has many applications, including business intelligence, resume harvesting, media analysis, sentiment detection, patent search, and email scanning. A particularly important area of current research involves the attempt to extract structured data out of electronically available scientific literature, especially in the domain of biology and medicine.

Information Extraction Architecture

Figure 7-1 shows the architecture for a simple information extraction system. It begins by processing a document using several of the procedures discussed in Chapters 3 and 5: first, the raw text of the document is split into sentences using a sentence segmenter, and each sentence is further subdivided into words using a tokenizer. Next, each sentence is tagged with part-of-speech tags, which will prove very helpful in the next step, **named entity recognition**. In this step, we search for mentions of potentially interesting entities in each sentence. Finally, we use **relation recognition** to search for likely relations between different entities in the text.

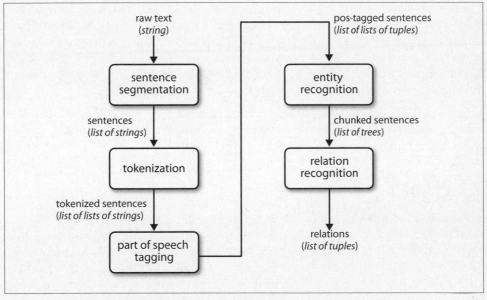

Figure 7-1. Simple pipeline architecture for an information extraction system. This system takes the raw text of a document as its input, and generates a list of (entity, relation, entity) tuples as its output. For example, given a document that indicates that the company Georgia-Pacific is located in Atlanta, it might generate the tuple ([ORG: 'Georgia-Pacific'] 'in' [LOC: 'Atlanta']).

To perform the first three tasks, we can define a function that simply connects together NLTK's default sentence segmenter ❶, word tokenizer ❷, and part-of-speech tagger ❸:

```
>>> def ie_preprocess(document):
...     sentences = nltk.sent_tokenize(document) ❶
...     sentences = [nltk.word_tokenize(sent) for sent in sentences] ❷
...     sentences = [nltk.pos_tag(sent) for sent in sentences] ❸
```

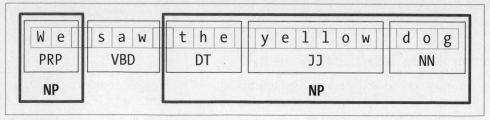

Figure 7-2. Segmentation and labeling at both the Token and Chunk levels.

Remember that our program samples assume you begin your interactive session or your program with `import nltk, re, pprint`.

Next, in named entity recognition, we segment and label the entities that might participate in interesting relations with one another. Typically, these will be definite noun phrases such as *the knights who say "ni"*, or proper names such as *Monty Python*. In some tasks it is useful to also consider indefinite nouns or noun chunks, such as *every student* or *cats*, and these do not necessarily refer to entities in the same way as definite NPs and proper names.

Finally, in relation extraction, we search for specific patterns between pairs of entities that occur near one another in the text, and use those patterns to build tuples recording the relationships between the entities.

7.2 Chunking

The basic technique we will use for entity recognition is **chunking**, which segments and labels multitoken sequences as illustrated in Figure 7-2. The smaller boxes show the word-level tokenization and part-of-speech tagging, while the large boxes show higher-level chunking. Each of these larger boxes is called a **chunk**. Like tokenization, which omits whitespace, chunking usually selects a subset of the tokens. Also like tokenization, the pieces produced by a chunker do not overlap in the source text.

In this section, we will explore chunking in some depth, beginning with the definition and representation of chunks. We will see regular expression and n-gram approaches to chunking, and will develop and evaluate chunkers using the CoNLL-2000 Chunking Corpus. We will then return in Sections 7.5 and 7.6 to the tasks of named entity recognition and relation extraction.

Noun Phrase Chunking

We will begin by considering the task of **noun phrase chunking**, or **NP-chunking**, where we search for chunks corresponding to individual noun phrases. For example, here is some *Wall Street Journal* text with NP-chunks marked using brackets:

---

(2) [The/DT market/NN] for/IN [system-management/NN software/NN] for/
    IN [Digital/NNP] ['s/POS hardware/NN] is/VBZ fragmented/JJ enough/RB
    that/IN [a/DT giant/NN] such/JJ as/IN [Computer/NNP Associates/NNPS]
    should/MD do/VB well/RB there/RB ./.

As we can see, NP-chunks are often smaller pieces than complete noun phrases. For
example, *the market for system-management software for Digital's hardware* is a single
noun phrase (containing two nested noun phrases), but it is captured in NP-chunks by
the simpler chunk *the market*. One of the motivations for this difference is that NP-
chunks are defined so as not to contain other NP-chunks. Consequently, any prepositional phrases or subordinate clauses that modify a nominal will not be included in the
corresponding NP-chunk, since they almost certainly contain further noun phrases.

One of the most useful sources of information for NP-chunking is part-of-speech tags.
This is one of the motivations for performing part-of-speech tagging in our information
extraction system. We demonstrate this approach using an example sentence that has
been part-of-speech tagged in Example 7-1. In order to create an NP-chunker, we will
first define a **chunk grammar**, consisting of rules that indicate how sentences should
be chunked. In this case, we will define a simple grammar with a single regular
expression rule ❷. This rule says that an NP chunk should be formed whenever the
chunker finds an optional determiner (DT) followed by any number of adjectives (JJ)
and then a noun (NN). Using this grammar, we create a chunk parser ❸, and test it on
our example sentence ❹. The result is a tree, which we can either print ❺, or display
graphically ❻.

Example 7-1. Example of a simple regular expression–based NP chunker.

```
>>> sentence = [("the", "DT"), ("little", "JJ"), ("yellow", "JJ"), ❶
... ("dog", "NN"), ("barked", "VBD"), ("at", "IN"),  ("the", "DT"), ("cat", "NN")]

>>> grammar = "NP: {<DT>?<JJ>*<NN>}" ❷

>>> cp = nltk.RegexpParser(grammar) ❸
>>> result = cp.parse(sentence) ❹
>>> print result ❺
(S
  (NP the/DT little/JJ yellow/JJ dog/NN)
  barked/VBD
  at/IN
  (NP the/DT cat/NN))
>>> result.draw() ❻
```

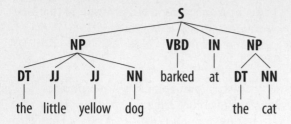

Tag Patterns

The rules that make up a chunk grammar use **tag patterns** to describe sequences of tagged words. A tag pattern is a sequence of part-of-speech tags delimited using angle brackets, e.g.,`<DT>?<JJ>*<NN>`. Tag patterns are similar to regular expression patterns (Section 3.4). Now, consider the following noun phrases from the *Wall Street Journal*:

```
another/DT sharp/JJ dive/NN
trade/NN figures/NNS
any/DT new/JJ policy/NN measures/NNS
earlier/JJR stages/NNS
Panamanian/JJ dictator/NN Manuel/NNP Noriega/NNP
```

We can match these noun phrases using a slight refinement of the first tag pattern above, i.e., `<DT>?<JJ.*>*<NN.*>+`. This will chunk any sequence of tokens beginning with an optional determiner, followed by zero or more adjectives of any type (including relative adjectives like `earlier/JJR`), followed by one or more nouns of any type. However, it is easy to find many more complicated examples which this rule will not cover:

```
his/PRP$ Mansion/NNP House/NNP speech/NN
the/DT price/NN cutting/VBG
3/CD %/NN to/TO 4/CD %/NN
more/JJR than/IN 10/CD %/NN
the/DT fastest/JJS developing/VBG trends/NNS
's/POS skill/NN
```

 Your Turn: Try to come up with tag patterns to cover these cases. Test them using the graphical interface `nltk.app.chunkparser()`. Continue to refine your tag patterns with the help of the feedback given by this tool.

Chunking with Regular Expressions

To find the chunk structure for a given sentence, the `RegexpParser` chunker begins with a flat structure in which no tokens are chunked. The chunking rules are applied in turn, successively updating the chunk structure. Once all of the rules have been invoked, the resulting chunk structure is returned.

Example 7-2 shows a simple chunk grammar consisting of two rules. The first rule matches an optional determiner or possessive pronoun, zero or more adjectives, then

---

a noun. The second rule matches one or more proper nouns. We also define an example sentence to be chunked , and run the chunker on this input .

Example 7-2. Simple noun phrase chunker.

```
grammar = r"""
  NP: {<DT|PP\$>?<JJ>*<NN>}    # chunk determiner/possessive, adjectives and nouns
      {<NNP>+}                 # chunk sequences of proper nouns
"""
cp = nltk.RegexpParser(grammar)
sentence = [("Rapunzel", "NNP"), ("let", "VBD"), ("down", "RP"), ❶
                ("her", "PP$"), ("long", "JJ"), ("golden", "JJ"), ("hair", "NN")]
>>> print cp.parse(sentence) ❶
(S
  (NP Rapunzel/NNP)
  let/VBD
  down/RP
  (NP her/PP$ long/JJ golden/JJ hair/NN))
```

>
> The $ symbol is a special character in regular expressions, and must be backslash escaped in order to match the tag PP$.

If a tag pattern matches at overlapping locations, the leftmost match takes precedence. For example, if we apply a rule that matches two consecutive nouns to a text containing three consecutive nouns, then only the first two nouns will be chunked:

```
>>> nouns = [("money", "NN"), ("market", "NN"), ("fund", "NN")]
>>> grammar = "NP: {<NN><NN>}  # Chunk two consecutive nouns"
>>> cp = nltk.RegexpParser(grammar)
>>> print cp.parse(nouns)
(S (NP money/NN market/NN) fund/NN)
```

Once we have created the chunk for *money market*, we have removed the context that would have permitted *fund* to be included in a chunk. This issue would have been avoided with a more permissive chunk rule, e.g., NP: {<NN>+}.

>
> We have added a comment to each of our chunk rules. These are optional; when they are present, the chunker prints these comments as part of its tracing output.

Exploring Text Corpora

In Section 5.2, we saw how we could interrogate a tagged corpus to extract phrases matching a particular sequence of part-of-speech tags. We can do the same work more easily with a chunker, as follows:

```
>>> cp = nltk.RegexpParser('CHUNK: {<V.*> <TO> <V.*>}')
>>> brown = nltk.corpus.brown
>>> for sent in brown.tagged_sents():
...     tree = cp.parse(sent)
...     for subtree in tree.subtrees():
...         if subtree.node == 'CHUNK': print subtree
...
(CHUNK combined/VBN to/TO achieve/VB)
(CHUNK continue/VB to/TO place/VB)
(CHUNK serve/VB to/TO protect/VB)
(CHUNK wanted/VBD to/TO wait/VB)
(CHUNK allowed/VBN to/TO place/VB)
(CHUNK expected/VBN to/TO become/VB)
...
(CHUNK seems/VBZ to/TO overtake/VB)
(CHUNK want/VB to/TO buy/VB)
```

 Your Turn: Encapsulate the previous example inside a function find_chunks() that takes a chunk string like "CHUNK: {<V.*> <TO> <V.*>}" as an argument. Use it to search the corpus for several other patterns, such as four or more nouns in a row, e.g., "NOUNS: {<N.*>{4,}}".

Chinking

Sometimes it is easier to define what we want to *exclude* from a chunk. We can define a **chink** to be a sequence of tokens that is not included in a chunk. In the following example, barked/VBD at/IN is a chink:

    [the/DT little/JJ yellow/JJ dog/NN] barked/VBD at/IN [the/DT cat/NN]

Chinking is the process of removing a sequence of tokens from a chunk. If the matching sequence of tokens spans an entire chunk, then the whole chunk is removed; if the sequence of tokens appears in the middle of the chunk, these tokens are removed, leaving two chunks where there was only one before. If the sequence is at the periphery of the chunk, these tokens are removed, and a smaller chunk remains. These three possibilities are illustrated in Table 7-2.

Table 7-2. Three chinking rules applied to the same chunk

	Entire chunk	Middle of a chunk	End of a chunk
Input	[a/DT little/JJ dog/NN]	[a/DT little/JJ dog/NN]	[a/DT little/JJ dog/NN]
Operation	Chink "DT JJ NN"	Chink "JJ"	Chink "NN"
Pattern	}DT JJ NN{	}JJ{	}NN{
Output	a/DT little/JJ dog/NN	[a/DT] little/JJ [dog/NN]	[a/DT little/JJ] dog/NN

In Example 7-3, we put the entire sentence into a single chunk, then excise the chinks.

Example 7-3. Simple chinker.

```
grammar = r"""
  NP:
    {<.*>+}          # Chunk everything
    }<VBD|IN>+{      # Chink sequences of VBD and IN
  """
sentence = [("the", "DT"), ("little", "JJ"), ("yellow", "JJ"),
      ("dog", "NN"), ("barked", "VBD"), ("at", "IN"),  ("the", "DT"), ("cat", "NN")]
cp = nltk.RegexpParser(grammar)
>>> print cp.parse(sentence)
(S
  (NP the/DT little/JJ yellow/JJ dog/NN)
  barked/VBD
  at/IN
  (NP the/DT cat/NN))
```

Representing Chunks: Tags Versus Trees

As befits their intermediate status between tagging and parsing (Chapter 8), chunk structures can be represented using either tags or trees. The most widespread file representation uses **IOB tags**. In this scheme, each token is tagged with one of three special chunk tags, I (inside), O (outside), or B (begin). A token is tagged as B if it marks the beginning of a chunk. Subsequent tokens within the chunk are tagged I. All other tokens are tagged O. The B and I tags are suffixed with the chunk type, e.g., B-NP, I-NP. Of course, it is not necessary to specify a chunk type for tokens that appear outside a chunk, so these are just labeled O. An example of this scheme is shown in Figure 7-3.

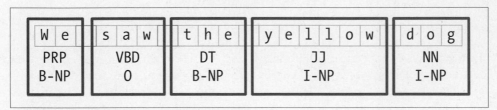

Figure 7-3. Tag representation of chunk structures.

IOB tags have become the standard way to represent chunk structures in files, and we will also be using this format. Here is how the information in Figure 7-3 would appear in a file:

```
We PRP B-NP
saw VBD O
the DT B-NP
little JJ I-NP
yellow JJ I-NP
dog NN I-NP
```

In this representation there is one token per line, each with its part-of-speech tag and chunk tag. This format permits us to represent more than one chunk type, so long as the chunks do not overlap. As we saw earlier, chunk structures can also be represented using trees. These have the benefit that each chunk is a constituent that can be manipulated directly. An example is shown in Figure 7-4.

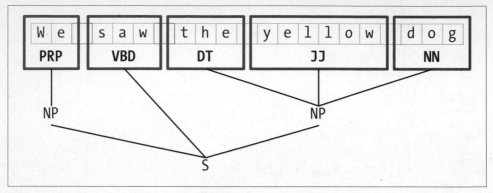

Figure 7-4. Tree representation of chunk structures.

 NLTK uses trees for its internal representation of chunks, but provides methods for converting between such trees and the IOB format.

7.3 Developing and Evaluating Chunkers

Now you have a taste of what chunking does, but we haven't explained how to evaluate chunkers. As usual, this requires a suitably annotated corpus. We begin by looking at the mechanics of converting IOB format into an NLTK tree, then at how this is done on a larger scale using a chunked corpus. We will see how to score the accuracy of a chunker relative to a corpus, then look at some more data-driven ways to search for NP chunks. Our focus throughout will be on expanding the coverage of a chunker.

Reading IOB Format and the CoNLL-2000 Chunking Corpus

Using the `corpora` module we can load *Wall Street Journal* text that has been tagged then chunked using the IOB notation. The chunk categories provided in this corpus are `NP`, `VP`, and `PP`. As we have seen, each sentence is represented using multiple lines, as shown here:

```
he PRP B-NP
accepted VBD B-VP
the DT B-NP
position NN I-NP
...
```

A conversion function `chunk.conllstr2tree()` builds a tree representation from one of these multiline strings. Moreover, it permits us to choose any subset of the three chunk types to use, here just for NP chunks:

```
>>> text = '''
... he PRP B-NP
... accepted VBD B-VP
... the DT B-NP
... position NN I-NP
... of IN B-PP
... vice NN B-NP
... chairman NN I-NP
... of IN B-PP
... Carlyle NNP B-NP
... Group NNP I-NP
... , , O
... a DT B-NP
... merchant NN I-NP
... banking NN I-NP
... concern NN I-NP
... . . O
... '''
>>> nltk.chunk.conllstr2tree(text, chunk_types=['NP']).draw()
```

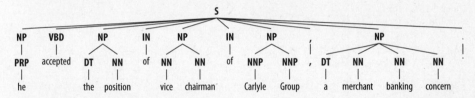

We can use the NLTK corpus module to access a larger amount of chunked text. The CoNLL-2000 Chunking Corpus contains 270k words of *Wall Street Journal* text, divided into "train" and "test" portions, annotated with part-of-speech tags and chunk tags in the IOB format. We can access the data using `nltk.corpus.conll2000`. Here is an example that reads the 100th sentence of the "train" portion of the corpus:

```
>>> from nltk.corpus import conll2000
>>> print conll2000.chunked_sents('train.txt')[99]
(S
  (PP Over/IN)
  (NP a/DT cup/NN)
  (PP of/IN)
  (NP coffee/NN)
  ,/,
  (NP Mr./NNP Stone/NNP)
  (VP told/VBD)
  (NP his/PRP$ story/NN)
  ./.)
```

As you can see, the CoNLL-2000 Chunking Corpus contains three chunk types: NP chunks, which we have already seen; VP chunks, such as *has already delivered*; and PP chunks, such as *because of*. Since we are only interested in the NP chunks right now, we can use the chunk_types argument to select them:

```
>>> print conll2000.chunked_sents('train.txt', chunk_types=['NP'])[99]
(S
  Over/IN
  (NP a/DT cup/NN)
  of/IN
  (NP coffee/NN)
  ,/,
  (NP Mr./NNP Stone/NNP)
  told/VBD
  (NP his/PRP$ story/NN)
  ./.)
```

Simple Evaluation and Baselines

Now that we can access a chunked corpus, we can evaluate chunkers. We start off by establishing a baseline for the trivial chunk parser cp that creates no chunks:

```
>>> from nltk.corpus import conll2000
>>> cp = nltk.RegexpParser("")
>>> test_sents = conll2000.chunked_sents('test.txt', chunk_types=['NP'])
>>> print cp.evaluate(test_sents)
ChunkParse score:
    IOB Accuracy:   43.4%
    Precision:       0.0%
    Recall:          0.0%
    F-Measure:       0.0%
```

The IOB tag accuracy indicates that more than a third of the words are tagged with O, i.e., not in an NP chunk. However, since our tagger did not find *any* chunks, its precision, recall, and F-measure are all zero. Now let's try a naive regular expression chunker that looks for tags beginning with letters that are characteristic of noun phrase tags (e.g., CD, DT, and JJ).

```
>>> grammar = r"NP: {<[CDJNP].*>+}"
>>> cp = nltk.RegexpParser(grammar)
>>> print cp.evaluate(test_sents)
ChunkParse score:
    IOB Accuracy:   87.7%
    Precision:      70.6%
    Recall:         67.8%
    F-Measure:      69.2%
```

As you can see, this approach achieves decent results. However, we can improve on it by adopting a more data-driven approach, where we use the training corpus to find the chunk tag (I, O, or B) that is most likely for each part-of-speech tag. In other words, we can build a chunker using a *unigram tagger* (Section 5.4). But rather than trying to determine the correct part-of-speech tag for each word, we are trying to determine the correct chunk tag, given each word's part-of-speech tag.

In Example 7-4, we define the `UnigramChunker` class, which uses a unigram tagger to label sentences with chunk tags. Most of the code in this class is simply used to convert back and forth between the chunk tree representation used by NLTK's `ChunkParserI` interface, and the IOB representation used by the embedded tagger. The class defines two methods: a constructor ❶, which is called when we build a new UnigramChunker; and the `parse` method ❸, which is used to chunk new sentences.

Example 7-4. Noun phrase chunking with a unigram tagger.

```
class UnigramChunker(nltk.ChunkParserI):
    def __init__(self, train_sents):  ❶
        train_data = [[(t,c) for w,t,c in nltk.chunk.tree2conlltags(sent)]
                         for sent in train_sents]
        self.tagger = nltk.UnigramTagger(train_data)  ❷

    def parse(self, sentence):  ❸
        pos_tags = [pos for (word,pos) in sentence]
        tagged_pos_tags = self.tagger.tag(pos_tags)
        chunktags = [chunktag for (pos, chunktag) in tagged_pos_tags]
        conlltags = [(word, pos, chunktag) for ((word,pos),chunktag)
                         in zip(sentence, chunktags)]
        return nltk.chunk.conlltags2tree(conlltags)
```

The constructor ❶ expects a list of training sentences, which will be in the form of chunk trees. It first converts training data to a form that's suitable for training the tagger, using `tree2conlltags` to map each chunk tree to a list of `word,tag,chunk` triples. It then uses that converted training data to train a unigram tagger, and stores it in `self.tagger` for later use.

The `parse` method ❸ takes a tagged sentence as its input, and begins by extracting the part-of-speech tags from that sentence. It then tags the part-of-speech tags with IOB chunk tags, using the tagger `self.tagger` that was trained in the constructor. Next, it extracts the chunk tags, and combines them with the original sentence, to yield `conlltags`. Finally, it uses `conlltags2tree` to convert the result back into a chunk tree.

Now that we have `UnigramChunker`, we can train it using the CoNLL-2000 Chunking Corpus, and test its resulting performance:

```
>>> test_sents = conll2000.chunked_sents('test.txt', chunk_types=['NP'])
>>> train_sents = conll2000.chunked_sents('train.txt', chunk_types=['NP'])
>>> unigram_chunker = UnigramChunker(train_sents)
>>> print unigram_chunker.evaluate(test_sents)
ChunkParse score:
    IOB Accuracy:  92.9%
    Precision:     79.9%
    Recall:        86.8%
    F-Measure:     83.2%
```

This chunker does reasonably well, achieving an overall F-measure score of 83%. Let's take a look at what it's learned, by using its unigram tagger to assign a tag to each of the part-of-speech tags that appear in the corpus:

```
>>> postags = sorted(set(pos for sent in train_sents
...                       for (word,pos) in sent.leaves()))
>>> print unigram_chunker.tagger.tag(postags)
[('#', 'B-NP'), ('$', 'B-NP'), ("'", 'O'), ('(', 'O'), (')', 'O'),
 (',', 'O'), ('.', 'O'), (':', 'O'), ('CC', 'O'), ('CD', 'I-NP'),
 ('DT', 'B-NP'), ('EX', 'B-NP'), ('FW', 'I-NP'), ('IN', 'O'),
 ('JJ', 'I-NP'), ('JJR', 'B-NP'), ('JJS', 'I-NP'), ('MD', 'O'),
 ('NN', 'I-NP'), ('NNP', 'I-NP'), ('NNPS', 'I-NP'), ('NNS', 'I-NP'),
 ('PDT', 'B-NP'), ('POS', 'B-NP'), ('PRP', 'B-NP'), ('PRP$', 'B-NP'),
 ('RB', 'O'), ('RBR', 'O'), ('RBS', 'B-NP'), ('RP', 'O'), ('SYM', 'O'),
 ('TO', 'O'), ('UH', 'O'), ('VB', 'O'), ('VBD', 'O'), ('VBG', 'O'),
 ('VBN', 'O'), ('VBP', 'O'), ('VBZ', 'O'), ('WDT', 'B-NP'),
 ('WP', 'B-NP'), ('WP$', 'B-NP'), ('WRB', 'O'), ('``', 'O')]
```

It has discovered that most punctuation marks occur outside of NP chunks, with the exception of # and $, both of which are used as currency markers. It has also found that determiners (DT) and possessives (PRP$ and WP$) occur at the beginnings of NP chunks, while noun types (NN, NNP, NNPS, NNS) mostly occur inside of NP chunks.

Having built a unigram chunker, it is quite easy to build a bigram chunker: we simply change the class name to BigramChunker, and modify line ❷ in Example 7-4 to construct a BigramTagger rather than a UnigramTagger. The resulting chunker has slightly higher performance than the unigram chunker:

```
>>> bigram_chunker = BigramChunker(train_sents)
>>> print bigram_chunker.evaluate(test_sents)
ChunkParse score:
    IOB Accuracy:   93.3%
    Precision:      82.3%
    Recall:         86.8%
    F-Measure:      84.5%
```

Training Classifier-Based Chunkers

Both the regular expression–based chunkers and the n-gram chunkers decide what chunks to create entirely based on part-of-speech tags. However, sometimes part-of-speech tags are insufficient to determine how a sentence should be chunked. For example, consider the following two statements:

(3) a. Joey/NN sold/VBD the/DT farmer/NN rice/NN ./.

   b. Nick/NN broke/VBD my/DT computer/NN monitor/NN ./.

These two sentences have the same part-of-speech tags, yet they are chunked differently. In the first sentence, *the farmer* and *rice* are separate chunks, while the corresponding material in the second sentence, *the computer monitor*, is a single chunk. Clearly, we need to make use of information about the content of the words, in addition to just their part-of-speech tags, if we wish to maximize chunking performance.

One way that we can incorporate information about the content of words is to use a classifier-based tagger to chunk the sentence. Like the n-gram chunker considered in the previous section, this classifier-based chunker will work by assigning IOB tags to the words in a sentence, and then converting those tags to chunks. For the classifier-based tagger itself, we will use the same approach that we used in Section 6.1 to build a part-of-speech tagger.

The basic code for the classifier-based NP chunker is shown in Example 7-5. It consists of two classes. The first class ❶ is almost identical to the ConsecutivePosTagger class from Example 6-5. The only two differences are that it calls a different feature extractor ❷ and that it uses a MaxentClassifier rather than a NaiveBayesClassifier ❸. The second class ❹ is basically a wrapper around the tagger class that turns it into a chunker. During training, this second class maps the chunk trees in the training corpus into tag sequences; in the parse() method, it converts the tag sequence provided by the tagger back into a chunk tree.

Example 7-5. Noun phrase chunking with a consecutive classifier.

```
class ConsecutiveNPChunkTagger(nltk.TaggerI):  ❶

    def __init__(self, train_sents):
        train_set = []
        for tagged_sent in train_sents:
            untagged_sent = nltk.tag.untag(tagged_sent)
            history = []
            for i, (word, tag) in enumerate(tagged_sent):
                featureset = npchunk_features(untagged_sent, i, history)  ❷
                train_set.append( (featureset, tag) )
                history.append(tag)
        self.classifier = nltk.MaxentClassifier.train(  ❸
            train_set, algorithm='megam', trace=0)

    def tag(self, sentence):
        history = []
        for i, word in enumerate(sentence):
            featureset = npchunk_features(sentence, i, history)
            tag = self.classifier.classify(featureset)
            history.append(tag)
        return zip(sentence, history)

class ConsecutiveNPChunker(nltk.ChunkParserI):  ❹
    def __init__(self, train_sents):
        tagged_sents = [[((w,t),c) for (w,t,c) in
                         nltk.chunk.tree2conlltags(sent)]
                        for sent in train_sents]
        self.tagger = ConsecutiveNPChunkTagger(tagged_sents)

    def parse(self, sentence):
        tagged_sents = self.tagger.tag(sentence)
        conlltags = [(w,t,c) for ((w,t),c) in tagged_sents]
        return nltk.chunk.conlltags2tree(conlltags)
```

The only piece left to fill in is the feature extractor. We begin by defining a simple feature extractor, which just provides the part-of-speech tag of the current token. Using this feature extractor, our classifier-based chunker is very similar to the unigram chunker, as is reflected in its performance:

```
>>> def npchunk_features(sentence, i, history):
...     word, pos = sentence[i]
...     return {"pos": pos}
>>> chunker = ConsecutiveNPChunker(train_sents)
>>> print chunker.evaluate(test_sents)
ChunkParse score:
    IOB Accuracy:  92.9%
    Precision:     79.9%
    Recall:        86.7%
    F-Measure:     83.2%
```

We can also add a feature for the previous part-of-speech tag. Adding this feature allows the classifier to model interactions between adjacent tags, and results in a chunker that is closely related to the bigram chunker.

```
>>> def npchunk_features(sentence, i, history):
...     word, pos = sentence[i]
...     if i == 0:
...         prevword, prevpos = "<START>", "<START>"
...     else:
...         prevword, prevpos = sentence[i-1]
...     return {"pos": pos, "prevpos": prevpos}
>>> chunker = ConsecutiveNPChunker(train_sents)
>>> print chunker.evaluate(test_sents)
ChunkParse score:
    IOB Accuracy:  93.6%
    Precision:     81.9%
    Recall:        87.1%
    F-Measure:     84.4%
```

Next, we'll try adding a feature for the current word, since we hypothesized that word content should be useful for chunking. We find that this feature does indeed improve the chunker's performance, by about 1.5 percentage points (which corresponds to about a 10% reduction in the error rate).

```
>>> def npchunk_features(sentence, i, history):
...     word, pos = sentence[i]
...     if i == 0:
...         prevword, prevpos = "<START>", "<START>"
...     else:
...         prevword, prevpos = sentence[i-1]
...     return {"pos": pos, "word": word, "prevpos": prevpos}
>>> chunker = ConsecutiveNPChunker(train_sents)
>>> print chunker.evaluate(test_sents)
ChunkParse score:
    IOB Accuracy:  94.2%
    Precision:     83.4%
    Recall:        88.6%
    F-Measure:     85.9%
```

Finally, we can try extending the feature extractor with a variety of additional features, such as lookahead features ❶, paired features ❷, and complex contextual features ❸. This last feature, called `tags-since-dt`, creates a string describing the set of all part-of-speech tags that have been encountered since the most recent determiner.

```
>>> def npchunk_features(sentence, i, history):
...     word, pos = sentence[i]
...     if i == 0:
...         prevword, prevpos = "<START>", "<START>"
...     else:
...         prevword, prevpos = sentence[i-1]
...     if i == len(sentence)-1:
...         nextword, nextpos = "<END>", "<END>"
...     else:
...         nextword, nextpos = sentence[i+1]
...     return {"pos": pos,
...             "word": word,
...             "prevpos": prevpos,
...             "nextpos": nextpos,                         ❶
...             "prevpos+pos": "%s+%s" % (prevpos, pos),    ❷
...             "pos+nextpos": "%s+%s" % (pos, nextpos),
...             "tags-since-dt": tags_since_dt(sentence, i)}  ❸
>>> def tags_since_dt(sentence, i):
...     tags = set()
...     for word, pos in sentence[:i]:
...         if pos == 'DT':
...             tags = set()
...         else:
...             tags.add(pos)
...     return '+'.join(sorted(tags))
>>> chunker = ConsecutiveNPChunker(train_sents)
>>> print chunker.evaluate(test_sents)
ChunkParse score:
    IOB Accuracy:   95.9%
    Precision:      88.3%
    Recall:         90.7%
    F-Measure:      89.5%
```

 Your Turn: Try adding different features to the feature extractor function `npchunk_features`, and see if you can further improve the performance of the NP chunker.

7.4 Recursion in Linguistic Structure

Building Nested Structure with Cascaded Chunkers

So far, our chunk structures have been relatively flat. Trees consist of tagged tokens, optionally grouped under a chunk node such as NP. However, it is possible to build chunk structures of arbitrary depth, simply by creating a multistage chunk grammar containing recursive rules. Example 7-6 has patterns for noun phrases, prepositional phrases, verb phrases, and sentences. This is a four-stage chunk grammar, and can be used to create structures having a depth of at most four.

Example 7-6. A chunker that handles NP, PP, VP, and S.

```
grammar = r"""
  NP: {<DT|JJ|NN.*>+}          # Chunk sequences of DT, JJ, NN
  PP: {<IN><NP>}               # Chunk prepositions followed by NP
  VP: {<VB.*><NP|PP|CLAUSE>+$} # Chunk verbs and their arguments
  CLAUSE: {<NP><VP>}           # Chunk NP, VP
  """
cp = nltk.RegexpParser(grammar)
sentence = [("Mary", "NN"), ("saw", "VBD"), ("the", "DT"), ("cat", "NN"),
    ("sit", "VB"), ("on", "IN"), ("the", "DT"), ("mat", "NN")]
>>> print cp.parse(sentence)
(S
  (NP Mary/NN)
  saw/VBD
  (CLAUSE
    (NP the/DT cat/NN)
    (VP sit/VB (PP on/IN (NP the/DT mat/NN)))))
```

Unfortunately this result misses the VP headed by *saw*. It has other shortcomings, too. Let's see what happens when we apply this chunker to a sentence having deeper nesting. Notice that it fails to identify the VP chunk starting at ❶.

```
>>> sentence = [("John", "NNP"), ("thinks", "VBZ"), ("Mary", "NN"),
...       ("saw", "VBD"), ("the", "DT"), ("cat", "NN"), ("sit", "VB"),
...       ("on", "IN"), ("the", "DT"), ("mat", "NN")]
>>> print cp.parse(sentence)
(S
  (NP John/NNP)
  thinks/VBZ
  (NP Mary/NN)
  saw/VBD ❶
  (CLAUSE
    (NP the/DT cat/NN)
    (VP sit/VB (PP on/IN (NP the/DT mat/NN)))))
```

The solution to these problems is to get the chunker to loop over its patterns: after trying all of them, it repeats the process. We add an optional second argument `loop` to specify the number of times the set of patterns should be run:

```
>>> cp = nltk.RegexpParser(grammar, loop=2)
>>> print cp.parse(sentence)
(S
  (NP John/NNP)
  thinks/VBZ
  (CLAUSE
    (NP Mary/NN)
    (VP
      saw/VBD
      (CLAUSE
```

```
(NP the/DT cat/NN)
(VP sit/VB (PP on/IN (NP the/DT mat/NN)))))))
```

 This cascading process enables us to create deep structures. However, creating and debugging a cascade is difficult, and there comes a point where it is more effective to do full parsing (see Chapter 8). Also, the cascading process can only produce trees of fixed depth (no deeper than the number of stages in the cascade), and this is insufficient for complete syntactic analysis.

Trees

A **tree** is a set of connected labeled nodes, each reachable by a unique path from a distinguished root node. Here's an example of a tree (note that they are standardly drawn upside-down):

(4)

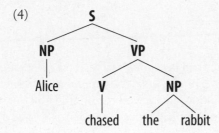

We use a 'family' metaphor to talk about the relationships of nodes in a tree: for example, S is the **parent** of VP; conversely VP is a **child** of S. Also, since NP and VP are both children of S, they are also **siblings**. For convenience, there is also a text format for specifying trees:

```
(S
    (NP Alice)
    (VP
        (V chased)
        (NP
            (Det the)
            (N rabbit))))
```

Although we will focus on syntactic trees, trees can be used to encode *any* homogeneous hierarchical structure that spans a sequence of linguistic forms (e.g., morphological structure, discourse structure). In the general case, leaves and node values do not have to be strings.

In NLTK, we create a tree by giving a node label and a list of children:

```
>>> tree1 = nltk.Tree('NP', ['Alice'])
>>> print tree1
(NP Alice)
>>> tree2 = nltk.Tree('NP', ['the', 'rabbit'])
>>> print tree2
(NP the rabbit)
```

We can incorporate these into successively larger trees as follows:

```
>>> tree3 = nltk.Tree('VP', ['chased', tree2])
>>> tree4 = nltk.Tree('S', [tree1, tree3])
>>> print tree4
(S (NP Alice) (VP chased (NP the rabbit)))
```

Here are some of the methods available for tree objects:

```
>>> print tree4[1]
(VP chased (NP the rabbit))
>>> tree4[1].node
'VP'
>>> tree4.leaves()
['Alice', 'chased', 'the', 'rabbit']
>>> tree4[1][1][1]
'rabbit'
```

The bracketed representation for complex trees can be difficult to read. In these cases, the draw method can be very useful. It opens a new window, containing a graphical representation of the tree. The tree display window allows you to zoom in and out, to collapse and expand subtrees, and to print the graphical representation to a postscript file (for inclusion in a document).

```
>>> tree3.draw()
```

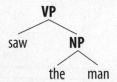

Tree Traversal

It is standard to use a recursive function to traverse a tree. The listing in Example 7-7 demonstrates this.

Example 7-7. A recursive function to traverse a tree.

```
def traverse(t):
    try:
        t.node
    except AttributeError:
        print t,

    else:
```

```
        # Now we know that t.node is defined
        print '(', t.node,
        for child in t:
            traverse(child)
        print ')',

>>> t = nltk.Tree('(S (NP Alice) (VP chased (NP the rabbit)))')
>>> traverse(t)
( S ( NP Alice ) ( VP chased ( NP the rabbit ) ) )
```

We have used a technique called **duck typing** to detect that t is a tree
(i.e., t.node is defined).

7.5 Named Entity Recognition

At the start of this chapter, we briefly introduced named entities (NEs). Named entities
are definite noun phrases that refer to specific types of individuals, such as organizations, persons, dates, and so on. Table 7-3 lists some of the more commonly used types
of NEs. These should be self-explanatory, except for "FACILITY": human-made artifacts in the domains of architecture and civil engineering; and "GPE": geo-political
entities such as city, state/province, and country.

Table 7-3. Commonly used types of named entity

NE type	Examples
ORGANIZATION	*Georgia-Pacific Corp., WHO*
PERSON	*Eddy Bonte, President Obama*
LOCATION	*Murray River, Mount Everest*
DATE	*June, 2008-06-29*
TIME	*two fifty a m, 1:30 p.m.*
MONEY	*175 million Canadian Dollars, GBP 10.40*
PERCENT	*twenty pct, 18.75 %*
FACILITY	*Washington Monument, Stonehenge*
GPE	*South East Asia, Midlothian*

The goal of a **named entity recognition** (NER) system is to identify all textual mentions of the named entities. This can be broken down into two subtasks: identifying
the boundaries of the NE, and identifying its type. While named entity recognition is
frequently a prelude to identifying relations in Information Extraction, it can also contribute to other tasks. For example, in Question Answering (QA), we try to improve
the precision of Information Retrieval by recovering not whole pages, but just those
parts which contain an answer to the user's question. Most QA systems take the

documents returned by standard Information Retrieval, and then attempt to isolate the minimal text snippet in the document containing the answer. Now suppose the question was *Who was the first President of the US?*, and one of the documents that was retrieved contained the following passage:

(5) The Washington Monument is the most prominent structure in Washington, D.C. and one of the city's early attractions. It was built in honor of George Washington, who led the country to independence and then became its first President.

Analysis of the question leads us to expect that an answer should be of the form *X was the first President of the US*, where *X* is not only a noun phrase, but also refers to a named entity of type PER. This should allow us to ignore the first sentence in the passage. Although it contains two occurrences of *Washington*, named entity recognition should tell us that neither of them has the correct type.

How do we go about identifying named entities? One option would be to look up each word in an appropriate list of names. For example, in the case of locations, we could use a **gazetteer**, or geographical dictionary, such as the Alexandria Gazetteer or the Getty Gazetteer. However, doing this blindly runs into problems, as shown in Figure 7-5.

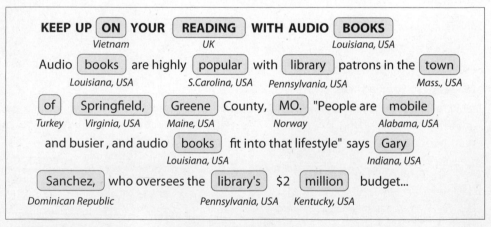

Figure 7-5. Location detection by simple lookup for a news story: Looking up every word in a gazetteer is error-prone; case distinctions may help, but these are not always present.

Observe that the gazetteer has good coverage of locations in many countries, and incorrectly finds locations like Sanchez in the Dominican Republic and On in Vietnam. Of course we could omit such locations from the gazetteer, but then we won't be able to identify them when they do appear in a document.

It gets even harder in the case of names for people or organizations. Any list of such names will probably have poor coverage. New organizations come into existence every day, so if we are trying to deal with contemporary newswire or blog entries, it is unlikely that we will be able to recognize many of the entities using gazetteer lookup.

Another major source of difficulty is caused by the fact that many named entity terms are ambiguous. Thus *May* and *North* are likely to be parts of named entities for DATE and LOCATION, respectively, but could both be part of a PERSON; conversely *Christian Dior* looks like a PERSON but is more likely to be of type ORGANIZATION. A term like *Yankee* will be an ordinary modifier in some contexts, but will be marked as an entity of type ORGANIZATION in the phrase *Yankee infielders*.

Further challenges are posed by multiword names like *Stanford University*, and by names that contain other names, such as *Cecil H. Green Library* and *Escondido Village Conference Service Center*. In named entity recognition, therefore, we need to be able to identify the beginning and end of multitoken sequences.

Named entity recognition is a task that is well suited to the type of classifier-based approach that we saw for noun phrase chunking. In particular, we can build a tagger that labels each word in a sentence using the IOB format, where chunks are labeled by their appropriate type. Here is part of the CONLL 2002 (`conll2002`) Dutch training data:

```
Eddy N B-PER
Bonte N I-PER
is V O
woordvoerder N O
van Prep O
diezelfde Pron O
Hogeschool N B-ORG
. Punc O
```

In this representation, there is one token per line, each with its part-of-speech tag and its named entity tag. Based on this training corpus, we can construct a tagger that can be used to label new sentences, and use the `nltk.chunk.conlltags2tree()` function to convert the tag sequences into a chunk tree.

NLTK provides a classifier that has already been trained to recognize named entities, accessed with the function `nltk.ne_chunk()`. If we set the parameter `binary=True` ❶, then named entities are just tagged as `NE`; otherwise, the classifier adds category labels such as PERSON, ORGANIZATION, and GPE.

```
>>> sent = nltk.corpus.treebank.tagged_sents()[22]
>>> print nltk.ne_chunk(sent, binary=True) ❶
(S
  The/DT
  (NE U.S./NNP)
  is/VBZ
  one/CD
  ...
  according/VBG
  to/TO
  (NE Brooke/NNP T./NNP Mossman/NNP)
  ...)
```

```
>>> print nltk.ne_chunk(sent)
(S
  The/DT
  (GPE U.S./NNP)
  is/VBZ
  one/CD
  ...
  according/VBG
  to/TO
  (PERSON Brooke/NNP T./NNP Mossman/NNP)
  ...)
```

7.6 Relation Extraction

Once named entities have been identified in a text, we then want to extract the relations that exist between them. As indicated earlier, we will typically be looking for relations between specified types of named entity. One way of approaching this task is to initially look for all triples of the form (X, α, Y), where X and Y are named entities of the required types, and α is the string of words that intervenes between X and Y. We can then use regular expressions to pull out just those instances of α that express the relation that we are looking for. The following example searches for strings that contain the word *in*. The special regular expression `(?!\b.+ing\b)` is a negative lookahead assertion that allows us to disregard strings such as *success in supervising the transition of*, where *in* is followed by a gerund.

```
>>> IN = re.compile(r'.*\bin\b(?!\b.+ing)')
>>> for doc in nltk.corpus.ieer.parsed_docs('NYT_19980315'):
...     for rel in nltk.sem.extract_rels('ORG', 'LOC', doc,
...                                      corpus='ieer', pattern = IN):
...         print nltk.sem.show_raw_rtuple(rel)
[ORG: 'WHYY'] 'in' [LOC: 'Philadelphia']
[ORG: 'McGlashan &AMP; Sarrail'] 'firm in' [LOC: 'San Mateo']
[ORG: 'Freedom Forum'] 'in' [LOC: 'Arlington']
[ORG: 'Brookings Institution'] ', the research group in' [LOC: 'Washington']
[ORG: 'Idealab'] ', a self-described business incubator based in' [LOC: 'Los Angeles']
[ORG: 'Open Text'] ', based in' [LOC: 'Waterloo']
[ORG: 'WGBH'] 'in' [LOC: 'Boston']
[ORG: 'Bastille Opera'] 'in' [LOC: 'Paris']
[ORG: 'Omnicom'] 'in' [LOC: 'New York']
[ORG: 'DDB Needham'] 'in' [LOC: 'New York']
[ORG: 'Kaplan Thaler Group'] 'in' [LOC: 'New York']
[ORG: 'BBDO South'] 'in' [LOC: 'Atlanta']
[ORG: 'Georgia-Pacific'] 'in' [LOC: 'Atlanta']
```

Searching for the keyword *in* works reasonably well, though it will also retrieve false positives such as `[ORG: House Transportation Committee] , secured the most money in the [LOC: New York]`; there is unlikely to be a simple string-based method of excluding filler strings such as this.

As shown earlier, the Dutch section of the CoNLL 2002 Named Entity Corpus contains not just named entity annotation, but also part-of-speech tags. This allows us to devise patterns that are sensitive to these tags, as shown in the next example. The method `show_clause()` prints out the relations in a clausal form, where the binary relation symbol is specified as the value of parameter `relsym` ❶.

```
>>> from nltk.corpus import conll2002
>>> vnv = """
... (
... is/V|    # 3rd sing present and
... was/V|   # past forms of the verb zijn ('be')
... werd/V|  # and also present
... wordt/V  # past of worden ('become')
... )
... .*       # followed by anything
... van/Prep # followed by van ('of')
... """
>>> VAN = re.compile(vnv, re.VERBOSE)
>>> for doc in conll2002.chunked_sents('ned.train'):
...     for r in nltk.sem.extract_rels('PER', 'ORG', doc,
...                             corpus='conll2002', pattern=VAN):
...         print nltk.sem.show_clause(r, relsym="VAN") ❶
VAN("cornet_d'elzius", 'buitenlandse_handel')
VAN('johan_rottiers', 'kardinaal_van_roey_instituut')
VAN('annie_lennox', 'eurythmics')
```

 Your Turn: Replace the last line ❶ with print show_raw_rtuple(rel, lcon=True, rcon=True). This will show you the actual words that intervene between the two NEs and also their left and right context, within a default 10-word window. With the help of a Dutch dictionary, you might be able to figure out why the result VAN('annie_lennox', 'eurythmics') is a false hit.

7.7 Summary

- Information extraction systems search large bodies of unrestricted text for specific types of entities and relations, and use them to populate well-organized databases. These databases can then be used to find answers for specific questions.

- The typical architecture for an information extraction system begins by segmenting, tokenizing, and part-of-speech tagging the text. The resulting data is then searched for specific types of entity. Finally, the information extraction system looks at entities that are mentioned near one another in the text, and tries to determine whether specific relationships hold between those entities.

- Entity recognition is often performed using chunkers, which segment multitoken sequences, and label them with the appropriate entity type. Common entity types include ORGANIZATION, PERSON, LOCATION, DATE, TIME, MONEY, and GPE (geo-political entity).

- Chunkers can be constructed using rule-based systems, such as the `RegexpParser` class provided by NLTK; or using machine learning techniques, such as the `ConsecutiveNPChunker` presented in this chapter. In either case, part-of-speech tags are often a very important feature when searching for chunks.

- Although chunkers are specialized to create relatively flat data structures, where no two chunks are allowed to overlap, they can be cascaded together to build nested structures.

- Relation extraction can be performed using either rule-based systems, which typically look for specific patterns in the text that connect entities and the intervening words; or using machine-learning systems, which typically attempt to learn such patterns automatically from a training corpus.

7.8 Further Reading

Extra materials for this chapter are posted at *http://www.nltk.org/*, including links to freely available resources on the Web. For more examples of chunking with NLTK, please see the Chunking HOWTO at *http://www.nltk.org/howto*.

The popularity of chunking is due in great part to pioneering work by Abney, e.g., (Abney, 1996a). Abney's Cass chunker is described in *http://www.vinartus.net/spa/97a .pdf*.

The word **chink** initially meant a sequence of stopwords, according to a 1975 paper by Ross and Tukey (Abney, 1996a).

The IOB format (or sometimes **BIO Format**) was developed for NP chunking by (Ramshaw & Marcus, 1995), and was used for the shared NP bracketing task run by the *Conference on Natural Language Learning* (CoNLL) in 1999. The same format was adopted by CoNLL 2000 for annotating a section of *Wall Street Journal* text as part of a shared task on NP chunking.

Section 13.5 of (Jurafsky & Martin, 2008) contains a discussion of chunking. Chapter 22 covers information extraction, including named entity recognition. For information about text mining in biology and medicine, see (Ananiadou & McNaught, 2006).

For more information on the Getty and Alexandria gazetteers, see *http://en.wikipedia .org/wiki/Getty_Thesaurus_of_Geographic_Names* and *http://www.alexandria.ucsb .edu/gazetteer/*.

7.9 Exercises

1. ○ The IOB format categorizes tagged tokens as I, 0, and B. Why are three tags necessary? What problem would be caused if we used I and 0 tags exclusively?

2. ○ Write a tag pattern to match noun phrases containing plural head nouns, e.g., `many/JJ researchers/NNS, two/CD weeks/NNS, both/DT new/JJ positions/NNS`. Try to do this by generalizing the tag pattern that handled singular noun phrases.

3. ○ Pick one of the three chunk types in the CoNLL-2000 Chunking Corpus. Inspect the data and try to observe any patterns in the POS tag sequences that make up this kind of chunk. Develop a simple chunker using the regular expression chunker `nltk.RegexpParser`. Discuss any tag sequences that are difficult to chunk reliably.

4. ○ An early definition of *chunk* was the material that occurs between chinks. Develop a chunker that starts by putting the whole sentence in a single chunk, and then does the rest of its work solely by chinking. Determine which tags (or tag sequences) are most likely to make up chinks with the help of your own utility program. Compare the performance and simplicity of this approach relative to a chunker based entirely on chunk rules.

5. ◑ Write a tag pattern to cover noun phrases that contain gerunds, e.g., `the/DT receiving/VBG end/NN, assistant/NN managing/VBG editor/NN`. Add these patterns to the grammar, one per line. Test your work using some tagged sentences of your own devising.

6. ◑ Write one or more tag patterns to handle coordinated noun phrases, e.g., `July/NNP and/CC August/NNP, all/DT your/PRP$ managers/NNS and/CC supervisors/NNS, company/NN courts/NNS and/CC adjudicators/NNS`.

7. ◑ Carry out the following evaluation tasks for any of the chunkers you have developed earlier. (Note that most chunking corpora contain some internal inconsistencies, such that any reasonable rule-based approach will produce errors.)

   a. Evaluate your chunker on 100 sentences from a chunked corpus, and report the precision, recall, and F-measure.

   b. Use the `chunkscore.missed()` and `chunkscore.incorrect()` methods to identify the errors made by your chunker. Discuss.

   c. Compare the performance of your chunker to the baseline chunker discussed in the evaluation section of this chapter.

8. ◑ Develop a chunker for one of the chunk types in the CoNLL Chunking Corpus using a regular expression–based chunk grammar `RegexpChunk`. Use any combination of rules for chunking, chinking, merging, or splitting.

9. ◑ Sometimes a word is incorrectly tagged, e.g., the head noun in `12/CD or/CC so/RB cases/VBZ`. Instead of requiring manual correction of tagger output, good chunkers are able to work with the erroneous output of taggers. Look for other examples of correctly chunked noun phrases with incorrect tags.

10. ◑ The bigram chunker scores about 90% accuracy. Study its errors and try to work out why it doesn't get 100% accuracy. Experiment with trigram chunking. Are you able to improve the performance any more?

11. ● Apply the n-gram and Brill tagging methods to IOB chunk tagging. Instead of assigning POS tags to words, here we will assign IOB tags to the POS tags. E.g., if the tag DT (determiner) often occurs at the start of a chunk, it will be tagged B (begin). Evaluate the performance of these chunking methods relative to the regular expression chunking methods covered in this chapter.

12. ● We saw in Chapter 5 that it is possible to establish an upper limit to tagging performance by looking for ambiguous n-grams, which are n-grams that are tagged in more than one possible way in the training data. Apply the same method to determine an upper bound on the performance of an n-gram chunker.

13. ● Pick one of the three chunk types in the CoNLL Chunking Corpus. Write functions to do the following tasks for your chosen type:

    a. List all the tag sequences that occur with each instance of this chunk type.

    b. Count the frequency of each tag sequence, and produce a ranked list in order of decreasing frequency; each line should consist of an integer (the frequency) and the tag sequence.

    c. Inspect the high-frequency tag sequences. Use these as the basis for developing a better chunker.

14. ● The baseline chunker presented in the evaluation section tends to create larger chunks than it should. For example, the phrase [every/DT time/NN] [she/PRP] sees/VBZ [a/DT newspaper/NN] contains two consecutive chunks, and our baseline chunker will incorrectly combine the first two: [every/DT time/NN she/PRP]. Write a program that finds which of these chunk-internal tags typically occur at the start of a chunk, then devise one or more rules that will split up these chunks. Combine these with the existing baseline chunker and re-evaluate it, to see if you have discovered an improved baseline.

15. ● Develop an NP chunker that converts POS tagged text into a list of tuples, where each tuple consists of a verb followed by a sequence of noun phrases and prepositions, e.g., the little cat sat on the mat becomes ('sat', 'on', 'NP')...

16. ● The Penn Treebank Corpus sample contains a section of tagged *Wall Street Journal* text that has been chunked into noun phrases. The format uses square brackets, and we have encountered it several times in this chapter. The corpus can be accessed using: for sent in nltk.corpus.treebank_chunk.chunked_sents(fil eid). These are flat trees, just as we got using nltk.cor pus.conll2000.chunked_sents().

    a. The functions nltk.tree.pprint() and nltk.chunk.tree2conllstr() can be used to create Treebank and IOB strings from a tree. Write functions chunk2brackets() and chunk2iob() that take a single chunk tree as their sole argument, and return the required multiline string representation.

    b. Write command-line conversion utilities bracket2iob.py and iob2bracket.py that take a file in Treebank or CoNLL format (respectively) and convert it to the other format. (Obtain some raw Treebank or CoNLL data from the NLTK

Corpora, save it to a file, and then use `for line in open(filename)` to access it from Python.)

17. ● An n-gram chunker can use information other than the current part-of-speech tag and the *n*-1 previous chunk tags. Investigate other models of the context, such as the *n*-1 previous part-of-speech tags, or some combination of previous chunk tags along with previous and following part-of-speech tags.

18. ● Consider the way an n-gram tagger uses recent tags to inform its tagging choice. Now observe how a chunker may reuse this sequence information. For example, both tasks will make use of the information that nouns tend to follow adjectives (in English). It would appear that the same information is being maintained in two places. Is this likely to become a problem as the size of the rule sets grows? If so, speculate about any ways that this problem might be addressed.

## CHAPTER 8

Analyzing Sentence Structure

Earlier chapters focused on words: how to identify them, analyze their structure, assign them to lexical categories, and access their meanings. We have also seen how to identify patterns in word sequences or n-grams. However, these methods only scratch the surface of the complex constraints that govern sentences. We need a way to deal with the ambiguity that natural language is famous for. We also need to be able to cope with the fact that there are an unlimited number of possible sentences, and we can only write finite programs to analyze their structures and discover their meanings.

The goal of this chapter is to answer the following questions:

1. How can we use a formal grammar to describe the structure of an unlimited set of sentences?
2. How do we represent the structure of sentences using syntax trees?
3. How do parsers analyze a sentence and automatically build a syntax tree?

Along the way, we will cover the fundamentals of English syntax, and see that there are systematic aspects of meaning that are much easier to capture once we have identified the structure of sentences.

8.1 Some Grammatical Dilemmas

Linguistic Data and Unlimited Possibilities

Previous chapters have shown you how to process and analyze text corpora, and we have stressed the challenges for NLP in dealing with the vast amount of electronic language data that is growing daily. Let's consider this data more closely, and make the thought experiment that we have a gigantic corpus consisting of everything that has been either uttered or written in English over, say, the last 50 years. Would we be justified in calling this corpus "the language of modern English"? There are a number of reasons why we might answer no. Recall that in Chapter 3, we asked you to search the Web for instances of the pattern *the of*. Although it is easy to find examples on the Web containing this word sequence, such as *New man at the of IMG* (see *http://www .telegraph.co.uk/sport/2387900/New-man-at-the-of-IMG.html*), speakers of English will say that most such examples are errors, and therefore not part of English after all.

Accordingly, we can argue that "modern English" is not equivalent to the very big set of word sequences in our imaginary corpus. Speakers of English can make judgments about these sequences, and will reject some of them as being ungrammatical.

Equally, it is easy to compose a new sentence and have speakers agree that it is perfectly good English. For example, sentences have an interesting property that they can be embedded inside larger sentences. Consider the following sentences:

(1)   a. Usain Bolt broke the 100m record.

         b. The Jamaica Observer reported that Usain Bolt broke the 100m record.

         c. Andre said The Jamaica Observer reported that Usain Bolt broke the 100m record.

         d. I think Andre said the Jamaica Observer reported that Usain Bolt broke the 100m record.

If we replaced whole sentences with the symbol S, we would see patterns like *Andre said* S and *I think* S. These are templates for taking a sentence and constructing a bigger sentence. There are other templates we can use, such as S *but* S and S *when* S. With a bit of ingenuity we can construct some really long sentences using these templates. Here's an impressive example from a Winnie the Pooh story by A.A. Milne, *In Which Piglet Is Entirely Surrounded by Water*:

> [You can imagine Piglet's joy when at last the ship came in sight of him.] In after-years he liked to think that he had been in Very Great Danger during the Terrible Flood, but the only danger he had really been in was the last half-hour of his imprisonment, when Owl, who had just flown up, sat on a branch of his tree to comfort him, and told him a very long story about an aunt who had once laid a seagull's egg by mistake, and the story went on and on, rather like this sentence, until Piglet who was listening out of his window without much hope, went to sleep quietly and naturally, slipping slowly out of the window towards the water until he was only hanging on by his toes, at which moment,

luckily, a sudden loud squawk from Owl, which was really part of the story, being what his aunt said, woke the Piglet up and just gave him time to jerk himself back into safety and say, "How interesting, and did she?" when—well, you can imagine his joy when at last he saw the good ship, Brain of Pooh (Captain, C. Robin; 1st Mate, P. Bear) coming over the sea to rescue him...

This long sentence actually has a simple structure that begins *S but S when S*. We can see from this example that language provides us with constructions which seem to allow us to extend sentences indefinitely. It is also striking that we can understand sentences of arbitrary length that we've never heard before: it's not hard to concoct an entirely novel sentence, one that has probably never been used before in the history of the language, yet all speakers of the language will understand it.

The purpose of a grammar is to give an explicit description of a language. But the way in which we think of a grammar is closely intertwined with what we consider to be a language. Is it a large but finite set of observed utterances and written texts? Is it something more abstract like the implicit knowledge that competent speakers have about grammatical sentences? Or is it some combination of the two? We won't take a stand on this issue, but instead will introduce the main approaches.

In this chapter, we will adopt the formal framework of "generative grammar," in which a "language" is considered to be nothing more than an enormous collection of all grammatical sentences, and a grammar is a formal notation that can be used for "generating" the members of this set. Grammars use recursive **productions** of the form S → S *and* S, as we will explore in Section 8.3. In Chapter 10 we will extend this, to automatically build up the meaning of a sentence out of the meanings of its parts.

Ubiquitous Ambiguity

A well-known example of ambiguity is shown in (2), from the Groucho Marx movie, *Animal Crackers* (1930):

(2) While hunting in Africa, I shot an elephant in my pajamas. How an elephant got into my pajamas I'll never know.

Let's take a closer look at the ambiguity in the phrase: *I shot an elephant in my pajamas*. First we need to define a simple grammar:

```
>>> groucho_grammar = nltk.parse_cfg("""
... S -> NP VP
... PP -> P NP
... NP -> Det N | Det N PP | 'I'
... VP -> V NP | VP PP
... Det -> 'an' | 'my'
... N -> 'elephant' | 'pajamas'
... V -> 'shot'
... P -> 'in'
... """)
```

This grammar permits the sentence to be analyzed in two ways, depending on whether the prepositional phrase *in my pajamas* describes the elephant or the shooting event.

```
>>> sent = ['I', 'shot', 'an', 'elephant', 'in', 'my', 'pajamas']
>>> parser = nltk.ChartParser(groucho_grammar)
>>> trees = parser.nbest_parse(sent)
>>> for tree in trees:
...     print tree
(S
  (NP I)
  (VP
    (V shot)
    (NP (Det an) (N elephant) (PP (P in) (NP (Det my) (N pajamas))))))
(S
  (NP I)
  (VP
    (VP (V shot) (NP (Det an) (N elephant)))
    (PP (P in) (NP (Det my) (N pajamas)))))
```

The program produces two bracketed structures, which we can depict as trees, as shown in (3):

(3) a.

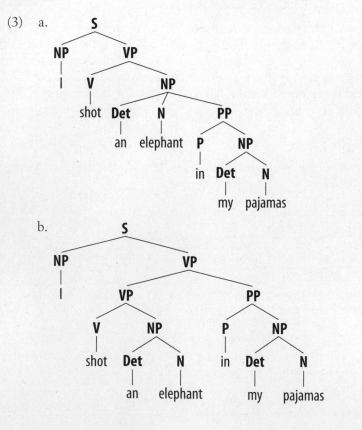

     b.

Notice that there's no ambiguity concerning the meaning of any of the words; e.g., the word *shot* doesn't refer to the act of using a gun in the first sentence and using a camera in the second sentence.

 Your Turn: Consider the following sentences and see if you can think of two quite different interpretations: *Fighting animals could be dangerous. Visiting relatives can be tiresome.* Is ambiguity of the individual words to blame? If not, what is the cause of the ambiguity?

This chapter presents grammars and parsing, as the formal and computational methods for investigating and modeling the linguistic phenomena we have been discussing. As we shall see, patterns of well-formedness and ill-formedness in a sequence of words can be understood with respect to the phrase structure and dependencies. We can develop formal models of these structures using grammars and parsers. As before, a key motivation is natural language *understanding*. How much more of the meaning of a text can we access when we can reliably recognize the linguistic structures it contains? Having read in a text, can a program "understand" it enough to be able to answer simple questions about "what happened" or "who did what to whom"? Also as before, we will develop simple programs to process annotated corpora and perform useful tasks.

8.2 What's the Use of Syntax?

Beyond n-grams

We gave an example in Chapter 2 of how to use the frequency information in bigrams to generate text that seems perfectly acceptable for small sequences of words but rapidly degenerates into nonsense. Here's another pair of examples that we created by computing the bigrams over the text of a children's story, *The Adventures of Buster Brown* (included in the Project Gutenberg Selection Corpus):

(4)   a. He roared with me the pail slip down his back

   b. The worst part and clumsy looking for whoever heard light

You intuitively know that these sequences are "word-salad," but you probably find it hard to pin down what's wrong with them. One benefit of studying grammar is that it provides a conceptual framework and vocabulary for spelling out these intuitions. Let's take a closer look at the sequence *the worst part and clumsy looking*. This looks like a **coordinate structure**, where two phrases are joined by a coordinating conjunction such as *and*, *but*, or *or*. Here's an informal (and simplified) statement of how coordination works syntactically:

Coordinate Structure: if v_1 and v_2 are both phrases of grammatical category X, then v_1 *and* v_2 is also a phrase of category X.

Here are a couple of examples. In the first, two NPs (noun phrases) have been conjoined to make an NP, while in the second, two APs (adjective phrases) have been conjoined to make an AP.

(5)   a. The book's ending was (NP *the worst part and the best part*) for me.

     b. On land they are (AP *slow and clumsy looking*).

What we *can't* do is conjoin an NP and an AP, which is why *the worst part and clumsy looking* is ungrammatical. Before we can formalize these ideas, we need to understand the concept of **constituent structure**.

Constituent structure is based on the observation that words combine with other words to form units. The evidence that a sequence of words forms such a unit is given by substitutability—that is, a sequence of words in a well-formed sentence can be replaced by a shorter sequence without rendering the sentence ill-formed. To clarify this idea, consider the following sentence:

(6)   The little bear saw the fine fat trout in the brook.

The fact that we can substitute *He* for *The little bear* indicates that the latter sequence is a unit. By contrast, we cannot replace *little bear saw* in the same way. (We use an asterisk at the start of a sentence to indicate that it is ungrammatical.)

(7)   a. He saw the fine fat trout in the brook.

     b. *The he the fine fat trout in the brook.

In Figure 8-1, we systematically substitute longer sequences by shorter ones in a way which preserves grammaticality. Each sequence that forms a unit can in fact be replaced by a single word, and we end up with just two elements.

the	little	bear	saw	the	fine	fat	trout	in	the	brook
the	bear		saw	the	trout			in	it	
He			saw	it				there		
He			ran					there		
He			ran							

Figure 8-1. Substitution of word sequences: Working from the top row, we can replace particular sequences of words (e.g., the brook*) with individual words (e.g.,* it*); repeating this process, we arrive at a grammatical two-word sentence.*

Det	Adj	N	V	Det	Adj	Adj	N	P	Det	N
the	little	bear	saw	the	fine	fat	trout	in	the	brook
Det	Nom		V	Det	Nom			P	NP	
the	bear		saw	the	trout			in	it	
NP			V	NP				PP		
He			saw	it				there		
NP			VP					PP		
He			ran					there		
NP			VP							
He			ran							

Figure 8-2. Substitution of word sequences plus grammatical categories: This diagram reproduces Figure 8-1 along with grammatical categories corresponding to noun phrases (NP), verb phrases (VP), prepositional phrases (PP), and nominals (Nom).

In Figure 8-2, we have added grammatical category labels to the words we saw in the earlier figure. The labels NP, VP, and PP stand for **noun phrase**, **verb phrase**, and **prepositional phrase**, respectively.

If we now strip out the words apart from the topmost row, add an S node, and flip the figure over, we end up with a standard phrase structure tree, shown in (8). Each node in this tree (including the words) is called a **constituent**. The **immediate constituents** of S are NP and VP.

(8)

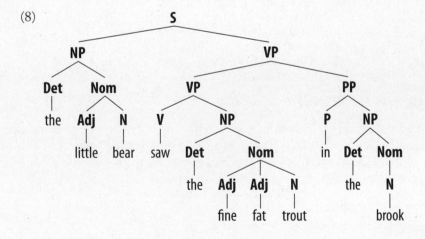

 As we saw in Section 8.1, sentences can have arbitrary length. Consequently, phrase structure trees can have arbitrary *depth*. The cascaded chunk parsers we saw in Section 7.4 can only produce structures of bounded depth, so chunking methods aren't applicable here.

As we will see in the next section, a grammar specifies how the sentence can be subdivided into its immediate constituents, and how these can be further subdivided until we reach the level of individual words.

8.3 Context-Free Grammar

A Simple Grammar

Let's start off by looking at a simple **context-free grammar** (CFG). By convention, the lefthand side of the first production is the **start-symbol** of the grammar, typically S, and all well-formed trees must have this symbol as their root label. In NLTK, context-free grammars are defined in the `nltk.grammar` module. In Example 8-1 we define a grammar and show how to parse a simple sentence admitted by the grammar.

Example 8-1. A simple context-free grammar.

```
grammar1 = nltk.parse_cfg("""
  S -> NP VP
  VP -> V NP | V NP PP
  PP -> P NP
  V -> "saw" | "ate" | "walked"
  NP -> "John" | "Mary" | "Bob" | Det N | Det N PP
  Det -> "a" | "an" | "the" | "my"
  N -> "man" | "dog" | "cat" | "telescope" | "park"
  P -> "in" | "on" | "by" | "with"
  """)
>>> sent = "Mary saw Bob".split()
>>> rd_parser = nltk.RecursiveDescentParser(grammar1)
>>> for tree in rd_parser.nbest_parse(sent):
...     print tree
(S (NP Mary) (VP (V saw) (NP Bob)))
```

The grammar in Example 8-1 contains productions involving various syntactic categories, as laid out in Table 8-1. The recursive descent parser used here can also be inspected via a graphical interface, as illustrated in Figure 8-3; we discuss this parser in more detail in Section 8.4.

Table 8-1. Syntactic categories

Symbol	Meaning	Example
S	sentence	*the man walked*
NP	noun phrase	*a dog*
VP	verb phrase	*saw a park*
PP	prepositional phrase	*with a telescope*
Det	determiner	*the*
N	noun	*dog*

Symbol	Meaning	Example
V	verb	*walked*
P	preposition	*in*

A production like VP -> V NP | V NP PP has a disjunction on the righthand side, shown by the |, and is an abbreviation for the two productions VP -> V NP and VP -> V NP PP.

If we parse the sentence *The dog saw a man in the park* using the grammar shown in Example 8-1, we end up with two trees, similar to those we saw for (3):

(9) a.

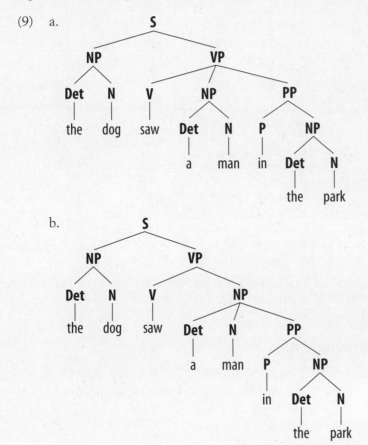

b.

Since our grammar licenses two trees for this sentence, the sentence is said to be **structurally ambiguous**. The ambiguity in question is called a **prepositional phrase attachment ambiguity**, as we saw earlier in this chapter. As you may recall, it is an ambiguity about attachment since the PP *in the park* needs to be attached to one of two places in the tree: either as a child of VP or else as a child of NP. When the PP is attached to VP, the intended interpretation is that the seeing event happened in the park.

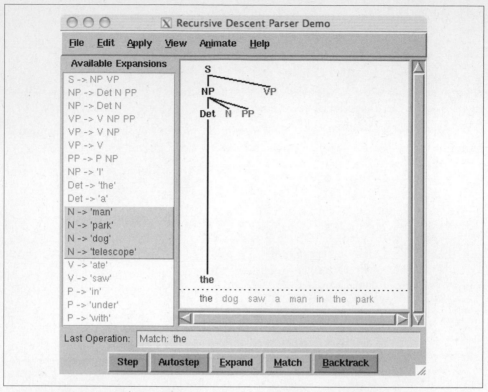

Figure 8-3. Recursive descent parser demo: This tool allows you to watch the operation of a recursive descent parser as it grows the parse tree and matches it against the input words.

However, if the PP is attached to NP, then it was the man who was in the park, and the agent of the seeing (the dog) might have been sitting on the balcony of an apartment overlooking the park.

Writing Your Own Grammars

If you are interested in experimenting with writing CFGs, you will find it helpful to create and edit your grammar in a text file, say, *mygrammar.cfg*. You can then load it into NLTK and parse with it as follows:

```
>>> grammar1 = nltk.data.load('file:mygrammar.cfg')
>>> sent = "Mary saw Bob".split()
>>> rd_parser = nltk.RecursiveDescentParser(grammar1)
>>> for tree in rd_parser.nbest_parse(sent):
...        print tree
```

Make sure that you put a *.cfg* suffix on the filename, and that there are no spaces in the string `'file:mygrammar.cfg'`. If the command `print tree` produces no output, this is probably because your sentence `sent` is not admitted by your grammar. In this case, call the parser with tracing set to be on: `rd_parser = nltk.RecursiveDescent`

`Parser(grammar1, trace=2)`. You can also check what productions are currently in the grammar with the command `for p in grammar1.productions(): print p`.

When you write CFGs for parsing in NLTK, you cannot combine grammatical categories with lexical items on the righthand side of the same production. Thus, a production such as `PP -> 'of' NP` is disallowed. In addition, you are not permitted to place multiword lexical items on the righthand side of a production. So rather than writing `NP -> 'New York'`, you have to resort to something like `NP -> 'New_York'` instead.

Recursion in Syntactic Structure

A grammar is said to be **recursive** if a category occurring on the lefthand side of a production also appears on the righthand side of a production, as illustrated in Example 8-2. The production `Nom -> Adj Nom` (where `Nom` is the category of nominals) involves direct recursion on the category `Nom`, whereas indirect recursion on `S` arises from the combination of two productions, namely `S -> NP VP` and `VP -> V S`.

Example 8-2. A recursive context-free grammar.

```
grammar2 = nltk.parse_cfg("""
  S  -> NP VP
  NP -> Det Nom | PropN
  Nom -> Adj Nom | N
  VP -> V Adj | V NP | V S | V NP PP
  PP -> P NP
  PropN -> 'Buster' | 'Chatterer' | 'Joe'
  Det -> 'the' | 'a'
  N -> 'bear' | 'squirrel' | 'tree' | 'fish' | 'log'
  Adj  -> 'angry' | 'frightened' |  'little' | 'tall'
  V ->  'chased'  | 'saw' | 'said' | 'thought' | 'was' | 'put'
  P -> 'on'
  """)
```

To see how recursion arises from this grammar, consider the following trees. (10a) involves nested nominal phrases, while (10b) contains nested sentences.

(10) a.

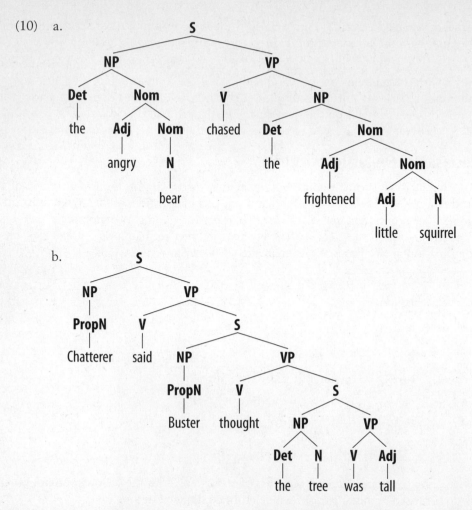

We've only illustrated two levels of recursion here, but there's no upper limit on the depth. You can experiment with parsing sentences that involve more deeply nested structures. Beware that the `RecursiveDescentParser` is unable to handle **left-recursive** productions of the form X -> X Y; we will return to this in Section 8.4.

8.4 Parsing with Context-Free Grammar

A **parser** processes input sentences according to the productions of a grammar, and builds one or more constituent structures that conform to the grammar. A grammar is a declarative specification of well-formedness—it is actually just a string, not a program. A parser is a procedural interpretation of the grammar. It searches through the space of trees licensed by a grammar to find one that has the required sentence along its fringe.

A parser permits a grammar to be evaluated against a collection of test sentences, helping linguists to discover mistakes in their grammatical analysis. A parser can serve as a model of psycholinguistic processing, helping to explain the difficulties that humans have with processing certain syntactic constructions. Many natural language applications involve parsing at some point; for example, we would expect the natural language questions submitted to a question-answering system to undergo parsing as an initial step.

In this section, we see two simple parsing algorithms, a top-down method called recursive descent parsing, and a bottom-up method called shift-reduce parsing. We also see some more sophisticated algorithms, a top-down method with bottom-up filtering called left-corner parsing, and a dynamic programming technique called chart parsing.

Recursive Descent Parsing

The simplest kind of parser interprets a grammar as a specification of how to break a high-level goal into several lower-level subgoals. The top-level goal is to find an S. The S → NP VP production permits the parser to replace this goal with two subgoals: find an NP, then find a VP. Each of these subgoals can be replaced in turn by sub-subgoals, using productions that have NP and VP on their lefthand side. Eventually, this expansion process leads to subgoals such as: find the word *telescope*. Such subgoals can be directly compared against the input sequence, and succeed if the next word is matched. If there is no match, the parser must back up and try a different alternative.

The recursive descent parser builds a parse tree during this process. With the initial goal (find an S), the S root node is created. As the process recursively expands its goals using the productions of the grammar, the parse tree is extended downwards (hence the name *recursive descent*). We can see this in action using the graphical demonstration nltk.app.rdparser(). Six stages of the execution of this parser are shown in Figure 8-4.

During this process, the parser is often forced to choose between several possible productions. For example, in going from step 3 to step 4, it tries to find productions with N on the lefthand side. The first of these is N → *man*. When this does not work it **backtracks**, and tries other N productions in order, until it gets to N → *dog*, which matches the next word in the input sentence. Much later, as shown in step 5, it finds a complete parse. This is a tree that covers the entire sentence, without any dangling edges. Once a parse has been found, we can get the parser to look for additional parses. Again it will backtrack and explore other choices of production in case any of them result in a parse.

NLTK provides a recursive descent parser:

```
>>> rd_parser = nltk.RecursiveDescentParser(grammar1)
>>> sent = 'Mary saw a dog'.split()
>>> for t in rd_parser.nbest_parse(sent):
...     print t
(S (NP Mary) (VP (V saw) (NP (Det a) (N dog))))
```

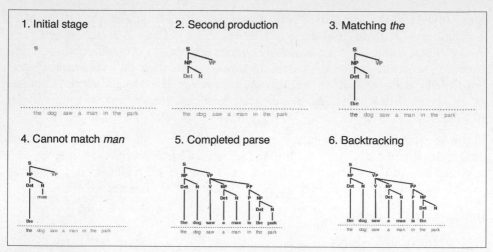

Figure 8-4. Six stages of a recursive descent parser: The parser begins with a tree consisting of the node S; at each stage it consults the grammar to find a production that can be used to enlarge the tree; when a lexical production is encountered, its word is compared against the input; after a complete parse has been found, the parser backtracks to look for more parses.

 RecursiveDescentParser() takes an optional parameter `trace`. If `trace` is greater than zero, then the parser will report the steps that it takes as it parses a text.

Recursive descent parsing has three key shortcomings. First, left-recursive productions like NP -> NP PP send it into an infinite loop. Second, the parser wastes a lot of time considering words and structures that do not correspond to the input sentence. Third, the backtracking process may discard parsed constituents that will need to be rebuilt again later. For example, backtracking over VP -> V NP will discard the subtree created for the NP. If the parser then proceeds with VP -> V NP PP, then the NP subtree must be created all over again.

Recursive descent parsing is a kind of **top-down parsing**. Top-down parsers use a grammar to *predict* what the input will be, before inspecting the input! However, since the input is available to the parser all along, it would be more sensible to consider the input sentence from the very beginning. This approach is called **bottom-up parsing**, and we will see an example in the next section.

Shift-Reduce Parsing

A simple kind of bottom-up parser is the **shift-reduce parser**. In common with all bottom-up parsers, a shift-reduce parser tries to find sequences of words and phrases that correspond to the *righthand* side of a grammar production, and replace them with the lefthand side, until the whole sentence is reduced to an S.

The shift-reduce parser repeatedly pushes the next input word onto a stack (Section 4.1); this is the **shift** operation. If the top *n* items on the stack match the *n* items on the righthand side of some production, then they are all popped off the stack, and the item on the lefthand side of the production is pushed onto the stack. This replacement of the top *n* items with a single item is the **reduce** operation. The operation may be applied only to the top of the stack; reducing items lower in the stack must be done before later items are pushed onto the stack. The parser finishes when all the input is consumed and there is only one item remaining on the stack, a parse tree with an S node as its root. The shift-reduce parser builds a parse tree during the above process. Each time it pops *n* items off the stack, it combines them into a partial parse tree, and pushes this back onto the stack. We can see the shift-reduce parsing algorithm in action using the graphical demonstration `nltk.app.srparser()`. Six stages of the execution of this parser are shown in Figure 8-5.

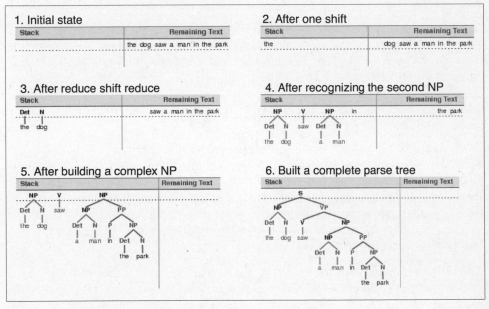

Figure 8-5. Six stages of a shift-reduce parser: The parser begins by shifting the first input word onto its stack; once the top items on the stack match the righthand side of a grammar production, they can be replaced with the lefthand side of that production; the parser succeeds once all input is consumed and one S item remains on the stack.

NLTK provides `ShiftReduceParser()`, a simple implementation of a shift-reduce parser. This parser does not implement any backtracking, so it is not guaranteed to find a parse for a text, even if one exists. Furthermore, it will only find at most one parse, even if more parses exist. We can provide an optional `trace` parameter that controls how verbosely the parser reports the steps that it takes as it parses a text:

```
>>> sr_parse = nltk.ShiftReduceParser(grammar1)
>>> sent = 'Mary saw a dog'.split()
>>> print sr_parse.parse(sent)
  (S (NP Mary) (VP (V saw) (NP (Det a) (N dog))))
```

 Your Turn: Run this parser in tracing mode to see the sequence of shift and reduce operations, using `sr_parse = nltk.ShiftReduceParser(gram mar1, trace=2)`.

A shift-reduce parser can reach a dead end and fail to find any parse, even if the input sentence is well-formed according to the grammar. When this happens, no input remains, and the stack contains items that cannot be reduced to an S. The problem arises because there are choices made earlier that cannot be undone by the parser (although users of the graphical demonstration can undo their choices). There are two kinds of choices to be made by the parser: (a) which reduction to do when more than one is possible and (b) whether to shift or reduce when either action is possible.

A shift-reduce parser may be extended to implement policies for resolving such conflicts. For example, it may address shift-reduce conflicts by shifting only when no reductions are possible, and it may address reduce-reduce conflicts by favoring the reduction operation that removes the most items from the stack. (A generalization of the shift-reduce parser, a "lookahead LR parser," is commonly used in programming language compilers.)

The advantages of shift-reduce parsers over recursive descent parsers is that they only build structure that corresponds to the words in the input. Furthermore, they only build each substructure once; e.g., `NP(Det(the), N(man))` is only built and pushed onto the stack a single time, regardless of whether it will later be used by the `VP -> V NP PP` reduction or the `NP -> NP PP` reduction.

The Left-Corner Parser

One of the problems with the recursive descent parser is that it goes into an infinite loop when it encounters a left-recursive production. This is because it applies the grammar productions blindly, without considering the actual input sentence. A left-corner parser is a hybrid between the bottom-up and top-down approaches we have seen.

A **left-corner parser** is a top-down parser with bottom-up filtering. Unlike an ordinary recursive descent parser, it does not get trapped in left-recursive productions. Before starting its work, a left-corner parser preprocesses the context-free grammar to build a table where each row contains two cells, the first holding a non-terminal, and the second holding the collection of possible left corners of that non-terminal. Table 8-2 illustrates this for the grammar from `grammar2`.

Table 8-2. Left corners in grammar2

Category	Left corners (pre-terminals)
S	NP
NP	Det, PropN
VP	V
PP	P

Each time a production is considered by the parser, it checks that the next input word is compatible with at least one of the pre-terminal categories in the left-corner table.

Well-Formed Substring Tables

The simple parsers discussed in the previous sections suffer from limitations in both completeness and efficiency. In order to remedy these, we will apply the algorithm design technique of **dynamic programming** to the parsing problem. As we saw in Section 4.7, dynamic programming stores intermediate results and reuses them when appropriate, achieving significant efficiency gains. This technique can be applied to syntactic parsing, allowing us to store partial solutions to the parsing task and then look them up as necessary in order to efficiently arrive at a complete solution. This approach to parsing is known as **chart parsing**. We introduce the main idea in this section; see the online materials available for this chapter for more implementation details.

Dynamic programming allows us to build the PP *in my pajamas* just once. The first time we build it we save it in a table, then we look it up when we need to use it as a sub-constituent of either the object NP or the higher VP. This table is known as a **well-formed substring table**, or WFST for short. (The term "substring" refers to a contiguous sequence of words within a sentence.) We will show how to construct the WFST bottom-up so as to systematically record what syntactic constituents have been found.

Let's set our input to be the sentence in (2). The numerically specified spans of the WFST are reminiscent of Python's slice notation (Section 3.2). Another way to think about the data structure is shown in Figure 8-6, a data structure known as a **chart**.

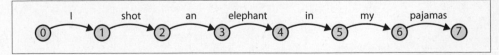

Figure 8-6. The chart data structure: Words are the edge labels of a linear graph structure.

In a WFST, we record the position of the words by filling in cells in a triangular matrix: the vertical axis will denote the start position of a substring, while the horizontal axis will denote the end position (thus *shot* will appear in the cell with coordinates (1, 2)). To simplify this presentation, we will assume each word has a unique lexical category, and we will store this (not the word) in the matrix. So cell (1, 2) will contain the entry V. More generally, if our input string is $a_1a_2 \dots a_n$, and our grammar contains a production of the form $A \rightarrow a_i$, then we add A to the cell $(i\text{-}1, i)$.

So, for every word in text, we can look up in our grammar what category it belongs to.

```
>>> text = ['I', 'shot', 'an', 'elephant', 'in', 'my', 'pajamas']
[V -> 'shot']
```

For our WFST, we create an $(n\text{-}1) \times (n\text{-}1)$ matrix as a list of lists in Python, and initialize it with the lexical categories of each token in the init_wfst() function in Example 8-3. We also define a utility function display() to pretty-print the WFST for us. As expected, there is a V in cell (1, 2).

Example 8-3. Acceptor using well-formed substring table.

```
def init_wfst(tokens, grammar):
    numtokens = len(tokens)
    wfst = [[None for i in range(numtokens+1)] for j in range(numtokens+1)]
    for i in range(numtokens):
        productions = grammar.productions(rhs=tokens[i])
        wfst[i][i+1] = productions[0].lhs()
    return wfst

def complete_wfst(wfst, tokens, grammar, trace=False):
    index = dict((p.rhs(), p.lhs()) for p in grammar.productions())
    numtokens = len(tokens)
    for span in range(2, numtokens+1):
        for start in range(numtokens+1-span):
            end = start + span
            for mid in range(start+1, end):
                nt1, nt2 = wfst[start][mid], wfst[mid][end]
                if nt1 and nt2 and (nt1,nt2) in index:
                    wfst[start][end] = index[(nt1,nt2)]
                    if trace:
                        print "[%s] %3s [%s] %3s [%s] ==> [%s] %3s [%s]" % \
                        (start, nt1, mid, nt2, end, start, index[(nt1,nt2)], end)
    return wfst

def display(wfst, tokens):
    print '\nWFST ' + ' '.join([("%-4d" % i) for i in range(1, len(wfst))])
    for i in range(len(wfst)-1):
        print "%d    " % i,
        for j in range(1, len(wfst)):
            print "%-4s" % (wfst[i][j] or '.'),
        print

>>> tokens = "I shot an elephant in my pajamas".split()
>>> wfst0 = init_wfst(tokens, groucho_grammar)
>>> display(wfst0, tokens)
WFST 1    2    3    4    5    6    7
0    NP   .    .    .    .    .    .
1    .    V    .    .    .    .    .
2    .    .    Det  .    .    .    .
3    .    .    .    N    .    .    .
```

```
4   .   .   .   .   P   .   .
5   .   .   .   .   .   Det .
6   .   .   .   .   .   .   N
>>> wfst1 = complete_wfst(wfst0, tokens, groucho_grammar)
>>> display(wfst1, tokens)
WFST 1   2   3    4   5   6    7
0    NP  .   .    S   .   .    S
1    .   V   .    VP  .   .    VP
2    .   .   Det  NP  .   .    .
3    .   .   .    N   .   .    .
4    .   .   .    .   P   .    PP
5    .   .   .    .   .   Det  NP
6    .   .   .    .   .   .    N
```

Returning to our tabular representation, given that we have Det in cell (2, 3) for the word *an*, and N in cell (3, 4) for the word *elephant*, what should we put into cell (2, 4) for *an elephant*? We need to find a production of the form $A \rightarrow$ Det N. Consulting the grammar, we know that we can enter NP in cell (0, 2).

More generally, we can enter A in (i, j) if there is a production $A \rightarrow B\ C$, and we find non-terminal B in (i, k) and C in (k, j). The program in Example 8-3 uses this rule to complete the WFST. By setting trace to True when calling the function complete_wfst(), we see tracing output that shows the WFST being constructed:

```
>>> wfst1 = complete_wfst(wfst0, tokens, groucho_grammar, trace=True)
[2] Det [3]   N [4] ==> [2] NP [4]
[5] Det [6]   N [7] ==> [5] NP [7]
[1]   V [2]  NP [4] ==> [1] VP [4]
[4]   P [5]  NP [7] ==> [4] PP [7]
[0]  NP [1]  VP [4] ==> [0]  S [4]
[1]  VP [4]  PP [7] ==> [1] VP [7]
[0]  NP [1]  VP [7] ==> [0]  S [7]
```

For example, this says that since we found Det at wfst[0][1] and N at wfst[1][2], we can add NP to wfst[0][2].

> To help us easily retrieve productions by their righthand sides, we create an index for the grammar. This is an example of a space-time trade-off: we do a reverse lookup on the grammar, instead of having to check through entire list of productions each time we want to look up via the righthand side.

We conclude that there is a parse for the whole input string once we have constructed an S node in cell (0, 7), showing that we have found a sentence that covers the whole input. The final state of the WFST is depicted in Figure 8-7.

Notice that we have not used any built-in parsing functions here. We've implemented a complete primitive chart parser from the ground up!

WFSTs have several shortcomings. First, as you can see, the WFST is not itself a parse tree, so the technique is strictly speaking **recognizing** that a sentence is admitted by a

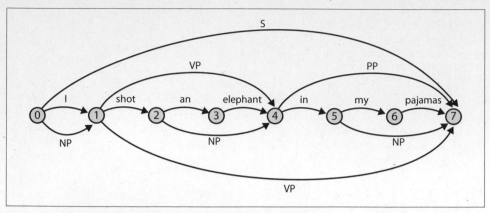

Figure 8-7. The chart data structure: Non-terminals are represented as extra edges in the chart.

grammar, rather than parsing it. Second, it requires every non-lexical grammar production to be *binary*. Although it is possible to convert an arbitrary CFG into this form, we would prefer to use an approach without such a requirement. Third, as a bottom-up approach it is potentially wasteful, being able to propose constituents in locations that would not be licensed by the grammar.

Finally, the WFST did not represent the structural ambiguity in the sentence (i.e., the two verb phrase readings). The VP in cell (2,8) was actually entered twice, once for a V NP reading, and once for a VP PP reading. These are different hypotheses, and the second overwrote the first (as it happens, this didn't matter since the lefthand side was the same). Chart parsers use a slightly richer data structure and some interesting algorithms to solve these problems (see Section 8.8).

> **Your Turn:** Try out the interactive chart parser application
> `nltk.app.chartparser()`.

8.5 Dependencies and Dependency Grammar

Phrase structure grammar is concerned with how words and sequences of words *combine* to form constituents. A distinct and complementary approach, **dependency grammar**, focuses instead on how words *relate* to other words. Dependency is a binary asymmetric relation that holds between a **head** and its **dependents**. The head of a sentence is usually taken to be the tensed verb, and every other word is either dependent on the sentence head or connects to it through a path of dependencies.

A dependency representation is a labeled directed graph, where the nodes are the lexical items and the labeled arcs represent dependency relations from heads to dependents. Figure 8-8 illustrates a dependency graph, where arrows point from heads to their dependents.

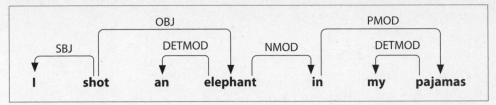

Figure 8-8. Dependency structure: Arrows point from heads to their dependents; labels indicate the grammatical function of the dependent as subject, object, or modifier.

The arcs in Figure 8-8 are labeled with the grammatical function that holds between a dependent and its head. For example, *I* is the `SBJ` (subject) of *shot* (which is the head of the whole sentence), and *in* is an `NMOD` (noun modifier of *elephant*). In contrast to phrase structure grammar, therefore, dependency grammars can be used to directly express grammatical functions as a type of dependency.

Here's one way of encoding a dependency grammar in NLTK—note that it only captures bare dependency information without specifying the type of dependency:

```
>>> groucho_dep_grammar = nltk.parse_dependency_grammar("""
... 'shot' -> 'I' | 'elephant' | 'in'
... 'elephant' -> 'an' | 'in'
... 'in' -> 'pajamas'
... 'pajamas' -> 'my'
... """)
>>> print groucho_dep_grammar
Dependency grammar with 7 productions
  'shot' -> 'I'
  'shot' -> 'elephant'
  'shot' -> 'in'
  'elephant' -> 'an'
  'elephant' -> 'in'
  'in' -> 'pajamas'
  'pajamas' -> 'my'
```

A dependency graph is **projective** if, when all the words are written in linear order, the edges can be drawn above the words without crossing. This is equivalent to saying that a word and all its descendants (dependents and dependents of its dependents, etc.) form a contiguous sequence of words within the sentence. Figure 8-8 is projective, and we can parse many sentences in English using a projective dependency parser. The next example shows how `groucho_dep_grammar` provides an alternative approach to capturing the attachment ambiguity that we examined earlier with phrase structure grammar.

```
>>> pdp = nltk.ProjectiveDependencyParser(groucho_dep_grammar)
>>> sent = 'I shot an elephant in my pajamas'.split()
>>> trees = pdp.parse(sent)
>>> for tree in trees:
...     print tree
(shot I (elephant an (in (pajamas my))))
(shot I (elephant an) (in (pajamas my)))
```

These bracketed dependency structures can also be displayed as trees, where dependents are shown as children of their heads.

(11)

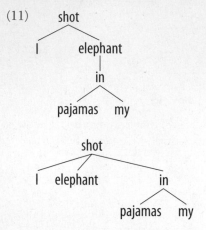

In languages with more flexible word order than English, non-projective dependencies are more frequent.

Various criteria have been proposed for deciding what is the head *H* and what is the dependent *D* in a construction *C*. Some of the most important are the following:

1. *H* determines the distribution class of *C*; or alternatively, the external syntactic properties of *C* are due to *H*.
2. *H* determines the semantic type of *C*.
3. *H* is obligatory while *D* may be optional.
4. *H* selects *D* and determines whether it is obligatory or optional.
5. The morphological form of *D* is determined by *H* (e.g., agreement or case government).

When we say in a phrase structure grammar that the immediate constituents of a PP are P and NP, we are implicitly appealing to the head/dependent distinction. A prepositional phrase is a phrase whose head is a preposition; moreover, the NP is a dependent of P. The same distinction carries over to the other types of phrase that we have discussed. The key point to note here is that although phrase structure grammars seem very different from dependency grammars, they implicitly embody a recognition of dependency relations. Although CFGs are not intended to directly capture dependencies, more recent linguistic frameworks have increasingly adopted formalisms which combine aspects of both approaches.

Valency and the Lexicon

Let us take a closer look at verbs and their dependents. The grammar in Example 8-2 correctly generates examples like (12).

---

(12)　a. The squirrel was frightened.

　　　b. Chatterer saw the bear.

　　　c. Chatterer thought Buster was angry.

　　　d. Joe put the fish on the log.

These possibilities correspond to the productions in Table 8-3.

Table 8-3. VP productions and their lexical heads

Production	Lexical head
VP -> V Adj	*was*
VP -> V NP	*saw*
VP -> V S	*thought*
VP -> V NP PP	*put*

That is, *was* can occur with a following Adj, *saw* can occur with a following NP, *thought* can occur with a following S, and *put* can occur with a following NP and PP. The dependents Adj, NP, S, and PP are often called **complements** of the respective verbs, and there are strong constraints on what verbs can occur with what complements. By contrast with (12), the word sequences in (13) are ill-formed:

(13)　a. *The squirrel was Buster was angry.

　　　b. *Chatterer saw frightened.

　　　c. *Chatterer thought the bear.

　　　d. *Joe put on the log.

 With a little imagination, it is possible to invent contexts in which unusual combinations of verbs and complements are interpretable. However, we assume that the examples in (13) are to be interpreted in neutral contexts.

In the tradition of dependency grammar, the verbs in Table 8-3 are said to have different **valencies**. Valency restrictions are not just applicable to verbs, but also to the other classes of heads.

Within frameworks based on phrase structure grammar, various techniques have been proposed for excluding the ungrammatical examples in (13). In a CFG, we need some way of constraining grammar productions which expand VP so that verbs co-occur *only* with their correct complements. We can do this by dividing the class of verbs into "subcategories," each of which is associated with a different set of complements. For example, **transitive verbs** such as *chased* and *saw* require a following NP object complement; that is, they are **subcategorized** for NP direct objects. If we introduce a new category label for transitive verbs, namely TV (for transitive verb), then we can use it in the following productions:

```
VP -> TV NP
TV -> 'chased' | 'saw'
```

Now *Joe thought the bear* is excluded since we haven't listed *thought* as a TV, but *Chatterer saw the bear* is still allowed. Table 8-4 provides more examples of labels for verb subcategories.

Table 8-4. Verb subcategories

Symbol	Meaning	Example
IV	Intransitive verb	*barked*
TV	Transitive verb	*saw a man*
DatV	Dative verb	*gave a dog to a man*
SV	Sentential verb	*said that a dog barked*

Valency is a property of lexical items, and we will discuss it further in Chapter 9.

Complements are often contrasted with modifiers (or adjuncts), although both are kinds of dependents. Prepositional phrases, adjectives, and adverbs typically function as modifiers. Unlike complements, modifiers are optional, can often be iterated, and are not selected for by heads in the same way as complements. For example, the adverb *really* can be added as a modifier to all the sentences in (14):

(14)   a. The squirrel really was frightened.

b. Chatterer really saw the bear.

c. Chatterer really thought Buster was angry.

d. Joe really put the fish on the log.

The structural ambiguity of PP attachment, which we have illustrated in both phrase structure and dependency grammars, corresponds semantically to an ambiguity in the scope of the modifier.

Scaling Up

So far, we have only considered "toy grammars," small grammars that illustrate the key aspects of parsing. But there is an obvious question as to whether the approach can be scaled up to cover large corpora of natural languages. How hard would it be to construct such a set of productions by hand? In general, the answer is: *very hard*. Even if we allow ourselves to use various formal devices that give much more succinct representations of grammar productions, it is still extremely difficult to keep control of the complex interactions between the many productions required to cover the major constructions of a language. In other words, it is hard to modularize grammars so that one portion can be developed independently of the other parts. This in turn means that it is difficult to distribute the task of grammar writing across a team of linguists. Another difficulty is that as the grammar expands to cover a wider and wider range of constructions, there is a corresponding increase in the number of analyses that are admitted for any one sentence. In other words, ambiguity increases with coverage.

Despite these problems, some large collaborative projects have achieved interesting and impressive results in developing rule-based grammars for several languages. Examples are the Lexical Functional Grammar (LFG) Pargram project, the Head-Driven Phrase Structure Grammar (HPSG) LinGO Matrix framework, and the Lexicalized Tree Adjoining Grammar XTAG Project.

8.6 Grammar Development

Parsing builds trees over sentences, according to a phrase structure grammar. Now, all the examples we gave earlier only involved toy grammars containing a handful of productions. What happens if we try to scale up this approach to deal with realistic corpora of language? In this section, we will see how to access treebanks, and look at the challenge of developing broad-coverage grammars.

Treebanks and Grammars

The `corpus` module defines the `treebank` corpus reader, which contains a 10% sample of the Penn Treebank Corpus.

```
>>> from nltk.corpus import treebank
>>> t = treebank.parsed_sents('wsj_0001.mrg')[0]
>>> print t
(S
  (NP-SBJ
    (NP (NNP Pierre) (NNP Vinken))
    (, ,)
    (ADJP (NP (CD 61) (NNS years)) (JJ old))
    (, ,))
  (VP
    (MD will)
    (VP
      (VB join)
      (NP (DT the) (NN board))
      (PP-CLR
        (IN as)
        (NP (DT a) (JJ nonexecutive) (NN director)))
      (NP-TMP (NNP Nov.) (CD 29))))
  (. .))
```

We can use this data to help develop a grammar. For example, the program in Example 8-4 uses a simple filter to find verbs that take sentential complements. Assuming we already have a production of the form VP -> SV S, this information enables us to identify particular verbs that would be included in the expansion of SV.

Example 8-4. Searching a treebank to find sentential complements.

```
def filter(tree):
    child_nodes = [child.node for child in tree
                   if isinstance(child, nltk.Tree)]
    return  (tree.node == 'VP') and ('S' in child_nodes)

>>> from nltk.corpus import treebank
>>> [subtree for tree in treebank.parsed_sents()
...          for subtree in tree.subtrees(filter)]
 [Tree('VP', [Tree('VBN', ['named']), Tree('S', [Tree('NP-SBJ', ...]), ...]), ...]
```

The PP Attachment Corpus, `nltk.corpus.ppattach`, is another source of information about the valency of particular verbs. Here we illustrate a technique for mining this corpus. It finds pairs of prepositional phrases where the preposition and noun are fixed, but where the choice of verb determines whether the prepositional phrase is attached to the VP or to the NP.

```
>>> entries = nltk.corpus.ppattach.attachments('training')
>>> table = nltk.defaultdict(lambda: nltk.defaultdict(set))
>>> for entry in entries:
...     key = entry.noun1 + '-' + entry.prep + '-' + entry.noun2
...     table[key][entry.attachment].add(entry.verb)
...
>>> for key in sorted(table):
...     if len(table[key]) > 1:
...         print key, 'N:', sorted(table[key]['N']), 'V:', sorted(table[key]['V'])
```

Among the output lines of this program we find offer-from-group N: ['rejected'] V: ['received'], which indicates that *received* expects a separate PP complement attached to the VP, while *rejected* does not. As before, we can use this information to help construct the grammar.

The NLTK corpus collection includes data from the PE08 Cross-Framework and Cross Domain Parser Evaluation Shared Task. A collection of larger grammars has been prepared for the purpose of comparing different parsers, which can be obtained by downloading the large_grammars package (e.g., python -m nltk.downloader large_grammars).

The NLTK corpus collection also includes a sample from the Sinica Treebank Corpus, consisting of 10,000 parsed sentences drawn from the *Academia Sinica Balanced Corpus of Modern Chinese*. Let's load and display one of the trees in this corpus.

```
>>> nltk.corpus.sinica_treebank.parsed_sents()[3450].draw()
```

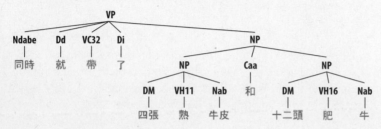

Pernicious Ambiguity

Unfortunately, as the coverage of the grammar increases and the length of the input sentences grows, the number of parse trees grows rapidly. In fact, it grows at an astronomical rate.

Let's explore this issue with the help of a simple example. The word *fish* is both a noun and a verb. We can make up the sentence *fish fish fish*, meaning *fish like to fish for other fish*. (Try this with *police* if you prefer something more sensible.) Here is a toy grammar for the "fish" sentences.

```
>>> grammar = nltk.parse_cfg("""
... S -> NP V NP
... NP -> NP Sbar
... Sbar -> NP V
... NP -> 'fish'
... V -> 'fish'
... """)
```

Now we can try parsing a longer sentence, *fish fish fish fish fish*, which among other things, means "fish that other fish fish are in the habit of fishing fish themselves." We use the NLTK chart parser, which is presented earlier in this chapter. This sentence has two readings.

```
>>> tokens = ["fish"] * 5
>>> cp = nltk.ChartParser(grammar)
>>> for tree in cp.nbest_parse(tokens):
...     print tree
(S (NP (NP fish) (Sbar (NP fish) (V fish))) (V fish) (NP fish))
(S (NP fish) (V fish) (NP (NP fish) (Sbar (NP fish) (V fish))))
```

As the length of this sentence goes up (3, 5, 7, ...) we get the following numbers of parse trees: 1; 2; 5; 14; 42; 132; 429; 1,430; 4,862; 16,796; 58,786; 208,012; .... (These are the **Catalan numbers**, which we saw in an exercise in Chapter 4.) The last of these is for a sentence of length 23, the average length of sentences in the WSJ section of Penn Treebank. For a sentence of length 50 there would be over 10^{12} parses, and this is only half the length of the Piglet sentence (Section 8.1), which young children process effortlessly. No practical NLP system could construct millions of trees for a sentence and choose the appropriate one in the context. It's clear that humans don't do this either!

Note that the problem is not with our choice of example. (Church & Patil, 1982) point out that the syntactic ambiguity of PP attachment in sentences like (15) also grows in proportion to the Catalan numbers.

(15) Put the block in the box on the table.

So much for structural ambiguity; what about lexical ambiguity? As soon as we try to construct a broad-coverage grammar, we are forced to make lexical entries highly ambiguous for their part-of-speech. In a toy grammar, *a* is only a determiner, *dog* is only a noun, and *runs* is only a verb. However, in a broad-coverage grammar, *a* is also a noun (e.g., *part a*), *dog* is also a verb (meaning to follow closely), and *runs* is also a noun (e.g., *ski runs*). In fact, all words can be referred to by name: e.g., *the verb 'ate' is spelled with three letters*; in speech we do not need to supply quotation marks. Furthermore, it is possible to *verb* most nouns. Thus a parser for a broad-coverage grammar will be overwhelmed with ambiguity. Even complete gibberish will often have a reading, e.g., *the a are of I*. As (Abney, 1996) has pointed out, this is not word salad but a grammatical noun phrase, in which *are* is a noun meaning a hundredth of a hectare (or 100 sq m), and *a* and *I* are nouns designating coordinates, as shown in Figure 8-9.

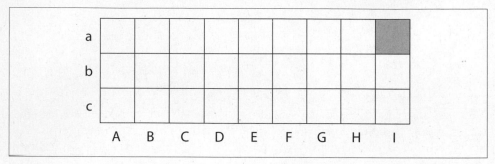

Figure 8-9. The a are of I: A schematic drawing of 27 paddocks, each being one are in size, and each identified using coordinates; the top-left cell is the a are of column A (after Abney).

Even though this phrase is unlikely, it is still grammatical, and a broad-coverage parser should be able to construct a parse tree for it. Similarly, sentences that seem to be unambiguous, such as *John saw Mary*, turn out to have other readings we would not have anticipated (as Abney explains). This ambiguity is unavoidable, and leads to horrendous inefficiency in parsing seemingly innocuous sentences. The solution to these problems is provided by *probabilistic parsing*, which allows us to *rank* the parses of an ambiguous sentence on the basis of evidence from corpora.

Weighted Grammar

As we have just seen, dealing with ambiguity is a key challenge in developing broad-coverage parsers. Chart parsers improve the efficiency of computing multiple parses of the same sentences, but they are still overwhelmed by the sheer number of possible parses. Weighted grammars and probabilistic parsing algorithms have provided an effective solution to these problems.

Before looking at these, we need to understand why the notion of grammaticality could be *gradient*. Considering the verb *give*. This verb requires both a direct object (the thing being given) and an indirect object (the recipient). These complements can be given in either order, as illustrated in (16). In the "prepositional dative" form in (16a), the direct object appears first, followed by a prepositional phrase containing the indirect object.

(16) a. Kim gave a bone to the dog.

b. Kim gave the dog a bone.

In the "double object" form in (16b), the indirect object appears first, followed by the direct object. In this case, either order is acceptable. However, if the indirect object is a pronoun, there is a strong preference for the double object construction:

(17) a. Kim gives the heebie-jeebies to me (*prepositional dative*).

b. Kim gives me the heebie-jeebies (*double object*).

Using the Penn Treebank sample, we can examine all instances of prepositional dative and double object constructions involving *give*, as shown in Example 8-5.

Example 8-5. Usage of give and gave in the Penn Treebank sample.

```
def give(t):
    return t.node == 'VP' and len(t) > 2 and t[1].node == 'NP'\
           and (t[2].node == 'PP-DTV' or t[2].node == 'NP')\
           and ('give' in t[0].leaves() or 'gave' in t[0].leaves())
def sent(t):
    return ' '.join(token for token in t.leaves() if token[0] not in '*-0')
def print_node(t, width):
        output = "%s %s: %s / %s: %s" %\
            (sent(t[0]), t[1].node, sent(t[1]), t[2].node, sent(t[2]))
        if len(output) > width:
            output = output[:width] + "..."
        print output

>>> for tree in nltk.corpus.treebank.parsed_sents():
...     for t in tree.subtrees(give):
...         print_node(t, 72)
gave NP: the chefs / NP: a standing ovation
give NP: advertisers / NP: discounts for maintaining or increasing ad sp...
give NP: it / PP-DTV: to the politicians
gave NP: them / NP: similar help
give NP: them / NP:
give NP: only French history questions / PP-DTV: to students in a Europe...
give NP: federal judges / NP: a raise
give NP: consumers / NP: the straight scoop on the U.S. waste crisis
gave NP: Mitsui / NP: access to a high-tech medical product
give NP: Mitsubishi / NP: a window on the U.S. glass industry
give NP: much thought / PP-DTV: to the rates she was receiving , nor to ...
give NP: your Foster Savings Institution / NP: the gift of hope and free...
give NP: market operators / NP: the authority to suspend trading in futu...
gave NP: quick approval / PP-DTV: to $ 3.18 billion in supplemental appr...
give NP: the Transportation Department / NP: up to 50 days to review any...
give NP: the president / NP: such power
give NP: me / NP: the heebie-jeebies
give NP: holders / NP: the right , but not the obligation , to buy a cal...
gave NP: Mr. Thomas / NP: only a `` qualified '' rating , rather than ``...
give NP: the president / NP: line-item veto power
```

We can observe a strong tendency for the shortest complement to appear first. However, this does not account for a form like give NP: federal judges / NP: a raise, where animacy may play a role. In fact, there turns out to be a large number of contributing factors, as surveyed by (Bresnan & Hay, 2008). Such preferences can be represented in a weighted grammar.

A **probabilistic context-free grammar** (or PCFG) is a context-free grammar that associates a probability with each of its productions. It generates the same set of parses for a text that the corresponding context-free grammar does, and assigns a probability to each parse. The probability of a parse generated by a PCFG is simply the product of the probabilities of the productions used to generate it.

The simplest way to define a PCFG is to load it from a specially formatted string consisting of a sequence of weighted productions, where weights appear in brackets, as shown in Example 8-6.

Example 8-6. Defining a probabilistic context-free grammar (PCFG).

```
grammar = nltk.parse_pcfg("""
    S    -> NP VP              [1.0]
    VP   -> TV NP              [0.4]
    VP   -> IV                 [0.3]
    VP   -> DatV NP NP         [0.3]
    TV   -> 'saw'              [1.0]
    IV   -> 'ate'              [1.0]
    DatV -> 'gave'             [1.0]
    NP   -> 'telescopes'       [0.8]
    NP   -> 'Jack'             [0.2]
    """)

>>> print grammar
Grammar with 9 productions (start state = S)
    S -> NP VP [1.0]
    VP -> TV NP [0.4]
    VP -> IV [0.3]
    VP -> DatV NP NP [0.3]
    TV -> 'saw' [1.0]
    IV -> 'ate' [1.0]
    DatV -> 'gave' [1.0]
    NP -> 'telescopes' [0.8]
    NP -> 'Jack' [0.2]
```

It is sometimes convenient to combine multiple productions into a single line, e.g., VP -> TV NP [0.4] | IV [0.3] | DatV NP NP [0.3]. In order to ensure that the trees generated by the grammar form a probability distribution, PCFG grammars impose the constraint that all productions with a given lefthand side must have probabilities that sum to one. The grammar in Example 8-6 obeys this constraint: for S, there is only one production, with a probability of 1.0; for VP, 0.4+0.3+0.3=1.0; and for NP, 0.8+0.2=1.0. The parse tree returned by parse() includes probabilities:

```
>>> viterbi_parser = nltk.ViterbiParser(grammar)
>>> print viterbi_parser.parse(['Jack', 'saw', 'telescopes'])
(S (NP Jack) (VP (TV saw) (NP telescopes))) (p=0.064)
```

Now that parse trees are assigned probabilities, it no longer matters that there may be a huge number of possible parses for a given sentence. A parser will be responsible for finding the most likely parses.

8.7 Summary

- Sentences have internal organization that can be represented using a tree. Notable features of constituent structure are: recursion, heads, complements, and modifiers.

- A grammar is a compact characterization of a potentially infinite set of sentences; we say that a tree is well-formed according to a grammar, or that a grammar licenses a tree.

- A grammar is a formal model for describing whether a given phrase can be assigned a particular constituent or dependency structure.

- Given a set of syntactic categories, a context-free grammar uses a set of productions to say how a phrase of some category A can be analyzed into a sequence of smaller parts $\alpha_1 \ldots \alpha_n$.

- A dependency grammar uses productions to specify what the dependents are of a given lexical head.

- Syntactic ambiguity arises when one sentence has more than one syntactic analysis (e.g., prepositional phrase attachment ambiguity).

- A parser is a procedure for finding one or more trees corresponding to a grammatically well-formed sentence.

- A simple top-down parser is the recursive descent parser, which recursively expands the start symbol (usually S) with the help of the grammar productions, and tries to match the input sentence. This parser cannot handle left-recursive productions (e.g., productions such as NP -> NP PP). It is inefficient in the way it blindly expands categories without checking whether they are compatible with the input string, and in repeatedly expanding the same non-terminals and discarding the results.

- A simple bottom-up parser is the shift-reduce parser, which shifts input onto a stack and tries to match the items at the top of the stack with the righthand side of grammar productions. This parser is not guaranteed to find a valid parse for the input, even if one exists, and builds substructures without checking whether it is globally consistent with the grammar.

8.8 Further Reading

Extra materials for this chapter are posted at *http://www.nltk.org/*, including links to freely available resources on the Web. For more examples of parsing with NLTK, please see the Parsing HOWTO at *http://www.nltk.org/howto*.

There are many introductory books on syntax. (O'Grady et al., 2004) is a general introduction to linguistics, while (Radford, 1988) provides a gentle introduction to transformational grammar, and can be recommended for its coverage of transformational approaches to unbounded dependency constructions. The most widely used term in linguistics for formal grammar is **generative grammar**, though it has nothing to do with generation (Chomsky, 1965).

(Burton-Roberts, 1997) is a practically oriented textbook on how to analyze constituency in English, with extensive exemplification and exercises. (Huddleston & Pullum, 2002) provides an up-to-date and comprehensive analysis of syntactic phenomena in English.

Chapter 12 of (Jurafsky & Martin, 2008) covers formal grammars of English; Sections 13.1–3 cover simple parsing algorithms and techniques for dealing with ambiguity; Chapter 14 covers statistical parsing; and Chapter 16 covers the Chomsky hierarchy and the formal complexity of natural language. (Levin, 1993) has categorized English verbs into fine-grained classes, according to their syntactic properties.

There are several ongoing efforts to build large-scale rule-based grammars, e.g., the LFG Pargram project (*http://www2.parc.com/istl/groups/nltt/pargram/*), the HPSG LinGO Matrix framework (*http://www.delph-in.net/matrix/*), and the XTAG Project (*http://www.cis.upenn.edu/~xtag/*).

8.9 Exercises

1. ○ Can you come up with grammatical sentences that probably have never been uttered before? (Take turns with a partner.) What does this tell you about human language?

2. ○ Recall Strunk and White's prohibition against using a sentence-initial *however* to mean "although." Do a web search for *however* used at the start of the sentence. How widely used is this construction?

3. ○ Consider the sentence *Kim arrived or Dana left and everyone cheered*. Write down the parenthesized forms to show the relative scope of *and* and *or*. Generate tree structures corresponding to both of these interpretations.

4. ○ The `Tree` class implements a variety of other useful methods. See the `Tree` help documentation for more details (i.e., import the `Tree` class and then type `help(Tree)`).

5. ○ In this exercise you will manually construct some parse trees.

a. Write code to produce two trees, one for each reading of the phrase *old men and women*.

b. Encode any of the trees presented in this chapter as a labeled bracketing, and use `nltk.Tree()` to check that it is well-formed. Now use `draw()` to display the tree.

c. As in (a), draw a tree for *The woman saw a man last Thursday*.

6. ○ Write a recursive function to traverse a tree and return the depth of the tree, such that a tree with a single node would have depth zero. (Hint: the depth of a subtree is the maximum depth of its children, plus one.)

7. ○ Analyze the A.A. Milne sentence about Piglet, by underlining all of the sentences it contains then replacing these with S (e.g., the first sentence becomes S *when* S). Draw a tree structure for this "compressed" sentence. What are the main syntactic constructions used for building such a long sentence?

8. ○ In the recursive descent parser demo, experiment with changing the sentence to be parsed by selecting Edit Text in the Edit menu.

9. ○ Can the grammar in `grammar1` (Example 8-1) be used to describe sentences that are more than 20 words in length?

10. ○ Use the graphical chart-parser interface to experiment with different rule invocation strategies. Come up with your own strategy that you can execute manually using the graphical interface. Describe the steps, and report any efficiency improvements it has (e.g., in terms of the size of the resulting chart). Do these improvements depend on the structure of the grammar? What do you think of the prospects for significant performance boosts from cleverer rule invocation strategies?

11. ○ With pen and paper, manually trace the execution of a recursive descent parser and a shift-reduce parser, for a CFG you have already seen, or one of your own devising.

12. ○ We have seen that a chart parser adds but never removes edges from a chart. Why?

13. ○ Consider the sequence of words: *Buffalo buffalo Buffalo buffalo buffalo buffalo Buffalo buffalo*. This is a grammatically correct sentence, as explained at *http://en.wikipedia.org/wiki/Buffalo_buffalo_Buffalo_buffalo_buffalo_buffalo_Buffalo_buffalo*. Consider the tree diagram presented on this Wikipedia page, and write down a suitable grammar. Normalize case to lowercase, to simulate the problem that a listener has when hearing this sentence. Can you find other parses for this sentence? How does the number of parse trees grow as the sentence gets longer? (More examples of these sentences can be found at *http://en.wikipedia.org/wiki/List_of_homophonous_phrases*.)

14. ◑ You can modify the grammar in the recursive descent parser demo by selecting Edit Grammar in the Edit menu. Change the first expansion production, namely

`NP -> Det N PP`, to `NP -> NP PP`. Using the Step button, try to build a parse tree. What happens?

15. ◑ Extend the grammar in `grammar2` with productions that expand prepositions as intransitive, transitive, and requiring a `PP` complement. Based on these productions, use the method of the preceding exercise to draw a tree for the sentence *Lee ran away home*.

16. ◑ Pick some common verbs and complete the following tasks:

   a. Write a program to find those verbs in the PP Attachment Corpus `nltk.cor` `pus.ppattach`. Find any cases where the same verb exhibits two different attachments, but where the first noun, or second noun, or preposition stays unchanged (as we saw in our discussion of syntactic ambiguity in Section 8.2).

   b. Devise CFG grammar productions to cover some of these cases.

17. ◑ Write a program to compare the efficiency of a top-down chart parser compared with a recursive descent parser (Section 8.4). Use the same grammar and input sentences for both. Compare their performance using the `timeit` module (see Section 4.7 for an example of how to do this).

18. ◑ Compare the performance of the top-down, bottom-up, and left-corner parsers using the same grammar and three grammatical test sentences. Use `timeit` to log the amount of time each parser takes on the same sentence. Write a function that runs all three parsers on all three sentences, and prints a 3-by-3 grid of times, as well as row and column totals. Discuss your findings.

19. ◑ Read up on "garden path" sentences. How might the computational work of a parser relate to the difficulty humans have with processing these sentences? (See *http://en.wikipedia.org/wiki/Garden_path_sentence*.)

20. ◑ To compare multiple trees in a single window, we can use the `draw_trees()` method. Define some trees and try it out:

```
>>> from nltk.draw.tree import draw_trees
>>> draw_trees(tree1, tree2, tree3)
```

21. ◑ Using tree positions, list the subjects of the first 100 sentences in the Penn treebank; to make the results easier to view, limit the extracted subjects to subtrees whose height is at most 2.

22. ◑ Inspect the PP Attachment Corpus and try to suggest some factors that influence PP attachment.

23. ◑ In Section 8.2, we claimed that there are linguistic regularities that cannot be described simply in terms of n-grams. Consider the following sentence, particularly the position of the phrase *in his turn*. Does this illustrate a problem for an approach based on n-grams?

   What was more, the in his turn somewhat youngish Nikolay Parfenovich also turned out to be the only person in the entire world to acquire a sincere liking to our "discriminated-against" public procurator. (Dostoevsky: The Brothers Karamazov)

24. ◑ Write a recursive function that produces a nested bracketing for a tree, leaving out the leaf nodes and displaying the non-terminal labels after their subtrees. So the example in Section 8.6 about Pierre Vinken would produce: `[[[NNP NNP]NP , [ADJP [CD NNS]NP JJ]ADJP ,]NP-SBJ MD [VB [DT NN]NP [IN [DT JJ NN]NP]PP-CLR [NNP CD]NP-TMP]VP .]S`. Consecutive categories should be separated by space.

25. ◑ Download several electronic books from Project Gutenberg. Write a program to scan these texts for any extremely long sentences. What is the longest sentence you can find? What syntactic construction(s) are responsible for such long sentences?

26. ◑ Modify the functions `init_wfst()` and `complete_wfst()` so that the contents of each cell in the WFST is a set of non-terminal symbols rather than a single non-terminal.

27. ◑ Consider the algorithm in Example 8-3. Can you explain why parsing context-free grammar is proportional to n^3, where n is the length of the input sentence?

28. ◑ Process each tree of the Penn Treebank Corpus sample `nltk.corpus.treebank` and extract the productions with the help of `Tree.productions()`. Discard the productions that occur only once. Productions with the same lefthand side and similar righthand sides can be collapsed, resulting in an equivalent but more compact set of rules. Write code to output a compact grammar.

29. ● One common way of defining the subject of a sentence S in English is as *the noun phrase that is the child of* S *and the sibling of* VP. Write a function that takes the tree for a sentence and returns the subtree corresponding to the subject of the sentence. What should it do if the root node of the tree passed to this function is not S, or if it lacks a subject?

30. ● Write a function that takes a grammar (such as the one defined in Example 8-1) and returns a random sentence generated by the grammar. (Use `grammar.start()` to find the start symbol of the grammar; `grammar.productions(lhs)` to get the list of productions from the grammar that have the specified lefthand side; and `production.rhs()` to get the righthand side of a production.)

31. ● Implement a version of the shift-reduce parser using backtracking, so that it finds all possible parses for a sentence, what might be called a "recursive ascent parser." Consult the Wikipedia entry for backtracking at *http://en.wikipedia.org/wiki/Backtracking*.

32. ● As we saw in Chapter 7, it is possible to collapse chunks down to their chunk label. When we do this for sentences involving the word *gave*, we find patterns such as the following:

```
gave NP
gave up NP in NP
gave NP up
gave NP NP
gave NP to NP
```

a. Use this method to study the complementation patterns of a verb of interest, and write suitable grammar productions. (This task is sometimes called **lexical acquisition**.)

b. Identify some English verbs that are near-synonyms, such as the *dumped/filled/ loaded* example from (64) in Chapter 9. Use the chunking method to study the complementation patterns of these verbs. Create a grammar to cover these cases. Can the verbs be freely substituted for each other, or are there constraints? Discuss your findings.

33. ● Develop a left-corner parser based on the recursive descent parser, and inheriting from ParseI.

34. ● Extend NLTK's shift-reduce parser to incorporate backtracking, so that it is guaranteed to find all parses that exist (i.e., it is **complete**).

35. ● Modify the functions `init_wfst()` and `complete_wfst()` so that when a non-terminal symbol is added to a cell in the WFST, it includes a record of the cells from which it was derived. Implement a function that will convert a WFST in this form to a parse tree.

Building Feature-Based Grammars

Natural languages have an extensive range of grammatical constructions which are hard to handle with the simple methods described in Chapter 8. In order to gain more flexibility, we change our treatment of grammatical categories like S, NP, and V. In place of atomic labels, we decompose them into structures like dictionaries, where features can take on a range of values.

The goal of this chapter is to answer the following questions:

1. How can we extend the framework of context-free grammars with features so as to gain more fine-grained control over grammatical categories and productions?

2. What are the main formal properties of feature structures, and how do we use them computationally?

3. What kinds of linguistic patterns and grammatical constructions can we now capture with feature-based grammars?

Along the way, we will cover more topics in English syntax, including phenomena such as agreement, subcategorization, and unbounded dependency constructions.

9.1 Grammatical Features

In Chapter 6, we described how to build classifiers that rely on detecting features of text. Such features may be quite simple, such as extracting the last letter of a word, or more complex, such as a part-of-speech tag that has itself been predicted by the classifier. In this chapter, we will investigate the role of features in building rule-based grammars. In contrast to feature extractors, which record features that have been automatically detected, we are now going to *declare* the features of words and phrases. We start off with a very simple example, using dictionaries to store features and their values.

```
>>> kim = {'CAT': 'NP', 'ORTH': 'Kim', 'REF': 'k'}
>>> chase = {'CAT': 'V', 'ORTH': 'chased', 'REL': 'chase'}
```

The objects kim and chase both have a couple of shared features, CAT (grammatical category) and ORTH (orthography, i.e., spelling). In addition, each has a more semantically oriented feature: kim['REF'] is intended to give the referent of kim, while chase['REL'] gives the relation expressed by chase. In the context of rule-based grammars, such pairings of features and values are known as **feature structures**, and we will shortly see alternative notations for them.

Feature structures contain various kinds of information about grammatical entities. The information need not be exhaustive, and we might want to add further properties. For example, in the case of a verb, it is often useful to know what "semantic role" is played by the arguments of the verb. In the case of *chase*, the subject plays the role of "agent," whereas the object has the role of "patient." Let's add this information, using 'sbj' (subject) and 'obj' (object) as placeholders which will get filled once the verb combines with its grammatical arguments:

```
>>> chase['AGT'] = 'sbj'
>>> chase['PAT'] = 'obj'
```

If we now process a sentence *Kim chased Lee*, we want to "bind" the verb's agent role to the subject and the patient role to the object. We do this by linking to the REF feature of the relevant NP. In the following example, we make the simple-minded assumption that the NPs immediately to the left and right of the verb are the subject and object, respectively. We also add a feature structure for *Lee* to complete the example.

```
>>> sent = "Kim chased Lee"
>>> tokens = sent.split()
>>> lee = {'CAT': 'NP', 'ORTH': 'Lee', 'REF': 'l'}
>>> def lex2fs(word):
...     for fs in [kim, lee, chase]:
...         if fs['ORTH'] == word:
...             return fs
>>> subj, verb, obj = lex2fs(tokens[0]), lex2fs(tokens[1]), lex2fs(tokens[2])
>>> verb['AGT'] = subj['REF'] # agent of 'chase' is Kim
>>> verb['PAT'] = obj['REF']  # patient of 'chase' is Lee
>>> for k in ['ORTH', 'REL', 'AGT', 'PAT']: # check featstruct of 'chase'
...     print "%-5s => %s" % (k, verb[k])
ORTH  => chased
REL   => chase
AGT   => k
PAT   => l
```

The same approach could be adopted for a different verb—say, *surprise*—though in this case, the subject would play the role of "source" (SRC), and the object plays the role of "experiencer" (EXP):

```
>>> surprise = {'CAT': 'V', 'ORTH': 'surprised', 'REL': 'surprise',
...             'SRC': 'sbj', 'EXP': 'obj'}
```

Feature structures are pretty powerful, but the way in which we have manipulated them is extremely *ad hoc*. Our next task in this chapter is to show how the framework of context-free grammar and parsing can be expanded to accommodate feature structures, so that we can build analyses like this in a more generic and principled way. We will start off by looking at the phenomenon of syntactic agreement; we will show how agreement constraints can be expressed elegantly using features, and illustrate their use in a simple grammar.

Since feature structures are a general data structure for representing information of any kind, we will briefly look at them from a more formal point of view, and illustrate the support for feature structures offered by NLTK. In the final part of the chapter, we demonstrate that the additional expressiveness of features opens up a wide spectrum of possibilities for describing sophisticated aspects of linguistic structure.

Syntactic Agreement

The following examples show pairs of word sequences, the first of which is grammatical and the second not. (We use an asterisk at the start of a word sequence to signal that it is ungrammatical.)

(1) a. this dog
     b. *these dog

(2) a. these dogs
     b. *this dogs

In English, nouns are usually marked as being singular or plural. The form of the demonstrative also varies: *this* (singular) and *these* (plural). Examples (1) and (2) show that there are constraints on the use of demonstratives and nouns within a noun phrase: either both are singular or both are plural. A similar constraint holds between subjects and predicates:

(3) a. the dog runs
     b. *the dog run

(4) a. the dogs run
     b. *the dogs runs

Here we can see that morphological properties of the verb co-vary with syntactic properties of the subject noun phrase. This co-variance is called **agreement**. If we look further at verb agreement in English, we will see that present tense verbs typically have two inflected forms: one for third person singular, and another for every other combination of person and number, as shown in Table 9-1.

Table 9-1. Agreement paradigm for English regular verbs

	Singular	**Plural**
1st person	*I run*	*we run*
2nd person	*you run*	*you run*
3rd person	*he/she/it runs*	*they run*

We can make the role of morphological properties a bit more explicit, as illustrated in (5) and (6). These representations indicate that the verb agrees with its subject in person and number. (We use 3 as an abbreviation for 3rd person, SG for singular, and PL for plural.)

(5)   the dog   run-s
         dog.3.SG run-3.SG

(6)   the dog-s   run
         dog.3.PL run-3.PL

Let's see what happens when we encode these agreement constraints in a context-free grammar. We will begin with the simple CFG in (7).

```
(7) S    ->    NP VP
    NP   ->    Det N
    VP   ->    V

    Det  ->    'this'
    N    ->    'dog'
    V    ->    'runs'
```

Grammar (7) allows us to generate the sentence *this dog runs*; however, what we really want to do is also generate *these dogs run* while blocking unwanted sequences like **this dogs run* and **these dog runs*. The most straightforward approach is to add new non-terminals and productions to the grammar:

```
(8) S -> NP_SG VP_SG
    S -> NP_PL VP_PL
    NP_SG -> Det_SG N_SG
    NP_PL -> Det_PL N_PL
    VP_SG -> V_SG
    VP_PL -> V_PL

    Det_SG -> 'this'
    Det_PL -> 'these'
    N_SG -> 'dog'
    N_PL -> 'dogs'
    V_SG -> 'runs'
    V_PL -> 'run'
```

In place of a single production expanding S, we now have two productions, one covering the sentences involving singular subject NPs and VPs, the other covering sentences with plural subject `NP`s and `VP`s. In fact, every production in (7) has two counterparts in (8). With a small grammar, this is not really such a problem, although it is aesthetically unappealing. However, with a larger grammar that covers a reasonable subset of English constructions, the prospect of doubling the grammar size is very unattractive. Let's suppose now that we used the same approach to deal with first, second, and third person agreement, for both singular and plural. This would lead to the original grammar being multiplied by a factor of 6, which we definitely want to avoid. Can we do better than this? In the next section, we will show that capturing number and person agreement need not come at the cost of "blowing up" the number of productions.

Using Attributes and Constraints

We spoke informally of linguistic categories having *properties*, for example, that a noun has the property of being plural. Let's make this explicit:

> (9) `N[NUM=pl]`

In (9), we have introduced some new notation which says that the category `N` has a (grammatical) **feature** called `NUM` (short for "number") and that the value of this feature is `pl` (short for "plural"). We can add similar annotations to other categories, and use them in lexical entries:

> (10) `Det[NUM=sg] -> 'this'`
>   `Det[NUM=pl] -> 'these'`
>
>   `N[NUM=sg] -> 'dog'`
>   `N[NUM=pl] -> 'dogs'`
>   `V[NUM=sg] -> 'runs'`
>   `V[NUM=pl] -> 'run'`

Does this help at all? So far, it looks just like a slightly more verbose alternative to what was specified in (8). Things become more interesting when we allow *variables* over feature values, and use these to state constraints:

> (11) `S -> NP[NUM=?n] VP[NUM=?n]`
>   `NP[NUM=?n] -> Det[NUM=?n] N[NUM=?n]`
>   `VP[NUM=?n] -> V[NUM=?n]`

We are using `?n` as a variable over values of `NUM`; it can be instantiated either to `sg` or `pl`, within a given production. We can read the first production as saying that whatever value `NP` takes for the feature `NUM`, `VP` must take the same value.

In order to understand how these feature constraints work, it's helpful to think about how one would go about building a tree. Lexical productions will admit the following local trees (trees of depth one):

(12) a. **Det[NUM=sg]**
         |
        this

      b. **Det[NUM=pl]**
         |
        these

(13) a. **N[NUM=sg]**
         |
        dog

      b. **N[NUM=pl]**
         |
        dogs

Now NP[NUM=?n] -> Det[NUM=?n] N[NUM=?n] says that whatever the NUM values of N and Det are, they have to be the same. Consequently, this production will permit (12a) and (13a) to be combined into an NP, as shown in (14a), and it will also allow (12b) and (13b) to be combined, as in (14b). By contrast, (15a) and (15b) are prohibited because the roots of their subtrees differ in their values for the NUM feature; this incompatibility of values is indicated informally with a *FAIL* value at the top node.

(14) a.   **NP[NUM=sg]**

        Det[NUM=sg]   N[NUM=sg]
              | |
             this   dog

      b.   **NP[NUM=pl]**

        Det[NUM=pl]   N[NUM=pl]
              | |
            these   dogs

(15) a.

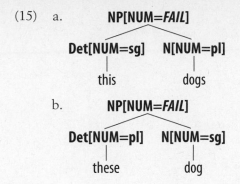

b.

Production `VP[NUM=?n] -> V[NUM=?n]` says that the NUM value of the head verb has to be the same as the NUM value of the VP parent. Combined with the production for expanding S, we derive the consequence that if the NUM value of the subject head noun is pl, then so is the NUM value of the VP's head verb.

(16)

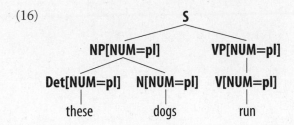

Grammar (10) illustrated lexical productions for determiners like *this* and *these*, which require a singular or plural head noun respectively. However, other determiners in English are not choosy about the grammatical number of the noun they combine with. One way of describing this would be to add two lexical entries to the grammar, one each for the singular and plural versions of a determiner such as *the*:

```
Det[NUM=sg] -> 'the' | 'some' | 'several'
Det[NUM=pl] -> 'the' | 'some' | 'several'
```

However, a more elegant solution is to leave the NUM value **underspecified** and let it agree in number with whatever noun it combines with. Assigning a variable value to NUM is one way of achieving this result:

```
Det[NUM=?n] -> 'the' | 'some' | 'several'
```

But in fact we can be even more economical, and just omit any specification for NUM in such productions. We only need to explicitly enter a variable value when this constrains another value elsewhere in the same production.

The grammar in Example 9-1 illustrates most of the ideas we have introduced so far in this chapter, plus a couple of new ones.

Example 9-1. Example feature-based grammar.

```
>>> nltk.data.show_cfg('grammars/book_grammars/feat0.fcfg')
% start S
# ####################
# Grammar Productions
# ####################
# S expansion productions
S -> NP[NUM=?n] VP[NUM=?n]
# NP expansion productions
NP[NUM=?n] -> N[NUM=?n]
NP[NUM=?n] -> PropN[NUM=?n]
NP[NUM=?n] -> Det[NUM=?n] N[NUM=?n]
NP[NUM=pl] -> N[NUM=pl]
# VP expansion productions
VP[TENSE=?t, NUM=?n] -> IV[TENSE=?t, NUM=?n]
VP[TENSE=?t, NUM=?n] -> TV[TENSE=?t, NUM=?n] NP
# ####################
# Lexical Productions
# ####################
Det[NUM=sg] -> 'this' | 'every'
Det[NUM=pl] -> 'these' | 'all'
Det -> 'the' | 'some' | 'several'
PropN[NUM=sg]-> 'Kim' | 'Jody'
N[NUM=sg] -> 'dog' | 'girl' | 'car' | 'child'
N[NUM=pl] -> 'dogs' | 'girls' | 'cars' | 'children'
IV[TENSE=pres, NUM=sg] -> 'disappears' | 'walks'
TV[TENSE=pres, NUM=sg] -> 'sees' | 'likes'
IV[TENSE=pres, NUM=pl] -> 'disappear' | 'walk'
TV[TENSE=pres, NUM=pl] -> 'see' | 'like'
IV[TENSE=past] -> 'disappeared' | 'walked'
TV[TENSE=past] -> 'saw' | 'liked'
```

Notice that a syntactic category can have more than one feature: for example, V[TENSE=pres, NUM=pl]. In general, we can add as many features as we like.

A final detail about Example 9-1 is the statement %start S. This "directive" tells the parser to take S as the start symbol for the grammar.

In general, when we are trying to develop even a very small grammar, it is convenient to put the productions in a file where they can be edited, tested, and revised. We have saved Example 9-1 as a file named *feat0.fcfg* in the NLTK data distribution. You can make your own copy of this for further experimentation using nltk.data.load().

Feature-based grammars are parsed in NLTK using an Earley chart parser (see Section 9.5 for more information about this) and Example 9-2 illustrates how this is carried out. After tokenizing the input, we import the load_parser function ❶, which takes a grammar filename as input and returns a chart parser cp ❷. Calling the parser's nbest_parse() method will return a list trees of parse trees; trees will be empty if the grammar fails to parse the input and otherwise will contain one or more parse trees, depending on whether the input is syntactically ambiguous.

Example 9-2. Trace of feature-based chart parser.

```
>>> tokens = 'Kim likes children'.split()
>>> from nltk import load_parser ❶
>>> cp = load_parser('grammars/book_grammars/feat0.fcfg', trace=2) ❷
>>> trees = cp.nbest_parse(tokens)
|.Kim .like.chil.|
|[----]    .    .| PropN[NUM='sg'] -> 'Kim' *
|[----]    .    .| NP[NUM='sg'] -> PropN[NUM='sg'] *
|[---->    .    .| S[] -> NP[NUM=?n] * VP[NUM=?n] {?n: 'sg'}
|.   [----]    .| TV[NUM='sg', TENSE='pres'] -> 'likes' *
|.   [---->    .| VP[NUM=?n, TENSE=?t] -> TV[NUM=?n, TENSE=?t] * NP[]
               {?n: 'sg', ?t: 'pres'}
|.    .   [----]| N[NUM='pl'] -> 'children' *
|.    .   [----]| NP[NUM='pl'] -> N[NUM='pl'] *
|.    .   [---->| S[] -> NP[NUM=?n] * VP[NUM=?n] {?n: 'pl'}
|.    [---------]| VP[NUM='sg', TENSE='pres']
               -> TV[NUM='sg', TENSE='pres'] NP[] *
|[==============]| S[] -> NP[NUM='sg'] VP[NUM='sg'] *
```

The details of the parsing procedure are not that important for present purposes. However, there is an implementation issue which bears on our earlier discussion of grammar size. One possible approach to parsing productions containing feature constraints is to compile out all admissible values of the features in question so that we end up with a large, fully specified CFG along the lines of (8). By contrast, the parser process illustrated in the previous examples works directly with the underspecified productions given by the grammar. Feature values "flow upwards" from lexical entries, and variable values are then associated with those values via bindings (i.e., dictionaries) such as {?n: 'sg', ?t: 'pres'}. As the parser assembles information about the nodes of the tree it is building, these variable bindings are used to instantiate values in these nodes; thus the underspecified VP[NUM=?n, TENSE=?t] -> TV[NUM=?n, TENSE=?t] NP[] becomes instantiated as VP[NUM='sg', TENSE='pres'] -> TV[NUM='sg', TENSE='pres'] NP[] by looking up the values of ?n and ?t in the bindings.

Finally, we can inspect the resulting parse trees (in this case, a single one).

```
>>> for tree in trees: print tree
(S[]
  (NP[NUM='sg'] (PropN[NUM='sg'] Kim))
  (VP[NUM='sg', TENSE='pres']
    (TV[NUM='sg', TENSE='pres'] likes)
    (NP[NUM='pl'] (N[NUM='pl'] children))))
```

Terminology

So far, we have only seen feature values like sg and pl. These simple values are usually called **atomic**—that is, they can't be decomposed into subparts. A special case of atomic values are **Boolean** values, that is, values that just specify whether a property is true or false. For example, we might want to distinguish **auxiliary** verbs such as *can*, *may*, *will*, and *do* with the Boolean feature AUX. Then the production V[TENSE=pres, aux=+] -> 'can' means that *can* receives the value pres for TENSE and + or true for AUX. There is a widely adopted convention that abbreviates the representation of Boolean features f; instead of aux=+ or aux=-, we use +aux and -aux respectively. These are just abbreviations, however, and the parser interprets them as though + and - are like any other atomic value. (17) shows some representative productions:

```
(17) V[TENSE=pres, +aux] -> 'can'
     V[TENSE=pres, +aux] -> 'may'

     V[TENSE=pres, -aux] -> 'walks'
     V[TENSE=pres, -aux] -> 'likes'
```

We have spoken of attaching "feature annotations" to syntactic categories. A more radical approach represents the whole category—that is, the non-terminal symbol plus the annotation—as a bundle of features. For example, N[NUM=sg] contains part-of-speech information which can be represented as POS=N. An alternative notation for this category, therefore, is [POS=N, NUM=sg].

In addition to atomic-valued features, features may take values that are themselves feature structures. For example, we can group together agreement features (e.g., person, number, and gender) as a distinguished part of a category, serving as the value of AGR. In this case, we say that AGR has a **complex** value. (18) depicts the structure, in a format known as an **attribute value matrix** (AVM).

```
(18) [POS = N           ]
     [                   ]
     [AGR = [PER = 3   ]]
     [      [NUM = pl  ]]
     [      [GND = fem ]]
```

In passing, we should point out that there are alternative approaches for displaying AVMs; Figure 9-1 shows an example. Although feature structures rendered in the style of (18) are less visually pleasing, we will stick with this format, since it corresponds to the output we will be getting from NLTK.

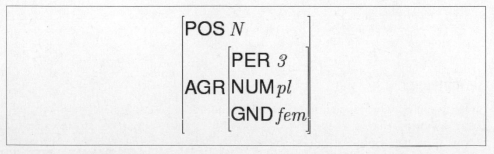

Figure 9-1. Rendering a feature structure as an attribute value matrix.

On the topic of representation, we also note that feature structures, like dictionaries, assign no particular significance to the *order* of features. So (18) is equivalent to:

```
(19) [AGR = [NUM = pl  ]]
     [       [PER = 3   ]]
     [       [GND = fem ]]
     [                   ]
     [POS = N            ]
```

Once we have the possibility of using features like AGR, we can refactor a grammar like Example 9-1 so that agreement features are bundled together. A tiny grammar illustrating this idea is shown in (20).

```
(20) S -> NP[AGR=?n] VP[AGR=?n]
     NP[AGR=?n] -> PropN[AGR=?n]
     VP[TENSE=?t, AGR=?n] -> Cop[TENSE=?t, AGR=?n] Adj

     Cop[TENSE=pres,  AGR=[NUM=sg, PER=3]] -> 'is'
     PropN[AGR=[NUM=sg, PER=3]] -> 'Kim'
     Adj -> 'happy'
```

9.2 Processing Feature Structures

In this section, we will show how feature structures can be constructed and manipulated in NLTK. We will also discuss the fundamental operation of unification, which allows us to combine the information contained in two different feature structures.

Feature structures in NLTK are declared with the `FeatStruct()` constructor. Atomic feature values can be strings or integers.

```
>>> fs1 = nltk.FeatStruct(TENSE='past', NUM='sg')
>>> print fs1
[ NUM   = 'sg'   ]
[ TENSE = 'past' ]
```

A feature structure is actually just a kind of dictionary, and so we access its values by indexing in the usual way. We can use our familiar syntax to *assign* values to features:

```
>>> fs1 = nltk.FeatStruct(PER=3, NUM='pl', GND='fem')
>>> print fs1['GND']
fem
>>> fs1['CASE'] = 'acc'
```

We can also define feature structures that have complex values, as discussed earlier.

```
>>> fs2 = nltk.FeatStruct(POS='N', AGR=fs1)
>>> print fs2
[       [ CASE = 'acc' ] ]
[ AGR = [ GND  = 'fem' ] ]
[       [ NUM  = 'pl'  ] ]
[       [ PER  = 3      ] ]
[                        ]
[ POS = 'N'              ]
```

```
>>> print fs2['AGR']
[ CASE = 'acc' ]
[ GND  = 'fem' ]
[ NUM  = 'pl'  ]
[ PER  = 3     ]
>>> print fs2['AGR']['PER']
3
```

An alternative method of specifying feature structures is to use a bracketed string consisting of feature-value pairs in the format feature=value, where values may themselves be feature structures:

```
>>> print nltk.FeatStruct("[POS='N', AGR=[PER=3, NUM='pl', GND='fem']]")
[           [ PER = 3     ] ]
[ AGR = [ GND = 'fem' ] ]
[           [ NUM = 'pl'  ] ]
[                                ]
[ POS = 'N'               ]
```

Feature structures are not inherently tied to linguistic objects; they are general-purpose structures for representing knowledge. For example, we could encode information about a person in a feature structure:

```
>>> print nltk.FeatStruct(name='Lee', telno='01 27 86 42 96', age=33)
[ age   = 33                ]
[ name  = 'Lee'            ]
[ telno = '01 27 86 42 96' ]
```

In the next couple of pages, we are going to use examples like this to explore standard operations over feature structures. This will briefly divert us from processing natural language, but we need to lay the groundwork before we can get back to talking about grammars. Hang on tight!

It is often helpful to view feature structures as graphs, more specifically, as **directed acyclic graphs** (DAGs). (21) is equivalent to the preceding AVM.

(21)

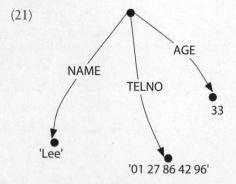

The feature names appear as labels on the directed arcs, and feature values appear as labels on the nodes that are pointed to by the arcs.

Just as before, feature values can be complex:

---

(22)

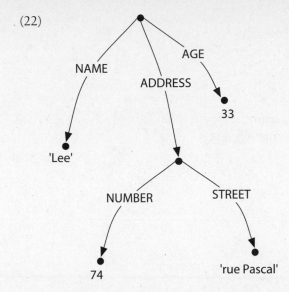

When we look at such graphs, it is natural to think in terms of paths through the graph. A **feature path** is a sequence of arcs that can be followed from the root node. We will represent paths as tuples of arc labels. Thus, (`'ADDRESS'`, `'STREET'`) is a feature path whose value in (22) is the node labeled `'rue Pascal'`.

Now let's consider a situation where Lee has a spouse named *Kim*, and Kim's address is the same as Lee's. We might represent this as (23).

(23)

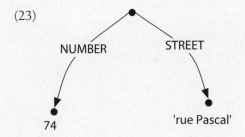

However, rather than repeating the address information in the feature structure, we can "share" the same sub-graph between different arcs:

(24)

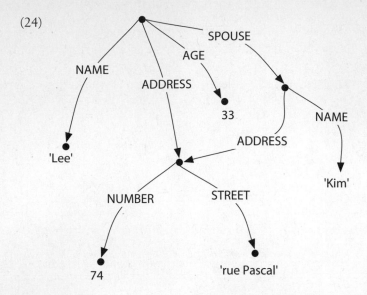

In other words, the value of the path (`'ADDRESS'`) in (24) is identical to the value of the path (`'SPOUSE'`, `'ADDRESS'`). DAGs such as (24) are said to involve **structure sharing** or **reentrancy**. When two paths have the same value, they are said to be **equivalent**.

In order to indicate reentrancy in our matrix-style representations, we will prefix the first occurrence of a shared feature structure with an integer in parentheses, such as (1). Any later reference to that structure will use the notation ->(1), as shown here.

```
>>> print nltk.FeatStruct("""[NAME='Lee', ADDRESS=(1)[NUMBER=74, STREET='rue Pascal'],
...                           SPOUSE=[NAME='Kim', ADDRESS->(1)]]""")
[ ADDRESS = (1) [ NUMBER = 74           ] ]
[               [ STREET = 'rue Pascal' ] ]
[                                         ]
[ NAME    = 'Lee'                         ]
[                                         ]
[ SPOUSE  = [ ADDRESS -> (1)   ]          ]
[           [ NAME    = 'Kim' ]          ]
```

The bracketed integer is sometimes called a **tag** or a **coindex**. The choice of integer is not significant. There can be any number of tags within a single feature structure.

```
>>> print nltk.FeatStruct("[A='a', B=(1)[C='c'], D->(1), E->(1)]")
[ A = 'a'            ]
[                    ]
[ B = (1) [ C = 'c' ] ]
[                    ]
[ D -> (1)           ]
[ E -> (1)           ]
```

Subsumption and Unification

It is standard to think of feature structures as providing **partial information** about some object, in the sense that we can order feature structures according to how general they are. For example, (25a) is more general (less specific) than (25b), which in turn is more general than (25c).

(25) a. `[NUMBER = 74]`

   b. `[NUMBER = 74          ]`
    `[STREET = 'rue Pascal']`

   c. `[NUMBER = 74          ]`
    `[STREET = 'rue Pascal']`
    `[CITY = 'Paris'       ]`

This ordering is called **subsumption**; a more general feature structure **subsumes** a less general one. If FS_0 subsumes FS_1 (formally, we write $FS_0 \sqsubseteq FS_1$), then FS_1 must have all the paths and path equivalences of FS_0, and may have additional paths and equivalences as well. Thus, (23) subsumes (24) since the latter has additional path equivalences. It should be obvious that subsumption provides only a partial ordering on feature structures, since some feature structures are incommensurable. For example, (26) neither subsumes nor is subsumed by (25a).

(26) `[TELNO = 01 27 86 42 96]`

So we have seen that some feature structures are more specific than others. How do we go about specializing a given feature structure? For example, we might decide that addresses should consist of not just a street number and a street name, but also a city. That is, we might want to *merge* graph (27a) with (27b) to yield (27c).

(27) a.

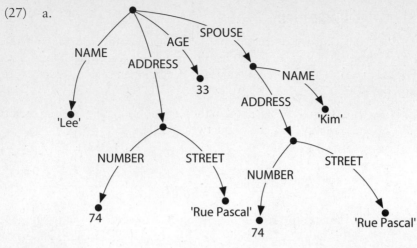

b.

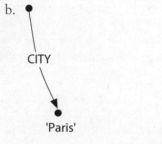

c.

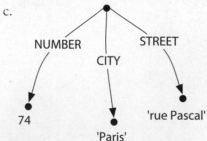

Merging information from two feature structures is called **unification** and is supported by the unify() method.

```
>>> fs1 = nltk.FeatStruct(NUMBER=74, STREET='rue Pascal')
>>> fs2 = nltk.FeatStruct(CITY='Paris')
>>> print fs1.unify(fs2)
[ CITY   = 'Paris'      ]
[ NUMBER = 74           ]
[ STREET = 'rue Pascal' ]
```

Unification is formally defined as a binary operation: $FS_0 \sqcup FS_1$. Unification is symmetric, so $FS_0 \sqcup FS_1 = FS_1 \sqcup FS_0$. The same is true in Python:

```
>>> print fs2.unify(fs1)
[ CITY   = 'Paris'      ]
[ NUMBER = 74           ]
[ STREET = 'rue Pascal' ]
```

If we unify two feature structures that stand in the subsumption relationship, then the result of unification is the most specific of the two:

(28) If $FS_0 \sqsubseteq FS_1$, then $FS_0 \sqcup FS_1 = FS_1$

For example, the result of unifying (25b) with (25c) is (25c).

Unification between FS_0 and FS_1 will fail if the two feature structures share a path π where the value of π in FS_0 is a distinct atom from the value of π in FS_1. This is implemented by setting the result of unification to be None.

```
>>> fs0 = nltk.FeatStruct(A='a')
>>> fs1 = nltk.FeatStruct(A='b')
>>> fs2 = fs0.unify(fs1)
>>> print fs2
None
```

Now, if we look at how unification interacts with structure-sharing, things become really interesting. First, let's define (23) in Python:

```
>>> fs0 = nltk.FeatStruct("""[NAME=Lee,
...                           ADDRESS=[NUMBER=74,
...                                    STREET='rue Pascal'],
...                           SPOUSE= [NAME=Kim,
...                                    ADDRESS=[NUMBER=74,
...                                             STREET='rue Pascal']]]""")
>>> print fs0
[ ADDRESS = [ NUMBER = 74            ]                 ]
[           [ STREET = 'rue Pascal'  ]                 ]
[                                                      ]
[ NAME    = 'Lee'                                      ]
[                                                      ]
[           [ ADDRESS = [ NUMBER = 74            ] ] ] ]
[ SPOUSE  = [           [ STREET = 'rue Pascal'  ] ] ] ]
[           [                                    ] ] ] ]
[           [ NAME    = 'Kim'                    ] ] ] ]
```

What happens when we augment Kim's address with a specification for CITY? Notice that fs1 needs to include the whole path from the root of the feature structure down to CITY.

```
>>> fs1 = nltk.FeatStruct("[SPOUSE = [ADDRESS = [CITY = Paris]]]")
>>> print fs1.unify(fs0)
[ ADDRESS = [ NUMBER = 74            ]                 ]
[           [ STREET = 'rue Pascal'  ]                 ]
[                                                      ]
```

```
[ NAME     = 'Lee'                              ]
[                                               ]
[                [           [ CITY    = 'Paris'     ] ] ]
[                [ ADDRESS = [ NUMBER = 74           ] ] ]
[ SPOUSE   = [              [ STREET = 'rue Pascal' ] ] ]
[                [                                   ] ]
[                [ NAME     = 'Kim'                  ] ]
```

By contrast, the result is very different if **fs1** is unified with the structure sharing version **fs2** (also shown earlier as the graph (24)):

```
>>> fs2 = nltk.FeatStruct("""[NAME=Lee, ADDRESS=(1)[NUMBER=74, STREET='rue Pascal'],
...                          SPOUSE=[NAME=Kim, ADDRESS->(1)]]""")
>>> print fs1.unify(fs2)
[                 [ CITY    = 'Paris'      ] ]
[ ADDRESS = (1) [ NUMBER = 74             ] ]
[                 [ STREET = 'rue Pascal' ] ]
[                                            ]
[ NAME     = 'Lee'                           ]
[                                            ]
[ SPOUSE   = [ ADDRESS -> (1)     ]          ]
[            [ NAME     = 'Kim'   ]          ]
```

Rather than just updating what was in effect Kim's "copy" of Lee's address, we have now updated *both* their addresses at the same time. More generally, if a unification involves specializing the value of some path π, that unification simultaneously specializes the value of *any path that is equivalent to* π.

As we have already seen, structure sharing can also be stated using variables such as ?x.

```
>>> fs1 = nltk.FeatStruct("[ADDRESS1=[NUMBER=74, STREET='rue Pascal']]")
>>> fs2 = nltk.FeatStruct("[ADDRESS1=?x, ADDRESS2=?x]")
>>> print fs2
[ ADDRESS1 = ?x ]
[ ADDRESS2 = ?x ]
>>> print fs2.unify(fs1)
[ ADDRESS1 = (1) [ NUMBER = 74           ] ]
[                [ STREET = 'rue Pascal' ] ]
[                                           ]
[ ADDRESS2 -> (1)                           ]
```

9.3 Extending a Feature-Based Grammar

In this section, we return to feature-based grammar and explore a variety of linguistic issues, and demonstrate the benefits of incorporating features into the grammar.

Subcategorization

In Chapter 8, we augmented our category labels to represent different kinds of verbs, and used the labels IV and TV for intransitive and transitive verbs respectively. This allowed us to write productions like the following:

(29)
```
VP -> IV
VP -> TV NP
```

Although we know that IV and TV are two kinds of V, they are just atomic non-terminal symbols in a CFG and are as distinct from each other as any other pair of symbols. This notation doesn't let us say anything about verbs in general; e.g., we cannot say "All lexical items of category V can be marked for tense," since *walk*, say, is an item of category IV, not V. So, can we replace category labels such as TV and IV by V along with a feature that tells us whether the verb combines with a following NP object or whether it can occur without any complement?

A simple approach, originally developed for a grammar framework called Generalized Phrase Structure Grammar (GPSG), tries to solve this problem by allowing lexical categories to bear a SUBCAT feature, which tells us what subcategorization class the item belongs to. In contrast to the integer values for SUBCAT used by GPSG, the example here adopts more mnemonic values, namely intrans, trans, and clause:

(30)
```
VP[TENSE=?t, NUM=?n] -> V[SUBCAT=intrans, TENSE=?t, NUM=?n]
VP[TENSE=?t, NUM=?n] -> V[SUBCAT=trans, TENSE=?t, NUM=?n] NP
VP[TENSE=?t, NUM=?n] -> V[SUBCAT=clause, TENSE=?t, NUM=?n] SBar

V[SUBCAT=intrans, TENSE=pres, NUM=sg] -> 'disappears' | 'walks'
V[SUBCAT=trans, TENSE=pres, NUM=sg] -> 'sees' | 'likes'
V[SUBCAT=clause, TENSE=pres, NUM=sg] -> 'says' | 'claims'

V[SUBCAT=intrans, TENSE=pres, NUM=pl] -> 'disappear' | 'walk'
V[SUBCAT=trans, TENSE=pres, NUM=pl] -> 'see' | 'like'
V[SUBCAT=clause, TENSE=pres, NUM=pl] -> 'say' | 'claim'

V[SUBCAT=intrans, TENSE=past] -> 'disappeared' | 'walked'
V[SUBCAT=trans, TENSE=past] -> 'saw' | 'liked'
V[SUBCAT=clause, TENSE=past] -> 'said' | 'claimed'
```

When we see a lexical category like V[SUBCAT=trans], we can interpret the SUBCAT specification as a pointer to a production in which V[SUBCAT=trans] is introduced as the head child in a VP production. By convention, there is a correspondence between the values of SUBCAT and the productions that introduce lexical heads. On this approach, SUBCAT can appear *only* on lexical categories; it makes no sense, for example, to specify a SUBCAT value on VP. As required, *walk* and *like* both belong to the category V. Nevertheless, *walk* will occur only in VPs expanded by a production with the feature SUBCAT=intrans on the righthand side, as opposed to *like*, which requires a SUBCAT=trans.

In our third class of verbs in (30), we have specified a category SBar. This is a label for subordinate clauses, such as the complement of *claim* in the example *You claim that you like children*. We require two further productions to analyze such sentences:

(31)
```
SBar -> Comp S
Comp -> 'that'
```

The resulting structure is the following.

(32)

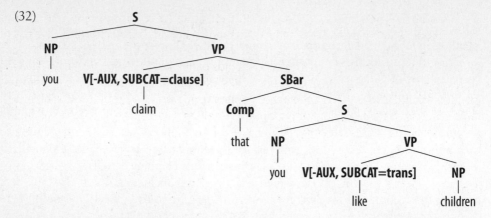

An alternative treatment of subcategorization, due originally to a framework known as categorial grammar, is represented in feature-based frameworks such as PATR and Head-driven Phrase Structure Grammar. Rather than using SUBCAT values as a way of indexing productions, the SUBCAT value directly encodes the valency of a head (the list of arguments that it can combine with). For example, a verb like *put* that takes NP and PP complements (*put the book on the table*) might be represented as (33):

(33) V[SUBCAT=<NP, NP, PP>]

This says that the verb can combine with three arguments. The leftmost element in the list is the subject NP, while everything else—an NP followed by a PP in this case—comprises the subcategorized-for complements. When a verb like *put* is combined with appropriate complements, the requirements which are specified in the SUBCAT are discharged, and only a subject NP is needed. This category, which corresponds to what is traditionally thought of as VP, might be represented as follows:

(34) V[SUBCAT=<NP>]

Finally, a sentence is a kind of verbal category that has *no* requirements for further arguments, and hence has a SUBCAT whose value is the empty list. The tree (35) shows how these category assignments combine in a parse of *Kim put the book on the table*.

(35)

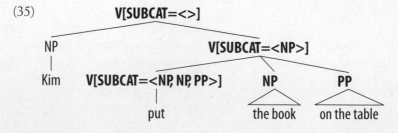

Heads Revisited

We noted in the previous section that by factoring subcategorization information out of the main category label, we could express more generalizations about properties of verbs. Another property of this kind is the following: expressions of category V are heads of phrases of category VP. Similarly, Ns are heads of NPs, As (i.e., adjectives) are heads of APs, and Ps (i.e., prepositions) are heads of PPs. Not all phrases have heads—for example, it is standard to say that coordinate phrases (e.g., *the book and the bell*) lack heads. Nevertheless, we would like our grammar formalism to express the parent/head-child relation where it holds. At present, V and VP are just atomic symbols, and we need to find a way to relate them using features (as we did earlier to relate IV and TV).

X-bar syntax addresses this issue by abstracting out the notion of **phrasal level**. It is usual to recognize three such levels. If N represents the lexical level, then N' represents the next level up, corresponding to the more traditional category Nom, and N'' represents the phrasal level, corresponding to the category NP. (36a) illustrates a representative structure, while (36b) is the more conventional counterpart.

(36) a.

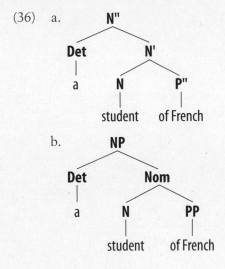

    b.

The head of the structure (36a) is N, and N' and N'' are called **(phrasal) projections** of N. N'' is the **maximal projection**, and N is sometimes called the **zero projection**. One of the central claims of X-bar syntax is that all constituents share a structural similarity. Using X as a variable over N, V, A, and P, we say that directly subcategorized *complements* of a lexical head X are always placed as siblings of the head, whereas *adjuncts* are placed as siblings of the intermediate category, X'. Thus, the configuration of the two P'' adjuncts in (37) contrasts with that of the complement P'' in (36a).

(37)

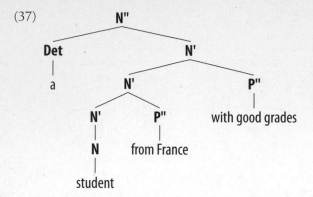

The productions in (38) illustrate how bar levels can be encoded using feature structures. The nested structure in (37) is achieved by two applications of the recursive rule expanding N[BAR=1].

```
(38) S -> N[BAR=2] V[BAR=2]
     N[BAR=2] -> Det N[BAR=1]
     N[BAR=1] -> N[BAR=1] P[BAR=2]
     N[BAR=1] -> N[BAR=0] P[BAR=2]
```

Auxiliary Verbs and Inversion

Inverted clauses—where the order of subject and verb is switched—occur in English interrogatives and also after "negative" adverbs:

(39)   a. Do you like children?

   b. Can Jody walk?

(40)   a. Rarely do you see Kim.

   b. Never have I seen this dog.

However, we cannot place just any verb in pre-subject position:

(41)   a. *Like you children?

   b. *Walks Jody?

(42)   a. *Rarely see you Kim.

   b. *Never saw I this dog.

Verbs that can be positioned initially in inverted clauses belong to the class known as **auxiliaries**, and as well as *do*, *can*, and *have* include *be*, *will*, and *shall*. One way of capturing such structures is with the following production:

```
(43) S[+INV] -> V[+AUX] NP VP
```

That is, a clause marked as [+inv] consists of an auxiliary verb followed by a VP. (In a more detailed grammar, we would need to place some constraints on the form of the VP, depending on the choice of auxiliary.) (44) illustrates the structure of an inverted clause:

(44)

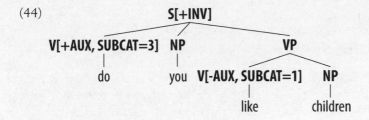

Unbounded Dependency Constructions

Consider the following contrasts:

(45)   a. You like Jody.

      b. *You like.

(46)   a. You put the card into the slot.

      b. *You put into the slot.

      c. *You put the card.

      d. *You put.

The verb *like* requires an NP complement, while *put* requires both a following NP and PP. (45) and (46) show that these complements are *obligatory*: omitting them leads to ungrammaticality. Yet there are contexts in which obligatory complements can be omitted, as (47) and (48) illustrate.

(47)   a. Kim knows who you like.

      b. This music, you really like.

(48)   a. Which card do you put into the slot?

      b. Which slot do you put the card into?

That is, an obligatory complement can be omitted if there is an appropriate **filler** in the sentence, such as the question word *who* in (47a), the preposed topic *this music* in (47b), or the *wh* phrases *which card/slot* in (48). It is common to say that sentences like those in (47) and (48) contain **gaps** where the obligatory complements have been omitted, and these gaps are sometimes made explicit using an underscore:

(49)   a. Which card do you put __ into the slot?

      b. Which slot do you put the card into __?

So, a gap can occur if it is **licensed** by a filler. Conversely, fillers can occur only if there is an appropriate gap elsewhere in the sentence, as shown by the following examples:

(50)   a. *Kim knows who you like Jody.

b. *This music, you really like hip-hop.

(51)   a. *Which card do you put this into the slot?

b. *Which slot do you put the card into this one?

The mutual co-occurrence between filler and gap is sometimes termed a "dependency." One issue of considerable importance in theoretical linguistics has been the nature of the material that can intervene between a filler and the gap that it licenses; in particular, can we simply list a finite set of sequences that separate the two? The answer is no: there is no upper bound on the distance between filler and gap. This fact can be easily illustrated with constructions involving sentential complements, as shown in (52).

(52)   a. Who do you like __?

b. Who do you claim that you like __?

c. Who do you claim that Jody says that you like __?

Since we can have indefinitely deep recursion of sentential complements, the gap can be embedded indefinitely far inside the whole sentence. This constellation of properties leads to the notion of an **unbounded dependency construction**, that is, a filler-gap dependency where there is no upper bound on the distance between filler and gap.

A variety of mechanisms have been suggested for handling unbounded dependencies in formal grammars; here we illustrate the approach due to Generalized Phrase Structure Grammar that involves **slash categories**. A slash category has the form Y/XP; we interpret this as a phrase of category Y that is missing a subconstituent of category XP. For example, S/NP is an S that is missing an NP. The use of slash categories is illustrated in (53).

(53)

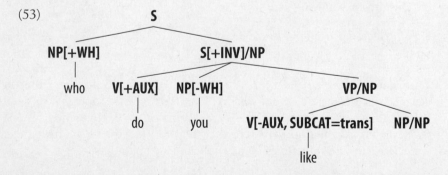

The top part of the tree introduces the filler *who* (treated as an expression of category NP[+wh]) together with a corresponding gap-containing constituent S/NP. The gap information is then "percolated" down the tree via the VP/NP category, until it reaches the category NP/NP. At this point, the dependency is discharged by realizing the gap information as the empty string, immediately dominated by NP/NP.

Do we need to think of slash categories as a completely new kind of object? Fortunately, we can accommodate them within our existing feature-based framework, by treating slash as a feature and the category to its right as a value; that is, S/NP is reducible to S[SLASH=NP]. In practice, this is also how the parser interprets slash categories.

The grammar shown in Example 9-3 illustrates the main principles of slash categories, and also includes productions for inverted clauses. To simplify presentation, we have omitted any specification of tense on the verbs.

Example 9-3. Grammar with productions for inverted clauses and long-distance dependencies, making use of slash categories.

```
>>> nltk.data.show_cfg('grammars/book_grammars/feat1.fcfg')
% start S
# ####################
# Grammar Productions
# ####################
S[-INV] -> NP VP
S[-INV]/?x -> NP VP/?x
S[-INV] -> NP S/NP
S[-INV] -> Adv[+NEG] S[+INV]
S[+INV] -> V[+AUX] NP VP
S[+INV]/?x -> V[+AUX] NP VP/?x
SBar -> Comp S[-INV]
SBar/?x -> Comp S[-INV]/?x
VP -> V[SUBCAT=intrans, -AUX]
VP -> V[SUBCAT=trans, -AUX] NP
VP/?x -> V[SUBCAT=trans, -AUX] NP/?x
VP -> V[SUBCAT=clause, -AUX] SBar
VP/?x -> V[SUBCAT=clause, -AUX] SBar/?x
VP -> V[+AUX] VP
VP/?x -> V[+AUX] VP/?x
# ####################
# Lexical Productions
# ####################
V[SUBCAT=intrans, -AUX] -> 'walk' | 'sing'
V[SUBCAT=trans, -AUX] -> 'see' | 'like'
V[SUBCAT=clause, -AUX] -> 'say' | 'claim'
V[+AUX] -> 'do' | 'can'
NP[-WH] -> 'you' | 'cats'
NP[+WH] -> 'who'
Adv[+NEG] -> 'rarely' | 'never'
NP/NP ->
Comp -> 'that'
```

The grammar in Example 9-3 contains one "gap-introduction" production, namely S[-INV] -> NP S/NP. In order to percolate the slash feature correctly, we need to add slashes with variable values to both sides of the arrow in productions that expand S, VP, and NP. For example, VP/?x -> V SBar/?x is the slashed version of VP -> V SBar and says that a slash value can be specified on the VP parent of a constituent if the same value is also specified on the SBar child. Finally, NP/NP -> allows the slash information on NP to be discharged as the empty string. Using the grammar in Example 9-3, we can parse the sequence *who do you claim that you like*:

```
>>> tokens = 'who do you claim that you like'.split()
>>> from nltk import load_parser
>>> cp = load_parser('grammars/book_grammars/feat1.fcfg')
>>> for tree in cp.nbest_parse(tokens):
...     print tree
(S[-INV]
  (NP[+WH] who)
  (S[+INV]/NP[]
    (V[+AUX] do)
    (NP[-WH] you)
    (VP[]/NP[]
      (V[-AUX, SUBCAT='clause'] claim)
      (SBar[]/NP[]
        (Comp[] that)
        (S[-INV]/NP[]
          (NP[-WH] you)
          (VP[]/NP[] (V[-AUX, SUBCAT='trans'] like) (NP[]/NP[] )))))))
```

A more readable version of this tree is shown in (54).

(54)

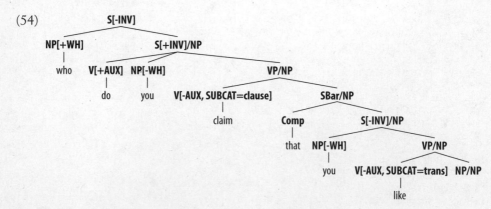

The grammar in Example 9-3 will also allow us to parse sentences without gaps:

```
>>> tokens = 'you claim that you like cats'.split()
>>> for tree in cp.nbest_parse(tokens):
...     print tree
(S[-INV]
  (NP[-WH] you)
  (VP[]
    (V[-AUX, SUBCAT='clause'] claim)
    (SBar[]
      (Comp[] that)
      (S[-INV]
        (NP[-WH] you)
        (VP[] (V[-AUX, SUBCAT='trans'] like) (NP[-WH] cats))))))
```

In addition, it admits inverted sentences that do not involve *wh* constructions:

```
>>> tokens = 'rarely do you sing'.split()
>>> for tree in cp.nbest_parse(tokens):
...     print tree
(S[-INV]
  (Adv[+NEG] rarely)
  (S[+INV]
    (V[+AUX] do)
    (NP[-WH] you)
    (VP[] (V[-AUX, SUBCAT='intrans'] sing))))
```

Case and Gender in German

Compared with English, German has a relatively rich morphology for agreement. For example, the definite article in German varies with case, gender, and number, as shown in Table 9-2.

Table 9-2. Morphological paradigm for the German definite article

Case	Masculine	Feminine	Neutral	Plural
Nominative	der	die	das	die
Genitive	des	der	des	der
Dative	dem	der	dem	den
Accusative	den	die	das	die

Subjects in German take the nominative case, and most verbs govern their objects in the accusative case. However, there are exceptions, such as *helfen*, that govern the dative case:

(55) a. Die   Katze   sieht   den   Hund
      the.NOM.FEM.SG cat.3.FEM.SG see.3.SG the.ACC.MASC.SG dog.3.MASC.SG
      'the cat sees the dog'

    b. *Die   Katze   sieht   dem   Hund
      the.NOM.FEM.SG cat.3.FEM.SG see.3.SG the.DAT.MASC.SG dog.3.MASC.SG

    c. Die   Katze   hilft   dem   Hund
      the.NOM.FEM.SG cat.3.FEM.SG help.3.SG the.DAT.MASC.SG dog.3.MASC.SG
      'the cat helps the dog'

    d. *Die   Katze   hilft   den   Hund
      the.NOM.FEM.SG cat.3.FEM.SG help.3.SG the.ACC.MASC.SG dog.3.MASC.SG

The grammar in Example 9-4 illustrates the interaction of agreement (comprising person, number, and gender) with case.

Example 9-4. Example feature-based grammar.

```
>>> nltk.data.show_cfg('grammars/book_grammars/german.fcfg')
% start S
# Grammar Productions
S -> NP[CASE=nom, AGR=?a] VP[AGR=?a]
NP[CASE=?c, AGR=?a] -> PRO[CASE=?c, AGR=?a]
NP[CASE=?c, AGR=?a] -> Det[CASE=?c, AGR=?a] N[CASE=?c, AGR=?a]
VP[AGR=?a] -> IV[AGR=?a]
VP[AGR=?a] -> TV[OBJCASE=?c, AGR=?a] NP[CASE=?c]
# Lexical Productions
# Singular determiners
# masc
Det[CASE=nom, AGR=[GND=masc,PER=3,NUM=sg]] -> 'der'
Det[CASE=dat, AGR=[GND=masc,PER=3,NUM=sg]] -> 'dem'
Det[CASE=acc, AGR=[GND=masc,PER=3,NUM=sg]] -> 'den'
# fem
Det[CASE=nom, AGR=[GND=fem,PER=3,NUM=sg]] -> 'die'
Det[CASE=dat, AGR=[GND=fem,PER=3,NUM=sg]] -> 'der'
Det[CASE=acc, AGR=[GND=fem,PER=3,NUM=sg]] -> 'die'
# Plural determiners
Det[CASE=nom, AGR=[PER=3,NUM=pl]] -> 'die'
Det[CASE=dat, AGR=[PER=3,NUM=pl]] -> 'den'
Det[CASE=acc, AGR=[PER=3,NUM=pl]] -> 'die'
# Nouns
N[AGR=[GND=masc,PER=3,NUM=sg]] -> 'Hund'
N[CASE=nom, AGR=[GND=masc,PER=3,NUM=pl]] -> 'Hunde'
N[CASE=dat, AGR=[GND=masc,PER=3,NUM=pl]] -> 'Hunden'
N[CASE=acc, AGR=[GND=masc,PER=3,NUM=pl]] -> 'Hunde'
N[AGR=[GND=fem,PER=3,NUM=sg]] -> 'Katze'
N[AGR=[GND=fem,PER=3,NUM=pl]] -> 'Katzen'
# Pronouns
PRO[CASE=nom, AGR=[PER=1,NUM=sg]] -> 'ich'
PRO[CASE=acc, AGR=[PER=1,NUM=sg]] -> 'mich'
PRO[CASE=dat, AGR=[PER=1,NUM=sg]] -> 'mir'
PRO[CASE=nom, AGR=[PER=2,NUM=sg]] -> 'du'
PRO[CASE=nom, AGR=[PER=3,NUM=sg]] -> 'er' | 'sie' | 'es'
PRO[CASE=nom, AGR=[PER=1,NUM=pl]] -> 'wir'
PRO[CASE=acc, AGR=[PER=1,NUM=pl]] -> 'uns'
PRO[CASE=dat, AGR=[PER=1,NUM=pl]] -> 'uns'
PRO[CASE=nom, AGR=[PER=2,NUM=pl]] -> 'ihr'
PRO[CASE=nom, AGR=[PER=3,NUM=pl]] -> 'sie'
# Verbs
IV[AGR=[NUM=sg,PER=1]] -> 'komme'
IV[AGR=[NUM=sg,PER=2]] -> 'kommst'
IV[AGR=[NUM=sg,PER=3]] -> 'kommt'
IV[AGR=[NUM=pl, PER=1]] -> 'kommen'
IV[AGR=[NUM=pl, PER=2]] -> 'kommt'
IV[AGR=[NUM=pl, PER=3]] -> 'kommen'
TV[OBJCASE=acc, AGR=[NUM=sg,PER=1]] -> 'sehe' | 'mag'
TV[OBJCASE=acc, AGR=[NUM=sg,PER=2]] -> 'siehst' | 'magst'
TV[OBJCASE=acc, AGR=[NUM=sg,PER=3]] -> 'sieht' | 'mag'
TV[OBJCASE=dat, AGR=[NUM=sg,PER=1]] -> 'folge' | 'helfe'
TV[OBJCASE=dat, AGR=[NUM=sg,PER=2]] -> 'folgst' | 'hilfst'
TV[OBJCASE=dat, AGR=[NUM=sg,PER=3]] -> 'folgt' | 'hilft'
TV[OBJCASE=acc, AGR=[NUM=pl,PER=1]] -> 'sehen' | 'moegen'
```

```
TV[OBJCASE=acc, AGR=[NUM=pl,PER=2]] -> 'sieht' | 'moegt'
TV[OBJCASE=acc, AGR=[NUM=pl,PER=3]] -> 'sehen' | 'moegen'
TV[OBJCASE=dat, AGR=[NUM=pl,PER=1]] -> 'folgen' | 'helfen'
TV[OBJCASE=dat, AGR=[NUM=pl,PER=2]] -> 'folgt' | 'helft'
TV[OBJCASE=dat, AGR=[NUM=pl,PER=3]] -> 'folgen' | 'helfen'
```

As you can see, the feature *objcase* is used to specify the case that a verb governs on its object. The next example illustrates the parse tree for a sentence containing a verb that governs the dative case:

```
>>> tokens = 'ich folge den Katzen'.split()
>>> cp = load_parser('grammars/book_grammars/german.fcfg')
>>> for tree in cp.nbest_parse(tokens):
...     print tree
(S[]
  (NP[AGR=[NUM='sg', PER=1], CASE='nom']
    (PRO[AGR=[NUM='sg', PER=1], CASE='nom'] ich))
  (VP[AGR=[NUM='sg', PER=1]]
    (TV[AGR=[NUM='sg', PER=1], OBJCASE='dat'] folge)
    (NP[AGR=[GND='fem', NUM='pl', PER=3], CASE='dat']
      (Det[AGR=[NUM='pl', PER=3], CASE='dat'] den)
      (N[AGR=[GND='fem', NUM='pl', PER=3]] Katzen))))
```

In developing grammars, excluding ungrammatical word sequences is often as challenging as parsing grammatical ones. In order to get an idea where and why a sequence fails to parse, setting the trace parameter of the load_parser() method can be crucial. Consider the following parse failure:

```
>>> tokens = 'ich folge den Katze'.split()
>>> cp = load_parser('grammars/book_grammars/german.fcfg', trace=2)
>>> for tree in cp.nbest_parse(tokens):
...     print tree
|.ich.fol.den.Kat.|
|[---]   .   .   .| PRO[AGR=[NUM='sg', PER=1], CASE='nom'] -> 'ich' *
|[---]   .   .   .| NP[AGR=[NUM='sg', PER=1], CASE='nom']
                    -> PRO[AGR=[NUM='sg', PER=1], CASE='nom'] *
|[--->   .   .   .| S[] -> NP[AGR=?a, CASE='nom'] * VP[AGR=?a]
                          {?a: [NUM='sg', PER=1]}
|.   [---]   .   .| TV[AGR=[NUM='sg', PER=1], OBJCASE='dat'] -> 'folge' *
|.   [--->   .   .| VP[AGR=?a] -> TV[AGR=?a, OBJCASE=?c]
                          * NP[CASE=?c] {?a: [NUM='sg', PER=1], ?c: 'dat'}
|.   .   [---]   .| Det[AGR=[GND='masc', NUM='sg', PER=3], CASE='acc'] -> 'den' *
|.   .   [---]   .| Det[AGR=[NUM='pl', PER=3], CASE='dat'] -> 'den' *
|.   .   [--->   .| NP[AGR=?a, CASE=?c] -> Det[AGR=?a, CASE=?c]
                          * N[AGR=?a, CASE=?c] {?a: [NUM='pl', PER=3], ?c: 'dat'}
|.   .   [--->   .| NP[AGR=?a, CASE=?c] -> Det[AGR=?a, CASE=?c] * N[AGR=?a, CASE=?c]
                    {?a: [GND='masc', NUM='sg', PER=3], ?c: 'acc'}
|.   .   .   [---]| N[AGR=[GND='fem', NUM='sg', PER=3]] -> 'Katze' *
```

The last two `Scanner` lines in the trace show that *den* is recognized as admitting two possible categories: `Det[AGR=[GND='masc', NUM='sg', PER=3], CASE='acc']` and `Det[AGR=[NUM='pl', PER=3], CASE='dat']`. We know from the grammar in Example 9-4 that Katze has category `N[AGR=[GND=fem, NUM=sg, PER=3]]`. Thus there is no binding for the variable `?a` in production:

    NP[CASE=?c, AGR=?a] -> Det[CASE=?c, AGR=? a] N[CASE=?c, AGR=?a]

that will satisfy these constraints, since the `AGR` value of `Katze` will not unify with either of the `AGR` values of *den*, that is, with either `[GND='masc', NUM='sg', PER=3]` or `[NUM='pl', PER=3]`.

9.4 Summary

- The traditional categories of context-free grammar are atomic symbols. An important motivation for feature structures is to capture fine-grained distinctions that would otherwise require a massive multiplication of atomic categories.

- By using variables over feature values, we can express constraints in grammar productions that allow the realization of different feature specifications to be interdependent.

- Typically we specify fixed values of features at the lexical level and constrain the values of features in phrases to unify with the corresponding values in their children.

- Feature values are either atomic or complex. A particular subcase of atomic value is the Boolean value, represented by convention as [+/- *feat*].

- Two features can share a value (either atomic or complex). Structures with shared values are said to be re-entrant. Shared values are represented by numerical indexes (or tags) in AVMs.

- A path in a feature structure is a tuple of features corresponding to the labels on a sequence of arcs from the root of the graph representation.

- Two paths are equivalent if they share a value.

- Feature structures are partially ordered by subsumption. FS_0 subsumes FS_1 when FS_0 is more general (less informative) than FS_1.

- The unification of two structures FS_0 and FS_1, if successful, is the feature structure FS_2 that contains the combined information of both FS_0 and FS_1.

- If unification specializes a path π in FS, then it also specializes every path π' equivalent to π.

- We can use feature structures to build succinct analyses of a wide variety of linguistic phenomena, including verb subcategorization, inversion constructions, unbounded dependency constructions, and case government.

9.5 Further Reading

Please consult *http://www.nltk.org/* for further materials on this chapter, including HOWTOs feature structures, feature grammars, Earley parsing, and grammar test suites.

For an excellent introduction to the phenomenon of agreement, see (Corbett, 2006).

The earliest use of features in theoretical linguistics was designed to capture phonological properties of phonemes. For example, a sound like /b/ might be decomposed into the structure [+labial, +voice]. An important motivation was to capture generalizations across classes of segments, for example, that /n/ gets realized as /m/ preceding any +labial consonant. Within Chomskyan grammar, it was standard to use atomic features for phenomena such as agreement, and also to capture generalizations across syntactic categories, by analogy with phonology. A radical expansion of the use of features in theoretical syntax was advocated by Generalized Phrase Structure Grammar (GPSG; [Gazdar et al., 1985]), particularly in the use of features with complex values.

Coming more from the perspective of computational linguistics, (Kay, 1985) proposed that functional aspects of language could be captured by unification of attribute-value structures, and a similar approach was elaborated by (Grosz & Stickel, 1983) within the PATR-II formalism. Early work in Lexical-Functional grammar (LFG; [Kaplan & Bresnan, 1982]) introduced the notion of an **f-structure** that was primarily intended to represent the grammatical relations and predicate-argument structure associated with a constituent structure parse. (Shieber, 1986) provides an excellent introduction to this phase of research into feature-based grammars.

One conceptual difficulty with algebraic approaches to feature structures arose when researchers attempted to model negation. An alternative perspective, pioneered by (Kasper & Rounds, 1986) and (Johnson, 1988), argues that grammars involve *descriptions* of feature structures rather than the structures themselves. These descriptions are combined using logical operations such as conjunction, and negation is just the usual logical operation over feature descriptions. This description-oriented perspective was integral to LFG from the outset (Kaplan, 1989), and was also adopted by later versions of Head-Driven Phrase Structure Grammar (HPSG; [Sag & Wasow, 1999]). A comprehensive bibliography of HPSG literature can be found at *http://www.cl.uni-bremen.de/HPSG-Bib/*.

Feature structures, as presented in this chapter, are unable to capture important constraints on linguistic information. For example, there is no way of saying that the only permissible values for NUM are sg and pl, while a specification such as [NUM=masc] is anomalous. Similarly, we cannot say that the complex value of AGR *must* contain specifications for the features PER, NUM, and GND, but *cannot* contain a specification such as [SUBCAT=trans]. **Typed feature structures** were developed to remedy this deficiency. A good early review of work on typed feature structures is (Emele & Zajac, 1990). A more comprehensive examination of the formal foundations can be found in

(Carpenter, 1992), while (Copestake, 2002) focuses on implementing an HPSG-oriented approach to typed feature structures.

There is a copious literature on the analysis of German within feature-based grammar frameworks. (Nerbonne, Netter & Pollard, 1994) is a good starting point for the HPSG literature on this topic, while (Müller, 2002) gives a very extensive and detailed analysis of German syntax in HPSG.

Chapter 15 of (Jurafsky & Martin, 2008) discusses feature structures, the unification algorithm, and the integration of unification into parsing algorithms.

9.6 Exercises

1. ○ What constraints are required to correctly parse word sequences like *I am happy* and *she is happy* but not **you is happy* or **they am happy*? Implement two solutions for the present tense paradigm of the verb *be* in English, first taking Grammar (8) as your starting point, and then taking Grammar (20) as the starting point.

2. ○ Develop a variant of grammar in Example 9-1 that uses a feature COUNT to make the distinctions shown here:

   (56)   a. The boy sings.

          b. *Boy sings.

   (57)   a. The boys sing.

          b. Boys sing.

   (58)   a. The water is precious.

          b. Water is precious.

3. ○ Write a function subsumes() that holds of two feature structures fs1 and fs2 just in case fs1 subsumes fs2.

4. ○ Modify the grammar illustrated in (30) to incorporate a BAR feature for dealing with phrasal projections.

5. ○ Modify the German grammar in Example 9-4 to incorporate the treatment of subcategorization presented in Section 9.3.

6. ◑ Develop a feature-based grammar that will correctly describe the following Spanish noun phrases:

   (59)   un   cuadro hermos-o
          INDEF.SG.MASC picture beautiful-SG.MASC
          'a beautiful picture'

   (60)   un-os   cuadro-s hermos-os
          INDEF-PL.MASC picture-PL beautiful-PL.MASC
          'beautiful pictures'

(61) un-a   cortina hermos-a
      INDEF-SG.FEM curtain beautiful-SG.FEM
      'a beautiful curtain'

(62) un-as   cortina-s hermos-as
      INDEF-PL.FEM curtain   beautiful-PL.FEM
      'beautiful curtains'

7. ◑ Develop a wrapper for the `earley_parser` so that a trace is only printed if the input sequence fails to parse.

8. ◑ Consider the feature structures shown in Example 9-5.

Example 9-5. Exploring feature structures.
```
fs1 = nltk.FeatStruct("[A = ?x, B= [C = ?x]]")
fs2 = nltk.FeatStruct("[B = [D = d]]")
fs3 = nltk.FeatStruct("[B = [C = d]]")
fs4 = nltk.FeatStruct("[A = (1)[B = b], C->(1)]")
fs5 = nltk.FeatStruct("[A = (1)[D = ?x], C = [E -> (1), F = ?x] ]")
fs6 = nltk.FeatStruct("[A = [D = d]]")
fs7 = nltk.FeatStruct("[A = [D = d], C = [F = [D = d]]]")
fs8 = nltk.FeatStruct("[A = (1)[D = ?x, G = ?x], C = [B = ?x, E -> (1)] ]")
fs9 = nltk.FeatStruct("[A = [B = b], C = [E = [G = e]]]")
fs10 = nltk.FeatStruct("[A = (1)[B = b], C -> (1)]")
```

Work out on paper what the result is of the following unifications. (Hint: you might find it useful to draw the graph structures.)

   a. `fs1` and `fs2`

   b. `fs1` and `fs3`

   c. `fs4` and `fs5`

   d. `fs5` and `fs6`

   e. `fs5` and `fs7`

   f. `fs8` and `fs9`

   g. `fs8` and `fs10`

Check your answers using NLTK.

9. ◑ List two feature structures that subsume `[A=?x, B=?x]`.

10. ◑ Ignoring structure sharing, give an informal algorithm for unifying two feature structures.

11. ◑ Extend the German grammar in Example 9-4 so that it can handle so-called verb-second structures like the following:

   (63) Heute sieht der Hund die Katze.

12. ◑ Seemingly synonymous verbs have slightly different syntactic properties (Levin, 1993). Consider the following patterns of grammaticality for the verbs *loaded*, *filled*, and *dumped*. Can you write grammar productions to handle such data?

(64)   a. The farmer *loaded* the cart with sand

       b. The farmer *loaded* sand into the cart

       c. The farmer *filled* the cart with sand

       d. *The farmer *filled* sand into the cart

       e. *The farmer *dumped* the cart with sand

       f. The farmer *dumped* sand into the cart

13. ● Morphological paradigms are rarely completely regular, in the sense of every cell in the matrix having a different realization. For example, the present tense conjugation of the lexeme *walk* has only two distinct forms: *walks* for the third-person singular, and *walk* for all other combinations of person and number. A successful analysis should not require redundantly specifying that five out of the six possible morphological combinations have the same realization. Propose and implement a method for dealing with this.

14. ● So-called **head features** are shared between the parent node and head child. For example, TENSE is a head feature that is shared between a VP and its head V child. See (Gazdar et al., 1985) for more details. Most of the features we have looked at are head features—exceptions are SUBCAT and SLASH. Since the sharing of head features is predictable, it should not need to be stated explicitly in the grammar productions. Develop an approach that automatically accounts for this regular behavior of head features.

15. ● Extend NLTK's treatment of feature structures to allow unification into list-valued features, and use this to implement an HPSG-style analysis of subcategorization, whereby the SUBCAT of a head category is the concatenation of its complements' categories with the SUBCAT value of its immediate parent.

16. ● Extend NLTK's treatment of feature structures to allow productions with underspecified categories, such as S[-INV] -> ?x S/?x.

17. ● Extend NLTK's treatment of feature structures to allow typed feature structures.

18. ● Pick some grammatical constructions described in (Huddleston & Pullum, 2002), and develop a feature-based grammar to account for them.

## CHAPTER 10

Analyzing the Meaning of Sentences

We have seen how useful it is to harness the power of a computer to process text on a large scale. However, now that we have the machinery of parsers and feature-based grammars, can we do anything similarly useful by analyzing the meaning of sentences? The goal of this chapter is to answer the following questions:

1. How can we represent natural language meaning so that a computer can process these representations?

2. How can we associate meaning representations with an unlimited set of sentences?

3. How can we use programs that connect the meaning representations of sentences to stores of knowledge?

Along the way we will learn some formal techniques in the field of logical semantics, and see how these can be used for interrogating databases that store facts about the world.

10.1 Natural Language Understanding

Querying a Database

Suppose we have a program that lets us type in a natural language question and gives us back the right answer:

(1)   a. Which country is Athens in?

  b. Greece.

How hard is it to write such a program? And can we just use the same techniques that we've encountered so far in this book, or does it involve something new? In this section, we will show that solving the task in a restricted domain is pretty straightforward. But we will also see that to address the problem in a more general way, we have to open up a whole new box of ideas and techniques, involving the representation of meaning.

So let's start off by assuming that we have data about cities and countries in a structured form. To be concrete, we will use a database table whose first few rows are shown in Table 10-1.

 The data illustrated in Table 10-1 is drawn from the Chat-80 system (Warren & Pereira, 1982). Population figures are given in thousands, but note that the data used in these examples dates back at least to the 1980s, and was already somewhat out of date at the point when (Warren & Pereira, 1982) was published.

Table 10-1. city_table: A table of cities, countries, and populations

City	Country	Population
athens	greece	1368
bangkok	thailand	1178
barcelona	spain	1280
berlin	east_germany	3481
birmingham	united_kingdom	1112

The obvious way to retrieve answers from this tabular data involves writing queries in a database query language such as SQL.

 SQL (Structured Query Language) is a language designed for retrieving and managing data in relational databases. If you want to find out more about SQL, *http://www.w3schools.com/sql/* is a convenient online reference.

For example, executing the query (2) will pull out the value `'greece'`:

(2) `SELECT Country FROM city_table WHERE City = 'athens'`

This specifies a result set consisting of all values for the column `Country` in data rows where the value of the `City` column is `'athens'`.

How can we get the same effect using English as our input to the query system? The feature-based grammar formalism described in Chapter 9 makes it easy to translate from English to SQL. The grammar *sql0.fcfg* illustrates how to assemble a meaning representation for a sentence in tandem with parsing the sentence. Each phrase structure rule is supplemented with a recipe for constructing a value for the feature SEM. You can see that these recipes are extremely simple; in each case, we use the string concatenation operation + to splice the values for the child constituents to make a value for the parent constituent.

```
>>> nltk.data.show_cfg('grammars/book_grammars/sql0.fcfg')
% start S
S[SEM=(?np + WHERE + ?vp)] -> NP[SEM=?np] VP[SEM=?vp]
VP[SEM=(?v + ?pp)] -> IV[SEM=?v] PP[SEM=?pp]
VP[SEM=(?v + ?ap)] -> IV[SEM=?v] AP[SEM=?ap]
NP[SEM=(?det + ?n)] -> Det[SEM=?det] N[SEM=?n]
PP[SEM=(?p + ?np)] -> P[SEM=?p] NP[SEM=?np]
AP[SEM=?pp] -> A[SEM=?a] PP[SEM=?pp]
NP[SEM='Country="greece"'] -> 'Greece'
NP[SEM='Country="china"'] -> 'China'
Det[SEM='SELECT'] -> 'Which' | 'What'
N[SEM='City FROM city_table'] -> 'cities'
IV[SEM=''] -> 'are'
A[SEM=''] -> 'located'
P[SEM=''] -> 'in'
```

This allows us to parse a query into SQL:

```
>>> from nltk import load_parser
>>> cp = load_parser('grammars/book_grammars/sql0.fcfg')
>>> query = 'What cities are located in China'
>>> trees = cp.nbest_parse(query.split())
>>> answer = trees[0].node['sem']
>>> q = ' '.join(answer)
>>> print q
SELECT City FROM city_table WHERE Country="china"
```

> **Your Turn:** Run the parser with maximum tracing on, i.e., `cp = load_parser('grammars/book_grammars/sql0.fcfg', trace=3)`, and examine how the values of SEM are built up as complete edges are added to the chart.

Finally, we execute the query over the database **city.db** and retrieve some results:

```
>>> from nltk.sem import chat80
>>> rows = chat80.sql_query('corpora/city_database/city.db', q)
>>> for r in rows: print r[0], ❶
canton chungking dairen harbin kowloon mukden peking shanghai sian tientsin
```

Since each row **r** is a one-element tuple, we print out the member of the tuple rather than the tuple itself ❶.

To summarize, we have defined a task where the computer returns useful data in response to a natural language query, and we implemented this by translating a small subset of English into SQL. We can say that our NLTK code already "understands" SQL, given that Python is able to execute SQL queries against a database, and by extension it also "understands" queries such as *What cities are located in China*. This parallels being able to translate from Dutch into English as an example of natural language understanding. Suppose that you are a native speaker of English, and have started to learn Dutch. Your teacher asks if you understand what (3) means:

(3) Margrietje houdt van Brunoke.

If you know the meanings of the individual words in (3), and know how these meanings are combined to make up the meaning of the whole sentence, you might say that (3) means the same as *Margrietje loves Brunoke*.

An observer—let's call her Olga—might well take this as evidence that you do grasp the meaning of (3). But this would depend on Olga herself understanding English. If she doesn't, then your translation from Dutch to English is not going to convince her of your ability to understand Dutch. We will return to this issue shortly.

The grammar *sql0.fcfg*, together with the NLTK Earley parser, is instrumental in carrying out the translation from English to SQL. How adequate is this grammar? You saw that the SQL translation for the whole sentence was built up from the translations of the components. However, there does not seem to be a lot of justification for these component meaning representations. For example, if we look at the analysis of the noun phrase *Which cities*, the determiner and noun correspond respectively to the SQL fragments `SELECT` and `City FROM city_table`. But neither of these has a well-defined meaning in isolation from the other.

There is another criticism we can level at the grammar: we have "hard-wired" an embarrassing amount of detail about the database into it. We need to know the name of the relevant table (e.g., `city_table`) and the names of the fields. But our database could have contained exactly the same rows of data yet used a different table name and different field names, in which case the SQL queries would not be executable. Equally, we could have stored our data in a different format, such as XML, in which case retrieving the same results would require us to translate our English queries into an XML query language rather than SQL. These considerations suggest that we should be translating English into something that is more abstract and generic than SQL.

In order to sharpen the point, let's consider another English query and its translation:

(4)   a. What cities are in China and have populations above 1,000,000?

  b. `SELECT City FROM city_table WHERE Country = 'china' AND Population > 1000`

Your Turn: Extend the grammar *sql0.fcfg* so that it will translate (4a) into (4b), and check the values returned by the query. Remember that figures in the Chat-80 database are given in thousands, hence `1000` in (4b) represents one million inhabitants.

You will probably find it easiest to first extend the grammar to handle queries like *What cities have populations above 1,000,000* before tackling conjunction. After you have had a go at this task, you can compare your solution to `grammars/book_grammars/sql1.fcfg` in the NLTK data distribution.

Observe that the *and* conjunction in (4a) is translated into an AND in the SQL counterpart, (4b). The latter tells us to select results from rows where two conditions are true together: the value of the Country column is 'china' and the value of the Population column is greater than 1000. This interpretation for *and* involves a new idea: it talks about *what is true in some particular situation*, and tells us that Cond1 AND Cond2 is true in situation *s* if and only if condition Cond1 is true in *s* and condition Cond2 is true in *s*. Although this doesn't account for the full range of meanings of *and* in English, it has the nice property that it is independent of any query language. In fact, we have given it the standard interpretation from classical logic. In the following sections, we will explore an approach in which sentences of natural language are translated into logic instead of an executable query language such as SQL. One advantage of logical formalisms is that they are more abstract and therefore more generic. If we wanted to, once we had our translation into logic, we could then translate it into various other special-purpose languages. In fact, most serious attempts to query databases via natural language have used this methodology.

Natural Language, Semantics, and Logic

We started out trying to capture the meaning of (1a) by translating it into a query in another language, SQL, which the computer could interpret and execute. But this still begged the question whether the translation was correct. Stepping back from database query, we noted that the meaning of *and* seems to depend on being able to specify when statements are true or not in a particular situation. Instead of translating a sentence *S* from one language to another, we try to say what *S* is *about* by relating it to a situation in the world. Let's pursue this further. Imagine there is a situation *s* where there are two entities, Margrietje and her favorite doll, Brunoke. In addition, there is a relation holding between the two entities, which we will call the *love* relation. If you understand the meaning of (3), then you know that it is true in situation *s*. In part, you know this because you know that *Margrietje* refers to Margrietje, *Brunoke* refers to Brunoke, and *houdt van* refers to the *love* relation.

We have introduced two fundamental notions in semantics. The first is that declarative sentences are *true or false in certain situations*. The second is that definite noun phrases and proper nouns *refer to things in the world*. So (3) is true in a situation where Margrietje loves the doll Brunoke, here illustrated in Figure 10-1.

Once we have adopted the notion of truth in a situation, we have a powerful tool for reasoning. In particular, we can look at sets of sentences, and ask whether they could be true together in some situation. For example, the sentences in (5) can be both true, whereas those in (6) and (7) cannot be. In other words, the sentences in (5) are **consistent**, whereas those in (6) and (7) are **inconsistent**.

(5)   a. Sylvania is to the north of Freedonia.

        b. Freedonia is a republic.

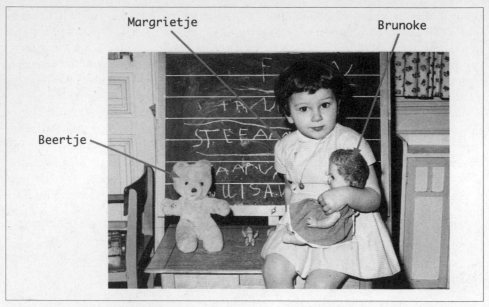

Figure 10-1. Depiction of a situation in which Margrietje loves Brunoke.

(6) a. The capital of Freedonia has a population of 9,000.

   b. No city in Freedonia has a population of 9,000.

(7) a. Sylvania is to the north of Freedonia.

   b. Freedonia is to the north of Sylvania.

We have chosen sentences about fictional countries (featured in the Marx Brothers' 1933 movie *Duck Soup*) to emphasize that your ability to reason about these examples does not depend on what is true or false in the actual world. If you know the meaning of the word *no*, and also know that the capital of a country is a city in that country, then you should be able to conclude that the two sentences in (6) are inconsistent, regardless of where Freedonia is or what the population of its capital is. That is, there's no possible situation in which both sentences could be true. Similarly, if you know that the relation expressed by *to the north of* is asymmetric, then you should be able to conclude that the two sentences in (7) are inconsistent.

Broadly speaking, logic-based approaches to natural language semantics focus on those aspects of natural language that guide our judgments of consistency and inconsistency. The syntax of a logical language is designed to make these features formally explicit. As a result, determining properties like consistency can often be reduced to symbolic manipulation, that is, to a task that can be carried out by a computer. In order to pursue this approach, we first want to develop a technique for representing a possible situation. We do this in terms of something that logicians call a "model."

A **model** for a set W of sentences is a formal representation of a situation in which all the sentences in W are true. The usual way of representing models involves set theory. The domain D of discourse (all the entities we currently care about) is a set of individuals, while relations are treated as sets built up from D. Let's look at a concrete example. Our domain D will consist of three children, Stefan, Klaus, and Evi, represented respectively as s, k, and e. We write this as $D = \{s, k, e\}$. The expression *boy* denotes the set consisting of Stefan and Klaus, the expression *girl* denotes the set consisting of Evi, and the expression *is running* denotes the set consisting of Stefan and Evi. Figure 10-2 is a graphical rendering of the model.

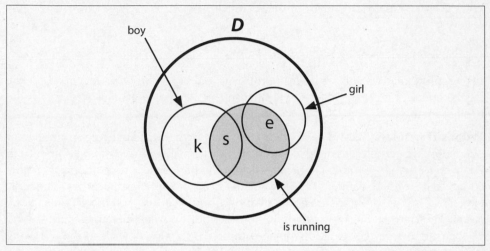

Figure 10-2. Diagram of a model containing a domain D and subsets of D corresponding to the predicates boy, girl, *and* is running.

Later in this chapter we will use models to help evaluate the truth or falsity of English sentences, and in this way to illustrate some methods for representing meaning. However, before going into more detail, let's put the discussion into a broader perspective, and link back to a topic that we briefly raised in Section 1.5. Can a computer understand the meaning of a sentence? And how could we tell if it did? This is similar to asking "Can a computer think?" Alan Turing famously proposed to answer this by examining the ability of a computer to hold sensible conversations with a human (Turing, 1950). Suppose you are having a chat session with a person and a computer, but you are not told at the outset which is which. If you cannot identify which of your partners is the computer after chatting with each of them, then the computer has successfully imitated a human. If a computer succeeds in passing itself off as human in this "imitation game" (or "Turing Test" as it is popularly known), then according to Turing, we should be prepared to say that the computer *can* think and can be said to be intelligent. So Turing side-stepped the question of somehow examining the internal states of a computer by instead using its *behavior* as evidence of intelligence. By the same reasoning, we have assumed that in order to say that a computer understands English, it just needs to behave as though it did. What is important here is not so much the specifics of Turing's imitation game, but rather the proposal to judge a capacity for natural language understanding in terms of observable behavior.

10.2 Propositional Logic

A logical language is designed to make reasoning formally explicit. As a result, it can capture aspects of natural language which determine whether a set of sentences is consistent. As part of this approach, we need to develop logical representations of a sentence φ that formally capture the **truth-conditions** of φ. We'll start off with a simple example:

(8) [Klaus chased Evi] and [Evi ran away].

Let's replace the two sub-sentences in (8) by φ and ψ respectively, and put & for the logical operator corresponding to the English word *and*: φ & ψ. This structure is the **logical form** of (8).

Propositional logic allows us to represent just those parts of linguistic structure that correspond to certain sentential connectives. We have just looked at *and*. Other such connectives are *not*, *or*, and *if..., then...*. In the formalization of propositional logic, the counterparts of such connectives are sometimes called **Boolean operators**. The basic expressions of propositional logic are **propositional symbols**, often written as *P*, *Q*, *R*, etc. There are varying conventions for representing Boolean operators. Since we will be focusing on ways of exploring logic within NLTK, we will stick to the following ASCII versions of the operators:

```
>>> nltk.boolean_ops()
negation        -
conjunction     &
disjunction     |
implication     ->
equivalence     <->
```

From the propositional symbols and the Boolean operators we can build an infinite set of **well-formed formulas** (or just formulas, for short) of propositional logic. First, every propositional letter is a formula. Then if φ is a formula, so is -φ. And if φ and ψ are formulas, then so are (φ & ψ), (φ | ψ), (φ -> ψ), and(φ <-> ψ).

Table 10-2 specifies the truth-conditions for formulas containing these operators. As before we use φ and ψ as variables over sentences, and abbreviate *if and only if* as *iff*.

Table 10-2. Truth conditions for the Boolean operators in propositional logic

Boolean operator	Truth conditions		
negation (*it is not the case that ...*)	-φ is true in *s*	iff	φ is false in *s*
conjunction (*and*)	(φ & ψ) is true in *s*	iff	φ is true in *s* and ψ is true in *s*

Boolean operator	Truth conditions		
disjunction (*or*)	$(\varphi \mid \psi)$ is true in *s*	iff	φ is true in *s* or ψ is true in *s*
implication (*if ..., then ...*)	$(\varphi \rightarrow \psi)$ is true in *s*	iff	φ is false in *s* or ψ is true in *s*
equivalence (*if and only if*)	$(\varphi \leftrightarrow \psi)$ is true in *s*	iff	φ and ψ are both true in *s* or both false in *s*

These rules are generally straightforward, though the truth conditions for implication depart in many cases from our usual intuitions about the conditional in English. A formula of the form (P -> Q) is false only when P is true and Q is false. If P is false (say, P corresponds to *The moon is made of green cheese*) and Q is true (say, Q corresponds to *Two plus two equals four*), then P -> Q will come out true.

NLTK's `LogicParser()` parses logical expressions into various subclasses of `Expression`:

```
>>> lp = nltk.LogicParser()
>>> lp.parse('-(P & Q)')
<NegatedExpression -(P & Q)>
>>> lp.parse('P & Q')
<AndExpression (P & Q)>
>>> lp.parse('P | (R -> Q)')
<OrExpression (P | (R -> Q))>
>>> lp.parse('P <-> -- P')
<IffExpression (P <-> --P)>
```

From a computational perspective, logics give us an important tool for performing inference. Suppose you state that Freedonia is not to the north of Sylvania, and you give as your reasons that Sylvania is to the north of Freedonia. In this case, you have produced an **argument**. The sentence *Sylvania is to the north of Freedonia* is the **assumption** of the argument, while *Freedonia is not to the north of Sylvania* is the **conclusion**. The step of moving from one or more assumptions to a conclusion is called **inference**. Informally, it is common to write arguments in a format where the conclusion is preceded by *therefore*.

(9) Sylvania is to the north of Freedonia.

  Therefore, Freedonia is not to the north of Sylvania.

An argument is **valid** if there is no possible situation in which its premises are all true and its conclusion is not true.

Now, the validity of (9) crucially depends on the meaning of the phrase *to the north of*, in particular, the fact that it is an asymmetric relation:

(10) if *x* is to the north of *y* then *y* is not to the north of *x*.

Unfortunately, we can't express such rules in propositional logic: the smallest elements we have to play with are atomic propositions, and we cannot "look inside" these to talk about relations between individuals *x* and *y*. The best we can do in this case is capture a particular case of the asymmetry. Let's use the propositional symbol SnF to stand for *Sylvania is to the north of Freedonia* and `FnS` for *Freedonia is to the north of Sylvania*. To say that *Freedonia is not to the north of Sylvania*, we write `-FnS`. That is, we treat *not* as equivalent to the phrase *it is not the case that* ..., and translate this as the one-place Boolean operator `-`. Replacing *x* and *y* in (10) by *Sylvania* and *Freedonia* respectively gives us an implication that can be written as:

(11) `SnF -> -FnS`

How about giving a version of the complete argument? We will replace the first sentence of (9) by two formulas of propositional logic: `SnF`, and also the implication in (11), which expresses (rather poorly) our background knowledge of the meaning of *to the north of*. We'll write `[A1, ..., An]` / `C` to represent the argument that conclusion `C` follows from assumptions `[A1, ..., An]`. This leads to the following as a representation of argument (9):

(12) `[SnF, SnF -> -FnS] / -FnS`

This is a valid argument: if `SnF` and `SnF -> -FnS` are both true in a situation *s*, then `-FnS` must also be true in *s*. By contrast, if `FnS` were true, this would conflict with our understanding that two objects cannot both be to the north of each other in any possible situation. Equivalently, the list `[SnF, SnF -> -FnS, FnS]` is inconsistent—these sentences cannot all be true together.

Arguments can be tested for "syntactic validity" by using a proof system. We will say a little bit more about this later on in Section 10.3. Logical proofs can be carried out with NLTK's `inference` module, for example, *via* an interface to the third-party theorem prover Prover9. The inputs to the inference mechanism first have to be parsed into logical expressions by `LogicParser()`.

```
>>> lp = nltk.LogicParser()
>>> SnF = lp.parse('SnF')
>>> NotFnS = lp.parse('-FnS')
>>> R = lp.parse('SnF -> -FnS')
>>> prover = nltk.Prover9()
>>> prover.prove(NotFnS, [SnF, R])
True
```

Here's another way of seeing why the conclusion follows. `SnF -> -FnS` is semantically equivalent to `-SnF | -FnS`, where `|` is the two-place operator corresponding to *or*. In general, $\varphi \mid \psi$ is true in a situation *s* if either φ is true in *s* or φ is true in *s*. Now, suppose both `SnF` and `-SnF | -FnS` are true in situation *s*. If `SnF` is true, then `-SnF` cannot also be true; a fundamental assumption of classical logic is that a sentence cannot be both true and false in a situation. Consequently, `-FnS` must be true.

Recall that we interpret sentences of a logical language relative to a model, which is a very simplified version of the world. A model for propositional logic needs to assign the values `True` or `False` to every possible formula. We do this inductively: first, every propositional symbol is assigned a value, and then we compute the value of complex formulas by consulting the meanings of the Boolean operators (i.e., Table 10-2) and applying them to the values of the formula's components. A `Valuation` is a mapping from basic symbols of the logic to their values. Here's an example:

```
>>> val = nltk.Valuation([('P', True), ('Q', True), ('R', False)])
```

We initialize a `Valuation` with a list of pairs, each of which consists of a semantic symbol and a semantic value. The resulting object is essentially just a dictionary that maps logical symbols (treated as strings) to appropriate values.

```
>>> val['P']
True
```

As we will see later, our models need to be somewhat more complicated in order to handle the more complex logical forms discussed in the next section; for the time being, just ignore the `dom` and `g` parameters in the following declarations.

```
>>> dom = set([])
>>> g = nltk.Assignment(dom)
```

Now let's initialize a model `m` that uses `val`:

```
>>> m = nltk.Model(dom, val)
```

Every model comes with an `evaluate()` method, which will determine the semantic value of logical expressions, such as formulas of propositional logic; of course, these values depend on the initial truth values we assigned to propositional symbols such as P, Q, and R.

```
>>> print m.evaluate('(P & Q)', g)
True
>>> print m.evaluate('-(P & Q)', g)
False
>>> print m.evaluate('(P & R)', g)
False
>>> print m.evaluate('(P | R)', g)
True
```

 Your Turn: Experiment with evaluating different formulas of propositional logic. Does the model give the values that you expected?

Up until now, we have been translating our English sentences into propositional logic. Because we are confined to representing atomic sentences with letters such as P and Q, we cannot dig into their internal structure. In effect, we are saying that there is no semantic benefit in dividing atomic sentences into subjects, objects, and predicates. However, this seems wrong: if we want to formalize arguments such as (9), we have to be able to "look inside" basic sentences. As a result, we will move beyond propositional logic to something more expressive, namely first-order logic. This is what we turn to in the next section.

10.3 First-Order Logic

In the remainder of this chapter, we will represent the meaning of natural language expressions by translating them into first-order logic. Not all of natural language semantics can be expressed in first-order logic. But it is a good choice for computational semantics because it is expressive enough to represent many aspects of semantics, and on the other hand, there are excellent systems available off the shelf for carrying out automated inference in first-order logic.

Our next step will be to describe how formulas of first-order logic are constructed, and then how such formulas can be evaluated in a model.

Syntax

First-order logic keeps all the Boolean operators of propositional logic, but it adds some important new mechanisms. To start with, propositions are analyzed into predicates and arguments, which takes us a step closer to the structure of natural languages. The standard construction rules for first-order logic recognize **terms** such as individual variables and individual constants, and **predicates** that take differing numbers of **arguments**. For example, *Angus walks* might be formalized as *walk(angus)* and *Angus sees Bertie as see(angus, bertie)*. We will call *walk* a **unary predicate**, and *see* a **binary predicate**. The symbols used as predicates do not have intrinsic meaning, although it is hard to remember this. Returning to one of our earlier examples, there is no *logical* difference between (13a) and (13b).

(13)   a. *love(margrietje, brunoke)*
        b. *houden_van(margrietje, brunoke)*

By itself, first-order logic has nothing substantive to say about lexical semantics—the meaning of individual words—although some theories of lexical semantics can be encoded in first-order logic. Whether an atomic predication like *see(angus, bertie)* is true or false in a situation is not a matter of logic, but depends on the particular valuation that we have chosen for the constants *see*, *angus*, and *bertie*. For this reason, such expressions are called **non-logical constants**. By contrast, **logical constants** (such as the Boolean operators) always receive the same interpretation in every model for first-order logic.

We should mention here that one binary predicate has special status, namely equality, as in formulas such as *angus = aj*. Equality is regarded as a logical constant, since for individual terms t_1 and t_2, the formula $t_1 = t_2$ is true if and only if t_1 and t_2 refer to one and the same entity.

It is often helpful to inspect the syntactic structure of expressions of first-order logic, and the usual way of doing this is to assign **types** to expressions. Following the tradition of Montague grammar, we will use two **basic types**: *e* is the type of entities, while *t* is the type of formulas, i.e., expressions that have truth values. Given these two basic types, we can form **complex types** for function expressions. That is, given any types σ and τ, ⟨σ, τ⟩ is a complex type corresponding to functions from 'σ things' to 'τ things'. For example, ⟨*e, t*⟩ is the type of expressions from entities to truth values, namely unary predicates. The `LogicParser` can be invoked so that it carries out type checking.

```
>>> tlp = nltk.LogicParser(type_check=True)
>>> parsed = tlp.parse('walk(angus)')
>>> parsed.argument
<ConstantExpression angus>
>>> parsed.argument.type
e
>>> parsed.function
<ConstantExpression walk>
>>> parsed.function.type
<e,?>
```

Why do we see `<e,?>` at the end of this example? Although the type-checker will try to infer as many types as possible, in this case it has not managed to fully specify the type of `walk`, since its result type is unknown. Although we are intending `walk` to receive type `<e, t>`, as far as the type-checker knows, in this context it could be of some other type, such as `<e, e>` or `<e, <e, t>`. To help the type-checker, we need to specify a **signature**, implemented as a dictionary that explicitly associates types with non-logical constants:

```
>>> sig = {'walk': '<e, t>'}
>>> parsed = tlp.parse('walk(angus)', sig)
>>> parsed.function.type
<e,t>
```

A binary predicate has type ⟨*e*, ⟨*e, t*⟩⟩. Although this is the type of something which combines first with an argument of type *e* to make a unary predicate, we represent binary predicates as combining directly with their two arguments. For example, the predicate *see* in the translation of *Angus sees Cyril* will combine with its arguments to give the result *see(angus, cyril)*.

In first-order logic, arguments of predicates can also be individual variables such as *x*, *y*, and *z*. In NLTK, we adopt the convention that variables of type *e* are all lowercase. Individual variables are similar to personal pronouns like *he*, *she*, and *it*, in that we need to know about the context of use in order to figure out their denotation. One way of interpreting the pronoun in (14) is by pointing to a relevant individual in the local context.

(14) He disappeared.

Another way is to supply a textual antecedent for the pronoun *he*, for example, by uttering (15a) prior to (14). Here, we say that *he* is **coreferential** with the noun phrase *Cyril*. In such a context, (14) is semantically equivalent to (15b).

(15)   a. Cyril is Angus's dog.

        b. Cyril disappeared.

Consider by contrast the occurrence of *he* in (16a). In this case, it is **bound** by the indefinite NP *a dog*, and this is a different relationship than coreference. If we replace the pronoun *he* by *a dog*, the result (16b) is *not* semantically equivalent to (16a).

(16) a. Angus had a dog but he disappeared.

   b. Angus had a dog but a dog disappeared.

Corresponding to (17a), we can construct an **open formula** (17b) with two occurrences of the variable *x*. (We ignore tense to simplify exposition.)

(17) a. He is a dog and he disappeared.

   b. *dog(x)* & *disappear(x)*

By placing an **existential quantifier** $\exists x$ ("for some x") in front of (17b), we can **bind** these variables, as in (18a), which means (18b) or, more idiomatically, (18c).

(18) a. $\exists x.(dog(x)$ & *disappear(x))*

   b. At least one entity is a dog and disappeared.

   c. A dog disappeared.

Here is the NLTK counterpart of (18a):

(19) `exists x.(dog(x) & disappear(x))`

In addition to the existential quantifier, first-order logic offers us the **universal quantifier** $\forall x$ ("for all x"), illustrated in (20).

(20) a. $\forall x.(dog(x) \rightarrow disappear(x))$

   b. Everything has the property that if it is a dog, it disappears.

   c. Every dog disappeared.

Here is the NLTK counterpart of (20a):

(21) `all x.(dog(x) -> disappear(x))`

Although (20a) is the standard first-order logic translation of (20c), the truth conditions aren't necessarily what you expect. The formula says that *if* some *x* is a dog, then *x* disappears—but it doesn't say that there are any dogs. So in a situation where there are no dogs, (20a) will still come out true. (Remember that `(P -> Q)` is true when `P` is false.) Now you might argue that *every dog disappeared* does presuppose the existence of dogs, and that the logic formalization is simply wrong. But it is possible to find other examples that lack such a presupposition. For instance, we might explain that the value of the Python expression `astring.replace('ate', '8')` is the result of replacing every occurrence of `'ate'` in `astring` by `'8'`, even though there may in fact be no such occurrences (Table 3-2).

We have seen a number of examples where variables are bound by quantifiers. What happens in formulas such as the following?

```
((exists x. dog(x)) -> bark(x))
```

The scope of the `exists` x quantifier is `dog(x)`, so the occurrence of x in `bark(x)` is unbound. Consequently it can become bound by some other quantifier, for example, `all` x in the next formula:

```
all x.((exists x. dog(x)) -> bark(x))
```

In general, an occurrence of a variable x in a formula φ is **free** in φ if that occurrence doesn't fall within the scope of `all` x or `some` x in φ. Conversely, if x is free in formula φ, then it is **bound** in `all` x.φ and `exists` x.φ. If all variable occurrences in a formula are bound, the formula is said to be **closed**.

We mentioned before that the `parse()` method of NLTK's `LogicParser` returns objects of class `Expression`. Each instance `expr` of this class comes with a method `free()`, which returns the set of variables that are free in `expr`.

```
>>> lp = nltk.LogicParser()
>>> lp.parse('dog(cyril)').free()
set([])
>>> lp.parse('dog(x)').free()
set([Variable('x')])
>>> lp.parse('own(angus, cyril)').free()
set([])
>>> lp.parse('exists x.dog(x)').free()
set([])
>>> lp.parse('((some x. walk(x)) -> sing(x))').free()
set([Variable('x')])
>>> lp.parse('exists x.own(y, x)').free()
set([Variable('y')])
```

First-Order Theorem Proving

Recall the constraint on *to the north of*, which we proposed earlier as (10):

(22) if *x* is to the north of *y* then *y* is not to the north of *x*.

We observed that propositional logic is not expressive enough to represent generalizations about binary predicates, and as a result we did not properly capture the argument *Sylvania is to the north of Freedonia. Therefore, Freedonia is not to the north of Sylvania*.

You have no doubt realized that first-order logic, by contrast, is ideal for formalizing such rules:

```
all x. all y.(north_of(x, y) -> -north_of(y, x))
```

Even better, we can perform automated inference to show the validity of the argument.

The general case in theorem proving is to determine whether a formula that we want to prove (a **proof goal**) can be derived by a finite sequence of inference steps from a list of assumed formulas. We write this as A ⊢ g, where A is a (possibly empty) list of assumptions, and g is a proof goal. We will illustrate this with NLTK's interface to the theorem prover Prover9. First, we parse the required proof goal ❶ and the two assumptions ❷ ❸. Then we create a `Prover9` instance ❹, and call its `prove()` method on the goal, given the list of assumptions ❺.

```
>>> NotFnS = lp.parse('-north_of(f, s)')   ❶
>>> SnF = lp.parse('north_of(s, f)')       ❷
>>> R = lp.parse('all x. all y. (north_of(x, y) -> -north_of(y, x))')   ❸
>>> prover = nltk.Prover9()                ❹
>>> prover.prove(NotFnS, [SnF, R])         ❺
True
```

Happily, the theorem prover agrees with us that the argument is valid. By contrast, it concludes that it is not possible to infer `north_of(f, s)` from our assumptions:

```
>>> FnS = lp.parse('north_of(f, s)')
>>> prover.prove(FnS, [SnF, R])
False
```

Summarizing the Language of First-Order Logic

We'll take this opportunity to restate our earlier syntactic rules for propositional logic and add the formation rules for quantifiers; together, these give us the syntax of first-order logic. In addition, we make explicit the types of the expressions involved. We'll adopt the convention that $\langle e^n, t \rangle$ is the type of a predicate that combines with n arguments of type e to yield an expression of type t. In this case, we say that n is the **arity** of the predicate.

1. If P is a predicate of type $\langle e^n, t \rangle$, and $\alpha_1, \dots \alpha_n$ are terms of type e, then $P(\alpha_1, \dots \alpha_n)$ is of type t.

2. If α and β are both of type e, then $(\alpha = \beta)$ and $(\alpha \mathrel{!=} \beta)$ are of type t.

3. If φ is of type t, then so is $-\varphi$.

4. If φ and ψ are of type t, then so are $(\varphi \mathbin{\&} \psi)$, $(\varphi \mid \psi)$, $(\varphi \mathbin{->} \psi)$, and $(\varphi \mathbin{<->} \psi)$.

5. If φ is of type t, and x is a variable of type e, then `exists x.`φ and `all x.`φ are of type t.

Table 10-3 summarizes the new logical constants of the `logic` module, and two of the methods of `Expression`s.

Table 10-3. Summary of new logical relations and operators required for first-order logic

Example	Description
=	Equality
!=	Inequality
exists	Existential quantifier
all	Universal quantifier

Truth in Model

We have looked at the syntax of first-order logic, and in Section 10.4 we will examine the task of translating English into first-order logic. Yet as we argued in Section 10.1, this gets us further forward only if we can give a meaning to sentences of first-order logic. In other words, we need to give a *truth-conditional semantics* to first-order logic. From the point of view of computational semantics, there are obvious limits to how far one can push this approach. Although we want to talk about sentences being true or false in situations, we only have the means of representing situations in the computer in a symbolic manner. Despite this limitation, it is still possible to gain a clearer picture of truth-conditional semantics by encoding models in NLTK.

Given a first-order logic language L, a model M for L is a pair $\langle D, Val \rangle$, where D is an non-empty set called the **domain** of the model, and *Val* is a function called the **valuation function**, which assigns values from D to expressions of L as follows:

1. For every individual constant c in L, $Val(c)$ is an element of D.
2. For every predicate symbol P of arity $n \geq 0$, $Val(P)$ is a function from D^n to $\{True, False\}$. (If the arity of P is 0, then $Val(P)$ is simply a truth value, and P is regarded as a propositional symbol.)

According to 2, if P is of arity 2, then $Val(P)$ will be a function f from pairs of elements of D to $\{True, False\}$. In the models we shall build in NLTK, we'll adopt a more convenient alternative, in which $Val(P)$ is a set S of pairs, defined as follows:

(23) $S = \{s \mid f(s) = True\}$

Such an f is called the **characteristic function** of S (as discussed in the further readings).

Relations are represented semantically in NLTK in the standard set-theoretic way: as sets of tuples. For example, let's suppose we have a domain of discourse consisting of the individuals Bertie, Olive, and Cyril, where Bertie is a boy, Olive is a girl, and Cyril is a dog. For mnemonic reasons, we use b, o, and c as the corresponding labels in the model. We can declare the domain as follows:

```
>>> dom = set(['b', 'o', 'c'])
```

We will use the utility function `parse_valuation()` to convert a sequence of strings of the form *symbol => value* into a `Valuation` object.

```
>>> v = """
... bertie => b
... olive => o
... cyril => c
... boy => {b}
... girl => {o}
... dog => {c}
... walk => {o, c}
... see => {(b, o), (c, b), (o, c)}
... """
>>> val = nltk.parse_valuation(v)
>>> print val
{'bertie': 'b',
 'boy': set([('b',)]),
 'cyril': 'c',
 'dog': set([('c',)]),
 'girl': set([('o',)]),
 'olive': 'o',
 'see': set([('o', 'c'), ('c', 'b'), ('b', 'o')]),
 'walk': set([('c',), ('o',)])}
```

So according to this valuation, the value of see is a set of tuples such that Bertie sees Olive, Cyril sees Bertie, and Olive sees Cyril.

 Your Turn: Draw a picture of the domain dom and the sets corresponding to each of the unary predicates, by analogy with the diagram shown in Figure 10-2.

You may have noticed that our unary predicates (i.e, boy, girl, dog) also come out as sets of singleton tuples, rather than just sets of individuals. This is a convenience which allows us to have a uniform treatment of relations of any arity. A predication of the form $P(\tau_1, \ldots \tau_n)$, where P is of arity n, comes out true just in case the tuple of values corresponding to $(\tau_1, \ldots \tau_n)$ belongs to the set of tuples in the value of P.

```
>>> ('o', 'c') in val['see']
True
>>> ('b',) in val['boy']
True
```

Individual Variables and Assignments

In our models, the counterpart of a context of use is a variable **assignment**. This is a mapping from individual variables to entities in the domain. Assignments are created using the `Assignment` constructor, which also takes the model's domain of discourse as a parameter. We are not required to actually enter any bindings, but if we do, they are in a (*variable*, *value*) format similar to what we saw earlier for valuations.

```
>>> g = nltk.Assignment(dom, [('x', 'o'), ('y', 'c')])
>>> g
{'y': 'c', 'x': 'o'}
```

In addition, there is a `print()` format for assignments which uses a notation closer to that often found in logic textbooks:

```
>>> print g
g[c/y][o/x]
```

Let's now look at how we can evaluate an atomic formula of first-order logic. First, we create a model, and then we call the `evaluate()` method to compute the truth value:

```
>>> m = nltk.Model(dom, val)
>>> m.evaluate('see(olive, y)', g)
True
```

What's happening here? We are evaluating a formula which is similar to our earlier example, `see(olive, cyril)`. However, when the interpretation function encounters the variable y, rather than checking for a value in `val`, it asks the variable assignment g to come up with a value:

```
>>> g['y']
'c'
```

Since we already know that individuals o and c stand in the *see* relation, the value `True` is what we expected. In this case, we can say that assignment g **satisfies** the formula `see(olive, y)`. By contrast, the following formula evaluates to `False` relative to g (check that you see why this is).

```
>>> m.evaluate('see(y, x)', g)
False
```

In our approach (though not in standard first-order logic), variable assignments are *partial*. For example, g says nothing about any variables apart from x and y. The method `purge()` clears all bindings from an assignment.

```
>>> g.purge()
>>> g
{}
```

If we now try to evaluate a formula such as `see(olive, y)` relative to g, it is like trying to interpret a sentence containing a *him* when we don't know what *him* refers to. In this case, the evaluation function fails to deliver a truth value.

```
>>> m.evaluate('see(olive, y)', g)
'Undefined'
```

Since our models already contain rules for interpreting Boolean operators, arbitrarily complex formulas can be composed and evaluated.

```
>>> m.evaluate('see(bertie, olive) & boy(bertie) & -walk(bertie)', g)
True
```

The general process of determining truth or falsity of a formula in a model is called **model checking**.

Quantification

One of the crucial insights of modern logic is that the notion of variable satisfaction can be used to provide an interpretation for quantified formulas. Let's use (24) as an example.

(24) exists x.(girl(x) & walk(x))

When is it true? Let's think about all the individuals in our domain, i.e., in dom. We want to check whether any of these individuals has the property of being a girl and walking. In other words, we want to know if there is some *u* in dom such that g[*u*/x] satisfies the open formula (25).

(25) girl(x) & walk(x)

Consider the following:

```
>>> m.evaluate('exists x.(girl(x) & walk(x))', g)
True
```

evaluate() returns True here because there is some *u* in dom such that (25) is satisfied by an assignment which binds x to *u*. In fact, o is such a *u*:

```
>>> m.evaluate('girl(x) & walk(x)', g.add('x', 'o'))
True
```

One useful tool offered by NLTK is the satisfiers() method. This returns a set of all the individuals that satisfy an open formula. The method parameters are a parsed formula, a variable, and an assignment. Here are a few examples:

```
>>> fmla1 = lp.parse('girl(x) | boy(x)')
>>> m.satisfiers(fmla1, 'x', g)
set(['b', 'o'])
>>> fmla2 = lp.parse('girl(x) -> walk(x)')
>>> m.satisfiers(fmla2, 'x', g)
set(['c', 'b', 'o'])
>>> fmla3 = lp.parse('walk(x) -> girl(x)')
>>> m.satisfiers(fmla3, 'x', g)
set(['b', 'o'])
```

It's useful to think about why fmla2 and fmla3 receive the values they do. The truth conditions for -> mean that fmla2 is equivalent to -girl(x) | walk(x), which is satisfied by something that either isn't a girl or walks. Since neither b (Bertie) nor c (Cyril) are girls, according to model m, they both satisfy the whole formula. And of course o satisfies the formula because o satisfies both disjuncts. Now, since every member of the domain of discourse satisfies fmla2, the corresponding universally quantified formula is also true.

```
>>> m.evaluate('all x.(girl(x) -> walk(x))', g)
True
```

In other words, a universally quantified formula ∀*x*.φ is true with respect to g just in case for every *u*, φ is true with respect to g[*u*/x].

 Your Turn: Try to figure out, first with pencil and paper, and then using `m.evaluate()`, what the truth values are for `all x.(girl(x) & walk(x))` and `exists x.(boy(x) -> walk(x))`. Make sure you understand why they receive these values.

Quantifier Scope Ambiguity

What happens when we want to give a formal representation of a sentence with *two* quantifiers, such as the following?

(26) Everybody admires someone.

There are (at least) two ways of expressing (26) in first-order logic:

(27) a. `all x.(person(x) -> exists y.(person(y) & admire(x,y)))`
       b. `exists y.(person(y) & all x.(person(x) -> admire(x,y)))`

Can we use both of these? The answer is yes, but they have different meanings. (27b) is logically stronger than (27a): it claims that there is a unique person, say, Bruce, who is admired by everyone. (27a), on the other hand, just requires that for every person *u*, we can find some person *u'* whom *u* admires; but this could be a different person *u'* in each case. We distinguish between (27a) and (27b) in terms of the **scope** of the quantifiers. In the first, ∀ has wider scope than ∃, whereas in (27b), the scope ordering is reversed. So now we have two ways of representing the meaning of (26), and they are both quite legitimate. In other words, we are claiming that (26) is *ambiguous* with respect to quantifier scope, and the formulas in (27) give us a way to make the two readings explicit. However, we are not just interested in associating two distinct representations with (26); we also want to show in detail how the two representations lead to different conditions for truth in a model.

In order to examine the ambiguity more closely, let's fix our valuation as follows:

```
>>> v2 = """
... bruce => b
... cyril => c
... elspeth => e
... julia => j
... matthew => m
... person => {b, e, j, m}
... admire => {(j, b), (b, b), (m, e), (e, m), (c, a)}
... """
>>> val2 = nltk.parse_valuation(v2)
```

The *admire* relation can be visualized using the mapping diagram shown in (28).

(28)

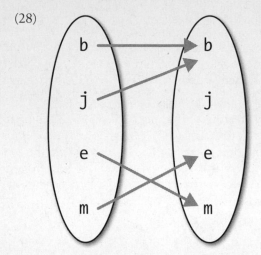

In (28), an arrow between two individuals *x* and *y* indicates that *x* admires *y*. So j and b both admire b (Bruce is very vain), while e admires m and m admires e. In this model, formula (27a) is true but (27b) is false. One way of exploring these results is by using the `satisfiers()` method of `Model` objects.

```
>>> dom2 = val2.domain
>>> m2 = nltk.Model(dom2, val2)
>>> g2 = nltk.Assignment(dom2)
>>> fmla4 = lp.parse('(person(x) -> exists y.(person(y) & admire(x, y)))')
>>> m2.satisfiers(fmla4, 'x', g2)
set(['a', 'c', 'b', 'e', 'j', 'm'])
```

This shows that `fmla4` holds of every individual in the domain. By contrast, consider the formula `fmla5`; this has no satisfiers for the variable y.

```
>>> fmla5 = lp.parse('(person(y) & all x.(person(x) -> admire(x, y)))')
>>> m2.satisfiers(fmla5, 'y', g2)
set([])
```

That is, there is no person that is admired by everybody. Taking a different open formula, `fmla6`, we can verify that there is a person, namely Bruce, who is admired by both Julia and Bruce.

```
>>> fmla6 = lp.parse('(person(y) & all x.((x = bruce | x = julia) -> admire(x, y)))')
>>> m2.satisfiers(fmla6, 'y', g2)
set(['b'])
```

 Your Turn: Devise a new model based on m2 such that (27a) comes out false in your model; similarly, devise a new model such that (27b) comes out true.

Model Building

We have been assuming that we already had a model, and wanted to check the truth of a sentence in the model. By contrast, model building tries to create a new model, given some set of sentences. If it succeeds, then we know that the set is consistent, since we have an existence proof of the model.

We invoke the Mace4 model builder by creating an instance of `Mace()` and calling its `build_model()` method, in an analogous way to calling the Prover9 theorem prover. One option is to treat our candidate set of sentences as assumptions, while leaving the goal unspecified. The following interaction shows how both [a, c1] and [a, c2] are consistent lists, since Mace succeeds in building a model for each of them, whereas [c1, c2] is inconsistent.

```
>>> a3 = lp.parse('exists x.(man(x) & walks(x))')
>>> c1 = lp.parse('mortal(socrates)')
>>> c2 = lp.parse('-mortal(socrates)')
>>> mb = nltk.Mace(5)
>>> print mb.build_model(None, [a3, c1])
True
>>> print mb.build_model(None, [a3, c2])
True
>>> print mb.build_model(None, [c1, c2])
False
```

We can also use the model builder as an adjunct to the theorem prover. Let's suppose we are trying to prove A ⊢ g, i.e., that g is logically derivable from assumptions A = [a1, a2, ..., an]. We can feed this same input to Mace4, and the model builder will try to find a counterexample, that is, to show that g does *not* follow from A. So, given this input, Mace4 will try to find a model for the assumptions A together with the negation of g, namely the list A' = [a1, a2, ..., an, -g]. If g fails to follow from S, then Mace4 may well return with a counterexample faster than Prover9 concludes that it cannot find the required proof. Conversely, if g *is* provable from S, Mace4 may take a long time unsuccessfully trying to find a countermodel, and will eventually give up.

Let's consider a concrete scenario. Our assumptions are the list [*There is a woman that every man loves*, *Adam is a man*, *Eve is a woman*]. Our conclusion is *Adam loves Eve*. Can Mace4 find a model in which the premises are true but the conclusion is false? In the following code, we use `MaceCommand()`, which will let us inspect the model that has been built.

```
>>> a4 = lp.parse('exists y. (woman(y) & all x. (man(x) -> love(x,y)))')
>>> a5 = lp.parse('man(adam)')
>>> a6 = lp.parse('woman(eve)')
>>> g = lp.parse('love(adam,eve)')
>>> mc = nltk.MaceCommand(g, assumptions=[a4, a5, a6])
>>> mc.build_model()
True
```

So the answer is yes: Mace4 found a countermodel in which there is some woman other than Eve that Adam loves. But let's have a closer look at Mace4's model, converted to the format we use for valuations:

```
>>> print mc.valuation
{'C1': 'b',
 'adam': 'a',
 'eve': 'a',
 'love': set([('a', 'b')]),
 'man': set([('a',)]),
 'woman': set([('a',), ('b',)])}
```

The general form of this valuation should be familiar to you: it contains some individual constants and predicates, each with an appropriate kind of value. What might be puzzling is the C1. This is a "Skolem constant" that the model builder introduces as a representative of the existential quantifier. That is, when the model builder encountered the `exists y` part of a4, it knew that there is some individual b in the domain which satisfies the open formula in the body of a4. However, it doesn't know whether b is also the denotation of an individual constant anywhere else in its input, so it makes up a new name for b on the fly, namely C1. Now, since our premises said nothing about the individual constants adam and eve, the model builder has decided there is no reason to treat them as denoting different entities, and they both get mapped to a. Moreover, we didn't specify that man and woman denote disjoint sets, so the model builder lets their denotations overlap. This illustrates quite dramatically the implicit knowledge that we bring to bear in interpreting our scenario, but which the model builder knows nothing about. So let's add a new assumption which makes the sets of men and women disjoint. The model builder still produces a countermodel, but this time it is more in accord with our intuitions about the situation:

```
>>> a7 = lp.parse('all x. (man(x) -> -woman(x))')
>>> g = lp.parse('love(adam,eve)')
>>> mc = nltk.MaceCommand(g, assumptions=[a4, a5, a6, a7])
>>> mc.build_model()
True
>>> print mc.valuation
{'C1': 'c',
 'adam': 'a',
 'eve': 'b',
 'love': set([('a', 'c')]),
 'man': set([('a',)]),
 'woman': set([('b',), ('c',)])}
```

On reflection, we can see that there is nothing in our premises which says that Eve is the only woman in the domain of discourse, so the countermodel in fact is acceptable. If we wanted to rule it out, we would have to add a further assumption such as `exists y. all x. (woman(x) -> (x = y))` to ensure that there is only one woman in the model.

10.4 The Semantics of English Sentences

Compositional Semantics in Feature-Based Grammar

At the beginning of the chapter we briefly illustrated a method of building semantic representations on the basis of a syntactic parse, using the grammar framework developed in Chapter 9. This time, rather than constructing an SQL query, we will build a logical form. One of our guiding ideas for designing such grammars is the **Principle of Compositionality**. (Also known as Frege's Principle; see [Partee, 1995] for the formulation given.)

Principle of Compositionality: the meaning of a whole is a function of the meanings of the parts and of the way they are syntactically combined.

We will assume that the semantically relevant parts of a complex expression are given by a theory of syntactic analysis. Within this chapter, we will take it for granted that expressions are parsed against a context-free grammar. However, this is not entailed by the Principle of Compositionality.

Our goal now is to integrate the construction of a semantic representation in a manner that can be smoothly with the process of parsing. (29) illustrates a first approximation to the kind of analyses we would like to build.

(29)

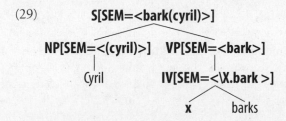

In (29), the SEM value at the root node shows a semantic representation for the whole sentence, while the SEM values at lower nodes show semantic representations for constituents of the sentence. Since the values of SEM have to be treated in a special manner, they are distinguished from other feature values by being enclosed in angle brackets.

So far, so good, but how do we write grammar rules that will give us this kind of result? Our approach will be similar to that adopted for the grammar *sql0.fcfg* at the start of this chapter, in that we will assign semantic representations to lexical nodes, and then compose the semantic representations for each phrase from those of its child nodes. However, in the present case we will use function application rather than string concatenation as the mode of composition. To be more specific, suppose we have NP and VP constituents with appropriate values for their SEM nodes. Then the SEM value of an S is handled by a rule like (30). (Observe that in the case where the value of SEM is a variable, we omit the angle brackets.)

(30) S[SEM=<?vp(?np)>] -> NP[SEM=?subj] VP[SEM=?vp]

(30) tells us that given some SEM value ?subj for the subject NP and some SEM value ?vp for the VP, the SEM value of the S parent is constructed by applying ?vp as a function expression to ?np. From this, we can conclude that ?vp has to denote a function which has the denotation of ?np in its domain. (30) is a nice example of building semantics using the principle of compositionality.

To complete the grammar is very straightforward; all we require are the rules shown here:

```
VP[SEM=?v] -> IV[SEM=?v]
NP[SEM=<cyril>] -> 'Cyril'
IV[SEM=<\x.bark(x)>] -> 'barks'
```

The VP rule says that the parent's semantics is the same as the head child's semantics. The two lexical rules provide non-logical constants to serve as the semantic values of *Cyril* and *barks* respectively. There is an additional piece of notation in the entry for *barks* which we will explain shortly.

Before launching into compositional semantic rules in more detail, we need to add a new tool to our kit, namely the λ-calculus. This provides us with an invaluable tool for combining expressions of first-order logic as we assemble a meaning representation for an English sentence.

The λ-Calculus

In Section 1.3, we pointed out that mathematical set notation was a helpful method of specifying properties P of words that we wanted to select from a document. We illustrated this with (31), which we glossed as "the set of all w such that w is an element of V (the vocabulary) and w has property P".

(31) $\{w \mid w \in V \,\&\, P(w)\}$

It turns out to be extremely useful to add something to first-order logic that will achieve the same effect. We do this with the **λ-operator** (pronounced "lambda"). The λ counterpart to (31) is (32). (Since we are not trying to do set theory here, we just treat V as a unary predicate.)

(32) $\lambda w. (V(w) \,\&\, P(w))$

 λ expressions were originally designed by Alonzo Church to represent computable functions and to provide a foundation for mathematics and logic. The theory in which λ expressions are studied is known as the λ-calculus. Note that the λ-calculus is not part of first-order logic—both can be used independently of the other.

λ is a binding operator, just as the first-order logic quantifiers are. If we have an open formula, such as (33a), then we can bind the variable x with the λ operator, as shown in (33b). The corresponding NLTK representation is given in (33c).

(33) a. $(walk(x)$ & $chew\_gum(x))$

    b. $\lambda x.(walk(x)$ & $chew\_gum(x))$

    c. `\x.(walk(x) & chew_gum(x))`

Remember that \ is a special character in Python strings. We must either escape it (with another \), or else use "raw strings" (Section 3.4) as shown here:

```
>>> lp = nltk.LogicParser()
>>> e = lp.parse(r'\x.(walk(x) & chew_gum(x))')
>>> e
<LambdaExpression \x.(walk(x) & chew_gum(x))>
>>> e.free()
set([])
>>> print lp.parse(r'\x.(walk(x) & chew_gum(y))')
\x.(walk(x) & chew_gum(y))
```

We have a special name for the result of binding the variables in an expression: **λ-abstraction**. When you first encounter λ-abstracts, it can be hard to get an intuitive sense of their meaning. A couple of English glosses for (33b) are: "be an x such that x walks and x chews gum" or "have the property of walking and chewing gum." It has often been suggested that λ-abstracts are good representations for verb phrases (or subjectless clauses), particularly when these occur as arguments in their own right. This is illustrated in (34a) and its translation, (34b).

(34) a. To walk and chew gum is hard

    b. `hard(\x.(walk(x) & chew_gum(x)))`

So the general picture is this: given an open formula φ with free variable x, abstracting over x yields a property expression $\lambda x.\varphi$—the property of being an x such that φ. Here's a more official version of how abstracts are built:

(35) If α is of type τ, and x is a variable of type e, then \x.α is of type $\langle e, \tau \rangle$.

(34b) illustrated a case where we say something about a property, namely that it is hard. But what we usually do with properties is attribute them to individuals. And in fact, if φ is an open formula, then the abstract $\lambda x.\varphi$ can be used as a unary predicate. In (36), (33b) is predicated of the term *gerald*.

(36) `\x.(walk(x) & chew_gum(x)) (gerald)`

Now (36) says that Gerald has the property of walking and chewing gum, which has the same meaning as (37).

(37) `(walk(gerald) & chew_gum(gerald))`

What we have done here is remove the \x from the beginning of \x.(walk(x) & chew_gum(x)) and replaced all occurrences of x in (walk(x) & chew_gum(x)) by gerald. We'll use α[β/x] as notation for the operation of replacing all free occurrences of *x* in α by the expression β. So

> (walk(x) & chew_gum(x))[gerald/x]

represents the same expression as (37). The "reduction" of (36) to (37) is an extremely useful operation in simplifying semantic representations, and we shall use it a lot in the rest of this chapter. The operation is often called **β-reduction**. In order for it to be semantically justified, we want it to hold that λ*x*. α(β) has the same semantic value as α[β/x]. This is indeed true, subject to a slight complication that we will come to shortly. In order to carry out β-reduction of expressions in NLTK, we can call the `simplify()` method ❶.

```
>>> e = lp.parse(r'\x.(walk(x) & chew_gum(x))(gerald)')
>>> print e
\x.(walk(x) & chew_gum(x))(gerald)
>>> print e.simplify()  ❶
(walk(gerald) & chew_gum(gerald))
```

Although we have so far only considered cases where the body of the λ-abstract is an open formula, i.e., of type *t*, this is not a necessary restriction; the body can be any well-formed expression. Here's an example with two λs:

(38) \x.\y.(dog(x) & own(y, x))

Just as (33b) plays the role of a unary predicate, (38) works like a binary predicate: it can be applied directly to two arguments ❶. The `LogicParser` allows nested λs such as \x.\y. to be written in the abbreviated form \x y. ❶.

```
>>> print lp.parse(r'\x.\y.(dog(x) & own(y, x))(cyril)').simplify()
\y.(dog(cyril) & own(y,cyril))
>>> print lp.parse(r'\x y.(dog(x) & own(y, x))(cyril, angus)').simplify()  ❶
(dog(cyril) & own(angus,cyril))
```

All our λ-abstracts so far have involved the familiar first-order variables: x, y, and so on —variables of type *e*. But suppose we want to treat one abstract, say, \x.walk(x), as the *argument* of another λ-abstract? We might try this:

> \y.y(angus)(\x.walk(x))

But since the variable y is stipulated to be of type *e*, \y.y(angus) only applies to arguments of type *e* while \x.walk(x) is of type ⟨*e*, *t*⟩! Instead, we need to allow abstraction over variables of higher type. Let's use P and Q as variables of type ⟨*e*, *t*⟩, and then we can have an abstract such as \P.P(angus). Since P is of type ⟨*e*, *t*⟩, the whole abstract is of type ⟨⟨*e*, *t*⟩, *t*⟩. Then \P.P(angus)(\x.walk(x)) is legal, and can be simplified via β-reduction to \x.walk(x)(angus) and then again to walk(angus).

When carrying out β-reduction, some care has to be taken with variables. Consider, for example, the λ-terms (39a) and (39b), which differ only in the identity of a free variable.

(39)   a. `\y.see(y, x)`

         b. `\y.see(y, z)`

Suppose now that we apply the λ-term `\P.exists x.P(x)` to each of these terms:

(40)   a. `\P.exists x.P(x)(\y.see(y, x))`

         b. `\P.exists x.P(x)(\y.see(y, z))`

We pointed out earlier that the results of the application should be semantically equivalent. But if we let the free variable x in (39a) fall inside the scope of the existential quantifier in (40a), then after reduction, the results will be different:

(41)   a. `exists x.see(x, x)`

         b. `exists x.see(x, z)`

(41a) means there is some x that sees him/herself, whereas (41b) means that there is some x that sees an unspecified individual z. What has gone wrong here? Clearly, we want to forbid the kind of variable "capture" shown in (41a).

In order to deal with this problem, let's step back a moment. Does it matter what particular name we use for the variable bound by the existential quantifier in the function expression of (40a)? The answer is no. In fact, given any variable-binding expression (involving ∀, ∃, or λ), the name chosen for the bound variable is completely arbitrary. For example, `exists x.P(x)` and `exists y.P(y)` are equivalent; they are called **α-equivalents**, or **alphabetic variants**. The process of relabeling bound variables is known as **α-conversion**. When we test for equality of `VariableBinderExpression`s in the `logic` module (i.e., using `==`), we are in fact testing for α-equivalence:

```
>>> e1 = lp.parse('exists x.P(x)')
>>> print e1
exists x.P(x)
>>> e2 = e1.alpha_convert(nltk.Variable('z'))
>>> print e2
exists z.P(z)
>>> e1 == e2
True
```

When β-reduction is carried out on an application f(a), we check whether there are free variables in a that also occur as bound variables in any subterms of f. Suppose, as in the example just discussed, that x is free in a, and that f contains the subterm `exists x.P(x)`. In this case, we produce an alphabetic variant of `exists x.P(x)`, say, `exists z1.P(z1)`, and then carry on with the reduction. This relabeling is carried out automatically by the β-reduction code in `logic`, and the results can be seen in the following example:

```
>>> e3 = lp.parse('\P.exists x.P(x)(\y.see(y, x))')
>>> print e3
(\P.exists x.P(x))(\y.see(y,x))
>>> print e3.simplify()
exists z1.see(z1,x)
```

 As you work through examples like these in the following sections, you may find that the logical expressions which are returned have different variable names; for example, you might see z14 in place of z1 in the preceding formula. This change in labeling is innocuous—in fact, it is just an illustration of alphabetic variants.

After this excursus, let's return to the task of building logical forms for English sentences.

Quantified NPs

At the start of this section, we briefly described how to build a semantic representation for *Cyril barks*. You would be forgiven for thinking this was all too easy—surely there is a bit more to building compositional semantics. What about quantifiers, for instance? Right, this is a crucial issue. For example, we want (42a) to be given the logical form in (42b). How can this be accomplished?

(42) a. A dog barks.

b. exists x.(dog(x) & bark(x))

Let's make the assumption that our *only* operation for building complex semantic representations is function application. Then our problem is this: how do we give a semantic representation to the quantified NPs *a dog* so that it can be combined with bark to give the result in (42b)? As a first step, let's make the subject's SEM value act as the function expression rather than the argument. (This is sometimes called **type-raising**.) Now we are looking for a way of instantiating ?np so that [SEM=<?np(\x.bark(x))>] is equivalent to [SEM=<exists x.(dog(x) & bark(x))>]. Doesn't this look a bit reminiscent of carrying out β-reduction in the λ-calculus? In other words, we want a λ-term M to replace ?np so that applying M to \x.bark(x) yields (42b). To do this, we replace the occurrence of \x.bark(x) in (42b) by a predicate variable P, and bind the variable with λ, as shown in (43).

(43) \P.exists x.(dog(x) & P(x))

We have used a different style of variable in (43)—that is, 'P' rather than 'x' or 'y'—to signal that we are abstracting over a different kind of object—not an individual, but a function expression of type $\langle e, t \rangle$. So the type of (43) as a whole is $\langle\langle e, t \rangle, t \rangle$. We will take this to be the type of NPs in general. To illustrate further, a universally quantified NP will look like (44).

---

(44) \P.all x.(dog(x) -> P(x))

We are pretty much done now, except that we also want to carry out a further abstraction plus application for the process of combining the semantics of the determiner *a*, namely (45), with the semantics of *dog*.

(45) \Q P.exists x.(Q(x) & P(x))

Applying (45) as a function expression to \x.dog(x) yields (43), and applying that to \x.bark(x) gives us \P.exists x.(dog(x) & P(x))(\x.bark(x)). Finally, carrying out β-reduction yields just what we wanted, namely (42b).

Transitive Verbs

Our next challenge is to deal with sentences containing transitive verbs, such as (46).

(46) Angus chases a dog.

The output semantics that we want to build is exists x.(dog(x) & chase(angus, x)). Let's look at how we can use λ-abstraction to get this result. A significant constraint on possible solutions is to require that the semantic representation of *a dog* be independent of whether the NP acts as subject or object of the sentence. In other words, we want to get the formula just shown as our output while sticking to (43) as the NP semantics. A second constraint is that VPs should have a uniform type of interpretation, regardless of whether they consist of just an intransitive verb or a transitive verb plus object. More specifically, we stipulate that VPs are always of type ⟨e, t⟩. Given these constraints, here's a semantic representation for *chases a dog* that does the trick.

(47) \y.exists x.(dog(x) & chase(y, x))

Think of (47) as the property of being a *y* such that for some dog *x*, *y* chases *x*; or more colloquially, being a *y* who chases a dog. Our task now resolves to designing a semantic representation for *chases* which can combine with (43) so as to allow (47) to be derived.

Let's carry out the inverse of β-reduction on (47), giving rise to (48).

(48) \P.exists x.(dog(x) & P(x))(\z.chase(y, z))

(48) may be slightly hard to read at first; you need to see that it involves applying the quantified NP representation from (43) to \z.chase(y,z). (48) is equivalent via β-reduction to exists x.(dog(x) & chase(y, x)).

Now let's replace the function expression in (48) by a variable X of the same type as an NP, that is, of type ⟨⟨e, t⟩, t⟩.

(49) X(\z.chase(y, z))

The representation of a transitive verb will have to apply to an argument of the type of X to yield a function expression of the type of VPs, that is, of type $\langle e, t \rangle$. We can ensure this by abstracting over both the X variable in (49) and also the subject variable y. So the full solution is reached by giving *chases* the semantic representation shown in (50).

(50) \X y.X(\x.chase(y, x))

If (50) is applied to (43), the result after β-reduction is equivalent to (47), which is what we wanted all along:

```
>>> lp = nltk.LogicParser()
>>> tvp = lp.parse(r'\X x.X(\y.chase(x,y))')
>>> np = lp.parse(r'(\P.exists x.(dog(x) & P(x)))')
>>> vp = nltk.ApplicationExpression(tvp, np)
>>> print vp
(\X x.X(\y.chase(x,y)))(\P.exists x.(dog(x) & P(x)))
>>> print vp.simplify()
\x.exists z2.(dog(z2) & chase(x,z2))
```

In order to build a semantic representation for a sentence, we also need to combine in the semantics of the subject NP. If the latter is a quantified expression, such as *every girl*, everything proceeds in the same way as we showed for *a dog barks* earlier on; the subject is translated as a function expression which is applied to the semantic representation of the VP. However, we now seem to have created another problem for ourselves with proper names. So far, these have been treated semantically as individual constants, and these cannot be applied as functions to expressions like (47). Consequently, we need to come up with a different semantic representation for them. What we do in this case is reinterpret proper names so that they too are function expressions, like quantified NPs. Here is the required λ-expression for *Angus*:

(51) \P.P(angus)

(51) denotes the characteristic function corresponding to the set of all properties which are true of Angus. Converting from an individual constant angus to \P.P(angus) is another example of type-raising, briefly mentioned earlier, and allows us to replace a Boolean-valued application such as \x.walk(x)(angus) with an equivalent function application \P.P(angus)(\x.walk(x)). By β-reduction, both expressions reduce to walk(angus).

The grammar *simple-sem.fcfg* contains a small set of rules for parsing and translating simple examples of the kind that we have been looking at. Here's a slightly more complicated example:

```
>>> from nltk import load_parser
>>> parser = load_parser('grammars/book_grammars/simple-sem.fcfg', trace=0)
>>> sentence = 'Angus gives a bone to every dog'
>>> tokens = sentence.split()
>>> trees = parser.nbest_parse(tokens)
```

```
>>> for tree in trees:
...     print tree.node['SEM']
all z2.(dog(z2) -> exists z1.(bone(z1) & give(angus,z1,z2)))
```

NLTK provides some utilities to make it easier to derive and inspect semantic interpretations. The function `batch_interpret()` is intended for batch interpretation of a list of input sentences. It builds a dictionary `d` where for each sentence `sent` in the input, `d[sent]` is a list of pairs (*synrep*, *semrep*) consisting of trees and semantic representations for `sent`. The value is a list since `sent` may be syntactically ambiguous; in the following example, however, there is only one parse tree per sentence in the list.

```
(S[SEM=<walk(irene)>]
  (NP[-LOC, NUM='sg', SEM=<\P.P(irene)>]
    (PropN[-LOC, NUM='sg', SEM=<\P.P(irene)>] Irene))
  (VP[NUM='sg', SEM=<\x.walk(x)>]
    (IV[NUM='sg', SEM=<\x.walk(x)>, TNS='pres'] walks)))
(S[SEM=<exists z1.(ankle(z1) & bite(cyril,z1))>]
  (NP[-LOC, NUM='sg', SEM=<\P.P(cyril)>]
    (PropN[-LOC, NUM='sg', SEM=<\P.P(cyril)>] Cyril))
  (VP[NUM='sg', SEM=<\x.exists z1.(ankle(z1) & bite(x,z1))>]
    (TV[NUM='sg', SEM=<\X x.X(\y.bite(x,y))>, TNS='pres'] bites)
    (NP[NUM='sg', SEM=<\Q.exists x.(ankle(x) & Q(x))>]
      (Det[NUM='sg', SEM=<\P Q.exists x.(P(x) & Q(x))>] an)
      (Nom[NUM='sg', SEM=<\x.ankle(x)>]
        (N[NUM='sg', SEM=<\x.ankle(x)>] ankle)))))
```

We have seen now how to convert English sentences into logical forms, and earlier we saw how logical forms could be checked as true or false in a model. Putting these two mappings together, we can check the truth value of English sentences in a given model. Let's take model `m` as defined earlier. The utility `batch_evaluate()` resembles `batch_interpret()`, except that we need to pass a model and a variable assignment as parameters. The output is a triple (*synrep*, *semrep*, *value*), where *synrep*, *semrep* are as before, and *value* is a truth value. For simplicity, the following example only processes a single sentence.

```
>>> v = """
... bertie => b
... olive => o
... cyril => c
... boy => {b}
... girl => {o}
... dog => {c}
... walk => {o, c}
... see => {(b, o), (c, b), (o, c)}
... """
>>> val = nltk.parse_valuation(v)
>>> g = nltk.Assignment(val.domain)
>>> m = nltk.Model(val.domain, val)
>>> sent = 'Cyril sees every boy'
>>> grammar_file = 'grammars/book_grammars/simple-sem.fcfg'
>>> results = nltk.batch_evaluate([sent], grammar_file, m, g)[0]
>>> for (syntree, semrel, value) in results:
...     print semrep
```

```
...     print value
exists z3.(ankle(z3) & bite(cyril,z3))
True
```

Quantifier Ambiguity Revisited

One important limitation of the methods described earlier is that they do not deal with scope ambiguity. Our translation method is syntax-driven, in the sense that the semantic representation is closely coupled with the syntactic analysis, and the scope of the quantifiers in the semantics therefore reflects the relative scope of the corresponding NPs in the syntactic parse tree. Consequently, a sentence like (26), repeated here, will always be translated as (53a), not (53b).

(52) Every girl chases a dog.

(53)   a. `all x.(girl(x) -> exists y.(dog(y) & chase(x,y)))`
       b. `exists y.(dog(y) & all x.(girl(x) -> chase(x,y)))`

There are numerous approaches to dealing with scope ambiguity, and we will look very briefly at one of the simplest. To start with, let's briefly consider the structure of scoped formulas. Figure 10-3 depicts the way in which the two readings of (52) differ.

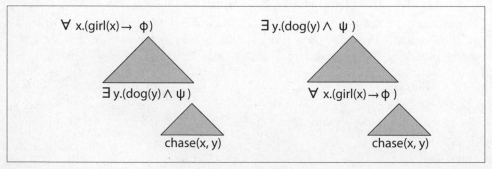

Figure 10-3. Quantifier scopings.

Let's consider the lefthand structure first. At the top, we have the quantifier corresponding to *every girl*. The φ can be thought of as a placeholder for whatever is inside the scope of the quantifier. Moving downward, we see that we can plug in the quantifier corresponding to *a dog* as an instantiation of φ. This gives a new placeholder ψ, representing the scope of *a dog*, and into this we can plug the "core" of the semantics, namely the open sentence corresponding to *x chases y*. The structure on the righthand side is identical, except we have swapped round the order of the two quantifiers.

In the method known as **Cooper storage**, a semantic representation is no longer an expression of first-order logic, but instead a pair consisting of a "core" semantic representation plus a list of **binding operators**. For the moment, think of a binding operator as being identical to the semantic representation of a quantified NP such as (44) or

(45). Following along the lines indicated in Figure 10-3, let's assume that we have constructed a Cooper-storage-style semantic representation of sentence (52), and let's take our core to be the open formula chase(x,y). Given a list of binding operators corresponding to the two NPs in (52), we pick a binding operator off the list, and combine it with the core.

```
\P.exists y.(dog(y) & P(y))(\z2.chase(z1,z2))
```

Then we take the result, and apply the next binding operator from the list to it.

```
\P.all x.(girl(x) -> P(x))(\z1.exists x.(dog(x) & chase(z1,x)))
```

Once the list is empty, we have a conventional logical form for the sentence. Combining binding operators with the core in this way is called **S-Retrieval**. If we are careful to allow every possible order of binding operators (for example, by taking all permutations of the list; see Section 4.5), then we will be able to generate every possible scope ordering of quantifiers.

The next question to address is how we build up a core+store representation compositionally. As before, each phrasal and lexical rule in the grammar will have a SEM feature, but now there will be embedded features CORE and STORE. To illustrate the machinery, let's consider a simpler example, namely *Cyril smiles*. Here's a lexical rule for the verb *smiles* (taken from the grammar *storage.fcfg*), which looks pretty innocuous:

```
IV[SEM=[CORE=<\x.smile(x)>, STORE=(/)]] -> 'smiles'
```

The rule for the proper name *Cyril* is more complex.

```
NP[SEM=[CORE=<@x>, STORE=(<bo(\P.P(cyril),@x)>)]] -> 'Cyril'
```

The bo predicate has two subparts: the standard (type-raised) representation of a proper name, and the expression @x, which is called the **address** of the binding operator. (We'll explain the need for the address variable shortly.) @x is a metavariable, that is, a variable that ranges over individual variables of the logic and, as you will see, also provides the value of core. The rule for VP just percolates up the semantics of the IV, and the interesting work is done by the S rule.

```
VP[SEM=?s] -> IV[SEM=?s]

S[SEM=[CORE=<?vp(?subj)>, STORE=(?b1+?b2)]] ->
   NP[SEM=[CORE=?subj, STORE=?b1]] VP[SEM=[core=?vp, store=?b2]]
```

The core value at the S node is the result of applying the VP's core value, namely \x.smile(x), to the subject NP's value. The latter will not be @x, but rather an instantiation of @x, say, z3. After β-reduction, <?vp(?subj)> will be unified with <smile(z3)>. Now, when @x is instantiated as part of the parsing process, it will be instantiated uniformly. In particular, the occurrence of @x in the subject NP's STORE will also be mapped to z3, yielding the element bo(\P.P(cyril),z3). These steps can be seen in the following parse tree.

```
(S[SEM=[CORE=<smile(z3)>, STORE=(bo(\P.P(cyril),z3))]]
  (NP[SEM=[CORE=<z3>, STORE=(bo(\P.P(cyril),z3))]] Cyril)
  (VP[SEM=[CORE=<\x.smile(x)>, STORE=()]]
    (IV[SEM=[CORE=<\x.smile(x)>, STORE=()]] smiles)))
```

Let's return to our more complex example, (52), and see what the storage style SEM value is, after parsing with grammar *storage.fcfg*.

```
CORE  = <chase(z1,z2)>
STORE = (bo(\P.all x.(girl(x) -> P(x)),z1), bo(\P.exists x.(dog(x) & P(x)),z2))
```

It should be clearer now why the address variables are an important part of the binding operator. Recall that during S-retrieval, we will be taking binding operators off the STORE list and applying them successively to the CORE. Suppose we start with bo(\P.all x.(girl(x) -> P(x)),z1), which we want to combine with chase(z1,z2). The quantifier part of the binding operator is \P.all x.(girl(x) -> P(x)), and to combine this with chase(z1,z2), the latter needs to first be turned into a λ-abstract. How do we know which variable to abstract over? This is what the address z1 tells us, i.e., that *every girl* has the role of chaser rather than chasee.

The module nltk.sem.cooper_storage deals with the task of turning storage-style semantic representations into standard logical forms. First, we construct a CooperStore instance, and inspect its STORE and CORE.

```
>>> from nltk.sem import cooper_storage as cs
>>> sentence = 'every girl chases a dog'
>>> trees = cs.parse_with_bindops(sentence, grammar='grammars/book_grammars/storage.fcfg')
>>> semrep = trees[0].node['sem']
>>> cs_semrep = cs.CooperStore(semrep)
>>> print cs_semrep.core
chase(z1,z2)
>>> for bo in cs_semrep.store:
...      print bo
bo(\P.all x.(girl(x) -> P(x)),z1)
bo(\P.exists x.(dog(x) & P(x)),z2)
```

Finally, we call s_retrieve() and check the readings.

```
>>> cs_semrep.s_retrieve(trace=True)
Permutation 1
   (\P.all x.(girl(x) -> P(x)))(\z1.chase(z1,z2))
   (\P.exists x.(dog(x) & P(x)))(\z2.all x.(girl(x) -> chase(x,z2)))
Permutation 2
   (\P.exists x.(dog(x) & P(x)))(\z2.chase(z1,z2))
   (\P.all x.(girl(x) -> P(x)))(\z1.exists x.(dog(x) & chase(z1,x)))

>>> for reading in cs_semrep.readings:
...      print reading
exists x.(dog(x) & all z3.(girl(z3) -> chase(z3,x)))
all x.(girl(x) -> exists z4.(dog(z4) & chase(x,z4)))
```

10.5 Discourse Semantics

A **discourse** is a sequence of sentences. Very often, the interpretation of a sentence in a discourse depends on what preceded it. A clear example of this comes from anaphoric pronouns, such as *he*, *she*, and *it*. Given a discourse such as *Angus used to have a dog. But he recently disappeared.*, you will probably interpret *he* as referring to Angus's dog. However, in *Angus used to have a dog. He took him for walks in New Town.*, you are more likely to interpret *he* as referring to Angus himself.

Discourse Representation Theory

The standard approach to quantification in first-order logic is limited to single sentences. Yet there seem to be examples where the scope of a quantifier can extend over two or more sentences. We saw one earlier, and here's a second example, together with a translation.

> (54)   a. Angus owns a dog. It bit Irene.
>
>   b. $\exists x.(dog(x)\ \&\ own(Angus, x)\ \&\ bite(x, Irene))$

That is, the NP *a dog* acts like a quantifier which binds the *it* in the second sentence. Discourse Representation Theory (DRT) was developed with the specific goal of providing a means for handling this and other semantic phenomena which seem to be characteristic of discourse. A **discourse representation structure** (DRS) presents the meaning of discourse in terms of a list of discourse referents and a list of conditions. The **discourse referents** are the things under discussion in the discourse, and they correspond to the individual variables of first-order logic. The **DRS conditions** apply to those discourse referents, and correspond to atomic open formulas of first-order logic. Figure 10-4 illustrates how a DRS for the first sentence in (54a) is augmented to become a DRS for both sentences.

When the second sentence of (54a) is processed, it is interpreted in the context of what is already present in the lefthand side of Figure 10-4. The pronoun *it* triggers the addition of a new discourse referent, say, u, and we need to find an **anaphoric antecedent** for it—that is, we want to work out what *it* refers to. In DRT, the task of finding the antecedent for an anaphoric pronoun involves linking it to a discourse referent already within the current DRS, and y is the obvious choice. (We will say more about anaphora resolution shortly.) This processing step gives rise to a new condition $u = y$. The remaining content contributed by the second sentence is also merged with the content of the first, and this is shown on the righthand side of Figure 10-4.

Figure 10-4 illustrates how a DRS can represent more than just a single sentence. In this case, it is a two-sentence discourse, but in principle a single DRS could correspond to the interpretation of a whole text. We can inquire into the truth conditions of the righthand DRS in Figure 10-4. Informally, it is true in some situation s if there are entities **a**, **c**, and **i** in s corresponding to the discourse referents in the DRS such that

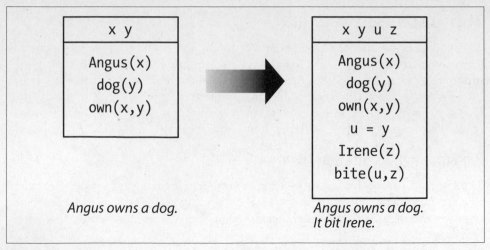

Figure 10-4. Building a DRS: The DRS on the lefthand side represents the result of processing the first sentence in the discourse, while the DRS on the righthand side shows the effect of processing the second sentence and integrating its content.

all the conditions are true in *s*; that is, **a** is named *Angus*, **c** is a dog, **a** owns **c**, **i** is named *Irene*, and **c** bit **i**.

In order to process DRSs computationally, we need to convert them into a linear format. Here's an example, where the DRS is a pair consisting of a list of discourse referents and a list of DRS conditions:

```
([x, y], [angus(x), dog(y), own(x,y)])
```

The easiest way to build a DRS object in NLTK is by parsing a string representation ❶.

```
>>> dp = nltk.DrtParser()
>>> drs1 = dp.parse('([x, y], [angus(x), dog(y), own(x, y)])') ❶
>>> print drs1
([x,y],[angus(x), dog(y), own(x,y)])
```

We can use the `draw()` method ❶ to visualize the result, as shown in Figure 10-5.

```
>>> drs1.draw() ❶
```

Figure 10-5. DRS screenshot.

When we discussed the truth conditions of the DRSs in Figure 10-4, we assumed that the topmost discourse referents were interpreted as existential quantifiers, while the conditions were interpreted as though they are conjoined. In fact, every DRS can be translated into a formula of first-order logic, and the `fol()` method implements this translation.

```
>>> print drs1.fol()
exists x y.((angus(x) & dog(y)) & own(x,y))
```

In addition to the functionality available for first-order logic expressions, DRT `Expressions` have a DRS-concatenation operator, represented as the + symbol. The concatenation of two DRSs is a single DRS containing the merged discourse referents and the conditions from both arguments. DRS-concatenation automatically α-converts bound variables to avoid name-clashes.

```
>>> drs2 = dp.parse('([x], [walk(x)]) + ([y], [run(y)])')
>>> print drs2
(([x],[walk(x)]) + ([y],[run(y)]))
>>> print drs2.simplify()
([x,y],[walk(x), run(y)])
```

While all the conditions seen so far have been atomic, it is possible to embed one DRS within another, and this is how universal quantification is handled. In `drs3`, there are no top-level discourse referents, and the sole condition is made up of two sub-DRSs, connected by an implication. Again, we can use `fol()` to get a handle on the truth conditions.

```
>>> drs3 = dp.parse('([], [(([x], [dog(x)]) -> ([y],[ankle(y), bite(x, y)]))])')
>>> print drs3.fol()
all x.(dog(x) -> exists y.(ankle(y) & bite(x,y)))
```

We pointed out earlier that DRT is designed to allow anaphoric pronouns to be interpreted by linking to existing discourse referents. DRT sets constraints on which discourse referents are "accessible" as possible antecedents, but is not intended to explain how a particular antecedent is chosen from the set of candidates. The module `nltk.sem.drt_resolve_anaphora` adopts a similarly conservative strategy: if the DRS contains a condition of the form `PRO(x)`, the method `resolve_anaphora()` replaces this with a condition of the form x = [...], where [...] is a list of possible antecedents.

```
>>> drs4 = dp.parse('([x, y], [angus(x), dog(y), own(x, y)])')
>>> drs5 = dp.parse('([u, z], [PRO(u), irene(z), bite(u, z)])')
>>> drs6 = drs4 + drs5
>>> print drs6.simplify()
([x,y,u,z],[angus(x), dog(y), own(x,y), PRO(u), irene(z), bite(u,z)])
>>> print drs6.simplify().resolve_anaphora()
([x,y,u,z],[angus(x), dog(y), own(x,y), (u = [x,y,z]), irene(z), bite(u,z)])
```

Since the algorithm for anaphora resolution has been separated into its own module, this facilitates swapping in alternative procedures that try to make more intelligent guesses about the correct antecedent.

Our treatment of DRSs is fully compatible with the existing machinery for handling λ-abstraction, and consequently it is straightforward to build compositional semantic representations that are based on DRT rather than first-order logic. This technique is illustrated in the following rule for indefinites (which is part of the grammar *drt.fcfg*). For ease of comparison, we have added the parallel rule for indefinites from *simple-sem.fcfg*.

```
Det[NUM=sg,SEM=<\P Q.([x],[]) + P(x) + Q(x)>] -> 'a'
Det[NUM=sg,SEM=<\P Q. exists x.(P(x) & Q(x))>] -> 'a'
```

To get a better idea of how the DRT rule works, look at this subtree for the NP *a dog*:

```
(NP[NUM='sg', SEM=<\Q.(([x],[dog(x)]) + Q(x))>]
  (Det[NUM'sg', SEM=<\P Q.((([x],[]) + P(x)) + Q(x))>] a)
  (Nom[NUM='sg', SEM=<\x.([],[dog(x)])>]
    (N[NUM='sg', SEM=<\x.([],[dog(x)])>] dog)))))
```

The λ-abstract for the indefinite is applied as a function expression to \x.([], [dog(x)]) which leads to \Q.((([x],[]) + ([],[dog(x)]) + Q(x)); after simplification, we get \Q.(([x],[dog(x)]) + Q(x)) as the representation for the NP as a whole.

In order to parse with grammar *drt.fcfg*, we specify in the call to `load_earley()` that SEM values in feature structures are to be parsed using `DrtParser` in place of the default `LogicParser`.

```
>>> from nltk import load_parser
>>> parser = load_parser('grammars/book_grammars/drt.fcfg', logic_parser=nltk.DrtParser())
>>> trees = parser.nbest_parse('Angus owns a dog'.split())
>>> print trees[0].node['sem'].simplify()
([x,z2],[Angus(x), dog(z2), own(x,z2)])
```

Discourse Processing

When we interpret a sentence, we use a rich context for interpretation, determined in part by the preceding context and in part by our background assumptions. DRT provides a theory of how the meaning of a sentence is integrated into a representation of the prior discourse, but two things have been glaringly absent from the processing approach just discussed. First, there has been no attempt to incorporate any kind of inference; and second, we have only processed individual sentences. These omissions are redressed by the module `nltk.inference.discourse`.

Whereas a discourse is a sequence $s_1, \ldots s_n$ of sentences, a *discourse thread* is a sequence $s_1\text{-}r_i, \ldots s_n\text{-}r_j$ of readings, one for each sentence in the discourse. The module processes sentences incrementally, keeping track of all possible threads when there is ambiguity. For simplicity, the following example ignores scope ambiguity:

```
>>> dt = nltk.DiscourseTester(['A student dances', 'Every student is a person'])
>>> dt.readings()
s0 readings: s0-r0: exists x.(student(x) & dance(x))
s1 readings: s1-r0: all x.(student(x) -> person(x))
```

When a new sentence is added to the current discourse, setting the parameter `consistchk=True` causes consistency to be checked by invoking the model checker for each thread, i.e., each sequence of admissible readings. In this case, the user has the option of retracting the sentence in question.

```
>>> dt.add_sentence('No person dances', consistchk=True)
Inconsistent discourse d0 ['s0-r0', 's1-r0', 's2-r0']:
s0-r0: exists x.(student(x) & dance(x))
s1-r0: all x.(student(x) -> person(x))
s2-r0: -exists x.(person(x) & dance(x))
>>> dt.retract_sentence('No person dances', verbose=True)
Current sentences are
s0: A student dances
s1: Every student is a person
```

In a similar manner, we use `informchk=True` to check whether a new sentence φ is informative relative to the current discourse. The theorem prover treats existing sentences in the thread as assumptions and attempts to prove φ; it is informative if no such proof can be found.

```
>>> dt.add_sentence('A person dances', informchk=True)
Sentence 'A person dances' under reading 'exists x.(person(x) & dance(x))':
Not informative relative to thread 'd0'
```

It is also possible to pass in an additional set of assumptions as background knowledge and use these to filter out inconsistent readings; see the Discourse HOWTO at *http://www.nltk.org/howto* for more details.

The `discourse` module can accommodate semantic ambiguity and filter out readings that are not admissible. The following example invokes both Glue Semantics as well as DRT. Since the Glue Semantics module is configured to use the wide-coverage Malt dependency parser, the input (*Every dog chases a boy. He runs.*) needs to be tagged as well as tokenized.

```
>>> from nltk.tag import RegexpTagger
>>> tagger = RegexpTagger(
...     [('^(chases|runs)$', 'VB'),
...      ('^(a)$', 'ex_quant'),
...      ('^(every)$', 'univ_quant'),
...      ('^(dog|boy)$', 'NN'),
...      ('^(He)$', 'PRP')
... ])
>>> rc = nltk.DrtGlueReadingCommand(depparser=nltk.MaltParser(tagger=tagger))
>>> dt = nltk.DiscourseTester(['Every dog chases a boy', 'He runs'], rc)
>>> dt.readings()
s0 readings:
s0-r0: ([],[(((([x],[dog(x)]) -> ([z3],[boy(z3), chases(x,z3)]))])
s0-r1: ([z4],[boy(z4), ((([x],[dog(x)]) -> ([],[chases(x,z4)]))])

s1 readings:
s1-r0: ([x],[PRO(x), runs(x)])
```

The first sentence of the discourse has two possible readings, depending on the quantifier scoping. The unique reading of the second sentence represents the pronoun *He* via the condition `PRO(x)`. Now let's look at the discourse threads that result:

```
>>> dt.readings(show_thread_readings=True)
d0: ['s0-r0', 's1-r0'] : INVALID: AnaphoraResolutionException
```

```
d1: ['s0-r1', 's1-r0'] : ([z6,z10],[boy(z6), (([x],[dog(x)]) ->
([],[chases(x,z6)])), (z10 = z6), runs(z10)])
```

When we examine threads d0 and d1, we see that reading s0-r0, where *every dog* out-scopes a boy, is deemed inadmissible because the pronoun in the second sentence cannot be resolved. By contrast, in thread d1 the pronoun (relettered to z10) has been bound via the equation (z10 = z6).

Inadmissible readings can be filtered out by passing the parameter filter=True.

```
>>> dt.readings(show_thread_readings=True, filter=True)
d1: ['s0-r1', 's1-r0'] : ([z12,z15],[boy(z12), (([x],[dog(x)]) ->
([],[chases(x,z12)])), (z17 = z15), runs(z15)])
```

Although this little discourse is extremely limited, it should give you a feel for the kind of semantic processing issues that arise when we go beyond single sentences, and also a feel for the techniques that can be deployed to address them.

10.6 Summary

- First-order logic is a suitable language for representing natural language meaning in a computational setting since it is flexible enough to represent many useful aspects of natural meaning, and there are efficient theorem provers for reasoning with first-order logic. (Equally, there are a variety of phenomena in natural language semantics which are believed to require more powerful logical mechanisms.)

- As well as translating natural language sentences into first-order logic, we can state the truth conditions of these sentences by examining models of first-order formulas.

- In order to build meaning representations compositionally, we supplement first-order logic with the λ-calculus.

- β-reduction in the λ-calculus corresponds semantically to application of a function to an argument. Syntactically, it involves replacing a variable bound by λ in the function expression with the expression that provides the argument in the function application.

- A key part of constructing a model lies in building a valuation which assigns interpretations to non-logical constants. These are interpreted as either n-ary predicates or as individual constants.

- An open expression is an expression containing one or more free variables. Open expressions receive an interpretation only when their free variables receive values from a variable assignment.

- Quantifiers are interpreted by constructing, for a formula $\varphi[x]$ open in variable x, the set of individuals which make $\varphi[x]$ true when an assignment g assigns them as the value of x. The quantifier then places constraints on that set.

- A closed expression is one that has no free variables; that is, the variables are all bound. A closed sentence is true or false with respect to all variable assignments.

- If two formulas differ only in the label of the variable bound by binding operator (i.e., λ or a quantifier) , they are said to be α-equivalents. The result of relabeling a bound variable in a formula is called α-conversion.

- Given a formula with two nested quantifiers Q_1 and Q_2, the outermost quantifier Q_1 is said to have wide scope (or scope over Q_2). English sentences are frequently ambiguous with respect to the scope of the quantifiers they contain.

- English sentences can be associated with a semantic representation by treating SEM as a feature in a feature-based grammar. The SEM value of a complex expressions, typically involves functional application of the SEM values of the component expressions.

10.7 Further Reading

Consult *http://www.nltk.org/* for further materials on this chapter and on how to install the Prover9 theorem prover and Mace4 model builder. General information about these two inference tools is given by (McCune, 2008).

For more examples of semantic analysis with NLTK, please see the semantics and logic HOWTOs at *http://www.nltk.org/howto*. Note that there are implementations of two other approaches to scope ambiguity, namely **Hole semantics** as described in (Blackburn & Bos, 2005), and **Glue semantics**, as described in (Dalrymple et al., 1999).

There are many phenomena in natural language semantics that have not been touched on in this chapter, most notably:

1. Events, tense, and aspect
2. Semantic roles
3. Generalized quantifiers, such as *most*
4. Intensional constructions involving, for example, verbs such as *may* and *believe*

While (1) and (2) can be dealt with using first-order logic, (3) and (4) require different logics. These issues are covered by many of the references in the following readings.

A comprehensive overview of results and techniques in building natural language front-ends to databases can be found in (Androutsopoulos, Ritchie & Thanisch, 1995).

Any introductory book to modern logic will present propositional and first-order logic. (Hodges, 1977) is highly recommended as an entertaining and insightful text with many illustrations from natural language.

For a wide-ranging, two-volume textbook on logic that also presents contemporary material on the formal semantics of natural language, including Montague Grammar and intensional logic, see (Gamut, 1991a, 1991b). (Kamp & Reyle, 1993) provides the definitive account of Discourse Representation Theory, and covers a large and interesting fragment of natural language, including tense, aspect, and modality. Another comprehensive study of the semantics of many natural language constructions is (Carpenter, 1997).

There are numerous works that introduce logical semantics within the framework of linguistic theory. (Chierchia & McConnell-Ginet, 1990) is relatively agnostic about syntax, while (Heim & Kratzer, 1998) and (Larson & Segal, 1995) are both more explicitly oriented toward integrating truth-conditional semantics into a Chomskyan framework.

(Blackburn & Bos, 2005) is the first textbook devoted to computational semantics, and provides an excellent introduction to the area. It expands on many of the topics covered in this chapter, including underspecification of quantifier scope ambiguity, first-order inference, and discourse processing.

To gain an overview of more advanced contemporary approaches to semantics, including treatments of tense and generalized quantifiers, try consulting (Lappin, 1996) or (van Benthem & ter Meulen, 1997).

10.8 Exercises

1. ○ Translate the following sentences into propositional logic and verify that they parse with `LogicParser`. Provide a key that shows how the propositional variables in your translation correspond to expressions of English.

   a. If Angus sings, it is not the case that Bertie sulks.

   b. Cyril runs and barks.

   c. It will snow if it doesn't rain.

   d. It's not the case that Irene will be happy if Olive or Tofu comes.

   e. Pat didn't cough or sneeze.

   f. If you don't come if I call, I won't come if you call.

2. ○ Translate the following sentences into predicate-argument formulas of first-order logic.

   a. Angus likes Cyril and Irene hates Cyril.

   b. Tofu is taller than Bertie.

   c. Bruce loves himself and Pat does too.

   d. Cyril saw Bertie, but Angus didn't.

   e. Cyril is a four-legged friend.

   f. Tofu and Olive are near each other.

3. ○ Translate the following sentences into quantified formulas of first-order logic.

   a. Angus likes someone and someone likes Julia.

b. Angus loves a dog who loves him.

c. Nobody smiles at Pat.

d. Somebody coughs and sneezes.

e. Nobody coughed or sneezed.

f. Bruce loves somebody other than Bruce.

g. Nobody other than Matthew loves Pat.

h. Cyril likes everyone except for Irene.

i. Exactly one person is asleep.

4. ○ Translate the following verb phrases using λ-abstracts and quantified formulas of first-order logic.

a. feed Cyril and give a capuccino to Angus

b. be given 'War and Peace' by Pat

c. be loved by everyone

d. be loved or detested by everyone

e. be loved by everyone and detested by no-one

5. ○ Consider the following statements:

```
>>> lp = nltk.LogicParser()
>>> e2 = lp.parse('pat')
>>> e3 = nltk.ApplicationExpression(e1, e2)
>>> print e3.simplify()
exists y.love(pat, y)
```

Clearly something is missing here, namely a declaration of the value of e1. In order for ApplicationExpression(e1, e2) to be β-convertible to exists y.love(pat, y), e1 must be a λ-abstract which can take pat as an argument. Your task is to construct such an abstract, bind it to e1, and satisfy yourself that these statements are all satisfied (up to alphabetic variance). In addition, provide an informal English translation of e3.simplify().

Now carry on doing this same task for the further cases of e3.simplify() shown here:

```
>>> print e3.simplify()
exists y.(love(pat,y) | love(y,pat))
```

```
>>> print e3.simplify()
exists y.(love(pat,y) | love(y,pat))
```

```
>>> print e3.simplify()
walk(fido)
```

6. ○ As in the preceding exercise, find a λ-abstract e1 that yields results equivalent to those shown here:

```
>>> e2 = lp.parse('chase')
>>> e3 = nltk.ApplicationExpression(e1, e2)
```

```
>>> print e3.simplify()
\x.all y.(dog(y) -> chase(x,pat))

>>> e2 = lp.parse('chase')
>>> e3 = nltk.ApplicationExpression(e1, e2)
>>> print e3.simplify()
\x.exists y.(dog(y) & chase(pat,x))

>>> e2 = lp.parse('give')
>>> e3 = nltk.ApplicationExpression(e1, e2)
>>> print e3.simplify()
\x0 x1.exists y.(present(y) & give(x1,y,x0))
```

7. ○ As in the preceding exercise, find a λ-abstract e1 that yields results equivalent to those shown here:

```
>>> e2 = lp.parse('bark')
>>> e3 = nltk.ApplicationExpression(e1, e2)
>>> print e3.simplify()
exists y.(dog(x) & bark(x))

>>> e2 = lp.parse('bark')
>>> e3 = nltk.ApplicationExpression(e1, e2)
>>> print e3.simplify()
bark(fido)

>>> e2 = lp.parse('\\P. all x. (dog(x) -> P(x))')
>>> e3 = nltk.ApplicationExpression(e1, e2)
>>> print e3.simplify()
all x.(dog(x) -> bark(x))
```

8. ◑ Develop a method for translating English sentences into formulas with binary **generalized quantifiers**. In such an approach, given a generalized quantifier Q, a quantified formula is of the form Q(A, B), where both A and B are expressions of type $\langle e, t \rangle$. Then, for example, all(A, B) is true iff A denotes a subset of what B denotes.

9. ◑ Extend the approach in the preceding exercise so that the truth conditions for quantifiers such as *most* and *exactly three* can be computed in a model.

10. ◑ Modify the sem.evaluate code so that it will give a helpful error message if an expression is not in the domain of a model's valuation function.

11. ● Select three or four contiguous sentences from a book for children. A possible source of examples are the collections of stories in nltk.corpus.gutenberg: bryant-stories.txt, burgess-busterbrown.txt, and edgeworth-parents.txt. Develop a grammar that will allow your sentences to be translated into first-order logic, and build a model that will allow those translations to be checked for truth or falsity.

12. ● Carry out the preceding exercise, but use DRT as the meaning representation.

13. ● Taking (Warren & Pereira, 1982) as a starting point, develop a technique for converting a natural language query into a form that can be evaluated more efficiently in a model. For example, given a query of the form (P(x) & Q(x)), convert it to (Q(x) & P(x)) if the extension of Q is smaller than the extension of P.

## CHAPTER 11

Managing Linguistic Data

Structured collections of annotated linguistic data are essential in most areas of NLP; however, we still face many obstacles in using them. The goal of this chapter is to answer the following questions:

1. How do we design a new language resource and ensure that its coverage, balance, and documentation support a wide range of uses?

2. When existing data is in the wrong format for some analysis tool, how can we convert it to a suitable format?

3. What is a good way to document the existence of a resource we have created so that others can easily find it?

Along the way, we will study the design of existing corpora, the typical workflow for creating a corpus, and the life cycle of a corpus. As in other chapters, there will be many examples drawn from practical experience managing linguistic data, including data that has been collected in the course of linguistic fieldwork, laboratory work, and web crawling.

11.1 Corpus Structure: A Case Study

The TIMIT Corpus was the first annotated speech database to be widely distributed, and it has an especially clear organization. TIMIT was developed by a consortium including Texas Instruments and MIT, from which it derives its name. It was designed to provide data for the acquisition of acoustic-phonetic knowledge and to support the development and evaluation of automatic speech recognition systems.

The Structure of TIMIT

Like the Brown Corpus, which displays a balanced selection of text genres and sources, TIMIT includes a balanced selection of dialects, speakers, and materials. For each of eight dialect regions, 50 male and female speakers having a range of ages and educational backgrounds each read 10 carefully chosen sentences. Two sentences, read by all speakers, were designed to bring out dialect variation:

(1)   a. she had your dark suit in greasy wash water all year

       b. don't ask me to carry an oily rag like that

The remaining sentences were chosen to be phonetically rich, involving all phones (sounds) and a comprehensive range of diphones (phone bigrams). Additionally, the design strikes a balance between multiple speakers saying the same sentence in order to permit comparison across speakers, and having a large range of sentences covered by the corpus to get maximal coverage of diphones. Five of the sentences read by each speaker are also read by six other speakers (for comparability). The remaining three sentences read by each speaker were unique to that speaker (for coverage).

NLTK includes a sample from the TIMIT Corpus. You can access its documentation in the usual way, using help(nltk.corpus.timit). Print nltk.corpus.timit.fileids() to see a list of the 160 recorded utterances in the corpus sample. Each filename has internal structure, as shown in Figure 11-1.

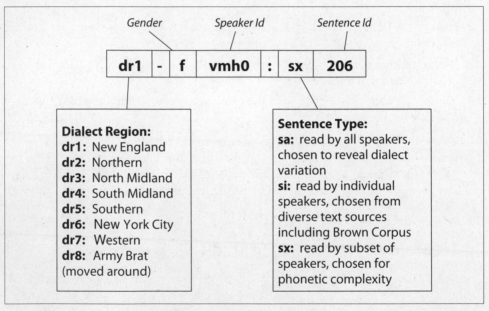

Figure 11-1. Structure of a TIMIT identifier: Each recording is labeled using a string made up of the speaker's dialect region, gender, speaker identifier, sentence type, and sentence identifier.

Each item has a phonetic transcription which can be accessed using the phones() method. We can access the corresponding word tokens in the customary way. Both access methods permit an optional argument offset=True, which includes the start and end offsets of the corresponding span in the audio file.

```
>>> phonetic = nltk.corpus.timit.phones('dr1-fvmh0/sa1')
>>> phonetic
['h#', 'sh', 'iy', 'hv', 'ae', 'dcl', 'y', 'ix', 'dcl', 'd', 'aa', 'kcl',
```

```
   's', 'ux', 'tcl', 'en', 'gcl', 'g', 'r', 'iy', 's', 'iy', 'w', 'aa',
   'sh', 'epi', 'w', 'aa', 'dx', 'ax', 'q', 'ao', 'l', 'y', 'ih', 'ax', 'h#']
>>> nltk.corpus.timit.word_times('dr1-fvmh0/sa1')
[('she', 7812, 10610), ('had', 10610, 14496), ('your', 14496, 15791),
('dark', 15791, 20720), ('suit', 20720, 25647), ('in', 25647, 26906),
('greasy', 26906, 32668), ('wash', 32668, 37890), ('water', 38531, 42417),
('all', 43091, 46052), ('year', 46052, 50522)]
```

In addition to this text data, TIMIT includes a lexicon that provides the canonical pronunciation of every word, which can be compared with a particular utterance:

```
>>> timitdict = nltk.corpus.timit.transcription_dict()
>>> timitdict['greasy'] + timitdict['wash'] + timitdict['water']
['g', 'r', 'iy1', 's', 'iy', 'w', 'ao1', 'sh', 'w', 'ao1', 't', 'axr']
>>> phonetic[17:30]
['g', 'r', 'iy', 's', 'iy', 'w', 'aa', 'sh', 'epi', 'w', 'aa', 'dx', 'ax']
```

This gives us a sense of what a speech processing system would have to do in producing or recognizing speech in this particular dialect (New England). Finally, TIMIT includes demographic data about the speakers, permitting fine-grained study of vocal, social, and gender characteristics.

```
>>> nltk.corpus.timit.spkrinfo('dr1-fvmh0')
SpeakerInfo(id='VMH0', sex='F', dr='1', use='TRN', recdate='03/11/86',
birthdate='01/08/60', ht='5\'05"', race='WHT', edu='BS',
comments='BEST NEW ENGLAND ACCENT SO FAR')
```

Notable Design Features

TIMIT illustrates several key features of corpus design. First, the corpus contains two layers of annotation, at the phonetic and orthographic levels. In general, a text or speech corpus may be annotated at many different linguistic levels, including morphological, syntactic, and discourse levels. Moreover, even at a given level there may be different labeling schemes or even disagreement among annotators, such that we want to represent multiple versions. A second property of TIMIT is its balance across multiple dimensions of variation, for coverage of dialect regions and diphones. The inclusion of speaker demographics brings in many more independent variables that may help to account for variation in the data, and which facilitate later uses of the corpus for purposes that were not envisaged when the corpus was created, such as sociolinguistics. A third property is that there is a sharp division between the original linguistic event captured as an audio recording and the annotations of that event. The same holds true of text corpora, in the sense that the original text usually has an external source, and is considered to be an immutable artifact. Any transformations of that artifact which involve human judgment—even something as simple as tokenization—are subject to later revision; thus it is important to retain the source material in a form that is as close to the original as possible.

A fourth feature of TIMIT is the hierarchical structure of the corpus. With 4 files per sentence, and 10 sentences for each of 500 speakers, there are 20,000 files. These are organized into a tree structure, shown schematically in Figure 11-2. At the top level

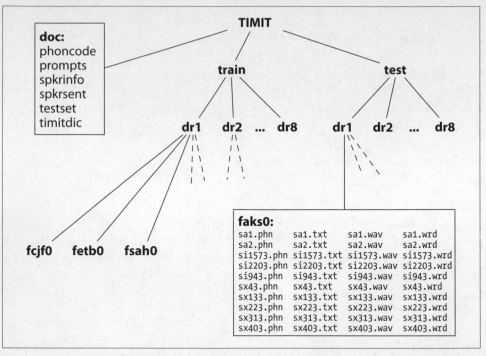

Figure 11-2. Structure of the published TIMIT Corpus: The CD-ROM contains doc, train, *and* test *directories at the top level; the* train *and* test *directories both have eight sub-directories, one per dialect region; each of these contains further subdirectories, one per speaker; the contents of the directory for female speaker aks0 are listed, showing 10* wav *files accompanied by a text transcription, a word-aligned transcription, and a phonetic transcription.*

there is a split between training and testing sets, which gives away its intended use for developing and evaluating statistical models.

Finally, notice that even though TIMIT is a speech corpus, its transcriptions and associated data are just text, and can be processed using programs just like any other text corpus. Therefore, many of the computational methods described in this book are applicable. Moreover, notice that all of the data types included in the TIMIT Corpus fall into the two basic categories of lexicon and text, which we will discuss later. Even the speaker demographics data is just another instance of the lexicon data type.

This last observation is less surprising when we consider that text and record structures are the primary domains for the two subfields of computer science that focus on data management, namely text retrieval and databases. A notable feature of linguistic data management is that it usually brings both data types together, and that it can draw on results and techniques from both fields.

Fundamental Data Types

Despite its complexity, the TIMIT Corpus contains only two fundamental data types, namely lexicons and texts. As we saw in Chapter 2, most lexical resources can be represented using a record structure, i.e., a key plus one or more fields, as shown in Figure 11-3. A lexical resource could be a conventional dictionary or comparative wordlist, as illustrated. It could also be a phrasal lexicon, where the key field is a phrase rather than a single word. A thesaurus also consists of record-structured data, where we look up entries via non-key fields that correspond to topics. We can also construct special tabulations (known as paradigms) to illustrate contrasts and systematic variation, as shown in Figure 11-3 for three verbs. TIMIT's speaker table is also a kind of lexicon.

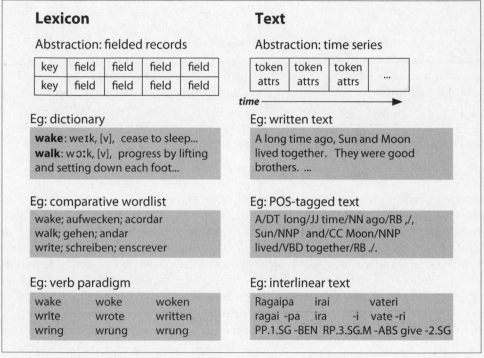

Figure 11-3. Basic linguistic data types—lexicons and texts: Amid their diversity, lexicons have a record structure, whereas annotated texts have a temporal organization.

At the most abstract level, a text is a representation of a real or fictional speech event, and the time-course of that event carries over into the text itself. A text could be a small unit, such as a word or sentence, or a complete narrative or dialogue. It may come with annotations such as part-of-speech tags, morphological analysis, discourse structure, and so forth. As we saw in the IOB tagging technique (Chapter 7), it is possible to represent higher-level constituents using tags on individual words. Thus the abstraction of text shown in Figure 11-3 is sufficient.

Despite the complexities and idiosyncrasies of individual corpora, at base they are collections of texts together with record-structured data. The contents of a corpus are often biased toward one or the other of these types. For example, the Brown Corpus contains 500 text files, but we still use a table to relate the files to 15 different genres. At the other end of the spectrum, WordNet contains 117,659 synset records, yet it incorporates many example sentences (mini-texts) to illustrate word usages. TIMIT is an interesting midpoint on this spectrum, containing substantial free-standing material of both the text and lexicon types.

11.2 The Life Cycle of a Corpus

Corpora are not born fully formed, but involve careful preparation and input from many people over an extended period. Raw data needs to be collected, cleaned up, documented, and stored in a systematic structure. Various layers of annotation might be applied, some requiring specialized knowledge of the morphology or syntax of the language. Success at this stage depends on creating an efficient workflow involving appropriate tools and format converters. Quality control procedures can be put in place to find inconsistencies in the annotations, and to ensure the highest possible level of inter-annotator agreement. Because of the scale and complexity of the task, large corpora may take years to prepare, and involve tens or hundreds of person-years of effort. In this section, we briefly review the various stages in the life cycle of a corpus.

Three Corpus Creation Scenarios

In one type of corpus, the design unfolds over in the course of the creator's explorations. This is the pattern typical of traditional "field linguistics," in which material from elicitation sessions is analyzed as it is gathered, with tomorrow's elicitation often based on questions that arise in analyzing today's. The resulting corpus is then used during subsequent years of research, and may serve as an archival resource indefinitely. Computerization is an obvious boon to work of this type, as exemplified by the popular program Shoebox, now over two decades old and re-released as Toolbox (see Section 2.4). Other software tools, even simple word processors and spreadsheets, are routinely used to acquire the data. In the next section, we will look at how to extract data from these sources.

Another corpus creation scenario is typical of experimental research where a body of carefully designed material is collected from a range of human subjects, then analyzed to evaluate a hypothesis or develop a technology. It has become common for such databases to be shared and reused within a laboratory or company, and often to be published more widely. Corpora of this type are the basis of the "common task" method of research management, which over the past two decades has become the norm in government-funded research programs in language technology. We have already encountered many such corpora in the earlier chapters; we will see how to write Python programs to implement the kinds of curation tasks that are necessary before such corpora are published.

Finally, there are efforts to gather a "reference corpus" for a particular language, such as the *American National Corpus* (ANC) and the *British National Corpus* (BNC). Here the goal has been to produce a comprehensive record of the many forms, styles, and uses of a language. Apart from the sheer challenge of scale, there is a heavy reliance on automatic annotation tools together with post-editing to fix any errors. However, we can write programs to locate and repair the errors, and also to analyze the corpus for balance.

Quality Control

Good tools for automatic and manual preparation of data are essential. However, the creation of a high-quality corpus depends just as much on such mundane things as documentation, training, and workflow. Annotation guidelines define the task and document the markup conventions. They may be regularly updated to cover difficult cases, along with new rules that are devised to achieve more consistent annotations. Annotators need to be trained in the procedures, including methods for resolving cases not covered in the guidelines. A workflow needs to be established, possibly with supporting software, to keep track of which files have been initialized, annotated, validated, manually checked, and so on. There may be multiple layers of annotation, provided by different specialists. Cases of uncertainty or disagreement may require adjudication.

Large annotation tasks require multiple annotators, which raises the problem of achieving consistency. How consistently can a group of annotators perform? We can easily measure consistency by having a portion of the source material independently annotated by two people. This may reveal shortcomings in the guidelines or differing abilities with the annotation task. In cases where quality is paramount, the entire corpus can be annotated twice, and any inconsistencies adjudicated by an expert.

It is considered best practice to report the inter-annotator agreement that was achieved for a corpus (e.g., by double-annotating 10% of the corpus). This score serves as a helpful upper bound on the expected performance of any automatic system that is trained on this corpus.

 Caution!

Care should be exercised when interpreting an inter-annotator agreement score, since annotation tasks vary greatly in their difficulty. For example, 90% agreement would be a terrible score for part-of-speech tagging, but an exceptional score for semantic role labeling.

The **Kappa** coefficient κ measures agreement between two people making category judgments, correcting for expected chance agreement. For example, suppose an item is to be annotated, and four coding options are equally likely. In this case, two people coding randomly would be expected to agree 25% of the time. Thus, an agreement of

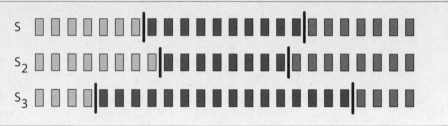

Figure 11-4. Three segmentations of a sequence: The small rectangles represent characters, words, sentences, in short, any sequence which might be divided into linguistic units; S_1 and S_2 are in close agreement, but both differ significantly from S_3.

25% will be assigned κ = 0, and better levels of agreement will be scaled accordingly. For an agreement of 50%, we would get κ = 0.333, as 50 is a third of the way from 25 to 100. Many other agreement measures exist; see `help(nltk.metrics.agreement)` for details.

We can also measure the agreement between two independent segmentations of language input, e.g., for tokenization, sentence segmentation, and named entity recognition. In Figure 11-4 we see three possible segmentations of a sequence of items which might have been produced by annotators (or programs). Although none of them agree exactly, S_1 and S_2 are in close agreement, and we would like a suitable measure. Windowdiff is a simple algorithm for evaluating the agreement of two segmentations by running a sliding window over the data and awarding partial credit for near misses. If we preprocess our tokens into a sequence of zeros and ones, to record when a token is followed by a boundary, we can represent the segmentations as strings and apply the `windowdiff` scorer.

```
>>> s1 = "00000010000000001000000"
>>> s2 = "00000001000000010000000"
>>> s3 = "00010000000000000001000"
>>> nltk.windowdiff(s1, s1, 3)
0
>>> nltk.windowdiff(s1, s2, 3)
4
>>> nltk.windowdiff(s2, s3, 3)
16
```

In this example, the window had a size of 3. The `windowdiff` computation slides this window across a pair of strings. At each position it totals up the number of boundaries found inside this window, for both strings, then computes the difference. These differences are then summed. We can increase or shrink the window size to control the sensitivity of the measure.

Curation Versus Evolution

As large corpora are published, researchers are increasingly likely to base their investigations on balanced, focused subsets that were derived from corpora produced for entirely different reasons. For instance, the Switchboard database, originally collected for speaker identification research, has since been used as the basis for published studies in speech recognition, word pronunciation, disfluency, syntax, intonation, and discourse structure. The motivations for recycling linguistic corpora include the desire to save time and effort, the desire to work on material available to others for replication, and sometimes a desire to study more naturalistic forms of linguistic behavior than would be possible otherwise. The process of choosing a subset for such a study may count as a non-trivial contribution in itself.

In addition to selecting an appropriate subset of a corpus, this new work could involve reformatting a text file (e.g., converting to XML), renaming files, retokenizing the text, selecting a subset of the data to enrich, and so forth. Multiple research groups might do this work independently, as illustrated in Figure 11-5. At a later date, should someone want to combine sources of information from different versions, the task will probably be extremely onerous.

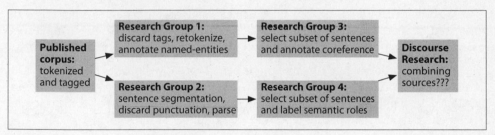

Figure 11-5. Evolution of a corpus over time: After a corpus is published, research groups will use it independently, selecting and enriching different pieces; later research that seeks to integrate separate annotations confronts the difficult challenge of aligning the annotations.

The task of using derived corpora is made even more difficult by the lack of any record about how the derived version was created, and which version is the most up-to-date.

An alternative to this chaotic situation is for a corpus to be centrally curated, and for committees of experts to revise and extend it at periodic intervals, considering submissions from third parties and publishing new releases from time to time. Print dictionaries and national corpora may be centrally curated in this way. However, for most corpora this model is simply impractical.

A middle course is for the original corpus publication to have a scheme for identifying any sub-part. Each sentence, tree, or lexical entry could have a globally unique identifier, and each token, node, or field (respectively) could have a relative offset. Annotations, including segmentations, could reference the source using this identifier scheme (a method which is known as **standoff annotation**). This way, new annotations could be distributed independently of the source, and multiple independent annotations of the same source could be compared and updated without touching the source.

If the corpus publication is provided in multiple versions, the version number or date could be part of the identification scheme. A table of correspondences between identifiers across editions of the corpus would permit any standoff annotations to be updated easily.

Caution!

Sometimes an updated corpus contains revisions of base material that has been externally annotated. Tokens might be split or merged, and constituents may have been rearranged. There may not be a one-to-one correspondence between old and new identifiers. It is better to cause standoff annotations to break on such components of the new version than to silently allow their identifiers to refer to incorrect locations.

11.3 Acquiring Data

Obtaining Data from the Web

The Web is a rich source of data for language analysis purposes. We have already discussed methods for accessing individual files, RSS feeds, and search engine results (see Section 3.1). However, in some cases we want to obtain large quantities of web text.

The simplest approach is to obtain a published corpus of web text. The ACL Special Interest Group on Web as Corpus (SIGWAC) maintains a list of resources at *http:// www.sigwac.org.uk/*. The advantage of using a well-defined web corpus is that they are documented, stable, and permit reproducible experimentation.

If the desired content is localized to a particular website, there are many utilities for capturing all the accessible contents of a site, such as GNU Wget (*http://www.gnu.org/ software/wget/*). For maximal flexibility and control, a web crawler can be used, such as Heritrix (*http://crawler.archive.org/*). Crawlers permit fine-grained control over where to look, which links to follow, and how to organize the results. For example, if we want to compile a bilingual text collection having corresponding pairs of documents in each language, the crawler needs to detect the structure of the site in order to extract the correspondence between the documents, and it needs to organize the downloaded pages in such a way that the correspondence is captured. It might be tempting to write your own web crawler, but there are dozens of pitfalls having to do with detecting MIME types, converting relative to absolute URLs, avoiding getting trapped in cyclic link structures, dealing with network latencies, avoiding overloading the site or being banned from accessing the site, and so on.

Obtaining Data from Word Processor Files

Word processing software is often used in the manual preparation of texts and lexicons in projects that have limited computational infrastructure. Such projects often provide templates for data entry, though the word processing software does not ensure that the data is correctly structured. For example, each text may be required to have a title and date. Similarly, each lexical entry may have certain obligatory fields. As the data grows in size and complexity, a larger proportion of time may be spent maintaining its consistency.

How can we extract the content of such files so that we can manipulate it in external programs? Moreover, how can we validate the content of these files to help authors create well-structured data, so that the quality of the data can be maximized in the context of the original authoring process?

Consider a dictionary in which each entry has a part-of-speech field, drawn from a set of 20 possibilities, displayed after the pronunciation field, and rendered in 11-point bold type. No conventional word processor has search or macro functions capable of verifying that all part-of-speech fields have been correctly entered and displayed. This task requires exhaustive manual checking. If the word processor permits the document to be saved in a non-proprietary format, such as text, HTML, or XML, we can sometimes write programs to do this checking automatically.

Consider the following fragment of a lexical entry: "sleep [sli:p] **v.i.** *condition of body and mind...*". We can key in such text using MSWord, then "Save as Web Page," then inspect the resulting HTML file:

```
<p class=MsoNormal>sleep
  <span style='mso-spacerun:yes'> </span>
  [<span class=SpellE>sli:p</span>]
  <span style='mso-spacerun:yes'> </span>
  <b><span style='font-size:11.0pt'>v.i.</span></b>
  <span style='mso-spacerun:yes'> </span>
  <i>a condition of body and mind ...<o:p></o:p></i>
</p>
```

Observe that the entry is represented as an HTML paragraph, using the `<p>` element, and that the part of speech appears inside a `<span style='font-size:11.0pt'>` element. The following program defines the set of legal parts-of-speech, `legal_pos`. Then it extracts all 11-point content from the *dict.htm* file and stores it in the set `used_pos`. Observe that the search pattern contains a parenthesized sub-expression; only the material that matches this subexpression is returned by `re.findall`. Finally, the program constructs the set of illegal parts-of-speech as the set difference between `used_pos` and `legal_pos`:

```
>>> legal_pos = set(['n', 'v.t.', 'v.i.', 'adj', 'det'])
>>> pattern = re.compile(r"'font-size:11.0pt'>([a-z.]+)<")
>>> document = open("dict.htm").read()
>>> used_pos = set(re.findall(pattern, document))
>>> illegal_pos = used_pos.difference(legal_pos)
>>> print list(illegal_pos)
['v.i', 'intrans']
```

This simple program represents the tip of the iceberg. We can develop sophisticated tools to check the consistency of word processor files, and report errors so that the maintainer of the dictionary can correct the original file *using the original word processor*.

Once we know the data is correctly formatted, we can write other programs to convert the data into a different format. The program in Example 11-1 strips out the HTML markup using `nltk.clean_html()`, extracts the words and their pronunciations, and generates output in "comma-separated value" (CSV) format.

Example 11-1. Converting HTML created by Microsoft Word into comma-separated values.

```
def lexical_data(html_file):
    SEP = '_ENTRY'
    html = open(html_file).read()
    html = re.sub(r'<p', SEP + '<p', html)
    text = nltk.clean_html(html)
    text = ' '.join(text.split())
    for entry in text.split(SEP):
        if entry.count(' ') > 2:
            yield entry.split(' ', 3)

>>> import csv
>>> writer = csv.writer(open("dict1.csv", "wb"))
>>> writer.writerows(lexical_data("dict.htm"))
```

Obtaining Data from Spreadsheets and Databases

Spreadsheets are often used for acquiring wordlists or paradigms. For example, a comparative wordlist may be created using a spreadsheet, with a row for each cognate set and a column for each language (see `nltk.corpus.swadesh` and `www.rosettapro ject.org`). Most spreadsheet software can export their data in CSV format. As we will see later, it is easy for Python programs to access these using the `csv` module.

Sometimes lexicons are stored in a full-fledged relational database. When properly normalized, these databases can ensure the validity of the data. For example, we can require that all parts-of-speech come from a specified vocabulary by declaring that the part-of-speech field is an *enumerated type* or a foreign key that references a separate part-of-speech table. However, the relational model requires the structure of the data (the schema) be declared in advance, and this runs counter to the dominant approach to structuring linguistic data, which is highly exploratory. Fields which were assumed to be obligatory and unique often turn out to be optional and repeatable. A relational database can accommodate this when it is fully known in advance; however, if it is not, or if just about every property turns out to be optional or repeatable, the relational approach is unworkable.

Nevertheless, when our goal is simply to extract the contents from a database, it is enough to dump out the tables (or SQL query results) in CSV format and load them into our program. Our program might perform a linguistically motivated query that cannot easily be expressed in SQL, e.g., *select all words that appear in example sentences for which no dictionary entry is provided.* For this task, we would need to extract enough information from a record for it to be uniquely identified, along with the headwords and example sentences. Let's suppose this information was now available in a CSV file *dict.csv*:

```
"sleep","sli:p","v.i","a condition of body and mind ..."
"walk","wo:k","v.intr","progress by lifting and setting down each foot ..."
"wake","weik","intrans","cease to sleep"
```

Now we can express this query as shown here:

```
>>> import csv
>>> lexicon = csv.reader(open('dict.csv'))
>>> pairs = [(lexeme, defn) for (lexeme, _, _, defn) in lexicon]
>>> lexemes, defns = zip(*pairs)
>>> defn_words = set(w for defn in defns for w in defn.split())
>>> sorted(defn_words.difference(lexemes))
['...', 'a', 'and', 'body', 'by', 'cease', 'condition', 'down', 'each',
'foot', 'lifting', 'mind', 'of', 'progress', 'setting', 'to']
```

This information would then guide the ongoing work to enrich the lexicon, work that updates the content of the relational database.

Converting Data Formats

Annotated linguistic data rarely arrives in the most convenient format, and it is often necessary to perform various kinds of format conversion. Converting between character encodings has already been discussed (see Section 3.3). Here we focus on the structure of the data.

In the simplest case, the input and output formats are isomorphic. For instance, we might be converting lexical data from Toolbox format to XML, and it is straightforward to transliterate the entries one at a time (Section 11.4). The structure of the data is reflected in the structure of the required program: a `for` loop whose body takes care of a single entry.

In another common case, the output is a digested form of the input, such as an inverted file index. Here it is necessary to build an index structure in memory (see Example 4.8), then write it to a file in the desired format. The following example constructs an index that maps the words of a dictionary definition to the corresponding lexeme ❶ for each lexical entry ❷, having tokenized the definition text ❸, and discarded short words ❹. Once the index has been constructed, we open a file and then iterate over the index entries, to write out the lines in the required format ❺.

```
>>> idx = nltk.Index((defn_word, lexeme) ❶
...                   for (lexeme, defn) in pairs ❷
...                   for defn_word in nltk.word_tokenize(defn) ❸
...                   if len(defn_word) > 3) ❹
>>> idx_file = open("dict.idx", "w")
>>> for word in sorted(idx):
...     idx_words = ', '.join(idx[word])
...     idx_line = "%s: %s\n" % (word, idx_words) ❺
...     idx_file.write(idx_line)
>>> idx_file.close()
```

The resulting file *dict.idx* contains the following lines. (With a larger dictionary, we would expect to find multiple lexemes listed for each index entry.)

```
body: sleep
cease: wake
condition: sleep
down: walk
each: walk
foot: walk
lifting: walk
mind: sleep
progress: walk
setting: walk
sleep: wake
```

In some cases, the input and output data both consist of two or more dimensions. For instance, the input might be a set of files, each containing a single column of word frequency data. The required output might be a two-dimensional table in which the original columns appear as rows. In such cases we populate an internal data structure by filling up one column at a time, then read off the data one row at a time as we write data to the output file.

In the most vexing cases, the source and target formats have slightly different coverage of the domain, and information is unavoidably lost when translating between them. For example, we could combine multiple Toolbox files to create a single CSV file containing a comparative wordlist, losing all but the \lx field of the input files. If the CSV file was later modified, it would be a labor-intensive process to inject the changes into the original Toolbox files. A partial solution to this "round-tripping" problem is to associate explicit identifiers with each linguistic object, and to propagate the identifiers with the objects.

Deciding Which Layers of Annotation to Include

Published corpora vary greatly in the richness of the information they contain. At a minimum, a corpus will typically contain at least a sequence of sound or orthographic symbols. At the other end of the spectrum, a corpus could contain a large amount of information about the syntactic structure, morphology, prosody, and semantic content of every sentence, plus annotation of discourse relations or dialogue acts. These extra layers of annotation may be just what someone needs for performing a particular data analysis task. For example, it may be much easier to find a given linguistic pattern if we can search for specific syntactic structures; and it may be easier to categorize a linguistic pattern if every word has been tagged with its sense. Here are some commonly provided annotation layers:

Word tokenization
> The orthographic form of text does not unambiguously identify its tokens. A tokenized and normalized version, in addition to the conventional orthographic version, may be a very convenient resource.

Sentence segmentation
> As we saw in Chapter 3, sentence segmentation can be more difficult than it seems. Some corpora therefore use explicit annotations to mark sentence segmentation.

Paragraph segmentation
> Paragraphs and other structural elements (headings, chapters, etc.) may be explicitly annotated.

Part-of-speech
> The syntactic category of each word in a document.

Syntactic structure
> A tree structure showing the constituent structure of a sentence.

Shallow semantics
> Named entity and coreference annotations, and semantic role labels.

Dialogue and discourse
> Dialogue act tags and rhetorical structure.

Unfortunately, there is not much consistency between existing corpora in how they represent their annotations. However, two general classes of annotation representation should be distinguished. **Inline annotation** modifies the original document by inserting special symbols or control sequences that carry the annotated information. For example, when part-of-speech tagging a document, the string `"fly"` might be replaced with the string `"fly/NN"`, to indicate that the word *fly* is a noun in this context. In contrast, **standoff annotation** does not modify the original document, but instead creates a new file that adds annotation information using pointers that reference the original document. For example, this new document might contain the string `"<token id=8 pos='NN'/>"`, to indicate that token 8 is a noun.

Standards and Tools

For a corpus to be widely useful, it needs to be available in a widely supported format. However, the cutting edge of NLP research depends on new kinds of annotations, which by definition are not widely supported. In general, adequate tools for creation, publication, and use of linguistic data are not widely available. Most projects must develop their own set of tools for internal use, which is no help to others who lack the necessary resources. Furthermore, we do not have adequate, generally accepted standards for expressing the structure and content of corpora. Without such standards, general-purpose tools are impossible—though at the same time, without available tools, adequate standards are unlikely to be developed, used, and accepted.

One response to this situation has been to forge ahead with developing a generic format that is sufficiently expressive to capture a wide variety of annotation types (see Section 11.8 for examples). The challenge for NLP is to write programs that cope with the generality of such formats. For example, if the programming task involves tree data, and the file format permits arbitrary directed graphs, then input data must be validated to check for tree properties such as rootedness, connectedness, and acyclicity. If the input files contain other layers of annotation, the program would need to know how to ignore them when the data was loaded, but not invalidate or obliterate those layers when the tree data was saved back to the file.

Another response has been to write one-off scripts to manipulate corpus formats; such scripts litter the filespaces of many NLP researchers. NLTK's corpus readers are a more systematic approach, founded on the premise that the work of parsing a corpus format should be done only once (per programming language).

Instead of focusing on a common format, we believe it is more promising to develop a common interface (see `nltk.corpus`). Consider the case of treebanks, an important corpus type for work in NLP. There are many ways to store a phrase structure tree in a file. We can use nested parentheses, or nested XML elements, or a dependency notation with a (*child-id, parent-id*) pair on each line, or an XML version of the dependency notation, etc. However, in each case the logical structure is almost the same. It is much easier to devise a common interface that allows application programmers to write code to access tree data using methods such as `children()`, `leaves()`, `depth()`, and so forth. Note that this approach follows accepted practice within computer science, viz. abstract data types, object-oriented design, and the three-layer architecture (Figure 11-6). The last of these—from the world of relational databases—allows end-user applications to use a common model (the "relational model") and a common language (SQL) to abstract away from the idiosyncrasies of file storage. It also allows innovations in filesystem technologies to occur without disturbing end-user applications. In the same way, a common corpus interface insulates application programs from data formats.

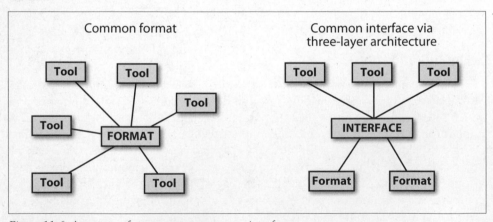

Figure 11-6. A common format versus a common interface.

In this context, when creating a new corpus for dissemination, it is expedient to use a widely used format wherever possible. When this is not possible, the corpus could be accompanied with software—such as an `nltk.corpus` module—that supports existing interface methods.

Special Considerations When Working with Endangered Languages

The importance of language to science and the arts is matched in significance by the cultural treasure embodied in language. Each of the world's ~7,000 human languages is rich in unique respects, in its oral histories and creation legends, down to its grammatical constructions and its very words and their nuances of meaning. Threatened remnant cultures have words to distinguish plant subspecies according to therapeutic uses that are unknown to science. Languages evolve over time as they come into contact with each other, and each one provides a unique window onto human pre-history. In many parts of the world, small linguistic variations from one town to the next add up to a completely different language in the space of a half-hour drive. For its breathtaking complexity and diversity, human language is as a colorful tapestry stretching through time and space.

However, most of the world's languages face extinction. In response to this, many linguists are hard at work documenting the languages, constructing rich records of this important facet of the world's linguistic heritage. What can the field of NLP offer to help with this effort? Developing taggers, parsers, named entity recognizers, etc., is not an early priority, and there is usually insufficient data for developing such tools in any case. Instead, the most frequently voiced need is to have better tools for collecting and curating data, with a focus on texts and lexicons.

On the face of things, it should be a straightforward matter to start collecting texts in an endangered language. Even if we ignore vexed issues such as who owns the texts, and sensitivities surrounding cultural knowledge contained in the texts, there is the obvious practical issue of transcription. Most languages lack a standard orthography. When a language has no literary tradition, the conventions of spelling and punctuation are not well established. Therefore it is common practice to create a lexicon in tandem with a text collection, continually updating the lexicon as new words appear in the texts. This work could be done using a text processor (for the texts) and a spreadsheet (for the lexicon). Better still, SIL's free linguistic software Toolbox and Fieldworks provide sophisticated support for integrated creation of texts and lexicons.

When speakers of the language in question are trained to enter texts themselves, a common obstacle is an overriding concern for correct spelling. Having a lexicon greatly helps this process, but we need to have lookup methods that do not assume someone can determine the citation form of an arbitrary word. The problem may be acute for languages having a complex morphology that includes prefixes. In such cases it helps to tag lexical items with semantic domains, and to permit lookup by semantic domain or by gloss.

Permitting lookup by pronunciation similarity is also a big help. Here's a simple demonstration of how to do this. The first step is to identify confusible letter sequences, and map complex versions to simpler versions. We might also notice that the relative order of letters within a cluster of consonants is a source of spelling errors, and so we normalize the order of consonants.

```
>>> mappings = [('ph', 'f'), ('ght', 't'), ('^kn', 'n'), ('qu', 'kw'),
...            ('[aeiou]+', 'a'), (r'(.)\1', r'\1')]
>>> def signature(word):
...     for patt, repl in mappings:
...         word = re.sub(patt, repl, word)
...     pieces = re.findall('[^aeiou]+', word)
...     return ''.join(char for piece in pieces for char in sorted(piece))[:8]
>>> signature('illefent')
'lfnt'
>>> signature('ebsekwieous')
'bskws'
>>> signature('nuculerr')
'nclr'
```

Next, we create a mapping from signatures to words, for all the words in our lexicon. We can use this to get candidate corrections for a given input word (but we must first compute that word's signature).

```
>>> signatures = nltk.Index((signature(w), w) for w in nltk.corpus.words.words())
>>> signatures[signature('nuculerr')]
['anicular', 'inocular', 'nucellar', 'nuclear', 'unicolor', 'uniocular', 'unocular']
```

Finally, we should rank the results in terms of similarity with the original word. This is done by the function rank(). The only remaining function provides a simple interface to the user:

```
>>> def rank(word, wordlist):
...     ranked = sorted((nltk.edit_dist(word, w), w) for w in wordlist)
...     return [word for (_, word) in ranked]
>>> def fuzzy_spell(word):
...     sig = signature(word)
...     if sig in signatures:
...         return rank(word, signatures[sig])
...     else:
...         return []
>>> fuzzy_spell('illefent')
['olefiant', 'elephant', 'oliphant', 'elephanta']
>>> fuzzy_spell('ebsekwieous')
['obsequious']
>>> fuzzy_spell('nucular')
['nuclear', 'nucellar', 'anicular', 'inocular', 'unocular', 'unicolor', 'uniocular']
```

This is just one illustration where a simple program can facilitate access to lexical data in a context where the writing system of a language may not be standardized, or where users of the language may not have a good command of spellings. Other simple applications of NLP in this area include building indexes to facilitate access to data, gleaning wordlists from texts, locating examples of word usage in constructing a lexicon, detecting prevalent or exceptional patterns in poorly understood data, and performing specialized validation on data created using various linguistic software tools. We will return to the last of these in Section 11.5.

11.4 Working with XML

The Extensible Markup Language (XML) provides a framework for designing domain-specific markup languages. It is sometimes used for representing annotated text and for lexical resources. Unlike HTML with its predefined tags, XML permits us to make up our own tags. Unlike a database, XML permits us to create data without first specifying its structure, and it permits us to have optional and repeatable elements. In this section, we briefly review some features of XML that are relevant for representing linguistic data, and show how to access data stored in XML files using Python programs.

Using XML for Linguistic Structures

Thanks to its flexibility and extensibility, XML is a natural choice for representing linguistic structures. Here's an example of a simple lexical entry.

```
(2) <entry>
      <headword>whale</headword>
      <pos>noun</pos>
      <gloss>any of the larger cetacean mammals having a streamlined
        body and breathing through a blowhole on the head</gloss>
    </entry>
```

It consists of a series of XML tags enclosed in angle brackets. Each opening tag, such as `<gloss>`, is matched with a closing tag, `</gloss>`; together they constitute an **XML element**. The preceding example has been laid out nicely using whitespace, but it could equally have been put on a single long line. Our approach to processing XML will usually not be sensitive to whitespace. In order for XML to be **well formed**, all opening tags must have corresponding closing tags, at the same level of nesting (i.e., the XML document must be a well-formed tree).

XML permits us to repeat elements, e.g., to add another gloss field, as we see next. We will use different whitespace to underscore the point that layout does not matter.

```
(3) <entry><headword>whale</headword><pos>noun</pos><gloss>any of the
      larger cetacean mammals having a streamlined body and breathing
      through a blowhole on the head</gloss><gloss>a very large person;
      impressive in size or qualities</gloss></entry>
```

A further step might be to link our lexicon to some external resource, such as WordNet, using external identifiers. In (4) we group the gloss and a synset identifier inside a new element, which we have called "sense."

```
(4) <entry>
      <headword>whale</headword>
      <pos>noun</pos>
      <sense>
        <gloss>any of the larger cetacean mammals having a streamlined
          body and breathing through a blowhole on the head</gloss>
        <synset>whale.n.02</synset>
```

```
        </sense>
          <gloss>a very large person; impressive in size or qualities</gloss>
          <synset>giant.n.04</synset>
        </sense>
      </entry>
```

Alternatively, we could have represented the synset identifier using an **XML attribute**, without the need for any nested structure, as in (5).

(5)
```
    <entry>
        <headword>whale</headword>
        <pos>noun</pos>
        <gloss synset="whale.n.02">any of the larger cetacean mammals having
            a streamlined body and breathing through a blowhole on the head</gloss>
        <gloss synset="giant.n.04">a very large person; impressive in size or
            qualities</gloss>
    </entry>
```

This illustrates some of the flexibility of XML. If it seems somewhat arbitrary, that's because it is! Following the rules of XML, we can invent new attribute names, and nest them as deeply as we like. We can repeat elements, leave them out, and put them in a different order each time. We can have fields whose presence depends on the value of some other field; e.g., if the part of speech is verb, then the entry can have a past_tense element to hold the past tense of the verb, but if the part of speech is noun, no past_tense element is permitted. To impose some order over all this freedom, we can constrain the structure of an XML file using a "schema," which is a declaration akin to a context-free grammar. Tools exist for testing the **validity** of an XML file with respect to a schema.

The Role of XML

We can use XML to represent many kinds of linguistic information. However, the flexibility comes at a price. Each time we introduce a complication, such as by permitting an element to be optional or repeated, we make more work for any program that accesses the data. We also make it more difficult to check the validity of the data, or to interrogate the data using one of the XML query languages.

Thus, using XML to represent linguistic structures does not magically solve the data modeling problem. We still have to work out how to structure the data, then define that structure with a schema, and then write programs to read and write the format and convert it to other formats. Similarly, we still need to follow some standard principles concerning data normalization. It is wise to avoid making duplicate copies of the same information, so that we don't end up with inconsistent data when only one copy is changed. For example, a cross-reference that was represented as <xref>headword</xref> would duplicate the storage of the headword of some other lexical entry, and the link would break if the copy of the string at the other location was modified. Existential dependencies between information types need to be modeled, so that we can't create elements without a home. For example, if sense definitions cannot exist independently of a lexical entry, the sense element can be nested inside the entry element. Many-to-many relations need to be abstracted out of hierarchical structures. For example, if a word can have many corresponding senses, and a sense can have several corresponding words, then both words and senses must be enumerated separately, as must the list of (*word*, *sense*) pairings. This complex structure might even be split across three separate XML files.

As we can see, although XML provides us with a convenient format accompanied by an extensive collection of tools, it offers no panacea.

The ElementTree Interface

Python's ElementTree module provides a convenient way to access data stored in XML files. ElementTree is part of Python's standard library (since Python 2.5), and is also provided as part of NLTK in case you are using Python 2.4.

We will illustrate the use of ElementTree using a collection of Shakespeare plays that have been formatted using XML. Let's load the XML file and inspect the raw data, first at the top of the file ❶, where we see some XML headers and the name of a schema called **play.dtd**, followed by the **root element** PLAY. We pick it up again at the start of Act 1 ❷. (Some blank lines have been omitted from the output.)

```
>>> merchant_file = nltk.data.find('corpora/shakespeare/merchant.xml')
>>> raw = open(merchant_file).read()
>>> print raw[0:168] ❶
<?xml version="1.0"?>
<?xml-stylesheet type="text/css" href="shakes.css"?>
<!-- <!DOCTYPE PLAY SYSTEM "play.dtd"> -->
<PLAY>
<TITLE>The Merchant of Venice</TITLE>
>>> print raw[1850:2075] ❷
<TITLE>ACT I</TITLE>
<SCENE><TITLE>SCENE I.  Venice. A street.</TITLE>
<STAGEDIR>Enter ANTONIO, SALARINO, and SALANIO</STAGEDIR>
<SPEECH>
<SPEAKER>ANTONIO</SPEAKER>
<LINE>In sooth, I know not why I am so sad:</LINE>
```

We have just accessed the XML data as a string. As we can see, the string at the start of Act 1 contains XML tags for title, scene, stage directions, and so forth.

The next step is to process the file contents as structured XML data, using Element Tree. We are processing a file (a multiline string) and building a tree, so it's not surprising that the method name is **parse** ❶. The variable merchant contains an XML element PLAY ❷. This element has internal structure; we can use an index to get its first child, a TITLE element ❸. We can also see the text content of this element, the title of the play ❹. To get a list of all the child elements, we use the getchildren() method ❺.

```
>>> from nltk.etree.ElementTree import ElementTree
>>> merchant = ElementTree().parse(merchant_file) ❶
>>> merchant
```

```
<Element PLAY at 22fa800> ❷
>>> merchant[0]
<Element TITLE at 22fa828> ❸       ·
>>> merchant[0].text
'The Merchant of Venice' ❹
>>> merchant.getchildren() ❺
[<Element TITLE at 22fa828>, <Element PERSONAE at 22fa7b0>, <Element SCNDESCR at 2300170>,
<Element PLAYSUBT at 2300198>, <Element ACT at 23001e8>, <Element ACT at 234ec88>,
<Element ACT at 23c87d8>, <Element ACT at 2439198>, <Element ACT at 24923c8>]
```

The play consists of a title, the personae, a scene description, a subtitle, and five acts.
Each act has a title and some scenes, and each scene consists of speeches which are
made up of lines, a structure with four levels of nesting. Let's dig down into Act IV:

```
>>> merchant[-2][0].text
'ACT IV'
>>> merchant[-2][1]
<Element SCENE at 224cf80>
>>> merchant[-2][1][0].text
'SCENE I.  Venice. A court of justice.'
>>> merchant[-2][1][54]
<Element SPEECH at 226ee40>
>>> merchant[-2][1][54][0]
<Element SPEAKER at 226ee90>
>>> merchant[-2][1][54][0].text
'PORTIA'
>>> merchant[-2][1][54][1]
<Element LINE at 226eee0>
>>> merchant[-2][1][54][1].text
"The quality of mercy is not strain'd,"
```

> **Your Turn:** Repeat some of the methods just shown, for one of the
> other Shakespeare plays included in the corpus, such as *Romeo and Ju-*
> *liet* or *Macbeth*. For a list, see nltk.corpus.shakespeare.fileids().

Although we can access the entire tree this way, it is more convenient to search for sub-
elements with particular names. Recall that the elements at the top level have several
types. We can iterate over just the types we are interested in (such as the acts), using
merchant.findall('ACT'). Here's an example of doing such tag-specific searches at every level of nesting:

```
>>> for i, act in enumerate(merchant.findall('ACT')):
...     for j, scene in enumerate(act.findall('SCENE')):
...         for k, speech in enumerate(scene.findall('SPEECH')):
...             for line in speech.findall('LINE'):
...                 if 'music' in str(line.text):
...                     print "Act %d Scene %d Speech %d: %s" % (i+1, j+1, k+1, line.text)
Act 3 Scene 2 Speech 9: Let music sound while he doth make his choice;
Act 3 Scene 2 Speech 9: Fading in music: that the comparison
Act 3 Scene 2 Speech 9: And what is music then? Then music is
Act 5 Scene 1 Speech 23: And bring your music forth into the air.
Act 5 Scene 1 Speech 23: Here will we sit and let the sounds of music
```

```
Act 5 Scene 1 Speech 23: And draw her home with music.
Act 5 Scene 1 Speech 24: I am never merry when I hear sweet music.
Act 5 Scene 1 Speech 25: Or any air of music touch their ears,
Act 5 Scene 1 Speech 25: By the sweet power of music: therefore the poet
Act 5 Scene 1 Speech 25: But music for the time doth change his nature.
Act 5 Scene 1 Speech 25: The man that hath no music in himself,
Act 5 Scene 1 Speech 25: Let no such man be trusted. Mark the music.
Act 5 Scene 1 Speech 29: It is your music, madam, of the house.
Act 5 Scene 1 Speech 32: No better a musician than the wren.
```

Instead of navigating each step of the way down the hierarchy, we can search for particular embedded elements. For example, let's examine the sequence of speakers. We can use a frequency distribution to see who has the most to say:

```
>>> speaker_seq = [s.text for s in merchant.findall('ACT/SCENE/SPEECH/SPEAKER')]
>>> speaker_freq = nltk.FreqDist(speaker_seq)
>>> top5 = speaker_freq.keys()[:5]
>>> top5
['PORTIA', 'SHYLOCK', 'BASSANIO', 'GRATIANO', 'ANTONIO']
```

We can also look for patterns in who follows whom in the dialogues. Since there are 23 speakers, we need to reduce the "vocabulary" to a manageable size first, using the method described in Section 5.3.

```
>>> mapping = nltk.defaultdict(lambda: 'OTH')
>>> for s in top5:
...     mapping[s] = s[:4]
...
>>> speaker_seq2 = [mapping[s] for s in speaker_seq]
>>> cfd = nltk.ConditionalFreqDist(nltk.ibigrams(speaker_seq2))
>>> cfd.tabulate()
     ANTO BASS GRAT  OTH PORT SHYL
ANTO    0   11    4   11    9   12
BASS   10    0   11   10   26   16
GRAT    6    8    0   19    9    5
 OTH    8   16   18  153   52   25
PORT    7   23   13   53    0   21
SHYL   15   15    2   26   21    0
```

Ignoring the entry of 153 for exchanges between people other than the top five, the largest values suggest that Othello and Portia have the most significant interactions.

Using ElementTree for Accessing Toolbox Data

In Section 2.4, we saw a simple interface for accessing Toolbox data, a popular and well-established format used by linguists for managing data. In this section, we discuss a variety of techniques for manipulating Toolbox data in ways that are not supported by the Toolbox software. The methods we discuss could be applied to other record-structured data, regardless of the actual file format.

We can use the toolbox.xml() method to access a Toolbox file and load it into an ElementTree object. This file contains a lexicon for the Rotokas language of Papua New Guinea.

```
>>> from nltk.corpus import toolbox
>>> lexicon = toolbox.xml('rotokas.dic')
```

There are two ways to access the contents of the lexicon object: by indexes and by
paths. Indexes use the familiar syntax; thus lexicon[3] returns entry number 3 (which
is actually the fourth entry counting from zero) and lexicon[3][0] returns its first field:

```
>>> lexicon[3][0]
<Element lx at 77bd28>
>>> lexicon[3][0].tag
'lx'
>>> lexicon[3][0].text
'kaa'
```

The second way to access the contents of the lexicon object uses paths. The lexicon is
a series of record objects, each containing a series of field objects, such as lx and ps.
We can conveniently address all of the lexemes using the path record/lx. Here we use
the findall() function to search for any matches to the path record/lx, and we access
the text content of the element, normalizing it to lowercase:

```
>>> [lexeme.text.lower() for lexeme in lexicon.findall('record/lx')]
['kaa', 'kaa', 'kaa', 'kaakaaro', 'kaakaaviko', 'kaakaavo', 'kaakaoko',
 'kaakasi', 'kaakau', 'kaakauko', 'kaakito', 'kaakuupato', ..., 'kuvuto']
```

Let's view the Toolbox data in XML format. The write() method of ElementTree expects a file object. We usually create one of these using Python's built-in open() function. In order to see the output displayed on the screen, we can use a special predefined
file object called stdout ❶ (standard output), defined in Python's sys module.

```
>>> import sys
>>> from nltk.etree.ElementTree import ElementTree
>>> tree = ElementTree(lexicon[3])
>>> tree.write(sys.stdout) ❶
<record>
    <lx>kaa</lx>
    <ps>N</ps>
    <pt>MASC</pt>
    <cl>isi</cl>
    <ge>cooking banana</ge>
    <tkp>banana bilong kukim</tkp>
    <pt>itoo</pt>
    <sf>FLORA</sf>
    <dt>12/Aug/2005</dt>
    <ex>Taeavi iria kaa isi kovopaueva kaparapasia.</ex>
    <xp>Taeavi i bin planim gaden banana bilong kukim tasol long paia.</xp>
    <xe>Taeavi planted banana in order to cook it.</xe>
</record>
```

Formatting Entries

We can use the same idea we saw in the previous section to generate HTML tables
instead of plain text. This would be useful for publishing a Toolbox lexicon on the
Web. It produces HTML elements <table>, <tr> (table row), and <td> (table data).

```
>>> html = "<table>\n"
>>> for entry in lexicon[70:80]:
...     lx = entry.findtext('lx')
...     ps = entry.findtext('ps')
...     ge = entry.findtext('ge')
...     html += "  <tr><td>%s</td><td>%s</td><td>%s</td></tr>\n" % (lx, ps, ge)
>>> html += "</table>"
>>> print html
<table>
  <tr><td>kakae</td><td>???</td><td>small</td></tr>
  <tr><td>kakae</td><td>CLASS</td><td>child</td></tr>
  <tr><td>kakaevira</td><td>ADV</td><td>small-like</td></tr>
  <tr><td>kakapikoa</td><td>???</td><td>small</td></tr>
  <tr><td>kakapikoto</td><td>N</td><td>newborn baby</td></tr>
  <tr><td>kakapu</td><td>V</td><td>place in sling for purpose of carrying</td></tr>
  <tr><td>kakapua</td><td>N</td><td>sling for lifting</td></tr>
  <tr><td>kakara</td><td>N</td><td>arm band</td></tr>
  <tr><td>Kakarapaia</td><td>N</td><td>village name</td></tr>
  <tr><td>kakarau</td><td>N</td><td>frog</td></tr>
</table>
```

11.5 Working with Toolbox Data

Given the popularity of Toolbox among linguists, we will discuss some further methods for working with Toolbox data. Many of the methods discussed in previous chapters, such as counting, building frequency distributions, and tabulating co-occurrences, can be applied to the content of Toolbox entries. For example, we can trivially compute the average number of fields for each entry:

```
>>> from nltk.corpus import toolbox
>>> lexicon = toolbox.xml('rotokas.dic')
>>> sum(len(entry) for entry in lexicon) / len(lexicon)
13.635955056179775
```

In this section, we will discuss two tasks that arise in the context of documentary linguistics, neither of which is supported by the Toolbox software.

Adding a Field to Each Entry

It is often convenient to add new fields that are derived automatically from existing ones. Such fields often facilitate search and analysis. For instance, in Example 11-2 we define a function cv(), which maps a string of consonants and vowels to the corresponding CV sequence, e.g., kakapua would map to CVCVCVV. This mapping has four steps. First, the string is converted to lowercase, then we replace any non-alphabetic characters [^a-z] with an underscore. Next, we replace all vowels with V. Finally, anything that is not a V or an underscore must be a consonant, so we replace it with a C. Now, we can scan the lexicon and add a new cv field after every lx field. Example 11-2 shows what this does to a particular entry; note the last line of output, which shows the new cv field.

Example 11-2. Adding a new cv field to a lexical entry.

```
from nltk.etree.ElementTree import SubElement

def cv(s):
    s = s.lower()
    s = re.sub(r'[^a-z]',    r'_', s)
    s = re.sub(r'[aeiou]',   r'V', s)
    s = re.sub(r'[^V_]',     r'C', s)
    return (s)

def add_cv_field(entry):
    for field in entry:
        if field.tag == 'lx':
            cv_field = SubElement(entry, 'cv')
            cv_field.text = cv(field.text)

>>> lexicon = toolbox.xml('rotokas.dic')
>>> add_cv_field(lexicon[53])
>>> print nltk.to_sfm_string(lexicon[53])
\lx kaeviro
\ps V
\pt A
\ge lift off
\ge take off
\tkp go antap
\sc MOTION
\vx 1
\nt used to describe action of plane
\dt 03/Jun/2005
\ex Pita kaeviroroe kepa kekesia oa vuripierevo kiuvu.
\xp Pita i go antap na lukim haus win i bagarapim.
\xe Peter went to look at the house that the wind destroyed.
\cv CVVCVCV
```

 If a Toolbox file is being continually updated, the program in Example 11-2 will need to be run more than once. It would be possible to modify `add_cv_field()` to modify the contents of an existing entry. However, it is a safer practice to use such programs to create enriched files for the purpose of data analysis, without replacing the manually curated source files.

Validating a Toolbox Lexicon

Many lexicons in Toolbox format do not conform to any particular schema. Some entries may include extra fields, or may order existing fields in a new way. Manually inspecting thousands of lexical entries is not practicable. However, we can easily identify frequent versus exceptional field sequences, with the help of a `FreqDist`:

```
>>> fd = nltk.FreqDist(':'.join(field.tag for field in entry) for entry in lexicon)
>>> fd.items()
[('lx:ps:pt:ge:tkp:dt:ex:xp:xe', 41), ('lx:rt:ps:pt:ge:tkp:dt:ex:xp:xe', 37),
```

```
        ('lx:rt:ps:pt:ge:tkp:dt:ex:xp:xe:ex:xp:xe', 27), ('lx:ps:pt:ge:tkp:nt:dt:ex:xp:xe', 20),
        ..., ('lx:alt:rt:ps:pt:ge:eng:eng:eng:tkp:tkp:dt:ex:xp:xe:ex:xp:xe:ex:xp:xe', 1)]
```

After inspecting the high-frequency field sequences, we could devise a context-free grammar for lexical entries. The grammar in Example 11-3 uses the CFG format we saw in Chapter 8. Such a grammar models the implicit nested structure of Toolbox entries, building a tree structure, where the leaves of the tree are individual field names. We iterate over the entries and report their conformance with the grammar, as shown in Example 11-3. Those that are accepted by the grammar are prefixed with a '+' ❶, and those that are rejected are prefixed with a '-' ❷. During the process of developing such a grammar, it helps to filter out some of the tags ❸.

Example 11-3. Validating Toolbox entries using a context-free grammar.

```
grammar = nltk.parse_cfg('''
  S -> Head PS Glosses Comment Date Sem_Field Examples
  Head -> Lexeme Root
  Lexeme -> "lx"
  Root -> "rt" |
  PS -> "ps"
  Glosses -> Gloss Glosses |
  Gloss -> "ge" | "tkp" | "eng"
  Date -> "dt"
  Sem_Field -> "sf"
  Examples -> Example Ex_Pidgin Ex_English Examples |
  Example -> "ex"
  Ex_Pidgin -> "xp"
  Ex_English -> "xe"
  Comment -> "cmt" | "nt" |
  ''')

def validate_lexicon(grammar, lexicon, ignored_tags):
    rd_parser = nltk.RecursiveDescentParser(grammar)
    for entry in lexicon:
        marker_list = [field.tag for field in entry if field.tag not in ignored_tags]
        if rd_parser.nbest_parse(marker_list):
            print "+", ':'.join(marker_list)  ❶
        else:
            print "-", ':'.join(marker_list)  ❷


>>> lexicon = toolbox.xml('rotokas.dic')[10:20]
>>> ignored_tags = ['arg', 'dcsv', 'pt', 'vx']  ❸
>>> validate_lexicon(grammar, lexicon, ignored_tags)
- lx:ps:ge:tkp:sf:nt:dt:ex:xp:xe:ex:xp:xe:ex:xp:xe
- lx:rt:ps:ge:tkp:nt:dt:ex:xp:xe:ex:xp:xe
- lx:ps:ge:tkp:nt:dt:ex:xp:xe:ex:xp:xe
- lx:ps:ge:tkp:nt:sf:dt
- lx:ps:ge:tkp:dt:cmt:ex:xp:xe:ex:xp:xe
- lx:ps:ge:ge:ge:tkp:cmt:dt:ex:xp:xe
- lx:rt:ps:ge:ge:tkp:dt
- lx:rt:ps:ge:eng:eng:eng:ge:tkp:tkp:dt:cmt:ex:xp:xe:ex:xp:xe:ex:xp:xe:ex:xp:xe:ex:xp:xe
- lx:rt:ps:ge:tkp:dt:ex:xp:xe
- lx:ps:ge:ge:tkp:dt:ex:xp:xe:ex:xp:xe
```

Another approach would be to use a chunk parser (Chapter 7), since these are much more effective at identifying partial structures and can report the partial structures that have been identified. In Example 11-4 we set up a chunk grammar for the entries of a lexicon, then parse each entry. A sample of the output from this program is shown in Figure 11-7.

```
<record>
  <lx>ceuv jiax</lx>
  <hm />
  <sense>
    <sn />
    <ps>vobj</ps>
    <dv>nzaeng jiax</dv>
    <ge>quarrel</ge>
    <de />
    <gn>吵架</gn>
    <gp>chao3 jia4</gp>
    <dn>争吵</dn>
    <example>
      <xv>Ninh mbuo i hmuangv mv ~ jiex jiax.</xv>
      <xe>That husband and wife have never quarrelled.</xe>
      <xn>他们夫妻俩从来不吵架。</xn>
    </example><example>
      <xv>Gorngv duh leiz mv duqv ~.</xv>
      <xe>Have some common sense, don't quarrel.</xe>
      <xn>讲道理，别吵架．</xn>
    </example><lexfunc>
      <lf />
      <lv />
    </lexfunc>
  </sense><dt>18/Feb/2004</dt>
</record>
```

Figure 11-7. XML representation of a lexical entry, resulting from chunk parsing a Toolbox record.

Example 11-4. Chunking a Toolbox lexicon: A chunk grammar describing the structure of entries for a lexicon for Iu Mien, a language of China.

```
from nltk_contrib import toolbox

grammar = r"""
    lexfunc: {<lf>(<lv><ln|le>*)*}
    example: {<rf|xv><xn|xe>*}
    sense:   {<sn><ps><pn|gv|dv|gn|gp|dn|rn|ge|de|re>*<example>*<lexfunc>*}
    record:  {<lx><hm><sense>+<dt>}
    """

>>> from nltk.etree.ElementTree import ElementTree
>>> db = toolbox.ToolboxData()
>>> db.open(nltk.data.find('corpora/toolbox/iu_mien_samp.db'))
>>> lexicon = db.parse(grammar, encoding='utf8')
>>> toolbox.data.indent(lexicon)
>>> tree = ElementTree(lexicon)
>>> output = open("iu_mien_samp.xml", "w")
>>> tree.write(output, encoding='utf8')
>>> output.close()
```

11.6 Describing Language Resources Using OLAC Metadata

Members of the NLP community have a common need for discovering language resources with high precision and recall. The solution which has been developed by the Digital Libraries community involves metadata aggregation.

What Is Metadata?

The simplest definition of metadata is "structured data about data." Metadata is descriptive information about an object or resource, whether it be physical or electronic. Although the term "metadata" itself is relatively new, the underlying concepts behind metadata have been in use for as long as collections of information have been organized. Library catalogs represent a well-established type of metadata; they have served as collection management and resource discovery tools for decades. Metadata can be generated either "by hand" or automatically using software.

The Dublin Core Metadata Initiative began in 1995 to develop conventions for finding, sharing, and managing information. The Dublin Core metadata elements represent a broad, interdisciplinary consensus about the core set of elements that are likely to be widely useful to support resource discovery. The Dublin Core consists of 15 metadata elements, where each element is optional and repeatable: Title, Creator, Subject, Description, Publisher, Contributor, Date, Type, Format, Identifier, Source, Language, Relation, Coverage, and Rights. This metadata set can be used to describe resources that exist in digital or traditional formats.

The Open Archives Initiative (OAI) provides a common framework across digital repositories of scholarly materials, regardless of their type, including documents, data, software, recordings, physical artifacts, digital surrogates, and so forth. Each repository consists of a network-accessible server offering public access to archived items. Each item has a unique identifier, and is associated with a Dublin Core metadata record (and possibly additional records in other formats). The OAI defines a protocol for metadata search services to "harvest" the contents of repositories.

OLAC: Open Language Archives Community

The Open Language Archives Community, or OLAC, is an international partnership of institutions and individuals who are creating a worldwide virtual library of language resources by: (i) developing consensus on best current practices for the digital archiving of language resources, and (ii) developing a network of interoperating repositories and services for housing and accessing such resources. OLAC's home on the Web is at *http://www.language-archives.org/*.

OLAC Metadata is a standard for describing language resources. Uniform description across repositories is ensured by limiting the values of certain metadata elements to the use of terms from controlled vocabularies. OLAC metadata can be used to describe data and tools, in both physical and digital formats. OLAC metadata extends the

Dublin Core Metadata Set, a widely accepted standard for describing resources of all types. To this core set, OLAC adds descriptors to cover fundamental properties of language resources, such as subject language and linguistic type. Here's an example of a complete OLAC record:

```
<?xml version="1.0" encoding="UTF-8"?>
<olac:olac xmlns:olac="http://www.language-archives.org/OLAC/1.1/"
            xmlns="http://purl.org/dc/elements/1.1/"
            xmlns:dcterms="http://purl.org/dc/terms/"
            xmlns:xsi="http://www.w3.org/2001/XMLSchema-instance"
            xsi:schemaLocation="http://www.language-archives.org/OLAC/1.1/
                http://www.language-archives.org/OLAC/1.1/olac.xsd">
  <title>A grammar of Kayardild. With comparative notes on Tangkic.</title>
  <creator>Evans, Nicholas D.</creator>
  <subject>Kayardild grammar</subject>
  <subject xsi:type="olac:language" olac:code="gyd">Kayardild</subject>
  <language xsi:type="olac:language" olac:code="en">English</language>
  <description>Kayardild Grammar (ISBN 3110127954)</description>
  <publisher>Berlin - Mouton de Gruyter</publisher>
  <contributor xsi:type="olac:role" olac:code="author">Nicholas Evans</contributor>
  <format>hardcover, 837 pages</format>
  <relation>related to ISBN 0646119966</relation>
  <coverage>Australia</coverage>
  <type xsi:type="olac:linguistic-type" olac:code="language_description"/>
  <type xsi:type="dcterms:DCMIType">Text</type>
</olac:olac>
```

Participating language archives publish their catalogs in an XML format, and these records are regularly "harvested" by OLAC services using the OAI protocol. In addition to this software infrastructure, OLAC has documented a series of best practices for describing language resources, through a process that involved extended consultation with the language resources community (e.g., see *http://www.language-archives.org/ REC/bpr.html*).

OLAC repositories can be searched using a query engine on the OLAC website. Searching for "German lexicon" finds the following resources, among others:

- CALLHOME German Lexicon, at *http://www.language-archives.org/item/oai: www.ldc.upenn.edu:LDC97L18*
- MULTILEX multilingual lexicon, at *http://www.language-archives.org/item/oai:el ra.icp.inpg.fr:M0001*
- Slelex Siemens Phonetic lexicon, at *http://www.language-archives.org/item/oai:elra .icp.inpg.fr:S0048*

Searching for "Korean" finds a newswire corpus, and a treebank, a lexicon, a child-language corpus, and interlinear glossed texts. It also finds software, including a syntactic analyzer and a morphological analyzer.

Observe that the previous URLs include a substring of the form: `oai:www.ldc.upenn.edu:LDC97L18`. This is an OAI identifier, using a URI scheme registered with ICANN (the Internet Corporation for Assigned Names and Numbers). These identifiers have the format `oai:`*`archive`*`:`*`local_id`*, where `oai` is the name of the URI scheme, *`archive`* is an archive identifier, such as `www.ldc.upenn.edu`, and *`local_id`* is the resource identifier assigned by the archive, e.g., `LDC97L18`.

Given an OAI identifier for an OLAC resource, it is possible to retrieve the complete XML record for the resource using a URL of the following form: `http://www.language-archives.org/static-records/oai:archive:local_id`.

11.7 Summary

- Fundamental data types, present in most corpora, are annotated texts and lexicons. Texts have a temporal structure, whereas lexicons have a record structure.
- The life cycle of a corpus includes data collection, annotation, quality control, and publication. The life cycle continues after publication as the corpus is modified and enriched during the course of research.
- Corpus development involves a balance between capturing a representative sample of language usage, and capturing enough material from any one source or genre to be useful; multiplying out the dimensions of variability is usually not feasible because of resource limitations.
- XML provides a useful format for the storage and interchange of linguistic data, but provides no shortcuts for solving pervasive data modeling problems.
- Toolbox format is widely used in language documentation projects; we can write programs to support the curation of Toolbox files, and to convert them to XML.
- The Open Language Archives Community (OLAC) provides an infrastructure for documenting and discovering language resources.

11.8 Further Reading

Extra materials for this chapter are posted at *http://www.nltk.org/*, including links to freely available resources on the Web.

The primary sources of linguistic corpora are the *Linguistic Data Consortium* and the *European Language Resources Agency*, both with extensive online catalogs. More details concerning the major corpora mentioned in the chapter are available: American National Corpus (Reppen, Ide & Suderman, 2005), British National Corpus (BNC, 1999), Thesaurus Linguae Graecae (TLG, 1999), Child Language Data Exchange System (CHILDES) (MacWhinney, 1995), and TIMIT (Garofolo et al., 1986).

Two special interest groups of the Association for Computational Linguistics that organize regular workshops with published proceedings are SIGWAC, which promotes the use of the Web as a corpus and has sponsored the CLEANEVAL task for removing HTML markup, and SIGANN, which is encouraging efforts toward interoperability of linguistic annotations. An extended discussion of web crawling is provided by (Croft, Metzler & Strohman, 2009).

Full details of the Toolbox data format are provided with the distribution (Buseman, Buseman & Early, 1996), and with the latest distribution freely available from *http:// www.sil.org/computing/toolbox/*. For guidelines on the process of constructing a Toolbox lexicon, see *http://www.sil.org/computing/ddp/*. More examples of our efforts with the Toolbox are documented in (Bird, 1999) and (Robinson, Aumann & Bird, 2007). Dozens of other tools for linguistic data management are available, some surveyed by (Bird & Simons, 2003). See also the proceedings of the LaTeCH workshops on language technology for cultural heritage data.

There are many excellent resources for XML (e.g., *http://zvon.org/*) and for writing Python programs to work with XML *http://www.python.org/doc/lib/markup.html*. Many editors have XML modes. XML formats for lexical information include OLIF (*http://www.olif.net/*) and LIFT (*http://code.google.com/p/lift-standard/*).

For a survey of linguistic annotation software, see the *Linguistic Annotation Page* at *http://www.ldc.upenn.edu/annotation/*. The initial proposal for standoff annotation was (Thompson & McKelvie, 1997). An abstract data model for linguistic annotations, called "annotation graphs," was proposed in (Bird & Liberman, 2001). A general-purpose ontology for linguistic description (GOLD) is documented at *http://www.lin guistics-ontology.org/*.

For guidance on planning and constructing a corpus, see (Meyer, 2002) and (Farghaly, 2003). More details of methods for scoring inter-annotator agreement are available in (Artstein & Poesio, 2008) and (Pevzner & Hearst, 2002).

Rotokas data was provided by Stuart Robinson, and Iu Mien data was provided by Greg Aumann.

For more information about the Open Language Archives Community, visit *http://www .language-archives.org/*, or see (Simons & Bird, 2003).

11.9 Exercises

1. ◑ In Example 11-2 the new field appeared at the bottom of the entry. Modify this program so that it inserts the new subelement right after the `lx` field. (Hint: create the new `cv` field using `Element('cv')`, assign a text value to it, then use the `insert()` method of the parent element.)

2. ◑ Write a function that deletes a specified field from a lexical entry. (We could use this to sanitize our lexical data before giving it to others, e.g., by removing fields containing irrelevant or uncertain content.)

3. ◑ Write a program that scans an HTML dictionary file to find entries having an illegal part-of-speech field, and then reports the headword for each entry.

4. ◑ Write a program to find any parts-of-speech (ps field) that occurred less than 10 times. Perhaps these are typing mistakes?

5. ◑ We saw a method for adding a cv field (Section 11.5). There is an interesting issue with keeping this up-to-date when someone modifies the content of the lx field on which it is based. Write a version of this program to add a cv field, replacing any existing cv field.

6. ◑ Write a function to add a new field syl which gives a count of the number of syllables in the word.

7. ◑ Write a function which displays the complete entry for a lexeme. When the lexeme is incorrectly spelled, it should display the entry for the most similarly spelled lexeme.

8. ◑ Write a function that takes a lexicon and finds which pairs of consecutive fields are most frequent (e.g., ps is often followed by pt). (This might help us to discover some of the structure of a lexical entry.)

9. ◑ Create a spreadsheet using office software, containing one lexical entry per row, consisting of a headword, a part of speech, and a gloss. Save the spreadsheet in CSV format. Write Python code to read the CSV file and print it in Toolbox format, using lx for the headword, ps for the part of speech, and gl for the gloss.

10. ◑ Index the words of Shakespeare's plays, with the help of nltk.Index. The resulting data structure should permit lookup on individual words, such as *music*, returning a list of references to acts, scenes, and speeches, of the form [(3, 2, 9), (5, 1, 23), ...], where (3, 2, 9) indicates Act 3 Scene 2 Speech 9.

11. ◑ Construct a conditional frequency distribution which records the word length for each speech in *The Merchant of Venice*, conditioned on the name of the character; e.g., cfd['PORTIA'][12] would give us the number of speeches by Portia consisting of 12 words.

12. ◑ Write a recursive function to convert an arbitrary NLTK tree into an XML counterpart, with non-terminals represented as XML elements, and leaves represented as text content, e.g.:

```
<S>
  <NP type="SBJ">
    <NP>
      <NNP>Pierre</NNP>
      <NNP>Vinken</NNP>
    </NP>
    <COMMA>,</COMMA>
```

13. ● Obtain a comparative wordlist in CSV format, and write a program that prints those cognates having an edit-distance of at least three from each other.

14. ● Build an index of those lexemes which appear in example sentences. Suppose the lexeme for a given entry is *w*. Then, add a single cross-reference field xrf to this entry, referencing the headwords of other entries having example sentences containing *w*. Do this for all entries and save the result as a Toolbox-format file.

Afterword: The Language Challenge

Natural language throws up some interesting computational challenges. We've explored many of these in the preceding chapters, including tokenization, tagging, classification, information extraction, and building syntactic and semantic representations. You should now be equipped to work with large datasets, to create robust models of linguistic phenomena, and to extend them into components for practical language technologies. We hope that the Natural Language Toolkit (NLTK) has served to open up the exciting endeavor of practical natural language processing to a broader audience than before.

In spite of all that has come before, language presents us with far more than a temporary challenge for computation. Consider the following sentences which attest to the riches of language:

1. Overhead the day drives level and grey, hiding the sun by a flight of grey spears. (William Faulkner, *As I Lay Dying*, 1935)

2. When using the toaster please ensure that the exhaust fan is turned on. (sign in dormitory kitchen)

3. Amiodarone weakly inhibited CYP2C9, CYP2D6, and CYP3A4-mediated activities with Ki values of 45.1-271.6 µM (Medline, PMID: 10718780)

4. Iraqi Head Seeks Arms (spoof news headline)

5. The earnest prayer of a righteous man has great power and wonderful results. (James 5:16b)

6. Twas brillig, and the slithy toves did gyre and gimble in the wabe (Lewis Carroll, *Jabberwocky*, 1872)

7. There are two ways to do this, AFAIK :smile: (Internet discussion archive)

Other evidence for the riches of language is the vast array of disciplines whose work centers on language. Some obvious disciplines include translation, literary criticism, philosophy, anthropology, and psychology. Many less obvious disciplines investigate language use, including law, hermeneutics, forensics, telephony, pedagogy, archaeology, cryptanalysis, and speech pathology. Each applies distinct methodologies to gather observations, develop theories, and test hypotheses. All serve to deepen our understanding of language and of the intellect that is manifested in language.

In view of the complexity of language and the broad range of interest in studying it from different angles, it's clear that we have barely scratched the surface here. Additionally, within NLP itself, there are many important methods and applications that we haven't mentioned.

In our closing remarks we will take a broader view of NLP, including its foundations and the further directions you might want to explore. Some of the topics are not well supported by NLTK, and you might like to rectify that problem by contributing new software and data to the toolkit.

Language Processing Versus Symbol Processing

The very notion that natural language could be treated in a computational manner grew out of a research program, dating back to the early 1900s, to reconstruct mathematical reasoning using logic, most clearly manifested in work by Frege, Russell, Wittgenstein, Tarski, Lambek, and Carnap. This work led to the notion of language as a formal system amenable to automatic processing. Three later developments laid the foundation for natural language processing. The first was **formal language theory**. This defined a language as a set of strings accepted by a class of automata, such as context-free languages and pushdown automata, and provided the underpinnings for computational syntax.

The second development was **symbolic logic**. This provided a formal method for capturing selected aspects of natural language that are relevant for expressing logical proofs. A formal calculus in symbolic logic provides the syntax of a language, together with rules of inference and, possibly, rules of interpretation in a set-theoretic model; examples are propositional logic and first-order logic. Given such a calculus, with a well-defined syntax and semantics, it becomes possible to associate meanings with expressions of natural language by translating them into expressions of the formal calculus. For example, if we translate *John saw Mary* into a formula *saw(j, m)*, we (implicitly or explicitly) interpret the English verb *saw* as a binary relation, and *John* and *Mary* as denoting individuals. More general statements like *All birds fly* require quantifiers, in this case $\forall$, meaning *for all*: $\forall x \, (bird(x) \rightarrow fly(x))$. This use of logic provided the technical machinery to perform inferences that are an important part of language understanding.

A closely related development was the **principle of compositionality**, namely that the meaning of a complex expression is composed from the meaning of its parts and their mode of combination (Chapter 10). This principle provided a useful correspondence between syntax and semantics, namely that the meaning of a complex expression could be computed recursively. Consider the sentence *It is not true that p*, where *p* is a proposition. We can represent the meaning of this sentence as *not(p)*.

Similarly, we can represent the meaning of *John saw Mary* as *saw(j, m)*. Now we can compute the interpretation of *It is not true that John saw Mary* recursively, using the foregoing information, to get *not(saw(j,m))*.

The approaches just outlined share the premise that computing with natural language crucially relies on rules for manipulating symbolic representations. For a certain period in the development of NLP, particularly during the 1980s, this premise provided a common starting point for both linguists and practitioners of NLP, leading to a family of grammar formalisms known as unification-based (or feature-based) grammar (see Chapter 9), and to NLP applications implemented in the Prolog programming language. Although grammar-based NLP is still a significant area of research, it has become somewhat eclipsed in the last 15–20 years due to a variety of factors. One significant influence came from automatic speech recognition. Although early work in speech processing adopted a model that emulated the kind of rule-based phonological **phonology** processing typified by the *Sound Pattern of English* (Chomsky & Halle, 1968), this turned out to be hopelessly inadequate in dealing with the hard problem of recognizing actual speech in anything like real time. By contrast, systems which involved learning patterns from large bodies of speech data were significantly more accurate, efficient, and robust. In addition, the speech community found that progress in building better systems was hugely assisted by the construction of shared resources for quantitatively measuring performance against common test data. Eventually, much of the NLP community embraced a **data-intensive** orientation to language processing, coupled with a growing use of machine-learning techniques and evaluation-led methodology.

Contemporary Philosophical Divides

The contrasting approaches to NLP described in the preceding section relate back to early metaphysical debates about **rationalism** versus **empiricism** and **realism** versus **idealism** that occurred in the Enlightenment period of Western philosophy. These debates took place against a backdrop of orthodox thinking in which the source of all knowledge was believed to be divine revelation. During this period of the 17th and 18th centuries, philosophers argued that human reason or sensory experience has priority over revelation. Descartes and Leibniz, among others, took the rationalist position, asserting that all truth has its origins in human thought, and in the existence of "innate ideas" implanted in our minds from birth. For example, they argued that the principles of Euclidean geometry were developed using human reason, and were not the result of supernatural revelation or sensory experience. In contrast, Locke and others took the empiricist view, that our primary source of knowledge is the experience of our faculties, and that human reason plays a secondary role in reflecting on that experience. Often-cited evidence for this position was Galileo's discovery—based on careful observation of the motion of the planets—that the solar system is heliocentric and not geocentric. In the context of linguistics, this debate leads to the following question: to what extent does human linguistic experience, versus our innate "language faculty," provide the basis for our knowledge of language? In NLP this issue surfaces in debates about the priority of corpus data versus linguistic introspection in the construction of computational models.

A further concern, enshrined in the debate between realism and idealism, was the metaphysical status of the constructs of a theory. Kant argued for a distinction between phenomena, the manifestations we can experience, and "things in themselves" which can never been known directly. A linguistic realist would take a theoretical construct like **noun phrase** to be a real-world entity that exists independently of human perception and reason, and which actually *causes* the observed linguistic phenomena. A linguistic idealist, on the other hand, would argue that noun phrases, along with more abstract constructs, like semantic representations, are intrinsically unobservable, and simply play the role of useful fictions. The way linguists write about theories often betrays a realist position, whereas NLP practitioners occupy neutral territory or else lean toward the idealist position. Thus, in NLP, it is often enough if a theoretical abstraction leads to a useful result; it does not matter whether this result sheds any light on human linguistic processing.

These issues are still alive today, and show up in the distinctions between symbolic versus statistical methods, deep versus shallow processing, binary versus gradient classifications, and scientific versus engineering goals. However, such contrasts are now highly nuanced, and the debate is no longer as polarized as it once was. In fact, most of the discussions—and most of the advances, even—involve a "balancing act." For example, one intermediate position is to assume that humans are innately endowed with analogical and memory-based learning methods (weak rationalism), and use these methods to identify meaningful patterns in their sensory language experience (empiricism).

We have seen many examples of this methodology throughout this book. Statistical methods inform symbolic models anytime corpus statistics guide the selection of productions in a context-free grammar, i.e., "grammar engineering." Symbolic methods inform statistical models anytime a corpus that was created using rule-based methods is used as a source of features for training a statistical language model, i.e., "grammatical inference." The circle is closed.

NLTK Roadmap

The Natural Language Toolkit is a work in progress, and is being continually expanded as people contribute code. Some areas of NLP and linguistics are not (yet) well supported in NLTK, and contributions in these areas are especially welcome. Check *http://www.nltk.org/* for news about developments after the publication date of this book. Contributions in the following areas are particularly encouraged:

Phonology and morphology

Computational approaches to the study of sound patterns and word structures typically use a finite-state toolkit. Phenomena such as suppletion and non-concatenative morphology are difficult to address using the string-processing methods we have been studying. The technical challenge is not only to link NLTK to a high-performance finite-state toolkit, but to avoid duplication of lexical data and to link the morphosyntactic features needed by morph analyzers and syntactic parsers.

High-performance components

Some NLP tasks are too computationally intensive for pure Python implementations to be feasible. However, in some cases the expense arises only when training models, not when using them to label inputs. NLTK's package system provides a convenient way to distribute trained models, even models trained using corpora that cannot be freely distributed. Alternatives are to develop Python interfaces to high-performance machine learning tools, or to expand the reach of Python by using parallel programming techniques such as MapReduce.

Lexical semantics

This is a vibrant area of current research, encompassing inheritance models of the lexicon, ontologies, multiword expressions, etc., mostly outside the scope of NLTK as it stands. A conservative goal would be to access lexical information from rich external stores in support of tasks in word sense disambiguation, parsing, and semantic interpretation.

Natural language generation

Producing coherent text from underlying representations of meaning is an important part of NLP; a unification-based approach to NLG has been developed in NLTK, and there is scope for more contributions in this area.

Linguistic fieldwork

A major challenge faced by linguists is to document thousands of endangered languages, work which generates heterogeneous and rapidly evolving data in large quantities. More fieldwork data formats, including interlinear text formats and lexicon interchange formats, could be supported in NLTK, helping linguists to curate and analyze this data, while liberating them to spend as much time as possible on data elicitation.

Other languages

Improved support for NLP in languages other than English could involve work in two areas: obtaining permission to distribute more corpora with NLTK's data collection; and writing language-specific HOWTOs for posting at *http://www.nltk .org/howto*, illustrating the use of NLTK and discussing language-specific problems for NLP, including character encodings, word segmentation, and morphology. NLP researchers with expertise in a particular language could arrange to translate this book and host a copy on the NLTK website; this would go beyond translating the discussions to providing equivalent worked examples using data in the target language, a non-trivial undertaking.

NLTK-Contrib

Many of NLTK's core components were contributed by members of the NLP community, and were initially housed in NLTK's "Contrib" package, `nltk_contrib`. The only requirement for software to be added to this package is that it must be written in Python, relevant to NLP, and given the same open source license as the rest of NLTK. Imperfect software is welcome, and will probably be improved over time by other members of the NLP community.

Teaching materials

Since the earliest days of NLTK development, teaching materials have accompanied the software, materials that have gradually expanded to fill this book, plus a substantial quantity of online materials as well. We hope that instructors who supplement these materials with presentation slides, problem sets, solution sets, and more detailed treatments of the topics we have covered will make them available, and will notify the authors so we can link them from *http://www.nltk.org/*. Of particular value are materials that help NLP become a mainstream course in the undergraduate programs of computer science and linguistics departments, or that make NLP accessible at the secondary level, where there is significant scope for including computational content in the language, literature, computer science, and information technology curricula.

Only a toolkit

As stated in the preface, NLTK is a *toolkit*, not a system. Many problems will be tackled with a combination of NLTK, Python, other Python libraries, and interfaces to external NLP tools and formats.

Envoi...

Linguists are sometimes asked how many languages they speak, and have to explain that this field actually concerns the study of abstract structures that are shared by languages, a study which is more profound and elusive than learning to speak as many languages as possible. Similarly, computer scientists are sometimes asked how many programming languages they know, and have to explain that computer science actually concerns the study of data structures and algorithms that can be implemented in any programming language, a study which is more profound and elusive than striving for fluency in as many programming languages as possible.

This book has covered many topics in the field of Natural Language Processing. Most of the examples have used Python and English. However, it would be unfortunate if readers concluded that NLP is about how to write Python programs to manipulate English text, or more broadly, about how to write programs (in any programming language) to manipulate text (in any natural language). Our selection of Python and English was expedient, nothing more. Even our focus on programming itself was only a means to an end: as a way to understand data structures and algorithms for representing and manipulating collections of linguistically annotated text, as a way to build new language technologies to better serve the needs of the information society, and ultimately as a pathway into deeper understanding of the vast riches of human language.

But for the present: happy hacking!

Bibliography

[Abney, 1989] Steven P. Abney. A computational model of human parsing. *Journal of Psycholinguistic Research*, 18:129–144, 1989.

[Abney, 1991] Steven P. Abney. Parsing by chunks. In Robert C. Berwick, Steven P. Abney, and Carol Tenny, editors, *Principle-Based Parsing: Computation and Psycholinguistics*, volume 44 of *Studies in Linguistics and Philosophy*. Kluwer Academic Publishers, Dordrecht, 1991.

[Abney, 1996a] Steven Abney. Part-of-speech tagging and partial parsing (*http://citeseer .ist.psu.edu/article/abney96partspeech.html*). In Ken Church, Steve Young, and Gerrit Bloothooft, editors, *Corpus-Based Methods in Language and Speech*. Kluwer Academic Publishers, Dordrecht, 1996.

[Abney, 1996b] Steven Abney. Statistical methods and linguistics (*http://www.vinartus .net/spa/95c.pdf*). In Judith Klavans and Philip Resnik, editors, *The Balancing Act: Combining Symbolic and Statistical Approaches to Language*. MIT Press, 1996.

[Abney, 2008] Steven Abney. *Semisupervised Learning for Computational Linguistics*. Chapman and Hall, 2008.

[Agirre and Edmonds, 2007] Eneko Agirre and Philip Edmonds. *Word Sense Disambiguation: Algorithms and Applications*. Springer, 2007.

[Alpaydin, 2004] Ethem Alpaydin. *Introduction to Machine Learning*. MIT Press, 2004.

[Ananiadou and McNaught, 2006] Sophia Ananiadou and John McNaught, editors. *Text Mining for Biology and Biomedicine*. Artech House, 2006.

[Androutsopoulos et al., 1995] Ion Androutsopoulos, Graeme Ritchie, and Peter Thanisch. Natural language interfaces to databases—an introduction. *Journal of Natural Language Engineering*, 1:29–81, 1995.

[Artstein and Poesio, 2008] Ron Artstein and Massimo Poesio. Inter-coder agreement for computational linguistics. *Computational Linguistics*, pages 555–596, 2008.

[Baayen, 2008] Harald Baayen. *Analyzing Linguistic Data: A Practical Introduction to Statistics Using R*. Cambridge University Press, 2008.

[Bachenko and Fitzpatrick, 1990] J. Bachenko and E. Fitzpatrick. A computational grammar of discourse-neutral prosodic phrasing in English. *Computational Linguistics*, 16:155–170, 1990.

[Baldwin & Kim, 2010] Timothy Baldwin and Su Nam Kim. Multiword Expressions. In Nitin Indurkhya and Fred J. Damerau, editors, *Handbook of Natural Language Processing*, second edition. Morgan and Claypool, 2010.

[Beazley, 2006] David M. Beazley. *Python Essential Reference*. Developer's Library. Sams Publishing, third edition, 2006.

[Biber et al., 1998] Douglas Biber, Susan Conrad, and Randi Reppen. *Corpus Linguistics: Investigating Language Structure and Use*. Cambridge University Press, 1998.

[Bird, 1999] Steven Bird. Multidimensional exploration of online linguistic field data. In Pius Tamanji, Masako Hirotani, and Nancy Hall, editors, *Proceedings of the 29th Annual Meeting of the Northeast Linguistics Society*, pages 33–47. GLSA, University of Massachussetts at Amherst, 1999.

[Bird and Liberman, 2001] Steven Bird and Mark Liberman. A formal framework for linguistic annotation (*http://arxiv.org/abs/cs/0010033*). *Speech Communication*, 33:23–60, 2001.

[Bird and Simons, 2003] Steven Bird and Gary Simons. Seven dimensions of portability for language documentation and description. *Language*, 79:557–582, 2003.

[Blackburn and Bos, 2005] Patrick Blackburn and Johan Bos. *Representation and Inference for Natural Language: A First Course in Computational Semantics*. CSLI Publications, Stanford, CA, 2005.

[BNC, 1999] BNC. British National Corpus, 1999. [http://info.ox.ac.uk/bnc/].

[Brent and Cartwright, 1995] Michael Brent and Timothy Cartwright. Distributional regularity and phonotactic constraints are useful for segmentation. In Michael Brent, editor, *Computational Approaches to Language Acquisition*. MIT Press, 1995.

[Bresnan and Hay, 2006] Joan Bresnan and Jennifer Hay. Gradient grammar: An effect of animacy on the syntax of *give* in New Zealand and American English. Lingua 118: 254–59, 2008.

[Budanitsky and Hirst, 2006] Alexander Budanitsky and Graeme Hirst. Evaluating wordnet-based measures of lexical semantic relatedness. *Computational Linguistics*, 32:13–48, 2006.

[Burton-Roberts, 1997] Noel Burton-Roberts. *Analysing Sentences*. Longman, 1997.

[Buseman et al., 1996] Alan Buseman, Karen Buseman, and Rod Early. *The Linguist's Shoebox: Integrated Data Management and Analysis for the Field Linguist*. Waxhaw NC: SIL, 1996.

[Carpenter, 1992] Bob Carpenter. *The Logic of Typed Feature Structures*. Cambridge University Press, 1992.

[Carpenter, 1997] Bob Carpenter. *Type-Logical Semantics*. MIT Press, 1997.

[Chierchia and McConnell-Ginet, 1990] Gennaro Chierchia and Sally McConnell-Ginet. *Meaning and Grammar: An Introduction to Meaning*. MIT Press, Cambridge, MA, 1990.

[Chomsky, 1965] Noam Chomsky. *Aspects of the Theory of Syntax*. MIT Press, Cambridge, MA, 1965.

[Chomsky, 1970] Noam Chomsky. Remarks on nominalization. In R. Jacobs and P. Rosenbaum, editors, *Readings in English Transformational Grammar*. Blaisdell, Waltham, MA, 1970.

[Chomsky and Halle, 1968] Noam Chomsky and Morris Halle. *The Sound Pattern of English*. New York: Harper and Row, 1968.

[Church and Patil, 1982] Kenneth Church and Ramesh Patil. Coping with syntactic ambiguity or how to put the block in the box on the table. *American Journal of Computational Linguistics*, 8:139–149, 1982.

[Cohen and Hunter, 2004] K. Bretonnel Cohen and Lawrence Hunter. Natural language processing and systems biology. In Werner Dubitzky and Francisco Azuaje, editors, *Artificial Intelligence Methods and Tools for Systems Biology*, page 147–174 Springer Verlag, 2004.

[Cole, 1997] Ronald Cole, editor. *Survey of the State of the Art in Human Language Technology (http://cslu.cse.ogi.edu/HLTsurvey/)*. Studies in Natural Language Processing. Cambridge University Press, 1997.

[Copestake, 2002] Ann Copestake. *Implementing Typed Feature Structure Grammars*. CSLI Publications, Stanford, CA, 2002.

[Corbett, 2006] Greville G. Corbett. *Agreement*. Cambridge University Press, 2006.

[Croft et al., 2009] Bruce Croft, Donald Metzler, and Trevor Strohman. *Search Engines: Information Retrieval in Practice*. Addison Wesley, 2009.

[Daelemans and van den Bosch, 2005] Walter Daelemans and Antal van den Bosch. *Memory-Based Language Processing*. Cambridge University Press, 2005.

[Dagan et al., 2006] Ido Dagan, Oren Glickman, and Bernardo Magnini. The PASCAL recognising textual entailment challenge. In J. Quinonero-Candela, I. Dagan, B. Magnini, and F. d'Alché Buc, editors, *Machine Learning Challenges*, volume 3944 of *Lecture Notes in Computer Science*, pages 177–190. Springer, 2006.

[Dale et al., 2000] Robert Dale, Hermann Moisl, and Harold Somers, editors. *Handbook of Natural Language Processing*. Marcel Dekker, 2000.

[Dalrymple, 2001] Mary Dalrymple. *Lexical Functional Grammar*, volume 34 of *Syntax and Semantics*. Academic Press, New York, 2001.

[Dalrymple et al., 1999] Mary Dalrymple, V. Gupta, John Lamping, and V. Saraswat. Relating resource-based semantics to categorial semantics. In Mary Dalrymple, editor, *Semantics and Syntax in Lexical Functional Grammar: The Resource Logic Approach*, pages 261–280. MIT Press, Cambridge, MA, 1999.

[Dowty et al., 1981] David R. Dowty, Robert E. Wall, and Stanley Peters. *Introduction to Montague Semantics*. Kluwer Academic Publishers, 1981.

[Earley, 1970] Jay Earley. An efficient context-free parsing algorithm. *Communications of the Association for Computing Machinery*, 13:94–102, 1970.

[Emele and Zajac, 1990] Martin C. Emele and Rémi Zajac. Typed unification grammars. In *Proceedings of the 13th Conference on Computational Linguistics*, pages 293–298. Association for Computational Linguistics, Morristown, NJ, 1990.

[Farghaly, 2003] Ali Farghaly, editor. *Handbook for Language Engineers*. CSLI Publications, Stanford, CA, 2003.

[Feldman and Sanger, 2007] Ronen Feldman and James Sanger. *The Text Mining Handbook: Advanced Approaches in Analyzing Unstructured Data*. Cambridge University Press, 2007.

[Fellbaum, 1998] Christiane Fellbaum, editor. *WordNet: An Electronic Lexical Database*. MIT Press, 1998. *http://wordnet.princeton.edu/*.

[Finegan, 2007] Edward Finegan. *Language: Its Structure and Use*. Wadsworth, Fifth edition, 2007.

[Forsyth and Martell, 2007] Eric N. Forsyth and Craig H. Martell. Lexical and discourse analysis of online chat dialog. In *Proceedings of the First IEEE International Conference on Semantic Computing*, pages 19–26, 2007.

[Friedl, 2002] Jeffrey E. F. Friedl. *Mastering Regular Expressions*. O'Reilly, second edition, 2002.

[Gamut, 1991a] L. T. F. Gamut. *Intensional Logic and Logical Grammar*, volume 2 of *Logic, Language and Meaning*. University of Chicago Press, Chicago, 1991.

[Gamut, 1991b] L. T. F. Gamut. *Introduction to Logic*, volume 1 of *Logic, Language and Meaning*. University of Chicago Press, 1991.

[Garofolo et al., 1986] John S. Garofolo, Lori F. Lamel, William M. Fisher, Jonathon G. Fiscus, David S. Pallett, and Nancy L. Dahlgren. *The DARPA TIMIT Acoustic-Phonetic Continuous Speech Corpus CDROM*. NIST, 1986.

[Gazdar et al., 1985] Gerald Gazdar, Ewan Klein, Geoffrey Pullum, and Ivan Sag (1985). *Generalized Phrase Structure Grammar*. Basil Blackwell, 1985.

[Gomes et al., 2006] Bruce Gomes, William Hayes, and Raf Podowski. Text mining. In Darryl Leon and Scott Markel, editors, *In Silico Technologies in Drug Target Identification and Validation*, Taylor & Francis, 2006.

[Gries, 2009] Stefan Gries. *Quantitative Corpus Linguistics with R: A Practical Introduction*. Routledge, 2009.

[Guzdial, 2005] Mark Guzdial. *Introduction to Computing and Programming in Python: A Multimedia Approach*. Prentice Hall, 2005.

[Harel, 2004] David Harel. *Algorithmics: The Spirit of Computing*. Addison Wesley, 2004.

[Hastie et al., 2009] Trevor Hastie, Robert Tibshirani, and Jerome Friedman. *The Elements of Statistical Learning: Data Mining, Inference, and Prediction*. Springer, second edition, 2009.

[Hearst, 1992] Marti Hearst. Automatic acquisition of hyponyms from large text corpora. In *Proceedings of the 14th Conference on Computational Linguistics (COLING)*, pages 539–545, 1992.

[Heim and Kratzer, 1998] Irene Heim and Angelika Kratzer. *Semantics in Generative Grammar*. Blackwell, 1998.

[Hirschman et al., 2005] Lynette Hirschman, Alexander Yeh, Christian Blaschke, and Alfonso Valencia. Overview of BioCreAtIvE: critical assessment of information extraction for biology (*http://www.biomedcentral.com/1471-2105/6/S1/S1*). *BMC Bioinformatics*, 6, May 2005. Supplement 1.

[Hodges, 1977] Wilfred Hodges. *Logic*. Penguin Books, Harmondsworth, 1977.

[Huddleston and Pullum, 2002] Rodney D. Huddleston and Geoffrey K. Pullum. *The Cambridge Grammar of the English Language*. Cambridge University Press, 2002.

[Hunt and Thomas, 2000] Andrew Hunt and David Thomas. *The Pragmatic Programmer: From Journeyman to Master*. Addison Wesley, 2000.

[Indurkhya and Damerau, 2010] Nitin Indurkhya and Fred Damerau, editors. *Handbook of Natural Language Processing*. CRC Press, Taylor and Francis Group, second edition, 2010.

[Jackendoff, 1977] Ray Jackendoff. *X-Syntax: a Study of Phrase Strucure*. Number 2 in Linguistic Inquiry Monograph. MIT Press, Cambridge, MA, 1977.

[Johnson, 1988] Mark Johnson. *Attribute Value Logic and Theory of Grammar*. CSLI Lecture Notes Series. University of Chicago Press, 1988.

[Jurafsky and Martin, 2008] Daniel Jurafsky and James H. Martin. *Speech and Language Processing*. Prentice Hall, second edition, 2008.

[Kamp and Reyle, 1993] Hans Kamp and Uwe Reyle. *From Discourse to the Lexicon: Introduction to Modeltheoretic Semantics of Natural Language, Formal Logic and Discourse Representation Theory*. Kluwer Academic Publishers, 1993.

[Kaplan, 1989] Ronald Kaplan. The formal architecture of lexical-functional grammar. In Chu-Ren Huang and Keh-Jiann Chen, editors, *Proceedings of ROCLING II*, pages 1–18. CSLI, 1989. Reprinted in Dalrymple, Kaplan, Maxwell, and Zaenen (eds), *Formal Issues in Lexical-Functional Grammar*, pages 7–27. CSLI Publications, Stanford, CA, 1995.

[Kaplan and Bresnan, 1982] Ronald Kaplan and Joan Bresnan. Lexical-functional grammar: A formal system for grammatical representation. In Joan Bresnan, editor, *The Mental Representation of Grammatical Relations*, pages 173–281. MIT Press, Cambridge, MA, 1982.

[Kasper and Rounds, 1986] Robert T. Kasper and William C. Rounds. A logical semantics for feature structures. In *Proceedings of the 24th Annual Meeting of the Association for Computational Linguistics*, pages 257–266. Association for Computational Linguistics, 1986.

[Kathol, 1999] Andreas Kathol. Agreement and the syntax-morphology interface in HPSG. In Robert D. Levine and Georgia M. Green, editors, *Studies in Contemporary Phrase Structure Grammar*, pages 223–274. Cambridge University Press, 1999.

[Kay, 1985] Martin Kay. Unification in grammar. In Verónica Dahl and Patrick Saint-Dizier, editors, *Natural Language Understanding and Logic Programming*, pages 233–240. North-Holland, 1985. Proceedings of the First International Workshop on Natural Language Understanding and Logic Programming.

[Kiss and Strunk, 2006] Tibor Kiss and Jan Strunk. Unsupervised multilingual sentence boundary detection. *Computational Linguistics*, 32: 485–525, 2006.

[Kiusalaas, 2005] Jaan Kiusalaas. *Numerical Methods in Engineering with Python*. Cambridge University Press, 2005.

[Klein and Manning, 2003] Dan Klein and Christopher D. Manning. A* parsing: Fast exact viterbi parse selection. In *Proceedings of HLT-NAACL 03*, 2003.

[Knuth, 2006] Donald E. Knuth. *The Art of Computer Programming, Volume 4: Generating All Trees*. Addison Wesley, 2006.

[Lappin, 1996] Shalom Lappin, editor. *The Handbook of Contemporary Semantic Theory*. Blackwell Publishers, Oxford, 1996.

[Larson and Segal, 1995] Richard Larson and Gabriel Segal. *Knowledge of Meaning: An Introduction to Semantic Theory*. MIT Press, Cambridge, MA, 1995.

[Levin, 1993] Beth Levin. *English Verb Classes and Alternations*. University of Chicago Press, 1993.

[Levitin, 2004] Anany Levitin. *The Design and Analysis of Algorithms*. Addison Wesley, 2004.

[Lutz and Ascher, 2003] Mark Lutz and David Ascher. *Learning Python*. O'Reilly, second edition, 2003.

[MacWhinney, 1995] Brian MacWhinney. *The CHILDES Project: Tools for Analyzing Talk*. Mahwah, NJ: Lawrence Erlbaum, second edition, 1995. [*http://childes.psy.cmu.edu/*].

[Madnani, 2007] Nitin Madnani. Getting started on natural language processing with Python. *ACM Crossroads*, 13(4), 2007.

[Manning, 2003] Christopher Manning. Probabilistic syntax. In *Probabilistic Linguistics*, pages 289–341. MIT Press, Cambridge, MA, 2003.

[Manning and Schütze, 1999] Christopher Manning and Hinrich Schütze. *Foundations of Statistical Natural Language Processing*. MIT Press, Cambridge, MA, 1999.

[Manning et al., 2008] Christopher Manning, Prabhakar Raghavan, and Hinrich Schütze. *Introduction to Information Retrieval*. Cambridge University Press, 2008.

[McCawley, 1998] James McCawley. *The Syntactic Phenomena of English*. University of Chicago Press, 1998.

[McConnell, 2004] Steve McConnell. *Code Complete: A Practical Handbook of Software Construction*. Microsoft Press, 2004.

[McCune, 2008] William McCune. Prover9: Automated theorem prover for first-order and equational logic (*http://www.cs.unm.edu/~mccune/mace4/manual-examples.html*), 2008.

[McEnery, 2006] Anthony McEnery. *Corpus-Based Language Studies: An Advanced Resource Book*. Routledge, 2006.

[Melamed, 2001] Dan Melamed. *Empirical Methods for Exploiting Parallel Texts*. MIT Press, 2001.

[Mertz, 2003] David Mertz. *Text Processing in Python*. Addison-Wesley, Boston, MA, 2003.

[Meyer, 2002] Charles Meyer. *English Corpus Linguistics: An Introduction*. Cambridge University Press, 2002.

[Miller and Charles, 1998] George Miller and Walter Charles. Contextual correlates of semantic similarity. *Language and Cognitive Processes*, 6:1–28, 1998.

[Mitkov, 2002a] Ruslan Mitkov. *Anaphora Resolution*. Longman, 2002.

[Mitkov, 2002b] Ruslan Mitkov, editor. *Oxford Handbook of Computational Linguistics*. Oxford University Press, 2002.

[Müller, 2002] Stefan Müller. *Complex Predicates: Verbal Complexes, Resultative Constructions, and Particle Verbs in German*. Number 13 in Studies in Constraint-Based Lexicalism. Center for the Study of Language and Information, Stanford, 2002. *http://www.dfki.de/~stefan/Pub/complex.html*.

[Nerbonne et al., 1994] John Nerbonne, Klaus Netter, and Carl Pollard. *German in Head-Driven Phrase Structure Grammar*. CSLI Publications, Stanford, CA, 1994.

[Nespor and Vogel, 1986] Marina Nespor and Irene Vogel. *Prosodic Phonology*. Number 28 in Studies in Generative Grammar. Foris Publications, Dordrecht, 1986.

[Nivre et al., 2006] J. Nivre, J. Hall, and J. Nilsson. Maltparser: A data-driven parser-generator for dependency parsing (*http://www.vxu.se/msi/users/nivre/papers/maltparser.pdf*). In *Proceedings of LREC*, pages 2216–2219, 2006.

[Niyogi, 2006] Partha Niyogi. *The Computational Nature of Language Learning and Evolution*. MIT Press, 2006.

[O'Grady et al., 2004] William O'Grady, John Archibald, Mark Aronoff, and Janie Rees-Miller. *Contemporary Linguistics: An Introduction*. St. Martin's Press, fifth edition, 2004.

[OSU, 2007] OSU, editor. *Language Files: Materials for an Introduction to Language and Linguistics*. Ohio State University Press, tenth edition, 2007.

[Partee, 1995] Barbara Partee. Lexical semantics and compositionality. In L. R. Gleitman and M. Liberman, editors, *An Invitation to Cognitive Science: Language*, volume 1, pages 311–360. MIT Press, 1995.

[Pasca, 2003] Marius Pasca. *Open-Domain Question Answering from Large Text Collections*. CSLI Publications, Stanford, CA, 2003.

[Pevzner and Hearst, 2002] L. Pevzner and M. Hearst. A critique and improvement of an evaluation metric for text segmentation. *Computational Linguistics*, 28:19–36, 2002.

[Pullum, 2005] Geoffrey K. Pullum. Fossilized prejudices about "however (*http://itre.cis.upenn.edu/~myl/languagelog/archives/001913.html*)", 2005.

[Radford, 1988] Andrew Radford. *Transformational Grammar: An Introduction*. Cambridge University Press, 1988.

[Ramshaw and Marcus, 1995] Lance A. Ramshaw and Mitchell P. Marcus. Text chunking using transformation-based learning. In *Proceedings of the Third ACL Workshop on Very Large Corpora*, pages 82–94, 1995.

[Reppen et al., 2005] Randi Reppen, Nancy Ide, and Keith Suderman. *American National Corpus* (*http://www.ldc.upenn.edu/Catalog/CatalogEntry.jsp?catalogId=LDC2005T35*). Linguistic Data Consortium, 2005.

[Robinson et al., 2007] Stuart Robinson, Greg Aumann, and Steven Bird. Managing fieldwork data with toolbox and the natural language toolkit (*http://nflrc.hawaii.edu/*

ldc/June2007/robinson/robinson.pdf). *Language Documentation and Conservation*, 1:44–57, 2007.

[Sag and Wasow, 1999] Ivan A. Sag and Thomas Wasow. *Syntactic Theory: A Formal Introduction*. CSLI Publications, Stanford, CA, 1999.

[Sampson and McCarthy, 2005] Geoffrey Sampson and Diana McCarthy. *Corpus Linguistics: Readings in a Widening Discipline*. Continuum, 2005.

[Scott and Tribble, 2006] Mike Scott and Christopher Tribble. *Textual Patterns: Key Words and Corpus Analysis in Language Education*. John Benjamins, 2006.

[Segaran, 2007] Toby Segaran. *Collective Intelligence*. O'Reilly Media, 2007.

[Shatkay and Feldman, 2004] Hagit Shatkay and R. Feldman. Mining the biomedical literature in the genomic era: An overview. *Journal of Computational Biology*, 10:821–855, 2004.

[Shieber, 1986] Stuart M. Shieber. *An Introduction to Unification-Based Approaches to Grammar*, volume 4 of *CSLI Lecture Notes Series*.CSLI Publications, Stanford, CA, 1986.

[Shieber et al., 1983] Stuart Shieber, Hans Uszkoreit, Fernando Pereira, Jane Robinson, and Mabry Tyson. The formalism and implementation of PATR-II. In Barbara J. Grosz and Mark Stickel, editors, *Research on Interactive Acquisition and Use of Knowledge*, techreport 4, pages 39–79. SRI International, Menlo Park, CA, November 1983. (*http://www.eecs.harvard.edu/ shieber/Biblio/Papers/Shieber-83-FIP.pdf*)

[Simons and Bird, 2003] Gary Simons and Steven Bird. The Open Language Archives Community: An infrastructure for distributed archiving of language resources. *Literary and Linguistic Computing*, 18:117–128, 2003.

[Sproat et al., 2001] Richard Sproat, Alan Black, Stanley Chen, Shankar Kumar, Mari Ostendorf, and Christopher Richards. Normalization of non-standard words. *Computer Speech and Language*, 15:287–333, 2001.

[Strunk and White, 1999] William Strunk and E. B. White. *The Elements of Style*. Boston, Allyn and Bacon, 1999.

[Thompson and McKelvie, 1997] Henry S. Thompson and David McKelvie. Hyperlink semantics for standoff markup of read-only documents. In *SGML Europe '97*, 1997. *http://www.ltg.ed.ac.uk/~ht/sgmleu97.html*.

[TLG, 1999] TLG. Thesaurus Linguae Graecae (*http://www.tlg.uci.edu/*), 1999.

[Turing, 1950] Alan M. Turing. Computing machinery and intelligence (*http://cogprints.ecs.soton.ac.uk/archive/00000499/00/turing.html*). *Mind*, 59(236):433–460, 1950.

[van Benthem and ter Meulen, 1997] Johan van Benthem and Alice ter Meulen, editors. *Handbook of Logic and Language*. MIT Press, Cambridge, MA, 1997.

[van Rossum and Drake, 2006a] Guido van Rossum and Fred L. Drake. *An Introduction to Python—The Python Tutorial*. Network Theory Ltd, Bristol, 2006.

[van Rossum and Drake, 2006b] Guido van Rossum and Fred L. Drake. *The Python Language Reference Manual*. Network Theory Ltd, Bristol, 2006.

[Warren and Pereira, 1982] David H. D. Warren and Fernando C. N. Pereira. An efficient easily adaptable system for interpreting natural language queries. *American Journal of Computational Linguistics*, 8(3-4):110–122, 1982.

[Wechsler and Zlatic, 2003] Stephen Mark Wechsler and Larisa Zlatic. *The Many Faces of Agreement*. Stanford Monographs in Linguistics. CSLI Publications, Stanford, CA, 2003.

[Weiss et al., 2004] Sholom Weiss, Nitin Indurkhya, Tong Zhang, and Fred Damerau. *Text Mining: Predictive Methods for Analyzing Unstructured Information*. Springer, 2004.

[Woods et al., 1986] Anthony Woods, Paul Fletcher, and Arthur Hughes. *Statistics in Language Studies*. Cambridge University Press, 1986.

[Zhao and Zobel, 2007] Y. Zhao and J. Zobel. Search with style: Authorship attribution in classic literature (*http://www.cs.rmit.edu.au/~jz/fulltext/acsc07yz.pdf*). In *Proceedings of the Thirtieth Australasian Computer Science Conference*. Association for Computing Machinery, 2007.

NLTK Index

We'd like to hear your suggestions for improving our indexes. Send email to *index@oreilly.com*.

nltk.sem.drt_resolve_anaphora, 399
nltk.tag, 401
nltk.tag.brill.demo, 210, 218
nltk.text.Text, 81
node, 170
nps_chat, 42, 105, 235

O

olac, 436
OrExpression, 369

P

packages, 154
parse, 273, 275, 320, 375, 398, 427
parsed, 51, 373
ParseI, 326
parse_valuation, 378
part_holonyms, 74
part_meronyms, 70, 74
path, 85, 94, 95, 96
path_similarity, 72
phones, 408
phonetic, 408, 409
PlaintextCorpusReader, 51
porter, 107, 108
posts, 65, 235
ppattach, 259
PPAttachment, 258, 259
productions, 308, 311, 320, 334
prove, 376
Prover9, 376
punkt, 112

R

RecursiveDescentParser, 302, 304
regexp, 102, 103, 105, 122
RegexpChunk, 287
RegexpParser, 266, 286
RegexpTagger, 217, 219, 401
regexp_tokenize, 111
resolve_anaphora, 399
reverse, 195
rte_features, 236

S

samples, 22, 44, 54, 55, 56
satisfiers, 380, 382
satisfy, 155
score, 115, 272, 273, 274, 276, 277
search, 177
SEM, 362, 363, 385, 386, 390, 393, 395, 396,
        403

sem, 363, 396, 400
sem.evaluate, 406
Senseval, 257
senseval, 258
ShiftReduceParser, 305
show_clause, 285
show_most_informative_features, 228
show_raw_rtuple, 285
similar, 5, 6, 21, 319
simplify, 388
sort, 12, 136, 192
SpeakerInfo, 409
sr, 65
State, 20, 187
stem, 104, 105
str2tuple, 181
SubElement, 432
substance_holonyms, 74
substance_meronyms, 70, 74
Synset, 67, 68, 69, 70, 71, 72
synset, 68, 69, 70, 71, 425, 426
s_retrieve, 396

T

tabulate, 54, 55, 119
tag, 146, 164, 181, 184, 185, 186, 187, 188, 189,
        195, 196, 198, 207, 210, 226, 231,
        232, 233, 241, 273, 275
tagged_sents, 183, 231, 233, 238, 241, 275
tagged_words, 182, 187, 229
tags, 135, 164, 188, 198, 210, 277, 433
Text, 4, 284, 436
token, 26, 105, 139, 319, 421
tokenize, 263
tokens, 16, 80, 81, 82, 86, 105, 107, 108, 111,
        139, 140, 153, 198, 206, 234, 308,
        309, 317, 328, 335, 352, 353, 355,
        392
toolbox, 66, 67, 430, 431, 434, 438
toolbox.ToolboxData, 434
train, 112, 225
translate, 66, 74
tree, 268, 294, 298, 300, 301, 311, 316, 317,
        319, 335, 352, 353, 355, 393, 430,
        434
Tree, 315, 322
Tree.productions, 325
tree2conlltags, 273
treebank, 51, 315, 316
trees, 294, 311, 334, 335, 363, 392, 393, 396,
        400
trigrams, 141
TrigramTagger, 205
tuples, 192

turns, 12
Type, 2, 4, 169

U

Undefined, 379
unify, 342
UnigramTagger, 200, 203, 219, 274
url, 80, 82, 147, 148

V

Valuation, 371, 378
values, 149, 192
Variable, 375
VariableBinderExpression, 389

W

wordlist, 61, 64, 98, 99, 111, 201, 424
wordnet, 67, 162, 170

X

xml, 427, 436
xml_posts, 235

General Index

We'd like to hear your suggestions for improving our indexes. Send email to *index@oreilly.com*.

regular expression metacharacter, 101

{ } (curly braces) in regular expressions, 100

| (pipe character)

 alternation in regular expressions, 100, 101

 or operator, 368

α-conversion, 389

α-equivalents, 389

β-reduction, 388

λ (lambda operator), 386–390

A

accumulative functions, 150

accuracy of classification, 239

ACL (Association for Computational
  Linguistics), 34

 Special Interest Group on Web as Corpus
   (SIGWAC), 416

adjectives, categorizing and tagging, 186

adjuncts of lexical head, 347

adverbs, categorizing and tagging, 186

agreement, 329–331

 resources for further reading, 357

algorithm design, 160–167

 dynamic programming, 165

 recursion, 161

 resources for further information, 173

all operator, 376

alphabetic variants, 389

ambiguity

 broad-coverage grammars and, 317

 capturing structural ambiguity with
   dependency parser, 311

 quantifier scope, 381, 394–397

 scope of modifier, 314

 structurally ambiguous sentences, 300

 ubiquitous ambiguity in sentence structure,
   293

anagram dictionary, creating, 196

anaphora resolution, 29

anaphoric antecedent, 397

AND (in SQL), 365

and operator, 24

annotated text corpora, 46–48

annotation layers

 creating, 412

 deciding which to include when acquiring
   data, 420

 quality control for, 413

 survey of annotation software, 438

annotation, inline, 421

antecedent, 28

antonymy, 71

apostrophes in tokenization, 110

appending, 11

arguments

 functions as, 149

 named, 152

 passing to functions (example), 143

arguments in logic, 369, 372

arity, 378

articles, 186

assert statements

 using in defensive programming, 159

 using to find logical errors, 146

assignment, 130, 378

 defined, 14

 to list index values, 13

Association for Computational Linguistics (see
  ACL)

associative arrays, 189

assumptions, 369

atomic values, 336

attribute value matrix, 336

attribute-value pairs (Toolbox lexicon), 67

attributes, XML, 426

auxiliaries, 348

auxiliary verbs, 336

 inversion and, 348

B

\b word boundary in regular expressions, 110

backoff, 200

backtracking, 303

bar charts, 168

base case, 161

basic types, 373

Bayes classifier (see naive Bayes classifier)

bigram taggers, 204

bigrams, 20

 generating random text with, 55

binary formats, text, 85

binary predicate, 372

binary search, 160

binding variables, 374

binning, 249

BIO Format, 286

book module (NLTK), downloading, 3

Boolean operators, 368

D

\d decimal digits in regular expressions, 110
\D nondigit characters in regular expressions, 111
data formats, converting, 419
data types
    dictionary, 190
    documentation for Python standard types, 173
    finding type of Python objects, 86
    function parameter, 146
    operations on objects, 86
database query via natural language, 361–365
databases, obtaining data from, 418
debugger (Python), 158
debugging techniques, 158
decimal integers, formatting, 119
decision nodes, 242
decision stumps, 243
decision trees, 242–245
    entropy and information gain, 243
decision-tree classifier, 229
declarative style, 140
decoding, 94
def keyword, 9
defaultdict, 193
defensive programming, 159
demonstratives, agreement with noun, 329
dependencies, 310
    criteria for, 312
    existential dependencies, modeling in XML, 427
    non-projective, 312
    projective, 311
    unbounded dependency constructions, 349–353
dependency grammars, 310–315
    valency and the lexicon, 312
dependents, 310
descriptive models, 255
determiners, 186
    agreement with nouns, 333
deve-test set, 225
development set, 225
    similarity to test set, 238
dialogue act tagging, 214
dialogue acts, identifying types, 235
dialogue systems (see spoken dialogue systems)
dictionaries

feature set, 223
    feature structures as, 337
    pronouncing dictionary, 63–65
    Python, 189–198
        default, 193
        defining, 193
        dictionary data type, 190
        finding key given a value, 197
        indexing lists versus, 189
        summary of dictionary methods, 197
        updating incrementally, 195
    storing features and values, 327
    translation, 66
dictionary
    methods, 197
dictionary data structure (Python), 65
directed acyclic graphs (DAGs), 338
discourse module, 401
discourse semantics, 397–402
    discourse processing, 400–402
    discourse referents, 397
    discourse representation structure (DRS), 397
    Discourse Representation Theory (DRT), 397–400
dispersion plot, 6
divide-and-conquer strategy, 160
docstrings, 143
    contents and structure of, 148
    example of complete docstring, 148
    module-level, 155
doctest block, 148
doctest module, 160
document classification, 227
documentation
    functions, 148
    online Python documentation, versions and, 173
    Python, resources for further information, 173
docutils module, 148
domain (of a model), 377
DRS (discourse representation structure), 397
DRS conditions, 397
DRT (Discourse Representation Theory), 397–400
Dublin Core Metadata initiative, 435
duck typing, 281
dynamic programming, 165

application to parsing with context-free grammar, 307

different approaches to, 167

E

Earley chart parser, 334

electronic books, 80

elements, XML, 425

ElementTree interface, 427–429

using to access Toolbox data, 429

elif clause, if . . . elif statement, 133

elif statements, 26

else statements, 26

encoding, 94

encoding features, 223

encoding parameters, codecs module, 95

endangered languages, special considerations with, 423–424

entities, 373

entity detection, using chunking, 264–270

entries

adding field to, in Toolbox, 431

contents of, 60

converting data formats, 419

formatting in XML, 430

entropy, 251

(see also Maximum Entropy classifiers)

calculating for gender prediction task, 243

maximizing in Maximum Entropy classifier, 252

epytext markup language, 148

equality, 132, 372

equivalence (<->) operator, 368

equivalent, 340

error analysis, 225

errors

runtime, 13

sources of, 156

syntax, 3

evaluation sets, 238

events, pairing with conditions in conditional frequency distribution, 52

exceptions, 158

existential quantifier, 374

exists operator, 376

Expected Likelihood Estimation, 249

exporting data, 117

F

f-structure, 357

feature extractors

defining for dialogue acts, 235

defining for document classification, 228

defining for noun phrase (NP) chunker, 276–278

defining for punctuation, 234

defining for suffix checking, 229

Recognizing Textual Entailment (RTE), 236

selecting relevant features, 224–227

feature paths, 339

feature sets, 223

feature structures, 328

order of features, 337

resources for further reading, 357

feature-based grammars, 327–360

auxiliary verbs and inversion, 348

case and gender in German, 353

example grammar, 333

extending, 344–356

lexical heads, 347

parsing using Earley chart parser, 334

processing feature structures, 337–344

subsumption and unification, 341–344

resources for further reading, 357

subcategorization, 344–347

syntactic agreement, 329–331

terminology, 336

translating from English to SQL, 362

unbounded dependency constructions, 349–353

using attributes and constraints, 331–336

features, 223

non-binary features in naive Bayes classifier, 249

fields, 136

file formats, libraries for, 172

files

opening and reading local files, 84

writing program output to, 120

fillers, 349

first-order logic, 372–385

individual variables and assignments, 378

model building, 383

quantifier scope ambiguity, 381

summary of language, 376

syntax, 372–375

theorem proving, 375
truth in model, 377
floating-point numbers, formatting, 119
folds, 241
for statements, 26
combining with if statements, 26
inside a list comprehension, 63
iterating over characters in strings, 90
format strings, 118
formatting program output, 116–121
converting from lists to strings, 116
strings and formats, 117–118
text wrapping, 120
writing results to file, 120
formulas of propositional logic, 368
formulas, type (t), 373
free, 375
Frege's Principle, 385
frequency distributions, 17, 22
conditional (see conditional frequency distributions)
functions defined for, 22
letters, occurrence in strings, 90
functions, 142–154
abstraction provided by, 147
accumulative, 150
as arguments to another function, 149
call-by-value parameter passing, 144
checking parameter types, 146
defined, 9, 57
documentation for Python built-in functions, 173
documenting, 148
errors from, 157
for frequency distributions, 22
for iteration over sequences, 134
generating plurals of nouns (example), 58
higher-order, 151
inputs and outputs, 143
named arguments, 152
naming, 142
poorly-designed, 147
recursive, call structure, 165
saving in modules, 59
variable scope, 145
well-designed, 147

G

gaps, 349

gazetteer, 282
gender identification, 222
Decision Tree model for, 242
gender in German, 353–356
Generalized Phrase Structure Grammar (GPSG), 345
generate_model ( ) function, 55
generation of language output, 29
generative classifiers, 254
generator expressions, 138
functions exemplifying, 151
genres, systematic differences between, 42–44
German, case and gender in, 353–356
gerunds, 211
glyphs, 94
gold standard, 201
government-sponsored challenges to machine learning application in NLP, 257
gradient (grammaticality), 318
grammars, 327
(see also feature-based grammars)
chunk grammar, 265
context-free, 298–302
parsing with, 302–310
validating Toolbox entries with, 433
writing your own, 300
dependency, 310–315
development, 315–321
problems with ambiguity, 317
treebanks and grammars, 315–317
weighted grammar, 318–321
dilemmas in sentence structure analysis, 292–295
resources for further reading, 322
scaling up, 315
grammatical category, 328
graphical displays of data
conditional frequency distributions, 56
Matplotlib, 168–170
graphs
defining and manipulating, 170
directed acyclic graphs, 338
greedy sequence classification, 232
Gutenberg Corpus, 40–42, 80

H

hapaxes, 19
hash arrays, 189, 190
(see also dictionaries)

head of a sentence, 310
    criteria for head and dependencies, 312
heads, lexical, 347
headword (lemma), 60
Heldout Estimation, 249
hexadecimal notation for Unicode string
        literal, 95
Hidden Markov Models, 233
higher-order functions, 151
holonyms, 70
homonyms, 60
HTML documents, 82
HTML markup, stripping out, 418
hypernyms, 70
    searching corpora for, 106
    semantic similarity and, 72
hyphens in tokenization, 110
hyponyms, 69

I

identifiers for variables, 15
idioms, Python, 24
IDLE (Interactive DeveLopment
        Environment), 2
if . . . elif statements, 133
if statements, 25
    combining with for statements, 26
    conditions in, 133
immediate constituents, 297
immutable, 93
implication (->) operator, 368
in operator, 91
Inaugural Address Corpus, 45
inconsistent, 366
indenting code, 138
independence assumption, 248
    naivete of, 249
indexes
    counting from zero (0), 12
    list, 12–14
    mapping dictionary definition to lexeme,
        419
    speeding up program by using, 163
    string, 15, 89, 91
    text index created using a stemmer, 107
    words containing a given consonant-vowel
        pair, 103
inference, 369
information extraction, 261–289

architecture of system, 263
    chunking, 264–270
    defined, 262
    developing and evaluating chunkers, 270–
        278
    named entity recognition, 281–284
    recursion in linguistic structure, 278–281
    relation extraction, 284
    resources for further reading, 286
information gain, 243
inside, outside, begin tags (see IOB tags)
integer ordinal, finding for character, 95
interpreter
    >>> prompt, 2
    accessing, 2
    using text editor instead of to write
            programs, 56
inverted clauses, 348
IOB tags, 269, 286
    reading, 270–272
is operator, 145
    testing for object identity, 132
ISO 639 language codes, 65
iterative optimization techniques, 251

J

joint classifier models, 231
joint-features (maximum entropy model), 252

K

Kappa coefficient (k), 414
keys, 65, 191
    complex, 196
keyword arguments, 153
Kleene closures, 100

L

lambda expressions, 150, 386–390
    example, 152
lambda operator (λ), 386
Lancaster stemmer, 107
language codes, 65
language output, generating, 29
language processing, symbol processing
        versus, 442
language resources
    describing using OLAC metadata, 435–437
LanguageLog (linguistics blog), 35

latent semantic analysis, 171
Latin-2 character encoding, 94
leaf nodes, 242
left-corner parser, 306
left-recursive, 302
lemmas, 60
    lexical relationships between, 71
    pairing of synset with a word, 68
lemmatization, 107
    example of, 108
length of a text, 7
letter trie, 162
lexical categories, 179
lexical entry, 60
lexical relations, 70
lexical resources
    comparative wordlists, 65
    pronouncing dictionary, 63–65
    Shoebox and Toolbox lexicons, 66
    wordlist corpora, 60–63
lexicon, 60
    (see also lexical resources)
    chunking Toolbox lexicon, 434
    defined, 60
    validating in Toolbox, 432–435
LGB rule of name resolution, 145
licensed, 350
likelihood ratios, 224
Linear-Chain Conditional Random Field
    Models, 233
linguistic objects, mappings from keys to
    values, 190
linguistic patterns, modeling, 255
linguistics and NLP-related concepts, resources
    for, 34
list comprehensions, 24
    for statement in, 63
    function invoked in, 64
    used as function parameters, 55
lists, 10
    appending item to, 11
    concatenating, using + operator, 11
    converting to strings, 116
    indexing, 12–14
    indexing, dictionaries versus, 189
    normalizing and sorting, 86
    Python list type, 86
    sorted, 14
    strings versus, 92

    tuples versus, 136
local variables, 58
logic
    first-order, 372–385
    natural language, semantics, and, 365–368
    propositional, 368–371
    resources for further reading, 404
logical constants, 372
logical form, 368
logical proofs, 370
loops, 26
    looping with conditions, 26
lowercase, converting text to, 45, 107

M

machine learning
    application to NLP, web pages for
        government challenges, 257
    decision trees, 242–245
    Maximum Entropy classifiers, 251–254
    naive Bayes classifiers, 246–250
    packages, 237
    resources for further reading, 257
    supervised classification, 221–237
machine translation (MT)
    limitations of, 30
    using NLTK's babelizer, 30
mapping, 189
Matplotlib package, 168–170
maximal projection, 347
Maximum Entropy classifiers, 251–254
Maximum Entropy Markov Models, 233
Maximum Entropy principle, 253
memoization, 167
meronyms, 70
metadata, 435
    OLAC (Open Language Archives
        Community), 435
modals, 186
model building, 383
model checking, 379
models
    interpretation of sentences of logical
        language, 371
    of linguistic patterns, 255
    representation using set theory, 367
    truth-conditional semantics in first-order
        logic, 377

what can be learned from models of
language, 255
modifiers, 314
modules
defined, 59
multimodule programs, 156
structure of Python module, 154
morphological analysis, 213
morphological cues to word category, 211
morphological tagging, 214
morphosyntactic information in tagsets, 212
MSWord, text from, 85
mutable, 93

N

\n newline character in regular expressions,
111
n-gram tagging, 203–208
across sentence boundaries, 208
combining taggers, 205
n-gram tagger as generalization of unigram
tagger, 203
performance limitations, 206
separating training and test data, 203
storing taggers, 206
unigram tagging, 203
unknown words, 206
naive Bayes assumption, 248
naive Bayes classifier, 246–250
developing for gender identification task,
223
double-counting problem, 250
as generative classifier, 254
naivete of independence assumption, 249
non-binary features, 249
underlying probabilistic model, 248
zero counts and smoothing, 248
name resolution, LGB rule for, 145
named arguments, 152
named entities
commonly used types of, 281
relations between, 284
named entity recognition (NER), 281–284
Names Corpus, 61
negative lookahead assertion, 284
NER (see named entity recognition)
nested code blocks, 25
NetworkX package, 170
new words in languages, 212

newlines, 84
matching in regular expressions, 109
printing with print statement, 90
resources for further information, 122
non-logical constants, 372
non-standard words, 108
normalizing text, 107–108
lemmatization, 108
using stemmers, 107
noun phrase (NP), 297
noun phrase (NP) chunking, 264
regular expression–based NP chunker, 267
using unigram tagger, 272
noun phrases, quantified, 390
nouns
categorizing and tagging, 184
program to find most frequent noun tags,
187
syntactic agreement, 329
numerically intense algorithms in Python,
increasing efficiency of, 257
NumPy package, 171

O

object references, 130
copying, 132
objective function, 114
objects, finding data type for, 86
OLAC metadata, 74, 435
definition of metadata, 435
Open Language Archives Community, 435
Open Archives Initiative (OAI), 435
open class, 212
open formula, 374
Open Language Archives Community
(OLAC), 435
operators, 369
(see also names of individual operators)
addition and multiplication, 88
Boolean, 368
numerical comparison, 22
scope of, 157
word comparison, 23
or operator, 24
orthography, 328
out-of-vocabulary items, 206
overfitting, 225, 245

P

packages, 59
parameters, 57
    call-by-value parameter passing, 144
    checking types of, 146
    defined, 9
    defining for functions, 143
parent nodes, 279
parsing, 318
    (see also grammars)
    with context-free grammar
        left-corner parser, 306
        recursive descent parsing, 303
        shift-reduce parsing, 304
        well-formed substring tables, 307–310
    Earley chart parser, parsing feature-based
        grammars, 334
    parsers, 302
    projective dependency parser, 311
part-of-speech tagging (see POS tagging)
partial information, 341
parts of speech, 179
PDF text, 85
Penn Treebank Corpus, 51, 315
personal pronouns, 186
philosophical divides in contemporary NLP,
    444
phonetics
    computer-readable phonetic alphabet
        (SAMPA), 137
    phones, 63
    resources for further information, 74
phrasal level, 347
phrasal projections, 347
pipeline for NLP, 31
pixel images, 169
plotting functions, Matplotlib, 168
Porter stemmer, 107
POS (part-of-speech) tagging, 179, 208, 229
    (see also tagging)
    differences in POS tagsets, 213
    examining word context, 230
    finding IOB chunk tag for word's POS tag,
        272
    in information retrieval, 263
    morphology in POS tagsets, 212
    resources for further reading, 214
    simplified tagset, 183
    storing POS tags in tagged corpora, 181

tagged data from four Indian languages,
    182
    unsimplifed tags, 187
    use in noun phrase chunking, 265
    using consecutive classifier, 231
pre-sorting, 160
precision, evaluating search tasks for, 239
precision/recall trade-off in information
    retrieval, 205
predicates (first-order logic), 372
prepositional phrase (PP), 297
prepositional phrase attachment ambiguity,
    300
Prepositional Phrase Attachment Corpus, 316
prepositions, 186
present participles, 211
Principle of Compositionality, 385, 443
print statements, 89
    newline at end, 90
    string formats and, 117
prior probability, 246
probabilistic context-free grammar (PCFG),
    320
probabilistic model, naive Bayes classifier, 248
probabilistic parsing, 318
procedural style, 139
processing pipeline (NLP), 86
productions in grammars, 293
    rules for writing CFGs for parsing in
        NLTK, 301
program development, 154–160
    debugging techniques, 158
    defensive programming, 159
    multimodule programs, 156
    Python module structure, 154
    sources of error, 156
programming style, 139
programs, writing, 129–177
    advanced features of functions, 149–154
    algorithm design, 160–167
    assignment, 130
    conditionals, 133
    equality, 132
    functions, 142–149
    resources for further reading, 173
    sequences, 133–138
    style considerations, 138–142
        legitimate uses for counters, 141
        procedural versus declarative style, 139

reentrancy, 340

references (see object references)

regression testing framework, 160

regular expressions, 97–106
- character class and other symbols, 110
- chunker based on, evaluating, 272
- extracting word pieces, 102
- finding word stems, 104
- matching initial and final vowel sequences and all consonants, 102
- metacharacters, 101
- metacharacters, summary of, 101
- noun phrase (NP) chunker based on, 265
- ranges and closures, 99
- resources for further information, 122
- searching tokenized text, 105
- symbols, 110
- tagger, 199
- tokenizing text, 109–112
- use in PlaintextCorpusReader, 51
- using basic metacharacters, 98
- using for relation extraction, 284
- using with conditional frequency distributions, 103

relation detection, 263

relation extraction, 284

relational operators, 22

reserved words, 15

return statements, 144

return value, 57

reusing code, 56–59
- creating programs using a text editor, 56
- functions, 57
- modules, 59

Reuters Corpus, 44

root element (XML), 427

root hypernyms, 70

root node, 242

root synsets, 69

Rotokas language, 66
- extracting all consonant-vowel sequences from words, 103
- Toolbox file containing lexicon, 429

RSS feeds, 83
- feedparser library, 172

RTE (Recognizing Textual Entailment), 32, 235
- exploiting word context, 230

runtime errors, 13

S

\s whitespace characters in regular expressions, 111

\S nonwhitespace characters in regular expressions, 111

SAMPA computer-readable phonetic alphabet, 137

Sanskrit meter, computing, 165

satisfies, 379

scope of quantifiers, 381

scope of variables, 145

searches
- binary search, 160
- evaluating for precision and recall, 239
- processing search engine results, 82
- using POS tags, 187

segmentation, 112–116
- in chunking and tokenization, 264
- sentence, 112
- word, 113–116

semantic cues to word category, 211

semantic interpretations, NLTK functions for, 393

semantic role labeling, 29

semantics
- natural language, logic and, 365–368
- natural language, resources for information, 403

semantics of English sentences, 385–397
- quantifier ambiguity, 394–397
- transitive verbs, 391–394
- λ-calculus, 386–390

SemCor tagging, 214

sentence boundaries, tagging across, 208

sentence segmentation, 112, 233
- in chunking, 264
- in information retrieval process, 263

sentence structure, analyzing, 291–326
- context-free grammar, 298–302
- dependencies and dependency grammar, 310–315
- grammar development, 315–321
- grammatical dilemmas, 292
- parsing with context-free grammar, 302–310
- resources for further reading, 322
- summary of important points, 321
- syntax, 295–298

sents( ) function, 41

syntactic agreement, 329–331
syntactic cues to word category, 211
syntactic structure, recursion in, 301
syntax, 295–298
syntax errors, 3

T

\t tab character in regular expressions, 111
T9 system, entering text on mobile phones, 99
tabs
  avoiding in code indentation, 138
  matching in regular expressions, 109
tag patterns, 266
  matching, precedence in, 267
tagging, 179–219
  adjectives and adverbs, 186
  combining taggers, 205
  default tagger, 198
  evaluating tagger performance, 201
  exploring tagged corpora, 187–189
  lookup tagger, 200–201
  mapping words to tags using Python
      dictionaries, 189–198
  nouns, 184
  part-of-speech (POS) tagging, 229
  performance limitations, 206
  reading tagged corpora, 181
  regular expression tagger, 199
  representing tagged tokens, 181
  resources for further reading, 214
  across sentence boundaries, 208
  separating training and testing data, 203
  simplified part-of-speech tagset, 183
  storing taggers, 206
  transformation-based, 208–210
  unigram tagging, 202
  unknown words, 206
  unsimplified POS tags, 187
  using POS (part-of-speech) tagger, 179
  verbs, 185
tags
  in feature structures, 340
  IOB tags representing chunk structures,
      269
  XML, 425
tagsets, 179
  morphosyntactic information in POS
      tagsets, 212
  simplified POS tagset, 183

terms (first-order logic), 372
test sets, 44, 223
  choosing for classification models, 238
testing classifier for document classification,
    228
text, 1
  computing statistics from, 16–22
  counting vocabulary, 7–10
  entering on mobile phones (T9 system), 99
  as lists of words, 10–16
  searching, 4–7
    examining common contexts, 5
text alignment, 30
text editor, creating programs with, 56
textonyms, 99
textual entailment, 32
textwrap module, 120
theorem proving in first order logic, 375
timeit module, 164
TIMIT Corpus, 407–412
tokenization, 80
  chunking and, 264
  in information retrieval, 263
  issues with, 111
  list produced from tokenizing string, 86
  regular expressions for, 109–112
  representing tagged tokens, 181
  segmentation and, 112
  with Unicode strings as input and output,
      97
tokenized text, searching, 105
tokens, 8
Toolbox, 66, 412, 431–435
  accessing data from XML, using
      ElementTree, 429
  adding field to each entry, 431
  resources for further reading, 438
  validating lexicon, 432–435
tools for creation, publication, and use of
    linguistic data, 421
top-down approach to dynamic programming,
    167
top-down parsing, 304
total likelihood, 251
training
  classifier, 223
  classifier for document classification, 228
  classifier-based chunkers, 274–278
  taggers, 203

About the Authors

Steven Bird is Associate Professor in the Department of Computer Science and Software Engineering at the University of Melbourne, and Senior Research Associate in the Linguistic Data Consortium at the University of Pennsylvania. He completed a Ph.D. on computational phonology at the University of Edinburgh in 1990, supervised by Ewan Klein. He later moved to Cameroon to conduct linguistic fieldwork on the Grassfields Bantu languages under the auspices of the Summer Institute of Linguistics. More recently, he spent several years as Associate Director of the Linguistic Data Consortium, where he led an R&D team to create models and tools for large databases of annotated text. At Melbourne University, he established a language technology research group and has taught at all levels of the undergraduate computer science curriculum. In 2009, Steven is President of the Association for Computational Linguistics.

Ewan Klein is Professor of Language Technology in the School of Informatics at the University of Edinburgh. He completed a Ph.D. on formal semantics at the University of Cambridge in 1978. After some years working at the Universities of Sussex and Newcastle upon Tyne, Ewan took up a teaching position at Edinburgh. He was involved in the establishment of Edinburgh's Language Technology Group in 1993, and has been closely associated with it ever since. From 2000 to 2002, he took leave from the University to act as Research Manager for the Edinburgh-based Natural Language Research Group of Edify Corporation, Santa Clara, and was responsible for spoken dialogue processing. Ewan is a past President of the European Chapter of the Association for Computational Linguistics and was a founding member and Coordinator of the European Network of Excellence in Human Language Technologies (ELSNET).

Edward Loper has recently completed a Ph.D. on machine learning for natural language processing at the University of Pennsylvania. Edward was a student in Steven's graduate course on computational linguistics in the fall of 2000, and went on to be a Teacher's Assistant and share in the development of NLTK. In addition to NLTK, he has helped develop two packages for documenting and testing Python software, epydoc and doctest.

Colophon

The animal on the cover of *Natural Language Processing with Python* is a right whale, the rarest of all large whales. It is identifiable by its enormous head, which can measure up to one-third of its total body length. It lives in temperate and cool seas in both hemispheres at the surface of the ocean. It's believed that the right whale may have gotten its name from whalers who thought that it was the "right" whale to kill for oil. Even though it has been protected since the 1930s, the right whale is still the most endangered of all the great whales.

The large and bulky right whale is easily distinguished from other whales by the calluses on its head. It has a broad back without a dorsal fin and a long arching mouth that begins above the eye. Its body is black, except for a white patch on its belly. Wounds and scars may appear bright orange, often becoming infested with whale lice or cyamids. The calluses—which are also found near the blowholes, above the eyes, and on the chin, and upper lip—are black or gray. It has large flippers that are shaped like paddles, and a distinctive V-shaped blow, caused by the widely spaced blowholes on the top of its head, which rises to 16 feet above the ocean's surface.

The right whale feeds on planktonic organisms, including shrimp-like krill and copepods. As baleen whales, they have a series of 225–250 fringed overlapping plates hanging from each side of the upper jaw, where teeth would otherwise be located. The plates are black and can be as long as 7.2 feet. Right whales are "grazers of the sea," often swimming slowly with their mouths open. As water flows into the mouth and through the baleen, prey is trapped near the tongue.

Because females are not sexually mature until 10 years of age and they give birth to a single calf after a year-long pregnancy, populations grow slowly. The young right whale stays with its mother for one year.

Right whales are found worldwide but in very small numbers. A right whale is commonly found alone or in small groups of 1 to 3, but when courting, they may form groups of up to 30. Like most baleen whales, they are seasonally migratory. They inhabit colder waters for feeding and then migrate to warmer waters for breeding and calving. Although they may move far out to sea during feeding seasons, right whales give birth in coastal areas. Interestingly, many of the females do not return to these coastal breeding areas every year, but visit the area only in calving years. Where they go in other years remains a mystery.

The right whale's only predators are orcas and humans. When danger lurks, a group of right whales may come together in a circle, with their tails pointing outward, to deter a predator. This defense is not always successful and calves are occasionally separated from their mother and killed.

Right whales are among the slowest swimming whales, although they may reach speeds up to 10 mph in short spurts. They can dive to at least 1,000 feet and can stay submerged for up to 40 minutes. The right whale is extremely endangered, even after years of protected status. Only in the past 15 years is there evidence of a population recovery in the Southern Hemisphere, and it is still not known if the right whale will survive at all in the Northern Hemisphere. Although not presently hunted, current conservation problems include collisions with ships, conflicts with fishing activities, habitat destruction, oil drilling, and possible competition from other whale species. Right whales have no teeth, so ear bones and, in some cases, eye lenses can be used to estimate the age of a right whale at death. It is believed that right whales live at least 50 years, but there is little data on their longevity.

The cover image is from the Dover Pictorial Archive. The cover font is Adobe ITC Garamond. The text font is Linotype Birka; the heading font is Adobe Myriad Condensed; and the code font is LucasFont's TheSansMonoCondensed.

Related Titles from O'Reilly

Scripting Languages

Essential PHP Security

Exploring Expect

Jython Essentials

Learning Python, *3rd Edition*

Learning PHP and MySQL, *2nd Edition*

Learning Ruby

Learning PHP 5

Learning Python, *3rd Edition*

PHP Cookbook, *2nd Edition*

PHP Hacks

PHP in a Nutshell

PHP Pocket Reference, *2nd Edition*

PHPUnit Pocket Guide

Programming PHP, *2nd Edition*

Programming Python, *3rd Edition*

Python & XML

Python Cookbook, *2nd Edition*

Python in a Nutshell, *2nd Edition*

Python Pocket Reference, *3rd Edition*

Python Standard Library

Ruby on Rails: Up and Running

The Ruby Programming Language

Upgrading to PHP 5

O'REILLY®

Our books are available at most retail and online bookstores.

To order direct: 1-800-998-9938 • *order@oreilly.com* • *www.oreilly.com*

Online editions of most O'Reilly titles are available by subscription at *safari.oreilly.com*